SHAKESPEARE AND THE ACTORS

Mrs. Barry as Constance
(From Bell's *Shakespeare*, 1774)

SHAKESPEARE AND THE ACTORS

THE ACTORS

The Stage Business in His Plays
(1660-1905)

BY

ARTHUR COLBY SPRAGUE

NEW YORK
RUSSELL & RUSSELL · INC
1963

PRINTED IN THE UNITED STATES OF AMERICA

To

J. FLETCHER SMITH

Preface

In August 1936, I read in the *Boston Herald* of a new piece of stage business (or was it new?) which had been introduced by Mr. Baliol Holloway in a performance of *A Midsummer Night's Dream* at Regent's Park. Bottom, it appeared, on awaking from his dream had discovered *hay* in his pouch. Later, I read, two persons had written to *The Observer* pointing out that George R. Weir, long a comedian in Sir Frank Benson's company, had employed the same business.

Meanwhile, I had been wondering where one could turn to find out about the "old business" in Shakespeare's plays. There was, I remembered, an article on Shakespearean stage traditions by Brander Matthews, first published in 1916. There was an admirable essay by W. J. Lawrence on the Gravedigger's waistcoats in *Hamlet*. I could find nothing more. Increasingly, the subject interested me, and a few months later I began to collect material for the book now about to be published.

Since English libraries were inaccessible, I was forced to confine my research to those in this country. Even a few more prompt books might have added appreciably to the information I have been able to collect about the business in a number of the less frequently acted plays. Whereas, with plays like *Hamlet*, *Macbeth*, and several others, my chief problem has been what to choose and what to reject.

Perhaps a word should be said about the later of the two dates on the title page. To have passed beyond the year of Irving's death would have been to intrude upon a time well within living memory, and to court repeated correction at the hands of those who had seen (and even taken part in) English productions which I had not attended. The appearance of Mr. Gordon Crosse's

delightful volume, *Fifty Years of Shakespearean Playgoing*, has
made me all the more certain that I did wisely.

I wish to acknowledge the privilege of consulting books, newspapers, and manuscripts in the following libraries: Harvard College; Yale University; the University of Pennsylvania; Hamilton
College; Folger; the Library Company of Philadelphia; "The
Players"; the Library of Congress; the Boston Athenaeum; the
New York Public Library; and the Boston Public Library. Many
persons have aided me in what has proved to be a long though a
very pleasant task. To some of them gratitude has been expressed
in the notes. I wish here to thank, most particularly, Professor
Samuel Claggett Chew; Mr. John Gassner, of the Theatre Guild;
Mr. Henry Herbert, once of Benson's company; Dr. William
Van Lennep, Curator of the Harvard Theatre Collection; Mr. J.
Fletcher Smith, formerly American representative of *The Stage*;
Miss Elisabeth Mignon of Bryn Mawr; and Mr. Roy Day, for
many years librarian of "The Players." The progress of my work
has been facilitated by several grants from the Madge Miller
Research Fund.

ARTHUR COLBY SPRAGUE

Bryn Mawr College.

Contents

INTRODUCTION xiii

CHAPTER I. THE COMEDIES 3

CHAPTER II. THE HISTORIES 76

CHAPTER III. HAMLET 127

CHAPTER IV. OTHELLO 185

CHAPTER V. MACBETH 224

CHAPTER VI. THE OTHER TRAGEDIES 281

Illustrations

MRS. BARRY AS CONSTANCE . . . . *Frontispiece*
  (From Bell's *Shakespeare*, 1774)

LEWIS AND MISS IRVING AS TOUCHSTONE AND AUDREY . . . 38
  (From a photograph in The Harvard Theatre Collection)

BURTON AS BOTTOM 52
  (From an engraving in The Harvard Theatre Collection)

THE KEMBLE FAMILY IN HENRY VIII 78
  (From an engraving after a painting by Harlow)

HAMLET'S START 138
  (From an illustration by Theodore Lane in Pierce Egan's *Life
  of an Actor*, 1825)

THE GHOST DESCENDING HIS TRAP 142
  (From an illustration by George Cruickshank in Raymond's
  Elliston, 1844)

THE CLOSET SCENE 162
  (From Rowe's *Shakespeare*, 1709)

BROOKE AND BENNETT IN THE COLLARING SCENE 198
  (From an engraving after a daguerreotype)

MACREADY AS MACBETH WITH TRUNCHEON 230
  (From an engraving after a painting by Tracey)

GARRICK IN THE MURDER SCENE 242
  (From Bell's *Shakespeare*, 1774)

THE STAGE ARRANGEMENT OF THE BANQUET SCENE . . . 252
  (From a drawing in Phelps's Promptbook at the Folger
  Library)

FORREST AS LEAR WITH STRAW SCEPTRE 294
  (From an engraving after a photograph by Brady)

Introduction

STAGE BUSINESS is a technical term meaning action. It refers to things seen, rather than things heard, to what the actors *do*, on the boards, when a play is performed. Business may accompany dialogue, or it may fill up moments of silence. Sometimes it is described by the dramatist in his stage directions; sometimes, as so often in Shakespeare's plays, it is implicit in the speeches of the characters.

Business is, or used to be, the actor's province; but a playwright neglects it — fails, that is, to think in terms of action and movement on the stage — only at the risk of laying himself open to charges of incompetence or merely literary aspiration. Volumnia urges Coriolanus to placate the aroused populace by an assumed humbleness of manner. She coaches him in the business of the rôle he is to perform before them, showing him how he is to handle his bonnet, how kneel, how bear his head. "Action," she says "is eloquence, and the eyes of th'ignorant/More learned than their ears." There is a patrician condescension in "th'ignorant." The words are perfectly in character. But if with a little violence we remove them from their context, may they not express, too, the quite natural resentment of one who was a poet as well as an infinitely accomplished theatrical craftsman? Shakespeare's realization of the importance of stage business needs no demonstration beyond what is afforded by scene after scene in his own plays.

"The more familiar an open-minded reader may be with the printed lines of a dramatic masterpiece," writes Brander Matthews, "the more likely is he to be delightfully surprized by the richness of detail and the fresh revelation of meaning when at last he has the privilege of seeing the play performed." Granted sincerity on the actors' part, with a measure of competence, and one's own experience will, I believe, testify to the truth of this. Moreover, unless I am greatly mistaken, it is precisely through action, through business, that the surprise is most likely to come. Not, of course, that one may not carry away the haunting inflection of some single phrase — in *Hamlet*, Walter Hampden's "Alas, poor ghost," shall we say, or John Gielgud's "Make her laugh at that." But Matthews is referring to our first seeing of great plays; and the full effect of things like Volumnia's kneeling to Coriolanus, or Regan's taking Goneril by the hand — of the mere physical presence of the little Prince Arthur while John and Hubert plot his death — is scarcely to be experienced from the printed page. Hazlitt, even in a bilious moment of revolt against the crudeness of stage representation, admits to something like this when he writes that "it is only the *pantomime* part of tragedy . . . which is sure to tell, and tell completely on the stage." [1]

During the period under review — before the rise of that tyrannical newcomer the modern stage director — business was almost wholly in the hands of the actors.[2] Through business, it was said, they filled in with light and shade the outlines furnished them by the playwright. Through business, actors became commentators, critics. Hamlet's conduct toward Ophelia in the Nunnery Scene might be inexplicable to a reader, but when visiting the theatre he saw Polonius, or the King, or both, peer through the curtains, and Hamlet catch sight of them, all difficulty vanished.[3] Shylock, returning lonely to a despoiled home, or as he quit the courtroom withering with one look the jeering Gratiano, became pitiful, or even heroic. Through business, Shakespeare's plays could be brought nearer us and our own experience — could be made more like "modern" plays. When, for example, the vogue of melodrama was at its height, the strong curtains and striking tableaux in which melodrama exulted replaced the quiet scene-endings which are a characteristic of Shakespearean technique; and Hamlet, bravely seconded by Horatio, now charged through the ranks of the enraged courtiers to strike down Claudius on the steps of his throne! It might even be maintained that with the growth of respect for Shakespeare's text, actors have turned more and more to business in order to effect such changes as seemed to them desirable. Had the Restoration decided, shall we say, that Shylock was, or should have been, a wronged gentleman, it would without hesitation have rewritten some of his scenes from this point of view — "improving" them, of course, in the process. But even when such frank dealing had ceased to be tolerated, and the lines which were not actually cut remained about as Shakespeare wrote them, the play might still be adapted — through business.

Shakespearean stage business is of different kinds and varying degrees of interest. Action of some sort may be called for by the lines themselves. Often, even without an Elizabethan stage direction, it is perfectly clear what the particular action is to be. Richard II asks for a looking glass. It is given him, and he cries:

> A brittle glory shineth in this face.
> As brittle as the glory is the face,
> For there it is, crack'd in a hundred shivers.

He must, then, before speaking the last line, break the glass, and break it with violence. Sometimes, however, though action is still demanded, there may be reasonable doubt as to its precise nature. Thus, in the same play, Richard is addressing Bolingbroke, who kneels before him:

> Up, cousin, up! Your heart is up, I know,
> Thus high at least, although your knee be low.

"Thus high" will be explained by the actor's gesture: but does he point to his own head or to the crown which he still wears? Business, again, may be appropriate to the lines without being demanded by them. A piece of byplay already mentioned, Hamlet's catching sight of Polonius behind the arras in the Nunnery Scene, would be cited by some critics as a good instance; or, for one springing rather from character than situation, there is the startling action introduced by the elder Booth, as Cassius, of striding over the mangled body of Caesar, near the close of the Assassination Scene. Finally, there is business out of keeping with the plain meaning of what Shakespeare wrote — business momentarily effective, it may be, but perverse or meretricious, none the less. Fechter's gazing in a mirror at his own blackened face, while speaking Othello's

> It is the cause, it is the cause, my soul,

is a case in point; or, for an awful example of quite recent date, Miss Bankhead's standing, as Cleopatra, while she applied the asps, then plunging forward to a sprawling, unlovely death!

In the following chapters I have felt free to include or reject stage business almost at pleasure. No distinction has been made between gesture and business — granted that there is a distinction. A gesture necessary to clarify the meaning of some passage will of course be included, but all other minor gestures — and some pretty elaborate ones, as well — will pass unnoticed. Robert Lloyd, in *The Actor* (1760), says wisely:

> The Word and Action should conjointly suit,
> But acting Words is labour too minute.

Woodward, the great Mercutio of Garrick's time, was, we are told, "after Rich . . . the best teller of a story in dumb shew, the English stage had ever seen," but "he never forgot it; if he mentioned an undertaker he flapped his hat, pursed up his brow, clasped his hands, and with a burlesque solemnity strode across the stage before he spoke: he would mimic the wiping of a glass, or the drawing of a cork at the word *waiter*, and would not say *mercer* till he had measured off several yards of cloth on the flap of his sleeve." [4] One is tempted to curse Hamlet — who is really not to blame — for what players have made of his advice to "suit the action to the word." (Watch almost any old-fashioned comedian, even today, when he tackles such a part as Sir Toby Belch!) Pageantry, as such, processions and the like — the triumph in *Coriolanus* and the interpolated "Dirge" in *Romeo and Juliet* — have been excluded, almost without exception. Business may be suggested or conditioned by the stage on which the play is represented, by scenery, costumes, and especially by properties — put a truncheon in Macbeth's hands, or a crutch stick in Shylock's, and there is no telling what he will do with it before long — but these matters concern us only as occasional influences. The business of foreign actors is not, as a rule, considered. There are, however, exceptions. Fechter and Salvini, Madame Ristori, Stella Colas, Rossi, and one or two others, belong, through their impersonations of certain rôles, to English and American stage history, and it would be absurd not to take account of their achievements. Finally, in deciding to include rather than reject a piece of business, I have usually been guided by one or more of the following considerations: that it possessed artistic merit in itself; or served to illustrate, or to enforce, the meaning of the lines; that it was early in time; that it had a place in the acting tradition of the play.

Even when it has seemed clear what to include and what reject, difficulties have remained in abundance. Variation in performance is one. Booth's performances, according to a writer in 1875, were "marked by ceaseless change," and rather in "details of 'business' than in expression of idea." [5] We may be sure in the case of some actor that he once did a particular thing in a particular way. But was this his common practice at the time? And, if so, was it never abandoned? At moments, too, though it is possible to date accurately the performance which is being described, we may lack confidence in the description. Amid the excitements and distractions of the theatre, it is only too easy to miss something that happens quickly on the stage, or to imagine we have seen what in point of fact did not happen at all. Hence the necessity, in my opinion, for an amount of documentation which to some readers will, doubtless, appear excessive. Memoirs are, perhaps, the least trustworthy source of information used; newspaper reviews are better; promptbooks, when they can be precisely identified, better still. The last difficulty is one which, unfortunately, is quite as likely to be in the reader's way as it has been in mine. The instant one begins to describe serious stage business in words, there is the gravest risk of its sounding ridiculous. And some of the accounts quoted in the following pages were composed by sneering critics, some by flowery sentimentalists, and a fair number by writers without adequate literary training or equipment. If we could see Charles Kean, as Hamlet, *sliding down the stage*, as he exclaimed, "Is it the King?" I am persuaded that, though we might not wholly like what he was doing, we should scarcely find it absurd. "All we really know about the great actors of the past," writes William Archer, "is the effect they produced upon their audiences." [6] It is a disquieting thought, but one which applies less clearly, perhaps, to an actor's business than to any other single aspect of his art.

Churchill in *The Rosciad* writes:

> Some errors, handed down from age to age,
> Plead Custom's force, and still possess the stage. . . .
>
> When Falstaff stands detected in a lye,
> Why, without meaning, rowls Love's glassy eye?
> Why? — There's no cause — at least no cause we know —
> It was the Fashion twenty years ago.[7]

The force of tradition in perpetuating business is hard to overestimate. The organization of the old stock companies, with their comparatively stable repertories, and the apprentice-like relationship of the younger actors to their elders, the flourishing, too, of great actor families like the Jeffersons and the Booths, contributed to foster tradition. Traditional stage business was once the pride of actors, the delight of audiences, and was handed down, orally, and through manuscript prompt copies and printed acting editions, from generation to generation.

The history of Shakespearean stage business falls almost of itself into curious patterns of convention and revolt. Every so often a great actor like Garrick or Irving comes forward with sweeping innovations, though it may turn out that as we learn more about the business of his predecessors these innovations will be found less numerous than they had once appeared to be. The degree of inventiveness in business is no sure measure, seemingly, of an actor's artistic stature. Fechter, in the words of Charles Dickens, made "a piratical swoop upon the whole fleet of little theatrical prescriptions without meaning, or, like Dr. Johnson's celebrated friend, with only one idea in them, and that a wrong one." [8] Edwin Booth, on the other hand, was conservative, taking a certain pride in keeping up the ways of his father and of Edmund Kean. Less distinguished players might find comfort in the mere fact of knowing "the business." Such knowledge, after all, was not readily to be acquired outside the profession, and they made the most of possessing it. The author of "A Few Words about Acting," in *The World: A Dramatic, Musical, and Literary Journal*, June 8, 1850, writes angrily against their pretensions:

These are the people among actors who now, at this present time, tell you about the great Mr. So-and-so, and the celebrated Mrs. A., and how the business of such a scene is after such a fashion, and how Mrs. C. dropped her pocket-handkerchief at such a passage . . . and who never for one moment ask you, or themselves, the simple questions, "What is the author's meaning?" or "What would be the conduct of a similar person in real life." The object of all this trash about business is to make a mystery about what is really very clear; and to enable dull people, who have stuffed their brains with a collection of stage directions and conventional rules, to get an engagement on the strength of their acquaintance with what is generally useless, often absurd; and to keep out of the theatre clever men who choose to think more of nature and the author's meaning than of the way Mr. Wrench sneezed, or Mr. Liston shrugged his shoulders.[9]

As for the audience, their interest in stage business was strongest, I think, about the beginning of the nineteenth century. Kemble had taught them to share something of his own enthusiasm for details. Kean — a pantomimic actor, as Kemble was a declamatory one — counted upon business for some of his greatest effects. Acting came to be judged, often mechanically, it would seem, in terms of "new readings," "points," bits of business. "False lights to the discernment of audiences," Macready calls them:

The instances have not been rare in the Drama's history [he continues], when the frequenters of theatres, on the occasion of an actor's or an actress's first essay in any popular character, have reserved their judgments for the effect to be produced by one line or one speech, the particular point rendered famous by some preceding player; and the artist has as often been betrayed into laboured efforts to give prominence to such isolated passages, instead of relying on his penetration into the full depth of the poet's intention.[10]

Thus we read, in *The Drama; Or Theatrical Pocket Magazine*, January 1823, of Mrs. Ogilvie's first appearance at Covent Garden, as Katherine in *Henry VIII*:

The challenge of *Wolsey*, in the passage —
"Lord Cardinal —
To you I speak,"
pointed with such powerful effect by Mrs. SIDDONS, was an awful crisis; and the breathless silence which marked its approach on the part of the audience, must have added greatly to the anxiety of the lady. She, however, bore the trial bravely.

Macready himself, playing Macbeth at Drury Lane a year later, got as far as the Banquet Scene: "when the ghost of Banquo appears for the second time, and he exclaims — '*Hence — hence horrible shadow*,' &c. Mr. Macready *retreated* to the chair, and hid his face. This varied style from that of another great tragedian, induced some fool to hiss." [11] Tradition has largely departed from our theatres today, in English-speaking countries, but it is strongly planted still in the older French and Italian operas. What, we wonder, will tonight's Mephistopheles do just before his exit in the Garden Scene in *Faust?* Or what will be the business of this new Tonio — with Nedda's whip, shall we say, or that eternal apple of his — at the end of the first act of *Pagliacci?* We know, of course, what is usually done. But often there is alternative business to choose from; and a great operatic actor can surprise and delight us by departing wholly from tradition, just as Kean surprised and delighted audiences in the Shakespearean parts they knew so well. Macready's complaints were fully justified, no doubt. But when he broke with tradition in that performance of *Macbeth*, and was hissed, one is glad to hear further that "the applauses of the audience soon made the silly critic inaudible."

In O'Keefe's *Recollections* (1826) are some curious verses on Wilde, the Covent Garden prompter, including these lines:

Stage properties, stage business, music, band,
Of stage arcana prompter holds the key.[12]

Prompters, in older times, seem to have been important functionaries, more important by far than they are today. The commemorative instinct was strong in them, too. Witness the careful inscriptions in many of the promptbooks which have been pre-

served for us. They were painstaking individuals, as a rule, setting down neatly the complicated marginalia it was their duty to
record. Often a prompt copy was used for more than one
production of a play — hence those later markings, hastily added
in pencil, which tantalize us today. If anyone in the old theatre
was fitted to be the repository of tradition, it was surely the
prompter.

Printed acting editions are, as a group, poor cousins to the
promptbooks. Some of them offer us merely a text cut for acting
purposes accompanied by the usual literary stage directions.
Others, containing stage business, are so derivative in character
that we can place little confidence in their claims to represent a
particular performance. Even the very good ones may suddenly
fail us. Winter writes of *The Shakespearean Plays of Edwin
Booth*, which he had edited:

> They prescribe some of the stage business that he [Booth] invented
> or employed. They might have contained more of it . . . but that
> Booth thought a more extensive and minute specification of such de-
> tails would prove wearisome, and also, though he was willing that
> other actors should use his acting arrangements of the plays, because
> he was averse to providing them with written specification of all his
> business.[13]

There can be no doubt that actors attached value to such indications of stage business as do appear in the printed texts. More
than once, in turning up a heavily marked copy of a Shakespearean play, I have been disappointed to find that the notes
were not, as at first they appeared to be, original prompt notes
but merely directions copied from some acting edition —
Oxberry's, for instance. Even clearer evidence of the respectful
attitude of players is afforded by those instances in which an
acting edition has served as the basis for a promptbook. The
most striking, perhaps, is an *Othello*, in the Harvard College
Library, inscribed "Chas. D. Herman. San Francisco Calif. Aug.
14th 1902," and representing without much doubt a performance
with Herman, as Iago, Antoinette Ashton, as Desdemona, and
Frederick Warde, as the Moor, at the California Theatre, August
8.[14] The printed text used in preparing this promptbook was one

published in "French's Standard Drama," c. 1845, which is under
debt to the still earlier and not very original *Othello* in Oxberry's
"New English Drama," c. 1819. In the course of making over
this antiquated version for performance, new business was added
and further cuts were introduced. But every single item of
stage business — except one, concerning the bearing out of
Roderigo, in v, 1 — is underscored in red to indicate that it was
to be retained in 1902!

Yet even before the death of Irving, tradition was tottering. A
new drama, profoundly different from what had gone before, was
establishing itself on the English stage during the eighteen-
eighties and nineties. The validity of the scenes-from-Shake-
speare-heavily-upholstered type of production was being attacked
frontally by Mr. Bernard Shaw, and subtly undermined by
William Poel's adventurous experiments with the Elizabethan
stage. More serious still, the resident stock company with its
stable repertory and comfortable ways was rapidly giving place,
both here and in England, to touring companies and the recent
metropolitan "hits" which they carried with them.[15] Not, of
course, that the old business is wholly absent from performances
of Shakespeare even today, but its appearances are haphazard at
best. Mr. Maurice Evans may still make splendid use of the
ancient miniatures in the Closet Scene in *Hamlet*, but tradition,
we may assume, had nothing to do with his decision to introduce
them.

Brander Matthews, in 1916, could write of the traditional stage
business in Shakespeare's plays that it had been "devised by successive generations of ingenious performers, every generation
retaining the best of the inventions of its predecessors and handing them along (augmented by its own contributions) to the
generation" that came after.[16] It would be gratifying to believe
that this rosy view was borne out by the pages which follow. To
what extent it is, will be left for the reader to decide. I must
admit, however, that the words "augmented by its own contributions" inevitably suggest to me the "Kitchen Scene" in *Twelfth
Night*, where item by item the antics of Sir Toby and Sir Andrew
might be amusing, but the sum of them is intolerable. Knowledge

of the traditional business had the obvious advantage of enabling the old stock companies to put on a Shakespearean play with the minimum of preparation. If, too, a good deal of the business was stuffy and uninspired, it might at least serve as a check on such extravagance as we have to put up with, at times, today. Mr. Orson Welles as Falstaff, in the Play Scene in *Henry IV*, chose to wear a saucepan on his head, as a crown. Surely, the cushion which Falstaff names and tradition might once have dictated is quite as funny — and Shakespearean, as well. Yet even here it may give us pause, when we have reached for French's acting edition or Kemble's, to find that the Play Scene itself — one of the glories of Shakespearean comedy as we know it — was regularly cut in the days when tradition flourished. But hear William Archer! He has just been told that Mrs. Patrick Campbell, the new Juliet, knows "nothing of the tradition of the part":

The more's the pity! It would need a genius comparable with Shakespeare's own to discern unaided all the delicate lights and shades of his conception, and to recognise . . . all the technical problems which he presents to his interpreter. Let it not be said that I am clamouring for a stagey, conventional Juliet. I do not erect tradition into a law, but simply assert its uses as a guide. If it does no more, it concentrates attention upon details, and reveals the existence of difficulties and opportunities.[17]

One last claim which might be advanced in favor of traditional business is still to be considered — that it may at certain points go back to Elizabethan days and represent Shakespeare's own intention. It cannot be too strongly insisted upon, at the outset, that the chances of our possessing such business will vary enormously from play to play. Thus *Hamlet*, revived early in the Restoration period and given with extraordinary continuity thereafter, is far more likely to have retained vestiges of Elizabethan practice than, say, *The Merchant of Venice*, which does not seem to have been played for two generations before its production, in Granville's adaptation, at the beginning of the eighteenth century. How Doggett, who then enacted Shylock, chose to play the part, will doubtless continue to be of interest to stage historians. It can have little bearing, however, on how Shakespeare intended Shylock to be represented. But suppose, in a play which was steadily popular before the death of Betterton, we know of some piece of business introduced, shall we say, fairly soon after. Is it likely to go back farther still, past Betterton to Burbage? There cannot be, I am afraid, a satisfactory answer to that question. Each case will have to be judged on its own merits. Assuming that no known change in the character of the stage is involved — that the business under consideration might have been employed with equal effectiveness at Shakespeare's Globe and Colley Cibber's Drury Lane — there is still the problem of changing styles in acting to be faced. Eighteenth century promptbooks of Shakespeare's plays contain as a rule few indications of stage business. Indeed, before Garrick, knowledge of Shakespearean business, from whatever source, is painfully hard to come by. May not stage business, at least as we have come to think of it, be a modern phenomenon, and acting before Garrick's time largely a matter of splendid speech? One question seems only to lead to another.

It is reasonably certain that the style of acting which Garrick's superseded was stilted to a degree. Even with Betterton, a great artist beyond question, it is well to remember that he belonged to an age in which tragedy was deliberately removed from life — or elevated above it, if you prefer. It is hard for me to believe that Betterton, returning to Shakespeare from the highly regarded plays of Dryden and Otway and Lee, did not carry over in his acting something of the style which would have been appropriate to them — that is to say, a rhetorical style. Nor, when one recalls the tendency of each age to make Shakespeare as much as possible like its own popular plays, is there reason to suppose that an approximation to this style would have been objected to by Betterton's audience. Rather, I should say, the contrary. Some Shakespearean business of a realistic sort may, accordingly, have been omitted in Betterton's time — in the tragedies, that is — whereas it seems unlikely that any appreciable amount would have been added. The scarcity of allusions to business, before Garrick's *début*, is reasonably explained if we assume that, being relatively stable, business was taken for granted. It must always be remembered, too, how little detailed criticism of Shakespearean acting — the only sort of criticism which is likely to yield evidence as to business being used — we possess for the whole stretch of years between the Restoration and the advent of Garrick. As for the tendency to omit stage business in early promptbooks, that seems to me rather a mere custom on the part of those who prepared them than evidence that stage business was not introduced in actual performances. If some of the eighteenth century promptbooks still available are to be taken literally, then acting, even after Garrick's time, was little more than entering P.S. instead of O.P., and speaking your lines! Uncertainty remains as to the character of Elizabethan acting. It is unlikely, I am convinced, to have been more formal than that of the Restoration, though difference of opinion here may be readily granted.[18] The extent to which business is implied, if not actually directed, in Shakespeare's own lines seems to me striking,[19] not to mention scene after scene, in his greater plays, which depends for its effectiveness largely upon action. Shakespeare's plays were written for performance, and surely, through performance, light has been shed on many dark places in them — often, it is my belief, by means of stage business. "I look upon a good Player," writes the anonymous author of *A Letter to Miss Nossiter*, "as the best Commentator." [20]

SHAKESPEARE AND THE ACTORS

I

The Comedies

NOT TOO LOGICALLY, I have taken up the comedies in the following order. First, *Twelfth Night*, *Much Ado about Nothing*, *The Merchant of Venice*, and *As You Like It*. These four plays one thinks of, instinctively, as a group. They have been very popular on the stage, and I have far more to tell about them than about any of the others. Next come, *The Tempest*, *The Merry Wives of Windsor*, *A Midsummer Night's Dream*, *The Taming of the Shrew*, *Cymbeline*, and *Measure for Measure* — all produced during the Restoration, though with varying degrees of success. These are followed, in turn, by *The Winter's Tale*, which waited longer for a revival. And last of all come *The Comedy of Errors*, *The Two Gentlemen of Verona*, *Love's Labour's Lost*, and *All's Well that Ends Well*, no one of them of much interest, historically, so far as stage business is concerned.

Twelfth Night

The fact that this most delightful of Shakespeare's comedies was on the boards in the sixteen-sixties, when Pepys saw it more than once — "a silly play," he calls it, "and not related at all to the name or day" — may well be misleading. For though, in 1703, *Twelfth Night* furnished ideas and a certain number of lines to a negligible piece by William Burnaby called *Love Betray'd*, it was not acted again until 1741, this time, we may be certain, without the slightest guidance from tradition.

It has long been customary for Viola, in the second scene, to be accompanied by two sailors carrying a "trunk" or "chest." Why, by the way, it is perfectly seemly for Viola, landing in Illyria, to have luggage, when it would be slightly ridiculous for Hamlet, setting out for England, to have any, is matter for thought.[1] Miss Helen Hayes, I recall, upon entering pretended to shake sand from her shoe.

Sir Andrew Aguecheek's demonstration of dancing and capering is the most notable bit of business in Scene 3. In one of two *Twelfth Night* promptbooks prepared by George Becks (this one identified by a reference to Adelaide Neilson), when Sir Toby says "Let me see thee caper," "Sir A does so — Sir Toby taps his cane on stage — higher &c. — Sir Toby laughing & applauding" — and the friends go out "laughing & capering." A "Walk⁸ Cane each" for the frolicsome knights is called for in Mrs. Shaw's promptbook (c. 1850). For a more subtle touch, one reads of Norman Forbes, the Aguecheek in Tree's production, that "his startled look when he caught sight of Maria over Sir Toby's shoulder as the knights embraced, was by itself worth the money." Equally happy was an idea of Kate Terry's in the next scene: Viola's "quick turn at the sound of [Orsino's] voice in the question 'Where's Caesario?' " [2]

Tree as Malvolio entered in state, attended by "four smaller Malvolios, who aped the great chamberlain in dress, in manners, in deportment. He had a magnificent flight of stairs on the stage; and when he was descending it majestically, he slipped and fell with a crash sitting." Mr. Bernard Shaw yet finds that this was not "mere clowning. . . . Tree, without betraying the smallest discomfiture, raised his eyeglass and surveyed the landscape as if he had sat down on purpose." Irving had entered with upturned nose, "and eyes half shut, as if with singular and moody contemplation." [3] Sent to admit Cesario, Malvolio has sometimes returned with him, to linger on the stage for whatever values might be obtained from his silent presence. Thus, Daly made Cesario's "some mollification for your giant, sweet lady" (1, 5, 218) apply to him and not to the little "wren," Maria — and was taken to task by Archer for doing so.[4] Two mid-nineteenth-century prompt notes of John Moore's may be quoted in passing. Sir Toby's entrance is "with slightly unsteady gait — Hat over eyes, and cloak awry," and, bèfore "A plague o' these pickle-herring!" "Pause slight Belch." Later, when Olivia says "I thank you for your pains," it is, "Retreating gradually to wing her eyes fixed on Viola — suddenly and eagerly advances to her and offers a purse."

Malvolio has long carried a wand; but it seems to have been Tree who first used the still familiar business of slipping Olivia's ring over the point of this wand and dropping it, churlishly enough, at Cesario's feet.[5] In Viola's soliloquy, which follows this incident in Act ii, Scene 2, Mrs. Charles Kean (Ellen Tree) is criticized by George Henry Lewes:

> The *look* with which she said "I am the man" was perfect; but that little saucy tap on her head, with the playful swagger which followed it, though they "brought down the house," appeared to us to betray a forgetfulness of Viola . . .

a passing into "the lower orbit of a soubrette." Julia Marlowe used regularly to check off on her fingers the several items in Viola's complicated account — "My master loves her dearly," etc.[6]

Voices have been raised from time to time in protest against the farcical extravagances of the so-called Kitchen Scene (ii, 3). Thus, Joseph Knight in 1878 was "almost certain" that the traditional business dated back "to the time of the Restoration" — though not to a still earlier period, because there were too few of the elder actors who survived the long years during which the theatres were closed. Even so, he found the behavior of the drunken knights "preposterous, unnatural, inartistic, and wholly out of keeping with the general scope of the play." Mr. G. R. Foss, in 1932, not only spoke out against the same ancient abuses, but advanced reasons for supposing that the scene does not take place in a kitchen at all. He even denies that it is a drinking scene! Rather, Sir Toby and Sir Andrew upon their return from carousing have ventured into a part of the great house where their uproar is audible. Twice they call to Maria "to bring drink, but she never does." The last point seems to me indemonstrable.[7]

Our first glimpse of the scene is pleasant enough. Dunlap saw *Twelfth Night* at Drury Lane about 1785.

The picture presented, when the two knights are discovered with their pipes and potations, as exhibited by Dodd and Palmer, is ineffaceable. . . . [Dodd's] thin legs in scarlet stockings, his knees raised nearly to his chin, by placing his feet on the front cross-piece of the chair (the degraded drunkards being seated with a table, tankards, pipes, and candles, between them), a candle in one hand and pipe in the other, endeavouring in vain to bring the two together; while, in representing the swaggering Sir Toby, Palmer's gigantic limbs outstretched seemed to indicate the enjoyment of that physical superiority which nature had given him.[8]

A generation later, the drunkenness of Liston's Sir Andrew made "his eyes dim and his feet tremble, without making his idiotism more senseless . . . his attempt to light his pipe was amusingly unsuccessful." Mrs. Shaw's promptbook calls for a "Long Pipe" each, for Sir Toby and his companion — and they were still smoking when Mr. Crosse saw them in Daly's production, and in Benson's wielded churchwardens.[9]

Shortly after Malvolio's entrance, comes this scrap of dialogue:

Clown [*sings*] "His eyes do show his days are almost done."
Mal. Is't even so?
To. "But I will never die."
Clown. Sir Toby, there you lie.

Capell, who thinks often in terms of the stage, calls the last speech "a waggish remark in tune upon a great stumble of sir Toby's which brings him almost upon his nose."[10] Bell's edition (1774) has Sir Toby fall down singing. Of course, Sir Andrew goes to his assistance, and of course, in time, he too falls down. Then, according to Becks's promptnotes ("1864"), "Maria & Clown assist them, put them back to back — &c &c — ad lib." "Mal gets L — Sir A X L tries to light his pipe at Mals candle — comic bus — blows it out"; and, as the intruder turns to go, "Clown crows, flaps his arms as though they were wings. . . ." Moore has Sir Toby cross to Malvolio: "fillips his fingers in his face — and Xes behind back to R.H. kissing his hand to Maria as he passes. Clown Xes in the same manner and round again to his place. Sir A. Xes, but is too drunk or stupid to say anything." Malvolio exits, "shaking his head & hand threateningly," and Sir Toby "throws his pipe" after him.

It would be tedious to dwell on such inanities. A general warning must, however, be offered. It is Malvolio who gives offense here; Malvolio who provokes vengeance. I well remember Maude Adams's angry walking up and down as the plan is taking shape in Maria's mind.[11] "Go shake your ears!" she had flung after him, as he went. If, on the contrary, an excess of physical abuse is meted out to the Steward, in this scene, he may, himself, become the injured party with much loss of meaning to what follows.

Near the end of the scene, Becks's "1864" promptbook has:

> Sir Andrew keeps repeating "Cut" as if it was the best joke in the world, laughing at it holding his sides — both Exeunt laughing loudly. or Sir Toby takes candle (also Sir A) from Table Comic bus — Toby mugs & holds candle to Sir A's face — he blows it out — then Toby tries to light it & fails — then make a desperate *thrust* — fails & both go up stairs — Sir Toby on hand & knees — when at top — rolls down.[12]

Of a performance by the Benson Company at the Lyceum, *The Athenaeum* (March 31, 1900) writes stuffily: "When Sir Andrew thrusts his long churchwarden tobacco-pipe through his belt as a sword, and when he and Sir Toby, after wild farcical business with their candles, stretch themselves out at full length . . . the effect is to us as depressing as it is inspiring to the uneducated portion of the public."

In the scene between Orsino and Viola (II, 4), Ada Rehan, upon receiving the chain which she is to give the Countess, "raised it to her lips and reverently kissed it." Julia Marlowe writes interestingly about another passage, the lines beginning "She never told her love." At one time, she had "endeavored to aid Shakespeare" and bring out the speaker's "shyness by coyly fingering Viola's little red cap. The result was that there was a great deal of red cap and not nearly enough of the maiden's perturbation." When, on the contrary, she had last played the part (this was written in 1901), she had "made an effort to keep everything still" — even to the ends of her fingers.

> Experience has taught me that . . . we cannot go far wrong if we let the lines have the center of the stage and allow them to show the poet's meaning. We cannot aid him by a multitude of gestures or by creating of intricate "business." [13]

On Malvolio's approach, in the Letter Scene, Moore's prompt-book has: "Sir A. goes to pick up the letter. Toby pulls him to bush, C." Sometimes, Sir Toby and Fabian have hidden themselves behind a tree, with Sir Andrew actually climbing the tree and putting his head out through the branches — a refinement of which Becks notes, "This is better after duel." [14] The Steward reads — and greatness is thrust upon him. "How he went smiling to himself," Lamb writes of Bensley, "with what ineffable carelessness would he twirl his gold chain; what a dream it was!" Or there was Charles Fisher, at Burton's Theatre in 1853: "When it comes home to him at last that he indeed is the favored of *Olivia* . . . he was inimitable. Already [in fancy] he is clothed in yellow-stockings and cross-gartered; and he smiles, as he struts." [15]

In the third act there is little to detain us until we come to the Duel Scene. Henry Austin Clapp, writing of a performance by Daly's Company at the Hollis Street Theatre, Boston, protests vigorously against

the impertinent and monstrously absurd introduction of Sir Andrew silently to threaten Viola with his sword in her chief scene with Olivia, as if Olivia's faintly ironical phrase, "Be not afraid, good youth," needed any explanation when followed without pause by "I will not have you." [16]

There could be no better example, indeed, of "business out of keeping with the plain meaning of what Shakespeare wrote." When, in Scene 4, Malvolio enters, no longer "sad and civil" but "in very strange manner," we hear again of Lamb's Mr. Bensley:

All his peculiarities of deportment . . . aided his exhibition of the steward — the sliding zig-zag advance and retreat of his figure fixed the attention to his stockings and his garters. His constrained smile, his hollow laugh, his lordly assumption, and his ineffable contempt of all that opposed him in the way to greatness were irresistibly diverting.

Fancy such a Malvolio exposed to the familiarity of Belch's "How dost thou, chuck?" accompanied as it sometimes was by a slap on the back! [17]

In the eighteenth-century theatre, two armed grenadiers were posted one on each side of the proscenium, where they remained throughout the performance mute and unregarded. On October 28, 1763, one of these sentries, at Drury Lane, behaved most strangely, falling down "in a kind of fit" during the encounter between Viola and Sir Andrew. Explanations were promptly offered: as that his collapse was due to fear; that it resulted from excessive laughter, which seems somewhat more probable; that it had been arranged beforehand since "it was proper for *Sir Andrew* to place himself in that part of the stage the soldier occupied." [18] Sir Andrew in later times has taken refuge in strange places. Mr. Liston, at Covent Garden in 1820, "violated the whole illusion of his duel-scene with *Viola*, by climbing up a part of the proscenium." Mr. Mason, in Edinburgh five years later, climbed up a rope-ladder — "but even that he makes in perfect keeping with the character." [19] In Moore's promptbook, at line 342, the duellists

advance towards centre — swords extended — but neither looking at his adversary. in centre the swords meet this frightens them, and they turn away ["causing Sir Toby and Fabian to bump together" inserted] & again are brought back by Sir Toby & Fabian — Advance as before Viola hits Sir Andrew on the leg — he holloas runs away and begin to climb tree L up stage.

By this time, however, if not before, he was more likely to postpone his climbing until Sir Toby crosses swords with Antonio. Then, when the brawl is over, Sir Toby calls him and he answers from among the branches — "Here I am." [20]

As for Viola, enough perhaps that Madame Modjeska realized that her antagonist was not in the least dangerous, had a good opportunity to hit him, and refrained from doing so, out of "womanly generosity"; whereas Julia Arthur beat her Sir Andrew first "with her sword, and then with her hands across his bent back." [21] One last glimpse of the knight comes from *The Examiner* June 5, 1808, and is probably by Leigh Hunt:

The fixed and trembling posture of Mr. MATHEWS . . . his hard breathing which tried to recover itself now and then by a heavy sigh, and his occasional side bend of the head accompanied with a munch of the lips, like a person who has just swallowed a crust that had stuck in his throat, presented a perfect picture of feeble despair.

At the beginning of the Dark Room Scene (IV, 2),[22] "Malvolio," according to Becks's notes, "gives a deep groan & passes his head by the window straw beruffled." The miserable man has "chains on wrists," too. Irving exhibited him in "a nerveless state of prostrate dejection . . . stretched on the straw of a dungeon worthy of *Fidelio*." [23]

For relief, there is an account of Sir Andrew's final exit. *John Bull*, September 8, 1839, is grateful to Buckstone, at the Haymarket,

for cheating us into hearty laughter by his whimsicalities in *Sir Andrew* . . . his parting look at *Olivia*, in the last scene, as if to ascertain whether there might not be a chance left for him, was characteristic, and in excellent keeping with his author.

Dyce, in 1853, could "well remember that, when *Twelfth Night* was revived at Edinburgh many years ago, Terry, who then acted Malvolio . . . had 'straw about him,' on his release from durance." Becks's "Neilson" Promptbook calls for "straws in his hair — one over hanging face — which annoys him for a time — finally pulls it out — Eyes red — terribly in earnest." His exit is a great moment. Phelps's restraint was striking. His Malvolio had gone through the play with half-closed eyes, as if there were "nothing in the world without that is worth noticing." Now "he opens his eyes on learning how he has been tricked," but

they close again in happy self-content, and he is retiring in state without deigning a word to his tormentors, when, as the fool had twitted him by noting how "the whirligig of time brings in his revenges," he remembers that the whirligig is still in motion. Therefore, marching back with as much increase of speed as is consistent with magnificence, he threatens all — including now Olivia in his contempt — "I'll be revenged on the whole pack of you!" [24]

Tree tore off his steward's chain — the chain Maria had referred to with derision, early in the play, the chain, too, which he had found himself fingering instinctively in the Letter Scene: "I frown the while, and perchance wind up my watch, or play with my — some rich jewel." Sothern preferred to tear the forged letter into bits, which he threw on the stage as he went. And "there was something of great dignity in the manner of that exit." [25]

Much Ado about Nothing

Benedick and Beatrice, removed from their accustomed surroundings, were exhibited on the Restoration stage in Davenant's strange piece, *The Law Against Lovers* (1662); but *Much Ado about Nothing* remained unacted till 1721, and did not really establish itself as a familiar play before Garrick's time. Its traditions are, accordingly, of no great antiquity.

Shortly after the appearance of Don Pedro and his company, in the opening scene, most of the characters leave the stage, with Benedick lingering, however, for his talk with Claudio. Byplay of some sort between Benedick and Beatrice has often been introduced here. Thus, when Vining played the part at the Haymarket, in 1833, "Benedick stands in RH Corner, as Beatrice walks up the Stage, Claudio hits him on the Shoulder and points to her, Benedick goes and offers to lead her out — She declines & goes off — Benedick is following when Claudio speaks." In Macready's production, "Ben and Beat. meet but turn from each other." And when George Becks saw Irving and Ellen Terry in 1884, Beatrice, going "last — playfully offers hand to Ben — who declines — she exits laughing Ben following when Claudio — 'Benedick.' " [26] On his own exit, Benedick has sometimes, after bowing to the Prince, put his hand to his heart and sighed — at Claudio.[27] More ambitious is the attempt made in several productions to connect with this scene the story Borachio later tells Don John (1, 3). Borachio appears "listening" soon after Benedick's departure. He hides behind a door or pillar; and, when the Prince and Claudio leave the stage, he follows, "dogging them." Fanny Davenport, when she toured in the play in 1886, ended the act with "a bevy of girls & children" (one of them blindfolded) scampering about the stage with much "laughing & noise." [28]

Lady Pollock writes of Macready's production of *Much Ado*: "I wish I could find a spell to bring back to its joyous life the scene of the masquerade . . . where they laughed, and talked, and danced, met and parted, assembled and dispersed without any

apparent art, where the frolic seemed quite spontaneous." No
spell exists, alas! But we who never saw these brave things can
come a little nearer to seeing them through studying the crabbed
notes of an old prompter:

> 30 Ladies, — 34 Gent^s — 6 pages —/ All masked, except pages —/ these
> enter from R, before the Char^s, — L, Ser^{ts} $\overline{w}$ Salvers, Ewers, & Goblets,
> Enter R. & L — at back/ and go about the Stage, — 8 Servants/ as
> Musicians/ enter $\overline{w}$ lutes & pipes, L, — and go up to the back to play,
> — the stage should appear as lively as possible, every one on, prome-
> nading to every part of the scene. — As the bits of dialogue terminate
> between the parties, the time should be occupied by the Masquers, in
> an ad lib dance, of the moment, — to stop instantly the Char^s are ready
> to speak, in front.

Presently, Benedick meets Beatrice, "and endeavours to avoid her,
but she pursues him," [29] as she was accustomed to do here — and
"*laughing*," too. Alexander's Benedick, in 1898, showed "his recal-
citrance by stamping his foot in the middle of the minuet"; and
"a charming little episode" in Ellen Terry's performance was her
noticing a "pretty child in the masked dance scene, kissing him,
and catching him up playfully in her arms."[30]

After Don John's entrance, Oxberry's *New English Drama*
(1824) introduces the stage direction, "*makes a sign to Borachio,
that he will now put his plot into practice, and then speaks with
affected loudness and emotion, in order to be observed by Claudio*" — "Sure my brother is amorous on Hero," etc. It is unlikely,
however, that the words are intended to be over-heard by
Claudio.[31] Finally, I cannot resist quoting from the notes on
Irving by George Becks, an actor of the old school. At line 192,
"has domino on his arm"; at line 209, "Throws Domino on chair
& sits . . . Irving 'Merry'! God forgive him. Hard — hard — dry
& blockish." [32]

Benedick's first soliloquy in the Orchard Scene (II, 3) was
spoken by Macready "walking up and down and eating cherries"
— which suggests the methods of much later actors. The slug-
gish boy whom Benedick sends after the book was allowed by
Daly to appear with it, during the same monologue. Tree brought
him back, too, and the graceless youth "dropped his hat over an

orange and picking them up together held the orange up behind him turning his back to the audience, so that it should not miss the joke." [33] Tree himself, as Benedick, after climbing a tree instead of hiding in the arbor, showered down oranges on the conspirators' heads.

As for the later soliloquy ("This can be no trick," etc.) the last lines used to be spoken as Benedick "walks about agitated," and, at "By this day, she's a fair lady!" he *"takes off his hat and wipes it — adjusts his dress."* [34] Hunt writes of Charles Kemble here:

> His utterance of his grand final reason for marrying — "The world must be peopled," — with his hands linked behind him, a general elevation of his aspect, and a sort of look at the whole universe before him, as if he saw all the future generations that might depend on his verdict, was a bit of the right masterly gusto — the true perception and relish of the thing.

Macready broke abruptly with tradition here. Taking one of the chairs which the conspirators had been occupying, and drawing it to the front, he sat down, and after a long pause began the speech, crossing and re-crossing his legs uneasily, as he proceeded.[35] It might be added, on the authority of the Macready Promptbook, that as Beatrice addressed him at the close of the scene, she "turns her back to him, — Ben, — before he speaks, walks round her, endeavouring to see her face, as he adv^s, she turns, till both in their original positions."

At the beginning of the third act, Hero bids Ursula

> look where Beatrice like a lapwing runs
> Close by the ground, to hear our conference —

and both Helen Faucit and Ellen Terry were thought to have done this "lapwing run" to perfection.[36] Then Hero and Ursula walk backwards and forwards and talk of how Benedick is "sick in love with Beatrice."

The Saturday Review, January 10, 1891, found Scene 2, in which Benedick is teased,

> Most happily played by Mr. Irving and his companions, and the snatching of his scented handkerchief and tossing it from one to another was devised by some one — whether it is Mr. Irving's "business"

or not we do not know — who thoroughly appreciated the spirit of the episode.

This business was old. Vining describes it, in its simplest form, in 1833. Benedick has his handkerchief to his face. He complains of toothache. Comments are made upon his hat ("'A brushes his hat o' mornings"), upon his indulgence in perfumes ("Nay, 'a rubs himself with civet"). "Pedro snatches away Benedick's handkerchief, throws it to Claudio, who tosses it back to Benedick." [37] As elaborated, Claudio first appropriates his hat, and, as this is being tossed about with Benedick trying to re-capture it, Don Pedro snatches the handkerchief. In the Macready Promptbook, the description of the business ends: "Note./ — If this is done quickly and neatly, it is sure to tell capitally with the audience!" At the end, Daly interpolated a scene of his own devising, in which Claudio sees Borachio waiting under Hero's window and Margaret appearing above when the villain calls "Hero!" "Hero!" [38]

Enter Dogberry and his ancient and most quiet watchmen. From the lines they speak it is clear that they carry bills, and a lanthorn, which Dogberry presently gives George Seacoal. Later, according to the Macready Promptbook, Seacoal drops it; but Borachio and Conrade, who are "both partly intoxicated," do not notice this. Dogberry and Verges are furnished with walking-staffs (in the same book); and George Wilson sent "as his memorial" to William Warren's funeral "a watchman's staff and crook of colored pampas grass, and, suspended from the crook, an old-fashioned lantern of red and white carnations, an appropriate tribute to Warren's inimitable impersonation of Dogberry." [39] When he is puzzled by the difficult questions put to them, Dogberry has sometimes turned for help to Verges, as has Verges to Dogberry. [40] Daly's stage direction, on their exit, is: "Verges *turns back to give further orders, but takes breath, then hobbles after* Dogberry."

When, in Scene 5, they come with their report to Leonato, the Warren-Wood Promptbook has: "Enter Dogberry & Verges OP. they knock at P. S. D. Enter Leonato PSD." Were the old proscenium doors still being used in Philadelphia? It would seem

so. The knocking is ingenious, too, for if Leonato had answered
it himself — and Dogberry would have thundered on the door —
he might have said as he does here: "What would you with me,
honest neighbour?" The fine comic acting of little Keeley as
Verges "culminated," we are told, "When his asinine chief patted
him on the head, and he first bent under the honour, and then
became the taller for it, gazing into his patron's face with an expression of fatuous contentment perfectly marvellous." [41] It is a
fair guess that the business was introduced at Dogberry's "an old
man, sir, and his wits are not so blunt as, God help, I would desire
they were; but, in faith, honest as the skin between his brows."
In the Barrett-Booth Promptbook, Verges crosses repeatedly to
the centre of the stage, during this scene, only to be 'put back'
each time by Dogberry.

In Irving's production, the characters upon entering at the
beginning of Act IV crossed themselves and bowed to the altar.
The fact that Hero's interrupted wedding takes place in a church
was endlessly illustrated, though, as Percy Fitzgerald observed
shrewdly, "the idea of Benedick and Beatrice making love in
front of the high altar is not to be thought of." [42] Many directions
in the Macready Promptbook — where, by the way, an "Altar"
is called for, and a "Boy $\overline{\overline{w}}$ incense on each side" — are concerned
with the wedding guests, who show a lively interest in what is
going on. Thus, when Claudio speaks ambiguously of "what men
daily do, not knowing what they do," "All exhibit surprise"; and,
when he rejects his bride, "All start astonished . . . turn^g to each
other, then all look at Hero, pressing forward"; and again, when
Leonato bids her speak, "All press forward to hear Hero's reply."
Pedro tells of what he has seen, and "All the company recede from
Hero, R&L." Finally, at line 97, "the Company break up, as if
departing, — some X to R — others, to L, — but all stop and turn
wherever they may be, when Claud speaks."

Though Hero may well kneel to her father at line 181 — as she
does in Oxberry's edition — little is to be said for Murdoch's
promptnote at the old man's exit, "Hero goes to Leonato who
waves her off." [43] On the other hand, in its review of Irving's
production, *The Athenaeum*, June 7, 1884, rightly insisted that

she "should not after the scene of denunciation and dishonour be clasped to her father's bosom so soon as the priest expresses his conviction of her innocence." In the same famous production at the Lyceum, characteristic points were made by Irving himself — the "quick, covert look" he gave Don John, early in the scene, as if to show that Benedick was suspicious of the man — and by Ellen Terry, whose Beatrice, "on the Friar's avowing his belief in Hero's innocence" flung herself on her knees and kissed his hand. Ada Rehan, it might be added, as the Friar was outlining his plan to "change slander to remorse," prostrated herself on the steps of the Altar, weeping.[44]

Much of the stage business which has accompanied the speeches of Benedick and Beatrice at the end of this scene goes back to Cumberland's *British Theatre* and is that, presumably, of Charles Kemble. After *"pausing"* before "I do love nothing in the world so well as you. Is not that strange?" Benedick *"takes her hand."* *"Follows and pulls her back,"* before "We'll be friends first," is logical enough. But the curious *"Puts on his hat,"* during the last speech of all, needs explaining. Here the Macready Promptbook has: "Beat with her hand resting on his shoulder, is now in front of Ben and looks up in his face delightedly, — their eyes meet, — he smiles, — and takes her hand"; and, a moment later, "Going with Beat to R, — still kiss[g] her hand, — when she is off he puts on his hat, — arranges his costume, &c — and, drawing on his glove, walks off, very self-satisfiedly."

In the same promptbook, an addition of a good deal of interest is "burst[g] into tears, & fall[g] on his shoulder," at Beatrice's startling "Kill Claudio!" But the older way was still followed. A critic in *The Illustrated London News*, July 10, 1852, becomes excited, indeed, over a "bit of by-play" he has just noticed in the Keans' performance, but he has in mind only "an expressive pause before the declaration of love, a surrender of the lady's hand, and the lover's action in pressing it to his lips."[45] J. H. Barnes as Benedick was left alone on the stage at the end. He "turns to pick up her gloves kisses it [*sic*] & puts in belt as curtain descends."[46]

The new scene (IV, 2) was regularly discovered. Oxberry's edition (1824) furnishes the "dissembly" with "*a table in centre, stool behind it: a great chair* R.H. *of table, and a stool* L. H. Dogberry, *Seated in a great chair*, Verges, *on the stool*, L. H." "If you have not room to discover table," a note in the Barrett-Booth Promptbook directs, "see it ready to be carried on from R 2 E" (The Church Scene, just before, had of course taken much space). Also, I read of a Mr. Miller at Edinburgh, early in 1824, that he "was sufficiently amusing as the informing watchman, only his idea of writing his information on the crown of his hat, was ridiculously extravagant and absurd." [47]

When Leonato exclaims, near the beginning of the last act,

> Nay, never lay thy hand upon thy sword,

Claudio protests,

> In faith, my hand meant nothing to my sword;

and in the Macready Promptbook he is taken at his word: "Claud, without intention, puts his L hand to his side." The young man has been so furiously abused by the critics that it is refreshing to find him getting the benefit of the doubt for once. Benedick now challenges him. "*Claudio bows to the Duke as if to ask assent,*" seems to me happily introduced, in Daly's edition, at "Shall I speak a word in your ear?" Frederick Reynolds, the playwright, had as a Westminster schoolboy seen Garrick as Benedick. Asked, next morning, by Harris, the Covent Garden Manager, in what scene he had liked the great actor best, he replied that it was "where he challenges Claudio," and went on to explain that,

"he there made me laugh more heartily than I ever did before; particularly on his exit, when sticking on his hat, and tossing up his head, he seemed to say as he strutted away, "Now, Beatrice, have I not cut a figure?" "You are right, my boy," rejoined Mr. Harris; "whilst other actors by playing this scene seriously, produce little or no effect, Garrick, by acting, as if Beatrice were watching him, delights, instead of fatiguing the audience." [48]

A glimpse of the Sexton crossing the stage with a paper in his hand was allowed Macready's audience at line 197, a little before Dogberry comes in with the prisoners. And this early entrance fits neatly with what we hear later of the Sexton's having "re-

formed Signior Leonato of the matter" while Dogberry was still
making no progress with his own explanation to Don Pedro.
Murdoch's promptbook has "Dogberry & Verges Bow" at Leonato's "Here stand a pair of honourable men" (line 275), mistak-
ing an ironic compliment bestowed upon their betters for a sincere
one paid to them. With somewhat more excuse, when Don Pedro
in addressing Borachio and Conrade mentions "this learned constable," Daly's edition has: "Verges *is stepping forward*, Dogberry *prevents him.*"

In Scene 2, Tree perversely jotted down on his tablets the
jingling lines beginning "The god of love." "And why should he
not?" asks A. B. Walkley. Only, one might answer, because it was
Shakespeare's clear intention that they should be sung, and because Benedick's next remark becomes meaningless if they are
not.[49] On the other hand, it is pleasant to learn that, in Fanny
Davenport's production, Beatrice's head was on Benedick's
shoulder when she answers his "And how do you?" "Very ill
too." Macready at the close of the scene ran across the stage to
his Beatrice — "I will live in thy heart, die in thy lap, and be
buried in thy eyes." But though "the run was as quick as if it had
been for a wager . . . there was no fervour, buoyancy, enthusiasm, or tender warmth in the act. . . . He was thinking how
he ran, instead of to whom he was running." [50]

As for the last scene of all, Irving, when he came to produce the
play, restudied and enlivened the episode of Benedick's search for
Beatrice. "The old fashion was to make the ladies, clad in horribly gaudy and ill-assorted satins, stand in a row, along which
Benedick stalked," till he found her. Finally, the two sets of
sonnets composed by the lovers are of course not returned to
them. Clara Fisher, in 1830, was praised for her acting here:

Watch her looks when she snatches the stanzas from *Benedick*, the
joy and triumph beaming in her eyes, and the light of successful vanity
and love gleaming altogether from her radiant face; then, when her
own verses are produced, and seized by *Benedick*, mark the change —
rapid and complete as the workings of thought — and then the gradual
yielding, as the archness and merriment break forth again, and she
accepts him — "out of pity, for they told me you were in a consump-
tion!" [51]

The Merchant of Venice

In 1701, Granville's adaptation, *The Jew of Venice* was produced at Lincoln's Inn Fields. Thomas Doggett, an excellent comedian, played Shylock. The ageing Betterton was Bassanio. This performance has been of great interest to stage historians. Was the Jew, in Doggett's hands, a merely farcical character? If so, the part was of course misinterpreted, just as it has been misinterpreted over and over again in the present century. What cannot be too strongly emphasized, however, is that the production of 1701 was a revival of a quite unfamiliar play. *The Merchant of Venice* had been unacted since the Restoration — perhaps for a long time before that. Doggett may have established a tradition. He was not following one.

There is little to report concerning the first two scenes. Charles Kean, in 1858, opened the play with atmosphere — a throng of picturesque Venetians, nobles, inquisitors, flower girls, water-carriers, the Doge, "in state procession," etc. At last Antonio and his friends emerged from the crowd and spoke the first lines. Ellen Terry lounged on a sofa during the discussion of her suitors, in Scene 2, as did Modjeska. Ada Rehan was discovered on a couch, but presently left it and "moved continually." [52]

A famous description of Edmund Kean's Shylock is that of George Henry Lewes: "From the first moment that he appeared and leant upon his stick to listen gravely while moneys are requested of him, he impressed the audience, as Douglas Jerrold used to say, 'like a chapter of Genesis.' " When Kean's theatrical effects were sold after his death, the stick he carried "in the character of Shylock, with curiously carved ivory handle, given to him by Alderman Cox," brought five guineas.[53]

Many of the notes which Edwin Booth contributed to the Furness Variorum *Merchant of Venice* have to do with details of business.

"Shylock enters," Booth writes, "with slow, shuffling gait; restless, half-closed eyes, and the fingers of his disengaged hand (one holds his staff) ever moving, as if from the constant habit of feeling and caressing the ducats that are passing through them." [54]

We read of Lawrence Barrett that "his richly jewelled hands" betrayed "the nervous eagerness" of Shylock, "as they clutch and twine upon his long knotted staff"; and of Irving that "the thumb and first two fingers of whichever hand happened to be free, — for he shifted his staff occasionally from one hand to the other, — were, from time to time, moved slowly, as though in the act of counting coins." Booth himself, when he came to Shylock's long aside, made two lines stand out sharply:

> "If I can *catch* him once upon the hip,
> I will *feed* FAT the ancient *grudge* I bear him."

And here "the hand clutches, rigidly as a claw, at the word *catch*, and dashes its prey toward a devouring maw as the idea of *feeding fat* upon it glances into the expression." [55]

Mansfield's Shylock when he first addressed Antonio,

> Your worship was the last man in our mouths,

spat — to express the Jew's loathing. But this "realistic" detail he later omitted. Another note of Booth's concerns line 111,

> "For suff'rance is the badge of all our tribe,"

where he showed his yellow cap: "I prefer the yellow cap to the cross upon the shoulder which other actors have worn, my Father among them. Cooke used the cap, and said Macklin also used it." Barrett laid "one hand upon his sleeve to show the red cross he wore there." [56] Later in the scene, Irving's Jew approached Antonio and touched him on the breast. Antonio recoiled, disgusted by the familiarity, and Shylock bowed low — not without a suggestion of sarcasm. Seemingly, this was at,

> Go with me to a notary, seal me there
> Your single bond. . . .[57]

Archer, noticing the same action used by Nutcombe Gould, Ben Greet's Shylock at the Olympic in 1897, felt "that it was this which suggested to Shylock the 'merry sport' about the pound of flesh. Mr. Gould had probably no such design, or he would have timed the touch differently and brought out the idea more clearly." At the end, the Christians went out together, leaving Shylock "watching after them" (Booth), or raising his stick and shaking it at them menacingly (Irving).[58]

Charles Kean used a single "set-scene" for Act II. It included

a bridge, under which gondolas pass and repass. . . . Old Gobbo with tottering steps climbs to the top of the bridge and carefully descends. . . . Lorenzo . . . from an elevated station on the bridge, receives the casket from Jessica's casement; the lady herself then comes down, and is carried off in a gondola. Other masquers follow. . . . Anon, there is a rush of illuminated gondolas, on which the curtain falls.[59]

Not only was the action in Kean's own production conditioned by these new scenic luxuries but, as we shall see, Irving took advantage of them in achieving what was probably his most celebrated effect as a Shakespearean actor.

Meanwhile, there is Young Gobbo to consider. Meadows, at Covent Garden, December 30, 1824, was scolded for "racing from O.P. to P. S. during the opening soliloquy of *Launcelot*." So, too, in Daly's production, seventy-five years later, was Wilfred Clarke, who ran "about the stage . . . instead of taking the centre, in the orthodox manner." On the other hand, Mr. A. G. Andrews — the Gardener in Maurice Evans's *Richard II* only a few years ago — when he played Launcelot with Mansfield, in 1893,

made his first entrance from his master's house hastily, then looked round fearfully and, finding himself unobserved, sat down upon the door-step and seriously held self-communion as to the justice of leaving his master's service.[60]

Presently, Old Gobbo appears, carrying a basket. In Pitman's promptbook he has also a staff and wears a "Green eye shade." Launcelot asks his blessing, and the blindman is astonished to find that his son has a great beard. Without action the passage is unintelligible. But Launcelot kneels with his back to his father, "who, of course, mistakes his long black hair for a beard, of which his face is perfectly innocent." [61] I do not know how early young Master Launcelot began to take his father by the shoulders and turn him about, in giving him the directions.[62] Nor have I been able to discover when Launcelot himself began to be bumped by

the young men. Mr. Henry Herbert tells me that the Benson
Company used this business, which was as follows. After delivering the letter to Lorenzo (in II, 4), Launcelot becomes confused.
In bowing to one of the young men he backs into another, bows
in turn to him — and does the same thing. The gentlemen bump
him each time. He takes off his hat to them, and they to him, and
the little farce goes on and on.[63]

In the next scene (II, 5), Launcelot's aside to Jessica requires
nice adjustment. In an acting edition of 1808, Shylock's hat and
cane are on a table, and just before the aside he goes to get them,
"coming forward" afterwards to inquire what the fool has said.[64]
Irving's Shylock went into the house, whence he reappeared carrying a lantern and staff. Hearing Launcelot's voice,

he swiftly advanced to his daughter, as *Launcelot* sped away, seized
her by the wrist, looked suspiciously upon her face and harshly put the
question to her, — pointing with his stick after the departed servant, —
"What says that fool of Hagar's offspring — ha?"

Mansfield's Jew, on the contrary, tenderly embracing Jessica,
kissed her on the forehead. It might be added that the "grotesque
activity" with which old Harley, as Launcelot, "skipped across"
Charles Kean's bridge, was noted at the time. Harley was then, in
1858, making his last appearance on the stage.[65]

Jessica elopes with her lover; and Shakespeare ends the scene
very quietly. There is to be no masque, after all, and Gratiano is
glad of it.[66] But quiet endings had long since gone out of fashion.
At the Lyceum, after Jessica had fled in a gondola, there was a
rushing in of revellers, and on a stage filled with lights, and noise,
and movement, the curtain descended. In response to the inevi-
table applause, it rose again. The stage was deserted now, and only
dimly lighted. You heard the tapping of a stick — Shylock's
stick — and presently the Jew appeared on the bridge, passed
across it, stood expectant at his own door, knocked perhaps, once
or twice, did not go in.[67]

Whatever is thought of the propriety of this interpolation, its
effectiveness is unquestionable. The externals were there before —
the gondola, the bridge, the maskers. The idea of a father's com-

ing to his own door and finding his daughter gone may conceivably have been suggested by Rigoletto's return to his despoiled home, in Verdi's opera. Even so, the business was strikingly original. Its reticence, and the appeal it makes to the imagination, are not to be denied. Irving's successors did not know when to stop. Mansfield's Shylock gave a "yell of surprise and agony" at his loss, and rushed into the street amid "the hoots of the delighted Christians." Nat Goodwin (in 1901) was heard crying out within the house, then appeared, once more, "distraught and dishevelled, bearing in his hand a letter." We are not compelled to trace the history of the business farther.[68]

Late in 1775, Lichtenberg saw Macklin at Covent Garden and describes graphically his entrance as Shylock at the beginning of the third act:

> In the scene where he first misses his daughter, he comes on hatless, with disordered hair, some locks a finger long standing on end, as if raised by a breath of wind from the gallows, so distracted was his demeanour. Both his hands are clenched, and his movements abrupt and convulsive.

When the elder Booth came to Shylock's grim answer —

Saler. Why, I am sure, if he forfeit, thou wilt not take his flesh. What's that good for?
Shy. To bait fish withal —

he would sometimes, "in his tamer moods" make "a gesture as if holding a fishing rod." At a performance in 1850, however, he accompanied the words "with a gesture inexpressibly violent and rapid," as if he were "tearing the flesh, and throwing it into the sea." Mansfield, for a time, pointed toward the canal, by way of illustration. For novelty, Sidney Herbert's Shylock, in Daly's production, entered pursued and jeered at by a mob of children.[69]

In the succeeding passage with Tubal a passionate climax is reached.

Tub. Yes, other men have ill luck too. Antonio, as I heard in Genoa —
Shy. What, what, what? Ill luck, ill luck?

"The impatience of a ravening appetite for the blood of the merchant" found expression in Cooke's manner of speaking the

words and in "the significant eagerness of his ghastly looks and
the clawing of his fingers." In the speech before, a brilliant
though not quite legitimate stroke was made by Kean. W. J. Fox
writes:

> At the exclamation, "I would my daughter were dead at my foot, and
> the jewels in her ear! would she were hearsed at my foot, and the
> ducats in her coffin!" he started back, as with a revulsion of paternal
> feeling from the horrible image his avarice had conjured up, and bor-
> rowing a negative from the next inquiry ("no news of them?"),
> gasped an agonising "No, no, no."

And, anticipating the ideas of certain recent Shakespearean critics,
Fox maintains that "the spirit of the scene is the alternation of the
two passions of anguished avarice and hopeful revenge. There is
no room for a third." [70] In Charles Kemble's performance, "the
suddenly falling on his knees when the intelligence is brought to
him of Antonio's losses, had a very striking effect." Gustavus
Brooke used the same business. Booth, we read,

> is at the back of the stage when he hears these tidings. He flings his
> arms over his head, he comes staggering down in mighty strides to the
> footlights, and sobbing in a delirium of revengeful joy, he flings him-
> self into Tubal's arms, crying all the while, "I thank God, I thank God
> — Is it true? Is it true?" [71]

Irving's Shylock, on hearing of the losses he had suffered, tore
open his robe and repeatedly smote his breast. "I will have the
heart of him if he forfeit." Winter pictures "the tall, attenuated
form, the ghastly, pallid face, the deep-sunken, dark eyes, blazing
with wrath, the jaws champing, the left hand turning the sleeve
up on the right arm as far back as the elbow, and the fingers of the
right hand stretched forth and quivering." It was "as if already
they were tearing out the heart" of Antonio.[72]

   The terms in which stage action is described inevitably color, at
times, our judgment of its worth. Witness the account given by
Margaret Stokes of Helen Faucit's Portia, at the moment Bassanio
is about to choose among the caskets of gold, silver, and lead:

> We seem still to see the upward gaze as of a St Cecilia, with which,
> in silent prayer, and with one knee scarce perceptibly drooped upon
> the cushioned footstool, she awaited the issue. . . . We felt how the

too tumultuous passion had been chastened by that prayer. Subdued, yet intensely happy, she rose from her seat and awaited the approach [of her lover].[73]

What we should have thought of Helen Faucit's business could we have seen it, is one thing. What we are tempted to think of it after reading Margaret Stokes, is quite another.

Ellen Terry in the same scene (III, 2), made departures which aroused criticism. Lady Pollock, indeed, rejoiced that this Portia "did not kneel to Bassanio at 'My Lord, my governor, my King.' I used to feel that too much like worship from any girl to her affianced." [74] But in *Blackwood's*, for December 1879, a different note was struck. During Portia's opening speech, we read, Miss Terry held Bassanio "caressingly by the hand, nay, almost in an embrace, with all the unrestrained fondness which is conceivable only after he had actually won her" — and more is added about " 'fingering of palms,' and laying of hands on arms." The anonymous author of a long paper on "The London Theatres," in *Scribner's Monthly Magazine* for January 1881, renews the attack:

When *Bassanio* has chosen·the casket . . . she approaches him, and begins to pat and stroke him. This seems to us an appallingly false note. "Good heavens, she's touching him!" a person sitting next to us exclaimed — a person whose judgment in such matters is always unerring.

Two additional pieces of business must be mentioned. Winter tells us that, after Bassanio had chosen, Ellen Terry "crumbled some roses and allowed the leaves to flutter down into the leaden casket . . . and then, bending over it, seemed to consecrate it with a kiss." [75] Also, it was usual, after Bassanio's choosing, for Gratiano and Nerissa to act out in pantomime a little courtship scene of their own. How early this byplay was introduced I do not know. "Nerissa gives her Ring to Gratiano" is written in an old hand on the margin of the Harvard copy of Kemble's 1797 edition of the play, just after Portia gives her ring to Bassanio, and a similar direction appears in Mrs. Vandenhoff's promptbook of about 1855.[76]

There is little more to tell until we come to the Trial Scene. At the beginning of the rarely acted Jailer Scene, Antonio in Granville's adaptation enters *"in Shackles."* At the end of the next scene (III, 4), Irving, not content with the simple setting off of Portia and Nerissa on their adventure, must needs introduce realistic detail — the appearance of servants "to correct the disorder of the room." [77]

A great deal of business has been introduced in the Trial Scene — some of it shoddy, or misconceived, some of it deeply impressive. It is curious to imagine what the scene would be like, were it played for once with the utmost austerity, no business being admitted save what is actually called for by the lines. Properties would still be needed: the bond itself, which first Portia and later Shylock asks to see; the money which Antonio's friends repeatedly offer the Jew; Shylock's knife, which at one appalling moment he is sharpening on the sole of his shoe; the scales, too, which he eagerly protests he has ready; Bellario's letter; Bassanio's gloves and ring. A few slight traces of legal ceremonial are perceptible: Portia is formally ushered in; she is assigned a particular place; Antonio and his enemy are told to "stand forth." Then, later, Antonio must 'bare his bosom.' "Give me your hand, Bassanio," he says steadily, when all hope seems gone.

The prosaic attempt to make this trial seem as much as possible like one taking place in an ordinary court of law will explain some of the added business. Even in Granville's version, Antonio *"as a Prisoner"* is attended by "Officers of the Court," and Nerissa as a lawyer's clerk carries a *"Bagg and Papers."* At Covent Garden, October 18, 1788, Mr. Fearon "comported himself perfectly in the Duke — his taking Notes, &c. was good." Helen Faucit first thought of turning to a large book and reading from it the crushing words beginning

It is enacted in the laws of Venice. . . .

Shakespeare's practice elsewhere makes it safe to assume that were this passage intended to be read it would have been in prose. But the book had an aura of legality about it. Ada Rehan even consulted it earlier in the scene when, in reply to Shylock's "Is that the law?" Portia says sternly, "Thyself shalt see the act." [78] I like rather better another idea of Helen Faucit's, that during the speeches of Bassanio and Antonio, beginning at line 264, Portia should quietly confer with the Duke.[79]

Friends of Shylock's have sometimes been admitted to the court-room, as for instance when Dowton acted in the play in 1815. Irving introduced "a knot of eager and interested Jews" among the spectators on the Lyceum stage, and Robert Ganthony, in his amusing reminiscences, tells us that as one of Shylock's friends he always "enlivened matters by offering to lend money to those who personated the Christian [*sic*], at, of course usurious rates of interest. . . . We also talked scandal about Gratiano, Salarino, and others." [80] When, in Mansfield's production, Shylock is offered the doubled and trebled sum, his friends inspected the ducats and pleaded with him to accept them. "There is a grim pause; and Shylock then finally dashes the gold upon the ground and claims his bond." [81]

Irving's Shylock, upon entering, looked about for his victim, at whom he gazed with evident satisfaction. Then, when Bassanio tendered the six thousand ducats, he tapped the open coins with his knife — as if even the sound of the gold was powerless to affect his resolve.[82] He laid no emphasis upon the whetting of the knife. This bit of business had been made much of by the older actors. *The Morning Post, and Daily Advertiser*, November 9, 1781, reports of a performance at Covent Garden the night before that when the scene was reached "where Shylock whets his knife . . . Mr. Macklin was so highly characteristic in the part, that a young man who was in the pit fainted away." Cooke was celebrated for "his savage and determined method of whetting his knife on the floor, and the fiend-like look that accompanied it." [83] And of Kean we read that

> He views *Antonio*, as he whets his knife, . . .
> There was a murderous smile upon his cheek,
> And from his eye some devil seem'd to speak.

He, too, sharpened his blade on the floor, not, as the lines imply, upon the sole of his shoe.[84] Booth directs: "Whet the knife on the sole of the shoe, — not too rapidly." He himself did not, we are assured, descend to the regular clap-trap·by coming down to the footlights and wearing out the boards with the steel blade and twisting up his face like the horribly tragic heads of Japanese sculpture. Rather did Mr. Booth retire up the stage and very quietly prepare to take the pound according to his bond without rant, fuss, or fury.[85]

Cooke's byplay during the "Quality of mercy" speech was justly admired. When Portia came to,

> It is an attribute to God himself,

Shylock reverently bent his head. "We do pray for mercy," she continued,

> And that same prayer doth teach us all to render
> The deeds of mercy.

But at this he only shook his head and waved his hand, as if to deny the application to himself, a Jew. According to Booth, when Cooke was complimented on the idea of Shylock's bowing, at the earlier line, "he said it was Macklin's 'business.'" Helen Faucit boldly appropriated it for Portia, removing her "barrister's cap" and pausing when she came to the words.[86]

It was customary for Shylock, in reply to Portia's "Are there balance here to weigh / The flesh," not only to say that he has them ready but to produce them eagerly. So, for instance, did Young, and Kean, and Irving — whose "grisly promptitude" in taking them from his bosom caused "an hysterical laugh." Just before, at "So says the bond . . . Nearest his heart," this Shylock had pointed to the words with his knife.[87]

At the climax of the scene, we hear praise of Mr. Graham, Charles Kean's Antonio at the Princess's: "Sinking back in a swoon, and held by his friends at the approach of the Jew to take his forfeit, he gradually awoke as from a terrible dream, opening his eyes in surprise at his safety." In Charles Calvert's Manchester production (1871), the influence of sensational melodrama is clearly perceptible:

When the Jew draws his knife, saying "a sentence; come, prepare!" a tableau is formed, accompanied by an orchestral crash and the sound of a gong! Antonio, clad in loose and sombre habiliments, open [*sic*] his vest, and retires into a dark recess conveniently exposed as the intended scene of the ghastly operation. There is too much clap-trap about this.

Antonio *"advances to C. and kneels. All shrink back,"* is the direction in Booth's edition.[88]

At the moment of his discomfiture, Shylock in Granville's adaptation *"starts surpriz'd"* and says "Humph." In later times he has often let his knife, or scales, or both, go crashing to the floor.[89] Irving still dropped them in 1879. In 1884, however, he appears to have given up this quite legitimate device, which goes back to Cooke, at least, if not farther, and merely stood motionless as if dazed by what he had heard.[90] On one occasion, he tore the bond, at

> Why, then the devil give him good of it!

and the words and action go well together. Moreover, as Poel has noted, in the old story in *Il Pecorone*, which Shakespeare knew, "the Jew seeing he could gain nothing, tore in pieces the bond in a great rage." Dowton's Shylock, in 1815, when he heard that he must become a Christian, fell back fainting into the arms of his friends.[91]

Gratiano exults over Shylock. I cannot discover that in early performances his happy crowing was attended by physical abuse — though he sometimes plucked Shylock by the sleeve in scoring his point about the godfathers.[92] In the Booth-Winter edition, however, Gratiano seizes the bag of money which the Jew has taken from Bassanio, at line 337; and when Shylock is *"about to kneel,"* before line 364, he *"holds him by the shoulder, during the rest of the speech, and then drops him."* In 1895, when Otis Skinner appeared as Shylock, Gratiano's behavior toward the defeated usurer was considered brutal, "and when he threw him to the floor . . . the harshness of the action seemed to jar on the nerves." [93]

The restraint of Kean's acting at the moment when Shylock leaves the court-room was striking.

"We are aware of Mr. Kean's idea," writes *The Theatrical Observer*, "he considers the Jew so completely overwhelmed . . . that he ought to represent the mind in calm though bitter anguish. This style . . . loses all effect on the stage, by the circumstance of the only power of expression to indicate this state of feeling, lying in the features . . . the perfect stillness of the frame, the clenched hands, and downcast eyes." [94]

But there was also the look of utter contempt which he gave Gratiano, a look very generally praised — though the provocative suggestion was offered, by one critic, that Shylock would have been unlikely "to bestow a thought on Gratiano, or even be supposed to have heard the jest." [95] Macready followed Kean closely. In Phelps's performance, "the utter prostration" of Shylock's "corporal and mental faculties" was brought out, and the Jew groped his way out, leaning against the wall of the court-room to keep himself from falling. Booth's exit, too, was made with his knees buckling and "shoulders pitifully drooping." [96] As for Irving, there can be no questioning the greatness of his acting at this moment — it was proclaimed over and over again. Like Kean he maintained Shylock's dignity in defeat. Like Kean he withered Gratiano with a look. Then, sighing heavily, he went slowly out.[97] It remains to mention that Richard Mansfield early in 1905 conceived the preposterous idea of having "*Shylock* place the point of his curved knife, inside his dress, at the throat, intimating the purpose or act of suicide, and he spoke the words, 'I am not well,' in a weak, thin voice, as though to signify that the *Jew* was bleeding to death." [98]

In a solemn article (possibly by Sir Theodore Martin) in *Blackwood's* for December 1879, something is said of the older comic treatment of Portia on the stage.

It is not very long since we have seen Mrs. Charles Kean, so far infected by the prevailing tradition . . . that she made her exit after the trial scene, tucking her arms under the back of her doctor's gown, and tripping with the affected gait of the Old Bailey barrister of the stage. We have fortunately got beyond the point where such a feat could be executed with impunity.

Yet Ellen Terry was to 'step jauntily,' or even 'swagger,' as she left the stage. Was it at this point, too, that she kissed her hand to Bassanio behind his back? To be sure, he would not give up her ring! [99]

In the last scene, Robert Ganthony tells of how, playing the small part of the Messenger, at the Lyceum, he used to come in "out of breath" and, while waiting, fix his spur as if it had been roughly used. Irving, he continues, never tired of making minute improvements in his productions and "months after we had been playing the 'Merchant' he called me to him and said, 'It would be better, Ganthony, if your spurs jingled a little more as you entered and crossed the stage ' " — and Ganthony saw to it that they did.[100]

Very rarely are we privileged to catch a glimpse of the business of Restoration players. One such glimpse may possibly be afforded by the stage direction in Granville's *Jew of Venice*, at v, 1 239: "*Walks about as in a Passion.*" It is pleasant to think that the business here referred to was that of the charming Mrs. Bracegirdle. A very different sort of stage business was that with which Charles Calvert chose to conclude the play. Portia's "It is almost morning" must needs be illustrated:

At the end of the speech the pages went round and quietly extinguished the lights; the guests dispersed to the sounds of song and music; the scene became gradually empty, dark, and silent; and the curtain slowly fell. This was a bold stroke of stage art, but it was exquisite in its quiet beauty.[101]

As You Like It

Early in 1723, Charles Johnson's *Love in a Forest*, a version of *As You Like It* with interpolated passages from other Shakespearean plays, especially *A Midsummer Night's Dream*, was put on at Drury Lane. Only some eighteen years later was *As You Like It* itself revived. The play prospered in the years to come, and of course accumulated traditions. But the oldest of these traditions go back only to a time long after any recollection of Elizabethan ways had vanished.

Almost at once we have a physical encounter. "Wilt thou lay hands on me?" Oliver cries. "Wert thou not my brother," says Orlando, "I would not take this hand from thy throat." Oliver, one is sure, is the first to pass from words to deeds; but what precisely he does, there is no way of telling. "Going to strike" is written, evidently by some early actor, in a copy of the 1794 acting edition. Most frequently, Oliver has 'advanced and laid hold of him.' In like manner, I have seen an attempt by Adam to help Oliver to his feet made the pretext for the latter's "Get you with him, you old dog!"

In 1890, exception was taken to Ada Rehan's "rushing rapidly on the stage with a face all smiles, followed, after an interval sufficient to give the audience time to applaud, by Celia coming on in much the same manner, as if the two ladies were playing at a lively game of hide-and-seek." But leading ladies like low comedians have their privileges. Another note concerns Le Beau, who, at the St. James's five years before, carried "a live falcon on his wrist." This bit of antiquarianism worked out badly, for the bird flapped its wings "persistently through all his speeches." [102]

The Duke's guards form a ring. This was sometimes done with ropes and spears, sometimes by the guards kneeling and crossing their spears.[103] Then the wrestling begins. Godfrey Turner, writing in 1883, could remember only two occasions upon which it was done successfully: once at Drury Lane, in Macready's time; once at Sadler's Wells. There "Marston, a Lancashire lad, wrestled superbly, and was as agile as a cat." He

allowed himself to be caught up by Charles, so as to lean over the wrestler's shoulder, while his own feet, being lifted clear above the ground, were coiled round the giant's firmly planted leg. For a few moments this statuesque position was retained; and then, just as Orlando appeared in utmost peril of being thrown, he suddenly regained his footing, reversed the situation, cross-buttocked Charles, and flung him heavily to earth.

Winter describes in detail Daly's arrangement of the bout. Hobart Bosworth, "who played *Charles*, was a large man of commanding presence, an athlete and a trained wrestler." He brought out "the savage animosity" Charles feels toward his adversary. After hurling Orlando from him twice, he rushed upon him "like a maddened bull." Whereupon, Orlando,

stepping suddenly forward . . . whirled upon his heel, reaching over his own shoulder, grasped *Charles* about the neck, and, using as an aid the momentum of that swiftly rushing attack, heaved his body aloft and seemed to dash it upon the ground, with killing force. The feat was, in reality, performed by Bosworth, using *Orlando's* shoulder to pivot upon.

Benson "in his earlier days . . . would lift Oscar Asche, even then no light weight, and throw him clear over his head." [104]
After the defeat of the wrestler come these speeches:

> *Duke.* How dost thou, Charles?
> *Le Beau.* He cannot speak, my lord.
> *Duke.* Bear him away.

But as early as 1774 (when Bell's edition appeared), Touchstone had appropriated Le Beau's line, and he continued in possession of it for more than a century. He even gagged it, in course of time, so that it became *"He says* he cannot speak, my lord." [105] Likewise, he took charge of the removal of Charles's body — and in one instance seems actually to have dragged it off himself.[106] Usually, however, following Kemble's direction (1810), the guards have carried away Charles, with Touchstone going, or rather, strutting before. In James Lewis's copy, the comedian wrote at "He cannot speak, my lord:" — "Puts End of Staff on Chas breast &c."

Rosalind rewards Orlando by hanging a chain about his neck. Helen Faucit stealthily kissed the chain in doing so. Mary Anderson, at Stratford in 1885, approached Orlando carrying a victor's wreath as well as her own chain, and, as she pressed the chain endearingly into his hand, Orlando let the wreath "drop unheeded to the ground." [107] One further variation comes from the so-called "William Warren Edition," based on Julia Marlowe's promptbook, where Orlando goes out at the end of the scene, *"kissing cross on chain."*

A single note must suffice for the next three scenes. When Celia pleads with her father (1, 3, 70), Julia Marlowe's Rosalind *"goes to bench and sits, weeping."* Rosalind must do something here — or do nothing very well. But the actress was criticized for abandoning "herself to such a prone state of sobbing as she did, lying prostrate . . . after the tyrannical Duke's stumping exit up the terrace-steps." She might have "taken her banishment with no less apprehension but with less collapse." [108]

Act II, Scene 3, begins with Adam saying "Who's there?" and
presently he warns Orlando not to come "within these doors."
Francis Gentleman, in 1770, speaks of the scene's changing "to
Oliver's house, Orlando appears knocking at the door, and is
answered by Adam." Orlandos not implausibly continued to
knock on doors for over a century.[109] In two early promptbooks,
Adam goes into the house for the gold. Later, he usually carried
it about with him in a bag, going in, however, to fetch a staff and
other small objects in preparation for his journey.[110]

Rosalind, Celia, and Touchstone find themselves in the Forest
of Arden, at the beginning of Scene 4. Rosalind has a boar-spear,
of course, and should have a cutlass, instead of the little axe she
was accustomed to wear at her belt in nineteenth century performances. Celia often carried a shepherd's crook — and leaned
heavily on Touchstone.[111] Touchstone has sometimes, indeed,
quite forgotten his place. Thus, Lionel Brough, in 1880, laid
Celia's "head on his shoulder, put his arm round her waist," and
patted her cheek, as they went out together, at the end of the
scene.[112] "Business and then Change Scene" is Buckstone's promptnote at this point. The word "Business" standing alone can be
most tantalizing — but not here! "Rosalind follows Corin off,"
reads the Howard Athenaeum (Boston) Promptbook, "Touchstone is following slowly when Celia calls. 'Touchstone.' he turns.
recollects. goes back for her and they Exit together." The same
pleasant bit of byplay turns up in at least three later acting
versions.[113]

Daly's treatment of the songs in Scene 5 was justly praised:

> Sung as they were by Amiens half lying on the ground, with his
> brother exiles stretched on the sward around him . . . they fitted
> naturally into the action. . . . As usually given by a gentleman who
> advances to the footlights and sings not to his companions but across
> the orchestra to the audience, all the dramatic value of these lyrics
> is lost.[114]

Next we have Orlando and Adam; and Orlando should carry
Adam off. Not infrequently, however, he has shirked his assign-
ment and merely led the old man away.[115] In the last scene in the
act, it may be worth noting that in Lester Wallack's promptbook:

"Duke — blesses — repast," just before Orlando rushes in; and "Jaq. Eats" after Orlando has forbidden it — which occasions his "but forbear, I say." At the end, it was usual for Amiens and Jaques to help Adam away, Orlando being now deeply engaged in talk with the Duke.[116]

As for the Seven Ages Speech, the old way was to accompany the "reading" of it with a full display of the actor's powers of mimicry. Darbyshire, in his *Art of the Victorian Stage*, describes a talk he had with Irving after a performance of *As You Like It* at the Prince's Theatre, Manchester, in 1902. " 'If these people are right,' " Irving is quoted as saying,

"how terribly wrong we must have been; who ever heard of or saw Jacques on a rustic stool at a table, from which he gave the seven age speech, and never rose from it, not even on the delivery of the final line." . . . I reminded Sir Henry . . . that he gave the "To be or not to be" speech from an arm chair.

Oscar Asche was to carry informality a step further, and munch an apple during the delivery of the lines — a feat which took, he observes, much rehearsing.[117]

Upon his entrance in the second scene in Act III, Orlando certainly hangs his verses on a tree — or, in Elizabethan performances, on one of "the pillars of the heavens" — and the natural sequence is for Rosalind, when she appears, to find these verses rather than bring others with her. So, at any rate, she does in *Love in a Forest* and in most of the later acting editions.[118] Winter, in a characteristic effusion, describes Ada Rehan's entrance:

When she dashed through the trees of Arden, snatching the verses of Orlando from their boughs, and cast herself at the foot of a great elm, to read those fond messages . . . her whole person, in its graceful abandonment of posture, seemed to express an ecstasy of happy vitality and of victorious delight; her hands that held the written scrolls trembled with eager, tumultuous, and grateful joy.[119]

Mary Anderson had entered singing and sauntering, continued to sing negligently after she saw Orlando's poem, then stopped singing as she read it. It may be added that Ben Greet's Touchstone, in 1896, was pounced upon by Mr. Bernard Shaw for picking up

and reading — as if they were still another of Orlando's composi-
tions — "the impromptu burlesque" beginning "If a hart do lack
a hind." [120]

Soon afterwards, Celia dismisses Corin and Touchstone. In
Daly's version, Touchstone has been impertinently *"looking over
her shoulder and reading in dumb show, winking at* Corin." At
Celia's "Shepherd, go off a little," Touchstone *"orders* Corin *off
with a gesture, when he turns — and is ordered off himself. He
goes with comic abruptness, first picking up the paper, which he
carries off, reading in dumb show."* In the "William Warren Edition" when Celia says "Go with him, sirrah," Touchstone *"points
to himself inquiringly;* Celia *points* L.; Corin *laughs."*

Celia names Orlando as the writer of the verses, and Rosalind
exclaims, "Alas the day! what shall I do with my doublet and
hose?" At this point, the Victorian actress was likely to make a
great to-do about her own legs. Mrs. Kendal put "her hands over
her face" at "Alas the day," then after a pause crossed to where
Celia was sitting and spoke, "half whispering in Celia's ear, 'What
shall I do with my doublet and hose?' " [121] To a writer in *Blackwood's* for September 1890, Rosalind's words are merely an expression

of natural embarrassment, suddenly to find that here is the man to
whom she has lost her heart, by whom "she would be woo'd, and not
unsought be won," and that her man's attire stands in the way of her
being so. . . . What can Miss Rehan mean by pulling down her
doublet as she speaks the words, as though she would accomplish the
impossible feat of hiding her legs under it, — an indelicacy of suggestion at which one can only shudder?

A. B. Walkley, playing "Devil's Advocate," complains that the
American actress "made as much fuss as though she had been
Susannah surprised by the Elders." [122] On the other hand, W.
Graham Robertson writes of Mrs. Langtry that, as Rosalind, she
gave "no new readings," spoke her lines

simply, not chopping them up with "business" or strangling them with
"suppressed emotion." . . . In short, she gave Shakespeare a chance.
. . . One bit of original business I remember which I have never
noticed in another Rosalind. She carefully avoided all vulgar clown-

ing in passages referring to her male attire, but when she spoke the line — "Here, on the skirts of the forest, like fringe on a petticoat," she put out her hand with a perfectly natural gesture to pick up her own petticoat, and finding none, paused awkwardly for half a second.[123]

Meanwhile, Jaques and Orlando have entered, and Rosalind has overheard their talk (Ada Rehan could not forbear clapping her hands "vivaciously, though softly, on hearing Orlando's sentiments"). On the departure of "Monsieur Melancholy," the lover may well begin to 'mar trees' once more [124] — and Rosalind will attract his attention with difficulty. Helen Faucit was praised for the manner in which she hugged Orlando's verses to her heart, as she talked with Orlando himself about them; and Mary Anderson used very similar business.[125]

On January 6, 1825, *The Edinburgh Dramatic Review*, in commenting upon a performance at the Theatre Royal the night before, praises the Audrey of Mrs. Nicol as

most rich and felicitous. There was perhaps an anachronism in her munching a turnip; but, to be sure, since Shakspeare treated the forest of *Ardennes* with a lion, a little thing like this may be overlooked; *argale*, we were very much pleased with the effect of the turnip.

From the terms used, it is conceivable that the eating of turnips was new to Audrey, in Edinburgh, at any rate, but once she had begun it was long indeed before she tired of them. In the Boston, Howard Athenaeum Promptbook, of 1852, she is furnished at her entrance — arm in arm with Touchstone — with a "clasp knife turnip and large sunflower." At "Well, the gods give us joy," Cumberland's old direction, "*Capers clumsily up the Stage*," is kept, with the added note: "during this Sc Audrey produces a knife & turnip and after peeling it cuts and eats it occasionally offering Touchstone a piece." And at the end: "He takes her arm and they go up and off R3E she dancing and singing 'The gods give us joy &c.' " [126]

The natural affinity existing between Audrey and her turnip is made the subject of some highly curious reflections by Arthur Matthison in his essay, "Theatrical Properties," in *The Era Almanack* for 1882. "Woe to the day for *As You Like It*," he exclaims, "should Audrey venture on alone, or the turnip in a rash moment rush on its fate discoupled from its Audrey." That day was fast approaching. In 1885, when Mary Anderson played Rosalind at Stratford, Audrey, indeed, not only "gnawed" a turnip, but one which "had been plucked near Anne Hathaway's cottage." But Marion Lea, Mrs. Langtry's Audrey in 1890, spoke "Is it honest in deed and word? Is it a true thing?" simply and well, instead of drawling it "with a leer between two bites at a property turnip." And in Isabel Irving's performance with the Daly Company, "for the first time *Audrey* became a possible mate for *Touchstone*, and no mere turnip-munching, cherry-cheeked clod." [127] Daly's acting edition has her in the course of devouring "*a huge turnip*," early in the scene. "*Touchstone, annoyed, snatches it and throws it off.*" Then she produces a succession of apples! In the "William Warren Edition" these apples again figure — but there is no turnip.

The scene of the mock marriage, early in Act IV, needs taste and tact if it is to be right. I fancy we should have liked the Orlando of Forbes-Robertson, which puzzled and somewhat offended *The Athenaeum* (October 27, 1888):

> What can we make of an Orlando who accepts his mistress's challenge to woo her in her disguise as a Girton graduate might accept a proposal to analyze a case of modern witchcraft; who declines, until compelled, to kiss the small gloved hand?

But we read, too, of Adelaide Neilson that "her utterance of the simple words 'Woo me! woo me!' to Orlando, as her cheek was laid upon his shoulder, and her arm stole coyly about his neck, was sweet as a blackbird's call to his mate." And when all allowance has been made for the sentimentality of the description, the action described still seems wrong. In Fanny Davenport's promptbook, when Rosalind, hearing that Orlando must be away from her until two o'clock, says " 'Tis but one cast away, and so, come death!" she "cries — Orlando taps her on shoulder — she turns laughing — he retreats"; and on his exit, "Ros. coughs — Orlando reenters — kisses her hand and then runs off." Both bits of business found their way into later acting texts.[128]

As for the episode of Rosalind's fainting near the end of the act, it is enough to note that Oliver had better not catch her, or do

Lewis and Miss Irving as Touchstone and Audrey
(From a photograph in The Harvard Theatre Collection)

more than Celia asks him to do, take her by the arm; that he has
sometimes slapped "Ganymede" cheerfully on the back, at "take
a good heart and counterfeit to be a man"; and that Rosalind has
occasionally indulged in a second (pretended) swoon, at "I pray
you tell your brother how well I counterfeited. Heigh-ho!"
Fanny Davenport, indeed, to get a strong curtain, closed with:
"Ros. faints on bank C. Oliver on R. & Celia on L. of bank. . . .
Picture." [129]

In the first scene in Act V, Touchstone has been accustomed to
follow William about, threateningly, during the speech beginning "He, sir, that must marry this woman," the clown shrinking
before him.[130]

In the concluding scene, Robson's Touchstone, at Cincinnati in
1885, is described with relish by Frederick Warde: "He strutted,
he crowed, and to continue the simile, he flapped his wings with
the triumphant satisfaction of a barnyard rooster." [131] "Salutation
and greeting to you all," says Touchstone — and James Lewis
wrote against the words, in his copy of *As You Like It*, "bows.
Makes Audrey curtsy &c." What she does to occasion his reprov-
ing, "Bear your body more seeming, Audrey" is for the actress to
decide. I have seen her hanging upon Touchstone here.[132] Or
perhaps she merely stands in some ungainly posture gaping at the
courtiers? The stage direction in Cumberland's edition, "*Audrey*,
L. *assumes a stiff and formal air*," presupposes some such display
of loutishness. On the other hand, the observant, if censorious
author of " '*As You Like It*' à l'Américaine," in *Blackwood's* for
September 1890, after remarking that the words are a hint to
Audrey "not to slouch in country fashion before the great folks,"
is shocked to find that in Daly's production Touchstone here
"turned round to Audrey, who is flirting with two courtiers
(*proh pudor!*) and with these words swings her round to him with
the roughness of an angry boor." [133]

Rosalind's final entrance, in early nineteenth century editions,
is slightly postponed. Hymen delivers his first stanza, then *goes
to the Top of the Stage, brings forward* Rosalind, *and presents her
to the* Duke." Anna Seward, in a letter dated July 20, 1786, describes Mrs. Siddons at this moment in the play:

One of those rays of exquisite and original discrimination, which her genius so perpetually elicits, shone out on her first rushing upon the stage in her own resumed person and dress; when she bent her knee to her father, the Duke, and said —

> "To you I give myself — for I am yours";

and when, falling into Orlando's arms, she repeated the same words, —

> "To *you* I give myself — for I am *yours!*" . . .

The tender joy of filial love was in the first [line]; the whole soul of enamoured transport in the second.

A century and more later, Julia Arthur was inspired to bring upon the stage "a lot of monks in an attempt to make the all-round marriage at the end realistic and spectacular." Norman Hapgood, who liked her production, calls this the "only impertinence" in it.[134]

The Tempest

As altered by Dryden and D'Avenant, or in the operatic version based on their disgraceful *rifacimento*, *The Tempest* was popular with Restoration theatre-goers. Those of the eighteenth century, to borrow Mr. Odell's words, "liked all kinds of *Tempests*" — even Shakespeare's at times. In 1838, the original play was restored to the stage by Macready. But even after the time had come when only Shakespeare's words were spoken, the treatment of the play remained insensitive, with suggestion giving place to representation, poetry to spectacle.

John Bull, October 21, 1838, finds fault with a detail in Macready's production, the entrance of Prospero and Miranda in Scene 2. Prospero had come "by a flight of rocky steps with *Miranda* at his heels," which precluded the possibility of her rushing to meet him and making her opening lines the passionate entreaty which the critic would have liked them to be. Tree's Prospero was discovered reading from his magical book. Kemble had Prospero take up his wand and charm Miranda to sleep — as he spoke line 184 — and then, before summoning Ariel, put on his mantle. Both bits of business are at least defensible. But such conjuring tricks as those resorted to by the Boston Prospero in 1856, who by waving his wand caused "*the trunk of a large tree*" to fall, forming "*a kind of rude arm chair*" for himself and Miranda, or by Daly's Prospero in 1897, who in the same fashion caused a young tree to spring up, "*upon which he hangs his robe and rests his wand*," are unworthy of Shakespeare's magician.[135]

Forster writes of George Bennett's Caliban, in 1838:

His first discovery in the hole where he is "styed" was singularly picturesque, nor less so was his manner of grabbling out of it to fly at Prospero, whose wand in a moment flung the danger of his fury down, and left him merely *dancing mad* with impotent fury.[136]

Benson as Caliban "always insisted on appearing with a real fish in his mouth." He also delighted in climbing trees and hanging head downward from their branches. The later Caliban of Beerbohm Tree also crawled from his den "*with a fish in his mouth*," tried to strike his master, at "The red plague rid you/ For learning me your language!" and was repelled, and forced to crouch, by Prospero's wand. Nevertheless, he lingered to hear Ariel's music, and, since Caliban too, like Shylock and Malvolio, could be sentimentalized, became "*transformed*" and was "*moved to dance, making inarticulate sounds as if attempting to sing.*"[137]

Ariel has sometimes waved Ferdinand after him, sometimes led him "*by the power of his wand*"; in Benson's Stratford production in 1891, the young man was "drawn by a silver thread, held by two tiny Cupids," and when Daly put on the comedy in 1897, Ariel entered "*floating in the air, attended by* Nymphs *and* Spirits, *playing and singing;* Ferdinand *following.*" He will do well to kneel at "Most sure the goddess" (line 421).[138] When, in Macready's production, he was disarmed by Prospero, *John Bull* complains that after Ferdinand had flourished his weapon, there was an "actual collision" between sword and wand: "the sword is made to fly over his head, and *Ferdinand* stands gazing at his hand."[139] Kemble has him merely drop "*his point to the ground*," which does very well. At the end of the act, Tree's stage direction is: "Prospero *leads* Miranda *slowly away, followed by* Ferdinand. Caliban *enters carrying wood, and watches the lovers; with hatred in his face he lifts a log to strike* Ferdinand, *but is charmed . . . by* Prospero, *and skulks into his rocky lair.*" Stage business is likely to be most extravagant just before the fall of a curtain.

In a "Memoir of the Late Mr. Emery," in *The Drama; Or, Theatrical Pocket Magazine*, for August 1822, there is a spirited account of the actor's performance at the beginning of Act ii, Scene 2. He approached

terrific tragedy when he described the various tortures inflicted on him by the magician, and the surrounding snakes that "*stare and hiss him into madness.*" This idea . . . was brought before the spectators with all the loathing and violence of desperate wretchedness; the monster, hugged and shrunk into himself, grew louder and shuddered more and more as he proceeded, and when he pictured the torment that almost turned his brain, glared with his eyes, and gnashed his teeth.

Kemble, in his edition of 1806, has Stephano enter with "*a keg in his hand,*" from which Caliban drinks with growing appreciation until at last, when Stephano says "Here, bear my bottle," and gives him the keg, Caliban "*drinks it empty.*" The keg figures also in Oxberry's edition (1823); and here, as Caliban is going out at the end of the scene, he turns his head "*scornfully towards the cell of* Prospero." Finally, Tree not only has Stephano fall over Caliban, soon after the butler's entrance, but when he is in the act of drinking (at line 57) sit on Caliban, "*who gives a cry.* Stephano *is surprised into sobriety.*"

Early in the third act, according to the Boston version of 1856, Ferdinand, after saying to Miranda "I do beseech you," "*bears log out . . . and returns again*" — to continue,

> Chiefly that I might set it in my prayers,
> What is your name?

Tree opens the second scene with Caliban "*discovered seated on the shore listening to sweet music in the air, and weaving a wreath of flowers wherewith to crown his new-found master.*" "*Falls upon his knees,*" is Kemble's direction for Trinculo, at "O, forgive me my sins," and Stephano does the same thing, after his "Mercy upon us!" Tree's Stephano "*strikes at* Ariel *with his staff*" just before this collapse of his courage. And, at the end of the scene, in the Boston version again, Trinculo speaks, "Wilt come? I'll follow, Stephano": "Caliban *is going off first* — Stephano *stops him, and turns him over to* L.H., *and exit* . . . Trinculo *on* L.H. *of* Caliban, *pushes him aside, and follows* Stephano . . . Caliban *takes up keg from* C. *of stage, puts to his mouth and staggers off.*" Tree's ending once more thrusts his own rôle into prominence: "Ariel *leads them about like a will-o'-the-wisp, then flies above them still playing in the air.* Caliban *attempts to dance and sing whilst the others watch him curiously.*"

In Shadwell's operatic *Tempest* of 1674, the episode of the vanishing banquet in Scene 3 is introduced as follows: "*Dance of fantastick Spirits, after the Dance, a Table furnish'd with Meat and Fruit is brought in by two Spirits.*" Alonso and his companions are about to eat when "*Two Spirits descend, and flie away with the Table.*" [140] Horace Walpole, in a letter of August 25, 1757, refers to "the devils in *The Tempest*, that whisk away the banquet from the shipwrecked Dukes"; and Bell's edition has "*Two Devils rise out of the stage with a Table decorated*" — only to "*vanish with the Table,*" a moment later. [141] Kemble has "*Three Spirits, in the shape of* Harpies, *descend on the table, and vanish with it, amidst flames and groans.*" Charles Kean replaced the " 'strange shapes' . . . hitherto represented by ludicrous and unmeaning monsters, with devils' heads and pitchforks," by "naiads, wood-nymphs, and satyrs . . . bearing fruit and flowers, with which they form a table." *The Athenaeum,* nevertheless, found his arrangements "too much like a transformation scene in a pantomime." Nor did the usual staging of a much later time satisfy Percy Fitzgerald. There was about it, he writes in 1908,

an extraordinary suggestion of prose. At a signal there is darkening, and a sort of box — that is, a table rises out of a trap with attendant clatter. . . . The carrying out of the table should not be the common process, lifting and struggling to carry it along. . . . Mr. Tree opened a trap-door and let it down. [142]

When in IV, 1, Prospero bids Ariel hang the glistering apparel "on this line," editors and actors have been at odds as to his meaning. Having decided that clotheslines were unpoetical, and ascer-

tained that "a line" might mean a lime tree, the editors have been
satisfied to believe that Prospero refers to a lime tree here.[143] Not
so, the actors. "Robes/behind/2 to hang em," is the preparatory
note in the Eighteenth Century Promptbook — and "the Robes
are hung on the Line by Devils." Kemble's 1819 edition is more
specific: "*The Spirits stretch a Cord across the mouth of the Cell,
and hang the garments on it.*" And in the Boston 1856 edition,
"Prospero *waves wand — a line appears on the instant, from
2 E. R., and crosses to 2 E. L. H., on which the robes which* Ariel
brings on and throws down on stage, appear hanging." [144]

Ariel's song, "Where the bee sucks," is retained in the 1674
opera, just before the close, and "*Song ended,* Ariel *speaks, hovering in the Air.*" But flyings, which were a feature of Restoration
performances of *The Tempest,*[145] at length passed out of fashion.
Macready was greatly excited over re-introducing them, for Miss
Horton as Ariel in 1838. "Our aim," he said at the end of his first
season of management, "has been fidelity of illustration. The
'delicate Ariel' is now no longer in representation a thing of earth,
but either 'a wandering voice' or a visible spirit of air, flitting in
his own element." [146] The innovation was widely praised. Robson, indeed, "the Old Play-Goer," looks back to the Kemble
days when "whole columns were given to the various beauties of
a Prospero, who . . . was not . . . concealed behind the pretty
scenery, or eclipsed by a little girl, ridiculously drawn across the
stage by ropes or wires or some such gear, making believe to
fly!" [147] But spectacular flights and ascents had become part of
the play. One even hears of Ariel's riding astride on "a 'practica-
ble' bat of huge size." [148]

Spectacle was likely to eclipse all else at the end of the play, as
in Charles Kean's production in which Prospero's ship was seen
to sail away, with Ariel, "alone in mid-air, watching the departure
of his late master," or at the Queen's Theatre in the autumn of
1871, when Prospero's ship again put to sea, but with Caliban this
time remembered at the last. Tree introduced a whole series of
pictures. The curtain fell, then rose again showing the ship on the
horizon, and Caliban "*stretching out his arms towards it in mute
despair.*" [149]

The Merry Wives of Windsor

This very popular comedy was frequently performed in the early Restoration years. It was revived in December 1692, and again, after the failure of a vicious alteration — Dennis's *Comical Gallant* — in the spring of 1704.[150] It has rarely been long from the boards in subsequent times.

Tree, in 1902, opened with a street scene and such inventions as Anne Page's greeting Fenton from her window and Falstaff's entering upon "a big white horse." Presently, we have the bullying of Slender by the knight's followers, and this used to be accomplished with almost stylized symmetry as each in turn stalked up to the poor witling — "you Banbury cheese!" etc. — and then returned to his place. Much the same ritual was performed anew just before their departure. Daly, however, varied the business. Bardolph merely shook his fist in Slender's face:

he is frightened and retreats a little. . . . Nym *then approaches* Slender, *draws his sword, and flourishes it over his head* . . . *as* Slender . . . *backs against* Pistol, *who glares at him, draws his finger across his throat, and exits.* . . . Slender, *greatly scared, runs to escape, and collides with* Simple . . . *then seeing who it is, seizes and shakes him.*[151]

Meanwhile, in Hackett's promptbook, Falstaff after putting Mrs. Ford's arm in his and kissing her, turns, and "seeing M^{rs} P — 'Ah' takes her arm too." Then, as he had been doing since early in the century, he went out with one of the merry wives on each arm.[152]

When, in I, 3, Falstaff turns away his followers, action regularly accompanied his words ("Rogues, hence, avaunt!" etc.). "*Driving them round the stage*," is Oxberry's direction here. By Hackett's time, this had become, "Drives Pistol & Nym all round Stage to R . . . They look at him as much as you couldn't come it"; and, at the end of the speech, "Ugh! kicks."[153] In Daly's edition, the scoundrels especially provoke Sir John by throwing down their letters, which they will not, and he cannot pick up.

At Dr. Caius's house, Mrs. Quickly has sometimes been busily sweeping when her master returns.[154] "Tarry you a littel-a-

while," he says to Simple, then begins to write. In Cumberland's
edition (c. 1827), he says, "Tarry you a little while *on that spot
all your life*" — and goes out. Simple of course edges away from
the designated spot, and runs back to it on the Doctor's reappearance. Then, when Caius starts to go, it is only to return again
"for' his scarlet Cloak." "Follow my heels, Rugby," he says — and
"Rugby *runs and treads on his heels.*" [155]

An ingratiating bit of realism in Act II, Scene 1, has to do with
the Host's setting forth to see the encounter between the Welshman and Dr. Caius. "Will you go, cavaleiros?" he says, at line
228. Then, according to Daly, he goes *"into Inn for his hat,"*
reappearing, *"with hat on,"* ten lines later — "Here, boys! here,
here! Shall we wag?" Scene 2, in which Falstaff entertains
Master Brook, is much richer in business. "French's Standard
Drama" is an excellent guide. The property-man and scene-
shifters were set to work at the beginning: "One oak chair and
large arm-chair carried on . . . and placed in centre. . . . Large
purse of money for Ford. Salver covered with a white napkin,
on it a tankard of ale, and a napkin folded up on it, ready . . . for
Bardolph. Purse for Falstaff." At the end of Falstaff's long speech
to Pistol ("Reason, you rogue, reason," etc.), the knight *"kicks
at him, goes up and sits in arm chair* L. *of table — a pause —*
Pistol *on* L. *goes entreatingly to* Falstaff." Then, after Mrs.
Quickly is announced by Robin, Sir John says (no longer in the
words of the text) "Hence, rogue, avaunt" and *"turns away from
Pistol, who approaches him on his* L. *as he nears him, he raises
cane to strike* Pistol *who runs off."* "Go steal and hang," Falstaff
flings after him. Much of this business (including the gag) lasted
on for years to come.[156] Master Brook is now called in. "Such
Brooks are welcome to me," Falstaff remarks, "that o'erflow such
liquor" — and, in Bartley's performance, he wiped his mouth.
Burton's manner of drinking was highly praised. "We have never
known a Sir John to pull away so heartily at his tankard of sack,"
a writer in 1853 protests, "his face emerges heated and flustered;
his breath is recovered with difficulty; his eyes roll with incipient
apoplexy." [157]

In the third scene, Caius of course fences a little with the helpless Rugby; and of course, at the Doctor's exit, Rugby again treads on his heels.[158]

That Evans and the Frenchman should actually fight, early in Act III, is unlikely. Nor is this implied in older accounts of the scene. A pleasant detail in Edwin's performance as Sir Hugh, at Covent Garden, October 9, 1789, is mentioned in one of the newspapers of the time:

> When Shakspere with such accumulated strength of phrase, said, "He hath, by wearisome petition, wrung from me my slow leave" — more compelled yielding is not implied, than was in Edwin's single action, when Sir Hugh drew the sword.

It was a "rusty rapier," too, as we learn from a poetical address spoken eight years later.[159] By about 1820, a fight was regularly introduced.[160] "Slender gets between them and gets hit and says 'Sweet Anne Page,' " according to Bartley's book; and, in Hackett's, decorum has vanished: "They fight & roll over & over C Caius supported on knee of Host Page assists Evans . . . Rugby & Simple fight." A climax of absurdity is reached in the version printed in "French's Standard Drama." The combatants are, it is true, deprived of their rapiers by Page and the Host, but *"they pull off each others wigs — throw them at each other"*— struggle, and roll about. After they have been separated, they thrice *"attempt to get at each other. . . . During the fight* Slender *ascends tree in* C. *and says,* 'Sweet Anne Page.' Rugby *and* Simple *go through the same business at back that is done in front by their masters."* When the fight is over, Caius and Evans *"pick up wigs, get the wrong ones, exchange them, put them on, etc."* At last, they embrace (as do Rugby and Simple) and go out arm in arm. Benson, it may be added, kept a great deal of this fooling — and Daly, also, even to Slender's climbing the tree! [161]

For comedy of a higher order, there is Mrs. Cowden Clarke's description of John Leech's Slender, in the famous Dickens-Lemon performance at the Haymarket in 1848:

> His mode of sitting on the stile, with his long, ungainly legs dangling down, during the duel scene . . . looking vacantly out across "the fields," as if in vapid expectation of seeing "Mistress Anne Page" . . .

ever and anon ejaculating his maudlin, cuckoo-cry . . . was a delectable treat.[162]

The business in the Buck-basket Scene is clear enough and lively enough, in itself, to make any exercise of invention on the actors' part unnecessary. As Falstaff addressing Mrs. Ford says, "This is the period of my ambition," he has sometimes kissed her hand.[163] Robin's entrance (in Hackett's book) interrupts him later, just as he is preparing to kiss her. Daly is to be blessed for one admirable idea:

Mrs. Page. Your husband's coming hither, woman, with all the officers in Windsor, to search for a gentleman that he says is here now. . . . You are undone!

Whereupon, "Falstaff *is seen running about uneasily behind the curtains.*" She "*digs at him in the basket*" is also attractive — "You dissembling knight!" And, finally, when Ford has gone to search the house, Bartley's promptnote is: "The two wives laugh & embrace."

Of the fifth scene (Falstaff and Brook, once more), it will be enough, perhaps, to note that, on Sir John's entrance, Bardolph is to "support him," according to the Bartley Promptbook; that the knight regularly threw himself into his great chair, at the end of his bitter reminiscences; and that Daly closed the scene with Bardolph removing the same chair, "*after tipsily stumbling over it.*" Was it, by the way, in this scene that Oscar Asche, with the Benson Company, devoured "an entire fowl . . . tearing it limb from limb with his fingers and throwing the drumsticks at Bardolph"? [164]

At the beginning of Act IV, Scene 2, French's edition calls for the discovery of the buck-basket, "*with plenty of linen, and a very large bundle tied up in a white sheet at bottom, a quantity of white muslin on top, to have the appearance as if* Falstaff *was in the basket when* Ford *comes on.*" Aside from this pleasant touch — and a Hackett promptnote, before line 66, enjoining the merry wives to "pull Falstaff from one to the other" — the business has to do, almost wholly, with the maltreatment of the old woman of Brainford. "I'll prat her," Ford cries furiously, then, in the Hackett book, "takes Mrs P^e by the hand turning her round to his L. & curtsies to Fal — at Fal 3d curtsy hit him a h-ll of a rap with stuffed stick follow to LH bus." Lewes gravely suggests to Charles Kean "that in one place he transgresses the limit set by good taste . . . I mean where he *kicks* the old woman of Brentford." [165] Daly's direction runs:

> *He makes a strike at him, and* Sir Hugh, *who has come round to peer into* Falstaff's *face, receives the blow intended for him.* Falstaff *courtesies again, and* Caius *this time receives the blow.* . . . . *Finally* Ford *seizes* Falstaff *by the shoulder and begins to beat him. He bellows, and is finally beaten round the stage and out of the door.*

As for Tree, he crawled on the floor, "encumbered with the dress of the old fat woman . . . while *Ford* belabors him over the buttocks." What was more, "by pulling a string, a quantity of vegetables, — turnips, carrots, etc., — fell from the woman's bag. Ellen [Terry] used to pick up some of them and pelt Falstaff." [166]

Sir John reads the letter brought him by Mrs. Quickly, and once more succumbs to temptation. Henderson's acknowledged excellence in byplay was shown in this scene:

> First, you saw, that he had "his belly full of Ford;" — her messenger even was an object of detestation. He glanced over the beginning of the letter, and pished at its apologies. He turned again to the messenger, to see how her air was in unison with the language of her mistress. The Cudgel of Ford then seemed to fall upon his shoulders, and he shrunk from the enterprise. He read a sentence or two of the letter,— a spark of lechery twinkled in his eye —

he looked again at Mrs. Quickly, and at length determined "to risk the *third* adventure." [167]

I have discovered very little business of interest in the concluding scenes. Kemble remembered to have Falstaff enter "*shaking*," or "*clanking a Chain.*" Cumberland has the fairies "*lay hold of each others garment, and run after* Evans *round the stage*" (in v, 4), and they beat Falstaff with wands. The rattles which the fairies are to carry have been sometimes sprung, alarmingly, just before they enter. Also, Caius has occasionally vented his chagrin upon his own hat, throwing it down and kicking it off, as he leaves the stage.[168]

A Midsummer Night's Dream

Pepys saw, and could not abide *A Midsummer Night's Dream* in 1662. Thirty years later, an operatic version, *The Fairy-Queen*, made its appearance, first of a long line of adaptations through which alone the play survived until the genuine revivals of the nineteenth century.

Although there is not much business in the first act, what there is gives a good idea of what is to come. There is spectacle. At the Broadway Theatre, in 1854, a procession began the play. *"Athenian soldiers with their officers . . . form on each side of the stage to receive the Duke,"* who appears, for no particular reason, in a galley.[169] There are attempts, through business, to make the lovers, Demetrius and Lysander, Helena and Hermia, as "real" as possible. Daly's edition is full of directions designed to this end. On seeing Lysander and Hermia, Helena *"starts with a pang, and* Hermia *advances smilingly."* At line 196, Hermia *"turns from* Lysander *pettishly, and crosses"*; at line 200, "Lysander *kneels at her feet and kisses her hand"*; at 201, Helena *"throws herself on seat and buries her head in her hands."* Against the success, and indeed the propriety of such attempts, is the deliberately formal character of the speeches. Nor is Helena to be transformed into a tragic heroine by such shifts as flinging her down repeatedly when, later in the play, she is pleading with Demetrius. There is, finally, business of a quite legitimate and edifying sort for Bully Bottom and his friends.

Quince. Here is the scroll of every man's name which is thought fit, through all Athens, to play in our enterlude . . .

and in Wright's promptbook, "they all crowd round Quince in centre looking over scroll which he holds in his hands." Even when Daly, by means of some characteristic shuffling of the lines, holds up Bottom's entrance (*"in a hurry"*) until his name is called, it is something, to remember that Hamlet's entrance, too, was sometimes retarded. And Bottom's exit reproduces in effect a celebrated bit of business in *Henry VIII* —*"The rest are hurrying to get out past him: he stops them, to pass before them."* [170]

At the beginning of Act II, the appearance of Robin Good-
fellow has often been contrived sensationally. He rises on a
mushroom; is discovered behind a fan, which suddenly disappears;
a fairy waves her wand at a "flower piece," which *opens and
Puck comes out.*[171] On the other hand, Robin's acquaintance,
the Fairy, entered in Daly's production *"plucking flowers"*—
since, as she says,

> I must go seek some dewdrops here![172]

Oberon and Titania have sometimes been provided with "cars",
and sometimes the Indian child has been conspicuous among
Titania's attendants.[173] At Oberon's

> I do but beg a little changeling boy
> To be my henchman,

Daly caused him to advance toward the canopy under which the
child had been shown *"reclining on a silver couch."* Instantly, *"at
a gesture from* Titania *the curtains are closed. . . .* Oberon *orders
his attendants to advance, and he dashes toward the couch to seize
the child. He tears aside the curtains, and finds that it has disappeared."*

In Phelps's promptbook, when Oberon is telling his "gentle
Puck" all about the flower he is to fetch, and asks him if he
remembers the time when the mermaid sang so sweetly, "Puck
pauses — scratches his ear, and appears to think." Then, when
he has received his orders, he "runs up bank RC. at back and
speaks his lines disappearing behind tree — at the same time Figure of Puck flies off L U. E." A similar contrivance was used in
Charles Kean's production, when Ellen Terry was Robin Good-
fellow.[174] Daly's production, at the Garrick, July 9, 1895, was
reviewed by Mr. Bernard Shaw. Miss Lillian Swain, he writes,

announces her ability to girdle the earth in forty minutes in the
attitude of a professional skater, and then begins the journey awkwardly in a swing, which takes her in the opposite direction to that in
which she indicated her intention of going.

And, summing up, Daly "swings Puck away on a clumsy trapeze
with a ridiculous clash of the cymbals in the orchestra, in the full-

est belief that he is thereby completing instead of destroying the effect of Puck's lines." [175]

A single note must suffice for II, 2. When Hermia, awaking from her dream, finds Lysander gone, Phelps showed her desperately searching for him, at the close: "Exits into 1EL. returns — goes a X to R.1.E. Exits and Returns — into R. 2. E. and returns finally Exits L. U. E. at which RING."

At the beginning of the third act, the hard-handed men are busily rehearsing. According to Wright's promptnotes, Davidge and his associates at the Broadway entered "studying their parts." When the question of lighting is raised, "all crowd around Quince" to hear what the almanac says. Presently, "they sit on stage studying their parts. Quince in Centre — back to Audience in front of footlights." And Bottom, after being corrected in his reading, first looks at his part, then at Quince, and begins again, "pronouncing the word 'odors' very strong & emphatic." Phelps's promptbook reads: "Bottom stops — then slowly refers to his part — scratches his head on finding his mistake — goes on with his part."

Then he is "translated" — and there is something to be said for Reynolds's idea in the 1816 adaptation that he should be *about to embrace* Thisby" when "Flute *and all look up, and show horror and astonishment.*" Near the end of the scene, when Titania cries,

Thou art as wise as thou art beautiful,

Phelps has Bottom bow "most profoundly — his ears working"; [176] and, a few lines later, "Embrace — Bottom rubbing his Asses head against her face — she patting his head." Sometimes, he has been garlanded, as he departs; and, in Wright, "when going off./Winks. when up L./turns and winks." [177]

Act III, Scene 2, has little for us. At Covent Garden in 1840 (the Vestris production), "Puck *waves his hand, and a thick fog pervades the scene. (gauzes 2nd and 3rd entrances).*" [178] Then one by one the lovers return, to lie down and await the coming of dawn. And the scene has often closed with a mustering of fairies, perhaps merely flying about, perhaps themselves "sinking into sleep" — which after what Oberon has just said is as wrong as possible.[179]

Burton as Bottom
(From an engraving in The Harvard Theatre Collection)

"Robin, take off this head," Oberon commands, early in the fourth act and, a few lines later, Robin says,

Now, when thou wak'st, with thine own fool's eyes peep.

"*He takes off the Ass's Head*" is quite properly the stage direction here, in *The Fairy-Queen* (1692). At the Broadway, Bottom conveniently rolls off the bank on which he has been sleeping, and is thus concealed when Theseus enters.[180] Daly was inspired to have this entrance made in a barge, and in due course of time the barge sets out again for Athens, a "panoramic illusion" of the Duke's passage to his capitol being introduced, which Mr. Shaw found "more absurd than anything that occurs in the tragedy of Pyramus and Thisbe." It may be added that Cooper, an actor of the Kemble school, when as Theseus he was describing his hounds, used "to count them, as in imagination, with his forefinger"; and that in the Broadway production certain hounds were actually brought upon the stage, for Theseus to pat.[181]

In *Notes and Queries*, December 12, 1868, appeared a letter from Brinsley Nicholson, in Australia, on the subject of Bottom's soliloquy as he is awaking from his dream.

"He then," writes Nicholson, "dreamingly and yawningly uses 'Heigh-ho,' the human particle of speech most nearly resembling a donkey's bray. . . . In like manner, when his vanity will not allow him to say in words what he bethought himself he was, and what he bethought himself he had, there can be no doubt but that he doubtingly, but half believingly, felt for the tips of his Midas ears."

To this came a reply, on January 2, suggesting that Nicholson had not seen Phelps in the part, since that fine actor had certainly felt musingly for his late adornments. So, indeed, *Punch* had remarked some years before: "He [Phelps] goes off thoughtfully and slowly, feeling in the air for his long ears and nose, which he cannot comprehend how he can have lost." [182] The engraving of Burton here reproduced, shows rather an explanation to the audience of what Bottom means than a gesture which Bottom himself might conceivably have made.[183] I have already noted, in my preface, the delightful idea, attributed to G. R. Weir, of Bottom's discovering hay in his pouch.[184]

As for the "tedious brief scene" of Pyramus and Thisby, **a great** deal of business has, of course, been invented to accompany its performance. One detail comes from Shakespeare's own time. In Edward Sharpham's comedy, *The Fleire* (1607), mention is made of one who "like *Thisbe* in the play . . . has almost kil'd himselfe with the scabberd." Furnival was convinced that "this bit of business . . . became a tradition on the Stage, and was followed by the actor [Mr. Saker] who playd Flute with Charles Kean between 1850 and 1860"; though Mr. Righton, "the last actor who playd Flute to Phelps's Bottom at the Gaiety in 1875 . . . stabd himself with the sword hilt, his own thumb, or anything that came handiest." I should greatly like to believe with Furnival in this matter, and it is possible that more Flutes may be discovered who have died "traditionally." [185]

When Madame Vestris gave the play at Covent Garden in 1840, some of the properties used were the following: a "lighted lantern hung by a pitchfork," as it was often to be, in later productions;[186] a "live dog of mongrel breed"; a "sponge with blood for lion," which seems to me a very happy thought; and a "deal quarter staff," to be wielded instead of a sword? Thisby *"dies — placing his head on* Bottom, *who pushes it off."* Wright's promptnote is:

> Takes Pyramus Sword up . . . stabs herself 3 times — (2d time a gutteral sound of, oh!) lies down alongside of Pyramus (having arranged her dress first) lays her head on his breast, he raises his head and removes her head from him and lies down again. Thisbe places her head again on his breast.[187]

Also, when Bottom, misunderstanding the Duke's aside, answers, "No, in truth, sir, he should not," he "takes his part from his pocket," and "looks over it for a moment," to make sure (Weir, in 1892, "thrust his *rôle* under Theseus's nose").[188] In Wright's book, finally, Moonshine, coming down stage to speak his first line, "treads on Lions tail. a Roar. The Lion tugging & pulling to remove it. Same time Moon is addressing the audience in action. Lion rises — and strikes Moon on shoulder, who removes off the Lion's tail — Lion then puts on head and lies down." [189]

Phelps's promptnotes deserve a paragraph to themselves. Pyramus has a "Roman Sword" and Moonshine a "wooden dog on wheels." At the end of the prologue, "Bottom is abstracted

— Quince nudges him — he starts and walks off — followed by Quince." Pyramus, after his imprecation, "pushes Wall more to R." But it is again in the way a little later: the lovers "take hands and are going off. but are impeded by Wall — they let go — pass Wall — rejoin their hands and go off." The Lion "enters on all fours . . . then stands up right and takes off his Lions head and bows R and L. — His tail curling and wagging — worked from R.U. E. by strings." And this action he repeats on his exit, "taking up his tail." After stabbing himself "on each side and on the breast," Pyramus falls. He raises "his head and cooly places his sword away from him — then lies again." Thisby, returning, "kneels beside him," and at "Speak, speak!" "bumps his head on stage." She now "takes up sword and stands in front of body — first crawling over Pyramus to get it" — stabs herself, and

falls across his feet. Pause — Pyramus. then raises his head. looks at Thisbe and tries to shake him off — after one or two efforts, does so; Thisbe turning heels over head backward — Pyramus then gets up — picks up his sword — and seeing Thisbe at his feet. Kicks him once or twice . . . they go off bowing — Pyramus giving him a push as they get up to R. U. E.[190]

As for the reappearance of the fairies, in the Vestris production they darted about carrying *"illuminated lamps of various colours."* Spectacle is again to the fore, with ascents through traps, flying on wires, and in Tree's production columns which became luminous "at the touch of Oberon's wand." [191]

The Taming of the Shrew

A grimy alteration, Lacy's *Sauny the Scot*, supplanted Shakespeare's comedy from 1667 until well into the eighteenth century. *Catharine and Petruchio*, Garrick's miniature version, acted in 1756, was much too popular in succeeding years to make demands for the revival of *The Taming of the Shrew* insistent, and it remained unacted until the productions of Webster and Phelps at the middle of the nineteenth century. In 1932, G. R. Foss could write of Shakespeare's play, that "if the principal plot . . . is apt to suffer from the amount of comic business traditionally associ-

ated with Garrick's version . . . . the underplot is handicapped by
having no traditions and no models on which to mould itself." [192]

Thus it is with the mysterious disappearance of Christopher
Sly. In Webster's interesting production without scenery, the
tinker gradually fell into a drunken stupor, during the fifth act,
and was carried away at the close. With Phelps and Daly, sleep
descended upon him sooner, and it became matter of course to
remove him at the end of the first act.[193] Only two bits of business concerning him are worth recording. At Sadler's Wells,
when it was suggested that he might like to wash his hands,
"Christopher, when he has grasped the fact that a basin is being
held before him . . . enters upon such a wash as sooty hands of
tinkers only can require, and, having made an end of washing and
bespattering, lifts up instinctively the corner of his velvet robe to
dry his hands upon." [194] And, in the promptbook made by Becks
for Daly's production, Sly's "Madam" curtsies, saying

> I am your wife in all obedience;

then, "when page rises from curtsy — he trips & as about to fall
— Sly — prevents her & comically (with Pride) passes her (him)
round to R chair!! Page enjoys it behind fan."

From Becks, likewise, comes a little business in Act I. When
Baptista has shown Bianca out, in the first scene, "Luc Xs at back
& peeks in & up & about the house & throws kisses"; and, at the
end, Tranio begins to put on airs: "Tranio — goes up — stamps
to call the attention of Bion — & in action 'follow *me*!' Bion
bows & follows both laughing." Daly postponed Katherina's
entrance until the second act when Ada Rehan, Winter writes,

> swept in, driving *Bianca* along with her. . . . As she moved to and
> fro, in tempestuous rage, it became easy to appreciate the dread of her
> which had previously been expressed. . . . After a moment, as *Bianca*
> ended her speech of supplication, she suddenly came to a menacing
> stand, towering over the frightened girl . . .
>
> > *Of all thy suitors*, here I charge thee, tell
> > Whom thou lov'st best.

Presently Hortensio appears "*with his forehead bloody, and a
broken lute in his hand.*" This direction goes back, indeed, to

Kemble's time, but Becks adds to it the words, "as if flung out —
he falls C — They aid him." [195] Kate of course is walking angrily
up and down while Petruchio talks of her limping — rather, "her
princely gait." *"Bends on one knee"* (a Cumberland direction)
is serviceable when he invites her to use him as a "join'd stool" —
"Come sit on me." [196]

In Kemble's own marked copy of *Catharine and Petruchio*, the
ominous words "whip for Petruchio" are written opposite the
Tamer's entrance in the Wedding Scene (iii, 2); and subsequent
Petruchios were to crack their whips almost continuously
throughout the remainder of the play, Ben Webster, for instance,
"with a hearty determination that always made an effect upon the
audience," and John Drew, it was said, 'orchestrally'.[197] Whether
the stately Kemble led the way in this matter, seems to me more
than doubtful. Petruchio has a fair amount of beating to do —
even in Shakespeare, let alone Garrick — and he has just dis-
mounted from the most decrepit of nags. As for his return from
the ceremony, he comes *"singing and dancing,"* in Kemble's edition (1815), and in the Sothern and Marlowe production, at the
very close of our period, shocked some of the critics by repeating
on the stage some of the excesses hitherto merely described —
seizing the vicar and throwing him against his clerk, etc.[198]

The scene has often been worked up to an exciting climax.
Even in Cumberland's edition (1828), Baptista *"draws his sword."*
In an acting text of 1839 ("Hind's English Stage"), *"the company
draw their swords."* The Walnut Street 1848 Promptbook reads:
"The Ladies give a faint scream and cling to the gentlemen. The
Servants retreat" — to which is added in a later hand, "Hortensio
& Baptista draw & attack Petr. who defends himself and at the
same time pulls Catherine up stage Business & change Scene."
Becks writes of Petruchio in the Daly performance: "he draws —
seizes Kate. she takes his whip from his belt — lashes him." Again,
the "Gentlemen draw . . . general confusion." Benson, finally,
"used to carry a kicking Katharine right off on one shoulder." [199]

On October 15, 1870, *The Athenaeum* initiated a series of
attacks which were to continue for a generation upon the manner
in which *The Taming of the Shrew* was performed on the English

stage. Petruchio's design is quite clearly one of deliberate mis-representation —

> As with the meat, some undeserved fault
> I'll find about the making of the bed. . . .
> This is a way to kill a wife with kindness —

Whereas, in the theatre, "Petruchio ceases to be unreasonable. The meat provided is indeed black as a coal, — so black, as to smurch the face and dress of the cook, at whom Petruchio throws it," and the gown "is a worn, faded, and ridiculous garment no woman of taste or reason would consent to wear." [200]

The blackening of the cook's face was only one of the enormities practised in the scene of Petruchio's home-coming. When, in the Walnut Street Promptbook, Petruchio is heard calling off-stage, " Servants retreat & form a line R. Grumio hides behind them"; and he is "peep[g] over Servants Shoulders. R. Cor[r]" when his master asks for him. Curtis, a female servant since the eighteenth century, does indeed help Kate off *"with her Fardingale,"* in "French's Standard Drama" (c. 1853). But, though Julia Marlowe's Shrew went behind a screen to receive similar attentions, she emerged wearing wooden shoes, the clatter of which was felt to add "appreciably to the general effectiveness." [201] Becks's promptnote tells us enough about the pulling off of Petruchio's boots: "Extends leg — a servant bestrides it to pull boot off. . . . Kicks him flat on his face Kate alarmed up L." Next comes a servant with water —

> Come, Kate, and wash, and welcome heartily.
> You whoreson villain! will you let it fall?

Walter Leman, in *Memories of an Old Actor*, tells engagingly of his first appearance on the stage. It was at the Tremont Street Theatre, Boston, in the season of 1827–1828. He had been promised the part of "Nicholas," in *Catharine and Petruchio*, and was much gratified, though he could learn little about it except that it was not very long and "principally *business*":

The rehearsal progressed as far as the scene in which Petruchio brings home his shrewish bride, and . . . administers his first lesson by whipping and beating his affrighted servants around the stage . . . while the scared wife stands trembling at the violence of a temper worse than her own. Doyne [the prompter] here shouted out to the property man to "bring the wash-bowl for Mr. Leman," and Mr. Leman found out that [Nicholas] was one of the mob of menials which Petruchio whips around the stage — not a word to say, but to come on . . . with a basin full of water, tumble over his master's legs, breaking the basin with a sprawl, and run off with a howl to avoid the angry thwacks and blows which fall impartially on all around.[202]

Finally, there is the episode of the mutton. Here gags began to be inserted early, as blame for the disaster was passed back and forth among the servants. "The cook," according to Becks, "is generally played with palatal tones — 'Muttle,' " etc.[203] In the Walnut Street Promptbook, Petruchio asks "What's this?" "Holding up leg of mutton," and "Cook sneaks behind servants." When his presence is demanded, "Gru. who has hid under the table C. pokes out his head & calls. 'Cook' Pet. beats him with the leg of mutton." At last he drives them out, and Becks writes: "They fall — stumble over each other — he storms & raves — & Kate runs behind . . . the settee & hides — Curtis screams & hurries off . . . & Grumio gets under table & as Pet looks to see if all have gone — Grumio walks off with table on his back."

Act IV, Scene 3 was almost as turbulent. Kate's assault upon Grumio is described thus, in the Walnut Street book: "takes his hand. beats him all round stage, on 3 feet of stage. Catches the eye of Pet as he comes in. Pause. Picture." Petruchio was long accustomed to elevate what he calls the "lewd and filthy cap" on the end of his whip; [204] and, at his

> Go hop me over every kennel home,

the stage direction in Cumberland's edition is *"Tailor hops over sword."* A fuller description is given by the invaluable Becks: "old bus. Pet made Tailor hop over sword (or wh[ip]) X stage — slapping his back — at each hop." A second attack on the wretched man was made a few lines later. And, just before his exit, Garrick added a fight between the Tailor and Grumio — about which much business collected. Since this last insertion is wholly un-Shakespearean, there is no occasion to consider it here.

Enough that the tailor at one point was accustomed to get into his band-box, whence he cried, "What! Strike a man in his own shop. . . ." [205]

A Bensonian invention at the end of the scene was to have Katherina "snatch up a knife and raise it to strike 'Petruchio,' when the sight of his mocking face, quite unruffled by her fury, breaks down her proud spirit, and plunging the knife into the table, she sinks sobbing at his feet." [206] I much prefer Julia Marlowe's holding two fingers behind her husband's back, as they went out. It was two o'clock, not seven! But was her signal to Hortensio, I wonder, or simply to the audience? [207]

Cymbeline

The Injured Princess, an adaptation of Shakespeare's tragicomedy by D'Urfey was produced not later than 1682 and turns up again in 1720 and 1738. In some form or other, *Cymbeline* was acted occasionally in the succeeding years, and with Garrick's revival in 1761 grew popular; nor was it by any means a forgotten play in the nineteenth century.

There is little business in the early scenes. *"King paces about in anger,"* a Cumberland (1829) stage direction at I, I, 128, calls perhaps for mention, as does Liston's habit, as Cloten, of 'whisking' off the stage "at the end of each scene." The Wager Scene begins in Bell's edition (1774) with Philario and the others *"at a Banquet"* — an idea which lasted.[208] Kemble has Philario hold a letter in his hand, containing, I suppose, praises of Posthumus.

When Miss Younge as Imogen in 1771 received Iachimo, she is reported to have dropped him "a solemn curtesy," quite missing "the highest joy and transport" which his coming — one with news from her lord! — should have called forth. Formality of another sort characterized the performance of Miss Phillips at Drury Lane in 1829:

> When she throws off the touch of Iachimo, which she does, indeed, as she should, with a thrilling and lion-like decision, she remains for several seconds with uplifted hand and poised foot, a spectacle of fixed magnificence.

Morley was to find Helen Faucit doing much the same thing —
"she remains with upraised arm throughout half the speech of
Iachimo that begins 'O happy Leonatus!' " [209] In rebuking the
villain, she either withdrew her hands from her face, or, after
standing with her back to him, suddenly wheeled round —

> Away! I do condemn my ears that have
> So long attended thee.

That "Away," Darbyshire writes, "brought Iachimo to his knees
and the audience to its feet." Julia Marlowe, on the other hand,
"listened with staring eyes of a childlike and innocent wonder; and she told with the lowering pitch of her voice as much
as with her contracting brows and lightening eyes the slow
growth of perception in her of the vileness of his thought."
Margaret Mather gave the rogue "a resounding slap on the
cheek." [210]

In the Chest Scene (II, 2), Helen Faucit has Imogen kiss the
bracelet (as she should do), before speaking her "brief prayer to
the gods for protection." [211] Then Iachimo issues forth. In
D'Urfey, he carries "*a Table-book,*" in which to "write all
down," [212] and just before his "O sleep . . . lie dull upon her!"
"*She stirs, and he starts back.*" Irving, who allowed "a piece of
red cloth" to hang from the chest — part of Iachimo's mantle, as
it proved — turned down Imogen's nightdress to discover the
"mole cinque-spotted." One reads, too, of Cooke's "gloating
eye," in this scene, and of his smile as he closed the lid of the
chest.[213]

Bell's edition makes Imogen's "How now, Pisanio" (II, 3, 141),
a summons occasioned by her "*missing her bracelet.*" To those
who feel that whatever is of consequence in a play should be
shown, not merely happen behind the scenes, this piece of business will no doubt commend itself. Helen Faucit was still using
it a long time later.[214] At the end of the next scene, Irving as
Iachimo walked slowly off the stage gazing with pleasure at the
ring he has just won from Posthumus. And from Clement Scott
comes a glimpse of Ellen Terry's Imogen in III, 2, as she is about
to set off for Milford Haven: "She bounds about the stage like a

young fawn, she kisses her hand, she kisses her dear lord's letter, she is a wilful madcap and a romp." [215]

Two scenes later, Imogen is reading her husband's letter and falling as if struck to the earth. She begs Pisanio to take her life, draws his sword for him, opens her breast, to find there

> The scriptures of the loyal Leonatus —

and at last Pisanio flings away his sword. The business is made perfectly clear by the lines themselves; and is none the less effective for being so — as the young Irving showed, playing Pisanio to Adelaide Neilson's Imogen, or Adelaide Neilson herself when she "dropped to the earth as if she had been shot." [216]

The business, first used by Helen Faucit, as Imogen enters the cave, is a different matter.

"She calls at the mouth of the unoccupied cavern," Morley writes, "and runs from the sound herself had made. The warning of her error might be found in the fact that her pantomime here excites rather general laughter, where surely Shakespeare never meant that even the dullest boor should grin."

Macready has expressed "many apprehensions" about this novelty of hers.[217] It succeeded, nevertheless, and was promptly adopted by actresses who saw nothing against making this scene a little like Viola's duel in *Twelfth Night*. Thus the Neilson Promptbook reads: "Draws her sword and thrusts awkwordly [sic] and fearfully before her as she enters cave." Madame Modjeska's touches of comedy, "her pretty bravado and her involuntary confession of her woman's fears," were much liked, as, in Ellen Terry's performance, were "the timid handling of the unaccustomed sword, the fearful glance into the depths of the unknown cave, the exquisite comedy of the entire performance at this point." [218]

The young princes, when Imogen first sees them in Act III, Scene 6, have often entered carrying game — as "*a Boar's Head*," in D'Urfey.[219] And Guiderius after slaying Cloten is directed in Kemble's editions of 1810 and 1815 to come in bearing Cloten's sword, instead of his severed head. Later in this scene (IV, 2), occurs the moment of Imogen's awaking and finding herself beside the headless body. John Drew, who himself once played

Cloten, explains that the actor's head is here covered with grass mats — a cloak' is another possibility. Drew's Imogen was Adelaide Neilson. In her performance, Winter speaks of the cry "with which she flung herself on the dead body of the supposed *Posthumus*, and the frenzy with which she kissed, again and again, the dead hands and senseless clothing." Mr. Bernard Shaw found that Ellen Terry presented faithfully and effectively

Imogen's bewilderment, between dreaming and waking, as to where she is; the vague discerning of some strange bedfellow there; the wondering examination of the flowers with which he is so oddly covered; the frightful discovery of blood on the flowers, with the hideous climax that the man is headless and that his clothes are her husband's.[220]

The detail of the blood on the flowers had been suggested by Shaw himself.[221] Kemble has Imogen still 'hanging over the body' at the close of her last speech in the scene, which ends with the Roman soldiers bearing the body away.[222]

In *The Universal Museum* for March 1762, one reads of Garrick that

while Iachimo is relating his villanous conduct to the King, Posthumus discovered the emotions of his soul . . . in his expressive face, when he comes forward and cries out

> Ay, so thou do'st,
> Italian fiend!

he speaks it in such an admirable manner that the souls of the audience are all suspence and attention.

Later the emphasis was changed. *"Rushing forward"* is Kemble's direction; [223] and in Cumberland's edition (1829), Posthumus advances *"throwing off his cloak"* — as Hamlet was accustomed to do when he discloses his identity in the Graveyard Scene. Murdoch writes of Charles Kean that while Iachimo is telling his story

Posthumus stands hidden behind the groups of courtiers and attendants, listening. . . . Iachimo, finishing the recital of his villainy, says, "Methinks I see him now." At this Kean suddenly darted from his concealment, and dashing down the stage struck his attitude and exclaimed, with a wild outburst of passion, sharp, harsh, and rattling in tone —

"Ay, so thou dost. . . ." [223a]

One further detail comes from "French's Acting Edition," of about 1864. Imogen, as she says,

> I see a thing
> Bitter to me as death. Your life, good master,
> Must shuffle for itself,

is *"looking intently at* Iachimo's *ring."* Only an expert reader would imagine for himself the action supplementing the words.

Measure for Measure

There is little continuity in the history of this comedy on the stage. The Restoration adaptations — by Davenant in the 'sixties and Gildon at the turn of the century — did not prosper. *Measure for Measure* was revived in 1720, in Garrick's time was often seen, and was given by Kemble with Mrs. Siddons as Isabella. The Victorians could scarcely be expected to enjoy it — though Phelps, for instance, produced it at Sadler's Wells.

Cumberland's edition (1826), which contains a Drury Lane cast of two years before, headed by Macready, is valuable for our purposes. At the beginning, the Duke, *"dressed as for his journey,"* is seated at a table on which is a green cloth. Presently Escalus and Angelo kneel to receive their commissions (as Kemble had had them do), and when the Duke addressing Angelo says "Give me your hand./I'll privily away," he signs to two attendants (recently christened Frederick and Leopold), who leave the room. Similarly, in Scene 3, the Friar *"goes up the Stage . . . and opens the Monastery Gates,"* in preparation for the Duke's exit *"into the Monastery."*

When the much maligned low comedy characters enter, early in the second act, and Escalus asks Froth "Where were you born, friend?" "French's Acting Edition" has Pompey push Froth *"across to* R.C." Froth soon *"gets behind Pompey"* and has to be pushed across again when Escalus says "Come hither." [224] And in the Sadler's Wells Promptbook is the direction, "Pompey thrusts off Froth," when Escalus bids the foolish gentleman farewell.

In the great scene between Isabella and Claudio (III, 1), I have again only one or two bits of business. At Isabella's "Dar'st thou die?" (line 77), French's edition calls for "*A pause. — Claudio averts his face*," and near the beginning of her next speech she "*embraces Claudio.*" Later, when Claudio says "Let me ask my sister pardon," Cumberland's edition has him cross to Isabella and kiss her hand.[225] A single detail deserves mention in III, 2: "Averting his face," in the Sadler's Wells Promptbook, before the Duke's reply to Lucio's "What news, friar, of the Duke?"

Robson writes of the Barnardine in Kemble's production: "When I saw Emery crawl from his den with the straws sticking in his clotted hair and filthy garments, growling out his remonstrance at being disturbed from his sleep, I absolutely started!" [226] Ragozine's head was not shown in this production, the Provost introducing it discreetly in a bag. Later, even his reference to it ("Here is the head") was expunged, and he merely tells the Duke, " 'Tis done, good sir." [227]

The last act began regularly with the ceremonious surrender of their commissions by Angelo and Escalus. At Sadler's Wells the Provost knelt behind them with "keys of City on Cushion . . . Duke places his hand on the Keys." When Isabella mentions Lucio, he takes off his cap to the Duke (in Cumberland), "That's I, an't like your Grace." Then he retires behind the Duke's chair of state, "*coming down*" and "*leaning over his shoulder*," to interject "Carnally, she says." At the right moment, he "*pulls off the Friar's habit, and discovers the* Duke. — Angelo *and* Escalus *start up from their seats, but do not quit their places.* — Lucio *goes* L.C. *and stands in amazement.*" "We'll borrow place of him," says the Duke, and Angelo, "*who has supported himself against the chair, moves one step from it. — The* Duke *places his hand on* Angelo's *arm, and gently pushes him to* R." — "Sir, by your leave".

"It is somewhat strange," Dr. Johnson writes, "that *Isabel* is not made to express either gratitude, wonder or joy at the sight of her brother"; and to Mr. Dover Wilson "this (dramatically speaking) inexplicable silence of Isabella" is of course evidence of revision. Yet the scene can be so played that we wholly forget the fact of her silence. "Claudio *discovers himself,* — Isabella *runs and embraces him,*" is Kemble's direction here. Mrs. Siddons was his Isabella. Perhaps, she originated the business. Or was it a boy-actress, some two centuries before? [228]

The Winter's Tale

This comedy was not seen during the Restoration, nor indeed until much later, and its stage traditions, such as they are, go back at best only to the middle years of the eighteenth century.

Charles Kean, who prided himself upon having lent substance, historical and geographical, to a very nebulous play, caused Leontes and his guests, *"crowned with Chaplets,"* to be *"discovered reclining on Couches, after the manner of the Ancient Greeks."* [229] A problem for the producer arises almost at once in the silence of Leontes while Hermione is persuading Polixenes to lengthen his visit. Kemble's edition directs Leontes to talk *"apart"* with Antigonus and Mamillius. Cumberland's (about 1827) has Leontes retire to one of three *"State-chairs in the background,"* where he seats himself, and Mamillius *"leans on his knee."* Other stage directions in old acting editions include: *"Lifting up Mamillius,"* at "To say this boy were like me" (line 135); *"Mamillius pulls him by the cloak,"* before "How now, boy?" (line 207); *"Goes up . . . and looks after them,"* immediately following the exit of Polixenes and Hermione; and "Camillo . . . *turns away . . . silently,*" on the return of Polixenes — an action which leads naturally to,

> *Pol.*   This is strange. Methinks
> My favour here begins to warp. Not speak? [230]

At the beginning of the second act, the Queen and her women have often been discovered at their needlework.[231] Mamillius, early in the nineteenth century, was contented with such playthings as a horse and drum. But Ellen Terry, playing the part in

Charles Kean's production, drew about a toy cart "from an actual one, in terra-cotta, preserved in the British Museum." [232] When Leontes cries, "bear the boy hence," he has frequently laid violent hands upon him, pushing him over to an attendant, or snatching him from Hermione.[233] Later, in replying to the expostulations of Antigonus, Leontes says:

> You smell this business with a sense as cold
> As is a dead man's nose; but I do see't and feel't,
> As you feel doing thus — and see withal
> The instruments that feel.

These lines, in Kemble's production and for a long time afterwards, he spoke striking or clapping *"his Hands together"* — instead of tweaking the courtier's nose or seizing his arm, as the literary editors would have him do.

In Act II, Scene 3, Antigonus must "swear by this sword" to do his master's bidding. *"Kisses the sword"* is the direction in Oxberry's edition (1824), and in French's, Leontes *"goes to Table, C., and draws sword, then advances to* Antigonus," who *"swears, his hand on sword."* [234]

A chair used to be brought in for Hermione in the Trial Scene; and Helen Faucit, doubtless with her own practice in mind, speaks of the Queen's sinking exhausted into this chair at the close of her defence.

> The Emperor of Russia was my father . . .

she goes on, "half to herself." In Charles Kean's production, *The Athenaeum* discovered "features of novelty. Hermione [Mrs. Kean] was borne in on a couch; and, on the announcement of her son's death, fell back on it, as if her own had suddenly followed, and thus gave the greater probability to Paulina's subsequent report." [235] But it is with the name of a later actress that this moment is rightly associated. Covering her face with a large white veil, as if "to hide from herself the light of a day so charged with horror," Mary Anderson's Hermione made a long pause, then with a cry fell headlong; and on this death-like fall, I am sorry to add, the curtain was rung down.[236] Kemble had of course continued the scene. "Hermione *is borne off by* Paulina, Emilia,

Lamia, *and* Hero, *followed by Officers,*" is his stage direction. And it is like Kemble to have remembered that the Queen was a prisoner — like him, too, to name her waiting-women and make her guards "Officers."

The bear which devours Antigonus seems more often than not to have been visibly presented. Dutton Cook recalls that in Charles Kean's production the animal "figured conspicuously, chasing the *Antigonus* of the time . . . with peculiar zest." Kean himself gravely noted that "the existence of bears in the East, is exemplified in the 2nd chapter of the Second Book of Kings"; and *Punch* had it upon authority that his bear was "an archaeological copy from the original bear of Noah's Ark." [237]

When, in III, 3, the Shepherd and his son find the baby, some of the directions in Oxberry's edition seem to me not without interest. As the Shepherd exclaims "What have we here?" he "*just opens the head of the mantle.*" The Clown enters "*running and frightened.*" "Here's a sight for thee," his father says, lifting "*the child and mantle from the ground*"; and, at "take up, take up, boy," "*Clown unfolds the mantle, as the shepherd holds the child to him in his arms.*" "It was told me I should be rich by the fairies," the Shepherd recalls, and as he speaks, "*the Clown takes the casket, and shakes it.*"

In an early prompt-copy of Garrick's adaptation, *Florizel and Perdita* (1756), the Clown, when he returns in Act IV, Scene 3, carries "Money in bag & paper wrote" — from which he reads some of the items he is to buy. The money does not remain long in his possession. "*Helps him up*" is the printed direction in *Florizel and Perdita* at line 73, and at "You ha' done me a charitable office," Autolycus "*picks his pocket.*" Having done so, he is of course embarrassed by the Clown's offer of money a moment later. "Clown *is about to take purse from his wallet,*" is the direction in French's edition at line 87, "Autolycus *hastily stops him.*" [238]

Late in the same scene, it is pleasant to read in the *Florizel and Perdita* promptbook that, when the Shepherd asks Autolycus if he is a courtier, the rogue's reply is made "strutting about." Certainly, too, the Shepherd and Clown should "*take off their hats*" to Autolycus before line 737 — as they do in Cumberland's edition.

In his Manchester production (1869), Charles Calvert chose as setting for Act v, Scene 1, a sacred grove and mausoleum, where Leontes was *"discovered offering oblations of incense and flowers to his dead Queen and Son."* There is, of course, nothing in the lines to imply such a place or action, but they gave opportunity for the sort of archaeological display in which Calvert, like Kean, delighted.[239]

At the beginning of the Statue Scene, the eighteenth century promptbook, already mentioned, calls for a "Saloon, Throne, Pedestal, Urn & Statue of Hermione. Curtain." One of these items reappears significantly in *A Parody of the Rosciad of Churchill* (1780):

> Reclining on an urn, I see
> The semblance of Hermione; . . .
>
> She breathes — she lives — behold her move,
> All sweetness, dignity, and love;
> 'Tis H[a]rtl[ey]'s spirit, sense, and mien
> Give life, Leontes, to thy queen.

Boaden writes of Mrs. Siddons that "upon the magical words . . . 'Musick; awake her: strike;' the sudden action of the head absolutely *startled* . . . and the descent from the pedestal was equally graceful and affecting." [240] Helen Faucit describes at length her first appearance in the part, with Macready, September 30, 1837. She had a pedestal upon which to lean, and this

was a slight help during the long strain upon the nerves and muscles, besides allowing me to stand in that "natural posture" which first strikes Leontes, and which therefore could not have been rigidly statuesque. By imperceptibly altering the poise of the body, the weight of it being on the forward foot, I could drop into the easiest position from which to move. . . . Towards the close of the strain [of music] the head slowly turned, the "full eyes" moved, and at the last note rested on Leontes.

Then, she continues, the music began again, and,

at a sign from Paulina . . . the arm and hand were gently lifted from the pedestal . . . the figure descended the steps that led up to the dais, and advancing slowly, paused at a short distance from Leontes. Oh, can I ever forget Mr. Macready at this point! At first he stood speech-less, as if turned to stone; his face with an awe-struck look upon it.

Encouraged by Paulina, he advanced, trembling, and

touched gently the hand held out to him. . . . His passionate joy at finding Hermione really alive seemed beyond control. Now he was prostrate at her feet, then enfolding her in his arms. I had a slight veil or covering over my head and neck. . . . This fell off in an instant. The hair, which came unbound, and fell on my shoulders, was rever-ently kissed and caressed. . . . It was the finest burst of passionate speechless emotion I ever saw.[241]

The Comedy of Errors

For the four remaining comedies, all of them seldom acted, I have discovered very little stage business. Kemble directs Aegeon to enter *"in Chains,"* in the first and last acts of *The Comedy of Errors*; [242] and, according to a property list in *Spencer's Boston Theatre* (1855), the brothers Antipholus carried a "small rattan" each, with which, beyond question, they belabored the brothers Dromio.

An American ("Ludlow and Smith") promptbook of the eighteen-forties, or thereabouts, keeps Dromio of Syracuse on the stage for a sensational curtain to Act III. Summoned, from a window, by the abhorred kitchen wench, now a cook, he speaks his concluding lines:

> As from a bear a man would run for life,
> So fly I from her that would be my wife.

"As he is running off the Cook enters d.f. and intercepts him, she beats him with Ladle, and he trips her up, and runs off L.H. — End Act Quick Drop."

Dr. Pinch, about whom every reader has desired to know more, has a little new business in Cumberland's *British Theatre* (1827). This is at the close of the fourth act, when, upon the exit of the Syracusan master and servant with drawn swords: *"Dr. Pinch runs across from R. to L. after them."* [243] The promptbook ends this act vigorously, at least. Dr. Pinch now says, "Away! Bear them all to my strong room!" Whereupon:

> 2 Servants drag off Ant. L.H.
> 2 — do — drag off officer L.H.
> 2 — do — drag off Dromio who

kicks at Dr Pinch, he following round from L·Corner as Dromio is dragged a cross — and pushes at him with his Cane — The Ladies X behind and run out RH.2E

The Two Gentlemen of Verona

Only a few bits of business need detain us in the early scenes of this comedy. At Sadler's Wells, Valentine and Proteus opened it by entering "hand in hand." The little episode of the glove, at the beginning of Act II, is taken care of quite satisfactorily by Kemble's stage direction, "*Enter* Valentine, *and* Speed *running after him.*" [244] In Benjamin Victor's version of the play, produced at Drury Lane in 1762, Silvia takes the letter which Valentine has written for her and "*looks at it,*" before saying,

> I thank you, gentle servant. 'Tis very clerkly done;

and shortly after, at line 118: "*All this while she is reading in the paper, but now and then looking over at* Valentine."

For business of somewhat livelier interest, one turns to the edition ("As Produced at the Park Theatre by Mr. and Mrs. Charles Kean") which appeared in Epes Sargent's "Modern Standard Drama" in 1846, and claims to have been prepared from Kean's own promptbook. Here, at the beginning of Act II, Scene 2, Proteus and Julia are discovered in an arbor. "*She is weeping — her head on his shoulder.*" And at the end of their farewells Julia "*makes an effort to speak, through her tears, then hurries out.*" "What, gone without a word?" he asks — then realizes how it has been. Here, also, are full and excellent directions concerning Launce, as he expostulates with his dog. Saying "I have receiv'd my proportion, like the Prodigious Son," he shows "*a small, dirty, leathern money-bag.*" At "no more pity in him than a dog," he "*fastens dog to a staple in stage.*" Then he "*takes off his shoes and kneels.*" "This staff is my sister" — he "*sticks staff up.*" "This hat is Nan, our maid" — "*Lays hat on the Stage.*" "Now should I kiss my father" — he "*kisses shoe, and lays it down.*" So it is with his mother. "Well, I kiss her" — he "*kisses other shoe*"; and "*embraces wand,*" for his sister. After Speed's entrance, he rises, "*puts on shoes, hat, &c.*"; and, at last, "*unties the dog.*" Warde writes of James Lewis, in Daly's production, that "he came upon the stage slowly, with an expression of extreme disgust on his face, leading his dog Crab by a cord." Presently, he "'led the dog to the base of a statue, or fountain on the scene, seated himself on the steps, the cur by his side, and enacted the domestic scene." [245]

"*Thu., anxious to attract Duke's notice, bows affectedly*" (at II, 4, 84), is again from the "Modern Standard Drama" edition. Proteus is there described as kneeling and kissing Silvia's hand, before he says,

> My duty will I boast of, nothing else.

He kisses her hand again, as she is going. Valentine "*looks after Silvia, then comes down to Proteus, and takes both his hands*" as he joyously addresses him —

> Now tell me, how do all from whence you came?

When, moreover, in III, i, Valentine is stayed by the Duke, the latter disconcertingly brings forward a chair and sits down, rising, and putting back the chair, only when he inquires about the rope-ladder.

At the end of Act IV, Scene I, the Outlaws, happy to have Valentine as their captain, crowd about him, "*waving their caps.*" In this scene, Blanchard who played Speed at Covent Garden, January 16, 1822, is praised for

an attention to the lighter shades, which denoted the *Master* — On being surrounded by the Robbers, Speed labours under the greatest fear, and, with much vehemency entreats Sir Valentine to accept their offer of electing him their Captain; on his doing which, the timid servant instantly became the courageous comrade, and Mr. B. giving the full effect to this, after a few minutes of examination, changed the cock of his hat to that assumed by the Banditti, and in other respects evinced a desire to imitate their manners and habits.[246]

Once more, through several scenes, there is no business of consequence except, occasionally, in the 1846 edition. One stage direction concerns Julia in the Serenade Scene: *"During the song Julia looks timidly at the faces of the Serenaders, going to Proteus last — on recognizing him, she retires sorrowful."* [247] Another prejudices us still further against Proteus who, with little excuse in the lines, *"drives dog with Launce round the Stage and off,"* at IV, 4, 64.

In Daly's edition, Act v, Scene 3 begins: *"The Forest — A Storm in progress —* Proteus *is seen plunging through the trees, and* Julia *follows at a distance. After a little while a woman's scream heard — A clash of swords ensues."* Then, after thunder and lightning, Silvia enters with the Outlaws. The Sadler's Wells Promptbook has the single word "Picture" after the following lines:

Val. Ruffian! let go that rude uncivil touch
      Thou friend of an ill fashion!
Pro.   Valentine!

For an explanation, one turns for a last time to the 1846 text: Proteus *"seizes her, but when Val. speaks, he goes* R., *draws his sword, and rushes forward to strike, when, recognizing his friend, he staggers back,* R, *and drops his sword."* He *"kneels to Val.,"* a moment later, and just at the close, when Valentine is beginning a reply to the Duke's innocent

> I think the boy hath grace in him; he blushes,

"Pro. in dumb show entreats Val. to silence."

Love's Labour's Lost

In the second scene of this comedy Don Armado has, in certain performances, taken Jaquenetta's hand as he promises to visit her at the lodge; and in Daly's acting editions, he looks after her and sighs before beginning his soliloquy.[248] Meanwhile, Moth has tyrannized over "the rational hind," her companion. He "displays great authority which alarms Costard," is a Sadler's Wells promptnote. And, again: "Moth stamps his foot Costard Exits hastily

Moth follows." Costard, by the way, has sometimes carried a
"folly staff," and Boyet, like Polonius, a "white wand." [249]

Early in the third act, Armado sends Moth out — "I shoot thee
at the swain" — and, according to the Sadler's Wells book, he
"takes one bound and Exits L.I.E.," then, a moment later, "runs
on followed by Costard who is rubbing his shin." James Lewis,
Daly's Costard, placed the letters with which he was intrusted on
opposite sides of his hat. And Daly's edition gives us, too, the
direction, "*Roguishly taking his arm*," for Rosaline, as she and
Boyet are leaving the stage near the close of IV, i, and she says or
sings,

> "Thou canst not hit it, hit it, hit it,
> Thou canst not hit it, my good man,"

lines which Boyet, "*detaining her*," caps with,

> "An I cannot, cannot, cannot,
> An I cannot, another can."[250]

Early in the last scene of all, Moth becomes confused, and
mangles the speech he was to deliver by way of introducing the
"Russians." A Sadler's Wells promptnote concludes the episode:
"Biron twists him to R.C. others follow the same business till he
is off." Later, seats are brought in, "2 Green Men draw on Platform," and the pageant begins. "A Banner bearer" precedes "each
worthy with a Banner," on which is inscribed his name. At Sir
Nathaniel's entrance, "Banner Bearer (inscription 'Alexander the
Great') comes from R.U.E. on Platform & stands L.H. until
pushed off by Costard," at line 583. Then Marcade enters and
kneels, and in response to Berowne's

> Worthies, away! The scene begins to cloud,

the green men draw off the platform, and "Super Lords" the seats.
In Daly's version, "*the curtains of the tent are lifted at back, disclosing a platform*," upon which the Worthies perform, and in
course of time fall out among themselves. Pompey is "*throwing
down his helmet*," before line 704; and, soon after, he and Armado
"*fight and exit. The curtain closes.*"

Spring and Winter have frequently been presented in "cars" —
at Sadler's Wells brought in by the useful men in green.[251] And,
after the songs, the ladies have reappeared as if setting out on their
journey. "They come down," according to the promptbook,
"and are saluted by — King — Biron — Dumain — Longaville . . .
as the last couple goes up bowing & curtseying adieu's — Ring
down." [252]

All's Well That Ends Well

The business which I have found concerning this rarely acted
play may be disposed of in a very few words. After Bertram's
grudging acceptance of Helena (ii, 3), the direction, "*Exeunt all
but Paroles* [sic] *and Lefeu* [sic] R. — *Paroles, who is following
them, passes by Lefeu conceitedly*," is about what is wanted to introduce Lafeu's "Do you hear, monsieur? A word with you."
And, at the beginning of the next scene, Helena will do well to
carry a letter, as she enters saying to the Clown, "My mother
greets me kindly. Is she well?" [253]

The Parolles scenes in the fourth act are eminently actable.
"Ten o'clock," the poor braggart begins, "within these three
hours 'twill be time enough to go home." Against the aside of the
First Lord, which follows, Harry Edwards's Australian promptbook of 1858 has the note: "During this dialogue Soldiers have
gradually closed down behind Parolles." At line 66, Dumain, in
Cumberland's edition, "*signs to a Soldier, who goes away*," to return an instant later, speaking the terrifying gibberish of the text.
Bell's edition (1774) begins a new scene at iv, 3, 133, with "*Parolles discovered, in the stocks, blindfolded*." The Second Lord
gives orders for him to be released and brought forward:

Int[*erpreter*]. *Damabous news* — you must down on your knees.
Par.   O dear!

Of this scene, Tom Davies wrote a few years later that it had
"always afforded much pleasure to the audience. Upon its last
revival . . . the unbiding Parolles, who looked about him with
surprize and terror, redoubled the bursts of laughter which
echoed round the theatre." [254]

II

The Histories

Henry VIII

OF Shakespeare's histories, the two in which Elizabethan stage business is most likely to have been perpetuated are *Henry VIII* and the *First Part of Henry IV*. When, in December 1663, *Henry VIII* was revived by the Duke's company Betterton played the part of the King, "being Instructed in it," Downes writes, "by Sir *William* [Davenant], who had it from Old Mr. *Lowen*, that had his Instructions from Mr. *Shakespear* himself." [1] The Restoration saw the play often — Betterton was again cast as the King in 1709 — and there is enough continuity in its subsequent history, despite one or two serious gaps, to make the preservation of acting traditions possible.

A turnip is intimately associated with Audrey. Wolsey in Charles Kean's production of *Henry VIII* carried an orange. For this there was warrant in history, since Cavendish describes the Cardinal as issuing from his privy chamber,

holding in his hand a very fair orange, whereof the meat or substance within was taken out, and filled up again with the part of a sponge, wherein was vinegar, and other confections against the pestilent airs; the which he most commonly smelt unto, passing among the press, or else where he was pestered with many suitors.[2]

Tree was again to carry an orange — and to make "excessive fastidiousness Wolsey's predominant trait." [3]

To an unusual extent, the original stage directions in *Henry VIII* include details of action. Thus in the first scene, "*The*

Cardinall in his passage, fixeth his eye on Buckingham, and Buck-
ingham on him, both full of disdaine." "Irving's great moment,"
to W. Graham Robertson, "was when, in his first passing across
the stage, he turned and looked for a long moment at Buckingham. How Buckingham survived that moment I could never
understand." The Duke's arrest follows swiftly. And here, in
some nineteenth century editions, *"he lets fall his hat,"* to show
that he has been startled by the Sergeant's words, then, saying
"I obey," *"Gives his Sword to the* Sergeant." [4] As for the second
scene — that in which Buckingham's Surveyor is questioned —
enough perhaps that the remarks of Wolsey on the gravity of the
Duke's offense have sometimes been accompanied by the porten-
tous unrolling of *"a scroll."* [5]

The scene of the Masque at York Place, with its constant movement, its grouping and re-grouping of the characters, is not easily
followed by a reader unfamiliar with the play in performance.
For sometime, Wolsey has only to look on at the festivities. But
Irving, sitting "in lonely state, his chin on his hand," at first bored
by the dancing, then, as he recognizes Henry among the shep-
herds, watching keenly, could make even this looking on memorable.[6] As the Cardinal says,

> By all your good leaves, gentlemen, here I'll make
> My royal choice,

Oxberry's edition (1824) directs him to kneel, and the King
crosses *"and raises him."* "As the King goes towards the Ladies,"
the Cooke-Cooper Promptbook tells us, "he starts at seeing Anne
Bullen & the instant Lord Sands gives place seats himself by her."
Oxberry explains that Sandys, who has been sitting between Anne
and Lady Denny, *"knows the King"* and *"rises and stands at Lady
Denny's* R. H. *The King takes Lord Sand's place."* Now Sandys
had long been played as a comic character — Theophilus Cibber
goes so far as to speak of Gardiner and Sandys as "debased . . .
into the *Zanys* of a *Bartholomew Droll"* — and his display of tact
at this moment lends itself to comic treatment. Oxberry, again, has
Sandys and Lady Denny *"salute with ceremonious formality and
affectation,"* a little later in the scene; and since Lady Denny re-

appears as the unidentified "Old Lady" who talks with Anne in
II, 3, she would have been a fit match for a comic old lord.[7] At
the close of the scene, Kemble has Wolsey *"with Lights"* precede
the King, and in Oxberry *"a Page gives two lights from the Cardinal's table to the Chamberlain, who gives them to Wolsey"* in
preparation for this formality.[8]

In Charles Kean's revival, Act II, Scene 1, began with *"The
Duke's Barge discovered . . . at the foot of the steps leading to the
river"*; and at the end, Buckingham walked *"guarded, into Barge,
which slowly moves off."* Forbes-Robertson, who as a child had
seen this production and remembered "John Ryder's 'archæologi-
cal figure,' as he himself was pleased to describe his person, towering above the devoted crowds, in his black habit against the
background of the river and distant houses," found the same
"wonderful scene" at the Lyceum when he began rehearsing
there. But "something was wrong." His "Buckingham would not
be able to dominate the throng as Ryder's had done." So he
asked for more steps "leading up to the barge," got three more, in
course of time, and was satisfied. Meanwhile, in the New York
production at Booth's in 1878 — one in which Kean's stage
arrangement had again been followed — the "Peasants Kneel" at
Buckingham's "Pray for me" (line 132), and

as Buckingham gets on step an old peasant advances from the crowd
& kisses the hem of Buckinghams cloak. Buckingham turns & blesses
him The two chaplains elevate their small crosses and scene changes
Buckingham with his hat in his LH his R hand elevated.[9]

In a copy of French's edition of *Henry VIII* in which the part
of Campeius has been marked by Russell Bassett — an actor who
at one time supported such stars as Charlotte Cushman and Lester
Wallack — this quaint note is pencilled at the end of scene 2:
"Bus. after Kings Exit — start to go L. I. E. stopped by Wolsey
step back — Bus. & Exit." In other words, Cardinal Campeius
attempts to take precedence over Cardinal Wolsey; Wolsey gives
him an awful look; Wolsey stalks out before him. This was,
with minor variations, Macready's business and Charles Kean's,
Phelps's, Booth's, and George Vandenhoff's.[10] Was it also Kem-

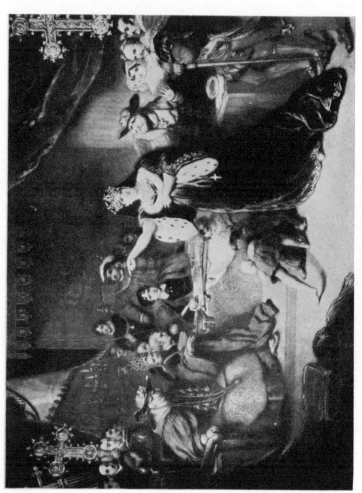

The Kemble Family in Henry VIII
(From an engraving after a painting by Harlow)

ble's? Calcraft the actor, who as "John William Cole" wrote the life of the younger Kean, says in effect that it was.[11] But I have found no further trace of it before Macready's time; and the Cooke-Cooper Promptbook (1811) has Henry exit "leaning on Wolsey." Irving introduced the skirmish between the cardinals at a later moment, where perhaps it is equally appropriate — at the end of the Trial Scene. And it is with this later moment, not unnaturally, that it is associated by H. M. Walbrook in *A Play-goer's Memories*. He is recounting the opinions of William Warren Vernon, "the right kind of playgoer," as he calls him:

"In one touch of business [Charles Kean] excelled all the Wolseys of my time. It was in the scene where the two cardinals, Wolsey and Campeius, at the end of the scene in the hall in Blackfriars (Act II, scene 2 — sic), followed the King in leaving the apartment, and a battle of politeness ensued as to which should take precedence. . . . At last, while they were in the act of bowing low to each other, Charles Kean, with an oily smile . . . and without raising his head, glided like an eel past the much disconcerted Campeius. Phelps used to throw up his arm in indignant defiance; Irving marched out first in contemptuous indifference; but Charles Kean's was the true manner of one Roman prelate to another Roman prelate." [12]

Although doubt may remain as to where, in the play, and how early the business was introduced, it was effective, in any case, and, though not remotely suggested by the lines, is neither incompatible with them nor with the stage for which the play was written.

Anne and the Old Lady (II, 3) may be summarily dismissed after noting that in the Jarrell and Palmer Promptbook (1878) they are "both seated at table," Anne behind a spinning wheel. The Trial Scene is another matter. Minor departures from the arrangements called for in the Folio were made early. A discovery replaced the procession. Katherine entered only when summoned.[13] She still knelt to the King; and, in Kemble's time and for many years after, the action was facilitated by Guildford's placing a cushion for her. Is it this cushion which the two little pages are removing, in Harlow's painting? [14] There, it will be noticed, Henry is seated toward the back of the stage, center. Cromwell sits below him at a table, on which is a mace. The two Cardinals are conspicuously placed, farther forward, Wolsey on the King's right, Campeius on his left.[15] Campeius has just risen. The Queen is pointing, however, toward Wolsey. It is the moment made famous by Mrs. Siddons. "Therefore, Madam," Campeius says,

> It's fit this royal session do proceed
> And that (without delay) their arguments
> Be now produc'd and heard.
> *Queen.*   Lord Cardinal,
> To you I speak.
> *Wolsey.*   Your pleasure, madam.

At "Lord Cardinal," Campeius rises; but the words were not, as he supposes, directed to him. "She turns from him impatiently," writes Bell, of Mrs. Siddons, "then makes a sweet bow of apology, but dignified. Then to Wolsey, turned and looking *from* him, with her hand pointing back to him, in a voice of thunder, 'to *you* I speak.' " [16] "The excitement of this outburst," Brander Matthews writes, "is so electric that it has been repeated in the subsequent revivals of 'Henry VIII,' as I can testify from my memory of Charlotte Cushman's performance, Modjeska's and Ellen Terry's; and in so arranging it Kemble" — for Matthews assumes that Kemble, "a most fertile deviser of points," invented this one — "made a permanent contribution to the staging of Shakspere." [17]

As Katherine is about to depart, she is again summoned by the Crier. Charlotte Cushman, we read,

pays no attention as she walks out until her attendant, walking backward before her, stops and says: "Madam, you are called back," when, with head erect, and the air of a lioness, she waves him forward with:
> What need you note it? Pray, you keep your way:
> When *you* are called, return. Now, the Lord help,
> They vex me past my patience! Pray you, pass on.
At this she sweeps out of the court. . . . Modjeska, on the other hand, starts to leave the court with her hands to her face, sobbing, and when the attendant seeks to stop her, lifts her head for a moment and, with convulsive sighs, motions him forward and utters the words of the text as though her heart was breaking.[18]

Of the two interpretations, that of the American actress seems to me far the more natural.

Henry is left with the ecclesiastics, and in the performance of William Terriss vented his spite against them on the royal footstool, which he kicked viciously out of the way, before rising: "These Cardinals trifle with me. . . . Break up the court." [19]

In Act III, Scene 1, Irving pointed up the Queen's exit. Wolsey, after offering Katherine his arm, which she declined, going instead with Campeius, watched her departure pitifully; then with a change of expression shrugged his shoulders and followed haughtily.[20] It would be pedantic to insist that the lines themselves carry no suggestion of her distinguishing between the "reverend fathers" here — rather the contrary. Scene 2 is richer in business. When, speaking figuratively, Wolsey says,

> This candle burns not clear. 'Tis I must snuff it,

Colley Cibber "imitated, with his fore-finger and thumb, the extinguishing of a candle with a pair of snuffers" — which was stupidly prosy, of course. Even Kemble "seemed to smell a stink," whereas Young attempted no illustration and "kept his arms folded." [21] Phelps's Cardinal held "his head erect when doing obeisance to the King at the very moment when disgrace is upon him." This was, I suppose, as Henry went out saying:

> Read o'er this;
> And after, this; and then to breakfast with
> What appetite you have.

Davies advises the actor to reserve his anger for the last line: "The tremendous look which [Barton] Booth put on, with his rapid and vehement expression, fully corresponded with the design of the author." Cooke's Henry, according to the 1811 Promptbook, banged the door after him.[22]

Finally, there is the baiting of the Churchman by Surrey. In "*Strictures on the late revived Tragedy of* Henry VIII," which appeared in *The Macaroni* for November 1772, Mr. Dyer's Surrey at Covent Garden is described as "truly *comical*"; he "has been justly compared, from his size and action, to a bantling cock, kept at a contemptible distance from the flap of a game cock's wing." "*Offers to draw his sword*," is Cumberland's direction for Surrey at "Thou art a proud traitor, priest." But from his edition, too, comes the pleasant detail that, whereas the noblemen "*go off smiling*," the Chamberlain at his exit "*bows respectfully*" to Wolsey.[23]

Katherine's vision (IV, 2), included in Restoration performances, then for long years banished in favor of a song sung by Patience,[24] was restored by Charles Kean "with some new machinery from Paris — used also in the apotheosis of Margaret [*sic*], at the end of 'Faust.'" [25] Mrs. Siddons was very great in this scene. In her performance, the sick Queen's restlessness found expression in many small actions: her pillows and the chair she sat in must be changed; or she bent forward, resting her hands upon her knees, or played with the folds of her drapery.[26] At the last,

she gives signs of a slight convulsion, but this is apparent only at the ends of her fingers: she nips up her robe; and the arm, in that action, suddenly seems numbed and powerless.[27]

Much of this remained traditional with later actresses; but one at least, Mrs. Charles Kean, gave over Katherine's tottering exit, supported by her attendants, and instead, "falling back, after an effort to rise," expired in her chair.[28]

For the last act, I have only a little stage business. At the beginning, indeed, Bell's edition (1774) and the Cooke-Cooper Promptbook have the "King *and* Suffolk *discover'd at play*" — which does well enough, provided the whole first part of the scene is sacrificed. Similarly, at the very end, "All Kneel as curtain signal is given" (in the Jarrett and Palmer Promptbook) will pass, if no attention is paid to Henry's "Lead the way, lords./ Ye must all see the Queen." The absurd antics of certain misguided comedians who have played Gardiner remain to be considered. Davies writes that Benjamin Johnson, early in the eighteenth century, "preserved all the decorum proper to the character of a bishop and privy-counsellor." With Hippisley there were approaches to farce. "But Taswell's Gardiner degenerated into absolute trick and buffoonery, and, when he followed Cranmer, at the close of the scene [v, 3], to make the upper gallery sport, he held his crutch over his head." [29] This was at Drury Lane about the middle of the century. From *The Macaroni* for November 1772 we learn that

the *immaculate* Ned Shuter, not content with degrading the mitre, by appearing in the character of a bishop, went a step farther, in *threatening to knock down Archbishop Cranmer with a clenched stick, as he passed before him.*

Parsons at the Haymarket, five years later, indulged in the same tomfoolery.[30] Finally, in the *Lincoln Dramatic Censor*, November 1, 1809, there is an illiberal attack on "*a* Mr. Brown," one of old Tom Robertson "the Mogul's" company. As Gardiner, "he twisted his fingers like an ideot, he grimaced every exit, he embraced Cranmer with distended features, he introduced all the mummery of Bartholomew fair. . . . Were these mountebank pranks introduced," it is asked, "to bring the sacred function of the clergy into contempt?" The last point told. *A Letter Addressed to the Authors of the Lincoln Censor* appeared promptly. And in it, among other arguments for the defense, theatrical custom is cited: "the part of the bloody-minded Gardiner has always been given to the first Comic actor in every Theatre; and . . . Munden, in particular, performs it in London with his usual buffoonery."

1 Henry IV

The First Part of King Henry the Fourth was acted in the autumn of 1660 and, though not one of Shakespeare's most popular plays, it has seldom in later years been absent long from the boards.

To Stephen Kemble (laughed at in his time as the *big*, not the *great* Kemble, and as a Falstaff without stuffing) is assigned the invention of one piece of business still current to-day. In 1804 Kemble visited Manchester. Commenting on his performance, *The Townsman* writes:

The discovery of Falstaff on a Couch, in his first scene, as if awaking, was an excellent idea of Mr. Kemble's; for his question, on the entry of the Prince, of "Now Hal! what time of the Day is it Lad?" — had a much better effect than the common method of walking on, from opposite sides, is able to produce.[31]

It is possible to dislike heartily the excessive use of discoveries in modern Shakespearean productions while retaining a fondness for this one. In the same scene, Falstaff regularly carried a stick and, what is less easy to accept, both the Prince and Poins often sported canes.[32] "*Tapping Falstaff's belly with his cane*," at "and is not a buff jerkin a most sweet robe of durance," is one of the many bits of business recorded in Cumberland's edition (1826). Another is when Hal asks, "Where shall we take a purse to-morrow, Jack?" Falstaff "*after a short pause eagerly shakes hands with the Prince*": "Zounds, where thou wilt, lad! I'll make one."

As for the scene in which Hotspur demands his prisoners, enough that when Kemble played the part at Drury Lane, January 11, 1802, he was told that perhaps it was "a refinement which had better be dropt, to halloo in *Worcester's* ear the name with which Hotspur threatens to disturb the King." Also,

> We wish the *carriers* had been less solicitous to wound the delicacy of the audience; for though they are "*stung like a tench*," there is no occasion to "*suit the action to the word*" so unequivocally and so repeatedly as was done.[32a]

Cumberland's direction at II, 1, 17 is: "*Catches fleas, and examines them by the light of his lantern.*"

The old arrangements for the Gadshill robbery are interesting. As soon as the travellers are attacked, they take to their heels, pursued by Bardolph, Peto, and Gadshill — thus leaving Falstaff alone on the stage, "*running about with his sword drawn*," and shouting defiance.[33] Then he follows them out. The Prince and Poins appear briefly — wearing "different Vizors," as Phelps notes. Falstaff and his companions return "*with Bags of Money*," and "*sit down on the ground*" to divide the spoils — it was Phelps's idea, again, that they should "assist Falstaff to sit." Stephen Kemble "succeeded admirably" here: "Nothing could be

better described than the gleam of contentment in his countenance, and his chuckling at being so fortunate, with so little danger
to himself." [34] The knight's happiness does not last long. Hal
and Poins — a multitude of men in buckram and men in Kendal
green — set upon him. "We caught him," an old actor is quoted
as saying in Henry Curling's *Recollections of the Mess-Table and
the Stage*, "and, one on each side, rained just such a shower of
blows upon him as Prince Hal and Poins inflicted upon poor Jack
at Gad's Hill; thrashing him unmercifully." [35] At times, I am sorry
to say, Sir John has literally *crawled* away. So, at any rate, did
Charles Kemble at Covent Garden in 1824; and so Mark Lemon
was advised to do when, as an amateur, he played Falstaff in 1869:
"Poor old — (mentioning an actor of considerable reputation)
was quite outraged because I would not go down on my face and
grovel in the robbery." It was "the recognized legitimate business." [36]

Hotspur reads his letter (II, 4) and afterwards, in both the
Wood and Sadler's Wells Promptbooks, he "throws himself into
a chair." Lady Percy, entering, would sometimes tap him on the
shoulder, "which arrests his attention." [37] Also, as Winter noticed,
it was the "stage custom" for her to sit on Hotspur's knee, while
she teases him and tries to discover his secret. And, as he says "I
care not for thee, Kate," he kisses her.[38]

We have reached the Tavern Scene. On Falstaff's entrance,
when the play was given at Sadler's Wells, Gadshill placed his
"Hat on Table Peto hangs Falstaff's Shield on the back of chair"
— a "Large Oak Arm Chair," be it noted. Then, as Sir John exclaimed against his liquor — "here's lime in this sack too!" — he
threw "the dregs in Francis's face." This business was old. Mr.
Knight at Drury Lane in April 1820 was criticized as " 'too fine
in his evidence' for the simplicity" of the drawer, who

could not possess sagacity enough to practice a prominent manoeuvre
which Mr. KNIGHT has adopted. *Falstaff*, on returning from Gad's-hill,
after quaffing his "cup of sack" throws the sediment in *Francis's* face;
on presenting another potation, this cautious skinker holds up his
apron to prevent the recurrence of that indignity, which *Falstaff* is
accordingly foiled in repeating.[39]

In *Garrick's Looking-Glass* (1776), the English Roscius is made to insist upon the importance of dress, properties, and the like:

> Fat FALSTAFF's shield, and mountain belly,
> Are half the battle, let me tell ye.

Behind this shield, Sir John used to hide his face at the moment when there seems no hope of his escaping an "open and apparent shame." Then, all at once, "*peeping over his Shield*," he speaks: "By the Lord, I knew ye as well as he that made ye."[40] A variation was introduced when the play was given, with W. F. Owen as Falstaff and Julia Marlowe as the Prince, in 1895. Brander Matthews writes that "after Falstaff had met the Prince's incredulity with abuse, he cried, 'O for breath to utter!'" and sank into "a spacious arm-chair" which stood with its back to the audience. When he "was convinced that his bluff was about to be called he shrank into the chair and the back of his head was no longer to be seen." At last,

> Henry paused for a reply and it was so long in coming, that Poins backed up the Prince, saying, "Come, let's hear, Jack." . . . Falstaff out of sight of the audience had twisted himself about in the chair until he was kneeling on it; and he slowly raised his face above its back — a face wreathed with smiles.

Matthews was much interested in the origins of this trick. Had Phelps introduced it? Forbes-Robertson could not remember that he had.[41] Such Jack-in-the-box devices have one grave disadvantage. We cannot watch the actor's face, cannot see the idea come to him, as we saw it, for instance, in Roy Byford's performance when Falstaff fairly hopped up and down with excitement — "the lion will not touch the true prince."

Falstaff's chair was, in itself, a notable property. Thus in Garrick's prologue to *Florizel and Perdita* (1756):

> But shou'd you call for Falstaff, *where to find him*,
> *He's gone — nor left one Cup of Sack behind him.*
> *Sunk in his Elbow Chair, no more he'll roam.* . . .

And in Kenrick's play, *Falstaff's Wedding* (1766), Mrs. Quickly, expecting the fat knight, cries, "Francis! What Francis! bring the great chair for Sir John!"[42] One even hears of its accompanying its owner to the field of Shrewsbury. Ireland, in 1786, writes of Quin:

in the scene of the battle, instead of the stump of a tree on which Falstaff sits to rest himself, I remember the then directors of the Theatre introduced a crimson velvet arm chair, with gilt claw feet and blue fringe.[43]

There is little more to detain us in this greatest, perhaps, of Shakespeare's comic scenes. The little play was seldom acted. Kemble introduced the enduring custom of having the Sheriff accompanied by two of the wronged travellers,

> Here are two gentlemen
> Have in this robbery lost three hundred marks

replacing Shakespeare's "There are two gentlemen," etc. It is worth mentioning, as well, that Phelps's Falstaff was not in the least flustered when he prepared to hide. Cool and sagacious still, he would leave no trace of his presence. "Falstaff goes and takes his Hat from Table," reads the Sadler's Wells Promptbook.[43a]

Passing now to Act III, Scene 2, we find Leigh Hunt commenting upon the pomps of dress at Drury Lane in 1830:

Mr. Cooper's costume as Henry IV. was a real historical picture. We saw the King himself before us, with his draperied head; and the performer, as he rose from his chair, and remained lecturing his son with his foot planted on the royal stool, displayed the monarch well — his ermined robe, stretched out by his elbow, making a back-ground to the portrait.[44]

But this king is a talker, and it is to Jack Falstaff and the madcap Prince that we must turn for stage business.

The Quarto stage direction at III, 3, 101, is as follows: *"Enter the prince marching, and Falstalffe meetes him playing upon his trunchion like a fife."* [45] Surely, it is Falstaff who does the playing, and in the epilogue to Gildon's *Measure for Measure; Or, Beauty's the Best Advocate* (1700), Shakespeare's Ghost is made to say of the Lincoln's Inn Fields playhouse:

> *Fat* Falstaff *here, with Pleasure, I beheld,*
> *Toss off his Bottle, and his* Truncheon *weild:*
> *Such as I meant him, such the* Knight *appear'd.*

Kemble, however, assigned the truncheon to Hal; and Mr. Jones's "playing upon the truncheon" (though not his fighting) won the approval of the *Edinburgh Dramatic Review*, April 17, 1824.

Just what significance a truncheon possessed for the Elizabethans is not too clear. At times, certainly, it was a mere symbol of command. For not only does the ghost of a king have a truncheon, in *Hamlet* — his marshal's baton, as it were — but so too does Cassio as Captain of the Guard, in *Othello*, while in Lant's engraving of Sir Philip Sidney's funeral, truncheons seem to be carried by "Two Corporalls" (or "Ductores ordinū eqestriū").[46] As a theatrical property, truncheons in the Restoration time came to be associated with tragedy. Mr. Bayes, asked what his heroic scene is to be, explains: "my design is guilded Truncheons, forc'd conceipt, smooth Verse, and a Rant." Steele's unfinished *School of Action* contains an amusing episode in which Buskin, a tragedian, is stripped of his high heels and towering plumes. He can no longer recite his speech. "Give me my truncheon at least," he whines, "I got it by heart with a stick in my hand."[47] It may be added that the phrase, to change your yardstick, your basting ladle, your quill, or what not, for a truncheon, occurs not infrequently in the eighteenth century, meaning to give up such-and-such a trade and become an actor.

Later in the same scene (III, 3), the Sadler's Wells Promptbook calls for some spirited byplay between the angry Hostess and Sir John. She "threatens Falstaff in action," as she addresses the Prince. "Falstaff by action tries to prevent Mrs Quickly from telling the Prince," a moment after. When, too, he insists that Henry is in his debt — "A thousand pound, Hal? A million! Thy love is worth a million; thou owest me thy love" — it is "seizing his hand and shaking it heartily — then laughs at Hostess trying as she speaks to put her down with his laughs." And at Dame Quickly's departure, "Falstaff kisses her then chuckles to Prince/ Hostess very pleased Exits." Far happier, however, is still another direction in the same book:

Prince. I am good friends with my father, and may do anything.
Fal.   Rob me the exchequer the first thing thou doest, and do it with unwash'd hands too.
Bard.   Do, my lord —

and, so saying, Bardolph "X's eagerly to Prince who rebukes him
— Bardolph retires up. . . ."
As Stephen Kemble spoke the concluding couplet,

> Rare words! brave world! Hostess, my breakfast, come.
> O, I could wish this Tavern were·my drum!

"instead of retiring from the Stage, he placed himself in a Chair,
and remained in that situation, till the scene shut him out; which,
though apparently new," *The Townsman* remarks, "was evidently natural, and is entitled to commendation." [48] In Miss Margaret Webster's production, we were permitted a glimpse of Sir
John actually getting his breakfast. It was brought to him on a
tray.

Kemble provided a flag of truce for the deputations which pass
between the camps in Act IV, Scene 3, and Act V, Scene 1. A
further bit of punctilio was introduced in Cumberland's edition
where, on Blunt's entrance, in the earlier scene, "*All take off their
hats*" — to put them on again when Blunt reminds them that they
"stand against anointed majesty." Phelps's promptnote, "The
Leaders all bow to Sir W. Blunt," is less naïve. In his production,
"3 Lady Pages Bearing the Kings and 2 Princes Shields" were in
attendance at the beginning of V, 1, and the scene was given a
stirring climax when, as Henry orders "every leader to his
charge," "The King. Prince Henry & John take their Shields
from Pages — Knights & (Sir John) draws. unsling their Shields &
swords &c." [49] For contrast, Francis Gentleman had written in
1770:

> There is a most contemptible piece of stage buffoonery introduced
> here, which ought to be repulsed, not laughed at; we mean Falstaff's
> sitting upon the same drum with the King, and tumbling down when
> Henry gets up.

It is good to hear that Cooke, appearing at Chester in the summer
of 1802, disclaimed "the hacknied paltry tricks of rolling off a
drum — of having several alarms, and falling down repeatedly
. . . he steadily adheres to the letter and spirit of the poet." [50]

When the Prince enters in the third scene, to ask help of Falstaff, it is "*with his Sword broken*," according to Kemble. Tree

was at fault, a moment before. "Pointing to Sir Walter Blunt's body, he says, 'There's honour for you!' and then taps his own breastplate as he proceeds, 'Here's no vanity!' " But, as Archer noted, "Here's no vanity" applies to Blunt quite as clearly as the previous phrase.[51]

Falstaff encounters Douglas and feigns death. The Prince, after killing Percy, says,

> But let my favours hide thy mangled face —

covering it with a scarf or, as I have seen it done on the stage, merely with his cloak. Meanwhile, Falstaff should be lying very still indeed. If, however, we are to credit Maurice Morgann, the actors of his time took outrageous liberties here:

> The painful Comedian lies spread out on his belly, and not only covers himself all over with his robe as with a shell, but forms a kind of round Tortoise-back by I know not what stuffing or contrivance; in addition to which, he alternately lifts up, and depresses, and dodges his head, and looks to the one side and to the other.[52]

When he is alone, as we read in Cumberland's edition, Falstaff *"makes several attempts to rise, but on hearing the drums drops under his shield again."* And this had been Charles Kemble's business in 1824, when he "elaborated some points far too much, particularly the *ducking* as he heard the rolling of the drum at a distance." [53]

Sir John rises — "with the assistance of Sword & Shield," in Phelps's performance. But an even more laborious task confronts him. "We conceive," Francis Gentleman writes, "the son of sack's rolling and tumbling about the stage, to get *Hotspur* on his back, is too much in the style of pantomime mummery," though, "it may, and certainly does, create laughter." Davies observes that

> Quin had little or no difficulty in perching Garrick upon his shoulders, who looked like a dwarf on the back of a giant. But oh! how he tugged and toiled to raise Barry from the ground. . . . At length this upper-gallery merriment was done away with by the difficulties which Henderson encountered in getting Smith on his shoulders. So much time was consumed in this pick-a-back business, that

the spectators grew tired, or rather disgusted. It was thought best, for the future, that some of Falstaff's ragamuffins should bear off the dead body.[54]

Later acting editions, indeed, often call for soldiers to perform the task; and "the martial style in which Mr. [Charles] Kemble strutted away before the soldiers who bore the body of *Hotspur*, as if *veni, vidi, vici*, had been emblazoned on his forehead, provoked great bursts of laughter." On the other hand, a Charleston newspaper in 1787 mentions the advisability of having "a stump of a tree on which *Falstaff* may rest the body of *Hotspur*, during his conversation with the Prince"; and Ryder and Dowton, in 1823, both executed the macabre directions of the text.[55]

2 Henry IV

When *The Second Part of King Henry the Fourth* was given at Drury Lane on December 17, 1720, it was described as "not acted 17 years," which suggests the likelihood of a production soon after the turn of the century. It seems to have been unacted, before, since the Restoration and subsequent revivals have not been numerous.

In a political essay in *The Craftsman*, June 19, 1731, a comparison is drawn between Verres and Falstaff. A statue, "raised to the perpetual Infamy" of the former, had, we are told, a small image "called *Plutus*, placed before him, pouring Money into his Lap, and endeavoring to screen him from *Justice.* . . . *Falstaff* places his *little Page* before him, to cover him from the Sight of my *Lord Chief Justice.*" Clearly, it would seem, this is an allusion to the play in performance. "Sir," says the Page, "here comes the nobleman that committed the Prince for striking him about Bardolph." And Falstaff: "Wait close. I will not see him." But in *The Sequel of Henry the Fourth* (c. 1721), this speech has been altered, and reads, "Sirrah, stand between us, I won't be seen." In Garrick's marked copy, the original words are retained, but with "Boy stand before me" added in manuscript; while in Bell's edition (1774), Falstaff is made to say, "Boy, stand before me, I would not be seen." The business implied is wholly delightful, and one would ask nothing better than to see it adopted when next the play is revived. It might be added that this rascally little page used to mock his master. "Your imitations of Shakespeare," Sir Fretful Plagiary hears, in *The Critic*, "resemble the mimicry of Falstaff's Page, and are about as near the standard of the original." [56]

At the beginning of the third scene, Kemble has the conspirators "*discovered, seated.*" Then they "*rise,*" and the Archbishop says,

> Thus have you heard our cause and known our means,

as if they had been conferring for a long time. But I have found little business concerning these distinctly unexciting characters.

It is in character for Falstaff to put Bardolph "*between himself and Fang,*" as Cumberland's edition directs him to do at ii, 1, 50. A scuffle follows "*between Bardolph, Fang, Snare, and Page*"; but presently "*Bardolph and Page, seeing the Chief Justice, run behind,*" and "*Fang and Snare seize hold of Falstaff.*" One further stage direction, this time from Lacy's edition, has to do with the appeasement of the Hostess. "Come, come, I know thou wast set on to this," Falstaff cries, "*holding both her hands and see-sawing her arms, playfully.*" [57]

In the later Tavern Scene (ii, 4), it seems a pity that Sir John should not be allowed sole credit for the ejection of Pistol — though admittedly he later asks whether Bardolph has "turn'd him out"— but Kemble would not have it so. "Falstaff, Bardolph, *and* Page, *drive* Pistol *out,*" is his stage direction here, preserved, regrettably, in later acting versions.[58] The Knight had entered, by the way, bearing "*a jug of sack*" (Kemble). As he is summoned away — "Well, sweet Jack, have a care of thyself"— Doll "*hugs him*" (Lacy).

Davies tells us that, as Justice Shallow,

> Cibber's transition from asking the price of bullocks, to trite, but grave, reflections on mortality, was ... attended with ... an unmeaning roll of his small pigs-eyes, accompanied with an important utterance of tick! tick! tick! not much louder than the balance of a watch's pendulum.

A *"table, pens, ink, paper, three chairs,"* are called for, in Cumberland's edition, at the beginning of the scene (III, 2), and these props Davy puts forward as Falstaff is announced. The board now sits, *"Falstaff,* L, *Shallow,* C, *and Silence,* R." Before them appear Mouldy, Bullcalf, and the rest; and, after each recruit has been examined, Bardolph *"puts"* him *"behind to* R." Mr. Gordon Crosse has seen Laurence Irving's Shallow at Manchester in 1898: "I laugh as I write at the remembrance of his showing Wart how to manage his caliver and then sinking onto a seat, panting with exhaustion." [59]

The early eighteenth century *Sequel of Henry the Fourth* is useful at several moments in the scenes which follow. *"Enter Officers with Wine,"* at IV, 2, 66, is practical and to the point, as is *"Gives him his Sword,"* of Coleville in IV, 3, when he surrenders to Falstaff. The removal of the sick King "into some other chamber" is accomplished without a change of scene. *"The King faints,"* at IV, 4, 111. "Pray bear me hence," he says,

> And lay me on my Bed – Softly I pray;

and presently *"He is laid on the Bed."* Similar slight liberties with the text are taken in all the later acting versions I have seen. Westmoreland (Kemble), or the Lord Chief Justice (Lacy), now puts the crown on the King's pillow. And, at the end of the long episode with the Prince, Lacy's edition calls for *"the organ without — the* King *is led up, supported by the* Prince of Wales, *and* Prince John. — *Tableau."*

Kemble supplied the delightful scene in Shallow's garden with business of obvious propriety. Thus, Bardolph and the Boy sit at a table, apart from their elders and betters, where they are supplied with *"a Dish of Apples"* by the factotum Davy. When, too, Davy tells of the arrival of "one Pistol come from the court with news" and Falstaff repeats, "From the court?"— *"They rise,"* excitedly. Finally, at Sir John's "Carry Master Silence to bed," *"Davy and the* Servants *remove the Tables, &c. and carry* Silence *away."* According to Lacy, he *"falls off his chair,"* just before, and Lady Benson recalls that James Fagan, as the Justice, "was much annoyed when H. O. Nicholson, as 'Davy,' threw a pot of beer full in his face as he lay prostrate on the stage." [60]

Another Bensonian note concerns the last scene of all. This is from a tribute to G. R. Weir which appeared shortly after his death. At the King's harsh words, "I know thee not, old man,"

the expression of the "old man's" face was wonderful. So sad was it, so full of pain, so filled with amazement, that . . . one felt pitiful towards him — very, very pitiful. And then the trembling hand clutching the arm of Shallow, the shaking voice, fighting against despair, "I shall be sent for soon at night." This is not a thing to be forgotten.[61]

It is possible to conceive of a quite different interpretation. Yet, after all, it is legitimate for the actor to look ahead here — "By my troth, he'll yield the crow a pudding one of these days. The King has kill'd his heart."

Richard III

The recent discovery of a manuscript list of actors — including Sandford as Richard, Mountfort as Richmond, and Kynaston as Clarence — makes it beyond doubt that at least one Restoration production of *Richard III* took place before the dazzling appearance of Colley Cibber's version in 1700.[62] One cannot believe, however, that much Pre-Restoration tradition can have survived, through Sandford and Cibber's recollections of Sandford, to affect later performances. A new chapter in the history of the play begins with 1700, a chapter which closes only with the reforms, none too securely achieved, of Samuel Phelps, Edwin Booth, and Sir Henry Irving. Meanwhile, the disentangling of Shakespeare from Cibber in the case of many recorded bits of business is not easy. Thus, to take a single instance, Act III, Scene 7, ends, in the original:

Rich. [*to the Bishops*] Come, let us to our holy work again. —
Farewell, my cousin; farewell, gentle friends.

Booth, in 1886–1887, did without the soliloquy which Cibber had added here ("Why, now my golden dream is out," etc.), but he still reversed the order of the two quoted lines. Hence the fol-

lowing business, as set down in his promptbook at "The Players":
"Gloster with joy embraces Buck — just then the 2 Clergymen
advance to C. Gloster perceiving them pushes Buck away — who
Exits L arch — Gloster then speak this line as he is going off R
with Clergymen." The words are still Shakespeare's; the business
belongs, rather, to Cibber?

Kean's entrance for the famous soliloquy attracted attention
— a rapid entrance. "Tumbling on the stage . . . he stops short"
and speaks,

> Now is the winter of our discontent. . . .[63]

In this, we are told, he departed from "the 'business' of Kemble
and Cooke . . . the 'martial stalk' of his predecessors. . . . The
audience ratified the new reading, and it was imitated by all succeeding candidates for fame in the same part —" by Forrest, certainly, who "burst upon the stage, cloaked and capped, waving
his glove in triumph over the downfall of the house of Lancaster,"
and by Davenport, "rushing on the stage" and breaking at once
"into a burst of passion." Very different was the entrance of the
elder Booth, as Walt Whitman describes it:

> I can, from my good seat in the pit, pretty well front, see again
> Booth's quiet entrance from the side, as, with head bent, he slowly and
> in silence (amid the tempest of boisterous hand-clapping), walks down
> the stage to the footlights with that peculiar and abstracted gesture,
> musingly kicking his sword, which he holds off from him by its sash.
> Though fifty years have pass'd since then, I can hear the clank, and
> feel the perfect following hush of perhaps three thousand people
> waiting.[64]

At least two lines in the soliloquy itself have been elaborately
illustrated. As Cooke began,

> "In the deep bosom — "

he lifted the right hand a little, with a gently sweeping motion, and
then turning the palm downwards, he continued

> " — of the ocean — "

and made a short pause, then sinking his hand (the palm parallel with
the earth) and his voice at the same time, finished the sentence by the
word,

> " — buried."

Kean, too, paused at "buried" and "pointed his finger downwards" (Doran speaks of "the murmur of approbation" with which the action was greeted).[65] When, a little later, Richard can think of no delight in these new, peaceful times —

> Unless to see my shadow in the sun
> And descant on mine own deformity —

Theophilus Cibber finds the idea one which "his hurt Imagination would naturally turn from, the Moment it occurs to him: — But for the sake of an Attitude, which is sure to be dwelt on 'till the Audience clap, — this Sentence is commonly closed with an Action of pointing to the Ground, and fixing the Eye thereon for some Time." [66] At the end of the succeeding dialogue with Clarence, Phelps's promptnote, "Gloster embraces Clarence," is exactly right, in view of the doomed man's later expostulation (1, 4, 250).

As Cibber arranged it, Richard is present when the funeral procession enters at the beginning of Scene 2. The grace of Kean's attitude as he leaned against a Gothic pillar while waiting his chance to speak was much commented upon. It was imitated by the elder Booth,[67] whence it passed to his son, in whose promptbook "leans on post" is written against the printed direction, "*Retires*." Mansfield, however, having shifted the scene from the London street to a country road, changed the business, too, and crouched "behind his cloak, lifting it to conceal his face from a sidewise view, while facing the audience." [68] Stopped by the guard, who raises his halbert, Richard, in "French's Acting Edition" (a Charles Kean text), strikes up the man's weapon and crosses to Anne.

"When *Richard* gets upon his knees to *Lady Anne* in this scene," writes the critic of *The Edinburgh Dramatic Review*, March 11, 1824, "there is, in the usual style of acting it, too much antithetical point to the discourse of *Richard*; — it is made all seesaw; and *Lady Anne* . . . is made to point the sword, or drop it, like a figure in a puppet show." It is arguable that the introduction of patterns of action to accompany the patterns of speech is appropriate here.[69] But such an idea would have seemed strange indeed to early nineteenth century actors and audiences. Kemble took pains at least. Sir Walter Scott finds that his

anxiety as a manager made him sometimes too busy; he was apt to be drilling the performers even during the time of the performance. . . . We ourselves remember to have seen a very pleasing looking young person much disturbed by Kemble's directions about lifting and lowering the sword in the scene betwixt the princess Anne and Richard.[70]

Nor was Booth above giving precise instructions. When Lady Anne offers to strike, he notes: "The handle of sword is held in her RH & she clutches blade with her left, raising it up to the right each time"; and when she drops it, at last, it is "with handle towards Gloster." This is from his promptbook. The acting version published in *The Shakespearean Plays of Edwin Booth*, which Winter edited, has also: "*He lays his breast open; she offers at it with his sword; as she does so he looks up sadly, when she slowly lowers the sword.*"

A few further details. Henry Crabb Robinson writes of Kean that "his finest scene was with Lady Anne . . . his mode of lifting up her veil to watch her countenance was exquisite." Booth, in putting on the ring, kissed her hand, as did Mansfield.[71] Booth's father, when he came to the concluding lines,

> Shine out, fair sun, till I have bought a glass,
> That I may see my shadow as I pass,

"looked down at his supposed shadow . . . he looked with lingering step, and, with pauses between the words, annihilated the singsong of the double ending —

> 'That I may see — my shadow — as — I pass.' "

Yet Theophilus Cibber, a century before, had derided a Richard of that day for "halting off, all the Way looking at, and admiring his supposed Shadow. . . . *Richard* is not such a Simpleton, seriously to intend" hiring the score or two of tailors; " 'tis Laughter all, and Mockery of the Widow's Weakness." [72]

Irving in Act I, Scene 3, instead of 'strutting' about, sat "thoroughly enjoying the railings of his royal relatives at each other, and at the point where the discussion comes loudest and nearest and most offensive to him goes to a table and, hearing everything all the time, writes out a warrant of arrest." Phelps, in Scene 4, has Clarence before telling of his dream point to "a rude seat which Brackenbury assists him to in front of stage," and later Brackenbury "removes the seat within the Opening of Flat" and helps Clarence off. Nor does the Duke re-enter, the murder taking place off-stage: "A noise without — Fall of a body/ and then a noise as if dragged along/ A heavy sack of shavings." Booth showed the murder. *"As Clarence falls, the 2nd Murderer kneels as if to raise and carry him. — The 1st Murderer throws down his dagger and turns in horror."* [73]

In the second scene in Act II, when Richard says to his mother "Humbly on my knee/ I crave your blessing,"

> Irving, with a refinement of mockery, lightly spreads his handkerchief on the ground at her feet before kneeling to her. This little touch is thrown in with such finish that it is not till he rises again with the ironical *aside* that follows that its ribald insolence is made clear. [74]

When we come to Act III, and the little princes, Cibber's stage direction, *"Embracing,"* when the Duke of York addresses his "dread lord," is not without poignancy. [75] York says,

> Uncle, my brother mocks both you and me:
> Because that I am little, like an ape,
> He thinks that you should bear me on your shoulders,

and here "French's Acting Edition (Late Lacy's)" has: *"puts up his right shoulder, going across to* Duchess." Kate Terry is York in the Princess's Theatre, 1854, cast printed at the beginning of this edition. "The feigned playfulness" with which Gustavus Brooke, as Richard, met "the sallies of the Infant York" found praise, and "the idea of patting the child's head," which was "original, and well imagined." [76] Then there was Joseph Haworth at the Castle Square, Boston, in 1895, of whom the *Transcript* writes that "his by-play was excellent . . . of especial force being the working of his hands about the little Duke of York's throat in the midst of a pretended caress." Almost at the end of this episode, Kean disappointed Hazlitt:

The manner in which, after his nephew said, "I fear no uncles dead," he suddenly turned round, and answered, "And I hope none living, sir," was, we thought, quite out of character. The motion was performed, and the sounds uttered, in the smallest possible time in which a puppet could be made to mimic or gabble the part.[77]

On the other hand, *The Examiner*, February 27, 1814, approves of "the familiar tap" on Buckingham's arm, with which Kean, laughing, accompanied the words "Chop off his head," at the close of the scene.

Shakespeare's fourth scene, containing the arrest of Hastings, was restored by Macready in 1821, when

the hurry of his step to the chair, his attitude of wrath, his sudden denunciation of the witchcraft, the stripping up the withered arm, were all conceived with the energy of strong passion, and were honoured with great applause.[78]

The Phelps Promptbook has at Richard's re-entrance: "he paces angrily to & fro the stage then seats himself at the head of Table." Hastings attempts to speak:

> If they have done this deed, my noble lord —
> *Rich.*   If?

"Strikes his hand violently on Table & Enter 4 English Guard who range OP." Booth stamped here. It is noteworthy, too, that in his acting edition the celebrated strawberries from the Bishop's Holborn garden are actually presented: *"Page enters with berries. Ely about to rise, Catesby goes quickly to prevent him — takes the dish and gives it to Gloster."* [79]

In Act III, Scene 7, Phelps has the Mayor and "4 Aldermen" arrive by barge ("A Barge pushed on 4 City Bargemen with Oars upraised"), while his citizens entered, less jerkily, no doubt, by the "PS3E." "All the Citizens . . . take off their Hats when Gloster appears," and when Buckingham cries

> Long live King Richard, England's worthy King!

"Every one kneels to Gloster." At this point, Forrest raised "Buck — with a knowing look & pressure of hand," and Irving "from behind the convenient shelter of that prayer-book, darted a triumphant look" at his accomplice.[80] Mansfield's Richard, on his entrance between the clergymen, had appeared to give all his attention, piously, to the same prayer-book; then, the moment the others looked away, turned it upside-down! At the end of the scene, he recurred to the old Cibber business of flinging the volume into the air — or even, upon one occasion, into the orchestra.[81]

Phelps's promptnotes are again of interest at the beginning of the fourth act. Thus, Brackenbury's exit, after the pleadings of the ladies, is "thro the Gates which he closes after him"; and during Richard's dialogue with Tyrrel, (IV, 2), "the Lords are conversing together not heeding it"— whereas when "Buckingham Enters all observe the conversation." Cumberland's *British Theatre* (1829) adds the graphic detail that when Buckingham reaches the climax of his importunity —

May it please you to resolve me in my suit —

he "*kneels and catches the King's robe, which the King dashes from his hand.*" So, too, in the Booth-Winter Edition, he "*kneels and takes Richard by the robe,*" but at an earlier moment, when it could not have been so telling.

Mansfield's inventiveness found scope in the next scene, that in which Richard learns of the murder of the little princes. Thus, at Tyrrel's exit, the actor "caused a commotion and a horrified, smothered cry to be heard," as if the wretched man "had been set upon and killed, outside of the throne room." [82] The usurper is now alone.

Filled with a sense of security and gratified ambition, he mounts the throne chair, and sits in it with every evidence of satisfaction. As he does so the red light streams through stained glass windows, and falls with the color of blood upon his face and hands. . . . Terror-stricken, he slides from the throne and sits brooding at its foot.[83]

George Becks, the actor and collector, has left full descriptive notes on Mansfield's production. An ardent admirer of Edwin Forrest, Becks was unimpressed by the modern Richard. At the end of the scene, he writes, the King "draws — all draw strong-tableau," and his comment is: "!They sharpen their glaves! o!"

The *Thespian Magazine*, for December 1793, contains a letter of advice to a young performer at the Haymarket. "During the reproaches of his Mother and the Queen, also on his way to battle," he is "to walk the stage in splenetic fretfulness to draw off the regard of his attendants from his mother's curses, and converse with the officers about him." "Paces up & down" is Ferrers's promptnote at

Thus will I drown your exclamations —

as if this were still in the eighteen-thirties the accepted business. Later in the same scene (IV, 4), the Booth-Winter Edition has the curious direction, "*Messenger enters* R.2.E, *and gives a paper to Richard,*" when the tyrant is frantically issuing orders (line 451). Something in this paper, we are to suppose, causes his veering about:

Rat.　What, may it please you, shall I do at Salisbury?
Rich.　Why, what wouldst thou do there before I go?
Rat.　Your Highness told me I should post before.
Rich.　My mind is chang'd.[84]

"Richmond with a Truncheon" appeared in Garrick's commemorative pageant, *The Jubilee* (1769), and in Cumberland's *British Theatre* (1829) he enters "*with a truncheon, having a written paper rolled round it.*"[85] At Sadler's Wells, the audience saw the setting up of the two tents, Phelps's promptnote, at V, 3, 1, reading: "The Soldiers bring in Tent which they pitch OP masked in by 6 English Archers — they Exit when finished." Shields hang on posts in front of this tent, which was Richard's and tall cressets were lighted on each side of it. Richmond's was similarly "masked" by soldiers while it was being erected.[86]

The despondency of Kemble's Richard on the eve of battle was so pronounced that

We do not wonder at the languor of the nerveless arm that drops overpowered by his sword's weight — it strikes against the ground — silence and darkness give louder tongue to the accident, and that accident carries to the heart a superstitious foreboding that tomorrow it may fall as powerless in his hand.[87]

It is with the name of a greater actor, however, that this scene is peculiarly associated.

> Kean's preparations for the dreadful fight
> The most fastidious critic must delight. . . .

Lingering at the entrance to his tent, Kean sketched on the ground, musingly, with the point of his sword, the plan of the morrow's engagement. Byron, it was suggested, remembered the business when he wrote the fourteenth stanza of the "Ode to Napoleon Buonaparte." Kean's own source was discovered in a speech of Young Norval's in *Douglas*.[88] But Cooke's practice is also to be taken into account. Of his Richard in Philadelphia, March 25, 1811, *The Mirror of Taste and Dramatic Censor* writes:

> Doubt — confidence — apprehension — disregard — defiance — and yet misgiving of the event of the next day, are successively displayed . . . by his restlessness, and walking backwards and forwards, — and by his sticking the point of his sword in the ground, and then recovering and flourishing it, — by his sighing and silent attempts to speak.[89]

Cooke's business, in other words, was given a wholly new meaning by Kean. As adapted by him — transformed, even — it was taken over by Barry Sullivan, but with a subtle variation of his own. Kean's sketch had been triumphantly completed: "with a sudden motion," he "drew another line across, as if he had just found his point of attack." Sullivan's would not satisfy him:

> Something is evidently lacking, has been overlooked. He retraces his movements, but halts again on reaching the same point. After a meaningful pause, he leaves the field, puzzled and in heavy doubt. It was a presage of "Richard's" defeat on the morrow at Bosworth Field.[90]

What follows is complicated alike by changes in staging and by the astonishing persistence of Colley Cibber's alterations. In early nineteenth century performances, for instance, the interior of Richard's tent was shown: "*Lamps down — Couch — Table (R.C.) with Pens, Ink, and Paper — Lamp, Truncheon. Shield, Hat and Feathers — Crown and Sceptre on Cushion — Drawn Sword.*"[91] Before retiring, Richard still spoke the soliloquy which Cibber had "conveyed" for him from *Henry V.* The ghosts were but four in number.

In the first edition of Cibber's play (1700), each of the ghosts *"rises"*— that is, through traps — and the last to speak *"sinks."* For well over a hundred years, they regularly appeared and disappeared after the same antique fashion.[92]   Those at the Theatre Royal, Edinburgh, near the close of the century, are an exception. Thus we read in "Jordan *versus* Jackson; Or, An Heroic Epistle from Mrs. Jordan to the Manager of the Theatre Royal, Edinburgh," as printed in *The Gazetteer and New Daily Advertiser,* November 12, 1789:

> To save a crown the trap-doors thou nail'st up,
> And bid'st the Carpenter go home and sup;
> While Ghosts, who from the burning ground should pop,
> Enter on either side, with skip and hop.

And "Timothy Plain," in *Letters Respecting the Performances at the Theatre Royal, Edinburgh,* has, under February 3, 1797: "By the bye, where *Ghosts* are introduced, I think it is a great improvement to make them walk on and off, instead of rising through squeaking trap-doors." [93]

On February 21, 1814, Hazlitt in *The Morning Chronicle* expressed the wish that "the introduction of the ghosts through the trap-doors of the stage were altogether omitted," adding the suggestion that the ghosts' speeches "might be delivered . . . from behind the scenes." [94] Reform was to come swiftly. On March 15, *The Times* observes that

> The raising of the ghosts through stage-traps was always a clumsy contrivance, and we are glad to see it laid aside. At Drury-lane they are now introduced behind a gauze or tissue, at the back of the tyrant's couch. At Covent-garden . . . the young Princes appear at the back, but the shades of *King Henry* and *Lady Anne* come in at the sides, within a sort of aerial mist.[95]

Thenceforward, a partial concealment of the ghosts behind gauzes became the rule.[96]

"Richard starts out of his dream." It has been a great moment for the actor. Wilkes, in 1759, could not "recollect any situation

in Tragedy" in which Garrick had appeared "to more advantage than that in which he rises and grasps his sword before quite awake." "A spectacle of horror," he advanced and fell upon his knees — "Have mercy, Jesu!" [97] Kemble elaborated. Darting first to the right, then to the left, he thrust with his sword at the objects of terror conjured up by his fancy, and at last dropped on his knees close to the footlights. Kean, as described by Tieck, in 1817, "staggered forward," leaning upon his sword, and

sank on one knee, then started back as if he wished to rise, holding high in the air his other arm, which shook violently even to the finger-tips; then trembling, staring with wide-open eyes, he advanced in silent anguish on his knees . . . still shaking with fright.[98]

Later actors were not, for a long time, to add appreciably to the business of Kemble and Kean. Alger should, perhaps, be quoted on Forrest:

He struggled on his couch with horrible phantoms. . . . Acting his dreams out he dealt his blows around with frightful and aimless energy, and . . . fell apparently cloven to the earth. He then arose like a man coming out of hell . . . and, struggling fiercely to awake, rushed to the footlights, sank on his knee, and spoke. . . .[99]

New ideas for the scene came at last with Irving. As he uttered the lines,

> There is no creature loves me;
> And if I die, no soul shall pity me,

his hands fell, as if by accident, on a crucifix. At the beginning, too, he had sat for some time studying a map; then, having placed it on a table, where a small lamp was burning, he limped about the tent and presently, coming to the entrance and drawing back the curtains, looked out at the night.[100] On the other hand, a much applauded *coup* of Mansfield's seems not to have been of his own invention. It is described in *The Boston Herald*, October 22, 1899:

Even Catesby, at first, to the rudely awakened King is another avenging spirit. Rapidly and repeatedly, in terror, he makes the sign of the cross, and finally reaches out and touches Catesby . . . then, satisfied, falls exhausted upon his friendly breast. The effect of this new business . . . was electrical.

As Becks puts it: " ! ! looks. afraid. at Catesby." [101] But Kemble, too, had fallen "almost lifeless . . . soliciting sympathy, into the arms of Catesby." Cooke had "started from his knees" at the man's entrance. And Kean's "start," and his "superstitious alarm on the sudden entrance of *Catesby*" won repeated praise.[102] That Mansfield should have been to this extent anticipated, is not in the least to his discredit. "Zounds, who's there?" Richard exclaims, the terror of his dream seizing him anew. Only his crossing himself, Mansfield's own contribution, is in the least questionable.

There can be little doubt, I am afraid, that to a great many Richards the chief attraction which the rôle possessed was the opportunity it afforded for a prolonged and terrific single combat with Richmond. To this fight and the tyrant's death we shall come in a moment. But first, a curious detail, Richard's reading of the doggerel verses. . . . Kemble treated them with disdain and struck aside the paper containing them, with his sword. Cooke, on the other hand, after reading the first line,

> Jockey of Norfolk, be not so bold,

"with the manner of curiosity," becomes grave as he goes on, and at last "slowly throws aside the scroll." And poor little Clara Fisher, appearing in Edinburgh in 1824, is told that "she ought, instead of returning it, to toss away" the offensive paper "with sovereign contempt." [103]

Francis Gentleman speaks of the "general murmur which the meeting of *Richmond* and *Richard* always occasions, followed by the eager applause that attends the tyrant's fall." Already, it would seem, there was much extravagance in the playing. Wilkinson finds Thomas Sheridan exceptional in that he performed the death scene "without the aid of a flounder-like flouncing." [104] An ironic epilogue printed in *The London Chronicle*, April 17–19, 1792, protests:

> The voice of Nature is too faint, and flat; ˙. . .
> He spoil'd the tent scene — 'Twas so tame! so dead!

Why when he dreams, he never quits his bed!
I love to see ferocious Dick the Third
Jump up, and cut the side scenes with his sword:
Rush on, with haggard eye, and bristling locks;
As if he meant to storm the music box.
I love to see him when you think he's slain,
Start up and stagger, and be kill'd again.[105]

Kean, ever fortunate in those who described his acting, has been pictured for us unforgettably in this last scene. "He fought like one drunk with wounds," Hazlitt writes, "and the attitude in which he stands with his hands stretched out, after his sword is taken from him, had a preternatural and terrific grandeur, as if his will could not be disarmed, and the very phantoms of his despair had a withering power." [106] In one of his ideas at least, the "glare of hate" which he fixed upon Richmond, he had been anticipated by Cooke. Cooke's business varied, indeed, from performance to performance:

One time . . . he makes an ineffectual effort to rise, and failing in it dashes away his sword in despair; another time he drops his sword, and, in making a vain effort to recover, falls again. . . . But that which gives the finishing stroke to the picture is the look which, raising himself on his elbow, he darts at Richmond. It was terrible . . . it looked a testamentary curse.[107]

Another idea of Kean's was to continue to push or lunge with his hand after he had dropped his sword.[108] After Kean, it was said,

Every personator of *Richard* must fight like a madman, and fence on the ground, and when disarmed and wounded, thrust with savage impotence with his naked hand. . . . Mr. Kean has passed this manner into a law, and woe be to him who breaks it. No one but Mr. Kemble can be allowed to parry like a schoolboy, and drop like a gentleman.[109]

Junius Brutus Booth adopted Kean's manner. He fought with savage fury. According to a story, often repeated, though it may be (alas!) no more than what his son termed it, "one of the myths of the stage," he even, on one occasion, refused to yield at all, and pursued his now terrified antagonist from the stage and out into the street.[110] Macready, in 1820, after receiving

his death-blow . . . retires to the side-scene, and then, with a super-
human energy, lifts himself to more than his natural height, and comes
pouring down upon his adversary till he reaches him, and then falls at
his feet like a spent thunderbolt.[111]

Sullivan's fight, punctuated by the gods with cries of "Go on,
Barry!" was thrilling. By way of innovation, he spat at Richmond; but also, he thrust at him "with his empty hands"[112]— as
Kean had done. Irving revived the excitements of an earlier day.
Again, there was novelty, in his clinging to Richmond's sword
"with hands and teeth," or "passionately tearing his gauntlet from
his stiffening fingers," to fling it "defiantly at the conqueror's
feet"; again, tradition, in "the glare of baffled hate and malignity,"
which he fixed upon his enemy.[113]

Much might be added of other Richards — of the substantial
armor, for instance, the hacking and hewing, which distinguished
Mansfield's combat. Rather, for its mere curiosity, I have set
down the following description, headed *"Richard fight"* from
Louis James's promptbook:

> 6 Shoulder blows & thrust to R cor — on *Richm.*
> 6 Round blows up *C* —
> 6 Head blows from Richm — on Richard — to *L. H.*
>   *Richm* runs up *C* — followed by *Rich* —
>   head blow on *Rich*, Rich *down* —
> 6 Prime blows (*double*) down *C* — thrust
>   and *picture* — X blows to *L* — stab *Rich*,
>   Double Shoulder blows *"ad Lib"*—
>   Rich. gives quick thrust on *Richm*
>   is disarmed, *stab — picture — Richm*
>   catch blow of Rich — hand —
>   Rich falls — *picture*
>   *& End*

As for the last scene of all, enough that in early nineteenth
century performances it was customary to introduce a waving of
banners while the concluding lines were being spoken; that at
Drury Lane, in 1823, Richard's soldiers did not even go through
the motions of surrendering before mingling with the victorious
army; and that Charles Kean had "Norfolk *brought in wounded
upon a shield.*" [114]

King John

The first performance of *King John* after the Restoration was in 1737. There is no need, this time, to reckon with the possibility that some part of the traditional business may go back to Shakespeare himself. Though now almost unknown as an acting play, *King John* yet contains scenes which are full of life and excitement on the stage — scenes, too, which depend largely upon action for their effectiveness. Nor is it a barren pleasure to read of the majestic Constance of Mrs. Siddons, the dashing, chivalrous Faulconbridge of her brother. Even King John himself may become interesting — once he is Kemble's John, or Macready's.

Regularly, the play began with a discovery, the King on his throne. His abrupt,

> Now say, Chatillon, what would France with us?

has sometimes been spoken only after Norfolk, "*who is discovered in the act of speaking to the King*," has gone out and returned again, formally ushering in the French ambassador. This was Charles Kean's idea.[115] More interesting is the early nineteenth century direction for Chatillon to enter bareheaded, then put on his hat as he addresses John:

> Thus, after greeting, speaks the King of France
> In my behaviour to the majesty,
> The borrowed majesty, of England here.

Tree, in 1899, chose to begin with a procession, and introduced not only "a little jester" (all mediaeval courts had jesters on the later Victorian stage?) but also monks "chanting a Mass." [116]

Stately, and practical too, is the introduction of the brothers Faulconbridge as Kemble arranged it. An English Herald, replacing Shakespeare's mere Sheriff, enters at line 38, while John and Elinor are still conferring, and "*whispers* Essex." Essex tells the King,

> My liege, here is the strangest controversy . . .

and the Herald, leaving the stage at "Let them approach," brings
in the two contestants. Near the end of the scene, Charles Kemble
was praised for his reading of,

> Sir Robert never holp to make this leg,

where "suiting the action to the word, as well he might, it had a
great effect upon the house." And Mrs. Cowden Clarke writes of
the same actor that

> in the scene with his mother . . . his manly tenderness, his filial coax-
> ing way of speaking and putting his arm round her as he thanks her for
> having made Richard Cœur de Lion his father, was something to be
> grateful for having witnessed.[117]

As the kings parleyed beneath the walls of Angiers, Mr. Bernard Shaw writes of Tree's production in 1899, "the queen mother
holds out her arms to little Arthur, and Constance reads in her
eyes all that would befall him in England." [118] The citizens open
their gates and, entering, kneel to present the keys of the city.
"*Exeunt into the gates, all but* Faulconbridge."

> Mad world! mad kings! mad composition!

he cries; then, after speaking the great lines on "Commodity," he
too goes in. A mere entrance . . . but made by Charles Kemble
with so much grace and meaning; "I can see him now," writes
the painter Frith, "as, with the elegant saunter appropriate to the
character, he disappears under the portcullis, and, the place being
new to him, he looks to the right and left with the insolence of a
conqueror." Edward FitzGerald is another who recalls with pleasure "his look up at Angiers' Walls as he went out in Act II." [119]
Charles Kean set the stage for the new scene in "*the French
King's Tent. A Dais with one chair on it . . . table with crucifix,
book, &c.,* R.— *Sentries patrolling before the entrance.*" On
John's entrance, "*The Attendants place the other chair on the
Dais*"; and at "England, I will fall from thee," Philip leaves the
throne. "*General excitement — Nobles prepare for battle, cross
R and L, and crowd round their respective kings.*" [120] It is Con-
stance's scene, none the less. Victor speaks of Mrs. Cibber's enter-

ing "with dishevel'd hair, and Wildness in her Eyes. . . . The Cardinal, and others attempting to comfort her — she sunk on the Ground — and looking round with a dignified Wildness and Horror! said,

> 'Here *I*, and *Sorrow* sit! — this is my *Throne!*' "

Joseph Cradock had heard from Davies that the house was "electrified when she threw herself upon the ground in agony. . . . Even Garrick expressed his astonishment." [121] This was a great moment, too, in the performance of Mrs. Siddons. Leigh Hunt compares her with her niece in the same scene:

> The passage in which Constance wildly seats herself upon the ground, and exclaims,
>> "Here I and sorrow sit: let kings come bow to me,"
> produced no effect last night. All who remember Mrs. Siddons must remember its electrical effect, and how marvellously she reconciled the mad impulse of it, with habitual dignity. Miss Kemble was almost stationary in her grief. Mrs. Siddons used to pace up and down, as the eddying gust of her impatience drove her.

Miss O'Neill "rooted one knee, as it were, to the ground, clasped her boy firmly with one hand, and dashed the other upon the limb before her, with a voice and look of unparalleled grandeur." Miss Faucit's Constance, "after throwing herself on the ground," played "with the ringlets of her boy," as he stood "drooping over her." Ellen Terry, as Arthur, was supposed to catch Mrs. Kean as "she sank down on to the ground." [122]

Large gestures were in order here. Helen Faucit, after "bending down to clasp her son, with the words,"

> And our oppression hath made up this league —

rose to her full height and flung up her hands, "in the majestic appeal,"

> Arm, arm, you heavens, against these perjur'd kings!
> A widow cries; be husband to me, heavens!

Mrs. Siddons, likewise, had raised clasped hands. Yet "she patted *Lewis* on the breast" when she came to "O, thine honour, Lewis, thine honour," which she spoke sarcastically with a laugh.[123] As for the Bastard's taunting of Austria, in early nineteenth century performances, he spoke

> And hang a calve's-skin on those recreant limbs

from behind King John's chair, then repeated it, "*Rushing down to the front of the stage.*" [124]

Austria's head might no longer be displayed by Faulconbridge, but an admirable substitute for it was discovered. After referring to the Bastard's return "as conqueror of Austria," Francis Gentleman suggests that "the lion's skin, as a trophy of honour worn by his father, should be worn by the Bastard through the remainder of the play." Kemble has Faulconbridge enter at the beginning of iii, 2, and say:

> Now, by my life, this day grows wondrous hot!
> Some airy devil hovers in the sky
> And pours down mischief.

Then: "*Enter* Austria; Faulconbridge *and* Austria *engage*; Faulconbridge *drives* Austria *off the Stage, and presently re-enters with the Lion's Skin in his Hand.*" "Austria's head lie there," he continues. It was a good arrangement, and lasted. In Tree's production, however, the audience saw Faulconbridge "fell his arch foe and snatch from his shoulders the lion skin of Richard." [125] A few lines later, at "Hubert, keep this boy," Arthur is of course taken into custody — or, as J. B. Addis's promptbook of the eighteen-forties puts it, "King John flings Arthur over to Hubert — who hurries him off."

The scene between Hubert and John, which follows, loses its full force if we have forgotten that even while they are plotting Arthur's murder the little prince himself is present. Elinor is there, too, entertaining Arthur, watching the faces of the others, guessing, it may be, what they are so earnestly discussing. Yet Mrs. Vining, at Covent Garden in 1831, neglected her opportunities, standing "like a stock at the front of the stage." Kemble's colloquy with Hubert was, we are told,

a master-piece. . . . His glances at the child, and the unconscious wandering of his malignant eye, till arrested by the sullen visage of his emissary, are too exquisite to acknowledge description. We must particularize the skill with which Mr. Kemble delivered the first line annexed:

> "Good Hubert, Hubert, Hubert, throw thine eye
> On yon young boy;" —

The arm of *Hubert* was cautiously drawn through his own, as he addressed him with courtesy, paused and *repeated* "Hubert!"

Kemble's "tiger-like prowl to and fro . . . as he eyed his young victim" was another point.[126] Macready, after uttering the word "death," "started back appalled by the sense of having overleaped all safety"; then gazed "in terror on the witness to the sound . . . in agony of suspense to know how he received it." Like Kemble he had glanced first at the young prince, and made this glance an "index to the dark deed." But "when he pronounces the word 'death!' he does not look in Hubert's face." Frith reports that when this John threw off the mask "and in two words, '*the grave*,'" made his meaning unmistakable, he "placed his mouth close to Hubert's ear" and whispered them; yet the whisper "could be heard at the back of Drury Lane gallery." [127] Tree, last of all, must needs invent business. In 1889, "the King, weary from battle, sets down his helmet encircled by the crown. Arthur takes it up and places it on his own head. John, seeing him, snatches the crown away"— and plots his murder with Hubert. Ten years later, Arthur was plucking daisies while they talked, and afterwards John lopped off the heads of the flowers with his sword.[128]

The manuscript part of Constance with Helen Faucit's pencilled annotations is preserved in the Furness Collection at the University of Pennsylvania. Many of the notes are now undecipherable; but against III, 4, 37, the actress wrote, "look about for Arthur during the scene — occasionally put out the hand as if expecting to meet his," and again, at line 102, "look for him" and "think of seeing and calling for him." Action of some sort is implied just before, when Constance cries:

> I will not keep this form upon my head
> When there is such disorder in my wit.

France had twice besought her to 'bind up her hairs' and seemingly she had done so —

> I envy at their liberty
> And will again commit them to their bonds —

only now, with a fresh impulse of grief, to tear them free. In the eighteenth century, however, a more decorous action was preferred. Mrs. Yates, it is said, "took off a thin cap which surmounted her head-dress, and merely placed it on the right side of the circumference of her hoop." An engraving in Bell's *Shakespeare* (1774), reproduced as the frontispiece to the present volume, shows Mrs. Barry in the act of removing something like a veil. Fanny Kemble tore off a "diadem"; Miss Glyn, a "coronet." [129] When, however, Julia Neilson was preparing to play Constance, in 1899, Maud Tree showed her "how to use the grand Emmelaiac gesture of the tearing down of the hair." [130]

The scene between Hubert and Arthur at the beginning of the fourth act used to be played with much realism of detail. "French's Standard Drama," a Charles Kean edition, as already noted, has especially full directions. In addition to *"an antique table and chair . . . towards the front,"* two doors are called for. A tapestry hangs before one of these doors. The other is locked, and there is *"a key in the lock."* Saying "Heat me these irons hot," Hubert gives them to the Attendants, and, after their exit, unlocks the door and calls to Arthur. Then he goes to the chair, *"sits, and leans on table."* At "You are sad," the Prince, *"who has been playing with his bow . . . suddenly looks at Hubert intently, then goes to him"* (Fifty years later, in Tree's production, Arthur still carried a crossbow). Hubert shows him the warrant. He

stamps. Re-enter Attendants, with cord, irons, &c., L. *Arthur runs shrieking to cling round Hubert,* R. *The 2d Attendant puts down the pan of fire, and gives the iron across to Hubert. 1st Attendant has the rope, and seizes Arthur. They both strive to disengage and drag him away as he says,* "Nay, hear me," &c.

When at last Hubert is dissuaded from his cruel purpose, there is a *"pause."* Hubert *"throws away the iron — kneels and embraces Arthur."* He *"goes,* L.*, listens, and returns,"* before saying

"Peace! no more!" At "O heaven! I thank you, Hubert," Arthur kisses him. It might be added that at least once — under Macready — Arthur was played realistically. Miss Newcombe at Drury Lane, October 24, 1842 — "an interesting child, with his plaything in his hand," was "made to kick and scream, and in the turbulence of infantine terror to banish the sweetness and the beauty of the poet." [131]

When John blames Hubert for Arthur's death and is shown the King's own hand and seal, Garrick "snatched the warrant from his hand; and, grasping it hard, in an agony of despair and horror . . . threw his eyes to heaven, as if self-convicted of murder, and standing before the great Judge." Tree, on the contrary, thought of the warrant simply as a piece of evidence against a criminal, which John proceeded to destroy. "While the king burns this parchment on the cresset, the monks file into their mass. . . . The king smiles, and then, still leaning by the cresset, folds his hands in prayer." [132]

Arthur leaps from the walls and is killed. Cibber's stage direction in his adaptation, *Papal Tyranny in the Reign of King John* (1745) reads: *"He leaps from the Walls, and is cover'd by a Parapet between his Body and the Audience."* A drawing by the Bowery prompter J. B. Addis (reproduced on page 115) will make clear how this action was contrived a century later.

"Set Castle piece with Bed behind it," is the accompanying note. "Arthur leaps down — on the bed — and crawls out — round the corner of the wall." *The Athenaeum*, October 29, 1842, finds that at Drury Lane under Macready "the death of Arthur" (Miss Newcombe) was "absurdly overdone: not content with his leaping from a high tower, he is made to roll over and over down the steps as if they were a sloping bank of turf." Kate Reignolds, who played Arthur in Brougham's revival of the play in 1856, writes that

a "double" was used for the fall, a limp, made-up figure, dressed exactly like Arthur, the battlements being so constructed that . . . I ran, as if to take the leap, past a turreted part of the wall. Behind that turret we changed places, the "double" was cast over the battlements and disappeared among the tangled grass beneath the wall, while I grasped the perpendicular rods, also behind the turret, and slid down. . . . The men, whose business it was, caught me a few feet from the ground. An opening was left in the scene which admitted of my being rolled through it, so, as the "double" disappeared, I took my place behind the "set piece" under the wall and raised my head to speak the last two lines. . . .[133]

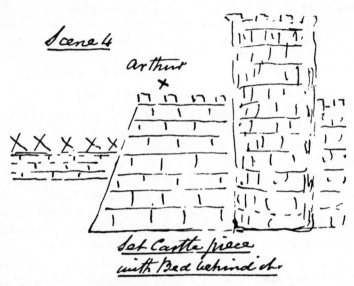

At the end of the scene, Hubert lifts the body of Arthur and bears it away in his arms —

How easy dost thou take all England up!

Kemble had regard to his author's clear intention here; and in performance this exit can be deeply affecting. Too often, however, the action was shirked, with Hubert merely stooping over the body, or being *sorrowfully engaged in raising it,*" as the curtain fell.[134] It is hard to guess why. The dread of ridicule, perhaps? In nineteenth century performances it was an actress, of course, who played Arthur.[135]

There is not much more of interest before John's death scene. At the beginning of Act v, Scene 1, the King was usually discovered kneeling before Pandulph, to whom he has just given his crown. Mr. Gordon Crosse writes of Louis Calvert, Tree's Pandulph, that "only once in the twitch of the hands as John approaches to make his submission, did the human nature of the man break out in his moment of triumph from under the immobility of the priest." Charles Kean had John's litter conspicuously carried across the stage, at the beginning of the third scene ("The lions on the curtains," Kean was at pains to note, "were introduced from King John's shield").[136] Moreover, he equipped Hubert with a crossbow at the beginning of Scene 6; and Hubert *"walks three or four times past the gate before he speaks"*—

> Who's there? Speak, ho! speak quickly, or I shoot!

Soon after the beginning of the last scene, according to Kemble's stage directions, Salisbury and "English Gentlemen" enter *"with a Couch."* John was not "brought in," and the *Examiner*, November 30, 1823, thought Kemble's "rush upon the stage in a paroxysm of burning fever . . . particularly fine." As Whitman recalled it, long afterwards, Charles Kean in the 'forties "rush'd in, gray-pale and yellow, and threw himself on a lounge in the open. His pangs were horribly realistic." [137] So must Macready's have been. Pemberton, writing in 1834, speaks of

the face, now blazing, now ashy pale . . . the hard tension of the arms, as the hands gripped in life's last agony to the cushions of the couch, the stony death of the position in which the *body* sat for some seconds ere it fell back across the couch; life as thought had no direction in that body's so falling; it was a corpse's momentum, — a weight let go.

Tree opened the scene with monks passing quietly to the chapel. John was "borne out in a chair." Presently, Faulconbridge "comes in hot haste, and the king, to receive his tidings, sits upright, and is crowned for the last time. He makes no answer to the tidings. One of the courtiers touches him, ever so lightly, on the shoulder and he falls back." Then the crown was "taken from his head and laid on the head of the child who is now king." [138]

King Henry the Fifth

As was the case with *King John*, the stage history of *Henry V* in Post-Restoration times begins late, not long before the middle

of the eighteenth century. On the other hand, the nineteenth
century revived the play a number of times, and the business used
in these later productions is often interesting.

It was a nicety in the performances at Sadler's Wells that the
"Constable and French Lords" upon entering were to "take off
their Hats & bow — the English return it." And when the Constable speaks in his character of Ambassador ("Thus then, in
few"), it is "putting on Hat" and "all the French Lords put on
their Hats." [139] Before Exeter makes known what the "tun of
treasure" really contains, "2 Attendants open the Chest — Exeter
takes out a Tennis ball holding it up to view. All express surprise.
Attendants take off Chest when Exeter has put back ball."

Act II, Scene I, introduces the comic characters, a sadly de-
pleted company. At the end, according to the Sadler's Wells
Promptbook, Pistol "Xs C taking their arms" —

> Let us condole the knight; for, lambkins, we will live —

and they go out. Even more appealing is the direction in Oxberry's *New English Drama* (1824), Exeunt Pistol and Nym,
"hand in hand."

The exposure of the conspirators, Cambridge, Scroop, and
Grey, takes place in Scene 2. As Exeter places them under arrest,
it was customary for each in turn to surrender his sword, either to
Exeter himself or to some Officer. In Mansfield's acting edition,
however, Exeter *"touches the shoulder of each with his baton.*
Gower *draws the sword of each."* Against line 95, Charles Kean
wrote: "Scroop drops face in hands."

Mrs. Quickly tells of Falstaff's death. Her husband and friends
are going to the wars:

Pist. Touch her soft mouth, and march.
Bard. Farewell, hostess.
Nym. I cannot kiss, that is the humour of it; but adieu!

Phelps caused Nym to "turn away whimpering"— at the thought
of parting, I suppose. Mansfield has him approach *"to kiss* Quickly.
Pistol *interferes."* There is still the Boy to dispose of. *The
Athenaeum*, April 2, 1859, finds that in Kean's production "the
heroism of the English character" is

the spirit that pervades the scenes. This is exemplified in the small as well as the great incidents. . . . Miss Kate Terry, as the impersonator of the brave youth, in the heroic and pleased attitude with which he listened to the sound of the drum, and the measured march with which he followed delightedly the spirit-stirring music, showed us at once the sympathetic gallantry of the English lad going to the wars.

In the last scene in Act II — the French King's reception of Henry's defiance — the ceremony of an ambassador's taking off and putting on his hat was introduced again. And, in Benson's production, this time, Shakespeare was so far sacrificed to History that the French King was turned into a half-wit, "playing with a bauble, and caring nothing for State affairs." [140]

For the scene before Harfleur, at the beginning of the third act, the resources of the stage were often taxed in the endeavour to show an actual siege in progress. Thus, at Sadler's Wells, the English troops advanced, then retreated. "The King rallies them, and they again rush to Attack." A "Panorama" was introduced, to aid illusion. "Henry ascends bridge heading the whole of the Army. with Colors." At Manchester, in 1872, the supers

rose each night to such a pitch of excitement, that as [Charles Calvert] rushed up the eminence, followed by the shouting soldiery, the moment he was out of sight of the audience, he had to jump down and get underneath the platform, or he would, most assuredly, have been mown down by his own men.[141]

Similarly, in Scene 3, the yielding of the town was regularly shown, with the Governor and Citizens issuing from the gates, to kneel and give up their keys; and, though there is no suggestion in the dialogue that the French leaders are at dice, in Scene 7, Charles Kean and other producers,[142] taking their hint from the subsequent words of the Chorus, so represented them.

For contrast,

> The poor condemned English,
> Like sacrifices, by their watchful fires
> Sit patiently. . . .

Mansfield began the fourth act with chanting off-stage. "*The monks confess and bless the soldiers. Retiring, they leave the young* Duke *of* Bedford *standing over the embers of a smoulder-ing fire. He is joined by his brothers,* King Henry *and the* Duke *of* Gloster." Charles Kean thought of having the King give back the borrowed cloak to Erpingham, on the "good old knight's" return after the episode with the soldiers; and Kemble scored at the end of the scene:

As a *coup de Theatre,* his starting up from prayer at the sound of the trumpet, in the passage where he states his attempted atonement to Richard the Second, formed one of the most spirited excitements that the stage has ever displayed.

Vandenhoff was using the same business at the Theatre Royal, Edinburgh, in 1825.[143]

A stage accident which befell Macready in 1833 was the break-ing of his truncheon during the great "St. Crispin's" speech in Scene 3. Charles Kean brought out the effect of the same speech on the listening soldiers by having them raise their hands and incline their weapons "to King" at

> We few, we happy few, we band of brothers,

and by introducing a similar demonstration at the end — "Shouts Kept up — Waving of Weapons." Mr. Crosse writes of Lewis Waller that

the climax of his performance was the last few lines of the Crispin speech which by a bold and happy device he spoke at the front of the stage with his back to the audience, while his followers knelt in a semi-circle facing him.[144]

Of the business in the succeeding scenes, it is enough to note: that in Mansfield's production Pistol entered, absurdly enough, drag-ging in his French Soldier *"by a halter"*; that Charles Kean caused *"the bodies of the* Duke of York *and* Earl of Suffolk" to be *"borne across the stage by soldiers"* just before the King's entrance in IV, 7; and that on the exit of Williams, a little later, Phelps's Henry dropped "the Glove of Williams. Fluellen picks it up and gives it to Henry Kneeling." [145] "Here Fluellen," the King says, "wear thou this favour for me and stick it in thy cap."

When the difference between Fluellen and Williams over the

matter of this glove has been adjusted (in IV, 8), it is satisfactory
to learn, from Phelps's Promptbook, that "Williams takes the
shilling. Flu offers his hand which Williams takes, and shakes."
For an impropriety, later in the same scene, Macready is taken to
task by *John Bull*, June 16, 1839:

> So far has this rage for over-embellishing his author led MR. MAC-
> READY that at the conclusion of the fourth act, which ends with these
> words, spoken by *King Henry* —
>> Do we all holy rites
>> Let there be sung *Non Nobis* and *Te Deum* . . .
> the actor literally kneels down with his soldiery, and the curtain falls
> to the solemn strains of an organ, brought from England we suppose
> for the purpose.

Charles Kean, as one might have guessed, was unable to resist the
same "*organ music*." Phelps closes with "Music and Te Deum . . .
when voices cease they all kneel in situations. Picture."

Ancient Pistol is made to eat the leek. Fluellen addresses him:
"God pless you, Aunchient Pistol! you scurvy, lousy knave, God
pless you!" Here the stage direction in Kemble's edition (1806)
is: "*Draws the leek across his nose.*" Pistol's reply thus becomes
one not simply of resentment at Fluellen's words but of outraged
personal dignity:

>> Ha! art thou bedlam? dost thou thirst, base Troyan,
>> To have me fold up Parca's fatal web?
>> Hence! I am qualmish at the smell of leek.

The Sadler's Wells promptnotes for this scene are wholly delightful. Upon entering, "Fluellen. winks intelligence to Gower. and
then addresses Pistol." During Pistol's third speech ("Base
Troyan, thou shalt die"), he is "affecting to be unable to draw his
Sword." A moment later, Fluellen is "beating him around Stage."
Yet after the Welshman's departure, Pistol rallies, "drawing his
sword & vaporing." Charles Kean's markings are even more full.
Again, as he salutes him, Fluellen "holds the leek close to Pistol"
— which is surely right! At first, he merely beats him "on back,"
but at line 39 he "strikes him on the back of his head," which
occasions Gower's quiet "Enough, Captain. You have astonish'd

him." "I say I will make him eat some part of my leek," Fluellen
replies, "or I will peat his pate four days"—"flourishing cudgel."
In Mansfield's production, when by the way Mr. A. G. Andrews
was the Welshman, Fluellen at the first blow struck the poor
wretch *"to his knees"*; and at "All hell shall stir for this," with
which, inexcusably enough, the scene now ended, Pistol *"struts
boldly off, but, perceiving* Fluellen, *lowers his sword and runs in
the opposite direction."* Finally, Frederick Warde, in his *Fifty
Years of Make-Believe*, tells a good story about this scene, as it
was played at Booth's Theatre in 1875. The leek-eating, Warde
writes,

has to be done near the footlights, and pretense is impossible. A property leek with a tube in which a piece of apple was inserted was the
usual method employed, and Mr. Bishop, who had a great aversion to
onions in any form, ate the apple without discomfort, but one night
the property leek was lost or misplaced; a real leek was substituted,
and poor Bishop had to eat the nauseating vegetable at which his
stomach revolted in full view of the audience.[146]

Of the business in the remaining scenes, I shall only point out
that Charles Kean had the French and English divided by "barriers," in v, 2, the scene beginning with the appearance of heralds
who "direct Serv[ts] to place barriers down stage, which they do —
8 of each & then return to places"; and that in Mansfield's edition
Henry is about to kiss Katherine again, when he sees the French
King — "Here comes your father."

Richard II

Tate's alteration of *Richard II*, in 1680, came to grief promptly.
The eighteenth century revived Shakespeare's play once or twice,
then forgot its existence. Even the nineteenth could find no place
for this *Richard* in the established repertory, though, just at the
end, it was beginning to be acted again.

Benson's Richard, at Stratford in 1896, is pictured for us in
the first scene, where the King, "young, beautiful, luxurious, and
self-centred, heard his cousin's quarrel with Mowbray, while he
played with his hounds and yawned." Like "roan Barbary," one

of these dogs, "a beautiful wolfhound, always attendant on the King," was to desert him presently and to fawn upon Boling-broke. This idea seems to have been adopted by a later actor. For to Mr. Bernard Shaw, "one of the most moving points," in Tree's performance, was when Richard's pet dog "turned to Bolingbroke and licked his hand." [147]

At Covent Garden in 1738, much was made of "the ancient ceremony which belonged to the single combat. . . . The com-batants were dressed in complete armour. Two chairs, finely adorned, were placed on opposite sides of the lists: to these they retired after each of them had stood forth and spoken." Charles Kean was, of course, much interested in the same ceremony, and in his production not only do the two chairs again figure but also the combatants *"mount their horses"* and, when *"a charge sounded . . . ride off*, R. and L. — *they approach each other — the* King *throws down his truncheon, and they stop suddenly, and throw up their spears,"* then *"dismount, and resume their chairs."* [148] How different was the management of the scene in the performance by the Elizabethan Stage Society!

It was, of course, impossible for the fight between Mowbray and Hereford to take place. All that could be done was to bring on the contending noblemen, put blunted lances in their hands, and make them, with the aid of their squires, don, and then at royal bidding doff their casques. For a moment it seemed as if they were going to fight without, but on the king's throwing down a superfluous warder they were haled back.

For a detail, Elizabeth Fagan, as one of the ladies attendant upon the Queen in Benson's production, "used weepingly to throw [Mowbray] a handkerchief, as — a banished man — he left the lists." And this bit of business, too, was taken over by Tree.[149]

In the Elizabethan Stage Society's production, *The Athenaeum* grumbles, John of Gaunt was "brought on the stage not even in a litter, but in the arms of his retainers, by whom he is placed in a chair and afterwards carried out." Charles Kean had caused him to die in sight of the audience.[150]

So little is known of Booth's business in this play that even the smallest detail assumes interest. At Richard's

> For God's sake let us sit upon the ground
> And tell sad stories of the death of kings!

Booth's promptnote is : "Lords take off their hats." A "truncheon for Bolingbroke" is called for in the next scene, that before Flint Castle.

Richard descends into the "base court." Henry kneels dutifully before him.

Rich. Up, cousin, up! Your heart is up, I know,
   Thus high at least.

Mr. Maurice Evans, at "Thus high", pointed to his crown. Edmund Kean had through his gesture given a similar meaning to the words, intimating "by a sign with his hand that Bolingbroke aims at the level of his crown." But the later and lesser Kean appears for once to have departed from his father's ways here, by "pointing significantly to his head when speaking the words." In Holinshed, Shakespeare had read that as the King went to the "vtter warde" he was "accompanied with the bishop of Carleill, the earle of Salisburie, and sir Stephan Scroope, knight, (who bare the sword before him)." [151] Richard, then, would be wearing his crown, too, the crown to which Bolingbroke aspired. . . . Which gesture was intended seems fairly clear.

As an instance of the excessive energy of Kean's Richard, Hazlitt cites "his dashing the glass down with all his might," in the Deposition Scene, "instead of letting it fall out of his hands, as from an infant's." [152] But all that is certain is that the glass should be "crack'd in a hundred shivers." Northumberland had insisted, a little earlier, that the King "dispatch" and "read o'er these articles." And, according to Cumberland's *British Theatre* — a Kean edition, seemingly — "*Richard takes the paper from Northumberland and gazes on it for a moment steadily.*"

> Mine eyes are full of tears; I cannot see,

he cries, and "*lets the paper fall.*" Booth waited till the end of the same speech. Then, as his promptbook tells us, he "dashes paper to ground." [153]

To Dickins, Benson's "finest moment" was in this scene. "In his impotent rage and despair, this Richard lay flat on the ground and kicked, and daring as was the conception, it perfectly conveyed the idea of the weak, miserable, angry, spoilt child." From another source, we learn that

after crowning Bolingbroke, he proceeds to examine himself in the glass, and in doing so mechanically ascends the steps to the vacant throne. Just as he is about to sit down, he suddenly remembers himself with a short laugh and an apologetic gesture.[154]

Viola Tree tells of playing the Queen to her father's Richard in 1903. In the first scene in Act v, she would look instinctively to see him come out,

very simply and rather tired, dressed in black, and each time it seemed as if he were surprised to see me standing there, and as if we were really to say good-bye. . . . Then I fell on his neck, and said my speech sobbing. . . . Aumerle and the super halberdiers had vanished like shadows to the dark corners.

Mrs. Kean was praised for "rushing towards the parapet and leaning over it to catch a last glimpse of the beloved object." [155]

When Richard attacks the Keeper, Charles Kean has him snatch "*a knife from the table.*" Booth's promptbook makes the weapon a craftily constructed stone seat. Also called for is a "small grated window, set deep in the wall, just high enough to rest the elbows on the sill" — where, I suppose, the long soliloquy at the beginning of the scene was spoken. After killing one of the servants, Richard is seized and stabbed by Exton, "staggers and falls on table." As this murderous struggle was recalled, years after, Booth was

"careful to keep all his sharp physical action and resistance subordinated to the expression of open-mouthed and all but speechless, horrified amazement and bewilderment. As one assassin plucks him by hair and pulls him half-bent, backward, and another stabs the handsome young king," he falls "with mouth still hanging open in the piteous fashion that is stamped forever on the mind."

C. E. Montague, in a finely sensitive review of Benson's performance at Manchester in 1899, writes that in uttering his concluding lines —

Mount, mount, my soul! thy seat is up on high;
Whilst my gross flesh sinks downward, here to die —

this Richard "half rises from the ground with a brightened face and repeats the two last words with a sudden return of animation and interest, the eager spirit leaping up, with a last flicker before it goes quite out, to seize on this new 'idea of' the death of the body." [156]

Henry the Sixth

I have found no business to record, in *The First Part of King Henry the Sixth*, and not much in the two later plays. They have, of course, been acted only rarely. An occasional stage direction in John Crowne's Restoration versions possesses a momentary interest. His "long Scrowles lying on a Table," at the beginning of *2 Henry VI*, ii, 2, might, one feels, be useful in the setting forth of York's title to the throne — but then, the setting is no longer a garden but "the Duke of *York*'s House." "*The Qu. swoons upon the Prince*," at *3 Henry VI*, v, 5, 42, is right enough — so right, indeed, as to be readily deducible from the lines themselves.[157]

The Benson Company did put on *The Second Part* successfully, and there was a production of it, also, at the Surrey in 1864, with James Anderson doubling York and Jack Cade. *The Athenaeum*, April 30, 1864, found Cade's fight with Iden exciting,

and Mr. Anderson threw considerable humour into it by indicating the weakness he suffered from a five days' fast, and buckling his belt tighter in order to strengthen himself for the task. He died boldly . . . and won our respect even in his fall.

A "gruesome bit of realism" in Benson's performance at Stratford, in 1899, was the bearing in of "the heads of Lord Say and Sir John Crome . . . on poles among the jeers of the rabble."

A story of Lady Benson's shows how an effective piece of business may originate in the inspiration of the moment. As Margaret in a revival of *The Third Part of King Henry the Sixth* at Stratford, in 1901, she found when she came to the last words in v, 4, that she had forgotten her sword. "Darting at 'King Henry' I snatched his sword from the scabbard, and flourishing it above my head, rushed off amid much applause, followed meekly by the weaponless King." It was, she read the next morning, "a magnificent exit." [158]

Certain passages in *The Third Part* have, as a matter of fact, been spoken on the boards a great many times. I am referring, of course, to the requisitions which Cibber made on this play for his own *Richard III*. Thus Macready writes of Edmund Kean that "as he uttered the line, 'To shrink my arm up like a withered shrub,' he remained looking on the limb for some moments with a sort of bitter discontent, and then struck it back in angry disgust." Forrest did the same thing.[159] But were a modern Shakespearean actor to introduce the business, it would be in Act III, Scene 2, of *Henry the Sixth, Part III*, whence Cibber had lifted it. Or there is the murder by Richard of the poor good King. While Cooke listened to his accuser, we read of

> the quivering of his lip and under jaw . . . the universal agitation produced throughout his whole frame by the violence of his passion. . . . His impatience and the fellness of his purpose were marked with more singular emphasis by his play with his sword, than by any other single circumstance: instead of putting his right hand to it every now and then as others do, he fiddled with the hilt with his left, his thumb beating upon it with convulsive agitation.

Mansfield's Richard upon entering paused before an oratory "to bow and make the sign of the cross." Then he looked off to make certain he was not being observed. Towse speaks of his coolly testing the tip of his sword, which he passed "through the body of his victim with the nonchalance of a poulterer skewering a fowl." [160]

> What? Will the aspiring blood of Lancaster
> Sink in the ground? I thought it would have mounted.

We read of "the unrelenting irony" with which Garrick looked at the blood on his sword, and of the elder Booth "towering erect, the head with the plumed hat thrown back, the eyes following the upturned point of the raised and outstretched sword." [161] "Shakes sword as if to throw off blood," is the direction in Edwin Booth's promptbook, where also, a few lines later, he "steps over body" — treating this dead king with the same contempt his father's Cassius had shown Caesar.[162]

III

Hamlet

THERE IS a great deal of action in *Hamlet*, and plenty of opportunities are afforded for adding, legitimately, to the business demanded by the lines and stage directions — in the ghost scenes, for instance. These opportunities cannot be said to have been neglected through the long stage history of the play, and some of the business may well be of great antiquity. John Downes writes of the revival of *Hamlet* at Lincoln's Inn Fields in 1661:

> The Tragedy of *Hamlet*; *Hamlet* being Perform'd by Mr. *Betterton*, Sir *William* (having seen Mr. *Taylor* of the *Black-Fryars* Company Act it, who being Instructed by the Author Mr. *Shaksepeur*) taught Mr. *Betterton* in every Particle of it; which by his exact Performance of it, gain'd him Esteem and Reputation, Superlative to all other Plays.[1]

What this amounts to (Downes was no stylist) is that through Davenant ("Sir *William*") the *Hamlet* tradition goes back to Shakespeare's own time. Betterton played the part for almost fifty years. Wilks succeeded Betterton. The line is unbroken, down to Forbes-Robertson and our own century. Much of Hamlet's business will depend, however, on the actor's idea of what the Prince of Denmark was really like, and no Shakespearean part has had more varied interpretations. What would Garrick have thought of Edwin Booth's Hamlet, or Irving of John Philip Kemble's? Tradition even at its strongest admits of innovation.

The scene of the nocturnal watch, with which the play begins, was often neglected in performance. It was thrust forward before "a front cloth, which is later to ascend and reveal the great

hall of state ready behind it." [2] Hamlet himself is not present, to
keep an eye on things; only minor actors are there — and the
"heavy" who plays the Ghost. To Warburton had come the
unpleasant idea that when, in reply to Bernardo's "What, is Horatio there?" Horatio says, "A piece of him," he should give his
hand. A stage direction to this effect got into Bell's Edition of
Shakespeare's Plays (1774); and, though Kemble rejected it,
"*Giving his hand*" lasted on, as the reading in "French's Standard
Drama," till the middle of the nineteenth century.[3] The Ghost's
entrance, in Elizabethan productions, was unquestionably through
a trap. Traps were regularly associated with the appearance of
ghosts; [4] they were the best available means for making a sudden,
surprising entrance; and since, on a later visit, this ghost is to 'cry
under the stage,' his ascent through a trap now — as if from
the "cellarage" — is peculiarly appropriate. Eighteenth century
spectres continued to enter thus. Aaron Hill writes, in *The
Prompter*, June 13, 1735:

THERE never rises a *Ghost*, but, instead of exciting our *Horror*, The
Poor Shade is sure to be *laugh'd at*, from the Aukwardness of these
Peoples Invention. — Had They only the Wit, in Place of *shewing* us
their TRAP, to conceal it, by contriving to *elevate*, at the same Time, a
proper Length of That Part of the *Stage*, that is between the *Ghost*,
and the *Audience*, No *Hole* being seen, for his Rising, he would *seem*
to ascend, *through the Floor*, and bring with him, in Consequence, the
Alarm he was sent to occasion.

The Ghost of Hamlet's father is not named here, it is true, but
since he was the best known of stage spirits I am afraid we must
believe that he was laughed at. Again, Mrs. Tabitha Bramble, in
Humphry Clinker, is gabbling to the great Quin, whom she calls
"Gwynn":

    "Mr Gwynn (said she the other day) I was once vastly entertained
with your playing the Ghost of Gimlet at Drury-lane, when you rose
up through the stage, with a white face and red eyes, and spoke of
quails upon the frightful porcofine — Do, pray, spout a little the Ghost
of Gimlet." "Madam (said Quin, with a glance of ineffable disdain)
the Ghost of Gimlet is laid, never to rise again." [5]

That accidents should befall the Ghost as he ascended was inevita-
ble. According to a story popular at the end of the eighteenth

century, "During the time of Mr. Garrick's performance in Goodman's-Fields,"

The stage, which rose very rapidly from the lamps, made it somewhat difficult for a performer to walk properly on it — and unfortunately it was the custom at that time for all Ghosts to appear in a complete suit — not of gilt leather — but of real armour.

On a particular night, this armour had "been borrowed from the Tower and was somewhat of the stiffest — the moment therefore he was put up at the trap-door — unable to keep his balance, he rolled down the stage to the lamps"— a mishap which occasioned waggish comments from the pit.[6]

When, exactly, the Ghost ceased to use trapwork, in making his entrance, is hard to say. But certainly, it would seem, by April 1824, when "The Ghost-player's Guide; Or, A Hint to Two Great Houses" was printed in *The London Magazine*. This guide — signed "Umbra"— is full of good things. The Ghost's costume, for example, is duly considered, and the suggestion thrown out that "a thin gauzy, sombre raiment thrown over the armour . . . would give a cloudy, indefined appearance to the figure." Ghosts did in fact veil themselves thus, for a long time to come. Professor Copeland remembers one of Booth's Ghosts who "solemnly lifting up his arm, disclosed, through the green gauze in which, twenty years ago, ghosts always travelled, that he had wisely put on a red flannel shirt." [7] "Umbra" does not refer to the trap, and he tells us that "under the present regime, the ghost marches in a mathematical right line across the stage, within truncheon's reach of the footlights." The course of his march across the stage is carefully plotted in Lawrence Barrett's promptbook, where, when Horatio says indulgently, "Well . . . let us hear Bernardo speak of this,"

They draw together, Horatio with L. hand on Bernar[do's] shoulder Marcellus leaning on his spear. . . . At the Ghost's Entrance, Bernardo swings around down stage, supporting himself on spea[r] Horatio & Marcellus spring to each other up C, the Gho[st] coming directly C, betw[een] them & Bernardo —

passing, as a diagram shows, from left to right.[8]

The Ghost steps softly, and he carries a truncheon. Tom Davies speaks of the "noiseless tread" of Barton Booth's Ghost, at the beginning of the eighteenth century, and this, we are told elsewhere, he achieved by wearing felt soles[9]— as Leigh Murray seems to advise Frank Archer to do, in a letter dated May 22, 1868:

am very pleased you have the "Ghost." Long may it be before you give it up, my dear boy! . . . "List, List, oh List" — if thou didst never that dear father play before, see that your boots or shoes creak not. Macready, when he played the Ghost to Charles Young's Hamlet, wore list or felt slippers under his mail-clad feet. You have no carpet on the platform, recollect.

The neglect of such precautions by Cooper, as the Ghost, led to his being told, on four several occasions in as many years, that 'the boards prated of his whereabout.' [10] The Ghost's truncheon is specifically mentioned by Horatio in Scene 2 ("Within his truncheon's length") and though we scarcely notice it nowadays, it was once an important property. "Abraham Thrifty," in *The Lady's Magazine; Or, Entertaining Companion for the Fair Sex*, for June 1789, complains that during his absence great preparations had been made by his family for a private performance of *Hamlet*:

They have made a prodigious large hole in the centre of the floor of the lesser room (now the stage) which I find was intended for the preternatural accomodation of a *ghost*. . . . Every thing was ready for representation . . . the ruler from the desk in the counting-house was employed as a truncheon.

And in Croker's *Familiar Epistles to Frederick J—s, Esq. on The Present State of the Irish Stage* (1804), we read:

>   The heroes brandish
>   Their swords . . .
>   Their truncheons ghosts, — their brooms the witches.[11]

Irving's promptbook (1877) calls for a "Glass Truncheon"; and, in 1882, readers of an article on properties were asked to "imagine Mead without" a truncheon — as if they scarcely could.[12] To what spectral use it was put we shall learn later.

The second exit of the Ghost, in this scene, is puzzling. Horatio calls to Marcellus to stop it, and Marcellus asks whether he shall "strike at it" with his weapon:

Hor. Do if it will not stand.
Ber.   'Tis here!
Hor.   'Tis here!
Mar. 'Tis gone!

They speak of its having "started, like a guilty thing" when the cock crew, and later tell Hamlet that it "shrunk in haste away, And vanish'd from our sight." W. J. Lawrence, for whose judgment on such matters I have the profoundest respect, held that on the Elizabethan stage two ghosts were set to work at this moment, the second entering just as the first is disappearing, only to vanish in his turn down a trap. In 1895, Winter spoke of "the double ghost," employed in E. S. Willard's production of the play, as "old." [13] Irving had introduced something very like it in 1883, when *The Athenaeum* (July 21) reported that "an innovation, happy enough in idea" had been "permitted":

On the first disappearance of the Ghost, Bernardo, Horatio, and Marcellus respectively exclaim, " 'Tis here! 'Tis here! 'Tis gone!" To convey the idea of this species of dispersal one or two figures dressed like the Ghost proceed in different directions.

But I can find no trace of the "double ghost" earlier. In November 1823, indeed, a writer in *The London Magazine* raised the question of how the lines beginning "Stop it, Marcellus" could be translated into action. He suggests *"machinery"*: "An effigy might be so constructed as to ubiquitate in the required manner, but a carnal ghost is manifestly unequal to the task. This is evident from the passage being always omitted in the performance of the tragedy." With the words " 'Tis here! 'Tis here! 'Tis gone!" cut — as they are in Bell's Edition of Shakespeare's Plays (1774) and many later acting versions — a simple descent on the part of the Ghost would be in order; and a cartoon in honor of Fielding's play *Pasquin* (1736) shows him in the act of going down his trap.[14] Later, when trapwork was falling into disrepute, I suppose he merely walked away. Ghosts, it was said, "never knew how to vanish till they learned to do so at Sadler's Wells." Fortunately, *The Theatrical Journal* has a detailed account of the arrangements there under Samuel Phelps:

Every one recollects the manner in which the *Ghost* used to stalk on and off in the first scene; at this little theatre the scene exhibits an extensive view of a castle by moonlight, with beacon pillars; the distant portions are lit up by the moon's rays, while the fore part lays [*sic*] in deep shadow. . . . The front of the stage forming a portion of the ramparts is kept very dark, the *Ghost* enters, moves slowly across the stage in an angular direction towards the beacon pillar, behind which it glides, when a burst of light shows it melting away in the far distance.[14a]

A few miscellaneous pieces of business remain to be mentioned. Kate Field in her rhapsody on the subject of Fechter in *The Atlantic*, for November 1870, writes:

Heretofore Horatios have senselessly *crossed the Ghost's path*, as if such a step would stay its progress. Not so with Fechter, whose Horatio makes the sign of the cross, at which the Ghost stops, as a Catholic ghost should. Once interpreted thus, intelligence exclaims "Of course"; and yet Horatios have been crossing the stage for three hundred years!

"I'll cross it, though it blast me," Horatio cries — and *crosses himself*, enlightened at last after "three hundred years"! Tradition does not come off so badly, after all. . . . Edward Lambert Stirling, as a young actor at Richmond and Dundee in the late eighteen-twenties, marked in his copy of *Hamlet*, "Makes the sign of the cross as he takes the stage," at the beginning of Horatio's speech about "th' extravagant and erring" spirits hastening away at cockcrow; and, at

> So hallow'd and so gracious is the time,

Booth's edition calls upon Horatio to uncover — and in each case the action is seemly and well imagined. Irving's promptbook has Horatio quit the stage first, "Marcellus and Bernardo following, when near the entrance; they turn, look towards where the Ghost has gone off, then Exeunt." There is a rightness about that which is refreshing. They might well look back!

For swift contrast, Claudius and Gertrude with their council-
lors — color and state. Hamlet himself, according to the Second
Quarto, comes last, after a pause, we may suppose, or through a
different door, since otherwise ceremonial usage would be disturbed. Actors have sometimes preferred a solemn procession,
sometimes a discovery with the King on his throne.[15] Kemble
chose the former method, making a striking appearance, "isolated
in the Danish revel court." [16] Macready was discovered: "Advancing slowly to the very front of the stage, he stood for a moment
with dejected eyes, then slowly raised them with a look . . . expressive of profound grief." [17] Charles Kean, on the contrary,
took part in a procession, then "stood in a bold upright attitude,
his arms folded and his handsome eyes turned up (so long that the
position must have been very painful)." [18] Forrest, in his later
years, was usually discovered. He sat, clutching the arms of his
chair, and glowered at Claudius.[19] Irving, who was "always" (in
Ellen Terry's words) "a tremendous believer in processions," had
one here, seating himself afterwards,

leaning on his elbow, motionless, making no show of grief, but gazing,
it would seem, half pensively, half cynically, not so much into vacancy
as into the heart of some oppressing mystery of sorrow.[20]

For novelty, Wilson Barrett, having entered through distant
arches, stood in the centre of the stage and petted a child; and
Forbes-Robertson kissed Gertrude's hand and then "paid attention" to some "elder ladies gathered round"—"that," Dame Madge
Kendal remarks, "was what only a real prince would do." [21]

Edwin Booth's Hamlet is memorably pictured in the eighteen-
sixties:

Before the splendid King and Queen bent a slight, lithe figure, robed
in black, which seemed to absorb gloomily into itself the brightness of
the place; and cast a shadow on it — so sad, so desolate, so intense, so
stricken it stood. When the King came toward it, with open palm and
loud "And now, my cousin Hamlet and *my son*," it started slightly
and moved away; the scornful "A little more than kin and less than
kind," falling in a half whisper from his lips.[22]

Presently, however, we begin to hear of an innovation of his —
very theatrical, very unlike Booth — the delaying of Hamlet's

entrance until just before the King addresses him. This belated appearance figures as a stage direction in Winter's edition of the actor's Shakespearean plays, and is the subject of a caustic footnote by Percy Fitzgerald:

> When Booth, that somewhat artificial performer, appeared in *Hamlet* he arranged his first entry in a thorough businesslike fashion, so as to produce a striking effect. The King was prosing on to the courtiers, as usual, when of a sudden there came a pause: the crowd of courtiers parted and formed a lane, while in came Hamlet, tripping it with much energy, smiling and bowing, till he found himself at the footlights.[23]

It is a relief to learn from Katherine Goodale's *Behind the Scenes with Edwin Booth* that by 1886–1887 the retarded entrance had been abandoned,[24] and to see Winter's stage direction cancelled in Booth's own promptbook (1890), where the Prince of Denmark is now "Dis[cd] Sitting RC." An actor's personality (Mr. Gielgud's for instance) can prevail with his audience even when Hamlet sits quietly well toward the side of the stage; and for sheer charm Booth can have had few rivals.

The old idea that Polonius was Lord Chamberlain at the court of Denmark determines some of the business in this scene. Kemble names Polonius first among the characters who take part in the procession, and probably allowed him to carry the white rod, frequently mentioned in later acting texts, and to indulge in a certain amount of comic bowing and backing.[25] At the departure of the King and his train, Fechter's Hamlet stood meditating, then, when the courtiers paused as if waiting to attend him, he perceived them and with a courteous gesture motioned them to proceed.[26] A Court Jester, the unhappy invention of Tom Taylor in his melodramatic version of the play in 1873, sometimes formed part of Claudius's retinue in Irving's performances, and, as the procession moved off, pointed jeeringly at Hamlet with his fool's bauble. Tree, on the other hand, made Ophelia the last to retire. Pitying Hamlet, she came back and touched his arm; whereupon he seized and kissed her hand, then turned sadly from her, "possessed with a larger passion." Shouts of "Long live the King!" were heard off-stage, and he covered his ears with his hands.[27]

Contrast with such elaborate by-play, a brief prompt note concerning "Mr. Young" at Brighton in 1809, who spoke

> Not so, my lord. I am too much i' th' sun,

"look^g at Kings Dress."

The soliloquy —

> Oh that this too too solid flesh would melt —

does not seem to have been accompanied by any very interesting business. Hamlet has often looked at the miniature of his father[28] — about which we shall hear a great deal presently — and there is a good opportunity for producing it at the words "So excellent a king." H. A. Clapp writes of Mounet-Sully, at the Tremont Theatre, Boston, in May 1894:

> Around his neck was a chain to which was attached a picture-in-little of his father, which he often observed and sometimes kissed. . . . [He] sat for a long time motionless, wordless, his eyes closed as if he were asleep, his mouth partly open, and presently began his first great soliloquy . . . with a direct handling of his arms and person on the word "flesh."

The Boston critic felt that this action "at once suggested the national conception of such a poetic passage." [29]

The clipped exchanges between Hamlet and the watchers follow. The American actor, Fennell, is cautioned by the Philadelphia *Theatrical Censor*, January 22, 1806, against looking upward, when Hamlet says musingly, "My father — methinks I see my father": "The mind oppressed by grief naturally directs the orbs of vision earthward, and 'the mind's eye' never seeks in vacant space the object of its contemplation." Yet Holman was keeping his eye "intently turned toward heaven," in Boston, seven years later.[30] George Becks in his manuscript notes on Forrest, describes him — "hand to head to soothe the pain — steps forward drops hand & with a far away look & *such* love in the voice, 'My father, &c.'" At Horatio's swift question, "O, where, my lord," the stage direction in Winter's edition of Booth's *Shakespearean Plays* is "*All start*"; and in his own "private" copy, Booth added — what no mere star-actor would ever have written — "The

effect of this rests wholly with Horatio." The "three solemn taps
on the brow with which Charles Kean always preluded the line,
'In my mind's eye, Horatio,'" must not pass unmentioned, sym-
bolizing as they do a tragic pomp, or pompousness, which is no
more. Fechter, the revolutionist, the leveller, in acting, 'crossed
his hands the moment his father was mentioned, as if praying for
the unhappy spirit.'[31] Two further passages in this scene have
been illustrated through business. At the end of Horatio's narrative —

> And we did think it writ down in our duty
> To let you know of it —

"Macready darted up the stage, turned suddenly and rushed down
to his starting point, and uttered

> 'Indeed, indeed, sirs, but this troubles me.'"[32]

How that was done, how adjusted to the conception of the character (in description it sounds splenetic), would determine its
value in performance. It might, I should think, be telling. Finally,
a much discussed point of John Kemble's was the strong emphasis
he placed upon "you," in Hamlet's "Did you not speak to it," as if
to single out Horatio, the scholar and his friend. This celebrated
"new reading" was not unaccompanied by action, if we are to
believe the following amusing lines from Leigh's *New Rosciad*
(1785):

> Sudden he starts! each feature turn'd awry,
> The lips contracted, vacant is the eye;
> The left hand without motion, wrist half bent,
> The right *slow* moves, as if he *something* meant;
> His head and hands affected airs display,
> Then opes his mouth, says nothing — walks away!
> Quickly returns — stops short — quite resolute —
> Exclaims "*Horatio did not* YOU *speak to 't?*"

In Scene 3, at Polonius's "There — my blessing with thee,"
Laertes is kneeling and the old man lays his hand on his son's head,
the words (as Theobald perceived) implying the action. Charlotte Porter writes of Wilson Barrett's production:

They make a pretty family picture, the dashing Laertes kneels to receive his silver-haired father's admonition, and the pink-robed maiden, with the baby face set in a glory of pale golden hair [Miss Eastlake], leans over him toying with his curls and returning the little caresses and laughing by-play, with which her brother consoles the tedium of the patriarch's harangue.

That is not to our taste today, nor is Ellen Terry's "placing a hand upon her brother's arm as though to add weight to the counsel given to him by Polonius"—but surely Ellen Terry had too much fun in her to do just that? [33] Attempts were often made to get something like a "strong curtain" for this scene which, as Shakespeare wrote it, ends so quietly. Lawrence Barrett's prompt-book, for instance, reads: "Ophelia remains L.C. with drooped head & dejected manner. Pol. turns from Entrance (R.1.) & says kindly — 'Come your ways' — She gladly runs to him." [34]

The two ghost scenes which follow are rich in stage business, much of it very old. An innovation of Fechter's, at the beginning of Scene 4, was to have Horatio and Marcellus met by Hamlet, who enters "from an opposite direction," since Hamlet has promised to visit them "upon the platform." The want of any exchange of salutation makes against acceptance of this rather prosy idea.[35] Henderson, Garrick's successor, a gifted actor about whom we know all too little, walked restlessly to and fro while he awaited the reappearance of the Ghost. This was Kemble's practice, I think, and certainly that of Macready, the elder Wallack, and Forbes-Robertson — a recognized tradition.[36] Cooper, the new Covent Garden Hamlet during the autumn of 1795, was criticized by the *Monthly Mirror* for his *caution*, on approaching the *platform.*"

Hamlet, though *troubled* . . . at the information he had received, does not *fear.* . . . Of course he would not *peep about*, as if appalled at his own shadow; therefore we think Mr. Cooper has been seduced by a novelty for the *sake* of novelty only. It has been usual with per-formers in this scene to *walk to and fro*, on the stage, and certainly the effect is improved by it . . . everybody knows, that the strongest symptom of a man's being agitated, is LOCOMOTION.

Irving's "glance roved over every discernible object and searched the darkness." [37]

"Look, my lord, it comes!" cries Horatio, at last, and Hamlet starts. For long years that start was, to actors, one of the great moments in the play. Colley Cibber's famous description of Betterton's Hamlet in the fourth chapter of the *Apology* does not mention business — only "a pause of mute amazement." Aaron Hill in *The Prompter*, October 24, 1735, in describing how the scene should be done, writes that "the Prince is suppos'd to turn eagerly toward the Spirit, with an unbelieving *Curiosity*, rather than a terrified *Apprehension*: But, upon the discover'd *Reality* of the Form, He *starts back*, a Step or two." He should kneel at the word "father," Hill continues.

Whoever remembers *Mr.* WILKS, in this Part of the Character, need not be put in mind, with what a *Lightness*, quite *improper* to the Occasion, *he anticipated* the *Place*, in which it would have been the Duty of his Friends, to *restrain* him; — causing them, (*immediately*, at his *first Sight* of the Apparition,) to *struggle* against his unreasonable Endeavours to break away, and *advance upon* the Ghost.[38]

It is interesting to find that Garrick's Hamlet was criticized for the same faulty anticipation of business to come. Those who disliked Garrick's start insisted, also, upon its artificiality. So *The Theatrical Examiner* (1757), in a paragraph on "Action" has: "The start at the ghost in the play of Hamlet may be picturesque, but it is grossly absurd to see a man fling himself into so exact an attitude, which it is impossible for him to remain steady in, without two supporters." [39] Dr. Johnson's opinion was sought and obtained. The subject of Partridge's visit to the play in *Tom Jones* came up for discussion, and Boswell asked, " 'Would not you, sir, start as Mr. Garrick does, if you saw a ghost?' He answered, 'I hope not. If I did, I should frighten the ghost.' " [40] For details, there is the admirable description by the German traveller Lichtenberg in 1775. Garrick's Hamlet had his back to the audience and was walking upstage when Horatio, crying "Look, my lord, it comes," pointed to where the Ghost (who had, I suppose, risen through his accustomed trap) was standing motionless before the audience was aware of his presence.

At these words Garrick turns sharply and at the same moment staggers back two or three paces with his knees giving way under him;

Hamlet's Start

(From an illustration by Theodore Lane in Pierce Egan's *Life of an Actor*, 1825)

his hat falls to the ground and both his arms, especially the left, are stretched out nearly to their full length, with the hands as high as his head, the right arm more bent and the hand lower, and the fingers apart; his mouth is open: thus he stands rooted to the spot, with legs apart, but no loss of dignity, supported by his friends.

Kemble, though he was not immediately held by Horatio and Marcellus, and though the naturalness of his start — which "was not preceded by any studied preparation"— found favor, yet seems to have come near reproducing Garrick's posture of alarm.[41] Gilbert Austin's strange work, *Chironomia; Or, A Treatise on Rhetorical Delivery*, in which a system of "notation for gesture" is invented and enthusiastically applied, assures us that "when Hamlet starts at his father's ghost he changes at once the entire position of both hands and feet. Mr. Kemble . . . standing in the quiet position of familiar observation with his face towards the spectators, suddenly turns aside into this strong position. $\frac{Bvhf}{st.L_{1}.x}$."[42] By this I understand that he stretched both arms horizontally forward, with the palms vertical, the fingers pointing upwards; that he started; that his left foot was advanced, his weight chiefly on his right, and his feet far apart. In the engraving from Pierce Egan's *Life of an Actor* (1825), Proteus, the hero, is shown in his friend Quill's garret rehearsing this start. He is being interrupted just as he "flattered himself that he had knocked off his hat with almost as much grace and elegance as a GARRICK" and had "placed himself in an attitude little inferior to JOHN KEMBLE" — though the position of his right arm seems scarcely correct.

Hamlet's hat is a subject in itself. There is the story, for instance, of the friendly country girl who, on a benefit night when benches were introduced on the stage itself, picked up the hat which Holland ("the pupil of Garrick") had just contrived to knock off and placed it solicitously on the actor's head.[42a] With Kemble is associated the distinctive hat with the sable plume which he wears in Lawrence's portrait; and this romantic item of dress is repeatedly mentioned in accounts of *Hamlet* down to the time of Fechter, and even later, for Irving was still wearing the hat — and flinging it off when he saw the spectre — in 1874. To the modern reader, the description of Mr. Wopsle's Hamlet in *Great Expectations* may sound absurdly exaggerated, but there is scarcely a detail in it which is not warranted by fact. So in this matter of the hat. Joe protests against the pelting of Wopsle "partickler when he sees the ghost":

if the ghost of a man's own father cannot be allowed to claim his attention, what can, Sir? Still more, when his mourning 'at is unfortunately made so small as that the weight of the black feathers brings it off, try to keep it on how you may.

It may be added that Hamlet has often divested himself of cloak as well as hat.[43]

Although Master Betty ("The Young Roscius") indulged in a tremendous start — which he was criticized for anticipating by removing his hat, instead of waiting and then knocking it off[44]— he also knelt to the Ghost at the word "Father."[45] This act of kneeling, practised by many subsequent Hamlets, is symbolic of an emotion beyond mere terror. Kean, we are told, was no longer frightened. Booth "dropped on one knee . . . and bowed his head, not in terror, but in awe and love." At sight of the spirit, Salvini's face was "illumined with an awe-struck joy"; and his Hamlet, "spontaneously, and one would almost say unconsciously, uncovers his head."[46] Such trends are easily exaggerated. Enough, perhaps, that pity and reverence are finding expression increasingly through Hamlet's action when he sees the Ghost.

The Ghost beckons and Hamlet follows, sword in hand. He has held it: with the point toward the spectre; or trailing; or towards his friends; or, by the blade, with the hilt raised to form a cross. Wilks addressed "I say, away!" to the Ghost, "with a Flourish of his drawn Sword"— a "most shocking *Indecorum*." Garrick broke with violence from Horatio and Marcellus, then followed the apparition slowly, pausing from time to time, with his sword held out before him, to be sheathed only at "I am thy father's spirit."[47] After all, Horatio had authorized Marcellus to strike at the Ghost if it would not stay. But critics insisted upon the fact of spectral invulnerability; and Kemble, turning his left hand toward the Ghost, trailed his sword behind him.[48] Kean, too, abandoned bravado, and kept his sword pointed at Marcellus and Horatio, as if to prevent them from following him.[49] Booth, in a manuscript note which he contributed to James Taylor's copy of *Hamlet*, now in the Harvard Theatre Collection, tells of how he came to alter the accepted business:

By accident I lost my grasp of my sword, when drawing it against my companions, and caught it by the blade — with the cross-hilt upward. Instantly it occurred to me as appropriate to hold it in that position while following the ghost — as a guard against any evil influence. Until then, from Garrick's time, the sword was either pointed at the ghost or pointed behind Hamlet.   E.B.

It might be supposed that the possibilities were now exhausted, but when Joseph Haworth was about to follow the Ghost, at the Castle Square Theatre, Boston, in 1895, he threw away his sword. Clapp calls it "a striking, noble and significant action befitting the character and the moment, even if the text made it necessary to find a sword to swear by after the departure of the spirit." [50]

Hamlet goes, leaving Horatio and Marcellus on the stage. They are not, however, without occupation, as Lawrence Barrett's Promptbook makes clear: "Mar. & Hor. do not move until Hamlet is off. Marcellus also as he is going picks up Hamlet's hat — 'Mar., do not forget this.' " Sometimes there was Hamlet's cloak to remember, as well.[51]

In Scene 5 we have: action (or, rather, the conspicuous lack of action) by the Ghost during the speaking of his narrative; Hamlet's business as he listens to the same speech; the Ghost's disappearance; action by Hamlet in the course of his soliloquy ("O all you host of heaven!"); his putting off an intrusive Marcellus; the swearing on Hamlet's sword; and the final exit. At the beginning, a simple entrance, as against a discovery, will bring out the sense of continuity — of Hamlet's having followed his father's shade for a long time. Fennell's leaning against a tree, in 1806, was much discussed. Booth, in the 'sixties, stumbled down "massive steps," then, crying

Whither wilt thou lead me? Speak! I'll go no further,

he sank upon his knees.[52]

"The speech of the ghost", according to a handbook on acting, published in 1807, "is to be spoken without action, very low and solemn." [53] That was the custom, certainly, from early in the eighteenth century. Critics have noticed it, occasionally, and have been surprised, or pretended to be surprised. The Ghost carries a truncheon in his hand, they observe, yet he merely holds it as a schoolboy might "when ordered to hold out the ruler at arm's length by way of punishment." [54] Mr. Bransby, at Drury Lane in 1768, did, for once, indulge in action. He 'sawed the air' — and was duly reminded of the abstinence of his ghostly predecessors.[55]

The *St. James's Chronicle* reports of "Gentleman" Smith, at Drury Lane in the autumn of 1774, that as Hamlet he followed Garrick, "except in one Passage, where the Ghost says, *I am thy Father's Spirit*; there he forgot himself, and made a very genteel Bow. A Gentleman who sate near me" (the critic adds) "was so struck with the Impropriety, that he whispered me, 'This is Monsieur Hamlet.'" Lichtenberg gives a garbled version of the same story. As a matter of fact, Garrick himself, when he first played the part, had made the Ghost "a very respectful bow" at this point.[56] Presumably, he had given the business up, meanwhile. Fechter once more bowed profoundly — but only later, at "Fare thee well at once." [57] Henderson dropped his sword, on learning that his father had been murdered, and the question was promptly raised how Hamlet could "with so much propriety talk of 'sweeping to his revenge' without it." Macready, according to a promptbook of 1848, used the same business; and Tree, in 1895, was praised for "the laying down of his sword . . . when the illusion proclaimed himself the father of the prince" and for "the taking up of it at mention of his uncle." [58] Finally, Emil Devrient, acting in London with a German company in 1851, covered his face with his cloak, at the mention of Gertrude's adultery. This daring gesture does not seem to have been adopted, however, by English actors. Wilson Barrett fell prone, as he heard the same words.[59]

The Ghost's mode of exit is next to be considered. His slow-paced valedictory line,

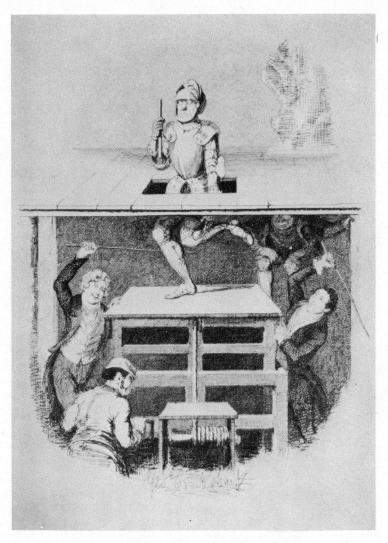

The Ghost Descending his Trap
(From an illustration by George Cruikshank in Raymond's *Elliston*, 1844)

Adieu, adieu, adieu! Remember me,

may well have been designed to be spoken descending, and he will presently be heard crying beneath the stage.[60] So the trap is particularly appropriate, and it was long employed here. Ryder, playing the Ghost to Macready's Hamlet in Charleston, was suddenly shot down a badly worked trap as late as January 1844; though later in the same year the Sadler's Wells Ghost was merely to glide away under shadowy arches.[61] A still simpler method was not unknown. The Folger promptbook inscribed "Mr Young. Brighton Septr 19. 1809" has, at the Ghost's departure: "if not sinking — Exit LH Hamlet looks after Ghost at Exit & seems to see him sink into the Earth." John Foster Kirk writes, in 1884:

down to a very recent period, the business of the ghost was very clumsily managed. We have all seen him descend by a trap-door, liable either to stick on its passage or to drop with a jerk before the final "Adieu" was uttered. On the last occasion on which I saw the play I found that all this had been changed. There was an ingenious and beautiful arrangement of blue lights, gauze curtains, and other paraphernalia, by which the mysterious figure was made to recede and vanish in a becoming and even marvellous manner.

This arrangement — which sounds very like that used by Fechter — Kirk found distracting, as it might well have been.[62] George Cruikshank's etching, here reproduced, was inspired by a practical joke played on Dowton by Elliston and another wag. They concealed themselves beneath the stage and, armed with rattan canes, belabored the unprotected calves of the shade, as he was slowly descending. Raymond's *Life of Elliston*, in which the anecdote is told, does not name the play in which Dowton was thus victimized. Cruikshank made it *Hamlet*, naturally enough, and furnished the spectre with armor and a truncheon.

Hamlet's first words after the Ghost's exit, "O all you host of heaven!" followed an instant later by the appeal to his sinews not to grow "instant old" but bear him "stiffly up," gain in relevance if he has fallen, whether prostrate or upon his knees, and now, rallying, looks up and with difficulty rises. Garrick, indeed, stood

"rooted to the spot and like one distraught." Of Kemble, however, we learn from *The Public Advertiser*, October 7, 1783, that

swearing to remember the Ghost — he flings himself on one Knee.
   In such Doating is John Bull for Novelty, that six Barbary Horses
shall be impawned, that if Hamlet, whether right or wrong, will kneel,
on the first shutting of the Trap-Door, he shall get a thundering *Clap
of Applause*!

Boaden adds that this "*kneeling* at the descent of the Ghost,"
which "had not been done before," was promptly adopted by
Henderson. On the Ghost's disappearance, Irving sank "in a
heap" at the foot of a tree, "thus making his 'sinews grow instant
old,' at the very moment when he calls upon them not to do so,"
it was said by *Punch*, stupidly.[63] Mr. Gielgud points out that it is
difficult for an actor to handle both his "tables" and his sword,
during this speech. If a choice has to be made, it seems to me that
Hamlet's sword, the use of which is comparatively modern here
and not called for by the lines — as that of the tables surely is! —
had better not be produced. The swearing on the sword will be all
the more impressive later.[64] Tree half drew his, at "O villain,"
then, abandoning the idea of instant action, took out his tables, or,
as he himself puts it, "turns from the sword to the pen." For
eccentricities, he rushed to embrace the spectre, only to beat himself "against the bare walls in impotent despair," and Cooper, in
1804, when he came to "while memory holds a seat In this distracted globe," "threw his arms abroad, as if applying the simile
to the *world*." [65]
   That Hamlet during the dialogue which follows, is prevented
from speaking out by the presence of Marcellus — a prying person who cannot be trusted — is a theory which we are likely to
think of as very recent indeed. Mr. J. Dover Wilson makes much
of it in his brilliant and provocative studies of *Hamlet*. Now Irving's name does, it is true, figure for a moment in the course of
Mr. Wilson's exposition. But that actors, from the later years
of the eighteenth century on, have repeatedly explored the possibilities of making Marcellus "Hamlet's problem in this scene"
passes unnoticed. *The Public Advertiser*, October 7, 1783, reviewing John Philip Kemble's first performance of Hamlet in

London, states that "Kemble, like Henderson, discriminates finely his Trust in Horatio's Secrecy, his doubt of Marcellus. . . . Yet strange to tell it, this Distinction, which as the Players call it, *tells* most forcibly, *Garrick overlooked!*" According to Boaden, Kemble (and also Henderson) made the distinction where Mr. Wilson would have it made: they gave up "the seeming intention of particular disclosure to Horatio —

> Yes, but there *is*, Horatio, — and much offence too;"

and "turned off from the pressing forward of Marcellus to partake the communication." [66] Forrest followed Kemble here, but introduced similar business, also, earlier in the scene where there is much less excuse for it. Becks writes at "Ay, by heaven, my lord":

> Marcel peering close to his face for the news — when Hamlet catches his eyes [*sic*] — & a momentary halt with his own — & he turns the subject — "There's ne'er &c" — Hor is a little piqued & turns — the pose is broken.[67]

Brooke, at the Olympic Theatre, March 2, 1848, had ideas of his own, such as they were. "Mr. Brooke," says *The Athenaeum*,

> after showing the usual reluctance to betray the spiritual communication which he had received, says to *Horatio* — "Touching this vision here, — it is an honest ghost, that let me tell *you*" (emphasizing the pronoun strongly,) and then withdraws his friend up the stage, as if whispering to him apart; which done, he addresses the next portion of the speech to *Marcellus* exclusively — "For *your* desire to know what is between *us*" — (that is between Hamlet and Horatio — not Hamlet and his Father) — "o'ermaster it as you may." [68]

One still hears it asserted, sometimes, that the star actors of older days spoke Shakespeare's verse as verse. Some of them unquestionably did, and admirably, too. But what hash Gustavus Vaughan Brooke was making of it in this passage! Fechter snubbed Marcellus at both places — and at the exit as well.[69] Booth followed Kemble, and once more anticipated Mr. Wilson.[70]

Charles Mayne Young's Hamlet, in 1807, swore Horatio and Marcellus on the cross hilt of an antique sword instead of on the blade of a modern dress sword, as Kemble had done; [71] and the innovation seems to have established itself as part of the business of the play. A manuscript note by Booth in James Taylor's copy of *Hamlet* runs:

> Many years ago my sword, as I knelt heavily with it in my hand, stuck so firmly in the stage that I could not easily withdraw it, and I left it there upright, forming the cross. Since when others have adopted this mode of using the cross at this point. E.B.

Booth was fond of telling members of his company about the accident, but what precisely resulted from it, is made none too clear.[72] Irving led his Marcellus and Horatio from the stage — as Macready seems first to have done — and his promptbook has, "Ring down as Mr Irving turns to where Ghost was." Salvini also looked round, apprehensively.[73] Hamlet's hat, by the way, is still being carried by Marcellus or Horatio; and George Becks, at the exit, has Marcellus offer it to the Prince as "Hor quietly be-cloaks him." Yet in the spring of 1905, H. B. Irving got credit for thinking of "shivering all forlorn after the interview with the ghost until Horatio takes off his cloak and wraps it about his friend, who says, affectionately, 'Let us go — together.' " Forrest, I take it, did not shiver.[74]

There is little stage business in Act II before Hamlet's interview with Polonius. Once or twice, Shakespeare has called upon the actors for an explanatory gesture. Ophelia, in describing the visit which has so frightened her, must show how Hamlet's hand was placed —"thus o'er his brow"— as he studied her face. Tom Taylor was convinced that "the hand . . . should be pressed hard on the forehead, not placed, as it usually is, by the actress, as if to shade the eyes from the light." [75] Similarly, Polonius must indicate through a gesture of some sort what he means by

> Take this from this, if this be otherwise.

But Dowden's suggestion that the old man refers to "his chamberlain's staff or wand and the hand which bears it" is tame; and Polonius will do wisely if, continuing to be guided by Theobald, he points to his own head and shoulder.

Mr. Wilson's early entrance for Hamlet while the plot to "loose" Ophelia is still being discussed seems to have been tried on the stage at least once before the appearance of *What Happens in Hamlet*. At any rate, Tree writes, in 1895:

> As presented on the stage, I conceive that Hamlet enters slightly before his cue, detects the King and Polonius in their conspiracy, vanishes for a moment behind the curtains, and then enters stark, staring mad to Polonius.

Tree was thinking, I hasten to add, merely of present advantages, real or supposed: of Hamlet's treatment of Polonius in what immediately follows, not of Hamlet's treatment of Polonius's daughter in the next act.[76] The book which the Prince is reading when Polonius boards him has now and again suggested business. Thus Irving's Promptbook (1877) has Hamlet *read* the objectionable phrase "being a god kissing carrion," whereupon "Polonius approaches, Hamlet, and tries to look over the book. Hamlet closes it." Also, Fechter, when he came to the words, "friend, look to 't," pointed at the open book in his hand, "and Polonius, literal in all things, runs his eye over the page." More picturesque and quite legitimate was Kemble's business of tearing out a leaf of the book at "Slanders, sir" (A much later, minor Hamlet, Joseph Haworth, did the same thing at "Words, words, words"). Barry Sullivan read the description of old men — that they have grey beards, etc. — pausing after each item to examine the specimen before him.[77] Polonius has had much to endure!

Rosencrantz and Guildenstern, once known in theatrical parlance as "the knife and the fork"— since of course they "feed" Hamlet — are an indistinguishable pair. Kean's taking them "under each arm, under pretence of communicating his secret to them, when he only means to trifle with them," brought out this idea; so, too, Madame Bernhardt's "execrable comic business" of knocking their heads together.[78] Just when Hamlet becomes suspicious of his old friends is not precisely indicated in the lines. At first, of course, he is almost pathetically cordial. Booth's 1890 Promptbook has at "Ah, Rosencrantz!" "Throws book on table & goes to them shakes their hands." When, however, he asks for the fifth time why they have come to Elsinore, the swift asides —

Ros. [*aside to Guildenstern*] What say you?
Ham. [*aside*] Nay then, I have an eye of you —

will reassure the audience that he has escaped the trap. Stirling's manuscript stage direction, "He observes them whispering," is a natural addition at this point, where further business will only be in the way. Business, on the other hand, will definitely ease an abrupt transition on the Prince's part, later in the scene:

Ham. Do the boys carry it away?
Ros. Ay, that they do, my lord — Hercules and his load too.
Ham. It is not very strange; for my uncle is King of Denmark, and those that would make mows at him while my father lived give twenty, forty, fifty, a hundred ducats apiece for his picture in little.

Here Booth's Hamlet lifted miniatures of Claudius from the breasts of both his schoolfellows; [79] whereas Fechter attempted to differentiate between knife and fork by having only Guildenstern so served. Fechter's Hamlet, too, noticed the picture sometime before, and, with a change of expression and manner, asked eagerly "Were you not sent for?" [80] Tree had recourse to physiology. Quoting "Beggar that I am, I am even poor in thanks; but I thank you," he suggests that here,

The meaning of the play may be illumined by stage business. Hamlet, in all the frankness of his nature, gives his hand to Rosencrantz. He finds it moist, with moistness of nervousness and treachery. He looks into Rosencrantz's eyes, and, reading in them a confirmation of the hand's betrayal, he suddenly asks, "Were you not sent for?" [81]

It took inventiveness beyond even that of the much abused commentators to discover that Rosencrantz had clammy hands!

Polonius bustles in, full of news. "I will prophesy he comes to tell me of the players," Hamlet remarks. Booth was "sitting on arm of chair" as he spoke the words, which suggests the informality of Shakespearean acting today. But informality is one thing, bad taste another. Incredible as it may seem, Madame Bernhardt, at "Buzz, buzz!" pursued and finally caught a fly, close to Polonius's nose, herself "buzzing vigorously" all the while.[82] After that, one longs for the eighteenth century! "Your accompanying the player," writes one of Garrick's correspondents, "by acting the speech while he repeats it, is judged to have too mean a look for the son of a king." Fechter also indulged in "unconscious pantomime and silent repetition of the words" the First Tragedian was declaiming.[83] And when Polonius interrupts, with "This is too long," the Lawrence Barrett Promptbook has him "Stroking his beard," which gives occasion for Hamlet's rude reply, "It shall to the barber's, with your beard."

Forbes-Robertson's method of introducing the great soliloquy which concludes the second act, by "conning a promptbook of the play handed him by the First Actor," is praised by no less an authority than Archer. On the other hand, Winter wrote sarcastically of Madame Bernhardt's obtaining the book in the same way that the First Actor must, "conveniently," have "carried his whole repertory in his belt." I have often seen Hamlet, as he cries "O Vengeance," lunge with his dagger at the empty throne. The frustrated rage implied in this action is right enough. But when Hamlet checks himself it is for unpacking his heart with words — for cursing "like a very drab, A scullion!" And the self-accusation will lose point if his fury has just found expression in deeds. The originator of this business was perhaps Charles Coghlan who, in New York, in 1877, "rushed up to the throne and fell to stabbing the empty chair, as if to glut his vengeance in this shadowy fashion." Tree's Hamlet also thrust at the throne; then "the drawn sword drops by his side." [84]

Finally, two pieces of stage business at the end of the soliloquy afford a striking contrast in the styles of acting implied. Gilbert Austin's encyclopedic work on gesture, *Chironomia*, has already been mentioned. In it is described what is called the "sweep", that is to say, "a curved movement descending from the opposite shoulder, and rising with velocity to the utmost extent of the arm, or the reverse." And Austin adds that "the sweep is sometimes doubled by returning the arm back again through the same arch," and, in a note, "Kemble used the double sweep with fine effect on these words:

> The play's the thing
> Will [*sic*] catch the conscience of the king. *Hamlet.*" [85]

Formal acting, of course. Yet conceivably Kemble's double sweep was not only dignified but expressive. The other piece of business is rightly associated with Irving, though quite clearly he did not originate it. In Henry B. Phillips's promptbook, containing an Astor Place cast of 1848, occurs this note: "ⓡ as Hamlet takes Pen to write"—"ⓡ" meaning ring for curtain. At Leicester, in the 'forties, Sam Butler, a tragedian in the Robertson company, when he came to the end of the soliloquy

rushed to the table, snatched up a pen, and with "eyes in a fine frenzy rolling" began, *coram populo*, to write the lines "with which to catch the conscience of the king." This was considered by Mr. Robertson [Tom's father] to be "an audacious and even idiotic innovation."

Coleman, who tells the story, adds that later he tried the business himself, but abandoned it as "rococo and ineffective." It was tried, too, by Henry Nicholls ("the dramatic reader") at the Soho Theatre in 1854.[86] Irving made it one of the great moments in the play. Rushing to a pillar, he set against it the same "tables" which he had produced after the Ghost's departure. Then he began to write, hysterically, as if (we are told) in letters "quite twelve inches high," the speech, Hamlet's own speech, which was to convert "The Murder of Gonzago" into "The Mousetrap."[87] Naturally, this brilliant stroke commended itself to later actors: to Tree, for instance, who modified it only in that he knelt, or rather squatted, and wrote by the sole light of a huge wood fire. It was, in his own words, "a purely pictorial effect."[88]

Lichtenberg writes of Garrick that, entering before the soliloquy, "To be, or not to be," he is

sunk in contemplation, his chin resting on his right hand, and his right elbow on his left, he gazes solemnly downwards. And then, removing his right hand from his chin, but, if I remember right, still supporting it with his left hand, he speaks.

Macready was less posed, entering with "his hands behind him, the right hand clasping the left wrist like a vice, the eyes fixed." Booth made a radical departure by sitting down. "In a discussion with Henry Tuckerman," Mrs. Clarke writes,

that gentleman, who had witnessed many of the old actors, observed to Booth that they all stood during the soliloquies, and inquired if it were not possible to alter this. On the next representation of "Hamlet," Booth, seated, began the soliloquy "To be, or not to be." Mr. Tuckerman, watching the play, could not conceive how *Hamlet* could rise from that chair with propriety and ease. When at the words, "to sleep, perchance to dream," after an instant of reflection . . . he rose with the horror of that terrible "perchance" stamped upon his features . . . his friend was satisfied.[88a]

As for H. B. Irving, in 1896, he carried a book, in which he was so engrossed that he stepped into a table on which he proceeded to sit, "swinging his leg," and warmed his hand over a brazier of coals. At last, he "withdrew his hand very hurriedly," put down the book — and spoke. Add that Hamlet's reference to the bare bodkin was precisely illustrated in Charles Kemble's performance by a "contracted nicety of the finger and thumb, as if holding the nominated implement," whereas Fechter brought a drawn sword with him, and Booth either handled or drew a dagger.[89]

Meanwhile, Polonius has told Ophelia where she is to "walk," and has given her a book. Fortunately, we are not concerned here with the staging of the scene at the Globe. If, for instance, Polonius and the King are concealed behind the "study" curtain, where it is a temptation to ensconce them, the assumption that Ophelia either walks, or kneels at a faldstool, on the inner stage, becomes untenable. Mr. Dover Wilson refers to "a theatrical tradition that she should be kneeling when Hamlet enters." But how old is this tradition? [90] The Phillips Promptbook does, indeed, supply a "Table . . . with Crucifix Book, & footstool before it" for Ophelia to kneel at, and Forrest's edition has her kneel at a prayer desk, as Polonius finishes his last speech before Hamlet's appearance. But I can find nothing about kneeling, earlier. When Barry Sullivan appeared at Stratford in 1879, it was proposed to have Ophelia kneel at "a beautiful little *prie-Dieu*" of carved wood, furnished with a "ruby lamp" and "an illuminated Missal." But Sullivan objected.

Her presence detracted from the importance of his "To be, or not to be," so she had to leave the stage, re-entering at the end of his speech (as used formerly to be done). After she had gone off, his eye fell upon the *prie-Dieu*, and he said, "And take that thing away. I don't want it there." It was removed.

When it reappeared in the Closet Scene, he spoke even more emphatically —"and the public never saw the beautiful thing." To Mrs. Calvert, who tells the story, Sullivan was merely in a bad mood as a result of some unkind press notices. But some years earlier, when Sullivan was acting in this country, he had made similar objection to the use of a "very fine mediaeval street scene" of Booth's. "Elaborate scenic display," he said, "attracts the attention of the audience from the play. As long as the scenery is not inappropriate their imagination will supply the details." For contrast, Tree built Ophelia a complete private oratory at the side of the stage, where, overhearing the soliloquy, she promptly knelt to pray for him. "Rushing out," he notices her, and "instantly his whole demeanour changes." [91]

The King and Polonius have hidden themselves behind the arras, where, it may be, Hamlet becomes aware that they are eavesdropping. But Ophelia's behavior — her face, too — may tell him much without recourse to such adventitious aids as the thrusting forth of heads or the dropping of staffs. Business may be desirable here — certainly actors found it so through a long period of time — but that it was intended by Shakespeare remains scarcely demonstrable. As for the moment at which it may be introduced to the best advantage, there is again doubt. Hamlet's sudden "Where's your father?" will gain in effectiveness if the old courtier's eagerness to hear has just led to some indiscretion on his part by which the audience is reminded of his presence. If, however, Hamlet only detects him here, at III, I, 134, then the pronounced change in his manner which we should expect is very inadequately reflected in the lines. Turning back, there is the Prince's wild denial that he ever gave Ophelia the gifts which she would now return to him —

> No, not I!
> I never gave you aught —

and, a better place still, his abrupt "Ha, ha! Are you honest?" which startles her, a little later. All three moments — and especially the first — have been tried repeatedly on the stage.

As for date, Hamlet began to notice Polonius, or Polonius and the King, only it would seem in the eighteen-twenties. On December 25, 1826, John Howard Payne suggested in *The Opera Glass* that at Ophelia's question, "What means your lordship,"

it would be but natural for the king and Polonius . . . to be drawn a little forward by their eagerness, — Polonius especially. . . . *Hamlet here might catch a glimpse of the intruders.* Indeed, we see no way in which the scene can be understood without.

Payne calls this a "new view" and urges its advantages: "Thus is the imputed unfeelingness of his [Hamlet's] subsequent speeches to Ophelia fully explained away by action." About two years later, Stirling wrote in his acting copy of the play (at "Where's your father"), "Looks round & perceives Polonius peeping UE. op." There is a good chance, however, that the business is slightly older. For, in praising J. B. Booth's Hamlet, the anonymous author of *The Actor* (1846) speaks of "the strange and startling burst of passion at the sight of the King (the introduction of whom, for a moment, was entirely new to us)" and the performance he has in mind was Booth's first in the part in New York — October 15, 1821.[92] James H. Hackett criticizes with a good deal of shrewdness Macready's "conception of causing both the *King* and *Polonius* . . . to reappear for a moment, and by their sudden retreat to their covert be supposed to make some noise or momentary exposure of their persons" — at "Where's your father." Hackett: (1) would have only Polonius show himself; (2) would have him do so when Ophelia is returning the gifts (since it is "immediately thereafter that *Hamlet* changes his tone and language"); and (3) expostulates against Macready's making Hamlet "walk up close to the *King's* place of concealment, and there *vociferate* his parting speech . . . the threat respecting the *King.*"[93]

From the 'twenties till the very end of our period, when Forbes-Robertson and Sir John Martin-Harvey suddenly dissented, the idea of Hamlet's detecting the eavesdroppers has been regularly accepted by those who played the Dane. Their practice has varied, however, at certain points. Edwin Booth caught a glimpse of the conspirators very early, just before Hamlet's

"No, not I." Becks's notes indicate that Forrest chose the same moment;[94] and Lawrence Barrett's promptbook has, at the end of the speech:

> The King & Polonius here appear from RUE on platform thro arch, watching — the moment they are seen by Hamlet, they appear in deep conversation & X the platform, disappearing L.U.E —

which I should think might have amused the audience. Irving, in "An Actor's Notes on Shakespeare," calls attention to the fact that in the Quarto of 1604 (as also in the First Quarto, where however the order of events is not the same) Hamlet's entrance is an early one, occurring before "the *exeunt* words of Polonius to the King." Hamlet is too much preoccupied with his own thoughts to take heed, at the moment, but a little later he "remembers — there is no need for him to have any reminder — the hidden presence of the King." In performance, nevertheless, Irving still allowed Hamlet to make the usual discovery at "Where's your father." [95] Wilson Barrett sometimes, at any rate, saw first the King, and then later Polonius.[96] Benson, in 1890, having "just caught a glimpse" of Ophelia's father, rushed to the curtains (at "it hath made me mad") and drew them aside to see if anyone was hiding.[97] And Tree played the first part of the scene, up to "Where's your father," tenderly, but after he had caught sight of Polonius became "as harsh as his words." To the *Athenaeum* it seemed only "a perverted ingenuity" which could find in the lines "any indication that Shakspeare intended the scene to be taken in two different keys." [98]

Hamlet's gifts to Ophelia were frequently returned to him in a "casket." There is no reason for showing them, and they might become distracting if seen.[99] Fechter illustrated the passage beginning "This was sometime a paradox, but *now* the time gives it proof," by looking "sadly at the letters in his hand." [100] A glance at them lent poignancy to Hamlet's next words —"I did love you once" — in Leslie Howard's performance, a few years ago.

At Hamlet's twice-spoken "Farewell," near the end of the scene, the actor has often left the stage for an instant, then suddenly returned. Ophelia's pitiful "O, help him, you sweet heavens," and again, "O heavenly powers, restore him" will cover such exits, and when they are introduced the abruptness with which the Prince resumes his attack "If thou dost marry"—"I have heard of your paintings too"— gains in meaning. Booth laid his hand on the girl's head and looked straight into her eyes, as he awaited her faltering "At home, my lord." Then he snatched away his hand. "The whole scene," writes Lucia Calhoun, "he plays like one distract. He is never still. He strides up and down the stage, in and out at the door, speaking outside with the same rapidity and vehemence." [101] In Kemble's time, this business of going and returning seems to have been abused. Thus Buckingham's *Polyanthos*, for January 1813, could praise Holman "for reforming the usual practice of turning to ridicule the scene with *Ophelia*, by going off at the stage doors at the end of each sentence." What was worse, the doors were being banged. Kemble himself is accused of treating Ophelia with "what threatening of fists, what ferocity of voice, what stamping of feet, what clattering of doors." [102] From this violence (which I suspect began with Garrick) the scene was rescued by Edmund Kean. By him "the slapping of doors, and a great part of Hamlet's ungallant and cruel deportment" was rejected; and at the end of the interview with Ophelia, he slowly returned and kissed her hand[103]— an act which Hazlitt called "the finest commentary that was ever made on Shakespear." [104] It was widely adopted, and such alternative business as was devised — Vandenhoff, for instance, merely "shook her hand with a look of affecting regret" [105]— attracted little interest. At last, in 1892, Tree carried sentiment a step further. Ophelia had sunk upon a couch. Tree's Hamlet stole back and, unseen by her, kissed "one of the tresses of her hair." "This is a beautiful idea," Clement Scott exclaimed. "It is right, it is true, it is effective." [106]

Finlay observes of Kean that at the beginning of Act III, Scene 2, he entered

with the players at his heels, speaking to them with his back to them; "speak the speech, I pray you;" as if it had been the continuation of an easy mannered conversation in which he had been engaged with them along the corridore.

Lawrence Barrett's promptbook calls for Hamlet to give a scroll
to the First Actor, at the conclusion of his directions to him.
Forbes-Robertson, retaining this manuscript (which Fechter
seems to have been the first to carry), called in Horatio. "He sits
reading over the play and, as Horatio enters, looks up intending
to point out the passage: as their eyes meet the idea occurs to him
and he speaks." [107] A pleasant detail in Benson's London production in 1890, was, we are told,

the face of the low comedian of the company, as, happening at the
moment to be prominent, he hears the Prince's words, "Let those that
play your clowns speak no more than is set down for them." The
player's features relax into a grin . . . though he shakes his head in
denial of the charge.

I recall in a Ben Greet performance that the clown and the boy-
actress quietly exchanged smiles when Hamlet spoke gravely to
their superior on the subject of ranting. Such by-play is innocent
and something of a relief, provided always that nothing is allowed
to interfere with our sense that these are excellent players quite
capable of doing justice to "The Mousetrap." [108]

"Something too much of this," Hamlet says, and in a few swift
words describes his plan. A note (by "Hand B") in the
Crow Street "Promptbook" points out that "as Hamlet is in the
pallace, he should look about cautiously before communicating
this Scheme to Horatio." [109] A second transition is bridged by the
Prince's

They are coming to the play. I must be idle.

Here the elder Booth retired

up the stage, passes from view, and reappears like a shadow; is lost in
the company that enters to witness the play. We find him next at
Ophelia's feet. [110]

Macready got more meaning out of "idle." There are at least two
accounts of his behavior which go back to a time before strange
and even very serious events had rendered impartial criticism of
it almost impossible. G. R. Pemberton wrote early in 1834:

there have been men of "renown" in Hamlet who did not exhibit so
much understanding of the true man . . . so much of the true poetic

spirit of dramatic life through the whole five acts . . . as Macready evinces in rocking his head, with such a volume of meaning, thought, feeling, and expectation in his look, as he paces to and fro when the king, queen, and courtiers are assembling to witness the play.

And Forster, in October 1835, praised "his quick and salient walk up and down the front of the stage, waving his handkerchief as if in idle and gay indifference, but ill concealing, at that instant, the sense of an approaching triumph." [111] For the waving of the handkerchief, Garrick's usage might have been cited, though, as we shall see, that great actor introduced it somewhat later in the play. On March 2, 1846, Edwin Forrest as a member of an Edinburgh audience hissed Macready's business, which he later dubbed "a fancy dance" or *"pas de mouchoir"* and "a desecration of the scene." The story of what followed, with its climax of bloodshed during the Astor Place Riot, fortunately does not concern us. Enough for our purposes that even if Macready's Hamlet behaved absurdly at this point in the play his excuse of assumed madness is sufficient to justify it. Winter, by the way, tells us that Barry Sullivan used the same business, and Forrest "hissed him, in Philadelphia, as he had hissed Macready in Edinburgh." [112]

During the performance of "The Mousetrap" Hamlet, lying at Ophelia's feet, used to toy with her fan, or turn the pages of a copy of the play. Then he crawled across the stage toward his enemy. Betterton "threw himself at *Ophelia's* Feet"; [113] but we first hear of the fan from Aaron Hill's *Prompter*, October 24, 1735. There Wilks is praised for

the *Gayety*, the unforc'd, soft, becoming, NEGLIGENCE, with which, reclining, at the Feet of *Ophelia*, and toying with her Fan, as if *genteely Insignificant*, He kept a *Guard* upon his *Uncle's* EYE: and *watch'd* (unnotic'd) the *Effect* of his *Play's Influence*.

When next the fan appears, Garrick is the Hamlet, and so fascinating that when he is on the stage it is impossible to see anyone else. Thus there really should have been a King in the Play Scene, "but the devil a king was there"— only "*Hamlet* sitting at the feet of *Ophelia*, and looking at something through her fan." Finlay made the point that, since Hamlet's excuse for sitting where he can observe the King's face is that he wants to be near Ophelia, he should be attentive to her. Kean, he writes, watched the play itself too closely, whereas Kemble

was in full possession of this idea, and whenever the eye of the king would fall on Hamlet in any of the questions which he put to him, the face of Hamlet was always toward Ophelia, and he answered the questions as to the name and plot of the play carelessly. . . .

Kemble plied the fan, too, and with it "artfully shaded his observation." [114] So did a great many of his successors in the part, Charles Kemble, for instance, whose business interested Paris at the time of the visit of the English actors in 1827. Dumas, indeed, refers to what we call the Play Scene as *"la scène de l'éventail."* [115] Only with the coming of Fechter is there a departure. Fechter, instead of "the specified fan" (it had by now got into the stage directions of acting editions like Cumberland's and French's), carried the text of the play, and at the climax tore out the pages and flung them in the air. Salvini used the same business, and later still, Tree — with the crude addition of thrusting "the leaves of the manuscript in the King's face." [116] Irving, however, restored the fan — and, for a particular reason, his fan was one of peacock's feathers.[117]

Hamlet's crawling across the stage is of a piece with such frequent blemishes in the treatment of this scene as the premature 'blenching' of Claudius and the shouting by Hamlet of lines which, if style can tell us anything, are to be spoken quietly:

He poisons him i' th' garden for's estate. His name's Gonzago. The story is extant, and written in very choice Italian. You shall see anon how the murtherer gets the love of Gonzago's wife.

Frank Marshall describes the customary business, in his *Study of Hamlet* (1875):

At this point most of the actors, that I have seen in the part of Hamlet, are wont to execute what I must venture to call the most vulgar piece of melodramatic absurdity which can be conceived. They crawl on their hands and knees from the feet of Ophelia to the King, whilst the poisoner is speaking his short speech on the stage; they then scream, or rant, in the King's ear . . . Tradition, deriving itself from Edmund Kean, is said to justify this astonishing piece of business.[118]

Cooper's "gradual relinquishment of his seat at Ophelia's feet, and advance towards the king," in 1795, are referred to as if they were a novelty. Kean played the scene daringly, but I have not read that he crawled. Whereas Vandenhoff *did*, "serpent-like" — and struck Claudius "a smart blow" on the knee "with *Ophelia's* fan." [119] As for later Hamlets, Macready and Charles Kemble, Booth (at least in the 'sixties), Irving, Benson, and Tree, all crawled. Walter Montgomery (in 1866) and Sothern (in 1900) both rudely seized the King; Barry Sullivan plucked his robe aside, and Sarah Bernhardt thrust a torch before his face. [120]

There is much less risk of over-acting when we come to Hamlet's hysterical outburst after the departure of the King. Garrick, while declaiming the first scrap of rhyme ("Why let the strucken deer go weep", etc.) always walked about the stage twirling a white handkerchief — business which, as we have seen, Macready in an ill hour borrowed. Davies who describes it was puzzled because of "its constant repetition." Garrick of all players he had ever seen "gave the greatest variety to action and deportment." Why, then should "so great an artist" in this instance "tie himself down to one particular mode, when his situation would admit of so many?" [121] Kemble, on the King's exit, threw himself into Horatio's arms. So did Young, and a great many other Hamlets in the early and middle years of the nineteenth century. [122] The Booth 1890 Promptbook has, immediately after the play: "Ham falls on Hor breast who gets to C to catch Ham when King rushes off R." Irving made this moment the most exciting in his performance. Staggering to his feet, he darted to the seats which Claudius and Gertrude had occupied and flung himself into the King's chair — the throne which should by right have been his. Then, leaving it, he chanted the wild verses,

> For thou dost know, O Damon dear,
>   This realm dismantled was
> Of Jove himself; and now reigns here
>   A very, very — pajock,

and at "pajock" (peacock) he looked at Ophelia's fan, which he was still carrying, and, as if it had suggested the word, threw it aside. Mr. Henry R. Pettitt, in the commemorative volume *We Saw Him Act*, writes that even though you had seen Irving's performance many times, and knew this moment was coming, "its thrill was never lessened." [123] Still another idea — and a good one — was Wilson Barrett's in 1884. Instead of seizing the King's throne he mounted the players' stage, whence he declaimed the rhymed verses. Hamlet asks: "Would not this, sir, and a forest of feathers . . . get me a fellowship in a cry of players, sir?" And Horatio answers dryly: "Half a share." [124]

Rosencrantz and Guildenstern bring the Queen's message. When, in 1896, H. B. Irving appeared as the Prince, "one of them" (Rosencrantz, I suppose) "held out his hands in a protesting way to him" and "he struck them down on the words, 'Nay, nay, by these pickers and stealers.'" Forrest's business of "working his fingers" was rather more natural, since Hamlet's phrase seems to be a mere "mad" variant on "by this hand." [125] The anonymity of the Folio's *Enter one with a Recorder*, a few lines later, was not kept in performance. Instead, Horatio would go out, quietly, at Hamlet's "Come, some music!" to return, at this moment, with the property pipe, or flute.[126] After all, he has nothing else to do for the rest of the scene. There was the possibility, too, of making a point. The Winter-Booth Edition has the direction, "*Hamlet takes one of the flutes, Guildenstern passes to the* R. *of Hamlet, as if to overhear what may pass between him and Horatio.*" Fechter substituted one of the musicians who had been present, in a gallery, during the performance of "The Mousetrap" and now entered carrying his instrument.[127] The Prince's question, "Why do you go about to recover the wind of me, as if you would drive me into a toil?" was sometimes prompted by his schoolfellows' following him —"Guil^n RH Ros^z LH"— as he goes up stage. We hear, too, of Kemble's "stately *march* from Guildenstern to Rosencrantz," as he urged them to play upon the pipe, "I do beseech you" being addressed to Rosencrantz.[128] On their refusal, Booth in his early years would fling the pipe into the flies at "though you can fret me, you cannot play upon me." There was no place for this exuberant action in the quieter performances of his maturity. Elizabeth Robins reports that he used "to snap the pipe across his knee and throw the pieces from him" [129]—business which Irving also employed. Indeed, it was held to be owing to "the antithetic influence of Irving" that Wilson Barrett merely handed the pipe to Horatio.[130]

There is little more to record of this long scene or, for that matter, of the Prayer Scene (often omitted) which succeeds it. Booth used to show Polonius the strangely shaped clouds through a window — though little could the old man have seen of them at this "witching time of night!" Cumberland's acting edition, earlier in the century, had the Prince *"leaning on the shoulder of Pol.,"* as he pointed them out. Wilson Barrett's Hamlet, who had staged his play *al fresco*, in a garden, looked "cautiously around him everywhere," when he was alone, then whipping out his sword struck at the shadows in the porch through which he must pass. Irving left the stage bearing a torch in his hand, and this torch he still carried in the Prayer Scene, thus stretching convention almost to the breaking-point.[131] Frank Marshall in his *Study of Hamlet* (1875) praises Rossi in the Prayer Scene at the expense of both Irving and Salvini, the only other Hamlets he had seen who gave the vengeful speech. Rossi entered "with his head down, as if deep in thought. . . . On seeing the King he starts and draws back; then the idea of killing the kneeling man strikes him suddenly"—

Now might I do it pat, now he is praying.

Salvini mimicked "the raised hands" of the praying King — which he was assured "Hamlet would never have done"— and Willard, concealing himself behind curtains, overheard the King's directions to Rosencrantz and Guildenstern and also the soliloquy "be fore the vain attempt at prayer." [132] To do so was, of course, completely destructive to the ironic conception of the episode.

At the beginning of the Closet Scene, we may have in the First Quarto *Hamlet* a hint of Elizabethan stage business. W. J. Lawrence points out that there the Prince, in reply to Gertrude's "How is't with you?" says "I'le tell you, but first weele make all safe —" at which point, Lawrence maintains, "he proceeded to lock the doors." [133] The likelihood that he did so is strengthened

by a line in *Fratricide Punished*, "But hush! are all the doors shut
fast?" But I can find no further trace of the business until it turns
up in Tom Taylor's acting edition of 1873, where, at

> Come, come and sit you down. You shall not budge!

Hamlet, as he had often done,[134] seizes her arm and forces her into
a seat. Then he "*bolts the door*." Upon entering, Macready (and
also Fechter) had laid his sword on the table, and the threat implied in this action is legitimate. Irving, having been last seen with
a torch, now appeared with a lamp; and this lamp he raised to look
in at poor Polonius at the close of the scene.[135] As a rule, this
piece of business had come earlier, when Hamlet ascertains that
it is Ophelia's father whom he has slain, not Claudius. Cumberland's influential acting edition (1826) has at "Ay, lady, 'twas my
word": "*Takes a candle, lifts up the arras, and sees* Polonius."
Sometimes, the tragedian actually left the stage for a moment,
returning it might be somewhat *paler* than before. Hence the anecdote of Macready's missing his dresser, one night, and frantically
crying "puff! . . . puff!" Whereupon his candles were blown out
by an officious scene-shifter.[136] Just before, when Hamlet demands of his mother, "Is it the King?" Charles Kean produced

> one of his most admired and applauded points . . . by making *Hamlet*,
> after he had thrust violently through the arras in 2nd stage entrance
> left, *slide* ten or twelve feet upon the floor-cloth down to the right-
> centre of the stage.

"Absurd as it may appear in description," Coleman writes,
"nothing more picturesque or striking could be imagined" than
this business.[137] Even so, one is not sorry to find that it got into a
late acting edition (Lacy's) of Poole's *Hamlet Travestie*: "Hamlet
draws, and stabs Polonius *behind the arras, then returns sliding
down the stage to* R.C."

Much of the remaining business in this scene has some connection with an engraving in Rowe's edition of Shakespeare (1709).
The precise degree to which this famous picture represents the
contemporary staging of the scene is doubtful. At certain points,
the artist seems to have had in mind the practice of his own day;
at others, he appears to have been merely "illustrating," without

The Closet Scene
(From Rowe's *Shakespeare*, 1709)

any great attempt at accuracy, the text before him. That some details in the engraving do in fact agree with what is known of eighteenth century stage customs is incontestable. That any single detail is to be accepted without additional evidence as showing what the practice of 1709 really was, does not in the least follow. The Ghost, it will have been noticed, is in armor, his "beaver up," a truncheon in his hand. Hamlet, bewigged and in contemporary costume, is standing with his mouth open, his legs far apart, the right leg advanced, and the right stocking sagging. His arms are stretched out, the left a good deal more raised than the right, and his fingers are extended. A chair lies overturned "down stage." On the rear wall hang two half-length portraits. The one to our right is fully visible, and the handsome subject of it is once more furnished with a truncheon. Finally, Gertrude sits uneasily on a second chair, beneath the portraits, and gazes at her son.[138]

The Ghost's wearing armor is clearly out of accord with the text. For Hamlet, when he would convince Gertrude of the reality of what he sees, cries:

> Why, look you there! Look how it steals away!
> My father, *in his habit as he liv'd!*

The practice of the stage is another matter; and I am not certain that in 1709 the Ghost wore a *"night gowne"* (as he does in the First Quarto) and not armor. Davies obviously thinks of him as still being in armor here[139]— and Davies thinks regularly in terms of the theatre. As for Hamlet's own costume, Professor Spencer is reluctant to believe that Ophelia's account of the hero's disordered dress was reproduced in performance: "No one supposes that he appears with one bare calf all through the play, and it seems most unlikely that he did so on either the Queen Anne or the Elizabethan stage." There is, however, abundant evidence to show that as early as the middle of the eighteenth century a black stocking, rolled half-way down the leg and showing a white one underneath, was regularly worn by stage Hamlets. In 1838, Charles Kean definitely gave up this eccentricity, and the retention of it by Mr. Wopsle, who "appeared with his stocking disordered (its disorder expressed, according to usage, by one neat fold in the top, which I suppose to be always got up with a flat iron)" was presumably out of loyalty to the customs of his youth.[140]

Hamlet's position and the overturned chair more directly concern us. Rowe's stage direction, "*Starting up,*" sounds theatrical rather than literary; and Gildon's *Betterton* (1710) states that

> In all regular Gestures of the Hands, they ought perfectly to correspond with one another, as in starting in a Maze, on a sudden Fright, as *Hamlet* in the Scene betwixt him and his Mother, on the Appearance of his Father's Ghost —
>> *Save me, and hover o'er me with your Wings,*
>> *You Heavenly Guards!*
> This is spoke with Arms and Hands extended, and expressing his Concern, as well as his Eyes, and whole Face.

So with Hamlet's legs. "In *Astonishment* and *Surprize,* arising from *Terror,*" Pickering wrote in 1755, "the *left Leg* is drawn back to some Distance from the other," and as an instance he cites "the Astonishment of HAMLET at the Sight of his FATHER's GHOST." [141] In the same year, "Sir" John Hill was praising Garrick's "kicking down the chair" when the Ghost "enters in the closet scene" as "a piece of bye-play introduced very happily in tragedy"; and, what was more, Garrick "had the moderation not to repeat it constantly; for then it becomes a stage-trick and is contemptible." His sitting in a chair "somewhat different from that appropriated to the queen, the cabriole feet being tapered, and placed so much under the seat, that it fell with a touch," no doubt facilitated the business. It was abandoned in 1777, and thereafter recourse was had to less sensational devices.[142] With Booth, indeed, the very emotion had changed:

> For an instant of time terror touches him. Then a passion of tenderness sweeps over him. He reaches out his hands to the shadowy figure. . . . When the ghost says: "Speak to her, Hamlet" . . . he puts his arm around the trembling woman of whose presence he has ceased to be aware.[143]

I am open to conviction as to how the Ghost should enter. Since he wears a new dress, Lawrence observes, he had better identify himself by using his old trap. But it has already been sug-

gested that on the stage he may have preferred not to "change."
Kelly's prologue to *The Romance of an Hour* (1774) tells us that,
though every line of Hamlet's upbraiding of Gertrude may deserve applause, the gods remain silent:

> But cas'd in canvass, let the dead stalk in,
> Then the loud pæans — then the claps begin —
> And pit, box, gall'ry, eagerly contend,
> Exalted strife! who loudest shall commend
> The frantic ha! The Bedlamite — "look there["] —
> The start — the heave — the stagger — and the stare.[144]

That is to say, the spectre wears stage-armor and "stalks in"—
in the Brighton Promptbook, at the "RHD^r." As for his exit, "he
goes even now out at the portal," Hamlet says, and to have him
there and then plunge down a trap would be ridiculous. Fielding,
I admit, allows Partridge to fancy that at this point the spirit
'sinks into the earth'; and in the early editions of Poole's *Hamlet
Travestie* (1810) he announces,

> Straight through the trap-door now I'm going,

and "*sinks.*" But since ghosts regularly went down traps — to the
amusement of many persons — a little license in this matter is
understandable in a novel and a burlesque. And if the Ghost really
did descend here — out of habit, as it were — one can only say
that he ought to have known better. When Tieck saw the play at
Covent Garden in 1817, the Ghost not only walked in and, having
crossed the stage, walked out again, but on his exit slammed the
door in Hamlet's face. This trick, as employed in a performance
with Kean in 1814, is attacked by John Finlay:

> Perhaps, the prompter will tell me, that it is necessary to slap the
> door, to create an obstruction to Hamlet from following the ghost.
> . . . If he must follow him to the portal, he might, as we have seen it
> done, fall and faint on the threshold. . . . Let him do anything, but let
> him not exhibit the dead, slapping doors in the face of the living, and
> Hamlet placing his ear to the door as if to invite the ghost to a *tete a
> tete* through the key-hole.[145]

Kemble had, indeed, thrown himself "passionately, yet fondly
forward, as if to catch and detain the form so revered, so

lamented," and this fall was part of the business in American performances with Cooper, Forrest, and Booth.[146] A little more will be said about the Ghost's ways when we come to the problem of the pictures.

But first, a word about Gertrude. In Hill's *Actor* (1755) a curious stage custom is described:

> When Hamlet bids his mother look at the ghost . . . she turns away for fear she should see it, because the poet makes her deny that she does. . . . Her true action is to look full upon the place, for Shakespear represents all his ghosts as visible only to the particular person they address —[147]

or, at any rate, he does so here and in *Macbeth*. If Garrick's Queen, Mrs. Pritchard, is meant, as seems likely, she profited from this counsel, for the look she gave here is vividly recalled by a writer in *St. James's Chronicle*, not long after her death: "She turned her Head slowly round, and with a certain *Glare* in her Eyes, which looked every where, and saw nothing, said, *Nothing at all, yet all that's here I see!*" Yet the careful avoidance of looking straight at the Ghost persisted. In the Cumberland and French acting editions — where so many Gertrudes have learned their parts — the direction at "What would your gracious figure?" is for Hamlet to look "*at the* Ghost — *the* Queen *looks a contrary way*"; and Mrs. Vezin, Booth's Gertrude at the Princess's Theatre in 1880, "fell into that feeblest of errors of never once following the direction of Hamlet's distracted gaze." [148]

When Hamlet bids his mother

> Look here upon this picture, and on this,
> The counterfeit presentment of two brothers,

the actor has regularly done one of three things: he has pointed at large portraits visible on the wall; he has examined two miniatures; or he has conjured up, by means of impassioned description, imaginary pictures. Something may be said in favor of each of these methods. For portraits, clearly, are referred to in *Fratricide Punished*, where one of Hamlet's pictures is hanging "in a gallery"; and portraits figure again in the Rowe engraving. Thereafter, they disappear, except occasionally in combination with miniatures, until Macready's time. In the engraving itself, they are half-lengths, and, as such, open to the very objection often raised, prosaically, as it seems to me, against the miniatures: that these are incapable of showing

> A station like the herald Mercury
> New lighted on a heaven-kissing hill.

What is more, the idea of such portraits of the two husbands hanging side by side in Gertrude's closet is a little improbable. And, on Shakespeare's stage, the place occupied by the portraits in Rowe's engraving would not have been visible to the audience if, as seems likely, Polonius and the King were at this moment concealed behind the inner stage curtain.[149] Irving, moreover, has remarked that in describing wall-portraits the actor will almost certainly have to "turn his back on the spectators, whose attention will thus be distracted from Hamlet's words." [150] And, finally, there is the grave objection that if the paintings shown are in the least like the description of their subjects, the audience may begin comparing, item by item, what it sees with what it hears.[151] Miniatures, by the same token, cannot be scrutinized by us, though we see them and may surmise that they give point to Hamlet's lesson. Hamlet has already mentioned the King's "picture in little": it is for purposes of the play a concrete fact. And, not least in importance, the use of miniatures in this scene goes far back in time — there is even the possibility of its having been imitated in *The Two Noble Kinsmen*.[152] The last method, that of imagined pictures, is without the disadvantages of the portraits and, equally, without the traditional authority of the miniatures. Certain phrases — Hamlet's "Look you now what follows," and Gertrude's "O, speak to me no more" — have been supposed to refer more naturally to what is seen only in the "mind's eye"; [153] but "counterfeit presentment" is, perhaps, quite as strong on the other side.

In 1784, Tom Davies wrote that it had been "the constant practice of the Stage, ever since the Restoration, for Hamlet, in this scene, to produce from his pocket two pictures in little . . . not much bigger than two large coins or medallions," and he praises

Wilks's Hamlet (a few pages later) for the reluctance with which he chided Gertrude, "when he presented the pictures." Davies himself is yet opposed to what he calls "these hand-pictures," and names "Dr. Armstrong" as one who had "long ago" pointed out the absurdity of using them. This Dr. Armstrong ("Launcelot Temple") had, indeed, written some twenty-five years before against "that Action of HAMLET producing the two Miniatures . . . out of his Pocket," suggesting as Davies was to do the substitution of wall portraits. In 1772, a writer in *St. James's Chronicle* had again taken up the question, but this time on the side of tradition and the miniatures.[154]

Henderson is the earliest known innovator. He tried whirling "the king's picture from his hand," and was duly reminded that Mr. Garrick never did this — and that, in the same scene, *he* had kicked down the chair. Kemble's Hamlet, too, flung away the miniature of his uncle — but now kissed that of his father.[155] Holman at Covent Garden, October 9, 1793, had Gertrude wear the miniature of "her existing husband, as a bracelet," and hung a portrait of the elder Hamlet on the wall. "By this means," it was urged, "what appeared a trick of premeditation, wears the better semblance of strong and immediate feeling." [156] But the business was swiftly and intelligently modified, so that Hamlet drew from his bosom a picture of his father while the Queen wore about her neck one of Claudius. This good arrangement, which was Cooper's and Edmund Kean's[157]— and in our time is Mr. Maurice Evans's — was disturbed by Macready in 1840. With him, Gertrude's closet came to resemble a Royal Picture Gallery containing full-length paintings of Claudius, the Queen, and both Hamlets, and the Ghost appeared and disappeared through his own portrait. Charles Kean remained loyal to the miniatures, however; and from his time on, the practice of actors varies, Phelps, for instance, following Macready, whereas Fechter works the miniatures hard,[158] and Booth at the close of his career tries Holman's way, once more.

"I now place the full-length portrait of the *old* king on the wall," he writes, "and take from the Queen's neck the 'picture in little' of the *new* one. Some *wise ones* insist that both should be together on the wall. . . . Criticism — Bosh!" [159]

Irving boldly dispensed with actual pictures, relying solely upon Hamlet's lines. Salvini did the same thing.[160] But Rossi used the miniatures still, and tearing off that worn by Gertrude flung it down, furiously, and stamped upon it. And H. B. Irving "by a happy trick" smashed the picture of Claudius "on to the taper, thus procuring the darkness necessary for the intrusion of the ghost." [161] It should be added that a "young Mr. Allerton," at the Princess's Theatre in June 1868, was the first of those silly Hamlets who have made the Ghost invisible to the audience as well as to the Queen.[162]

The anonymous author of *Some Remarks on the Tragedy of Hamlet* (1736) writes of Hamlet's "*tugging*" of Polonius "into another Room" that it is "unbecoming the Gravity of the rest of the Scene, and is a Circumstance too much calculated to raise a Laugh, which it always does." [163] Through lopping off everything after the couplet,

> I must be cruel, only to be kind;
> Thus bad begins, and worse remains behind,

and introducing a tableau, this macabre ending was got rid of, yielding place to one either sentimental or sternly self-righteous. Hackett describes the scene as he had always known it on the stage:

> When *Hamlet* utters the words —
> "So again, good night!"
> the Queen is required to approach *Hamlet* and to offer a parting *embrace*, at which *Hamlet* seems shocked, and shudders, and shrinks back with averted palms . . . The Queen then seems convulsed, bursts into tears, and rushes off one way whilst *Hamlet* goes in the opposite direction.[164]

This was certainly Macready's way, and Forrest's, Fechter modifying it only to the extent that he confronted the wretched woman with the miniature of his father. He then kissed it, ("I must be cruel" . . .) and, "taking light in hand and raising the arras," looked in at Polonius —

Thus bad begins, and worse remains behind.[165]

Booth, on the other hand, though he had shrunk from his mother when she attempted to bless him, now took her in his arms as the curtain descended; while Louis James's promptbook gags, as follows:

>   Ham — says — Mother!
>   Queen — "   My son —
>   Embrace

— and "Ring on Picture." [166] Irving, in 1874, dared to be "seen dragging the body of Polonius from behind the arras," though later he seems merely to have raised his "lamp over the body." And Sothern's curtain fell, in 1900, on Hamlet weeping *"over body of* Polonius." [167]

The fourth act has fared shabbily in many performances of the play. Hamlet must, indeed, be sent to England — and, accordingly, some of Scene 3 will be included — and Ophelia insists upon having her Mad Scene, or part of it. Otherwise, the sooner those droll fellows the gravediggers are brought on, the better — or so it was thought. Instead of the sudden flight implied in the Folio's "Hide fox, and all after," at the end of Scene 2, the Crow Street "Promptbook" has in "Hand B":

Hamlet points to Rosencrantz to shew him the way to the K., as Guildenstern follows Hamlet, the prince stops & just gives him a look of dreadful contempt, G sinks as it were under it, & goes off as if confounded.

In one or two early acting editions (Bell's, for instance), Hamlet is specifically furnished with *"Guards,"* when he next enters. Booth wisely has them, too; and in his 1890 promptbook the hero comes with "2 guards who divide and x spears Hamlet comes through." In the light of subsequent happenings, they were needed. Wilson Barrett's Hamlet stamped upon the King's picture (for the second time in the play) and, when Claudius rushed toward him (at "seek him i' th' other place yourself"), held up before his eyes the medallion of the murdered brother — at sight of which the villain shrank back "like a cowed beast." Sothern, early in his career, went even further, catching up a naked sword which the King had just placed "on a convenient chair," and attempting to kill him then and there.[168] As against such broad effects, Booth looked intently into his enemy's eyes, at "I see a cherub that sees them":

"Therein," as it was explained to Booth's daughter, "*Hamlet* sees his own face reflected in miniature, and my father, by pointing upward, with special stress upon the word 'cherub,' merely indicated *Hamlet's* preconceived idea of playing upon the King's superstitious fancies, and thus still more deeply convincing him of his own madness." [169]

In Poel's memorable performance of the First Quarto *Hamlet* in 1881, Miss Maud Holt, his Ophelia, appeared "*playing on a Lute,*" as the Quarto directs her to do.[170] Rowe has Ophelia enter, the second time, "*fantastically drest with Straws and Flowers*"— and the straws are interesting. Perhaps the reference to her spurning "enviously at straws" was taken literally? But there were practical considerations, as well, especially when the play was acted in winter, and the pathos of the scene may well have been enhanced. At any rate, Ophelia's straws belong to theatrical history for many years to come. Lloyd's *Actor* (1760) has these lines:

> In vain *Ophelia* gives her Flowrets round,
> And with her Straws fantastic strews the Ground;
> In vain now sings, now heaves the desp'rate Sigh,
> If Phrenzy sit not in the troubled Eye.
> In *Cibber's* Look commanding Sorrows speak. . . .

Lichtenberg, in describing Mrs. Smith, Garrick's Ophelia in 1775, speaks of her as holding "a bunch of loose straw" in her left hand; and, in 1789, "Abraham Thrifty" mentions among the objectionable designs of his family — who were preparing to do *Hamlet*, during his absence — that "Ophelia was to go mad with straw from one of the packages in the warehouse." When, too, in 1827, Paris was excited over Miss Smithson's Ophelia, "*une coiffure à la Miss Smithson, dite à la folle*" was introduced. "*Elle consiste en un voile noir et en fétus de paille artistement entremêlés aux cheveux.*" As late as 1855, *Punch* included among its "illustrations to Shakspeare" one of Ophelia (at "There's fennel for you") presenting straws to the King. Ellen Terry, however, always had real flowers —"no matter what the cost"— and perhaps under Pre-Raphaelite influence carried, in 1883, "a lily branch in her hand." [171] After that, of course, one hears no more about straws.

Besides her straws (*"long wheat Straws"*, in the Cumberland and French editions), Ophelia had a scarf or veil. Stirling, in his copy of *Hamlet*, added to the printed stage direction *"Kneeling,"* just before the song,

> And will he not come again?

the note, "Spreads her veil as a Coffin"; and of Miss Glover's Ophelia at Covent Garden, October 16, 1826, it was remarked that "her action, when she formed her scarf into a shroud, and laid herself down beside it, excited loud and earnest applause." [172] Mr. Wopsle's Ophelia

> was a prey to such slow musical madness, that when, in course of time, she had taken off her white muslin scarf, folded it up, and buried it, a sulky man . . . growled, "Now the baby's put to bed, let's have supper!"

A later variation is described in Lawrence Barrett's promptbook: "The usual bus here is for Ophelia to make a cross ~}~ of the flowers she has in veil tied about her waist." A photograph of Julia Marlowe, in 1903, shows her kneeling over a similar cross of flowers.[173]

A pitiful half-recognition of Laertes was sometimes allowed Ophelia. Helen Faucit, in one of the essays in her book, *On Some of Shakespeare's Female Characters*, elaborates upon this idea. Or, for a simpler expression of it, there is the Barrett Promptbook, once more:

> The Queen assists her to rise, & in backing up stage — Laertes steps forward thus intercepting her (Ophelia's) view of the flowers — she — [?gets] sight of him — starts & runs to him as though about to recognize him b[ut] it passes from her — she sadly shakes her head & backs up — looking back at cross — kissing her hand to it — & if inclined — can sing last verse of song as she exits . . . Queen follows her off.[174]

The Queen's exit here is worth noticing. She has nothing further to do in the scene and may as well go now — or so actors seem to have felt, from Kemble's time on.

One last piece of stage business in this act is still familiar in performances today. This is the quiet bringing in of Ophelia's body on a bier while the manner of her death is, even at that moment, being recounted by the Queen. At the Porte-Saint-Martin, in March 1886, a novelty which attracted wide interest was the substitution of Ophelia herself (Madame Bernhardt), "borne to the grave on a bier," for the lay figure, or untenanted coffin, which had ordinarily been employed.[175] It seems to me likely that the introduction of the open bier in the earlier scene was suggested by accounts of this Parisian innovation. At any rate, "the presentation of the body of the drowned *Ophelia*" in the Booth-Barrett production, late in 1887, was objected to by H. M. Ticknor;[176] and the Booth 1890 Promptbook has "4 guards . . . bring on bier carry down C & turn it setting it crosswise" and "immediately exeunt," just as the Queen begins her story — and Laertes "throws himself on Ophelia's body — back of bier," at the curtain. Similarly, in England, "most of Mr. Benson's new business" was regarded with dislike by the *Athenaeum* (March 15, 1890); and "no reason presents itself for bringing in the body of the drowned Ophelia in the fourth act."[177] The sight of the bier is impressive, however, and it had come to stay.[178] Against it is to be urged chiefly that it takes from a later, and this time Shakespearean, effect — "What, the fair Ophelia?"

The ingenuous Partridge "expressed much surprise at the number of skulls thrown upon the stage" by the Gravedigger. They were real skulls, too — no doubt of that. In 1755, a minor critic (Paul Hiffernan) did, indeed, object. He is addressing his man of straw "Eugenius":

You agree, that . . . *Water* represented by *Water* is a Fault; and further add, that you have always been offended at the real *Skulls* and *Bones* in the Grave-digging Scene of *Hamlet*, to which a wooden Substitution might be easily made by a Carpenter. I join with you.

Almost a century later, *The Theatrical Journal*, in reviewing one of the many amateur performances to which it paid attention, protested "against the using of real skulls upon the stage — it is highly indecent, at the same time repulsive to the audience." [179] Except, however, on rare occasions, actors have consistently represented skulls by skulls. Irving assured a Dundee audience, in 1904, that when he had visited their city with the Edinburgh Company, early in his career, the Gravedigger had handed Hamlet "a small, attenuated, consumptive, and rather grimy turnip"; and a turnip figured also, on one occasion, during Booth's southern tour of 1876.[180] Very familiar is the grim story of how Dr. Francis, visited "at a late hour." by a subordinate from the Park Theatre "was compelled" to lend him the skull of George Frederick Cooke, to be fondled and knocked about by the players. One hears, too, of the elder Booth's obtaining for stage purposes the skull of a man named Lovett whom he had known in jail before Lovett's execution, and of "Pop" Reed, gas man at the Walnut Street Theatre, Philadelphia, who bequeathed his own skull "to be used in the graveyard scene of HAMLET after his death." Finally, *The Gazetteer and New Daily Advertiser*, September 22, 1783, notes the discovery "during the repair of Drury-lane Theatre in the summer" of

a human scull in the earth under the stage. . . . An old scene shifter unravelled the mystery, by declaring it was no other than Yorick's scull used in Hamlet, and that he remembered it being lost many years since in Mr. Garrick's time.

The omission of the Gravedigger's Scene in Garrick's version of the play may perhaps explain how so important a property could have been mislaid.[181]

When the Gravedigger would demonstrate what suicide really is, he turns inevitably to action. The water will perhaps be a coil of rope; the man, a pickaxe stood on end with the Gravedigger's hat added for the sake of verisimilitude. This arrangement, which becomes exciting when the water comes to the man, might be thought to go far back in time. But as introduced by Benson's Gravedigger, G. R. Weir, in 1890, it was hailed as a novelty — and "it is very hard to import anything approaching to novelty into *Hamlet*." [182] A simpler demonstration is called for, in the

Lawrence Barrett and Louis James Promptbooks, by which a shovel is laid on the ground for the water, and the pickaxe stands upright for the man, this time bareheaded. A Mr. Vail, at the Surrey in 1829, illustrated the passage by spitting on the stage.[183]

Louis Simond tells in his *Journal* of seeing *Hamlet*, at Covent Garden, on April 20, 1811:

> After beginning their labour, and breaking ground for a grave, a conversation begins between the two grave-diggers. The chief one [Fawcett] takes off his coat, folds it carefully, and puts it by in a safe corner; then, taking up his pickaxe, spits in his hand, — gives a stroke or two, — talks, — stops, — strips off his waistcoat, still talking, — folds it with great deliberation and nicety, and puts it with the coat, — then an under-waistcoat, still talking, — another and another. I counted seven or eight, each folded or unfolded very leisurely, in a manner always different, and with gestures faithfully copied from nature. The British public enjoys this scene excessively, and the pantomimic variations a good actor knows how to introduce in it, are sure to be vehemently applauded.[184]

That the business here described was not, as had sometimes been fancied, traditional business handed down by generations of pious low comedians from perhaps Shakespeare's own day, was shown pretty conclusively by W. J. Lawrence in one of the happiest of his many studies, "The Folly of the Grave-Digger's Waistcoats." He calls attention to the silence of persons like Voltaire and Davies who might have been expected to mention the abuse, had it existed when they wrote. What is more, he quotes a letter written by Tom King, October 12, 1796, stating in effect that throughout his long career "as a member of the Theatres Royal in London and Dublin" he (King) had never seen the Gravediggers eat bread and cheese beside Ophelia's grave or sink to the degradation of the many waistcoats. There is, thus, a good deal of evidence against an early date, and no real evidence for one.[185] Lawrence suggests that the "trick" originated in some country theatre soon after Garrick's death (in 1779) and the popular restoration of the fifth act, omitted in his version of *Hamlet*. And there do seem to have been provincial performances in which the waistcoats were removed, at about this time. Boaden records one in which Suett played Rosencrantz and the First Gravedigger,

April 8, 1780: "The joy of the galleries to see him in Goodman
Delver's dozen waistcoats . . . may be readily conceived." Boaden
may, of course, be ascribing to Suett the customary misbehavior
of a later day; but the German traveller, Carl Gottlob Küttner,
saw a production of *Hamlet* in Manchester during the winter of
1783–1784 in which ten or a dozen waistcoats were pulled off—
"while the gallery shrieked with laughter." [186] By 1800, certainly,
the business had reached Drury Lane.[187]

It was long before the Gravedigger recovered his sanity. Possibly, the following passage from *The Roscius*, February 1, 1825,
may mean that the same comedian whom Simond saw take off so
many waistcoats had now got down to one:

> FAWCETT . . . besides other excellencies, displays the judgment of
> Solomon himself, wearing only half the number of waistcoats to ac-
> comodate both parties – in another month we recommend another
> division.

In 1831, Leigh Hunt in *The Tatler* expressed pleasure at the dis-
continuance of the abuse, only to be sharply called to account by
one of his correspondents, who refused to grant that it was an
abuse; and in January 1838 Compton, appearing with Charles
Kean at Drury Lane, was lauded "for not following the absurd
custom." Boston's great comedian, William Warren, made the
same reform on October 5, 1846 — of all places at the Howard
Athenaeum! [188] References to the now venerable tomfoolery
become scarce after this.[189] But Mr. Henry Herbert assures me
that he has seen the many waistcoats, once, in the present century.
It was in the north of England, and the old comedian who wore
them had sunk to the rank of super. He gagged the part a great
deal, too — and the audience liked him.

When Hamlet enters he will do well to wear a cloak and not
appear as he seems regularly to have done in the seventeen-fifties
"every way as nicely dressed as at court, and . . . without any
alteration of garb, when it is plain he is not known till he discovers himself." So Kemble, wearing "a long robe" in this scene,
flung it off, with a splendid flourish, no doubt, at "This is I,/Ham-
let the Dane." [190] Stirling, too, threw off his cloak, and Mr.
Wopsle wore "a comprehensive black" one. Contrast, for its

modern informality, Fechter's sitting down comfortably on a tombstone and nursing his knee, as he listened to the Grave-digger.[191]

Booth had his own ideas about the bones and Yorick's skull. "The bones," he wrote in Taylor's copy of the play, "sh^d be tossed by *hand* not shovelled from the grave; the former action suggests the game of loggats, the latter does not" (Hamlet suggests that the gravedigger was playing "at loggats with 'em"). As for the skull, Booth would have it identified "*by the remnant of a leather fool's cap which adheres to it.*" Also, his Gravedigger patted it "in a kindly, jocose way" before handing it to the Prince; but that detail (at "A pestilence on him for a mad rogue") was old.[192] Hamlet, in his turn, after examining the skull must get rid of it. "Hand B" in the Crow Street "Promptbook" has him lay it down "with delicacy and respect"— often he has given it to Horatio — but sometimes loathing has overmastered him, and Macready in his early days "literally tossed" the disgusting object "over his back to the gravedigger." Barry Sullivan, we read, "after handing over Yorick's skull to Horatio . . . takes out his handkerchief and carefully wipes his fingers"; [193] and Mr. Wopsle "could not possibly have returned the skull . . . without dusting his fingers on a white napkin taken from his breast; but even that innocent and indispensable action did not pass without the comment, 'Wai-ter!'"

The funeral procession — often far more pompous than the text warrants[194]— comes in, and Hamlet learns for whom the grave has been made ready. Here the elder Booth, turning "What, the fair Ophelia?" into "a wild inarticulate cry," "muffled his face in his cloak"; whereas Forrest "staggered, and bent his head for a moment on the shoulder of his friend Horatio"; and Edwin Booth covered his face with his hands and threw himself upon Horatio's breast. Fechter sank upon his knees — and he, too, buried his face in his hands.[195] With a lay-figure as Ophelia, careful masking is of course necessary when the body is placed in the grave. Wallack's Promptbook (1856) takes care of this:

Bell — Attendants raise pall, & hold it up in front while Gravediggers lower coffins [*sic*] — they then place pall on bier, and Exit with it.

Similar maneuvering is called for in a number of later acting texts.[196] In 1886, as already noted, Ophelia herself was shown on her bier at the Porte-Saint-Martin; and before long Benson made a similar innovation at the Globe. The *Athenaeum* (March 15, 1890) protested at once: "the depositing of the real Ophelia, in the presence of the audience, in the grave into which her brother jumps, we resent as little short of an offence." [197] And into the same grave Hamlet, too, is expected to jump.

Whether this action, which is called for in the queer First Quarto text, is in point of fact what Mr. Granville-Barker considers it, "Shakespeare's betrayal by his actors," does not have to be decided here. It was Burbage's business, is called for in Rowe's edition, and aroused "sympathetic Anguish" as practised by Wilks.[198] There is no break in the tradition until we come to Kemble, who did not jump into the grave but made Laertes spring out of it and seize Hamlet. Young, after having used the business at Manchester in 1804, gave it up, presumably out of respect for his master; and Vandenhoff, too, was criticized for staying out of Ophelia's grave. The pantomimic Kean leaped into it, indeed, though without achieving "the tumultuous and overpowering effect" which Hazlitt expected the action to produce.[199] But many later Hamlets of note — Booth and Irving, Fechter and Salvini — have followed Kemble, as have the editors of nineteenth century acting texts, almost without exception.[200] Near the close of the scene, Booth, with a fine instinct, knelt beside Ophelia's grave, at "Nay, an thou'lt mouth,/I'll rant as well as thou." And Tree, for a sentimental curtain, returned to the now deserted grave, upon which he cast flowers. That was to pervert Shakespeare, as even Winter realized, though he found the act itself "gracious and sweet." [201]

The beginning of the second scene — Hamlet and Horatio, Hamlet and Osric — is played with little or no business; and we may pass at once to the whirlwind conclusion — to the poisoned cup, first of all, and the fencing. The King calls for "cups," and,

Set me the stoups of wine upon that table;

but actors, from Kemble's time on, have made it their practise, seemingly, to use only one cup, into which Claudius drops the poison, as he cries "Hamlet, this pearl is thine," and *"pretends to drink."* [201a] Mr. Granville-Barker's idea that we be allowed to see Laertes anoint his weapon had occurred to Booth, and was introduced for a time in his performance.[202]

The "brother's wager"— a triumphant little drama in itself, with a thrill of its own in the theatre and plenty of problems for the student —.seems to have been left by early critics pretty much to the actors, to do with it what they chose. We hear at last of Kemble, who has been called to task for the "attitude in which he places himself, to parry off the weapon of his antagonist," which is considered "too mechanical and artificial." In his defense, is urged that Hamlet "only handles his weapon as a trial of skill," and "the peculiar grace with which Mr. Kemble makes his first pass at Laertes shews excellent skill in the art of fencing." "When he took off his sword and gave it to Horatio's care," another writer tells us,

his gesture was all elegance — he took the foil with equal grace — he turned to the king when uttering his compliments. He stood so proudly graceful, his air and head so lofty, that the inimitable bow that thanked the flattery was doubly gracious from the fine attitude he bent from.

In the Brighton 1809 Promptbook, there are full directions for the "Salute with M^r Y[oung]" but the actual fencing notes are simple and brief, "Laertes lunge 2/ 3 Hamlet hits," doing for the first "exchange"; "Laertes hits H^t/Disarm — scufflin[g]/Laertes hit," for the last.[203] Macready was accustomed "when trying his foil . . . to make a spring and a lunge together, hitting the edge of the wing nearest the footlights with unerring accuracy." It is, again, Hamlet's mere "skill in fence" which is remembered.[204] It was Salvini who, in 1875, "delighted and surprised" English audiences by introducing an elaborate piece of stage business, which seems to have been quite new to them. His Hamlet, feeling the prick of the "unbated" foil, clapped his hand to his side, and looked, astonished, at his fingers, as if he had found blood on them. Then he pressed his attack on Laertes, "disarmed him in *seconde*," and, setting his foot upon the poisoned weapon, offered his adversary with a low bow his own foil, useful only for defense. The contest was resumed and Laertes mortally wounded.[205] Hamlet's realization during the fencing that he is the victim of foul play is questionable.

> The treacherous instrument is in thy hand,
> Unbated and envenom'd,

Laertes tells him later, though perhaps without distinguishing precisely between what Hamlet already knows and what as yet he cannot know. Rossi believed that the Prince was unaware of having been wounded:

> As soon as Laertes feels that his dastardly purpose has been accomplished, his grasp of the foil slackens, and Hamlet disarms him with ease, offering him, with the courtesy of a high-bred gentleman, his own (Hamlet's) foil, and retaining for his own use the one he had just wrested from his (Laertes's) hand. . . . This is my view of the encounter, and thus do I invariably play it.

With Booth, as described by Furness in 1877,

> Hamlet secures Laertes's foil by a powerful parry of his thrust in *carte*, by which Hamlet disarms him; catching his foil as it leaves his grasp with the left hand, Hamlet uses it as a dagger, being too close to him for a free use of his own weapon.

Mr. Dover Wilson has learned from "fencers" who saw Irving in 1878 that in his performance Laertes attacked Hamlet treacherously at the end of the second bout.[206] That may have been the business, but according to a description of the scene in *The Theatre*, April 1, 1891, the exchange of weapons was clearly not forced by Irving's Hamlet who, after disarming Laertes, merely tossed his own foil to him, "as a man of unsuspicious nature . . . might do." In 1894, Winter writes of E. S. Willard's Hamlet, that the fencing was "played with both 'rapier and dagger' "— as perhaps it had not been, before, since Shakespeare's own day.[207]

"*While the Queen drinks*," runs the stage direction in Winter's acting edition of Booth's plays, "*Osric and others approach the King.*" That is puzzling at first sight. For why should Gertrude's drinking need to be masked? Claudius asks her not to drink, and she does so, for whatever reason, deliberately:

I will, my lord; I pray you pardon me.

The explanation lies in a small change in the text, one quite beneath the notice of literary editors: "have" for "will" ("I have, my lord"), introduced in Bell's edition (1774) and handed down through the Kemble, Cumberland, and French editions, to Booth's time. For Gertrude to drink of the poisoned cup without the King's noticing it, calls indeed for masking! As for Hamlet's courteous refusal to drink, at this moment, Laurence Barrett's promptbook explains this, dramatically, by making Laertes beat the *rappel* "with his foot — signifying a desire to begin"— just as Hamlet "raises cup to his lips." [208]

The Queen, dying, has often been led from the stage; but this is post-Kemble and sophisticated, and Hamlet's "Wretched Queen, adieu!" will lose force and direction if she is no longer there when it is spoken.[209] In the Booth Edition, once more, Claudius goes out with her, then, returning, "*calls his lords around him on the throne.*" And presently they "*draw their swords to defend the King. Hamlet rushes through the crowd and stabs him.*" The idea underlying these energetic proceedings — that the King should not die without something like a battle — is old. In a letter to Garrick on the subject of his alteration of *Hamlet*, Steevens in 1771 urged the actor to give attention to the stabbing of Claudius:

I beg, for your own sake, you will take care that this circumstance is not on his part awkwardly represented. . . . A stab given to an unarmed or a defenceless man has seldom a very happy effect. An Englishman loves a spirited, but abhors a phlegmatic exit.

If we are to believe Davies, Garrick followed this advice: Claudius, in the alteration, "defends himself, and is killed in the rencounter." And Davies adds: "Garrick, if I remember right, used to say, that, before his alteration of Hamlet, the King used to be stuck like a pig on the stage." [210] How much resistance Kemble's Kings were expected to offer, I am uncertain — though one of them, a Mr. Waddy in 1800, is accused of not waiting to be killed but dying, "most composedly, before *Hamlet* has time to make a single pass at him." Macready's monarchs put up something of a fight. Walter Leman tells an amusing anecdote of how, playing Claudius in Philadelphia, in the autumn of 1843, he had left off his sword between the acts and, remembering almost too late, snatched "a fencing-foil" from the property man and, thus armed, went on for the last scene. "The play progressed to its close — Hamlet disarmed and slew the King, and the curtain fell." Whereupon Macready, a painstaking artist, justly incensed, had Leman on the carpet:

"Where did you get — where, sir, did you con-trive to get"— here he gave a great gasp —"that awful tool, that skewer, that-that-a-a kitchen spit, to draw it on me for a regal weapon, whipping it out from beneath your robe like a ramrod; oh, sir!" [211]

As Fechter arranged the scene, "a gallery ran at the back of the stage, with short flights of stairs on either side." During the confession of Laertes, Claudius stole toward one of these stairways, up which he darted at "the King's to blame." But Hamlet was too quick for him. Mounting the other staircase, he encountered him at the centre of the gallery, and there "despatched him." [212] Tom Taylor's edition (1873) calls for even more sensational action. At "Then, venom, to thy work," Hamlet rushes through the group of courtiers and stabs the King. That was, by now, pretty familiar. [213] But when Claudius cries,

Oh, yet defend me friends! I am but hurt,

the Lords now

form round the King, *and draw to repel* Hamlet. *He, after a moment's pause, rushes on the* King *again, followed by* Horatio, *who, trussing his mantle round his left arm, takes the left-hand blows on it, guarding* Hamlet *with his right from the swords of the* Lords *on that side.*

A real battle, at last! On the other hand, Shakespeare's intention may actually have been carried out in the Mounet-Sully version of 1894: "*Hamlet s'élance sur le roi; quelques-uns des seigneurs s'avancent pour l'arrêter, mais reculent devant l'épée empoisonnée.*" Fear of the poisoned rapier explains in an instant why Claudius found no one to defend him. But we are not yet done with eccentricity. For Benson's Hamlet, like a Scandinavian retiarius, enmeshed his foe in a fisherman's net, which he had been carrying with him since the beginning of the act, and then slew him.[214]

As for the grim detail of Hamlet's forcing the King to drink — 'commending the ingredience of his poisoned chalice to his own lips'—it was regularly omitted by English actors. A possible exception is Kemble. Tieck, writing of a performance at Covent Garden in June 1817, declared that he had learned nothing from it, except that while Hamlet is saying,

> Here, thou incestuous, murd'rous, damned Dane,
> Drink off this potion! Is thy union here?

he "thrusts the poisoned chalice to the king's mouth, and forces him, as he dies, to drink it, which I take to be the right thing." [215] The second of the two lines is omitted in Kemble's editions of *Hamlet* — as it had been in stage texts since Davenant's time — but Kemble was the sort of actor who might conceivably have dared to introduce the business, just at the close of his career. Rossi, in 1876, caused Hamlet "to stab the King, holding the foil half-way by its blade, as a dagger is held," then forced the goblet to the wretch's lips. Winter, shocked by the savage literalness of this suiting of the action to the word, cried out that Rossi was applying "realism to poetry — and realism applied to Hamlet is a desecration." [216] Irving, it might be noted in passing, had "bosses fixed below the rim" of his "massive metal goblet," so that it could not roll when Hamlet, struggling with Horatio, desperately flings it down. "There is a sort of fascination," Bram Stoker comments, "in the uncertain movement of an inanimate object." "In flinging away the goblet in *Hamlet*, are you disturbed by having to aim it so that it may be caught by the prompter?" was one of the items in the curious questionnaire circulated among actors by William Archer, in preparation for his book *Masks or Faces?* [217]

Hamlet's death scene has been played very differently by different actors. Kean, for example, illustrated in detail the effects of the poison. His limbs shook, his eye dilated, and he gnawed his hand "in the vain effort to repress emotion." Macready fell prostrate, after snatching the cup from Horatio, and his death was "a violent, and next to an instantaneous one." Forrest, on the other hand, died slowly, supported by Horatio. Lewes wrote of Salvini's performance in the summer of 1875:

> No more pathetic death has been seen on the stage. Among its many fine touches there was the subtle invention of making the dying Hamlet draw down the head of Horatio to kiss him before sinking into silence. . . . And this affecting motive was represented by an action as novel as it was truthful — namely, the uncertain hand blindly searching for the dear head, and then faintly closing on it with a sort of final adieu.

But Irving's business had been very similar, before the coming of the great Italian. Rossi's Hamlet died on the throne which was his by right. Wilson Barrett brought out Hamlet's love for his father, by searching with "fumbling fingers . . . for what Horatio guesses, finds, and lifts before his eyes — his father's picture." [218] Last of all, Forbes-Robertson (in 1897) went "feebly to the empty throne," there died; Horatio placed the crown upon the dead Prince's knees.[219] Then, for the first time in an English performance for generations, Fortinbras and his soldiers entered, and bore Hamlet away on their shields. Mr. Bernard Shaw had described to Forbes-Robertson how it should all be done; but to many critics of the time, the restoration of Shakespeare's heroic ending was unwelcome. An anti-climax, they called it! [220]

IV

Othello

THE POPULARITY of *Othello* during the Restoration Period was second, perhaps, only to that of *Hamlet*, among Shakespeare's plays, and the tragedy has never been long from the stage in later times. What is more, *Othello* was not adapted, or "improved," though as early as Mr. Spectator's time it was severely cut in performance.[1] Both of the leading parts have been played in radically different ways. Fechter's Moor in the eighteen-sixties, Salvini's in the eighteen-seventies, departed almost wholly from the traditions of the rôle in England, Fechter's production, likewise, giving cause for alarm to those who held with the past. His business is minutely set down in what is really the first "modern" acting edition (1861) of a Shakespearean play, while Salvini's business is described with equal fullness of detail in E. T. Mason's book, *The Othello of Tommaso Salvini* (1890). So complete, indeed, are these two records that it is a temptation to give to the performances of Fechter and Salvini even more attention, in the pages which follow, than is their due. Salvini was a very great though not, perhaps, a very "right" Othello. Fechter was neither the one nor the other.

The elder Booth when, as Iago, he urged Roderigo to arouse Brabantio, spoke with "a devilish unconcern, as if pleased with the fancy of terror and dismay, and playing meanwhile with his sword-hilt, or pulling at his gauntlets." Then he struck "on the door of Brabantio's house, and speaking through the key-hole," cried "What, ho, Brabantio!" There had been knocking at the old man's door, earlier, when Cooke played Iago.[2] "Here is her father's house," Roderigo says; and presently (according to the Quarto direction), Brabantio appears "*at a window.*" A thunderous knocking at the stage door might well accompany the "terrible summons." Soon after, when in reply to Brabantio's "Thou art a villain," Iago says "You are — a senator," the hiatus has sometimes been explained by Roderigo's "putting his hand over Iago's mouth" or otherwise checking him. And it is easier to accept Iago's deferring to his dupe here than to suppose such a master of self-control to have been caught off his guard even momentarily.[3]

Fechter's Othello, at the beginning of Scene 2, displayed "*a golden key,*" opening the door of "the Sagittary" with it, and then, after pausing on the threshold to confer with Iago, shutting the door quickly, at sight of Cassio, and *locking* it. Later, he gave Iago the same key, when he sent him to fetch Desdemona. "Mr. Macready and other authorities," it was remarked "used to be content to make their entrance and exit at one of the right wings — our modern Roscius gives countenance to a door with a 'golden key' "; and Lewes felt that although Fechter aimed no doubt at "an air of reality," the effect was "to make us forget the 'noble Moor,' and to think of a sepoy."[4] The contrast between old ways and new is seen again when we come to the fray, narrowly averted by Othello, between his followers and those of Brabantio. Bell's edition (1774) has the direction, "*They fight,*" just before Othello's "Hold your hands"; and Clarke's Forrest Promptbook adds "X swords" both here and earlier, at

> Keep up your bright swords, for the dew will rust them.

Booth, on the other hand, would have the hero's friends no more than "motion to draw," at the line just quoted; and later, instead of striking up the swords, as was sometimes done, his Othello merely stood "between the two parties with sheathed scimetar held up."[5] Business to conclude a scene is to be expected in nineteenth century performances; and John Moore's promptbook of the 'forties has Othello stop on his way out, and turn toward Cassio, whom he calls "by a wave of the head, and Exit. with his hand on Cassio's shoulder." This unobtrusive action — ironic in the light of subsequent happenings — is much to be preferred to Salvini's ending:

Upon Brabantio's exit with his party, Iago starts forward, as if to attack them, but is restrained by Othello, who lays his hand upon Iago's arm, and then motions him, and the rest, to follow him . . . and exit.[6]

One of Kemble's contributions to Shakespeare was an attention to ceremonial. Thus, at the beginning of the Senate Scene, the Messenger who brings news that the Turks are headed for Rhodes, after speaking his first lines, now *"gives Letters to Marco"* (Kemble was fond of christening the unnamed characters of Shakespeare) and Marco in his turn *"delivers them to the Duke."* That the Messenger carried letters is a perfectly natural assumption;[7] but if he does carry them, he will not, as Kemble knew, walk straight up to the Duke and hand them to him. Hence Marco! Glimpses of Quin's business are rare. But Francis Gentleman speaks of "one stroke" as "not amiss"— his "coming on in white gloves, by pulling off which the black hands became more realized."[8] Brabantio, who enters with Othello, is unnoticed by the Duke —"I did not see you"— and the actor must explain this through introducing business of some sort, as for instance the Duke's being shown papers just as Brabantio comes in.[9] When, a little later, Iago is sent for Desdemona, he has usually been accompanied by Roderigo (Iago beckons to him, and in a promptbook of the eighteen-thirties he "follows him out on tip toe").[10] The elder Booth had Brabantio make a "gesture of dissent" when Othello says "Her father lov'd me," and if this is not too pronounced it can do no harm. Contrast Fechter's treatment of the Moor's earlier speech, where at

> The very head and front of my offending
> Hath this extent, no more,

he uttered

the "no more" as one violently repelling a foul imputation on his honour, with fierce gesture of advance towards the table. Upon this senators rise as if they almost expected an attack, and Othello gives the next eight or nine lines, "Rude am I in speech," etc., as a special apology called for by that show of violence.[11]

Edwin Booth abstained from hurrying to greet Desdemona when she entered, and would even have Othello avoid looking at her. "Othello," he argues, "must not 'give a loop to hang a doubt on' respecting his influence over Desdemona. . . . He must turn his back towards her until she announces him as her husband, then let him turn and face her and the whole Court." [12] Out of the eighteenth century comes the following tribute to Mrs. Pope in this scene. "The stroke was slight," we read, "but it was electrical."

> It was not any word she spoke . . . but it was her polite and tender manner of saluting her husband from the opposite side of the stage, when answering her father's sharp interrogation, she says,
> "I do perceive here a divided duty."
> The grace and delicacy of her action, at that moment, has not only not been equalled, but it has never been attempted by any other. OTHELLO generally stands as much unnoted by his fair Bride, except perhaps by a glance of the eye, whilst she recites this speech, as any other individual present.

I do not know what to think of Brabantio's actually joining the hands of his daughter and the Moor, at

> I here do give thee that with all my heart
> Which, but thou hast already, with all my heart
> I would keep from thee.

Certainly, this piece of business, which is called for in a number of promptbooks, could only be carried out with the bitterest irony.[13] Salvini's Othello, according to Mason, here "instantly responds to what he deems magnanimity on Brabantio's part. He bends towards him, extending his right hand." But when the Senator "continues, 'Which, but thou hast already,' etc. Othello draws himself up to his full height, gazes a moment at Brabantio with grief and indignation; then turns from him." [14] From early in the nineteenth century, Desdemona has knelt to her father on his exit. "He puts her from him," or "throws her off," and the Moor "raises her." Salvini elaborated upon this action, his Othello starting back at Brabantio's warning ("Look to her, Moor"), and following the old man threateningly up the stage; then returning

to Desdemona and, at the close of his final speech, embracing
her.[15]

Iago and Roderigo are left alone on the stage. And here Fechter's production became very modern indeed. "The furniture
was so disposed that it was available to histrionic purposes"; and
John Ryder, the Iago, actually sat on the council table and coolly
swung his leg —"*à la Captain Macheath*," it was said at the time.[16]
Later, after Roderigo had '*run out at the door at the back*,' to sell
all his land, Iago spoke his soliloquy once more sitting "*on the
angle of the table*." Presently he leaned "*his forehead on his
hands, thoughtfully*," thus concealing his face, and "How? how?
let's see," he spoke "*slowly raising his head, and showing his face,
which gradually brightens with a diabolical smile*." Years later
Irving, too, "covered his face with his two hands" and then after
a long pause "slowly drew down his hands, revealing a face all
alive with the devilish scheme which had come into his mind."
"Only an actor of rare imagination would have thought of it,"
writes H. M. Walbrook, "and only an actor with a face as expressive as Irving's would have dared to do it" [17] — or, rather, could
have made it memorable.

In Cyprus, Othello's coming is anxiously awaited (II, 1).
Fechter was again modern in the informality and realistic detail
of his stage arrangements. A capstan was introduced, with bales
of goods beside it. Iago "leans cross-armed on the top of the
capstan," speaking his "old, fond paradoxes" about women, and
stares now at his wife, now at Desdemona, who are sitting on the
bales.[18] A little later in the scene, Shakespeare has set a task for
his actors as Iago comments aside on the civilities exchanged in
dumb show between Cassio and Desdemona —"He takes her by
the palm. Ay, well said, whisper!" Kemble made this byplay
easier to carry out by enlarging the group concerned in it, Cassio
taking Desdemona by the hand, "*to introduce her to the Gentlemen of Cyprus*." [19] But it is not Cassio or even Desdemona whom
we are closely watching. Irving as he spoke Iago's words plucked
and slowly ate a bunch of purple grapes, "spitting out the seeds,
as if each one represented a worthy virtue." Mowbray Morris is
alone, perhaps, in preferring Booth's "still, respectful attitude,

leaning against the sun-dial, alert to execute any command, seeming careless what goes on so long as he is ready when wanted,
yet ever watching his prey with sly, sleepless, vigilance." [20]

Back in the days before Garrick, Aaron Hill would have had
Mr. Stephens at Covent Garden bring out

that conscious superiority, inseparable from a character, so dignified
as *Othello's*. . . . When, at your arrival in *Cyprus*, you ran so eagerly
to the arms of *Desdemona*, that *love* (as is commonly the case) made
you unmindful of your *greatness*, which might, however, be well
enough preserved here, by a certain stately, yet tender, *advance*, not
tripping lightly, to her *embrace*; but a little quickening the *step*, more
strongly extending the arms, gently *inclining* the *breast*, not the head.

Whether Hill's admonitions produced any effect upon the performance of Mr. Stephens, I am at a loss to say — the actor
proved to be a mere nine days' wonder — but Spranger Barry,
the great Othello of Garrick's time, 'rushed' into Desdemona's
arms.[21] From American promptbooks of a century later come
two details of stage business which are appealing: Othello's taking Montano by the hand at

How does my old acquaintance of this isle;

and Roderigo's start and "look of disapprobation" when Iago
mentions Cassio's quick temper and the possibility of his striking
at the poor gull. The Iago of the elder Booth looked "up to
heaven with defiant forehead and gesture, and with a cold and
mocking smile," as in his soliloquy he spoke of loving Desdemona
not out of absolute lust —"though peradventure/I stand account-
ant for as great a sin." [22] Of the rightness or wrongness of that,
only those who saw it are in a position to judge.

If knowledge of the stage business of a Shakespearean play
does no more than remind a reader of the imaginative activity
demanded of him, it should be worth acquiring. Let him try
himself on the Drinking Scene, for instance, and, having done so,
glance then at Edwin Booth's notes in the *Furness Variorum
Othello*. "Remember," wrote John Marston of his own comedies,
"the life of these things consists in action." At Cassio's "To the
health of our general!" Booth's Iago emptied his glass on the
ground; and Montano's instant

I am for it, Lieutenant, and I'll do you justice,

fits neatly if Iago has avoided drinking the toast.[23] "Well, God's
above all," Cassio observes profoundly. Whereupon, "Officers
begin to titter and look at each other," according to Moore's
promptbook. Cassio turns and sees them laughing, a moment
later, and "they shrink a little away." He "feels his sword to discover his right hand." "This is my right hand," he says, "and this
is my left." Another way —"said to be Charles Kemble's"— was
for Cassio to drop his handkerchief and "in his effort to recover
it" fall on his knees;

to account for this position to his companions, he attempts to pray
["God forgive us our sins!"]. His clothes being awry, his sword has
slipped to his right side, and this confuses him for a moment as to
which is his right or his left hand.

"Caricature" is Kittredge's word for this bit of business, and the
degree of Cassio's intoxication is often exaggerated on the stage.[24]
Roderigo's sudden entrance, and equally abrupt exit after Iago's
aside to him — "I pray you after the Lieutenant, go!" — must
somehow be covered, and there is elaborate though somewhat
awkward contrivance for this in two of the promptbooks: "A
Laugh L.H. which occasions Mont to look off & as he turns again
to Ia Rod X behind & Exit L.H." A little before is the quaint
direction, "Ready Laugh L.H." [25]
   In Iago's character Irving found "a slight dash of the bull-
fighter, and during the brawl between Cassio and Montano," he
used (he says) "to enjoy a mischievous sense of mastery by flick-
ing at them with a red cloak, as if they were bulls in the arena."
Iago tells Othello that in the course of the quarrel he pursued "the
crying fellow," who outran him. Assuming that the Ancient told
truth — as he does so often when it suits his purposes — Booth
took pains to follow Roderigo out, at

> Away, I say' go out and cry a mutiny,

returning, of course, immediately afterwards. Macready may
even have crossed swords with Roderigo here. "Acted Iago," he
writes in his *Diary*, November 16, 1850, "cut up by Roderigo;
beyond my ability to fence him off; it was literally disgusting;

the stupid absence of all meaning or semblance of the character!" [26] The moment at which Montano is wounded is not precisely indicated, and in Lewis's Promptbook "Mont & Cassio continue fighting till Othello comes down between them — Cassio then gives the stab behind Othello." This arrangement explains readily enough how Cassio, deep in his cups as he is, could ever have got the better of Montano; nor would Cassio have been as likely as Montano to perceive Othello's presence and give over the combat. The business is, at least, ingenious. Othello's entrance in this scene might be thought sufficiently dramatic in itself. Yet Kean's "rushing with cimeter in hand through the centre gates, shouting 'Hold for your lives'" is recalled by Davidge; [27] and Gustavus Brooke, with the same exclamation (Othello's earlier and quieter, "What is the matter here?" was regularly cut), rushed down between the combatants and "as his scimitar swept through the air it collided with their swords, making a fiery circle in its flight." In Brooke's time, too, it was customary for the brawlers to exaggerate the dramatic change of speed by falling into attitudes, "as though cast in marble." [28] The tableaux of melodrama come to mind, once more. Desdemona's appearance was often omitted, but Salvini included it and, snatching "a cloak from his own shoulders," wrapped it tenderly about her.[29] Details of business from nineteenth century promptbooks include Cassio's dropping his sword when he hears the sentence of dismissal, and Iago's leaving the stage when he is told to "look with care about the town"— he returns, a moment later, and Cassio takes his hand when they part. Fechter's Iago, as he urged Roderigo to be patient, stretched himself on one of Othello's coffers — there were several of them about the stage and also a cannon on which the Ancient had perched earlier in the scene — and Roderigo in the same production was rubbing his own back when Iago asks:

> Does't not go well? Cassio hath beaten thee,
> And thou by that small hurt hath cashier'd Cassio.[30]

Early accounts of the great third act scene between Othello and Iago are disquieting. Rymer in 1693 refers sneeringly to "the Mops and the Mows, the Grimace, the Grins and Gesticulation" as the only reason for the success of this "top scene" in the tragedy. In 1734, Cibber, as Iago,

> when he is working up *Othello* to his ends, shrugs up his shoulders, shakes his noddle, and, with a fawning motion in his hands, drawls out these words,
> > *Good name. in man or woman, good my lord,* &c.
> From which gestures, and drawling manner of speaking, *Othello* must be supposed a fool, a stock, if he does not see thro' him.

And in a detailed summary of the plot of the play in *The Dramatic Historiographer*, a year later, we read that "the perfidious *Jago* . . . by Shrugs, Grimaces, and half Sentences, inflames the *Moor* with Jealousy." [31] Such descriptions as these are not, it appears, to be taken too seriously. Rymer's bias is notorious. Cibber, as his enemies were never tired of telling him, was unhappy in tragic parts. Recollections of his performance may even account for the gratuitous details in the *Historiographer*, though these seem to me a good deal harder to explain away.

As cut in representation, the third act usually began with the entrance, or rather discovery, of Desdemona and Emilia. Fechter had the lady winding off silk, which Emilia "*holds to her*." This would seem to be an innocent employment, but it was resented at the time, less I suspect for the reasons which Fechter's critic advances — Desdemona's continuing any occupation, especially one "so trivial," while she listened to Cassio's suit, he calls an offense against "common courtesy"— than because the action savored of realistic innovation. Cassio, too, stood "over her, leaning his hand upon her chair!" [32]

Othello's entrance "*reading a paper*" dates back to Cumberland's edition (1829). Older still, but less attractive, is for the Moor to exchange a look with Iago when Desdemona says it was Cassio who had just left her.[33] Fechter's Othello now sat down to attend to his papers, and was thus occupied while Desdemona pleaded with him for Cassio, Iago, at the same time, making a show of talking with Emilia and "*pointing out to her the handkerchief which* Desdemona *holds; while the latter kneels on the stool before* Othello." Her pleading was, on the Victorian stage, ac-

companied by many small acts of coquetry or endearment. Fechter
played with her curls; in Wilson Barrett's production she plucked
away a paper which her husband was signing; and, in Salvini's,
took his pen from him.[34] Othello may be expected to embrace
Desdemona when she leaves the stage (though Salvini's Moor,
suddenly conscious of the presence of Emilia and Iago, did not do
so) and to stand, for a moment, looking after her.[35] Then he
returns to his papers.

Charles Dillon, at the Lyceum in December 1856, seems to have
been the first Othello on the English stage to use a piece of business still familiar to playgoers today. "Quietly seated," he was
"perusing some state document" when Iago began his poisonous
insinuations.[36] Fechter used the same business, and since Fechter
was a controversial figure, a revolutionist, it attracted attention.
Lewes, for instance, found it admirable in itself, though disliking
the manner in which it was executed. This Othello, he complains,
answered Iago carelessly, for some time, playing with his pen as
he spoke, and was at last "*suddenly* convinced." The business
established itself, in any case, Salvini, Booth, and Irving being
others who used it.[37]

At this point in the tragedy, or perhaps a little later, a striking
effect had been obtained by George Frederick Cooke. This brilliant but eccentric performer had refused Kemble's summons to
rehearsal.

> "Let *Black Jack*"— so he called Kemble —"come to me." So they
> went on the boards without previous rehearsal. In the scene in which
> Iago instils his suspicion, Cooke grasped Kemble's left hand with his
> own, and then fixed his right, like a claw, on his shoulder. In this
> position, drawing himself up to him with his short arm, he breathed
> his poisonous whispers. Kemble coiled and twisted his hand, writhing
> to get away — his right hand clasping his brow, and darting his eye
> back on Iago.

Later, when Cooke was in New York, Washington Irving spoke
to him about the scene. " 'Didn't I play up to Black Jack!' he
exclaimed. 'I saw his dark eye sweeping back upon me.' "[38]
What follows, down to Iago's exit (line 257), may well seem
colorless, after that! Yet some of Kean's great moments were

here: his "Not a jot, not a jot," as he "clung to the side-scene . . . as if trying to steady himself against the heart-blow he was receiving"; or when, bidding Iago leave him, he walked "to the back of the stage, raising his hands, and then bringing them down upon his head with clasped fingers," and stood thus "with his back to us." He had made the same gesture, at "O misery!" and

when Iago says: —
    "My lord, beware of jealousy,"
there was a sudden spasmodic contraction of the body, as if he had been abruptly stabbed; his hands were tightly clenched, his features were horribly contracted, his eyes rolled, his shoulders were drawn up, and his frame writhed.[39]

A lesser Othello, Wilson Barrett in the eighteen-nineties, chose at this point to catch sight of "a picture of Desdemona, a draped canvas on an easel," at which he gazed; and to this picture he addressed " 'Tis not to make me jealous/To say my wife is fair," etc., "lightly laying his hand upon the canvas, with a caressing touch." [40]

Fechter's Othello, as already noted, was not easily jealous. Only when his wife's 'deception' of Brabantio is mentioned did his imagination take fire. "And so she did," he says — and "stands aside with his eye fixed on vacancy, as one reasoning out in contemplation the path shown him to the hell whither it leads." [41] With Salvini, whose performance of this part of the scene was notably sound and artistic, realization came not as a flash but very slowly; and, when Iago says of Brabantio, "he thought 'twas witchcraft," Othello's hand moved toward his sword-hilt — as it did again at

    Foh! one may smell in such a will most rank.[42]

One further detail, this time in the performance of the elder Booth who, while speaking

        And yet, how nature erring from itself,

glanced at his own hand "as it passed down before his eyes from his forehead," is a curious illustration of how through action a particular meaning may be imposed upon Shakespeare's words.

Without the gesture, Othello is more likely to be referring to the possibility of Desdemona's adultery than to the fact of her marriage. [43]

At "My lord, I take my leave," Iago goes, or makes a pretence of going, and then returns. The Cooke Promptbook has merely "looks at Othello" here — though with what an expression of malignity, one can well imagine. Booth would allow "a quick, fiendish smile of triumph and a rapid clutch of the fingers, as though squeezing his very heart (Othello's face is buried in his hands) . . . but do it unobtrusively." And of Fechter's Iago, when he left the Moor, we read that "his fingers cast at him behind his back a swift Italian gesture of contempt, instantly followed"— deplorably enough — "by servile obeisance at the threshold as Othello turns his face." [44] Left alone, Salvini's Othello, tried pitifully to resume his work, then cast away his pen, and paced the floor. Fechter, before speaking "Haply, for I am black" . . . had caught a glimpse of his own face in a mirror!

Another "modernism" in this actor's production was for Emilia to be arranging flowers in vases (not very well, I feel sure), while Othello talks with her mistress.[45] He speaks of the "pain upon my forehead, here"— the cuckold's horns, of course — and Desdemona offers to bind his head. "Your napkin is too little," he says, "let it alone." Edwin Forrest, according to the hostile Forster, in 1836,

made a "point" here, as usual. He thrust the handkerchief from her hand — pointed at it emphatically —"Your *napkin*"— (with the rigid Kean accent) — passed the forefinger with which he had been pointing at it over his brow —"is — too *little!*" [46]

Fechter also threw down the handkerchief. But Emilia speaks later of Desdemona's having "let it drop by negligence." Booth had Othello put it aside gently and Desdemona drop it. Salvini, more elaborately, showed her that it would not go round his head, then returned it, and she let it fall as she left the stage.[47] As for Othello's "let it alone," the meaning will again depend upon the action. Forrest took "it" to refer not to the General's aching head but to the handkerchief, his promptbook having "She is about to take it up" just before the words are spoken. Louis

James was later scolded for using the same business: "If Mr. James be right in his interpretation," Alfred Ayres writes, "then Desdemona should know just where to look for the object of her search"—which, of course, she doesn't. Helen Faucit recalls Macready's exit: "He took my face in both his hands, looked long into my eyes, and then the old look came back into his, and it spoke as plainly as possible, 'My life upon her faith!'" [48]

Iago has got the handkerchief from Emilia sometimes by stratagem (Booth), sometimes by coaxing, and taking her in his arms (Fechter). In each case, a preliminary snatch at it might well have been dispensed with, as likely to put her on her guard. Booth paused "mysteriously" after "Why"—"Why, what's that to you?"—"as if about to give her some wonderful reason" for wanting the handkerchief—then snatched it. A promptbook direction in George Becks's hand, and presumably referring to a Forrest performance, has her walk to the wing, just before going, and turn to him "imploringly—he—'leave me!' She exits." [49]

When Kean's Othello re-entered, he came with "abrupt and wandering step. . . . The sound of *Iago's* voice broke his meditation. He suddenly raised his eye, and pronounced the words 'avaunt, begone,' with the haughty and resentful glance of a man accustomed to authority." Then, at the end of what all who heard it agreed was his greatest speech—the "Farewell"—he used once more the gesture, already described, of bringing down his clasped hands upon his head.[50] Macready "threw himself on a chair at the back of the stage," to deliver the same "apostrophe to Content. . . . This might be a relief to him," Hazlitt remarks, "but it distressed the audience." Salvini, too, spoke part of the "Farewell" while seated, and, at the close of it, fell forward upon a table, where he lay "sobbing, his head upon his outstretched arms." Booth and Fechter each sank upon a chair, and though Forrest, I believe, remained standing it was with "form and limbs drooping . . . as if everything had been taken from him and he was all gone." [51]

Tate Wilkinson in his *Memoirs* (1790) speaks of the "collaring scene" in *Othello*. He was thinking of a piece of stage business still regularly used today—Mr. Paul Robeson employed it

memorably in his recent performance — and in all probability as
old as the play itself. It is appropriate to the lines rather than
implied in them. A full stop has been reached with the close of
the great speech —

>   Farewell! Othello's occupation's gone.

Then Iago:

>   Is't possible, my lord?
> *Oth.* Villain, be sure thou prove my love a whore!
>   Be sure of it; give me the ocular proof. . . .

And, a moment later, he cries that if Iago is slandering her he is
never to pray more:

>   On horror's head horrors accumulate;
>   Do deeds to make heaven weep, all earth amąz'd;
>   For nothing canst thou to damnation add
>   Greater than that.
> *Iago.*   O grace! O heaven forgive me!

The change in speed is striking, and that it should be accompanied
by physical action is most natural. Othello has suddenly rushed
upon the villain, collared him, throttled him, flung him down, or
across the stage, threatened his very life. Rowe's direction,
"Catching hold on him" (at "give me the ocular proof"), may
record the stage practice of his own time. Barton Booth, whose
assumption of the part dates back to a time before the death of
Betterton, is described as having caught Iago by the throat, while
his voice "went through all the scale of rage." [52] Quin and Barry
are compared as Othello in Foote's curious *Treatise on the Passions* (1747). In the "great Scene of Business" in the third act,
Foote writes,

> B's Action and Attitude, with the Totterings of *Iago*, convey to my
> Mind a pretty strong Idea of Wrestling, but do not disturb my Tran-
> quillity [*sic*] with any Emotions of Terror; nor does Q's Method of
> Collaring and quitting, and then collaring again, correspond with my
> Conception of the Passage —

as one "climactick Speech," that is, with Iago's interjections serv-
ing merely as "breathing Places for *Othello*"—

Brooke and Bennett in the Collaring Scene
(From an engraving after a daguerreotype)

There is a Connection through the whole Speech; and, to give the Mind an Opportunity of cooling by a Walk cross the Stage, is an Error that I could not have thought Mr. *Q*'s Experience would have committed.[53]

So familiar had the business become by now that it could be glanced at, effectively, in a farce. The stage-struck hero of Arthur Murphy's *Apprentice* (1756) is addicted to declaiming passages from plays, often with extreme inappropriateness. In the course of his elopement with Gargle's daughter he has encountered a Porter, who complains afterwards that "he took hold un me here by the Collar, and called me Villain and bid me prove his Wife a Whore — Lord help him, I never see'd the Gentleman's Spouse in my born Days before." [54] Or there is Foote again. In the second act of his "*Diversions of the Morning* as Performed at the Theatre Royal Drury Lane, 1758–9" Macklin (as "Puzzle") is introduced with his actor-pupils. He is showing off Bounce (who may be Barry): "begin at 'Othello's occupation's gone.' Now catch at me, as you would tear the very strings and all — keep your voice low — loudness is no mark of passion — mind your attitude." Bounce proceeds, continually interrupted by Puzzle:

Bounce. "Do deeds to make Heaven weep."
Puz.   Now terror.
Bounce. "All earth amazed! for nothing canst thou to damna —"
Puz.   Grind "na-na-na-nation."
Bounce. "Na — na — nation add, greater than that."
Puz.   Now throw me from you and I'll yield — very well! keep
    that attitude — your eye fixed — there's a figure! there's a contrast!
    His majestic rage — and my timorous droop — um —"Are you a
    man — have you a soul of sense?" [55]

Nineteenth century Othellos seem always to have taken their Iagos by the throat. Kean made this a great moment in his performance, as did Forrest.[56] Once, when Macready was appearing in Liverpool and used the same business, "a gentleman in the upper boxes" is said to have "started up and exclaimed, loud enough for all around to hear, 'Choke the devil! choke him!' " [57] Stories of this sort are particularly numerous in the case of *Othello*, and furnish a curious tribute to its tragic intensity.

Minor variations in the collaring business were, of course, introduced. Booth snatched Iago's own dagger and threatened to stab
him with it. The "gasping struggles" of Iago "heightened the
effect" of McCullough's fury. Wilson Barrett, after hurling
the villain across the chamber, suddenly turned to the picture of Desdemona, already mentioned, and vented his rage
upon it, knocking it down, or even hacking the canvas into
pieces.[58]

It is with Salvini, however, that the "Collaring Scene" will always be associated. The Italian's "colossal physique," as much as
the animal ferocity with which he indued Shakespeare's hero, no
doubt contributed to the extraordinary effect which he produced
here. In two respects he added to what had been done before.
Having taken Iago by the throat, shaken him, and dashed him to
the ground, he lifted his foot as if to trample on him.[59] Then he
recoiled. Iago flung up his arm, as if to protect himself from a
fresh attack; but instead, the Moor took his hand and "penitently,
yet with a species of loathing," helped him to his feet.[60] Dumas,
in his *Souvenirs Dramatiques* (1868) protests against the practice
of *"certains acteurs"* (he does not name Salvini) who *"renversent
Iago à terre, et lèvent le pied comme pour l'écraser."* Besides the
fact that there is no warrant in the text for their doing so (*"Taking him by the throat"* Dumas supposes to be Shakespeare's own
direction); there is, he argues, the certainty that after such humili-
ation Iago would, as a soldier, seek vengeance — and Othello
would know this. More subtle is Kirk's criticism. Salvini's "display of passion is unsurpassable," but it is based "on a miscon-
ception":

> The sudden access of rage . . . gives place to the thought of the
> stupendous guilt of the baseless slander, if such it be, and Iago is bid-
> den to go on without remorse, since, after such an act, he can neither
> hope for grace nor incur a deeper damnation. The idea of vengeance
> has faded under the perception that no adequate vengeance can be
> conceived of. . . . It is this reflux of emotion that relieves Iago from
> his momentary terror and arms him with audacity to turn upon his
> victim. . . . This is a very effective piece of "business," but it pre-
> supposes a gap where none had ever been detected, and interpolates
> an emotion of which there is no indication or suggestion in the text.[61]

Gould in his book *The Tragedian* had written of the elder Booth's Iago that, when he referred to Cassio's wiping his beard on Desdemona's handkerchief, he used "to lay his hand on his heart," and, in doing so, "tuck away" the same handkerchief a little more securely in his own doublet. Edwin Booth is certain, however, that Gould was wrong. "Father never did anything of the kind," he writes Furness, "*I* formerly did, and G. got confused, supposing I followed my father's business closely." It was "an old stage-trick," he concludes, which Iago should not condescend to use.[62]

Before kneeling to take the oath, Fechter's Moor (who, at "blood, blood, blood!" had rushed about, "*as if seeking his prey*") now caught Iago by the arm and brought him forward, "*pointing to the sky*." Booth knelt, "both hands above the head, with upturned palms and fingers towards the back," which was found "suggestive of the Orient." A glimpse of Cooke's business is afforded us, too, this time by Dunlap. Othello accepts Iago's profession of love:

> Within these three days let me hear thee say
> That Cassio's not alive.

Mr. Cooke used then to start, and the spectator might read plainly in his expressive face, "What! murder my friend and companion?"— he then covered his face with his hands, and gradually lifting his head, when he withdrew his hands his face and eyes were turned upward — he then started again . . . and after a second mental struggle, said, as if submitting to necessity . . .

"My friend is dead!" [63]

At the end of the scene a point is made which is likely to escape any but the most attentive readers: Iago gets the promotion he desired. On the stage, the importance of this has been brought out in various ways: by the newly-made Lieutenant's kneeling to kiss the General's hand, for instance, while "his face reveals his triumph" (Booth); by Othello's returning and striking Iago "*on the shoulder, with a savage smile*" (Fechter); or merely by his extending his hand to him and uttering "the words in a loud, exultant tone" (Salvini). Brought out, it should be, in any case.[64]

The last scene in Act III, that in which Othello demands the handkerchief, is for our purposes far less interesting. We hear, indeed, of a bit of old-fashioned illustrative action used by the elder Booth, who, when he spoke of Desdemona's hand as requiring

Much castigation, exercise devout,

held it up "between his two, in momentary but fervent attitude of prayer." Madge Kendal recalls playing Desdemona to the Othello of Ira Aldridge, the "African Roscius." He "made a very great point," she writes, "of opening his hand and making you place yours in it; and the audience used to see the contrast. He always made a point of it, and got a round of applause, — how, I do not know." At the beginning of the scene (the brief exchanges with the Clown have been very consistently omitted), Fechter showed Desdemona *"turning over her work and materials to find"* the missing handkerchief — a fussy, prosaic thought. Morley, however, praises a later moment:

> When Othello demands the handkerchief . . . the scene is enriched with some new touches of tenderness. His [Fechter's] face is averted when she says, "It is not lost", and he turns suddenly with all his love and trust flowing back on him, to take her in his arms, when she repels him with the addition, "but what an' if it were?" [65]

Just before the Moor's exit, Fechter's edition calls for melodramatic action: *"seizes her violently, and raises his hand as if to strike her*; Emi. *appears suddenly at the tapestry on the right. He lets go* Desd., *and retires repulsing her."* Emilia had been sent away on Othello's entrance, to return now in the very nick of time.[66] As for Salvini, after violently repelling Desdemona, he had 'retreated, backward, from her,' then had paused and become conscious of Emilia's presence. Seeing the substituted handkerchief on the floor, he pointed to it, and made as if to question Emilia; 'thought better of this,' and at last 'stalked moodily away,' wagging his head as he went.[67] Finally, it is to Fechter's credit that he included the passages, often excised, between Cassio and Bianca at the end of the scene. She was dismissed at last in what was criticized at the time as "the coarsest possible fashion": —

conducts her to the arcade, embracing her. Iago *appears at the door on the left and breaks into a loud laugh as he kisses the hand of* Bianca, *who runs off at the noise.*

"I'll see you soon," he calls after her. Then he *"returns towards* Iago, *making him signs to be silent.* Iago, *with comical gravity, puts his finger on his lips, stretching out his hand, as if to make oath. The curtain falls."* [68]

The fourth act of *Othello* has suffered greatly at the hands of actors. Among the scenes "left out" or "barbarously mangled" in Addison's time was "that which confirms Othello's jealousy, when he sees the handkerchief in Cassio's hands." "Othello's trance," which had once, we are told, given "great satisfaction" had also gone by the board.[69] These two episodes are almost invariably lacking in later acting texts, as is the beautiful passage between Desdemona and Emilia, near the end. In Booth's carefully edited acting text, Scene 2 has alone survived, with a little of the Willow Scene sometimes added, sometimes not.[70] In Fechter's edition, Othello is discovered *"stretched, unconscious on the divan.* Iago, *behind, contemplating him with a diabolical sneer."* Presently, Cassio enters, and the Moor listens from behind a *"tapestry on the left."* In leaving the stage, Bianca *"treads on the handkerchief,"* which Cassio *"takes up."* Othello *"violently draws the tapestry as if to rush on him,"* but is stayed by Iago. Cassio *"runs off, without seeing* Oth., *who, shuddering, holds himself by the tapestry."* [71] The blow which the Moor gives Desdemona later in the scene ("What, strike his wife!" Lodovico exclaims), must once have been a very perfunctory one indeed. Furness ruefully admits that a blow of some sort must be given: "FECHTER strikes with the letter which he holds; this is a shade better than the backhanded blow which SALVINI delivers full on those sweet lips, and which makes your own lips grow white as death, at the sight." But even Salvini struck her only with the paper: "he does not touch her with his hand." Years later, A. C. Bradley wrote courageously that the blow seems certainly to have been something more than the "tap on the shoulder with a roll of paper," which "some actors, feeling the repulsive-

ness of the passage, have made it." [72] For details, Fechter, when
he came to Cassio's name in the document, angrily tore the page
— something which Othello would have been unlikely to do —
and, later in the scene, Iago is directed by the same actor to touch
his own forehead significantly, when the General's strange behavior is being discussed, as if to intimate that he thought Othello
mad.[73]

The second scene, that in which the Moor comes to Desdemona
as if, he tortures himself by pretending, he were visiting the in-
mate of a brothel, is the one scene in the act which was always
performed. As a result, there is now a somewhat larger amount
of stage business to describe, and it is better distributed among
actors of different periods. On Emilia's exit —

> Cough or cry hem if anybody come.
> Your mystery, your mystery! Nay, dispatch! —

Othello used sometimes to lock the door, unlocking it again on
her return later in the scene.[74] In a letter of Benjamin Victor's to
Garrick, March 14, 1744, the point is made that

in the fourth act . . . when *Desdemona* enters to you, and (taking her
hand) you say —
> "Let me see your eyes["] —
it is evident the words that follow —
> "Look in my face"—
are spoken in anger; *Othello*, at that instant, observing the attentive
eye of *Emilia* upon him, quits his wife with these words —
> "Some of your function, mistress, &c."
and pushes her out of the room — you will easily observe this must
not be spoken in anger, but in a peevish, smothered contemptuous
tone — and exactly the same when he calls her in and throws the
money at her, this you did last night not only in a wrong tone of
voice, but in too much hurry.

The manner in which Spranger Barry, Garrick's successful rival
in the part, "gave the words,

> 'Oh, Desdemona — away — away — away!' "

was recalled, years later: "Instead of blustering them out . . . he looked a few seconds in Desdemona's face, as if to read her feelings and disprove his suspicions; then, turning away, as the adverse conviction gathered in his heart, he spoke them falteringly" — and wept.[75] Fechter's edition has, at "Oh, Desdemona": "*she rises with a cry of joy, and throws herself on the breast of* Oth., *who disengages himself, repulses her; and falls, sobbing, on the divan*"— a crudely theatrical effect.[76] More praiseworthy was his placing his hand on Desdemona's head, which he caressed "*unconsciously,*" as he began the speech "Had it pleased Heaven/To try me with affliction." Then, as she still sat at his feet, he took her face between his hands —

> O thou weed,
> Who art so lovely fair, and smells't so sweet,
> That the sense aches at thee. . . .[77]

In Salvini's production, Desdemona, who had been kneeling, started up in terror, as the Moor bending over her uttered his final taunt:

> I cry you mercy then.
> I took you for that cunning whore of Venice
> That married with Othello.

Turning to Emilia, he bowed low to her —"inclining his whole body, and bending his head, smiling at her"— his fingers knit, his hands held downward —"a picture of the most obsequious mock-politeness." Taking a purse from his girdle, he jingled the coins for her to hear; repeated the action, as she turned away; then 'furiously dashed the purse at her feet.' This last point was old.[78] "Don't use a purse," cautions Booth, "it is absurd, and 'tis not likely that Iago would pass it by. . . . This purse once tempted me so annoyingly that I picked it up, and very properly was reproved for it, — but I could not help it." A happy variation on the business was introduced recently by Miss Margaret Webster as Emilia, who picked up the purse scornfully and threw it after Othello.[79]

Forrest, in 1833, was told that there was "no occasion for his striking the door open with his fist," when he made his exit in this scene. The critic (was it William Leggett?) might be supposed a little hard up for things to tell him, were it not that the detail mentioned seems to have been chosen merely as an instance of Forrest's over-violence. Fechter got rid of Emilia's exit and her almost immediate return with Iago by having the villain, unseen by the spectators, lurking *"at the back"*— as he might be in a melodrama — and Emilia now signs to him without leaving the stage. In the same production, she spoke the lines about the unknown wretch who may have slandered her lady, *"suspiciously eyeing* Iago." Many another Emilia must have been tempted to do so! But Booth's direction is quite rightly: *"This is spoken without intended reference to Iago."* [80] Meanwhile, Iago may perhaps do as Vandenhoff did in 1839:

> He here advanced to the front, and his features disclosed alternate emotions of rage and fear; at length, overpowering both, cunning resumes its sway, as he answers —
>
> "Fye! there is no such man."

How he should behave, a moment later, while Desdemona, kneeling, protests her innocence, is uncertain. Mr. Wilson Knight would have him do nothing at all. "The effect on Iago" he writes, "is left by Shakespeare unregistered. To follow Shakespeare, let Iago turn up-stage after Desdemona's exit, and stand with his back to the audience." Irving, having been moved to the extent of shedding real tears here by the pathos of Ellen Terry's acting, promptly exploited them as the crocodile tears of a hypocritical villain — and "blew his nose with much feeling." [81]

The sudden appearance of Roderigo — he has the *entrée*, seemingly, into all sorts of unexpected places — is immediately followed in one of the earlier promptbooks by his slapping Iago on the shoulder, which seems scarcely in character. Booth has them "run against each other." [82] When Iago offers to shake hands with him, Roderigo has often 'turned away', or 'sulkily declined' at first.[83] But "Iago wheedles, and gets his hand laughingly" (Booth), or retains it *"in spite of him"* (Fechter). Then Iago, in Fechter's version once more, leads Roderigo mysteriously forward, to tell him of Othello's having been deprived of his command. The silly gentleman replies in a loud tone, and Iago puts "*his finger on his lips,*" and "*looks round again cautiously.*" "He goes into Mauritania," Iago says, "unless his abode be linger'd here by some accident; wherein none can be so determinate as" — and he used "*an expressive action*" — "the removing of Cassio."

Roderigo. "How do you mean"— (*imitating the action*) "removing of him?" [84]

I have nothing to tell about the business in Act IV, Scene 3.[85] The first scene in Act V is crowded with action. Roderigo attacks Cassio, and both men are wounded, Cassio treacherously by Iago, who makes off to avoid being found on the scene of the crime. Othello appears briefly. He learns that Iago has been true to his word, and leaves to carry out his own part in their compact, the murder of Desdemona. Cassio and Roderigo cry out for help; and presently Lodovico and Gratiano enter. They hesitate to approach the wounded men for fear of being waylaid, them-selves, in the darkness. Iago reappears, carrying a light. He recognizes his "dear friend" Cassio lying hurt, and stabs Roderigo. Bianca comes in and, a moment later, Emilia. Iago accuses Bianca of complicity in the attempted assassination of Cassio, and she is placed under arrest. Cassio has been carried away in a "chair."

When the play was given, however — as witness the acting editions from Bell's, in 1774, onwards — all this was greatly sim-plified. Rowe, indeed, had Othello enter, "*above at a Window,*" which implies I think that he had seen him appear there, in the theatre. But later the Moor's entrance was regularly omitted, as was that of Bianca, which is wanting even in Fechter's edition where the scene in which Cassio gives her the handkerchief had been restored. Finally, the entrance of Lodovico and Gratiano was postponed until after the stabbing of Roderigo. "Kill men i' th' dark?" Iago exclaims, "Where be these bloody thieves?/How silent is this town!" Then, as he hears footsteps approaching, "Ho! murther! murther!" This last change probably suggested the most interesting piece of stage business in the whole scene.

The Cooke-Cooper Promptbook has Iago enter, "dragging Rod°"; and in Fechter's edition Roderigo, during the speaking of Iago's aside, "*goes to the door, which he half-opens, to facili-*

tate a retreat." Booth, as Iago at the Princess's in 1881, was using
business which was new to the *Athenaeum* critic:

[he] knocks up, after the fashion of Mephisto dealing with Valentine, the sword of Roderigo, and lays him open to the lunge of his
adversary, and then, while Cassio's sword is still in the body of his
antagonist, deals him the traitorous blow in the back.

The possibility that this method of conducting the fight came
from *Faust* is interesting. Irving, it may be recalled, was pretty
certainly indebted to *Rigoletto* for his celebrated pantomime
scene in *The Merchant of Venice*.[86] In Fechter's production
Cassio, after wounding Roderigo, had turned "*abruptly to fly*,"
only to find himself "*face to face with Iago, who was about to
enter his house. Iago makes a violent sword-cut at his head, which
Cassio parries, but is wounded in the thigh with a back stroke.*"

Early in the nineteenth century, it became customary for Cassio
to bandage his wound with Desdemona's handkerchief. As we
shall see, there is reason to suppose that this well-imagined detail
had not been introduced earlier. Perhaps, Cooke first thought of
it.[87]

An ancient gag of Roderigo's—"Oh, help me first!"—and
the condemnation of Dodd in 1793 for buffoonery in "the dying
scene" may be mentioned in passing, though I do not know of
any particular antics in which the poor "snipe" indulged after
being stabbed.[88] According to *The Examiner*, June 5, 1814, Kean
brought out the idea that Iago's

whole fortune hinges on this event. . . . The actors of this part in general seem to be of a different opinion: they stab *Roderigo*, and then
walk away with perfect ease and satisfaction. Mr. KEAN . . . gives
and repeats the atrocious thrust, till it may be supposed no life remains; but he feels this to be a matter too important to be left in doubt.
He therefore, though he at the same time converses coolly with those
about him, throws his eye perpetually towards the prostrate body . . .
sometimes he walked by it carelessly, and surveyed it with a glance
too rapid to be observed: sometimes he deliberately approached it,
and looked at it with his candle . . . and thus he continued to hover
over and watch it till he leaves the stage.

Irving's Iago, after "*running Roderigo through the body and*

drawing out his sword slowly," kicked the corpse "contemptu-
ously out of his path . . . as if it had been carrion"; or, according
to another account, which sounds a good deal more convincing,
he turned over the body "with his foot, in indolent and mocking
curiosity . . . to see if life were extinct." [89]

Winter assures us that Booth was the inventor of a piece of
business, not in any strict sense of the word Shakespearean though
it is effective enough in its way. It was employed also by Fechter
and Irving, and as recently as December 25, 1936, by Mr. Brian
Aherne in Robert Edmond Jones's queerly old-fashioned production, at the Forrest Theatre, Philadelphia. Roderigo is dead, Cassio only hurt. There is no one about. "How silent is this town,"
Iago whispers. He stoops over the wounded man, realizes that
he is at his mercy, is about to stab him. Booth's acting here "could
not be surpassed for its blood-curdling horror." Then Iago sees
Lodovico and Gratiano approaching — and the thrust is not
given.[90] Fechter, in whose performance the villain rushed on
Cassio "with his sword, as if with a sudden inspiration to despatch
him," now crowded the stage with people suddenly aroused and
appearing half-dressed at their doors.[91] And from the lines themselves it is clear that Lodovico, Gratiano, and Iago are not the
only men present at the end of the scene. A "chair" is summoned
and brought, to bear away Cassio, and there is Roderigo's body to
be attended to. John Palmer's ancient promptbook calls naively
for "2 Scene Men to take off Roderigo"; and in the Warde-
Herman Book, "Ring on Picture" makes it unnecessary to remove
the body at all.

Montague Summers remembers a nineteenth century performance of *Othello* at the Theatre Royal, King Street, Bristol, in
which the Moor, upon entering his wife's bedroom on the prompt
side by one of the old proscenium doors, made a point of locking
it. Mr. Summers speaks of how effective this action was,[92] as one
might have guessed it would be; but it does not seem to have been
long traditional. Lacy's acting edition, which contains among
several casts one headed by Gustavus Brooke at the Olympic,
February 4, 1850, does indeed call for the locking of the door
immediately after Othello's entrance, "L.," and Fechter conspicu-

ously bolted a door which led "from within the house," though leaving other doors by which there might be "entry from without . . . wide open." But I have found no trace of the business earlier — though Salvini was also to use it.[93] A note in Oxberry's edition (1819) refers to the "modern practice" of Othello's appearing "with a drawn sword, which must be incorrect and unnecessary," in view of his "determination to 'strangle her [Desdemona] in bed.'" But when in soliloquy the Moor says,

> Yet I'll not shed her blood,
> Nor scar that whiter skin of hers than snow,
> And smooth as monumental alablaster,

the words will not inappropriately be accompanied by his laying down his sword — as Theobald had perceived back in the eighteenth century.[94]

In a note on

> Put out the light, and then put out the light,

Theobald tells us something, too, about stage practices in the bad period before the coming of Garrick:

"The *players*," he writes, "in all the companies wherever I have seen this tragedy perform'd, commit an absurdity here, in making *Othello* put out the candle. . . . If there were any other lights burning in the room, where would be the drift of putting out *his*? If there were no others, and that he puts *his* out, how absurd is it for *Desdemona* in the dark to talk of his *eyes rowling*, and his *gnawing his nether lip*?" [95]

Forrest, according to the minute description by Gabriel Harrison, was discovered musing at a table on which a single candle was burning. After speaking the first lines of the soliloquy,

> It is the cause, it is the cause, my soul,

"he rose from his chair, walked over to the bed of Desdemona, and pulling aside the one-half of the curtain, the moonlight fell upon her sweet face." He looked at her for an instant, then returned to the table and went on, "Yet I'll not shed her blood." Saying, "else she'll betray more men," he "dropped himself into the chair and, in a condition of despair, as he raised his head, his eyes happened to fall upon the flaming candle, and, in a moment, he rose, took the candle as if to puff it out, and do the murder by the moonlight," then spoke the second "put out the light" as a question, and presently replaced the candle, still lighted of course, on the table.[96]

Fechter not only disturbed the old arrangement by which Desdemona's bed was placed at the back of the stage, centre[97] — where it may well have stood since Elizabethan days — but introduced one of the most ludicrous bits of illustrative action which has ever disfigured a Shakespearean performance. Coming slowly forward toward Desdemona's bed, he accidentally touched a small looking-glass which had *"fallen from her hand"* and lay near her. In this he gazed, and exclaimed:

> It is the cause, it is the cause, my soul.

He looked in it again, after returning to the window —

> Let me not name it to you, you chaste stars! —

then violently threw it *"into the sea."* "I had not imagination strong enough to conceive what he meant," Morley writes, "now Mr. Fechter's explanatory book shows me that here Othello looks at his face in the glass, and is telling his soul that his skin is the cause of his misfortunes! It is his skin that he will not name to the chaste stars!" [98]

During the succeeding dialogue with Desdemona, Othello, in Kean's later years and for some time after, used to seat himself on a sofa. Forster objected to this custom, explaining its introduction as due to the mere fact of Kean's exhaustion at this point in the play.[99] After saying, "be brief; I will walk by," the Moor paced up and down the stage, and in Salvini's performance this action became truly memorable. William Story saw the Italian at the Teatro Valle, Rome, before his American and English appearances:

> In the last interview with Desdemona Salvini is wonderful. Like a tiger weaving across his cage, he ranges to and fro along the furthest limits of the stage, now stealing away from her with long strides and

avoiding her approaches, and now turning fiercely round upon her and rolling his black eyes, by turns agitated by irresolution, touched by tenderness, or goading himself into rage.[100]

In murdering his wife, the Moor from quite early times employed a pillow. "When the stifling pillow was uplifted" . . . is a phrase used in describing a performance of the tragedy in one of the *Original and Genuine Letters Sent to the Tatler and Spectator*, first printed in 1725.[101] In the *Town and Country Magazine* for April 1773, it is coolly stated that

we are *Methodists* with regard to Shakespeare; we carry our enthusiasm so far, that we entirely suspend our senses towards his absurdities . . . devoutly view *Desdemona stifled to death, then so perfectly restored to life, as to speak two or three sentences, then die again, without another oppressive stroke from the pillow.*

And in *Garrick's Looking Glass*, three years later, "DESDEMONA'S strangling pillow" is listed, with Lear's straw crown, as an important stage property. Charles Kemble, at the Odéon in 1827, pressed down the pillow "*de ses deux mains pendant plus d'une minute*," and his contemporary, Macready, also used it as an instrument of death.[102]

Rossi remains an exception. Appearing at Booth's Theatre, October 31, 1881, this actor murdered Desdemona

in full view of the audience . . . by strangling her with his hands after twisting her long hair about her neck, as he shook her violently and then dragged her about the bed and finally tossed her down upon the pillows. . . . Murmurs of dissatisfaction were audible in the house.[103]

The inclusion of such grisly details appears to have been of comparatively recent date. The *Theatrical Censor* (Philadelphia) writes of Mrs. Wignell (formerly Mrs. Merry) who played Desdemona to Fennell's Moor, February 3, 1806, that "she displayed, perhaps, as much nature as the circumstances allow. This would be a frightful scene, indeed, were it fully represented." And the writer goes on to suggest that "if anything like a real *smothering* were to be exhibited, the audience, unable to contain themselves, would rush upon the stage to stop the murder."

Fanny Kemble was very anxious before her first appearance as

Desdemona, at the Princess's Theatre, February 25, 1848. "I think I shall make a desperate fight of it," she writes, "for I feel horribly at the idea of being murdered in my bed. The Desdemonas that I have seen, on the English stage, have always appeared to me to acquiesce with wonderful equanimity in their assassination. On the Italian stage they run for their lives." But against that possibility was the "bedgown" she was wearing — and then "Shakespeare's text gives no hint of any such attempted escape." At rehearsal she found to her great relief that Macready, who had pinched her black and blue in *Macbeth*, "lets down the bed-curtains before he smothers me, and, as the drapery conceals the murderous struggle, and therefore he need not cover my head at all, I hope I shall escape alive." [104] Macready's decorous veiling of the murder had been noted when he gave *Othello* in Paris, in 1828. At that time, it was suggested to Miss Smithson, *"elle aurait dû fermer elle-même le rideau du lit pour s'en faire un rempart"*; and years later, this proposal was brilliantly executed at a Haymarket performance in which the younger J. W. Wallack played the lead:

> when the enraged husband rushes to the bed, Desdemona, with a cry of terror, grasps the curtain, which, descending, shrouds the fearful act from the gaze of the audience, and imparts to it a far greater appearance of reality than if they had really witnessed the deed.[105]

As for Phelps, " 'tradition' is so closely adhered to at Sadler's Wells, that the strangling takes place behind curtains in an alcove at the back of the stage." What is more, it is "preceded by no struggle between Othello and Desdemona, in which the latter rushes to the door and is carried back to the bed by the former, according to the directions laid down in M. Fechter's 'acting edition'." [106]

It is noteworthy that these directions were not literally carried out in Fechter's performance. Desdemona, we read, leaves her bed, falls terrified at Othello's feet, seizes his hands and tries to kiss them. *"She rushes to the door,"* but he bars her way. *"In mad fury, he whirls round his sword"* over her head. Again she attempts to escape, and again *"he stops her passage."* He *"carries*

*her to the bed on which he throws her; then stifles her cries with
the pillow, which he presses with both hands,*" and at last gives her
the *coup de grâce,* "*pressing his poignard under the pillow, and
turning away his eyes.*" "These stage directions," writes Sir Theodore Martin, "make one think rather of the murder of Nancy
by Bill Sikes, than of Othello and Desdemona"; no English audience would have endured them in representation.

Even now there is too much violence. Why should Desdemona
spring out of bed, to be brutally thrust back into it? . . . "Tradition"
was right in placing Desdemona's couch at a remote part of the stage:
Mr. Fechter is wrong in bringing it so far forward that every detail is
thrust painfully on our senses. "Tradition" was right in confining
Desdemona to her couch: Mr. Fechter is wrong in hazarding the
ludicrous effects of the opposite course.[107]

When, nevertheless, four years later, Madge Kendal was appearing with Ira Aldridge, she found that "he used to take Desdemona
out of bed by her hair and drag her round the stage before he
smothered her." The Haymarket audience thought the business
brutal, she adds, and "loudly hissed." [108] Salvini's tiger-like pacing
back and forth has already been mentioned. Desdemona in his
performance had quit her bed to expostulate with Othello, and
she knelt saying "Then Lord have mercy on me!" At length, her
equivocal words,

> Alas, he is betray'd, and I undone!

madden him:

he drags her to her feet, as she kneels, facing him; he then clutches her
right arm with his right hand, and grasps her neck and head with his
left hand, knotting his fingers in her loose hair; and pulling back her
head, as if to break her neck. Holding her thus, he swiftly forces her
up the stage, and through the curtains which close behind them. . . .
Muffled sounds of the last fatal act are heard.[109]

Propriety, however, was not yet a thing of the past. In Louis
James's production at the Fifth Avenue Theatre, April 23, 1888,
Desdemona was not "carried out struggling" but "partially smothered behind a curtain, and then her husband's dagger [was] employed to put her out of her pain." [110]

This death stroke with a dagger goes back to the eighteenth century. Rymer, who is always most offensive when he is jocose, had quoted Desdemona's dying words, with the comment, "we may learn here, that a Woman never loses her Tongue, even tho' after she is stifl'd," and a French writer in 1717 suggested:

si elle allait expirer par l'effet de l'épée ou du poison, la chose serait probable; mais une personne étouffée doit être privée de tout sentiment, ou si elle retrouve la force de parler elle peut bien en revenir tout à fait.[111]

The same objection was raised anew in *Lloyd's Evening Post*, January 10–13, 1766; and also by Francis Gentleman in *The Dramatic Censor*, 1770, who approves of "Othello's stabbing her with a dagger, after the words —

> 'I that am cruel [am yet merciful;
> I would not have thee linger in thy pain.
> So, so.]' "[112]

It was left, however, for Steevens in his edition of Shakespeare, three years later, to offer as an explanation of the difficulty the loss of an original stage direction — one which might, we may imagine have been supplied at rehearsal by word of mouth —"I suspect that some play-house direction has been omitted; and that when [Othello] says,

> *I would not have thee linger in thy pain.*
> *So, so.*

He then stabs her, repeating the two last words, as he repeats the blow."

A muddled reply to Steevens, by "D" in *St. James's Chronicle*, December 7–9, 1773, has the postscript, "After all, as I am sending this away, I am told that Powell really used the Dagger in this Scene." Powell, an excellent actor, something of a *protégé* of Garrick's, had died in 1769. In view of "D's" postscript and the remark of Gentleman's, just quoted, one begins to wonder whether the dagger may not have belonged to stage tradition long before its need was discovered by the critics. But this does not seem too probable.

One of Garrick's correspondents has heard, January 1, 1774, that Barry "is very much approved in playing [the scene] according to Mr. Steevens's idea, which, however, is not to my best judgment equal to yours." [113] For almost a century thereafter, the dagger was regarded as obligatory. Salvini, at length, demurred. "So, so," in his opinion indicated the "action of his putting his knees on her breast to accelerate her end." [114] What Shakespeare's intention really was is not to be asserted dogmatically. "There lies your niece," Othello cries, later in the scene,

> Whose breath, indeed, these hands have newly stopp'd.

And after the Duchess of Malfi has been strangled, in Webster's play, she speaks twice, albeit but a word each time, before giving up the ghost.[115] A dagger may be convenient for the actor to use, effective, too, and not in the least inappropriate to the words he speaks; but it is neither called for by them, nor necessary to introduce, 'in order to save Shakespeare from absurdity.'

Towse describes graphically the murder of Desdemona as it was represented by Salvini:

> "It was awful," he concludes, "utterly, abominably un-Shakespearean if you will, but supremely, paralyzingly real. . . . Then came a long pause. Emilia knocked at the door, once, twice, thrice, louder and louder, as she called Othello's name. Presently, the curtains opened a little and Othello's face, wild eyed, was thrust out, and withdrawn. The tension was almost insufferable."

Years before, Macready's "thrusting of his dark despairing face through the curtains" had been found "thrilling in its effect." [116] The same action had been introduced by Forrest and Phelps, and was to be remembered as a striking detail in the famous Lyceum production, with Booth and Irving, in the spring of 1881.[117]

At "Let me the curtains draw," Othello suits the action to the word and, closing them, conceals Desdemona's body.[118] Clearly, too, he unlocks the door, in admitting Emilia — Fechter's Othello, *"in his agitation"* attempted *"to open [it] at the hinges"* [119]— and Emilia "undraws curtains" just before she finds her mistress slain, at line 119. It became customary for her to leave the stage when, a little later, she raises the alarm. As a young actress, Clara Morris, in the eighteen-sixties, found an opportunity to score heavily at this point in the play. She had noticed, she writes,

that many *Emilias* . . . cried out their "Murder! Murder!" against all the noise of the tolling bells, and came back upon the stage spent, and without voice or breath left to finish their big scene with. . . . A long hanging bar of steel is generally used for the alarm, and blows struck upon it send forth a vibrating clangor that completely fills a theatre.

So she arranged with the Cleveland prompter that these strokes should come only as she signalled for them, by raising her hand. They were thus timed to fill up the intervals in her prolonged out-cries, which continued after she had made her exit, until at last she "burst upon the stage, and with one last long full-throated cry of 'Murder! the Moor has killed my mistress!' stood waiting" (in her own words) "for the applause to let me go on." [120] If, however, Emilia remains on the stage — as Shakespeare pretty certainly meant her to do — she may actually struggle with Othello, as in Fechter's melodramatic rendering of the scene, or be allowed to summon help while the Moor, stunned, "*goes up the stage and leans upon the bed*," which was, I think, Kean's way.[121]

When Othello "*runs at Iago*," only to be disarmed, he "seizes sword from Montano or from Table," says Ferrers's promptbook. Moore's has him go "to table R for sword. Montano perceives and follows him. Iago stabs Emilia as she kneels"— she has been protesting "by heaven" that she is telling the truth.[122] Dying, she begs to be laid by her "mistress' side," but the line was regularly cut and the favor denied her. Miss Huddard, later Mrs. Warner, the Sadler's Wells actress, appearing with Forrest at Drury Lane in 1836, "tried a novelty which improved the effect, instead of dying on a couch . . . and having afterwards to lie a long time, she was supported off the stage." This new idea caught on, so that in 1849 *The Athenaeum* found it equally a novelty for Miss Glyn to expire "in the arms of her attendants, instead of being, as usual led out dying." [123] Thereafter, practice varied, neither Forrest nor Booth being wholly consistent in their own performances.[124] Fechter, by the way, employs "Julio," Kemble's added character of that name, still after all these years a member of the cast: "Julio *places her at the foot of the prie-Dieu, in the oratory; then draws the curtain."*

The sword of which Othello speaks later —

> I have another weapon in this chamber;
> It is a sword of Spain, the ice-brook's temper.
> O, here it is —

was much on the minds of harassed prompters, who were responsible for having it ready for the Moor to find. Nor was it always kept in the same place. *The Theatrical Censor* (Philadelphia) writes of Mr. Fennell, February 3, 1806: "It struck us as singular, in this scene, that Mr. F. left the room, to fetch a sword." Cooper, in the Harvard Promptbook of five years later, "takes sword from RH2E," where it was still kept for Murdoch in 1845, while Booth found it in a *"recess near the bed."* [125]

A "modern" touch in Fechter's acting edition is having Iago, when he is brought back as a prisoner, *"followed by common people who threaten [him] violently, but are kept back by the* Guards. *Behind, in the doorway, women press forward, looking over their shoulders."* Booth's instant closing of the curtains, "that Desdemona's corpse may not be polluted by Iago's gaze," is far more truly imagined. In Salvini's version, there is no wounding of Emilia, and only now at last does the Moor attack Iago. Henry James speaks of the Italian's "tiger like spring":

he traverses the chamber to reach Iago, with the mad impulse of destruction gathered into a single blow. He has sighted him, with the intentness of fate, for a terrible moment, while he is still on one knee beside Desdemona; and the manner in which the spectator sees him — or rather feels him — rise to his avenging leap is a sensation that takes its place among the most poignant the actor's art has ever given us.[126]

Finally, a thoughtful essay in the Philadelphia *Port Folio*, for March 1809, comparing Cooper, the emotional, with Fennell, the studious actor, tells us that when Othello would learn the motive which has prompted "that demi-devil" to ensnare his soul and body, Cooper "uttered this sentence with the querulous accent of piercing agony: his knees bending under him and knocking against each other, as if borne down by the accumulated pressure of misery and guilt."

On March 7, 1751, a group of aristocratic amateurs, "superintended" by old Macklin, put on *Othello* at Drury Lane. Horace Walpole wrote of them, "they really acted so well, that it is astonishing they should not have had sense enough not to act at all." "The manner·in which Mr. [Francis] DELAVAL," who headed the cast, "took the hand of the man he had injured," as he spoke

> I do believe it, and I ask your pardon,

"had" (we are told) "something in it so like the man of honour, and so unlike all that we see in imitation of it in the player, that we shall not easily be reconciled to the bearing it from any body else again." [127] Some gracious action on Cassio's part would be in keeping with his words,

> Dear General, I never gave you cause.

Pattie's edition tells him to take off his hat here; in Fechter's, Othello, "*bowing his head*," offers the wounded man "*his hand without daring to look up*," and "Cassio *bends over his hand, which he kisses*"; and in the Warde-Herman Promptbook "Othello gives his hand to Cassio and [? Cassio] is about to kiss it — when he is stopped by Othello."

The fatal handkerchief, when for the last time it is spoken of, is likely to be shown for the Moor to see. The older and simpler way of doing this is the one recorded in Kemble's editions, where, as Cassio says "I found it in my chamber," he takes the handkerchief from his pocket. But when, as may be remembered, Cassio is wounded, he sometimes used the same handkerchief as a bandage, and in the Cooke-Cooper Promptbook he appears now with his "Knee bound by Handf." Kean, also, asked,

> How came you, Cassio, by that handkerchief
> That was my wife's?

"*pointing to the handkerchief bound round Cassio's leg.*" [128] Forrest was much more elaborate. With him, Lodovico shows Othello the letter which has been found on Roderigo. Then, according to the reliable Becks: "Oth drops letter. RC Cassio picks it up. & presents it to Oth. & he then ·discerns hdkf." [129]

Kean and the elder Booth were at unnecessary pains to show how Othello obtained the dagger with which he effects his sudden suicide. "This did I fear," Cassio says afterwards, "but thought he had no weapon." As Booth began the great apologia,

Soft you! a word or two before you go . . .

he took up "a silken robe," flinging it carelessly over his shoulder, "then reaches for his turban, possessing himself of a dagger he had concealed therein." [130] Kean had stolen to the bed and recovered thence the dagger with which he killed Desdemona, then had come forward, if we are to believe a protesting letter in *The Theatrical Inquisitor*, "with the naked weapon in his hand." [131]

John Finlay criticizes another detail in Kean's death scene:

when Othello stabs himself the by-standers look on without affording him the slightest assistance; this was most unnatural. We may be told that this is not the fault of Mr. Kean; but Mr. Kemble always spent as much time at rehearsal, in marshalling and disciplining the corps dramatique, as in any other occupation. They surely would have done any thing which Mr. Kean directed them to do.

As for the manner of his death, it was by stabbing himself to the heart: "he literally dies standing; it is the dead body of Othello that falls, heavily and at once; there is no *rebound*." [132] Dumas, in his *Souvenirs Dramatiques* makes a curious comparison:

On ne croirait pas qu'il y ait tant de façons de se frapper d'un poignard. . . . Kean et [? Charles] Kemble s'enfonçaient horizontalement et à deux mains le poignard dans le cœur. Macready se l'enfonçait au-dessous des côtes, et de bas en haut.
Puis Macready ajoutait une chose d'un grand effet: une fois frappé, il se sentait encore la force d'aller jusqu'au lit, et, en râlant le nom de Desdemona, il allait tomber et mourir la bouche sur la main de sa victime.[133]

Macready, from quite early in his career, had made much of Othello's attempt to reach the bed, staggering, or dragging himself, toward it from close to the footlights, supporting himself against the furniture. Even so. the usually sympathetic Kirk found it an effect which "did not reach the mark, being simply of the stage, stagey." [134] Phelps, the younger James William Wallack, and Edwin Booth all died in attempting to reach the bed, or just after reaching it; while for a variation on what was by now the traditional business, Gustavus Brooke, after staggering to the bed, "clutched the heavy curtains of it, which, giving way, fell upon his prostrate body as a kind of pall, disclosing, at the same time, the dead form of Desdemona." [135]

With Fechter and Salvini came revolution. The miserable claptrap of the former may be dismissed in a very few words. His Othello made *Iago* the "malignant" and "turban'd Turk"— the "circumcised dog"— of the tragic anecdote, seizing him and forcing him, bound as he was, to kneel before the bed on which Desdemona lay murdered; then, instead of driving his dagger into the wretch — stabbed himself, and threw down the weapon at Iago's feet. Macready in his retirement read of this business in Fechter's edition of the play. "There is frequent perversion of the author's meaning," was his comment, "and complete blindness as to the emotions of his characters — *e.g.*, the demission of his lofty nature to bestow a thought upon that miserable thing, Iago, when his great mind had made itself up to die! To me it was in the worst taste of a small melodramatic theatre." [136]

Salvini's Moor, instead of stabbing himself to the heart with a dagger, cut his own throat across with a short curved sword. In justification of this departure from tradition, he urged the customs "of the people of Africa, who usually execute their criminals and enemies in this way" and whose arms "are of a curved form" — archæology, in other words, of the same sort which had been exploited to the point of absurdity in the "upholstered" productions of Charles Kean, twenty years before. That Shakespeare's lines,

> I took by th' throat the circumcised dog
> And smote him — thus,

imply a quite different action, was easy to demonstrate. Only Lewes, however, in his essay, *On Actors and the Art of Acting*, got beyond such demonstration into the formulating of a principle:

no actor is to be blamed for not presenting *your* conception of Hamlet, Othello, or Macbeth; but he is justly blamed when he departs from the text such as all men understand it. You may not think Othello was a man of fierce animal passion, but you know that Othello stabbed himself and did *not* cut his throat.

With some at least of the others whose voices were raised in anger or ridicule, one cannot help feeling that the violation of "Shakespeare's intention" could not have been a matter of particular consequence. Rather, it was the shocking realism of this death scene — a realism hitherto unapproached in Shakespearean representation — which had caused offense. Salvini's leaning backwards, and violently sawing at his throat across and across, cutting and hacking it, the quivering of his body and limbs, above all, the simulation of such sounds as "escaping blood and air" together might make, seemed disgusting to critics of the 'seventies and 'eighties. It was "a blot," in Joseph Knight's words, "upon an otherwise magnificent performance." [137]

Meanwhile, Booth as Iago had spoken

> Demand me nothing. What you know, you know.
> From this time forth I never will speak word,

with a horrible grinding of clenched teeth —"not," the actor writes, "because it 'takes,' but because I feel that it expresses determination never to speak again." And though Mrs. Goodale had seen him in the part "over forty times," this action of "self-imposed lockjaw" never seemed studied, nor did she ever miss the sense of "Iago's unspoken gloating over those who would try to open his jaw, and fail." [138]

In Bell's acting edition, and Kemble's, the villain exits "*guarded*," a little before the beginning of Othello's apologia, the words "Away with him" being interpolated (at line 335) to get him off. Here Hazlitt might not approve "Mr. Kean's pointing to the dead bodies," since though Iago "may feel no remorse, he would feel no triumph"; whereas, to Miss Williams-Wynn the look with which Kean's Iago "directs the eye of the miserable Othello to his murdered Desdemona" was unforgettable.[139] The business of the elder Booth was similar to Kean's, but much elaborated. A press cutting of 1817, quoted in Mrs. Clarke's book, *The Booths*, assures us that here he looked at *Othello* with a significant gaze, then pointed to his own wife, as if to express that her violation by the *Moor* was the cause of all his perfidy. He then struck his breast in a triumphant manner, meaning that his vindication was complete and gratifying.

"If this pantomime had been abbreviated," the critic added, "it would be more consistent with the dignity of tragedy, and . . . the judgment of the actor." In 1817, "three rounds of approbation" were bestowed upon "the shaking head and twisted thumb with which he quitted the stage"; when in 1836, the same tragedian, newly returned from America, was again appearing at Drury Lane, his studied display of pantomimic art "called forth peals of derisive laughter." [140] Many other Iagos distinguished themselves at the same moment in the play by their looks of hate or triumph. The "keen gaze" which Young took, "past those on the stage, at the dead body of *Desdemona*" was found to be "vampire-like," as if the wretch were

taking the last draught of pleasure, the draught that was to sustain him in his torments. . . . It had not all the meaning of *Cooke's* pointing with his finger to the body; but it had more character and effect.

Macready's "demoniacal smile" showed that "even now" Iago's heart was filled with "a joy that his designs have worked destruction on him he hated"; and Phelps's "final exit was equal to any other feature of the performance. Glancing round with one look of ineffable scorn, he reared himself erect and strode out of the room, defiant to the last." [141]

Edwin Booth gave up the un-Shakespearean exit and the added words. Iago is now removed, to stand waiting beside Emilia's body, "*at the window.*" But when he sees his enemy fall, he "*starts forward*" to gloat over him, only to be seized by an officer, "*who forces him to his knee.*" Such, at any rate, is the description in Winter's edition. Yet, in London, with Irving, the same Iago "brought down the final curtain standing over Othello, pointing . . . at the dead body and gazing up at the gallery with a malignant smile of satisfied hate." [142] Kean's business, once more — and Cooke's — though shifted, a little way, now, to end the tragedy. Iago triumphs still!

V

Macbeth

THE MACBETH tradition is strong and continuous. The play has never been long from the boards. Pepys saw it often in the sixteen-sixties, and through Davenant and his Restoration version a certain amount of Elizabethan stage business may well have been preserved for us. Differences in the interpretation of the characters do not seem to have been drastic. Macbeth, though he might be somewhat more or somewhat less robust, was never, I think, before Irving's time a craven; and whatever Lady Macbeth was like before Mrs. Siddons, the practice of that great actress, if not her theory, stood for many years as a fixed ideal. The witch scenes are a different matter. Spectacle, "divertisement," the ludicrous and the grotesque, long encumbered performances of the play, coarsening its texture and reducing its dimensions as a tragedy. Thus, "Dunscotus" in *St. James's Chronicle*, January 19–21, 1768, contrasts with "The uncommon Taste and Propriety in the Habits of *the Witches*," at a Covent Garden production which he had just seen, "the torn Mobs, Checked Aprons, and high-crowned Hats, heretofore worn, by which, and by their Birch Brooms, those high-wrought Characters of Enchantment were sunk into Burlesque"; and as late as February 18, 1833, Fanny Kemble could write in her *Journal*:

> It has been always customary, — heaven only knows why, — to make low comedians act the witches, and to dress them like old fish-women . . . with as due a proportion of petticoats as any woman, letting alone witch, might desire, jocose red faces, peaked hats, and broomsticks.[1]

The veteran Macklin is represented satirically in *St. James's Chronicle*, October 19–21, 1773, as interrupting a rehearsal of his production of *Macbeth* with "And hark you, you Witches! Manage your Broomsticks with Dignity, and be d---n'd to you!"— which brings us to the business of the play.

> Fair is foul, and foul is fair,

chant the Sisters,

> Hover through the fog and filthy air.

Perhaps there is a hint of action in that "hover." At any rate, Davenant's version has the Sisters "*Ex. flying*"; and old John Downes recalls, in describing a production of the play about 1672–1673, that it was "drest in all it's Finery, as new Cloath's, new Scenes, Machines, as flyings for the Witches." [2] That was one way. Another is suggested by some lines from "A Fable" in *The Gentleman's Magazine* for October 1760:

> Say, ladies, have you never been
> Spectators of the magic scene?
> Whether the fate of great *Macbeth*
> Or *Harlequin's* love, birth, or death,
> When after many a thunder clap,
> Grim witches vanish through a trap;
> Or haply the confed'rate hags
> Use broomsticks for aerial nags;
> But whether they may sink or soar,
> The beldames are beheld no more.

Now risings and sinkings through trapdoors had long been associated with the supernatural — in *Hamlet*, for instance, as we have seen — and they seem definitely called for in at least two later scenes in *Macbeth*. Why not, then, here? "Ring G. Trap" is the direction in a manuscript Promptbook "Adapted to yᵉ Edinburgh Theatre Anno 1761," "Stage dark Lamps down." And the Witches "rise"; though at the end of the scene they still (as in Rowe's edition, 1709) "rise from the stage and fly away." [3] But what more natural than that they should go as they had come, and presently one finds that literal minded critic Francis Gentleman complaining, in his *Dramatic Censor*, 1770, that they were doing so: "We know not why they should *sink* under the stage, immediately after pronouncing these words, '*Hover* through the fog and filthy air';" though he admits that "their sudden disappearance gains a desire in the spectators to see them again." [4]

Kemble has the hags "*discovered*," and they "*Exeunt severally*" — Kemble would think of that! And in two American prompt-books — one a Boston (Howard Athenaeum) book dated 1852; the other containing notes by George Becks descriptive of Edwin Forrest's later practice — the Sisters have their heads together, quite literally, on being discovered, then move apart.[5] The First Witch, but not her companions, leaves the stage by means of a trap: in Boston, she used a "vampire in the flat C."; while "Ring Trap C for 1st W." heralded her departure in Forrest's performances. Against that last direction, however, is pencilled (in Becks's own hand, I think) the laconic "never should." By the eighteen-sixties, when these Forrest notes were made (if they were not made even later) better ways of getting her on and off had been discovered. Samuel Phelps had been doing wonders with gauze screens and a greater use of darkness, at Sadler's Wells. There at his revival of the play in 1847 — as Shakespeare wrote it, without Davenant adulteration — the Weird Sisters seemed to grow out of a supernaturally induced mist and to merge once more into it.[6] Phelps's staging has often a suggestion of poetry. By the way, his hags too were "disc^d their heads close together — arms on each others shoulder." [7]

John Coleman has vivid, and I hope accurate, memories of the second scene in *Macbeth*, as Charles Kean gave the play at the Princess's Theatre in 1853.

"I recall with pleasure", he writes, "Duncan's camp at Forres. The scene was discovered in night and silence, a couple of semi-savage armed kerns were on guard prowling to and fro with stealthy steps. A distant trumpet-call was heard, another in reply, another and yet another; a roll of the drum — an alarum. In an instant the whole camp was alive with kerns and gallowglasses, who circled round the old king and the princes of the blood. The Bleeding Sergeant was carried in upon a litter, and the scene was illuminated with the ruddy glare of burning pine-knots." [8]

After reading that description, one has no further doubt, I fancy, as to the ancestry of Sir Henry Irving's productions. The "rude litter" for the Sergeant attracted attention; formerly, he had been able to walk, supported, it might be, by two guards.[9] In certain Phelps and Forrest promptbooks, Duncan addresses "Go get him surgeons" to the Physician;[10] and, on the same principle of using what you have got, the doomed Chamberlains of Duncan have sometimes appeared in this scene, preceding their master on his entrance. They carry wands.[11]

The reappearance of the Weird Sisters at the beginning of Scene 3 was arranged about as before. That is, they entered *"fly-ing"* in Davenant's version; later frequently rose through traps; and under Phelps's management were discovered behind gauzes the gradually thickening folds of which produced the effect of the Sisters' vanishing, when the time for that came.[12] A Boston promptbook direction, at "Look what I have" (line 26) is attractive at first glance: "The 3RD witch leaves the others, goes up-stage and listens"—for Macbeth's drum, of course. But Phelps, doing without this sentry, has, far more impressively, before

> A drum, a drum!
> Macbeth doth come,

"Witches all assume an attitude of attention — pause — but do not look back or off."[13] As for the lines which immediately follow, spoken by all three of the Sisters, they have for a long time regularly accompanied some sort of mysterious turning or walking round, with joined hands. The acting text in Cumberland's *British Theatre* (c. 1829) describes a more elaborate movement:

> *The Witches join hands and turn whilst they repeat these lines; they continue turning, until the second gets into the C., facing the audience; she then bends her head thrice over the hands of the other two, and speaks; after which the third and first do the same, and part hands as they retire to R.*[14]

That this ritual was not always performed in a seemly fashion is, I am sorry to say, hinted in a letter to *The Examiner*, November 13, 1814. Of the Witches who had appeared with Edmund Kean at Drury Lane the week before, only Dowton "wound up the charm in an awful manner, and did not jerk back his head to make the galleries laugh: they should bend forward as if swearing a solemn oath." Clarke's Edwin Forrest Promptbook has them "Waving Wands" in the course of this speech. Wands, it might be observed, are a far cry from broomsticks; the Sisters are gradually taking on more and more of their true character. But "Cuthbert Bede" (Edward Bradley) in his full and exciting account of Charles Kean's production, tells us that just before Macbeth's entrance "the three witches joined their crutches and went round in a circle, then stood still, pointing to Macbeth." Crutches seem to me definitely reactionary.[15]

The Harvard Theatre Collection has recently acquired an extra-illustrated copy of Kirkman's *Life of Macklin* containing two large double column pages of manuscript notes made by Macklin in preparation, obviously, for his celebrated production of *Macbeth* at Covent Garden in 1773. They are the jottings of an old man, abounding in false starts, in painful returnings to thoughts imperfectly formulated. He writes:

> At the first entrance of Macbeth he should be preceeded by officers drums Fifes standards, & other warlike characters & Insignia of the van of an army on their march. he must be booted in russet broadsword pistols, at his girdle, dirk a cap imitating a Bonnet, — a ruff. — hair tied behind ["or" scored through] but short. — soldiers half stockinged.[16]

Now in *St. James's Chronicle*, October 28–30, 1773, is an unsigned letter, addressed to Garrick, grumbling about the stage arrangements in this scene. "The Procession before the *Thane* of the other House," we read, "was every Way improper. The advanced Guards of the Army ought to have remained . . . without the Door; and not to have been placed within Sight and Hearing of all that passed between *Macbeth*, *Banquo*, and the *Wierd Sisters*." And the writer goes on: "I always regarded the spurious Line with which hitherto you have begun your Part, as an Apology for the Non-appearance of the Soldiers. *Macklin* spoke the same Line, but his Army followed within Sight." The spurious line was Davenant's. In his version Macbeth, entering with Banquo and Attendants, says:

Command; they make a halt upon the Heath.

And in course of time his command had come to be literally executed, so that one heard the staccato "Halt, halt, halt," spoken
off-stage. (In the curious "William Warren Edition," a reprint,
prepared by Kate Reignolds-Winslow, of the old Boston Museum
Promptbook, the Prompter speaks the words). Davenant's idea
of suggesting the presence of an army near at hand — which has a
certain warrant, after all, in the rumbling drum heard by the
witches — had a lasting appeal. Rowe, who of course prints
neither the "spurious line" nor the echoing halts, does yield to it,
to the extent of describing Macbeth and Banquo as accompanied
by *"Soldiers and other Attendants"*— by their army, in fact. So
Sir Walter Scott, thinking of an old friend, could write: "Who
crosses the blighted heath of Forres without beholding in imagination the stately step of Kemble as he descended the stage at the
head of his victorious army?" [17] In Clarke's Edwin Forrest
Promptbook, the soldiers are lined up across the back of the stage.
At the order, halt, they "stroll of [*sic*] leisurely either side," and
Macbeth, taking off his shield, gives it to one of them, before
speaking

So foul and fair a day I have not seen.

Later, when the noblemen arrive to greet their general, the soldiers return. They "manifest great interest" in what is going on
and "look their congratulations" when Macbeth is told he is
Thane of Cawdor.

Forrest in this scene carried a truncheon, which seems to have
been regarded as the thing to do.[18] With it, when he came to
Macbeth's long aside ("Two truths are told") he smote his armed
breast, either at "I am Thane of Cawdor" or, worse still, at

And make my seated heart knock at my ribs.[19]

Booth did without a truncheon, I think, and seems to have entered
alone with Banquo. John McCullough told Winter of having
gone once with Forrest to see Booth, who was then acting in
Philadelphia with Charlotte Cushman:

At *Macbeth's* first entrance Forrest snorted with disgust. Booth, preoccupied and moody, was gazing toward the ground. "What's the damn' fool doing?" Forrest asked: "He looks like a super hunting for a sixpence." [20]

Finally, Irving was praised for the artistic disposal of his troops in this scene —"an endless procession," straggling by in small groups — and in 1874, at any rate, as his own marked copy of the play shows, he could not get along without

> Command they make a halt upon the heath.

He carried a ponderous sword. Mr. John Gielgud, impressed by Partridge's picture of Irving with that sword borne on one shoulder, tried carrying a similar weapon himself. Then arose the problem of getting rid of it, and he found that he could drop it effectively at the third "hail" of the witches —

> All hail, Macbeth, that shalt be king hereafter! [21]

It is worth adding that when J. H. Barnes appeared at Drury Lane with Madame Ristori, July 3, 1882, Davenant's line was retained, and the stage was filled with soldiers. "Surely," wrote Clement Scott at the time, "not a human being should know of this mysterious meeting except Banquo. . . . Effect is all very well, but it should be justifiable effect." [22]

The ceremonial hailing of Macbeth by the Weird Sisters is again described at length in Cumberland's Edition. When Banquo asks:

> Live you? or are you aught
> That man may question?

"*Each Witch lays the fore-finger of her right hand on her lips, and, with her left hand, points to Macbeth.*" And before speaking, each in turn "*takes her finger quickly from her lips.*" Then, at the last hail: "*Each Witch drops on her knee. They continue to point at Macbeth, till Banquo adjures them* 'I' the name of truth,' *at which they all start up.*" The kneeling of the Witches is at least as early as Kemble's time, when John Williams complained of it in reviewing a Covent Garden performance with Kemble and

Macready as Macbeth with Truncheon
(From an engraving after a painting by Tracey)

Mrs. Siddons, September 18, 1811. Williams found it ridiculous that "these preternatural hags" should be so "full of loyalty, and good breeding." [23] Later, instead of kneeling, each Witch raised both arms as she addressed the hero.[24]

As for Macbeth, Macready in this scene was somewhat captiously attacked by Leigh Hunt for "looking cheerily up at the sky" while speaking

> So foul and fair a day I have not seen.

After all, "foul" does refer to the weather! Edward FitzGerald, writing to Fanny Kemble years after Macready's retirement, is unkind too:

> Megreedy, with his flat face, managed to look well as Virginius, didn't he? And, as I thought, well enough in Macbeth, except where he *would* stand with his mouth open (after the Witches had hailed him), till I longed to pitch something into it out of the Pit, the dear old Pit.

Charles Kean started when Ross addressed him as Cawdor, "his right hand clenched against his breast, the fingers of his left hand opening convulsively." Forrest's arrangements interest me, finally: At the Sisters' vanishing, the stage became "suddenly dark"; there was "a 'whirring' sound, after which turn lights full on," and Macbeth "looks up (Banquo also) with searching amazement into the air." [25] By the way, is not some sort of apposite business called for at Macbeth's "I thank you, gentlemen," just as he begins his long aside? Phelps thought so, and had Macbeth bow "to Lords who do the same." But something better than that might, I fancy, be devised.[26]

Act I, Scene 4, yields only one piece of business which need detain us; and that comes tenuously, I admit, and by means of inference from an anecdote told by John Coleman. At Bristol, it seems, an actor whom they called "The Big Pot" made a wager that Macready when he came there for his farewell engagement would, at rehearsal, shake his ("The Big Pot's") hand. He counted, Coleman explains, on its being customary "when Macbeth first encounters Malcolm . . . for 'Bellona's Bridegroom' to shake hands with the Heir Apparent." But when the rehearsal

began and the moment came when "The Big Pot" expected to
have tradition followed and win his bet — Macready avoided his
hand. For Macbeth to avoid taking Malcolm's hand just after
Malcolm has been proclaimed Prince of Cumberland would it
seems to me, be not ineffective. Macready's notorious snobbish-
ness furnishes a simpler explanation, of course; but then, rehearsals were with him a matter of deadly seriousness.[27]

Coming now to Lady Macbeth's Letter Soliloquy, we hear from
Leigh Hunt of the gesture splendidly executed in the grand style,
with which Mrs. Siddons accompanied her speaking of the concluding lines:

Mrs. Siddons used to elevate her stature, to smile with a lofty and
uncontrollable expectation, and, with an arm raised beautifully in the
air, *to draw the very circle she was speaking of*, in the *air about her
head*, as if she ran her finger round the gold.[28]

William T. W. Ball, in his reminiscences of Charlotte Cushman,
tells us that, though she invented very few "new points in her
delineation of the character," she broke tradition here. Lady
Macbeth has been told to lay the letter to her heart; and Charlotte
Cushman put it "into her bosom, instead of holding it in her
hand" as had been customary "with all the other representatives
of the part" Ball had seen. Madame Ponisi, Forrest's Lady Macbeth, merely folded the letter and placed it under her girdle.
Madame Ristori, after reading it, walked to the side of the scene
and carelessly threw it away.[29] But the Ristori could be very
subtle, too. At the end of her soliloquy, she was accustomed to
turn towards that side of the stage where Macbeth would enter,
signifying through this action that Lady Macbeth's plan had
already begun to take shape in her mind. Reflection was over.[30]

An even more exacting test for the actress follows swiftly, in
Lady Macbeth's invocation to the spirits of evil. According to
"Cuthbert Bede," whose description is based on notes made at
the time of the Princess's Theatre production in 1853, Mrs.
Charles Kean at "Come to my woman's breasts," "drew herself
up, crossing her hands on her breasts and looking upwards. (Mrs.
Siddons did the same, so I was told by a lady who had seen her in

the part)." Madame Ristori's "white hands clutched her ample bosom," likewise. As for Charlotte Cushman, we hear rather of "the wild, roving, inspired glances, comprehending earth and air" with which she spoke the invocation.[31]

Dame Madge Kendal has a pleasant story to tell of how as a young actress she played Lady Macbeth at Hull with Samuel Phelps. Phelps left the rehearsal to his manager to conduct — the careful rehearsals at Sadler's Wells were now a thing of the past with him — and he had the unexpected to contend with when the performance took place.

"I had always been told," Madge Kendal writes, "that a subject knelt in the presence of his sovereign and, therefore, after greeting Macbeth as 'Great Glamis! worthy Cawdor!' when I spoke the line, 'Greater than both, by the all-hail hereafter,' I went down on my knees and prostrated myself before him."

Phelps, much surprised "at what was to him an unaccustomed piece of 'business,'" nevertheless, "held out his hands and bent down to assist me to my feet again"; and afterwards told the young actress's father, "Robertson, she's original." I am not certain as to what the accustomed business at Macbeth's entrance was. Rowe's direction is *"Embracing him,"* and it may be that, before Mrs. Siddons, this was the practice.[32] Phelps's own, "1860" Promptbook has Lady Macbeth "Xing to R and turns immediately to meet Macbeth — advances to him and places her hands, on each shoulder." [33]

We have not yet done with this scene. James Rees in his *Life of Forrest* — a bumptious and spread-eagle book — tells at length of a suggestion of his own as to how a subsequent passage was to be given. Lady Macbeth should answer Macbeth's "Duncan comes here to-night"

in the same tone, but with a decided marked emphasis, with the eyes fixed on those of her husband, as if to read his inmost soul, she exclaims:
"And when goes hence?"

Macbeth sees not the deep hellish glare — feels not the presence of a demon . . . and he naturally replies, "tomorrow." At that moment he meets the eye of his wife — like an electric shock, the infernal spark acts upon his already overcharged brain — he starts, gazes as if upon the fabled basilisk, and mutters in fear and dread, as if in the presence of a supernatural being,

"As he purposes."

Here it is they fully understand each other.[34]

Rees quotes Forrest as praising the idea and saying that he had called it to the attention of Miss Wemyss (a Lady Macbeth of his, I take it) and had endeavored to put it into practice. That he did so is borne out by Clarke's Promptbook where, at "Tomorrow," we find: "Lady Macbeth suddenly grasps his arm & looks him in the eye — a pause — then he says —'as he purposes'" [35]

Any detail which adds appreciably to our knowledge of the stage business of Mrs. Siddons is precious. J. H. Stocqueler, who claims to be her kinsman, remembers "peeping through one of the old doors which then flanked the fore-part of the stage," while she acted Lady Macbeth. At

> Your face, my Thane, is as a book where men
> May read strange matters,

"John Kemble, who played Macbeth, hung his head as if he could not withstand her penetrating gaze or the language which interpreted aright the ambitious whisperings of his own heart." [36] But we have a better witness. The famous notes of Professor G. J. Bell, made seemingly in the theatre during a performance, at Edinburgh, late in Mrs. Siddons's career, are by far the most vivid record of her acting we possess. Of the exit at the end of this scene Bell writes: "Leading him out, cajoling him, her hand on his shoulder clapping him." And his comment is: "This vulgar — gives a mean conception of Macbeth, unlike the high mental working by which he is turned to her ambitious purpose." [37] The Forrest Promptbook marked by George Becks concludes the scene with Lady Macbeth "taking hold of him, to lead him off"; and Henry Morley, under the date July 25, 1857, writes of Madame Ristori:

The manner of exit is peculiar; she has her hands upon him, and with a persuasive yet compelling force urges him on, smiling the while with firm-set lips and nodding satisfaction at her work. He is in her power; he moves at her urging.

This action she employed anew in the scene of the murder, and there was "a ghostly repetition" of it when she left the stage at the close of the Sleepwalking Scene.[38]

The next scene, that in which Duncan is received by Lady Macbeth and enters the Castle, yields just two bits of stage business. Professor Bell's note on Mrs. Siddons's exit is: "Bows gracefully to the King, when she gives him the *pas* in entering. Then graciously and sweetly to the nobles before she follows the king." That is one. The other, which is more interesting, concerns Charlotte Cushman. It was noticed as one of the "subtle beauties" in her last performance in New York — as Lady Macbeth at Booth's, November 7, 1874 — that she shrank from taking Duncan's hand when he offered it ("give me your hand"), to escort her into the castle.[39]

In the Macklin Manuscript, already referred to, we read:

> Scene the last of the first act — *If it were done*, — In this scene there should be table & chairs, Macbeth should sit down sometimes in this soliloquy, — then start up — traverse — it would diversifie the actors positions — & better mark his perturbation.

The latter part of that seems to me noteworthy. Recall that standing during the speaking of soliloquies was still well-nigh obligatory as late as the middle of the next century.[40] The use of gestures to enforce the supposed meaning of some Shakespearean phrase is capitally illustrated by Edmund Kean's "pressing his hand on his heart at the closing '*here*'" in the soliloquy ("We still have judgment here") and by Mrs. Siddons's "bowing with her hands down, the palms upward" at "We fail." The words were spoken with a "strong downward inflection."[41] Leigh Hunt writes of her brother,

> With what a trembling hand, confessing irresolution of purpose, did [Kemble] grasp his contemptuous wife, and decline to proceed "further in this business," while his eye yet seemed to gloat and glisten at the visionary crown.

Madame Modjeska introduced a "new" piece of business in this scene, which Winter found "infelicitous: she produced one of *Macbeth's* letters and showed it to him, as documentary evidence that he had sworn to kill the *King*." Modjeska had added Lady Macbeth to her repertory in 1888, when a very different style of acting from that of the Kembles had established itself. It is not surprising, therefore, to hear Mrs. Langtry praised, the next year, for "the wonderfully winning way in which she crept into Macbeth's arms while whispering to him her plan for the assassination." The reviewer calls it "a novel point" and assures us that it "fairly thrilled the audience." [42]

At the beginning of Act II, Banquo bids Fleance take his sword, adding a moment later "Take thee that too." Now to say dogmatically what the "that" refers to —"his dagger," for instance, or "a jewel box containing a diamond"— is to confound art with reality. For "that" is precisely what the actor who plays Banquo hands to the actor (or actress) who plays Fleance —"*his dagger*" in Booth's production; "his hat" in Phelps's.[43] And when, as has too often been the case, the lines are cut, we are reduced to the plight of the student of metaphysics who, according to the familiar definition, spends his time looking in the corner of a dark room for a black cat which isn't there. The diamond which Duncan had given Banquo for Lady Macbeth is quite another matter. That has been, consistently, I believe, a ring. Macready was naturally vexed when, playing at Shrewsbury, September 29, 1836, he discovered that his provincial Banquo had no ring. The poor man "*pretended* to pull one off his finger and give it me, but I would not take it," Macready writes; adding, "I was not so cross as I have often been with less provocation." [44] Finally, a letter of Arthur Murphy's gives us a glimpse of Garrick in this scene:

I will tell you how I have seen you do it: — you dissembled indeed, but dissembled with difficulty. Upon the first entrance the eye glanced at the door; the gaiety was forced, and at intervals the eye gave a momentary look towards the door, and turned away in a moment. . . . After saying, "Good, repose the while;" the eye then fixed on the door, then after a pause in a broken tone, "Go, bid thy mistress, &c." [45]

Macklin was troubled by the stage arrangements at this point in the play, finding many difficulties and, so far as we can judge from his notes, no solution. The most interesting passage is as follows:

In this scene. the Servant comes on with two candles, he goes off & leaves his master in the dark that is a breach of manners even to absurdity. to remedy this the scene must lie in a Hall, or anti-chamber, in which there must be a Table in the appartment and when the Servant goes off he must leave the candles on the Table, on which I think Macbeth must put them out.

This scene must [*sic*] reconsidered, for the absurdity must not remain.

One of his ideas, later discarded, was to have Macbeth go out when the servant does, though by a different door, and the scene change "from the outside to the inside of the Palace." Of the soliloquy itself, he writes merely:

Dagger Scene/ *Drop the Dagger* at — thou marshelest me the way that I was going/ take it up/ after there is no such thing.

Notice that it is a dagger to which Macklin refers, as in all conscience one might expect! Yet Kenrick, in a Shakespearean lecture described in *The Monthly Miscellany; Or, Gentleman and Lady's Complete Magazine* for April 1774, had called attention to the fact that, when Macbeth speaks of the dagger "which now I draw," "The player draws from his scabbard — not a *dagger*, but a *long toledo.* 'Mr. Macklin (said the Doctor) in his late performance of this character, judiciously avoided so gross a blunder; but he fell into one considerably greater, by not entirely avoiding the performance of the part.'" Kemble continued to draw "half-way out of the scabbard the sword he wore," not a dagger, and could never be persuaded that he was wrong.[46] And Young fell into the same error, which was at length corrected by Macready, of whom it was said "that he never likes to do what is done by other actors." [47]

John Kemble, as Macbeth, having forgotten the presence of the servant, started at sight of him. His brother Charles stole to the door of Duncan's chamber, where he listened a moment, retired, and then spoke.[48] Young, after dismissing the servant ("*Seyton*", who since Davenant's time had been a hard-worked functionary),

turns his eyes to the several parts of the hall in an inquisitive yet perturbed manner — he then fixes them on the door that leads to Duncan's chamber — . . . he turns from it as if it were the way to perdition — he is deeply agitated, and his eyes wander unconsciously around, till suddenly, he fixes them on the air, and starts.[49]

Both Kemble and Kean were accused of seeing the dagger too quickly.[50] According to Professor Bell's notes, Kemble "renews his walk, throws up his face, sick, sighs, then a start theatric and then the dagger. Why can't he learn from his sister?"[51] By contrast, the elder Vandenhoff, a good actor of the same school, took his own time. In *The Edinburgh Theatrical Observer, and Musical Review*, March 9, 1824, we read that

he seemed first to view the "fantasy of his brain" slowly and reluctantly; he fixed his eye upon it until the image seemingly acquired a reality of existence in his bewildered and troubled mind; he shrunk from the belief of this reality, but still returned to it with a struggling conviction of its existence.

Some twenty years later, a London newspaper printed a strikingly similar description of Phelps who again, instead of starting at once when he saw the dagger, "kept his eyes fixed on the 'painting of his fear' " until he came at length to accept its reality.[52] It is not surprising, therefore, to read of Irving's acting, in this scene, that at first it seemed disappointing,

but therein lay one of its chief excellencies. So much the apparition accorded with Macbeth's thought that he scarcely seemed to notice it. . . . It was not until the direction it took gave a practical hint of its terrible meaning, that the man became appalled, and the true power of the actor became apparent.[53]

A cycle is nearing its close. In 1908, just beyond our stopping-point, Percy Fitzgerald complained that the lines were regularly spoken "slowly and deliberately, the eyes fixed on vacancy." "If one saw a spectral dagger," he asks, would there not rather be "a sudden start, with drawing back, rubbing of the eyes, and hurried, agitated words."[54]

Macbeth, then, sees the dagger, starts, or abstains from starting, and draws his own dagger or, heretically, his sword. He attempts to seize the phantom dagger ("Come, let me clutch thee!"). David Garrick's *Essay on Acting* (1744) is a puzzling performance which one uses at one's peril. There can be no question, however, but that the recommendations for Macbeth which follow are ironical:

Now in this visionary Horror, he should not rivet his Eyes to an *imaginary* Object, as if it *really* was there, but should shew an *unsettled Motion* in his Eye, like one not quite awak'd from some disordering Dream; his *Hands* and *Fingers* should not be *immoveable*, but restless, and endeavouring to disperse the Cloud that over shadows his optick Ray, and bedims his Intellects. . . . *Come let me clutch thee!* is not to be done by *one* Motion only, but by several *successive Catches* at it, first with one Hand, and then with the other, preserving the same Motion, at the same Time, with his Feet, like a Man, who out of his Depth, and half drowned in his Struggles, *catches* at *Air* for *Substance*: This would make the Spectator's Blood run cold.

It was considered an innovation on Macready's part that, at a Haymarket performance, October 28, 1850, he gave "the effect of the fatal weapon wavering about in the air." And Forrest, if "J. W. C's" article "Stage Trick," in *Tallis's Dramatic Magazine* is to be trusted, followed Garrick's prescriptions almost to the letter. On perceiving the dagger, we are told, he started forward "to the front of the stage," where he stood, "with eyes starting and mouth gasping, for fully five minutes . . . all the time groping, with his outstretched hand, in the air, as if . . . he were engaged in the innocent pursuit of chasing a buterfly." [55] It is refreshing to turn from that description — which is not, I suppose, to be taken too literally — to one of an infinitely greater artist. *The Daily News*, September 27, 1875, has this to say of Irving:

We believe it has always been customary in the dagger scene to confront the audience looking upwards, as if the imaginary weapon were hovering in the air somewhere between the performer and the audience. Mr. Irving, on the contrary, sees the dagger at a much lower point as he follows it across the stage, drawn as it were by its fascination towards the arched entrance to the chamber of the King — a fine point being his averted hands, as if the man, "infirm of purpose," and conscious of the spell that is around and about him, could not trust himself to "clutch" the airy weapon save in words.[56]

That stirs us, I think, even on the printed page.

One more point must, I think, be made about the stage business in this scene before we come to Macbeth's exit. At "There's no such thing," Kemble covered his eyes with his hands. That might certainly have been impressive, but as Kemble did it we are told emphatically that it was not. He looked up, according to Professor Bell's notes, "peeping first over then under his hand, as if for an insect whose buzzing had disturbed him, he removes his hand, looks more abroad, and then recovers — very poor." In New York, some years before, Cooper had hidden his face "in his mantle"; then he too had looked apprehensively about to see whether or not the dagger was still there. Hodgkinson, with whom Cooper is compared in the same newspaper account — one of those gleaned by Mr. Odell for his *Annals* — gazed "with a fixed eye upon the ideal weapon," and while it was "still full in his view" gave up credit in its existence.[57]

Macbeth's exit to kill his king is a progress attended by all the pomps of poetical description. Murder himself,

> Thus with his stealthy pace
> With Tarquin's ravishing strides, towards his design
> Moves like a ghost.

That lies beyond the possibility of realization, and the actor will do well, I think, if, perceiving that it is, he denies himself a little. So, I should judge, Young did when Leigh Hunt saw him at the Haymarket in January 1809. "He managed," Hunt writes, "to give a personal character to the idea of the ghost, by just rising slowly and shrinkingly as if preparing to glide, without precisely acting the description, which would have been unseasonable and unnatural." Macready, on the contrary, tried only too hard.

"Had not one been entirely carried away by the cunning of the scene," Coleman tells us, "his exit into Duncan's chamber must have excited derision. Up to that moment he had reached the highest pitch of tragic horror, but his desire to over-elaborate made him pause, and when his body was actually off the stage, his left foot and leg remained trembling in sight, it seemed, fully half a minute."

The younger James W. Wallack imitated Macready in this matter of the reluctant left leg, and it has been suggested that Dickens had Macready in mind when, in Chapter XI of *Edwin Drood*, the leg of the flying waiter is described as "always lingering after he and the tray had disappeared, like Macbeth's leg when accompanying him off the stage with reluctance to the assassination of Duncan." [58] Forrest had recourse to adventitious aids: a peal of thunder, as he stole into the chamber, which made him start back gasping; or (at some later performance, I gather), a supererogatory appearance of the Weird Sisters, rising "above the fretted battlements" of the courtyard as if coming "to preside and exult over" this evil act.[59] Irving, last of all, brought out the mere physical weakness of his Macbeth, "his feet, as it were," feeling "for the ground, as if he were walking with difficulty a step at a time on a reeling deck." [60]

Scene 2 begins with Lady Macbeth, waiting for the accomplishment of the deed. Mrs. Siddons bent toward the door, her ear close to it, listening. Charlotte Cushman, too, crouched "against the door-post." [61] Macbeth returns, carrying the daggers, and here we are fortunate. For in the March 1810 issue of the Philadelphia *Mirror of Taste and Dramatic Censor* there is a full account of how actors had played this scene before the innovations of Kemble and Kemble's disciple, Cooper, Philadelphia's most recent Macbeth. The writer inspires confidence by admitting that he had not seen Garrick as Macbeth. But he had seen Sheridan, Mossop, Reddish, and Henderson, he says, and pictures of Garrick in the part. All these actors had followed, "with more or less success," the same plan. "The noise of a hasty foot was heard within" and as Lady Macbeth said, after a pause,

> "Had he not resembled
> My father as he slept, I had done 't" . . .

the door opened and Macbeth appeared, a frightful figure of horror, rushing out sideways with one dagger, and his face in consternation, presented to the door, as if he were pursued, and the other dagger lifted up as if prepared for action. Thus he stood as if transfixed, seeming insensible to every thing but the chamber, unconscious of any presence else, and even to his wife's address of "my husband."

He spoke only in whispers, remaining in the same attitude, "with eyes still fixed upon the chamber door." Only when Lady Macbeth says "Donalbain" did he move:

Then for the first time he drew his hands together with the daggers in them, and in the most heart-rending accents exclaimed,

"This is a sorry sight."

Thus represented by Mr. Sheridan, this scene was perhaps the most interesting in the drama.[62]

One detail at least in this vivid description can be substantiated. Macbeth as he left Duncan's chamber did use to carry one dagger in each hand. Garrick so bears them in the frontispiece to Bell's *Shakespeare* and Spranger Barry in the print ("Jackson after James Gwinn") reproduced in R. W. Lowe's edition of Churchill's *Rosciad*. The acting version published at Edinburgh in 1853 calls for Macbeth to enter *"disorder'd and bloody, with a dagger in each hand"* and the author of "Notes, Explanatory, &c. on the Tragedy of Macbeth" in *The European Magazine*, for February 1815, assures us that "it hath been the custom (for many years) with the representatives of Macbeth to return from Duncan's chamber with a DAGGER IN EACH HAND." Even Phelps at Sadler's Wells, "like Macready and others . . . followed the traditional business, the daggers clicking like castanets in his palsied hands." [63]

Edmund Kean "instead of beating violently at the door, and rushing on with gigantic strides"— which someone must have been doing —

crept on with the stealthy pace of fear, as if every faculty were for the time unstrung. When his timid eye first rested on Lady Macbeth, his frame was convulsed and wound up to the highest pitch of terror; even upon recognizing her he is but half assured.[64]

Kean's idea of Macbeth's being startled at sight of Lady Macbeth was adopted by Forrest who, without exactly refining upon it, made it very much his own. At Drury Lane, December 2, 1836,

He retired from the chamber of the murdered King with his face turned towards the scene of slaughter, and on *Lady Macbeth* [Miss Huddard] touching his arm, a thrill of fear and horror shook his whole frame, this point, which we do not recollect any previous *Macbeth* to have made, was seized by the audience and loudly applauded.[65]

Garrick in the Murder Scene
(From Bell's *Shakespeare*, 1774)

Yet, so far as I can see, it differed from Kean's way only in the touching of Macbeth's arm. Later, Forrest made Macbeth lift a dagger as if to stab his lady, at this moment. The business is thus described in Becks's Promptbook: "he 1/2 backs on — she touches him — he (ugh!) starts & 1/2 turns as if to strike: she takes (stopping him) his wrist, 'my husband,' &c." [66] Edwin Booth adopted this melodramatic expedient. In his acting version, edited by Winter, the stage direction is: *"Re-enter Macbeth. In his fright and frenzy, he makes as if to stab her."* [67] As for Irving, he "partly added, partly substituted, an idea of tremendous physical prostration"— just as he had done when Macbeth went out, earlier in the scene. "He reels, he totters, he can barely support himself." The daggers are but half held. "His body sways as if already hanging on a gibbet." [68]

As Maebeth tells of the mutterings of the sleepers, the prayer to which he could not respond, Mrs. Siddons listened —"her arms about her neck and bosom, shuddering." [69] Even finer in its way, because more suggestive, is the manuscript note, "Don't look at each other," which stands in Irving's copy of the play against the lines immediately preceding. From Becks's Forrest Promptbook, I gather that it was in the act of attempting to lead Macbeth away, so that he might rid himself of the evidence of guilt, that Lady Macbeth first noticed the daggers. The direction, opposite lines 45–47, is: "puts her R arm round him, & L hand on his (L) wrist as if to draw him to her — sees daggers." That too is well imagined, growing naturally out of the lines themselves. "Give me the daggers," Lady Macbeth says: but she has never, in any printed account I have read, been merely given them. On the contrary, she has "seized" them, or "grasped" them, has "snatched," "wrested," or "wrenched" them from her husband's hands, from as early as Mrs. Siddons's time — earlier still, for Mrs. Pritchard "snatched" them — to as late, at least, as Ellen Terry's. [70] The words themselves do, indeed, suggest action: 'And he gives them to her,' the reader supplies mentally, and thinks no more about it. It is for the player to decide upon the precise quality of the action, and then so represent it that we are satisfied of its rightness. Madame Janauschek had something to add to the stage business at this point. Of her Lady Macbeth, at the Boston Theatre, May 5, 1888, we read: "The woman's nature (for she cannot be all unsexed) is indicated with a beautiful and vivid insight by the sudden gesture of disgust with which she turns away from the bloody daggers." [71] The next moment, she had, indeed, recovered — and no doubt seized the daggers.[72] The traditional conception of Lady Macbeth as an heroic character was passing, even so. Mrs. Langtry, a year later, had the scene so arranged that "a winding stair" led to Duncan's chamber. After snatching the daggers, Lady Macbeth

dashes up the stair as if fearing her resolution may fail her. When she reappears, breathless, panting, overcome with the struggle against herself, she leans against a pillar and says "I shame to wear a heart so white," not as a reproach to Macbeth, but as an apology for her repugnance to the sight of blood.

Mrs. Siddons, according to Professor Bell's notes, had spoken the grim lines before the exit, "As stealing out she turns towards him stooping, and with the finger pointed to him with malignant energy says, 'If he do bleed,' &c." [73]

Macbeth is left alone on the stage. Gould, in *The Tragedian*, pictures his hero, the elder Booth, as "looking on his hands with starting eyes . . . and wiping one hand with the other *from* him, with intensest loathing"—a daring anticipation of Lady Macbeth's later action. Kemble had merely stood

motionless; his bloody hands near his face; his eye fixed, agony in his brow; quite rooted to the spot. She [Mrs. Siddons] at first directs him with an assured and confident air. Then alarm steals on her, increasing to agony. . . . Strikes him on the shoulder, pulls him from his fixed posture, forces him away, he talking as he goes.[74]

The dragging of Macbeth from the stage established itself firmly as part of the business of the play.[75] Westland Marston, for instance, remembers Macready, "as, with his face averted from his wife, and his arms outstretched, as it were, to the irrecoverable past, she dragged him from the stage." Charlotte Cushman (says Ball) "dragged — I may say almost lifted — the broken-down *Macbeth* from the stage." One wonders about the Herculean

Forrest. A compromise, one feels, might well have been effected in his case; but none was, seemingly.[76] Charles Kean and his wife did indeed go out "sorrowfully, she regarding him as though pitying his suffering." But Irving followed tradition and was "slowly dragged" from the stage. Madame Ristori, finally, would have her by-play at the exit bring out the influence which Lady Macbeth possessed over her husband. Macbeth was conceived of as wishing to question her anew. To stop him, she drew his arm about her waist and took his hand. Then, putting her finger to her lips, to impose silence, she led him gently off, all the while plying him with such glances that he might well succumb.[77]

As for the Porter, Davenant dispensed with his services, and he remained out of the play for something like two centuries. Booth, re-employing him, on part time, equipped him with a *"lanthorn and keys,"* which are what he might well be expected to carry.[78]

Sir Walter Scott's essay on Kemble is full of praise of his acting during the dialogue with Macduff and Lennox. The efforts of Kemble's Macbeth "to appear composed," Scott writes,

his endeavours to assume the attitude and appearance of one listening to Lennox's account of the external terrors of the night, while in fact he is expecting the alarm to arise within the royal apartment, formed a most astonishing piece of playing. . . . When Macbeth felt himself obliged to turn towards Lennox and reply to what he had been saying, you saw him, like a man awaking from a fit of absence, endeavour to recollect at least the general tenor of what had been said, and it was some time ere he could bring out the general reply, " 'Twas a rough night." [79]

When Macbeth says, "This is the door," Cumberland's Edition (1829) has him throw it open for Macduff to go in. Charles Kemble, playing in New York, February 18, 1833, was praised for "his manner of ushering Macduff into the chamber, and his shrinking away so guilty-like on uttering 'this is the door,' as if afraid to encounter again the image of his slaughtered monarch." [80]

As a matter of fact, the door meant is probably one that led to the stairs which Macbeth had "descended" after the murder.[81]

Mr. G. Wilson Knight observes that "Macbeth offers to take Macduff up, but his nerve fails, and he points: 'This is the door'." Macduff returns and arouses the household. At Sadler's Wells this was an exciting moment indeed. "Macduff goes to various Entrances giving the alarm"; then, according to the Phelps promptbooks, there was a

> Buzz of voices off R and L, trampling of feet, &c. —when Lady Macbeth is on Lords rush on from 2 E R — as they rush on others from 2 E L. again, as they are on others Enter from 3 E R, others again from 3 EL. and others after them from behind R & L of Arch. Everybody expressing by action "What's the matter &c" turning to one another, till Macbeth [*sic*] exclaims "Our royal Master's murdered," when there is a general expression of horror and alarm.[82]

At the Princess's Theatre, under Charles Kean, there was again a tumultuous thronging-in —"while in the centre of the seething crowd, with pale face and flashing eye, the murderer held aloft his blood-stained sword!" [83]

The question of whether Lady Macbeth does actually faint, as she might well do, under the circumstances, or merely pretends to faint, in order to distract attention from her husband, is one which, fortunately, does not directly concern us. In Davenant's version, the stage direction is "*Faints*"; in Rowe's Edition (1709), it is "*Seeming to faint*." Now Davenant's "*Faints*," as anyone familiar with the fragmentary directions in old plays will, I trust, agree, may be no more than a clipped way of saying what Rowe says. Whereas Rowe's "*Seeming to faint*" can only admit of one interpretation. Tom Davies seems, in a measure, to support Rowe. Observing that Lady Macbeth had long been denied participation in this scene, he finds it hard to believe that, were she restored, there would not be the same display of merriment on the part of some in the audience as had been occasioned, in point of fact, when the experiment of having her present was hazarded, at a performance "many years since." Mr. Macklin, he adds, was "of opinion, that Mrs. Porter alone could have credit with an audience, to induce them to endure the hypocrisy of Lady Macbeth." [84] When, well on in the next century, actresses once more appeared in this scene, their practice varied. Helen Faucit

fainted; and Professor Morley — writing of a late appearance of
the actress — felt that he knew why. It was at the "recurrence
to the image which recalled her father when he slept . . .

> 'Here lay Duncan
> His silver skin laced with his golden blood. . . .' " [85]

Madame Ristori fainted by design, after what must have been
an extraordinary piece of silent acting; [86] whereas Mrs. Langtry
really swooned, but this time only "because a procession of priests
has entered and she sees before her the Holy Cross which she has
rendered herself unworthy hereafter to worship." [87] "Improving
Shakespeare" did not stop with the Restoration!

Ellen Terry stood behind Banquo, "nervously assenting by
unconscious nods and gestures and inarticulate lip-movements to
her lord's story." Then her strength failed her and, falling, she
was "raised and carried out with her fair head thrown back over
a thane's shoulder, and her red hair streaming in the torchlight."
Madame Ristori had been merely "removed by her attendants." [88]
Phelps at Sadler's Wells set the Physician to work —"Physician
and Gentlewoman carry off Lady Macbeth," says the promptbook. Benson arranged a more romantic exit. He used, in his
own words, "to pick up Lady M. with my left arm, carrying her
off the stage on my left shoulder, whilst I kept at bay with my
right sword-arm the infuriated Thanes." [89]

I have little more to tell about the stage business in this scene
and nothing about that in the quiet expository scene (Macduff,
Ross, and the Old Man) which follows. One further note from
Becks's Forrest Promptbook. Against Banquo's solemn assevera-
tion ("In the great hand of God I stand," etc.) in which Macduff
and the rest join, appears the direction, "all swords raised as if in
oath." One wonders how Forrest's Macbeth raised his — slowly
and reluctantly, or with a fine bravado? [90]

Early in the third act come the important questions which
Macbeth asks Banquo, so casually: "Ride you this afternoon? . . .
Is't far you ride?" And then, the one which concerns us, "Goes
Fleance with you?" Now Fleance has often been present when
the question is asked (according to Kemble's arrangement, which

long persisted, he entered with his father at the beginning of the scene), and Macready made a point of his presence. "We have now to notice," writes a critic in *John Bull*, May 26, 1839, "the actor's fondling of *Fleance*, as inferring a cat-like propensity to play with his victim, very foreign from *Macbeth's* nature." In Becks's Forrest Promptbook, just before the question: "Mac passes Lady M over to R door. . . . In passing — M see Fleance: goes towards him & pats his head." When, in December 1864, Helen Faucit was playing Lady Macbeth to the Macbeth of Phelps, she boldly took over this sinister piece of business herself. Professor Morley gives it a thoroughly Victorian interpretation:

"We have seen Miss Faucit praised," he writes, "for representation of smooth treachery in the tender playing of her fingers about the head of the child Fleance while Macbeth is sending father and child into the toils set for them. Miss Faucit knows her Shakespeare better than that. The fingers of the woman who has been a mother, and has murder on her soul, wander sadly and tenderly over the type of her lost innocence." [91]

I find it equally curious that Helen Faucit should have wanted to use the business and that Phelps should have let her appropriate it. In the Booth-Winter Edition, at the line before, is the direction: *"Banquo and Fleance cross to L. — Fleance pauses, to kiss the hand which Macbeth extends to him."* [91a]

Banquo goes, soon after, and the stage is cleared in preparation for Macbeth's talk with the Murderers. The literary stage directions here — an *"Exeunt,"* shall we say, followed by *"Manent Macbeth and a Servant"*— are not very helpful to the imagination. For contrast, I quote one from "The William Warren Edition," that rare thing a printed promptbook, recording the practice of the famous Boston Museum Company, c. 1860–1865: "Exeunt Lady Macbeth *and ladies and pages*, R. 1 E., Lords, *etc.*, C. *door, which* Seyton *closes and is going* L. *when King stops him."* [92] Seyton, hard at work, once more! But we do get, I think, a fair notion of what really happens at this point when the play is acted. As for the Murderers, Winter writes of Salvini's performance in New York in 1881:

At the close of *Macbeth's* colloquy with the villains whom he employs to murder *Banquo* those wretches tried, with fawning servility, to seize the hem of his regal robe, and thereupon he repulsed them with a deportment of imperial disdain and a momentary shudder.[93]

By reducing these characters to the level of the "shag-ear'd" assassins who set upon Lady Macduff, the difficulties of the Banquet Scene are, as we shall see, greatly enhanced. Macbeth treats the Murderers as gentlemen, albeit somewhat decayed gentlemen, and exploits their personal grudge against Banquo instead of merely tossing them a purse. Kemble made them "Officers."

On September 3, 1853, in reviewing a performance of *Macbeth* at Sadler's Wells, *The Athenaeum* grumbled about an "old and objectionable uncertainty" in the second scene, that in which Macbeth gives veiled hints to Lady Macbeth of his design against Banquo, or, as the *Athenaeum* critic assumes, "seeks to screen his lady from a guilty participation" in it. "We require," he writes, "a definition of what Macbeth's own purpose really is in saying all these fine things," whereas the actors — every actor the critic has seen — leave their interpretation in doubt. (At least, then, we may assume that there had been no melodramatic over-playing of this scene!) And on October 22, *The Athenaeum* found comfort in a Marylebone production by the Wallacks (J. W. Wallack, Junior, and his wife, Ann Sefton):

The mingled tenderness and importance assumed by Macbeth in the mysterious announcement of the intended murder, were well conceived, — and his sudden exit from the stage, leaving his wife in a perplexed attitude of mute wonder, to follow him with slow and unsteady steps, was appropriate and effective.

Helen Faucit made it equally clear that Lady Macbeth was not an accomplice. At Macbeth's

> Be innocent of the knowledge, dearest chuck,
> Till thou applaud the deed —

she stood "averted as he crosses, and mechanically follows as he leads." [94] That was Irving's idea, too. In his own marked copy, he wrote, at the end of the scene: "She doesn't understand — & he

goes off abruptly"; and again, "no knowledge of his scheme."
Some of his other annotations seem to me well worth preserving.
Lady Macbeth "puts her arms round him," as Macbeth begins to
speak, removing them before line 16—"But let the frame of
things disjoint." At his reference to the "terrible dreams that
shake us nightly," the note is: "Hand to head & sigh"; and at
"Thou marvell'st at my words," "pause—look at her & smile."
Madame Modjeska took the harsher, and far more probable view
that Lady Macbeth was not in the least puzzled.

> "Be innocent of the knowledge, dearest chuck, till thou applaud the
> deed" is accepted by her deep, sad eyes with perfect intelligence, with-
> out approval, but without a murmur. . . . During part of the interview
> Macbeth is seated, and she bends round him, behind his chair, leaning
> upon him, compassionating his overwrought fancies, his nightly
> dreams . . . with the extreme tenderness alone possible to a thoroughly
> disillusionized woman.[95]

A few scattered bits of business remain to be mentioned. One is
Madame Ristori's "shrinking away" from Macbeth "with haggard
weariness," at the words "Duncan is in his grave"; another, Macbeth's gesture when he speaks of the crow's making "wing to the
rooky wood." Macready was accused of sacrificing the imaginative to "what is supposed to be the real," at this moment, by
"turning to look off the stage"—as if to see the crow. Booth, on
the contrary, pictured it "by a waving of hand and forearm." [96]
I am not in the least certain as to how Banquo's murder was
managed on the Elizabethan stage. There is no stage direction in
the Folio. Of course the "twenty trenched gashes" may have
been given him in sight of the spectators with all the vengeful
fury that should accompany them. But then, how comes it that
nothing is said about the disposal of the body? Perhaps, the murderers bear it away, at the end of the scene, but if so the action
has not been caught up into the lines. Davenant is unhelpful,
since he chose to revise the speeches extensively. And his general
arrangement—a sound of clashing swords within, following
Banquo's exit; then a sight of Fleance running, with one of the
Murderers in pursuit—was frequently adopted, or only slightly
modified, in later times, when the scene was acted at all.[97]

There is a quantity of stage business in the Banquet Scene, far more than in any other scene in the play; and it may be helpful, at the outset, to indicate the several topics which are to be taken up. First is the arrangement of the stage — and this must not detain us long. Next, the business which has to do with Macbeth's stealthy interview with the Murderer. Next, the two appearances of the Ghost — unfortunately, he has frequently been forbidden to appear at all, a matter which must be gone into. After this comes Macbeth's business while he is confronted by the Ghost — especially, his dropping the cup, an action of great antiquity. Then there is the behavior of Lady Macbeth and the guests, for this scene proceeds on several levels. And finally we reach the quiet, pitiful episode with which the scene concludes.

Suggestions as to how the stage is to be arranged are not wanting in the lines themselves. Lady Macbeth "keeps her state." Macbeth, on the contrary, "will mingle with society," like the "humble host" at an inn or ordinary; and, at an otherwise "full" table, where "both sides are even," he will "sit i' th' midst," and has a place reserved there. This table will be thrust well forward, so that we may watch Macbeth's face. Lady Macbeth's "state" need not be — and it has been assigned to the Elizabethan inner stage. As for the "stool" which the Ghost is to occupy, it is quite in keeping with the text to place it at the head of the table.[98] We are now ready for the good description which Fanny Kemble gives, in telling of a performance, with Macready, in 1848:

> From time immemorial, the banquet scene . . . has been arranged after one invariable fashion: the royal dais and throne, with the steps leading up to it, holds the middle of the stage, sufficiently far back to allow of two long tables, at which the guests are seated on each side, in front of it, leaving between them ample space for Macbeth's scene with Banquo's ghost, and Lady Macbeth's repeated rapid descents from the dais and return to it, in her vehement expostulations with him, and her courteous invitations to the occupants of both the tables to "feed, and regard him not." [99]

A diagram in Oxberry's Edition (1822) bears out the accuracy of this description at most points.[100] The guests sit only on the outer side of the two "decorated" tables which Fanny Kemble mentions, and "A Chair" for Macbeth is at the head of left-hand table, down stage. It is, thus, very conspicuous, and easy of access, for the Ghost. That the same important chair should

58   MACBETH.

Music to open Scene = Lights up.

SCENE 4. 6

A Room of State in the Palace.

A Banquet prepared. Enter MACBETH. *Lady* MAC-
BETH, ROSSE, LENOX, *Lords, and Attendants.* disc -

Macb. You know your own degrees, sit down: at
first,
And last, the hearty welcome [39].
Lords. /bowing/   Thanks to your majesty. /sit/
Macb. Ourself will mingle with society, /rises/
And play the humble host.
Our hostess keeps her state ; but, in best time,
We will require her welcome.
Lady M. Pronounce it for me, sir, to all our friends;
For my heart speaks, they are welcome. /all bow to Lady M/

      Enter first Murderer, to the door. R. 1 E

Macb. See, they encounter thee with their hearts'
thanks :—
Both sides are even : Here I'll sit i'the midst :
Be large in mirth ; anon, we'll drink a measure
The table round.—There's blood upon thy face.
Mur. 'Tis Banquo's then.
Macb. 'Tis better thee without, than he within.
Is he despatch'd ?
R _Mur._ My lord, his throat is cut ; that I did for him.
R.C _Macb._ Thou art the best o'the cut-throats : Yet he's
good,

The Stage Arrangement of the Banquet Scene
(From a drawing in Phelps's Promptbook at the Folger Library)

sometimes gravitate toward the center of the stage is, I suppose, only natural. The author of an unsigned letter in *The Drama; Or, Theatrical Pocket Magazine*, for October 1824, asks bitterly how Macbeth can "exclaim 'the table's full,'" when the seat which *Macbeth* should occupy, and which the ghost takes, is not at either table . . . but is placed in the middle of the stage, entirely apart from them." Phelps aroused comment by moving the chair farther back and altering the position of the two tables, now

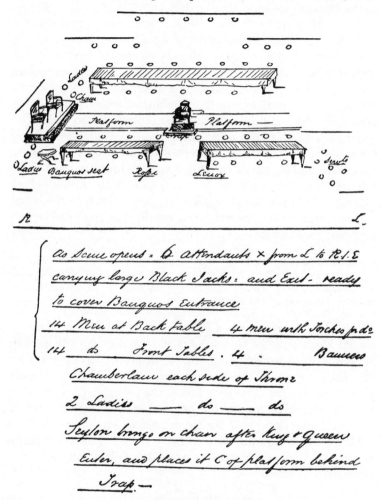

placed across the stage with a convenient division between them.[101] The dais, with chairs of state for Macbeth and his Queen, is now to the side. Notice also, in the drawing reproduced from

Phelps's promptbook, "Banquo's Seat" at the head of the right-hand table, and the "Trap" immediately in front of Macbeth's chair. Both objects will be worth remembering when we come to the Ghost.

As for Macbeth's talk with the Murderer, once grant that the latter is not a mere "bravo," and half the difficulty is over. Grant, too, a certain primitive informality in a court of long ago, and, with only a small allowance for Elizabethan stage conventions, Macbeth may step to the door for a moment and speak, aside, to a person dressed, shall we say like a minor courtier. When, however, it is unmistakably a professional cutthroat who comes, his presence is troublesome; and, during the Restoration period and for some time after, the Murderer's make-up seems to have been distinctive, and he wore a very black wig.[102] In the Booth-Winter Edition he enters *"with the Servants, who bring dishes. — First Murderer has a few drops of blood upon his cheek. — He brings a goblet of wine to Macbeth,"* and kneels, speaking. Before bidding him go, Macbeth

is about to drink; but the colour of the wine sickens him, and he gives the goblet back to the Murderer, who places it on the table, and, at Macbeth's next words, spoken simultaneously with this action, quietly slinks out of the room.

When Joseph Proctor — a "first-rate melodramatic actor"— played Macbeth at the Howard Athenaeum, Boston, early in 1867, he was scolded for adopting "the absurdity of having the *First Murderer* appear in the banquet scene as a species of Gaelic Ganymede, instead of meeting him at the [door]." Irving in 1875 had the Murderer "peep from behind the arras and whisper to *Macbeth*, who stood as if leaning against an adjoining pillar." [103]

Henry Higden in his *Modern Essay on the Thirteenth Satire of Juvenal* (licensed November 11, 1685) tells of one who had committed a crime:

> If to divert his Pangs he try
> Choice Musick, Mirth or Company,
> Like *Bancoe's* Ghost, his ugly Sin,
> To marre his Jollity, stalks in. . . .[104]

That "stalks in" and the spelling *"Bancoe"* suggest that Higden
was recalling a play he had seen rather than one he had read.
Davenant's stage directions for the Ghost are as follows: *"Enter
the Ghost of* Banquo *and sits in* Macbeth's *place"* (as he is directed
to do in the Shakespeare Folio); *"The Ghost descends"*; then,
dramatically, *"The Ghost of* Banq. *rises at his feet"*; and, last of
all, a mere *"Ex. Ghost."* I have already referred to West Digges's
promptnotes in his copy of the Edinburgh 1753 edition of the
play. That had called for the Ghost's rising, on his first appearance. Digges scores through *"rises"* and inserts "Enters OP," and
for *"Ghost sinks"* he gives us "Exit PS." On the other hand, when
the Ghost reappears, Digges's "Ring up Trap OP" is an appropriate promptnote to accompany the printed direction *"The ghost
rises at his feet,"* and, accepting (I take it) the final *"Exit"* for
what the word regularly means, Digges merely adds "OP." Traps,
in other words, as might be expected when one remembers the
goings up and down of the Ghost in *Hamlet*, are being regularly
employed in this scene. But as Digges's markings show clearly,
there need be nothing monotonous about their use. A Ghost who
has walked on and off the first time will startle us all the more if,
at the moment when Macbeth is about to drink, he *"rises just before him."*[105] Finally, to anticipate for a moment, it will be established, when we come to Macbeth's business in this scene, that
the Ghost's second exit was often not only walking but retreating.

His very existence as a stage character was becoming insecure.
On March 19, 1752, Bonnell Thornton in *Have At You All; or,
The Drury Lane Journal*, wrote threateningly against him:

There is a circumstance in this play of Macbeth, which I always
thought might be manag'd to more advantage. I would willingly confine all dumb ghosts beneath the trap-doors: the ghost in HAMLET is a
particular exception . . . otherwise, their mealy faces, white shirts, and
red rags stuck on in imitation of blood, are rather the objects of ridicule than terror. I cannot help imagining that if the audience were
not coldly let into the cause by the rising of the mangled MACDUFF
(*sic*), our surprise would be much greater, and our terror more alarm-
ing, while the imagination of MACBETH conjur'd up an airy form before him, though he were really looking only on a chair. There is no
reason why a bloody dagger might not with as much propriety be let

down . . . over MACBETH's head, when . . . he creates the air-drawn dagger of the mind. — At present, I am sure by far the greatest part of the audience is chiefly taken up in contemplating the odd figure of MACDUFF and marking the opening or closing of the trap-doors; — as I once overhea[r]d an honest citizen in the first gallery observing to her neighbor, *he looks deadly like a ghost.*

Eight years later, in a work dedicated to Thornton, the attack was renewed with marked success. Robert Lloyd's poem, *The Actor*, was regularly cited, by those who found the Ghost objectionable. In it occur these lines:

> But in Stage-Customs what offends me most
> Is the Slip-door, and slowly-rising Ghost. . . .
>
> When chilling Horrors shake th' affrighted King
> And Guilt torments him with her Scorpion Sting . . .
>
> Why need the Ghost usurp the Monarch's Place,
> To frighten Children with his mealy Face?
> The King alone should form the Phantom there,
> And talk and tremble at the vacant Chair.

Into the controversy as to whether or not the Ghost should actually appear on the boards, there is no need to enter. It was fought out, in desultory fashion, for many years — is not, perhaps, quite closed even now. On the one side is Shakespeare's clear intention. On the other, there are the supposed prejudices of sophisticated audiences; unprofitable conjectures as to what *Macbeth* might have been like had its author lived in a less credulous age; the false analogy of the "air-drawn dagger"; and the crudeness and substantiality of stage expedients for representing the insubstantial.

On April 21, 1794, at the opening of the new Theatre Royal in Drury Lane, Shakespeare's tragedy was acted with Kemble and Mrs. Siddons in the chief parts and Macbeth now bent "his eye on vacancy — an alteration" (to quote *The Morning Chronicle*) "in which every classical mind must agree with Mr. KEMBLE." At Covent Garden the Ghost still carried on, indeed, but his days seemed numbered. In the autumn of 1803, Kemble moved there, and summarily dispensed with his services. But though the weight of critical authority remained poised against his return, John Bull

wanted the Ghost, and at last Kemble gave in. Joseph Farington
dined with the actor, November 8, 1811, and records:

Kemble was decidedly for not introducing the *figure* of *Banquo* in
the *Feast Scene*, but to let it be expressed by Macbeth as the image of
His disturbed imagination. During 7 years, He said, He had so acted
it, but it was then called for by a few persons in the gallery, & the cry
being supported, He had been obliged to comply contrary to His
judgment, & the figure of Banquo again appears in Macbeth's chair.[106]

Forrest did without a ghost (though not, I think, for long), and
Edwin Booth, in spite of the fact that his father had used one.[107]
R. M. Sillard, praises as an "innovation" of Barry Sullivan's, at
Liverpool in March 1851, "the abolition . . . of the visible ghost
of Banquo. It was the first time such an idea was introduced on the
British stage." [108] Sillard adds that when Sullivan appeared in
Chicago, some years later, "the newspapers animadverted severely
upon the *absence* of the actor set down for Banquo at this critical
moment"— the actor in question was, it appears, addicted to the
bottle.[109] Irving, after experimenting in his earlier productions
— with a sudden dimming of lights, for instance, accompanying
the spectre's entrance — quietly gave up representing the ghost
at all and instead addressed "a seat with a bluish light falling upon
it" ("With a visible ghost," was a comment at the time, "the
actor can only attitudinise; without it he can 'create, vivify, and
appal' ").[110]

Meanwhile, the Ghost had still been appearing at many per-
formances, sometimes using a trap, sometimes not. In "What the
Play-Bill will come to," *Punch* in 1858 (doubtless, with a glance
at Charles Kean's ways), suggested as an appropriate item: "The
Trap that Raises Banquo's Ghost Will be presided over by Mr.
Wheeler, assisted by Master T. Wheeler." [111] But a new method
of getting the Ghost on had been discovered. The German
Prince, Pückler-Muskau, writes on November 28, 1827, of a recent
Drury Lane performance with Macready:

The entrance of the ghost is so cleverly concealed by the bustle of
the guests taking their seats at several tables, that it is not till the King
prepares to sit down that the dreadful form seated in his place, is
suddenly visible to him and to the audience. Two bloody wounds

deface his pale countenance . . . and when he looks up fixedly at the King from the festive tables, surrounded by the busy tumult of the guests, then nods to him, and slowly sinks into the earth, the illusion is as perfect as the effect is fearful and thrilling.[112]

Screening of the Ghost is carefully provided for in the invaluable Phelps Promptbook. When Macbeth says grace — it is almost that —

> Now good digestion wait on appetite,
> And health on both!

"Rosse and Lenox in front of Tables & 2 Lords at back, groupe forward as in conversation — masking Banquo as he rises on trap"; and, three lines later, "Pull for Trap" and the "Ghost rises." When he "disappears," it is again by means of the trap. His next appearance is differently arranged. At line 87, "Macbeth passes up C thro tables and gets to Chair on platform." Seyton "gives him goblet"; then, I think at "Would he were here," "Banquo Enters R.1.E. covered by 4 [changed in pencil to "6"] Attendants who Enter with wine. . . . Banquo sits on Stool R." The presence of these attendants, "carrying large Black Jacks," may perhaps have been noticed in the reproduction of a page from this prompt-book, given above. Phelps's arrangements commended themselves, as well they might, for use in other theatres; and, as early as 1852, the Boston, Howard Athenaeum Promptbook was calling, this time at the ghost's first appearance, for a "Banq. trap" and four attendants "with large jugs" who meet four others "with goblets passing in front of trap. they fill the goblets and when Banquo up, they go quietly to guests." Two of Phelps's actresses, Miss Addison and Mrs. Warner, had been at the Howard the autumn before, and presumably brought word of how things were done at Sadler's Wells.[113] As for Charles Kean, I know nothing about the Ghosts of his early years. At the Haymarket, May 21, 1841, he had one who wore "noisy, high-heeled boots" (the Ghost in *Hamlet* had been warned against squeaking, it will be remembered),[114] and at the same theatre, in the spring of 1849, a Ghost who was "reduced to the minimum of effect; the rear of his head only, above the tall back of a chair, being made visible to the audience in the first instance, and his entrance in the second re-

maining almost unobservable at the wing." [115] Kean's importance as a producer belongs, however, to the 'fifties during his
tenancy of the Princess's Theatre. There, when he gave *Macbeth*,
February 14, 1853, he exhibited bards with harps in a gallery
above — a characteristic bit of detail. "When Banquo's ghost
was first seen it appeared on the double seat of state by the side
of Lady Macbeth. The head of Banquo was illuminated by a
strong pale blue light." When it came the second time, a pillar,
close to Macbeth, "suddenly became illuminated, Banquo's ghost
being seen within it." [116] After such hocus-pocus as this, one
would like to hear of simpler proceedings. Salvini's, none the less,
will scarcely do. In his performances, we are told, "the ghost of
Banquo, in the first instance, scrambled up from under a table,
tumbled down again, and re-appeared from a front-trap, jerked
up like a Harlequin." [117]

But what of Macbeth in this scene? David Garrick's correspondents were forever sending him suggestions as to how he
might better his performances. So, for instance, early in his
career, he was urged to bring out the natural intrepidity of Shakespeare's hero. The Ghost "should have stepped back much
quicker" and "Macbeth should likewise have followed him step
for step. I remember to have seen it acted in that manner, and it
had a very good effect." Eighteen years later, H. H. takes exception to Garrick's playing of the scene on quite different grounds.
"When," he writes, "you utter . . .

> 'Be alive again,
> And dare me to the desert with thy sword, &c.'

You recollect a degree of resolution, and advancing on the Ghost,
pronounce the passage in a firm tone of voice. I apprehend the
whole situation supposes a fixed immovable attitude of horror
and amazement." Garrick replies that he does "certainly . . .
recollect a degree of resolution, but I never advance an inch, for,
notwithstanding my agitation, my feet are immovable." [118] In his
Essay on Acting (1744), he recommends ironically that

Macbeth should draw his Sword, and put himself in a Posture of
Defence; and when he comes to, *Hence horrid Shadow!* he should

make a home Thrust at him, recover upon the *Ghost's* moving, and keep passing at him till he has got quite out of the Room: The Manner it has been done *heretofore*, which is keeping the Hand upon the Sword, and following him out, is not so natural and effecting, as the Way I propose.

That "the Manner it has been done heretofore" persisted, is made clear by the criticism in *The London Chronicle*, November 11–13, 1784, of young Holman's first appearance as Macbeth at Covent Garden: "Why he should, when the spirit recedes, follow with his hand on his sword, in the act of threatening, we cannot conceive." The ghost seems regularly to have retreated at this time — and, I believe, walked backwards. *The Entertainer*, November 12, 1754, tells of startling a friend in the act of reading the Banquet Scene, and being taken for the ghost. So, he says, he

vanished away by walking backwards to the door, as I had seen Mr. Ross do in that character; no soener [*sic*] had I disappeared, than I heard him say in a triumphant tone,

> *I am a man again.*

"Lately," reports "Spiritualis" in *St. James's Chronicle*, May 15–18, 1773, "the Ghost of Banquo, instead of making good his Retreat backwards to his Chair, fell upon his Rump, to the great Surprise and Astonishment of Macbeth, and all his Train." [119] Young continued to "follow up" the Ghost, after it had become unfashionable to do so,[120] and the business got into Cumberland's Edition. Thence it passed to French's, where it long stood a curious reminder of the practices of other days — "*Exit Ghost, R., Macbeth following to the door.*"

Even Kemble had bullied the spectre. But Kean "retired" from it "with a head averted and in fear." [121] And Macready, improving upon Kean, made this one of his own great moments. Already unnerved by the Ghost's earlier appearance, Macready's Macbeth glanced fearfully at the vacant seat as he pledged Banquo. When the Ghost came again, he faced it at first with a sort of desperation; then, as he gazed, his strength failed him, and at last, uttering a cry, he flung his mantle over his face, and fell back into a chair.[122] Forrest, it seems to me, attempted to combine the older business with the new. According to the reliable George Becks,

"Mr. Forrest used to throw his robe under his R. arm (which was left free for action) into his L. hand — which held up the robe as if to shield him from seeing the ghost & would then advance upon it — as if to waft it away" repeating " 'hence' . . . four or five times — until it was off the stage — rising to great power of passion of fear & horror — & then fell back for support against the tormentor." [123]

Irving, in 1875, scored heavily here. Like Macready, he flung his mantle over his face, but instead of sinking back into a chair he fell — at the foot of the throne. On the Ghost's earlier appearance, according to one account, he "had plucked off his crown," as if Banquo had come to challenge his possession of it. [124]

One detail in the stage business of this scene is not only natural and effective when one sees it — and old, in any case — but may well have been introduced when the play was first performed. Early in the last act of *The Knight of the Burning Pestle*, Jasper, made up to resemble his own ghost, is threatening the Merchant:

> When thou art at thy Table with thy friends,
> Merry in heart, and fild with swelling wine,
> I'll come in midst of all thy pride and mirth,
> Invisible to all men but thy self,
> And whisper such a sad tale in thine ear
> Shall make thee let the Cup fall from thy hand,
> And stand as mute and pale as Death it self.

One would like to suppose that we have in the last two lines an allusion, in a nearly contemporary play (c. 1607), to a bit of "the original business" in *Macbeth*. [125] I find it next referred to, several times, at the middle of the eighteenth century. Garrick, in his *Essay on Acting* (1744), advises, "the Glass of Wine in his [Macbeth's] hand should not be dash'd to the Ground, but it should fall *gently* from him, and he should not discover the least Consciousness of having such a Vehicle in his Hand." *The Connoisseur*, July 4, 1754, in describing certain country actors, says of them:

Macbeth himself carries a rolling-pin in his hand for a truncheon; and, as the breaking of glasses would be very expensive, he dashes down a pewter pint pot at the sight of Banquo's ghost. [126]

In the Edinburgh, 1753, acting edition occurs the direction for
Macbeth, "*Going to drink, drops the glass,*" at the Ghost's second
appearance. Now comes a break in the record though not, I am
inclined to believe, in the tradition. But Genest had heard that
during a performance at Brighton, in 1809, Mrs. Siddons narrowly
escaped serious injury: "Charles Kemble, who was Macbeth,
threw the cup from him in the Banquet scene with such violence,
that it broke the arm of a glass chandelier, which stood on the
table, and sent it very near to Mrs. Siddons' face." The great
actress, nevertheless, "sat as if she had been made of marble." [127]
Again silence. Then in 1854, Mr. Punch, stirred by the publication in a London newspaper of a letter describing excavations at
"the supposed site of MACBETH's Castle at Dunsinane," announced
discoveries of his own there, including: "The goblet *Macbeth* let
fall when he saw the Ghost — rim a good deal indented, and the
vessel still smelling of whiskey." Becks writes in his promptbook
that Forrest "threw the goblet off R2 or 3 generally caught — by
prop man." And the "William Warren Edition" warns: "GOBLET
square and loaded, not to roll."

   Lady Macbeth, through all this, has been kept in the back-
ground — it is Macbeth's scene, not hers. Things there are for
her to do, manifestly, but most of them she must be contented to
do unobtrusively, or the scene will suffer. Davies, it is true, describes "the admirable art" of Mrs. Pritchard (Garrick's Lady
Macbeth)

in endeavouring to hide Macbeth's frenzy from the observation of the
guests, by drawing their attention to conviviality. She smiled at one,
whispered to another, and distantly saluted a third. . . . Her reprov-
ing and angry looks, which glanced towards Macbeth, at the same
time were mixed with marks of inward vexation and uneasiness.
When, at last, as if unable to support her feelings any longer, she rose
from her seat, and seized his arm, and, with a half-whisper of terror,
said, "*Are you a man!*" she assumed a look of such anger, indignation,
and contempt, as cannot be surpassed.

That has always sounded strangely remote to me — almost as if
someone were retelling the *story* of a play and embroidering
upon the details. As James Boaden says crossly — jealous, I fancy,

for the fame of an actress far greater than Mrs. Pritchard —"I should think Mr. Davies, from his minuteness of observation, must have figured there as one of the nobles, only a few covers from the royal state." Yet Mrs. Siddons in her "Remarks upon the Character of Lady Macbeth" has very much the same idea of how the scene should be played. Lady Macbeth, she writes,

having tottered up the steps to her throne . . . entertains her wondering guests with frightful smiles, with over-acted attention, and with fitful graciousness; painfully, yet incessantly, labouring to divert their attention from her husband. Whilst writhing thus under her internal agonies, her restless and terrifying glances towards *Macbeth*, in spite of all her efforts to suppress them, have thrown the whole table into amazement.[128]

And Mrs. Siddons's own acting here was ever esteemed one of her greatest achievements.[129] The business of her successors has seldom attracted attention. Madame Ristori, soon after the Ghost's first departure, drank

from a large bowl of wine; the cup is in her hand when she tries to recall her husband to the guests; she does not lay it down until after the next appearance of the spectre. On the night of Duncan's murder she had made addition to her courage by the help of wine. She feels it sinking now.[130]

A little earlier in the scene — just before the Ghost's exit, I think — Madame Janauschek had drawn "the head of the conscience-stricken Thane to her bosom, as if to shut out his vision, and held it there, while she turned upon the audience a face bloodless, drawn, and lined with despairing pity." [131] As for the guests, enough that from time to time they have been scolded for going about their eating and drinking too unconcernedly.[132] And, finally, two curiosities: When Lady Macbeth bids the guests "sit, worthy friends," the "William Warren Edition" has servants (headed by Seyton, of course) passing *"in front of table pouring out wine so that the guests do not see* Macbeth"; and at the Haymarket, October 8, 1849 (Macready playing the lead), "some new business was introduced" which to the *Athenaeum* seemed "of questionable propriety. During the confusion caused by Macbeth's strange behaviour, the Physician (Mr. Tilbury) came forward and gesticulated extravagantly before the Queen, as if giving a medical opinion on Macbeth's sanity."

The desolate close of this scene does not appear to have been emphasized by the older actors. Perhaps, they counted upon the mere reading of Shakespeare's lines to prevail and felt no need for inventing business? At any rate, one begins to hear of business only in Macready's time. Then Helen Faucit, after bowing low to the last guest and standing, for a moment more, with "her figure bent . . . staggered and grew faint." She "tottered to a table and sat down, resting her forehead on her hand. In doing this she touched her crown, then lifted this symbol of her misery from her head." [133] Booth at the end of the scene "slowly took the coronet from his head and sat gazing at it with a look of unutterable wretchedness and despair." [134] And one more note, of five words only, from Irving's own marked copy of the play. Against the lines in which Macbeth speaks of his intention of visiting the Weird Sisters—"for now I am bent to know By the worst means the worst"—Irving wrote: "Look at empty table pause." The table had not been empty, a little while before, but "full." [135]

In making his exit, Charles Kean leaned for support against a pillar. Helen Faucit led her Macbeth off, "never once looking at him, turning aside her head, as if in dread of meeting his glance." Forrest takes Madame Ponisi's hand and "leads her off — both drooping & subdued." Madame Janauschek, with a "weary gesture . . . bows her head over her husband as the curtain falls." And Madame Ristori's "simple action of laying Macbeth's hand upon her shoulder, as she leads him from the stage" is described as "never to be forgotten." [136] Better that alone, one feels, than the elaborate by-play described in the Ristori's *Memoirs* — Macbeth frightened anew by getting his cloak caught between his feet, as, supported by his wife, he nears the wings, and needing to be controlled by her and pushed off the stage! [137] Irving's exit, too, was at one time sensational. Taking up a torch, he suddenly hurled it "blazing to the ground," then flung his robe over his face and leaned against a pillar. Later, he merely paused, in ascending the steps by which he was to leave the stage, and looked back once more, fascinated, at the Ghost's chair.[138]

Since I am convinced that the Hecate passages are not Shakespeare's, the stage business which has accompanied them I shall not record. Otherwise, the reader might have heard much of Kemble's celebrated production in 1794, when Hecate and her companions flew backwards, "on account of the Machinery being necessary to be kept out of sight of the audience," and "new groups" were "introduced to personify the black spirits and white, blue spirits and grey"— in the same production, mind, in which Banquo's ghost had been forced to assume invisibility! [139] Lennox and another Lord (III, 6) have regularly been cut in performance — they are mere talkers anyway — and we can proceed at once to Shakespeare's witches and the Cauldron Scene. At the beginning of it, Macready had them "crouching . . . at distant corners of the cavern, each awaiting the signal of her own familiar"— which seems to me an excellent idea. Rowe's stage direction, *"They march round the Cauldron, and throw in the several Ingredients as for the Preparation of their Charm"* leaves nothing to be desired as a description of what should follow, though at York, March 10, 1788, an unhappy variation seems to have been effected, a local theatrical magazine protesting that when the Witches "encircled the caldron, they should have thrown *something* into it, which would have rendered the piece more natural; for, if you discriminate accurately, the very incantation was lost by the non-observance of this custom." [140] It is reassuring to read in the Boston, Howard Athenaeum, Promptbook (1852), "give witches plenty of charms." The Edinburgh acting edition of 1753 has the Sisters *"marching round and stirring it"* (the cauldron) at the first "Double, double"; and *"stirring its contents with their sticks"* is the corresponding stage direction in the Winter-Booth edition.[141] Broomsticks would be perfectly suitable for this purpose — or, on a pinch, crutches — but not wands. One more hint comes from a criticism of *The School for Scandal* in *The Edinburgh Dramatic Review*, April 27, 1824. Mr. Mason as Sir Peter and Mrs. Davison as Lady Teazel, we learn,

in pronouncing simultaneously the words "never, never, never," did not join hands, and raise and sink them to the cadence of the words, after the manner of *Macbeth's* witches over the enchanted Cauldron, as used to be done in our Theatre.

Finally, at Macbeth's entrance, Clarke's Forrest Promptbook has:

1st witch peering into caldron
2nd " on her knees blowing fire
3rd " in attitude, looking up.

The three apparitions which the Weird Sisters show Macbeth rose and descended by means of traps.[142] Whether they actually came through the cauldron, in older days, is much less certain. Digges's prompt notes may even imply, it seems to me, the use of different traps for the First and Second Apparitions, that for the First being merely "Trap OP," whereas "Hobs Trap" serves the Second. *The Monthly Mirror*, after discussing a number of innovations made by Kemble, when he gave the play at Covent Garden, December 12, 1803, goes on:

the apparitions rise from the mouth of the cauldron . . . but here again the effect and the interest suffer, since, from the glare of the cauldron, it is not easy to distinguish one apparition from another.[143]

And *The Theatrical Inquisitor*, for November 1814, asks, in connection with a recent Drury Lane performance in which Kean played Macbeth, why "the apparitions start from the cauldron? it is the agent of their [the Witches'] incantation, but it by no means follows that shadows are to rise from it." When they have done so, it may be added, their approach from below has sometimes been by means of a stepladder.[144] Katherine Goodale (Kitty Molony), who was a member of Booth's Company during the season of 1886–1887, tells a good deal about the "ascending-the-trap-through-the-cauldron robe" which she wore as the Second Apparition. "The 'armed head,' " she continues,

went up first; the "Child Apparition" followed me. This trap business is a scamper. The first and last apparitions had time for cautious one-way traffic — the first for getting on, the last for getting off — but the middle one to connect with the cues, needs to jump lively both ways.

No wonder stage accidents have so often happened in the course of this scene! Booth's practice, it may be added, was to have the armed head made up to look like Macbeth; and at the Howard

Athenaeum, in 1852, the crowned Child carried, stupidly, an olive branch.[145]

Presently the cauldron sinks, through a trap of course, and a show of kings passes before Macbeth's eyes.[146] Here gauzes — Phelps's favorite device for softening the glare of reality — have often been found serviceable. Indeed, we have Scott's word for it that their use goes back at least to Kemble, who "by causing the descendants of the murdered thane to pass behind a screen of black crape . . . diminished their corporeal appearance." [147] The shadowy Kings seem to have marched by, as a rule. "The fellows tramp past," Percy Fitzgerald complains, at the very end of our period; and in Philadelphia, a hundred years before, "their procession was anything but regular. One of them actually took a skip." [148] On the other hand, "Dunsinane" in *The James's Chronicle*, February 18–20, 1768, has a good word to say for the show, as it had appeared to Mr. Powell's Macbeth at Drury Lane, January 20:

I was particularly pleased with the slow Motion of Banquo when he follows the Vision of his Posterity, and his remaining in Sight till Macbeth has finished his Speech. This Part used to be hurried over in a very slovenly Manner.

At Covent Garden in the autumn of 1842, when the elder Vandenhoff was Macbeth, we are told that "instead of the spirits passing under Macbeth's review, like so many soldiers, they were made to glide almost imperceptibly through the air." For a strong curtain, Salvini "became insensible and fell, headlong, and *Hecate* and the *Three Witches* reappeared and hovered over him." [149] In the acting editions published under Salvini's name, he faints and the Witches dance, earlier, just before the vanishing; but presumably the quiet passage with Lennox, which should follow, was cut in performance.

Act IV, Scene 2, the butchering of Lady Macduff and her son used regularly to be omitted in performance. Phelps restored it, at Sadler's Wells, and the directions in his 1847 Promptbook (the scene is wanting in that of 1860) are thus of peculiar interest. They include: "falling on her knees" for Lady Macduff, when she begins to talk with the little boy (she rises at line 45, "Ay, that he was"); "Lady M. rushes and clings to her son," at the messenger's injunction, "Hence with your little ones!" "1st Murderer Snatches up young Macduff and bears him off he screaming 'Murder'—&c. thro opening LH," at "young fry of treachery"; and, finally, "The 2nd Murderer drags off Lady Macduff thro openg LH screaming 'Murder' A pause then whistle" — i.e. for the change of scene.

The long dialogue between Malcolm and Macduff — long, and slow but working up to a fine climax — yields less than might, perhaps, be expected. It is a declamatory scene, after all, and no star actor is present to invent and impose his own stage business. Coleman, indeed, tells an instructive story of how, playing Macduff at Bristol about 1850 he had "rushed over" to Ross, on the latter's entrance, and, exclaiming "My ever gentle cousin, welcome hither" . . . "clasped his hand in both mine." Whereupon,

Mrs. Macready's manager and son-in-law, James Chute . . . interposed and raised the strongest objection to the hand-shaking, stating that it was unusual, that it imparted vulgar and common-place realism to a great and lofty theme. He was very angry when I persisted in carrying out my views, and dubbed me "a young iconoclast." [150]

George Becks gives us a good idea of the minor excitements of a Forrest performance — minor, indeed, only since Forrest himself was absent from the stage. At

> O, I could play the woman with mine eyes
> And braggart with my tongue! —

Macduff "flings his hat down on the ground — draws his claymore and appeals to the heavens!" And at "Heaven forgive him too," he "rushes off. Mal picks up the bonnet" — thus doing for Macduff what Horatio used to do for Hamlet.[151]

The Sleepwalking Scene had been played by distinguished actresses before Mrs. Siddons established a new tradition, but how little we know of them! Of the distant Mrs. Betterton, for instance, and "those quick and careless Strokes of Terror" which marked her performance, or the much nearer Mrs. Pritchard, whom old-fashioned persons did not cease to extol even after the advent of her great successor! "It is difficult to perform this scene," writes Francis Gentleman in Bell's *Shakespeare* (1774), "she should speak in a low, anxious voice, keep moving slowly about, with fixed, glaring, open eyes, and horror-struck features." That is better than nothing, we say, but it is little enough, in all conscience. Or there is Samuel Jackson Pratt's amusing story, "The Distresses of a Father," which turns up more than once in periodical literature, after its first publication in *The Westminster Magazine*, January 1777.[152] "Delia Drama," the heroine, has in a regrettable moment been taken to see Mrs. Yates in *Macbeth*, and comes home stage-struck. Her father assures us he had no sooner given her her candle,

than she rose up, shut her eyes, held the light at arms-length, and began to rub her hand Lady Macbeth-like.

> "Yet here's a spot — Out damned spot!
> All the perfumes of Arabia will not sweeten
> This little hand."

Get away then, and wash it, said I, and be cursed to you, and don't put me in a passion. Here she sighed most bitterly,

> "Oh! Oh! Oh!"

Sometime after this she made towards the door, which I opened, and then she run side-long out of the room, still shutting her eyes, and cried

> "There's knocking at the gate;
> Go, go, go, go, go!
> Come, come, come, come, come!
> To bed, to bed, to bed, to bed, to bed!"

How closely Delia succeeded in copying Mrs. Yates — if she copied her at all — is indemonstrable, I am afraid. The side-long exit may be thought to savor of reality; but what of the closed eyes?

Two of Professor Bell's notes on Mrs. Siddons's business in the Sleepwalking Scene go far toward summing up the respects in which it differed from that of her predecessors. Of her entrance, he writes: "She advances rapidly to the table, sets down the light, and rubs her hand, making the action of lifting up water in one hand at intervals." And, again, while she spoke the words "One, two," she was "Listening eagerly." [153]

First of all, then, she set down the candle. Small as that detail may seem to us, it occasioned a great stir. Thus, *The European Magazine* for February 1785, asks: "When she sets down the candle, who does not perceive she varies from her predecessors only that her hands may be more at liberty to imitate the process of ablution? — *Artis est celare artem.*" And by the next month it had become to this critic "an error, which would be inexcusable in the youngest performer." The actress herself tells of how Sheridan had come into her dressing-room just before the performance (February 2, 1785):

> He told me he had heard with the greatest surprise and concern that I meant to act it ["the sleeping scene"] without holding the candle in my hand; and, when I urged the impracticability of washing out that "*damned spot*," with the vehemence that was certainly implied by both her own words, and by those of her gentlewoman, he insisted, that if I did put the candle out of my hand, it would be thought a presumptuous innovation, as Mrs. Pritchard had always retained it in hers.

Afterwards, she adds, he was converted, "and most ingenuously congratulated me on my obstinacy." [154] Mrs. Melmoth, playing Lady Macbeth in Philadelphia, March 17, 1806, to the Macbeth of Cooper, fared badly when she in turn set down the candle, *The Theatrical Censor* condemning the action (unaware seemingly of its origin) as one "ill calculated to maintain the audience in the belief that she was asleep." [155] A few months later, Washington Irving, in *Salmagundi*, ridiculed such insistence upon "points" by gravely assuring Mrs. Villiers that "she would have given a greater effect to the night-scene, if, instead of holding the candle in her hand, or setting it down on the table . . . she had stuck it in her night-cap." [156] Cumberland's Edition contains the direction, "*Enter Lady Macbeth, with a taper, R., which she places on the table, and slightly advances.*" A new tradition had been established. When Geneviève Ward made her *début* as Lady Macbeth, at the Theatre Royal, Manchester, October 1, 1873,

> an envious attempt was made to disconcert her, by leaving out the table on which the candle is to be set. . . . She saw this just at the moment of going on, and exclaimed, in despair, "Oh! what shall I

do? —" "You can drop it," was the taunting reply; but, seeing a three-legged stool in the wing, she quickly placed it where the table should have been, and was just out of sight in time as the curtain rose.[157]

Again, Mrs. Siddons was far more active, more vigorous, in all she did, than had been customary in this scene. Earlier actresses, Boaden writes,

rather *glided* than walked; and every other action had a *feebler* character than is exhibited by one awake. Their figure, too, was kept perpendicularly *erect*, and the eye, though open, studiously avoided motion. . . . Mrs. Siddons seemed to conceive the fancy as having equal power over the whole frame . . . she laded the water from the imaginary ewer over her hands — bent her body to listen to the sounds presented by her fancy, and hurried to resume the taper where she had left it, that she might with all speed drag her pallid husband to their chamber.[158]

There was, especially, her mode of rubbing, or washing, her hands — both words are used of Lady Macbeth, in the play. Deploring Mrs. Siddons's departure from custom in this matter —"she goes through all the process of washing in as great a degree as a washer-woman would with a tub before her"— *The Monthly Mirror* cites the opinion of "a gentleman well competent to judge," that Mrs. Pritchard "exhibited far more stupendous powers" in the Sleepwalking Scene — and she "kept her finger perpetually applied to the *'damned spot'*." [159] Leigh Hunt writes fastidiously of one further detail:

Mrs. Siddons's refinement was not on a par with her loftiness. We remember . . . when she washed her hand and could not get the blood off, she made "a face" in passing them [*sic*] before her nose, as if she perceived *a foul smell*. We venture to think that she should have shuddered and looked in despair, as recognizing *the stain on her soul*.[160]

As for her exit, "the great actress used, as it were, to *feel* for the light; that is, while stalking backwards, and keeping her eyes glaring on the house." [161]

The business of at least two later actresses, Helen Faucit and Adelaide Ristori, must be considered briefly before we leave Lady Macbeth. When Helen Faucit first played the part in 1842, Macready praised her for giving the idea of sleep, disturbed by fearful dreams, but still it was sleep. It was to be seen even in [her] walk, which was heavy and inelastic, marking the distinction — too often overlooked — between the muffled voice and seeming-mechanical motion of the somnambulist, and the wandering mind and quick fitful gestures of the maniac.

In other words, she was turning away from Mrs. Siddons —turning back, if you will, to the Pre-Siddons actresses who "rather *glided* than walked." Also, in Helen Faucit's performance, "the final flight to bed was weird and startling, wholly unlike the usual stilted exit." [162] Madame Ristori's exit was with a "ghostly repetition" of her earlier action of "urging Macbeth on before her." It came as climax to a prolonged piece of miming, which began during the asides of the Doctor and Gentlewoman —"What a sigh is there," etc. — as she seemed once more to be listening at Duncan's door, welcomed the murderer with a cry of joy, then, as if startled by the knocking, hurried him away. Like Mrs. Siddons, she had set down the candle on entering; and she simulated the act of taking up water in the palms of her hands as she washed them. Her walk, however, was slow and automaton-like, and she dragged her feet as if they were weighted down with lead. All the while, she breathed deeply — though, we are assured, without any "horrible and conventional gasping"— and kept her eyes wide open, not closing them throughout.[163]

Stage business is conditioned by personality and is inadequately described in words. Mrs. Langtry "made a quick exit . . . as if dragging off Macbeth." This, as we now know, was not what it was called at the time, "new business"; but as she employed it the effect was doubtless subtly different from what it had been before.[164] Geneviève Ward, too, "went through the whole scene without moving an eyelid"; Madame Bernhardt, too, ran from the stage; Lady Benson, too, breathed deeply[165]— it would be unprofitable to go on. Nor need we pause for the rarely acted second scene, in which the good and not very interesting legitimists, aided by England, made head against the usurper. Macbeth is being armed, in the third, and the lines themselves vividly reflect the process, just as they do in the later and perhaps greater arming scene in *Antony and Cleopatra* (IV, 4). Macbeth's order,

Come, put mine armour on. Give me my staff,

has at least from Kemble's time, and presumably from the beginning, been answered by Seyton's bringing him his truncheon
(until, that is, truncheons inexcusably went out of fashion —
Mantell still carried one) and a gentleman's bringing him his
armor.[166] By the late eighteen-sixties, "Seyton brings on to Mr
Forrest, Hat, Truncheon & Gloves which he hands to Mr F., on
motion." At "Seyton, send out" (line 49), "Seyton motions to
2nd officer, who exits . . . Seyton then puts on Mr Forrest's gloves
for him during speech," and, at "Bring it after me," "offers shield
& Axe" [167] — just what is "brought" does not seem to have been
determined by tradition. One more glimpse of this scene is
afforded in that fine essay of John Foster Kirk's, "Shakespeare's
Tragedies on the Stage," to which attention has been called more
than once in these pages. Kirk, in order to get for once "the
actor's point of view," asked Macready to be allowed to appear
as the Doctor, and Macready consented.

Macbeth, at my entrance, left the attendants . . . and, striding across
the stage with a step that seemed to shake the boards, stationed himself
so near me that all the lines in his face appeared to be magnified, like
those of a picture to the close gaze of a short-sighted man. In tones that
sounded like thunder,

he made his demands, "How does your patient, doctor," etc.

On receiving my disclaimer of . . . power, he turned his back upon me
. . . (and) strode back to have his armor buckled on, turning, in the
intervals of his stormy chidings, to direct some inquiry or splenetic
remark to me, and at last rushing off to meet the approaching foe.

It is worth noticing that the Doctor came on after the scene had
begun. The postponement of his entrance is as old as the Edinburgh 1753 edition, and a regular part of the acting tradition of
the play.[168] There is much to be said for it.

Macready made much of the literal coming of Birnam Wood.
In his dignified production of the play at Covent Garden, November 6, 1837, an "immense improvement was," we are told,
"the approach of the English Army, which really was a *moving
grove*, as if Birnham (*sic*) Wood had come to Duncinane (*sic*),

not as heretofore, a dozen men with small branches of laurel which did not half cover their faces." [169] Phelps's "1860" Prompt-book calls for "Troops behind openings, covered by boughs leaves, Laurels &c," and, at "your leavy screens throw down And show like those you are," "The Troops give a loud shout and discover themselves by throwing down the boughs." [170] Years later, it was asserted that Salvini "was the first actor who ever played Macbeth in Boston who literally followed out the stage direction. . . . Malcolm's army, amounting to about a dozen, came marching on, with large green branches in their hands." [171]

Between the two Birnam Wood scenes (v, 4 and v, 6), we have another devoted to Macbeth. Dame Madge Kendal's father remembered an effect of Edmund Kean's at the beginning of it:

> When Macbeth rushed on the stage and spoke, "Hang out our banners on the outward walls," he shouted the command in a voice like thunder. Suddenly he paused, dropped his double-handed sword to the ground and leaning on it, whispered, "The cry is still come, they come," at the same time seeming to become ashy grey with fear.[171a]

Good "Kean," whatever one thinks of it as business! Soon after comes the *"cry within of women"*— Lady Macbeth is dead and Macbeth can only brood on the meaningless "to-morrows" of our lives. And here occurs a curious discrepancy between two accounts of something which actors used to do by way of illustrating, or supplementing, Shakespeare's lines. The first is from a letter of FitzGerald's to Fanny Kemble (April 9, 1875): "Macready used to drop his Truncheon when he heard of the Queen's death, and stand with his Mouth open for some while — which didn't become him." The second is from an article called "Stage Trick," by "J. W. C.", in Tallis's *Dramatic Magazine*, June 1851. Here, classed with the hissing speech of the villain and "the low, doleful groan with which almost every actor preludes the soliloquies of Hamlet," we find:

> The fall of the royal truncheon from the hand of Macbeth, at the close of the famous reflective passage beginning with "She should have died hereafter;" a pretty little effective bit of stage trick studiously presented by three or four very distinguished actors I could name —

who perhaps remembered the dropping of Corporal Trim's hat in *Tristram Shandy*. Now FitzGerald was writing of old memories, whereas J. W. C.'s article came out only a few months after Macready's retirement. Moreover, I cannot help feeling that to drop your truncheon at "signifying nothing . . ." might be far more impressive than to do so at the earlier moment. But FitzGerald was almost certainly right. For, not only did Phelps introduce the same business at "The Queen, my lord, is dead," but also, both Davenport and the younger James W. Wallack who, we are told expressly, were here copying Macready. Charles Kean dropped his sword, not his truncheon, at "She should have died hereafter"; and, at the same words, Salvini sank into a chair and for an instant buried his face in his hands.[172] As for Forrest, if we are to believe a pungent review of Forster's, "he stalked about the stage rattling his truncheon at the 'To-morrow — and to-morrow — and to-morrow,' as if Macbeth should not at this speech stand rooted to the spot!" Another hostile critic refers to "the vibration of the tremulous truncheon . . . which he wields in Macbeth"— whatever that means! [173]

But we have not yet done with truncheons in this scene. In describing another employment to which they were sometimes put, I shall begin with two letters in *The St. James's Chronicle*. The earlier of these (unsigned) was printed in the issue of October 28–30, 1773. It concerns Macklin's Macbeth and is addressed to Garrick:

> The chief Applause which your unsuccessful Competitor either deserved or met with, arose from the Manner in which he received the Messenger who brought Word that *Birnam* Wood was in Motion. Instead of snapping the half-sawed Truncheon on the Caitiff's Elbow, *Macklin* seized his Arm, and bent him to the Ground in the Posture of vanquished *Jachimo*. . . .

"Eumenes" in the second letter (November 2–4) replies to this:

> The Gentleman has surely not seen Mr. Garrick act Macbeth these ten Years, else he could not have charged him with breaking a Truncheon upon a Messenger's Arm. This absurd Practice was humorously ridiculed by Mr. Murphy, in his Farce of the Apprentice. . . . There can be no Doubt that Mr. Garrick took the Hint from the Farce; for in his

late Representation of that Character, when the Messenger informed him of the Marching of Birnam Wood, he put his Hand upon his Sword, and, with a Look of Terror mixed with Dispondency, pronounced his Threat to him.

In Murphy's amusing play, produced in 1756, the father of the stage-struck hero cries: "Zookers! you Blockhead, you'd better stick to your Business, than turn Buffoon, and get Truncheons broke upon your Arm." [174] Kemble in his essay on *Macbeth and King Richard the Third* wrote strongly against Rowe's stage direction "*Striking him*" at "Liar and slave," finding it "irreconcileable to Macbeth's emotions at the moment." Then, employing a kind of evidence unfamiliar at the time, he urged that the absence of the direction in Davenant's alteration implies that neither the usage of Elizabethan actors nor that of Betterton "had invited its insertion." [175] Instead of striking the messenger, Kemble himself "staggered," and could barely ejaculate "Liar and slave!" [176] What Macready's own practice was, is less clear. Usually, I believe, he abstained from striking the man, but sometimes did. Charnock's Promptbook, used during Macready's Boston visit in 1826, crosses out the printed stage direction calling for the blow, and a critic in *Tallis's Dramatic Magazine*, November 1850, was impressed "as of old, by his terrific look and action, as he stands, half-drawing his sword, over the messenger." But there are stories concerning individual messengers whom he did strike, not without some provocation.[177] Forrest, after speaking "the terrible imprecation against the officer"— beginning "if thou speak'st true"— lifted him "bodily from the ground and fairly flung him off the stage." Barry Sullivan whirled a "great two-handed sword above his head," as he shouted "Liar and slave!" [178] In Irving's 1888 production, finally, one of the many illustrative details was the introduction of three soldiers staring "in through the door in a peeping attitude, with fright in their eyes, while their comrade . . . tells the King of the moving wood." More dignified, and quite as fully imagined, seems to me the arrangement at the Boston Museum by which the "Officer," after Macbeth has done with him — and he is not struck — "*goes up R. The others ask him the tidings eagerly*." [179]

A battle is waged during the concluding scenes, though as a rule one hears little about it in accounts of the play. Macklin, however, as his memoranda show, gave thought to it: to the weapons —"Bows and arrows," definitely, for the English, whatever the Scots finally got ("broad swords pistols Targets," was one idea) — and to the fluctuations of fortune:

> The fight must be so manoeuvred as to make the Scotch seem first to defeat the English & drive them off the stage — the English must beat them back and totally rout the Scotch. —
> English — Scotch, English
> Macbeth must appear in the front of the battle when the Scotch drives the English off.

More than a century later, Augustus Pitou, an American actor of wide experience, found pleasure in the battle as Irving staged it in London:

> The fighting was not all in sight of the audience; it seemed to be raging as fiercely off the stage in the distance. From every angle of sight the audience could see men fighting off the stage as well as on it. The distant clash of arms, the cries and cheers, and the rushing on and off the scene of fighting groups gave the illusion of a great battle.

"This appeal to the imagination," he adds, "was something new to me in stage management." [180] One further detail — for the battle itself is no more than a detail — before we come to Macbeth's meeting with Macduff. The Sadler's Wells Promptbooks make it clear that Phelps rushed down stage, at "Why should I play the Roman fool," and presented "his sword against his own breast" — in 1847 "sinking on his Knee," as well. I am afraid that this was his own invention.

As Macduff, Otis Skinner, "seeing Macbeth about to fly," dealt him "a down-swinging blow" with his heavy broadsword, and on one occasion nearly hurt Booth badly.[180a] Even on the printed page the combat which follows is almost uniquely dramatic. They fight and are interrupted, or pause. Macbeth's last hope fails him: those in whom he has trusted are "juggling fiends," and he will not fight with Macduff. Then, at thought of the indignities which will be meted out to him if he yields, he becomes himself once more.

Though Birnam Wood be come to Dunsinane —

the words have the ring of high courage, not merely of desperation. *"Exeunt fighting"* reads the Folio. But though Macbeth's death seems clearly to have taken place off-stage, and though his severed head is later brought in and shown, another stage direction — *"Enter Fighting, and Macbeth slaine,"* immediately following the *"Exeunt"* just quoted — may suggest, even so, that a change was made early in the play's history, and the fight fought out for all to see. So of course it has regularly been in later times, a furious encounter, to be ranked among stage combats only, perhaps, with that in *Richard III*, and leading up to Macbeth's death, usually as violent as possible, on the boards.

This interpolated death-scene need not, of course, be treated exhaustively. If the detailed description in Noverre's *Lettres sur la Danse, et sur les Ballets*, does indeed refer to it, as seems likely, Garrick carried realism to shocking lengths:

> *Il grattoit la terre, il creusoit en quelque façon son tombeau; mais le moment approchoit, on voyoit réellement la mort. . . il expiroit enfin; le hoquet de la mort & les mouvements convulsifs de la Physionomie, des bras et de la poitrine, donnoient le dernier coup à ce Tableau terrible.*[181]

Edmund Kean, after falling mortally wounded, crawled toward his sword (or, it might be, his dagger) and died as he touched it.[182] Forster tells of "the easy triumph" with which Macready's Macbeth "throws off his sword and talks of his charmed life; the agonised and hopeless despair with which he afterwards avoids [Macduff]; the fiend-like desperation with which he rushes back upon his weapon." Dying, he thrust his sword into the ground and, raising himself, glared into his enemy's face.[183] Barry Sullivan gloried in the contest and, after losing his sword, stabbed on with a dagger, which, at the last, stuck "harmlessly in the ground." Booth went even farther, "stabbing the air with his hand" — as Kean had done in *Richard III*. "On receiving the death-blow," he "reared himself for a moment in agony, and then plunged forward, dead, at the feet of his antagonist."[184] Irving, in 1888, was falling "face forwards, after dashing his dagger point

downwards at his antagonist's feet"— which could scarcely have
seemed unfamiliar. Later, however, he was conveying a sense of
Macbeth's growing recklessness — in other words, dramatizing
the fight. And he struck "wildly as one in whom only the desire
to strike . . . is left." [185]

After a perusal of such accounts as these, the showing of a mere
property head — a symbol, really, or not much more than that —
seems by comparison an almost chaste device. "Timothy Plain" in
his *Letters Respecting the Theatre Royal, Edinburgh*, writes on
April 14, 1800, of a recent performance "by a person assuming the
name of Langford," that in the last act

he adopted the original text, and went off fighting with Macduff, instead of giving us the dying speech introduced by Garrick — and if his
conqueror had also followed the author, by exhibiting his head upon a
pike, Melpomene would have had no cause to grieve on the occasion.[186]

The Theatrical Inquisitor, for November 1814, objects to the
retention of the dying speech, in Kean's representation: "The
bringing on the usurper's head upon a pole might not be much
better; perhaps it would be as well to substitute the crown and
regalia of royalty." Phelps made no such compromise when at
Sadler's Wells he restored the original ending. His 1847 Promptbook reads:

All the Forces — Macbeth's Head on a Pole borne by an Officer —
[&?] Flags of England & Scotland surrounding the head — Troops fill
the Stage characters down R & L — Macduff up Stage Centre pointing
to head — Malcolm in Front Centre back to audience.

The critics disagreed sharply as to the propriety of showing the
head[187]— and the business was not retained. The head itself "did
not look deathly," anyway; and "it was too small," and "bore no
facial resemblance to the actor." Phelps is to be commended, none
the less. As Westland Marston writes, "To relinquish the usual
close, in which the death of Macbeth in his desperate fight with
Macduff concentrates attention on the former, was a piece of self-
sacrifice, from an actor's point of view, that cannot well be over-

rated."[188] By contrast, Charles Kean's Edition has no dialogue after Macbeth's death. Instead Malcolm, re-entering, *"is raised on a shield in C. Shouts. Flourish."*[189] The shield was, I have no doubt, a shield "of the period"—and the ceremony, so much more interesting than forty lines more by William Shakespeare!

VI

The Other Tragedies

King Lear

THE POSSIBILITY, always fascinating, that Elizabethan stage business may have been perpetuated by means of tradition in some of
Shakespeare's plays is not so strong in the case of *King Lear* as in
that of the three tragedies already considered. *King Lear* as
Shakespeare wrote it was given at least once or twice between
1660 and 1681. We know next to nothing about these early
Restoration performances. Did Betterton play Lear? It appears
likely, but we cannot be certain that he did.[1] Nahum Tate's
notorious version flourished, after 1681, and there is no want of
continuity in the play's subsequent stage history down to, or for
that matter after, the revival of Shakespeare's original by Macready in 1838. But in Tate's *Lear*, be it remembered: "heart interest" is added in the form of a love affair between Edgar and Cordelia; there is a happy ending; and Shakespeare's Fool is omitted.
Furthermore, Shakespeare's language is villainously tampered
with — has endured "Tatification." Much of the business in
eighteenth and early nineteenth century performances has, as a
result of these changes, no real connection with Shakespeare's
tragedy and will not, of course, be discussed in the pages which
follow. On the other hand, it is noteworthy that a good deal of
stage business which accompanied the Shakespearean parts of
Tate's *Lear* lasted on after the restoration of the original. By the
same token, may not a similar carrying over of appropriate business, this time from Shakespeare's original, have occurred when
Tate's alteration was first acted? If Shakespeare's *Lear* had been

firmly established as an "old stock play" there would be little doubt of it.

When the King himself first speaks, it used to be literally from the throne, where he was seated as early as Colman's eighteenth century acting version. When, however, Shakespeare's text came to be used, a procession very often replaced the discovery. Irving, bringing up the rear of a long procession, is well pictured for us by Mr. Gordon Crosse:

> Here he comes down the steps, a striking figure with masses of white hair. He is leaning on a huge scabbarded sword which he raises with a wild cry in answer to the shouted greetings of his guards. His gait, his looks, his gestures, all reveal the noble, imperious mind already degenerating into senile irritability. . . .[2]

Instead of this sheathed sword, earlier Lears had often carried a stick. When Cooke, addressing Albany and Cornwall, cried "this coronet part between you," he had struck the coronet with his stick; and Forrest, who bore a long staff, had pointed out with it the boundaries of their new possessions on the map. Both map and coronet are of course indispensable properties. Kemble assigned "2 Gents." to look after each — later they usually fell to the custody of Pages. Booth, at "this coronet part between you," introduced the impressive, almost sacramental gesture of taking the crown from a Page and holding it *above the heads of Goneril, Regan, Albany and Cornwall, who kneel in front of throne*"; and Charles Kean, rising in anger, threw down the map as Kent asked courageously,

> Thinks't thou that duty shall have dread to speak
> When power to flattery bows? [3]

By this time, Lear had usually left his throne, descending "supported by Kent L. and Gloster R.," just before he addresses Cordelia. Kemble chose the moment wisely, since through this action the youngest daughter is appropriately distinguished from her sisters. Salvini's Lear, when Cordelia declined to make protestation of her love, "leaned backward on the throne and gazed at her in blank amazement." Irving was thought to have been too mild when, saying, "almost coaxingly,"

> Mend your speech a little,
> Lest it may mar your fortunes,

he put his arm about Cordelia's waist.[4]

That some at least of the directions in Rowe's *Shakespeare* may reflect stage usage in the early years of the eighteenth century, when the great Betterton was still alive, seems very probable. Thus, Lear's "*Laying his hand on his sword*," as, infuriated by Kent's defiance, he exclaims "O vassal! miscreant!" goes beyond the needs of a mere reader, determining as it does the kind of threatening action which accompanied the words. "Betterton's business," we say — with a fair chance of being right. Later Lears were more violent. In their promptbooks: Kemble, "attempting to draw his sword, is withheld by Albany . . . & Gloster"; Forrest "lets his staff fall — in trying to unsheath"; the younger J. W. Wallack "Seizes his sword from Physician — Alb R Corn L take hold of him & take the sword — he throws them off"; and Charles Kean "[? seizes] a battleaxe from Lord/James"— a supernumerary. In this last production, it may be added, Kent makes his exit "after shaking hands with one or two of the Lear Knights, who all extend their hands to him" — and "One to kiss Kent hand."

"Gloster Backwards" preceded Lear, in Forrest's performance, as the old monarch ceremoniously left the stage.[5] Just before this exit, Macready's Cordelia (Helen Faucit) had knelt and seized his mantle and for doing so was scolded in *John Bull:*

> We totally object to the usual stage affectation of kneeling to *Lear* when he exclaims,
>
> > "Therefore begone
> > Without our grace, our love, our benizon."
>
> *Cordelia* is fixed as a statue in her woe: she has no share, no art or part in effects.

But here she was only doing what earlier Cordelias had done when Tate's words were still spoken on the stage. "Then leave her, sir," Lear had said to Burgundy, "for by a father's rage, I tell you all her wealth. . . . Away!" and here, quite appropriately, Kemble in his edition had inserted the direction, "Cordelia *throws*

herself at King Lear's feet." [6] In Irving's sentimental treatment
of the same episode, Ellen Terry as Cordelia "hides her face in
the abandonment of grief while the royal train passes out, [and]
the Fool stoops with quick, reverent motion, and touches the hem
of her gown with his lips." The same business was used by Frederick Warde, who writes complaisantly that he "always had the
Fool present in the opening scene," listening to what went on,
and making "hardly suppressed gestures of protest and appeal." [7]
But to introduce the Fool here is to sacrifice, in great measure,
the effectiveness of his entrance, carefully prepared for by Shakespeare, in Scene 4.

With the entrance of Lear and his Knights, early in that scene,
there is again business to describe. From Ferrers's promptbook
we learn that in Kean's performance "The 16 Knights always form
near & at the 2EL so as to give the idea of the hundred being
placed in continuation." Wallack has "4 Super Knights" cross
the stage "bearing a buck" before the appearance of the King,
who now carries a spear. Charles Kean saw to it that his knights
were listening attentively. When, later in the scene, Goneril
refers to them as

> Men so disorder'd, so debosh'd, and bold,

"Knts turn slowly & look at each other in intense surprise," and,
when she suggests that some of them be discharged, "Knts
indign[antly] strike their spears on stage."

Hackett criticizes Forrest's business at the moment when Kent
mentions the "authority" in Lear's face which he "would fain call
master":

> Mr. Forrest paused here some seconds, wagged his head about and
> smiled very significantly as though *Lear's* vanity was particularly
> pleased that his features had indicated to a poor-service-beggar, an
> *autocratic rule* — one to which *Lear* (be it remembered!) had been
> born, ever been used, and then had never yet had disputed.

Speaking the same word, "authority," McCullough's Kent "takes
off hat"— a good and seemly thing for him to do. Oswald, on the
contrary, "generally enters the stage," says Davies, "in a careless
disengaged manner, humming a tune, as if on purpose to give

umbrage to the King . . ." and with Forrest he eyed him "from top to toe before speaking." [8]

Tate had Oswald brought back by Kent — and the idea is not without a superficial appeal. Of course, the actor made the most of his chances. In Kemble's marked copy of *King Lear*, "Kent throws Oswald over to the King"; in Forrest's promptbook, "Kent swings him roughly to C & then knocks his hat off"; and in Wallack's promptbook — for this bit of business lasted on after the restoration of the original play —"Kent pulls him on by the Ears." But, once more, this was to anticipate what should be a far happier moment.

Lear. Do you bandy looks with me, you rascal?
　　　　　　　　　[*Strikes him.*
Osw. I'll not be strucken, my lord.

Whereupon, Kent, coming forward just when we were forgetting him: "Nor tripp'd neither, you base football player? [*Trips up his heels.*]" Irving's prolonged rehearsing of this episode, his insistence that Oswald be tripped "on the right syllable of the right word" (the first syllable of "neither") and that the tripping be accomplished by means of "a very slight motion" of Kent's "right foot (chiefly the toe part of the said foot)" was described at some length in Gordon Craig's book, *Henry Irving* (1930). Mr. Bernard Shaw in *The Observer*, October 26, 1930, took exception to what he considered Irving's waste of time "over the trumpery business of tripping up the steward" and the "torturing" of the actor involved — a deliberate breaking of his nerve — and was answered in turn by Sir John Martin-Harvey.[9] It may be added that Oswald (the character, not the actor) has often suffered further indignity on his exit. Here Theobald supplied a direction for Kent to push him out — which may have been Shakespeare's intention. In Kemble's marked copy, "Kent pursues Oswald with his Staff, till he is off the Stage," and in Forrest's promptbook the Steward is beaten and goes out crying "Help! Help!" [10]

Lear's great moment, with the old actors, was the cursing of Goneril —

Hear, Nature, hear! dear goddess, hear!

Tate shifted the position of the speech, so that in his version it
concluded the first act; and after Shakespeare had come into his
own again — as far as mere words are concerned — it was not
always replaced where it belongs by Phelps, by Booth, or even by
Irving. Until quite recent years, it was spoken kneeling. Aaron
Hill, in blaming an actor of his own time (1735) for coldness, tells
of his advancing deliberately "to the Lamps in Front of the Pit,"
where he knelt and, "with elevated Eyes, and Arms," pronounced
the terrifying words "with the *Calmness*, and *the Reverie of a*
PRAYER." [11] The same action, though now introduced with no
want of passion, accompanied Garrick's delivery of the speech.
In *An Examen of the New Comedy, Call'd the Suspicious Husband* (1747), Garrick himself is addressed:

> You fall precipitately upon your Knees, extend your Arms — clench
> your Hands — set your Teeth — and with a savage Distraction in your
> Look — trembling in all your Limbs — and your Eyes pointed to Heaven
> . . . begin . . . with a *broken, inward, eager* Utterance; from thence
> rising every Line in Loudness and Rapidity of Voice,

and at last "bursting into Tears." [12] Whether Garrick might not
have been too deliberate in his whole treatment of the speech was
sharply debated.[13] Davies, in his well-known description of the
great actor in this scene, adds the point that he threw away his
"crutch" as he knelt. Bannister is quoted as remarking of Garrick
that his "very stick acted." [14]

In cursing their Gonerils, later Lears regularly did as Garrick
had done. Kemble, after throwing away both his hat and stick
(they were picked up later by the First Gentleman), came to the
front, knelt, "strongly clasped" his hands, and strained his eyes
upwards.[15] Cooke, too, got rid of his hat and stick before kneeling with tottering limbs. Kean, kneeling, "lifted up his arms"
and "threw his head quite back," as did Macready, whose action
was so like Kean's that *The Theatrical Journal*, in describing it,
quietly borrowed from Hazlitt's account of the earlier actor.
Charles Kean flung down a hunting spear, instead of a staff, but
he too knelt; [16] and Forrest struck his brow and beat his breast

before casting away the staff and falling on his knees. He was criticized (by Forster) for not throwing his head "completely back," as Edmund Kean had done; and his quivering limbs and palsied head did not pass unridiculed. Hackett writes that he shook "from head to toe" like one suffering from "what is called St. Vitus's Dance." [17] At last, in January 1883, Salvini broke with the tradition. Instead of kneeling, he "seemed to wander about the stage without control. It was very grand," writes the critic of *The Boston Herald*, "it was thrilling, but we think a more powerful effect would have been produced had he concentrated his effect more upon the object of his wrath." Garrick's business was still being followed to the letter by William E. Sheridan (an "actor of the old school") in Philadelphia the following December, when it seemed to Charlotte Porter "rather a trick to effect admiration than a means to compel emotion." [18]

Such was the concentration of interest upon Lear that Goneril whom he was cursing is seldom remembered. But in Forrest's promptbook Becks notes that she "is very much agitated during curse and at the End Shrieks & rushes to Lear imploringly who throws her off — She falls into Albanys arms & faints — Ladies & pages cluster round her"; and in a description of Irving's perform-ance it was observed that Goneril might well "shrink from the old man kneeling in the centre of the throng, and after a harrow-ing shriek hide her face in her husband's shoulder." [19]

In Act II, Scene 2, Oswald, according to Kemble's markings, "sidles round from L. to R. to avoid Kent, who still pursues him," as he bids him draw and defend himself.[20] Becks, who had him-self played Oswald, adds several details here. At "I care not for thee," the Steward "fillips." Kent, however, soon "backs him to L Corner"; "gives him a blow X chest," a little later, and "another slap" when he bids him draw. It must always have been a satisfac-tion to see the wretch well beaten! When (in Wallack's prompt-book) Kent is interrupted by the entrance of other characters, he "chases Oswald round stage . . . Oswald runs into LH Cor." Phelps's promptbook reads here: "N.B. Directly the characters are on — Oswald draws his sword and vapours about." Robert Ganthony tells an anecdote to illustrate what he calls "the fanati-

cal adherence to old business on the stage which characterised
the management in the provinces a few years back." While he
was playing at Birmingham soon after Charles Calvert's death
(in 1879) he got into trouble with a conservative stage manager
there:

> When Kent says of Oswald, "His countenance likes me not [line 96],"
> I made the coxcomb Oswald look at himself in his sword blade to see
> what was the matter. I don't reason out a character, but, by becoming
> familiar with what he says, become that character, and this action was
> what I felt, as Oswald, that he would do.[21]

The business was new, no doubt, but it was also fussy, and not too
readily comprehensible, I should think, to an audience, and my
sympathies are wholly on the side of the stage manager.

Francis Gentleman writes, in *The Dramatic Censor* (1770),
that he had seen Oswald "make a very pantomimical stroke, by
pushing at Kent when his legs are fast" in the stocks: "such a
manœuvre cannot fail of causing laughter, but are such violations
of the finer feelings sufferable?" And, returning to the same
"strange piece of buffoonery," in his notes to Bell's *Shakespeare*
(1774), he concludes that "it is beneath an actor of merit to adopt
it." [22] Kemble, however, as his copy of *Lear* shows, still allowed
it — "Oswald remains on the Stage, to indulge in a few vapouring
anticks with Kent, and then follows Gloster into the Castle."
Phelps, employing similar business at Sadler's Wells in 1861, has,
in his promptbook, "Oswald struts up to Kent. mockingly — Kent
aims a blow at him with his quarterstaff — Oswald runs into
Castle"; in the Booth-Winter Edition, "*Oswald approaches
Kent with drawn sword; Kent strikes at him; Oswald runs into
castle*"; and the wretch's hardihood reaches its lowest ebb in
Barrett's manuscript copy of McCullough's promptbook, where
the scene ends, "Business of Oswald, when Kent throws his cap
at him." [23]

One further instance of the painstaking attention which Kemble
gave to detail occurs in the fourth scene. "*Kent here set at liberty,*" the Folio reads, just after Cornwall and Regan, summoned
by Lear, have at last appeared. This direction might do for a
reader, scarcely for an actor. "Cornwall signs to the Captain, and

the Captain to the Guards: — they set Kent at liberty" (in Kemble's own copy of *King Lear*) is at once practical and ceremonious. More exciting is a notice of George Frederick Cooke's recent *Lear* in the Philadelphia *Mirror of Taste and Dramatic Censor*, for August 1811. Cooke had not satisfied the critic at one point — the reply of Lear to Regan's suggestion that he return to Goneril and "ask her forgiveness" —

> Do you but mark how this becomes the house:
> "Dear daughter, I confess that I am old.
> > [*Kneels.*]
> Age is unnecessary. On my knees I beg
> That you'll vouchsafe me raiment, bed, and food."

Here "all the living actors vary from their predecessors" by addressing the speech to Regan, "as if it was a serious petition to her," whereas,

the bare proposition is at once so insulting and so ludicrous, so replete with turpitude and folly, that the old king is filled with a compound of real anger and affected levity, in which he has recourse to the practical trope of falling on his knees, in order to mark to all around the abject degradation to which Regan's advice would incite him. Thus Barry, thus Mossop and Sheridan, thus Henderson, and, of course, thus Garrick read it.

The critic, said to be S. C. Carpenter, had seen all of these great early actors.

"Nor do we know," he continues, "one passage in the whole play, the curse itself not excepted, which had so piercing an effect upon the audience.

> Ask her forgiveness? — [*to Regan.*

Then turning round to all the attendants, Henderson, soliciting their attention, said, in a tone of solemnity,

> Do *you* but mark how this becomes the house. . . .

Then taking off his hat, and, when he kneeled, dropping it and his cane on the ground, in a tone of biting irony directed to Regan, he affectedly said,

> Dear daughter, I confess that I am old:
> Age is unnecessary, &c.

And having said it rose hastily, filled with resolution as well as rage." [26]

In passing, a variation on the same business, this time from Wallack's promptbook, may be noted: "As Lear is about to Kneel — Regan runs to him — prevents him & speaks quickly."

Another opportunity for manhandling Oswald was found, on the Steward's re-appearance later in the scene. "Out, varlet, from my sight!" Lear cries, and Kemble's printed stage direction is "*Strikes* Oswald." To this, in his marked copy, he added: "Oswald turns off, and runs away, crying out, R.U.E. — as he goes Kent gives him a hint of their acquaintance." Cooke's promptbook is even more specific: "Oswald is tripping past the King when Lear strikes him on the stomach & Oswald rushes into the Castle." Similar business lasted for a long time. In Wallack's promptbook, Oswald "Scoots off." [25]

Macready's "noble conception of shame as he *hides his face* on the arm of Goneril," saying,

> I'll go with thee.
> Thy fifty yet doth double five and twenty,
> And thou art twice her love   [line 261],

was considered by Forster his greatest moment in the whole second act — one "surpassing . . . in deep simplicity as well as agony of pathos." [26] At Goneril's brutal question, "What should you need of more? / Yea, or so many?" the same actor took off his hat and threw it on the ground. I see no particular objection to this piece of business, but it inherits once more from an earlier time when Tate's text was still used. Then, Lear had thrown down his hat, and Kent had taken it up, for the good and sufficient reason that in the next scene Kent was to make a great to-do over the King's refusal

> to 'bide
> This poor slight Cov'ring [the hat] on his aged head.

Wallack, who followed Macready in preferring Shakespeare to Tate, again threw down the hat, and "Kent picks up Lear's hat." [27]

At the end of the act, Garrick was criticized by Theophilus Cibber for dropping, "almost lifeless, into the Arms of his Attendants." What was more, they did not carry him off.

Relaxed as we may suppose his whole Machine — (for his Head and
Body are both thrown extravagantly behind, as if his Neck and Back
were broke) yet his Knees (which in Nature, would most likely falter
first) are still so able to support him, in that odd-bent Condition, that
he walks off.

With the restoration of the original play, Macready here leaned
his head upon the Fool's shoulder — "O fool, I shall go mad!" So,
too, did Booth, who made the action at once "very simple" and
deeply moving, and Irving, who, falling "upon the shoulders of
the Fool," sobbed aloud.[28]

When, in the first of the three Storm Scenes (iii, 2), Lear con-
sents to go with Kent to the hovel, Wallack's promptbook has the
direction, "As Lear Xs towards L— Kent places a cloak over his
shoulders," thus doing for his master what Horatio has often done
for Hamlet at the end of the Ghost Scene. Salvini, presumably at
the same moment in the play, chose rather to emphasize Lear's own
solicitude for another, by taking off his cloak and sharing it with
the "poor fool and knave" for whom he could still feel pity.[29]

Tate ran together Scenes 4 (in front of the hovel) and 6 (within
the farmhouse), and this arrangement, together with the woeful
absence of the Fool, will make the scenes difficult to treat. Thus,
to take a single instance, Edgar's "throwing out Straw" from the
hovel, before speaking, is no longer useful when the Fool has already entered the hovel and is about to rush out of it in a panic.[30]
On the other hand, "strikes on diff^t sides with his staff," a prompt
note of George Frederick Cooke's time, might still accompany
Edgar's "There could I have him now — and there — and there
again — and there!" though it may be that he is merely catching
vermin. Booth's Lear, asking

> Is it the fashion that discarded fathers
> Should have thus little mercy on their flesh?

drew "*a thorn, or wooden spike, from Edgar's arm*" and in his
madness attempted to "*thrust it into his own*" — an act which
Edgar prevented by seizing his hand.[31] A little further on, Lear
refuses to take shelter until he has talked "with this philosopher,"
and here Cooke's promptbook has them sit down, as no doubt they

should, and Lear "takes the straw from his [Edgar's] budget." This straw — sometimes Edgar wore a coronet of it — has long been a source of fascination to Lear. Foote would have Garrick's representation of madness kept within the bounds of dignity: "Every Motion, every Look, should express an Extravagance of State and Majesty; and when mad *Tom* is consulted as a learned *Theban*: *Lear* should not . . . pull his Rags, play with his Straws." [32] A further detail, from Wallack's promptbook, is wholly logical. "Let me ask you one word in private," Lear says to Edgar — then "whispers in his ear," and presently "Lear Laughs."

Early in Scene 6, when Edgar in his feigned madness says, "Frateretto calls me, and tells me Nero is an angler in the lake of darkness," he may well put his ear to the ground, as he did in Macready's time. In pretending to drive away the dogs which Lear fancies are barking at him — "Tom will throw his head at them. Avaunt, you curs!" — Edgar used to fling either his hat or his straw head-dress at them.[33] Then, when he says, "Come, march to wakes and fairs and market towns. Poor Tom, thy horn is dry," Forrest's promptbook has: "Marches like a soldier X Stage to L stops at horn — holds it up & says sorrowfully — 'is Dry'."

At the end of the scene, Lear is carried out, by Kent, it would seem, and the Fool; though on the stage servants have sometimes been introduced as bearers, not without dramatic loss. Charles Kean employed a litter here — one historically correct, I make no doubt — and Kemble thought of having Gloster bring a "Roquelaure," in which the King was wrapped forthwith. Macklin, by the way, had objected to the sleeping episode as "one of Shakespeare's weak redundancies" and had suggested that Garrick retained it only because "he knew that Barry, on account of his size, could not be carried off the Stage with the same ease that he could." Yet many persons wept at "the sad tableau" of Lear's exit when Irving produced the tragedy.[34]

I have no stage business relating to the scene in which Gloster is blinded. In the Bridges-Adams production, I remember, no attempt was made to hide its brutality, but, wisely, it was played with the utmost swiftness; one had scarcely time to shudder before it was over.[35] In Act IV, Scene 1, Gloster of course has his eyes bandaged. Presently, he bids the Old Man leave him alone with poor Tom, and Forrest's promptbook has the queer direction, "Edgar marches & tramps & watches Gloster: that he may Know." What? "Where he is," I suppose, since the line just before is slightly changed in Tate's version, reading:

Gloster.　　Where is the lunatic?
Old Man.　　Here, my lord.

As for Gloster's attempted suicide, a discreet compromise was usually made, in nineteenth century performances, with the plain implications of Shakespeare's lines. It involved, to be sure, a good deal of cutting. Gloster plunges forward, or is about to plunge forward, when Edgar catches him, and at the same moment Lear enters to interrupt them.[36] More helpful is a bit of business just before this. As Edgar bids his father farewell, he "*seems to go,*" according to Rowe, and how this was done is clearly explained in Forrest's promptbook, where after retiring a little way Edgar "stamps stick on ground then creeps back again." Phelps's book is only a shade less explicit: "makes noise as if walking away."

Like Ophelia's flowers, the "idle weeds," the "hardocks, hemlock, nettles, cuckoo flow'rs," with which Lear was crowned, become straws. Lear's "straw-made crown" was already, by Garrick's time, a famous property.[37] Addressing Garrick, the author of *The Examen of the New Comedy, Call'd the Suspicious Husband* (1747) is at pains to justify the employment of straws. Lear, he writes,

takes the Weeds for his Regalia, and therefore makes a Crown of them; . . . and therefore he may very naturally fancy a Handful of Straw his Scepter; and this is the Use you make of it. . . . You throw yourself into many various Attitudes of Command, and tho' you have Straw in your Hand, yet we very plainly see, that you take it for a *Scepter, Bow, Gauntlet,* &c. as the different Ideas rise in your Imagination.[38]

Kemble, too, had "a Sceptre of Straw," as well as "a straw crown as large, massive, and elaborately constructed as a bee-hive." Cooke accomplished much with the "straw in his hand," paying money with it and presenting it as the "challenge" which he would have Gloster read — "mark but the penning of it." [39] Forrest, who delighted in the now familiar regalia, "forgot," we are told, "the delusions of his madness," and when he spoke "the noble lines on Sin in the rich and poor . . . pointed with a straw at the words 'A pigmy straw will pierce it'." Phelps's "delivery of —

'Every inch a King'

was superb; at each word he rises his form higher, and waves the straw around his head." Booth, too, is praised for "the fashion in which he played with his straw sceptre." [40] And once more the break comes with Salvini. Henry James found his reply to Gloster's inquiry, "Is't not the King,"

a wonderfully bold piece of business. He stares for a moment . . . while he takes in the meaning of the question; then, as a pang of recollection comes over him, he rushes to a neighboring tree, tears off a great twig, grasps it as a sceptre, and, erecting himself for a moment in an attitude intended to be royal, launches his majestic answer. . . . I do not say that this touch will commend itself to every taste. Many people will find it too ingenious, and feel that the noble simplicity of the words is swallowed up in the elaboration of the act. But it produces a great effect.[41]

The ghostly influence of the execrable Tate affects still another piece of business — a clever stroke of Edwin Booth's a little later in this scene. "I will preach to thee," Lear says; but after making a beginning,

When we are born, we cry that we are come
To this great stage of fools . . .

he breaks off:

This' a good block.
It were a delicate stratagem to shoe
A troop of horse with felt.

As Kittredge notes, "the action here is left to the discretion of the actor." Wallack's Lear went over to Gloster and took his hat. Irving's Lear preferred Edgar's. But Tate had shifted the lines beginning "This' a good block," so that in his version they immediately precede Lear's mad exit, at

Then kill, kill, kill, kill, kill, kill!

Forrest as Lear with Straw Sceptre
(From an engraving after a photograph by Brady)

This re-arrangement persisted after two centuries, and in Booth's acting text the allusion to the hat follows these lines:

Lear. Come, come, I am a king.
Gentleman. You are a royal one, and we obey you.

"*Curan* [Shakespeare's *Gentleman*] *and attendants uncover and fall back.*" Lear's eye is attracted by the hat which one of them removes. Taking Curan's hat, he says, "This' a good block. . . ." Winter praises the business as "unique and skilful," which of course it is — but not in the least Shakespearean.[42]

Irving's " 'scuttle' from the stage," writes a critic in the *Liverpool Daily Post*, "is such an exit — so scared, so eccentric, so simply lunatic — as probably no other actor would dare"; and Mr. Gordon Crosse remembers "the shambling run of his exit" as "the most heart-rending moment of the play." [43] Gloster, left alone with Edgar, is presently attacked by the Steward. Mr. Granville-Barker has argued that Edgar's " 'Chill pick your teeth, sir,' suggests that he stabs him, either with a knife he wears, or, possibly, with Oswald's own dagger, wrested after a tussle"; and something very like this was in fact done in Forrest's performance, where "Edgar closes with Oswald & wrests his sword from him — (throwing his Staff up Stage —) & stabs him." [44] The body is well looked after in Bell's edition by Edgar's drawing "*the Steward off the stage.*" If the text is not cut, Gloster's lines, "The King is mad," etc. thus become a covering soliloquy, and Edgar will return with the effectively abrupt "Give me your hand. . . ." [45]

"*Enter Lear in a chaire carried by Servants*" is a Folio direction in the last scene of this act. But Tate has him discovered "*a Sleep on a Couch,*" and Tate's way prevailed. Garrick's kneeling to Cordelia was a memorable point in his performance, as was "the simplicity of his saying, 'Be these tears wet? — yes, faith,' putting his finger on the cheek of Cordelia, and then looking at his finger," which O'Keefe found "exquisite." [46] Irving's Lear, having gently touched Cordelia's wet cheek — Ellen Terry shed real tears — carried his finger to his lips; and, at the end, this Cordelia went "supporting and protecting the feeble old man," who clung to her.[47] "They lead him to L. H." is a note in Cooke's promptbook, "he turns round & pats Cordelia's Cheek." Kean's Lear, speaking

> For (as I am a man) I think this lady
> To be my child Cordelia,

had "staggered faintly into Cordelia's arms, and his sobs of tender-ness, and his ecstasy of joy commingled" drew tears from the audience. And Booth, "sitting in his bed . . . folds her round in his arms . . . and rocks her from side to side," sobbing as he does so.[48]

When Macready staged the judicial combat between Edgar and Edmund, "the soldiers in an instant formed the lists with their spears and banners in a most picturesque manner; which elicited great applause." At Sadler's Wells, under Phelps, "as the Herald enters the front rank face about and march to form single file," and "at the first sound of the trumpet the soldiers form a chevaux de freze with their spears. . . . When Edmund falls into the arms of Herald — Soldiers recover arms." It was Kemble's idea to have the Herald — and the Trumpeter — catch Edmund as he falls. Some-one will do well to support the dying villain since he has much still to say.[49]

In 1823, Kean tried playing Shakespeare's last scene, instead of Tate's, and entered with Cordelia dead in his arms. Then, saying "She's gone forever," he knelt on his right knee and placed her across his left, laying her *on the ground, and kneeling on both knees,* a little before the entreaty, "Pray you undo this button," which he spoke *placing his hand to his throat, as if choaking.*[50] Phelps's business cannot have been very different. Morley speaks of his "nursing and rocking of the body of Cordelia" and "the ten-derness with which he lays her down, as for an instant, while he lifts his hands to the throat in which the last convulsive throe of death is rising," as also of "his quiet death, with his eyes, his point-ing hands, and his last words directed to her lips." Salvini, instead of lifting Cordelia, entered dragging her "with exhausted force and painful effort, as a weak old man must bear a lifeless body."[51]

Two stage properties, called for in Booth's typescript prompt-book at "The Players," are a "Piece of rope with hangman knot in it for Cordelia," and a "Feather for Kent." Booth's "catching and playing, in his half-witless grief, with the rope's end dangling from

Cordelia's neck" was a grim detail in his performance. Irving, too, toyed vacantly with the rope, as if "half-awed, half-puzzled." [52] "This feather stirs; she lives!" It had been an imaginary feather with Forrest; whereas "one of the finest effects" Oscar Wilde had "ever seen on the stage was Salvini, in the last act of *Lear*, tearing the plume from Kent's cap and applying it to Cordelia's lips." Booth, he continues, "plucked, I remember, some fur from his archæologically incorrect ermine for the same business." [53] What, then, of the property-man's "Feather for Kent"? Perhaps, a change had been made here; perhaps Booth's property man had been negligent? Even promptbooks are not infallible guides to what actually happens on the stage.

Lear's death, in comparison with that of other Shakespearean heroes, is quiet and almost painless. Macready, we learn from *The Theatrical Journal*, October 31, 1840, "does not fall suddenly to the ground, as though the tyrant had come quickly on him, but sinks slowly back, as though nature, completely exhausted, gave way without a struggle." Phelps and even Forrest died so. Wallack, according to his own promptbook: "Falls with head to R— Edgar & Alb make a step towards him as he falls. Kent gets behind the bodies & extending his arms keeps them off." At Sadler's Wells, the curtain was rung down "as Characters groupe round Lear. Roll of Muffled Drums. Soldiers & Officers lower their weapons"; and at the Lyceum the crowds of barbaric soldiers stood with bent heads, pointing their spears toward the dead King.[54]

Romeo and Juliet

The Restoration stage history of *Romeo and Juliet* is not unlike that of *King Lear*. Again, we hear of the play not long after the reopening of the theatres — Pepys saw and disliked it on March 1, 1662 — again, an alteration is produced, this time by Otway in 1679–1680, which drives the original from the boards. There is less certainty, however, as to the form in which the tragedy was acted in the early Restoration years — Downes refers to an alteration even then by one of the Howards — and Otway's *Caius Marius* contains less Shakespeare than Tate's *Lear*. On the other hand, the troublesome vogue of the former play was not prolonged to anything like the same extent, and *Romeo and Juliet*, only mildly adapted, was being given again by the middle of the eighteenth century.

Irving, in 1882, used local color in abundance at the beginning of the play. His donkeys and children are, however, like his "sloping bridge" and "picturesque conduit," scarcely our concern here. When the fighting got under way, Bram Stoker writes, many persons,

> mostly apprentices of the Capulet faction, entered, at first slowly, but coming quicker and quicker till quite a mass had gathered on the hither side of the bridge. The strangers were being easily worsted. Then over the bridge came a rush of the Montagues armed like their foes with sticks or swords according to their degree . . . and for a few minutes such a scene of fighting was enacted as I have never elsewhere seen on the stage.[55]

In the production designed by Lewis Wingfield for Mary Anderson, two years later, the quarrel had become "a regular insurrection," with "windows opening and the alarmed inhabitants looking out, etc." ("A matron recognizes with a shriek her husband in one of the victims, and the guards carry away the bodies of other victims.")[56] More clearly within the field of our present interests are two pieces of business, a little further on. The first is thoroughly melodramatic. Charlotte Cushman's promptbook (1852) ends the scene with the Prince's exit: "Flourish / Exit Prince and train C others / are following him. At the top / Tybalt and Benvolio encounter / each others glances. They each draw / their swords and remain in attitude / Shut in on Picture." The second, from Rossi's acting edition (c. 1881), explains naturally the sudden change which comes into Romeo's voice, as he says:

> Alas that love, whose view is muffled still,
> Should without eyes see pathways to his will!
> Where shall we dine? *O me! What fray was here?*

For he has noticed on the ground — swords and cloaks.[57]

There is little more of importance until we come to the meeting of the lovers. At Sadler's Wells, Peter, who is of course the stupid

"Servant" entrusted with the list of guests, "bows ad libetum [*sic*]" before leaving Romeo and Benvolio, in the second scene. And when Romeo comes to "Rosaline" among those invited to Capulet's feast, he "unperceived kisses the name" — a detail borrowed, or happened upon independently, by Irving, many years afterwards.[58] Early in the next scene, that of the Nurse's reminiscences, Lady Capulet says:-

> Nurse, give leave awhile,
> We must talk in secret. Nurse, come back again;
> I have rememb'red me, thou's hear our counsel.

At "in secret," the Cushman promptbook notes: "Nurse is going sulkily away L appears much pleased when she is recalled." She speaks of Susan —

> Susan and she (God rest all Christian souls!)
> Were of an age. . . .

Mr. Oliver Elton recalls of the famous Angelica, Mrs. Stirling, at the Lyceum, that here she lowered her voice, spoke absently, and crossed herself." As the scene ends, Juliet is likely to be kind to the Nurse, leading her fondly out (Phelps), or turning back to assist her (Cushman). Mary Anderson did something new. "When the servant announces the arrival of the guests, dance music is faintly heard from the hall beyond," and, "catching the sound of this music," Juliet's eyes "kindle gradually" and she "makes a little dance movement with her feet as she follows her mother to the ball." [59]

The action leading up to the begging and giving of the kiss is not too easy to follow. When Romeo first notices Juliet she would seem to be dancing — with Paris, no doubt — and, "the measure done" (she says), he will "watch her place of stand." Tybalt's threatening and Capulet's scolding may cover some such happening as Juliet's dropping her fan and Romeo's handing it to her, as in Madame Modjeska's performance,[60] though that is a little commonplace. Romeo "would not dance," it is noted later. The kiss is not, then, merely part of the ritual of their dancing together. In Cumberland's acting edition (1829), Romeo "*goes and sits by*

Juliet," just before the "pilgrim" speech, then leads her "*from her chair towards* C." Phelps's promptbook has them exit, separately, during the asides of Tybalt and Capulet, and return together — how they had met being left to the imagination. It may be added that Irving's Romeo looked first for Rosaline:

> Once found she is the cynosure of his rapt gaze. But presently, as if in fatigue, he turns listlessly from this wistful melancholy contemplation, and then and there is, as it were, struck statue-like by the beauty and charm of the unknown girl.[61]

Of a performance at the Globe with Otis Skinner and Adelaide Moore, *The Athenaeum* notes, June 21, 1890: "Among the restorations which are judiciously made are the kisses bestowed in Act 1 ... by Romeo upon the lips of Juliet, which modern squeamishness has constantly excised." There seems little doubt that for a long time Juliet was not kissed on the lips. The "pilgrim" speeches are, in such representative acting editions as Bell's, Kemble's, and French's, a good deal cut, and Romeo's last line, as it now runs,

> Thus then, dear saint, let lips put up their prayers,

implies no more than that he is about to kiss her hand. Some verses, too, "*Written after seeing Miss* F. H. Kelley, *in the Character of* Juliet," point to the same comparatively decorous action:

> I mark'd her tremulous hope, and fear
> At the Masquerade, when her lover drew near:
> And the downcast glance, and the smile of bliss,
> When her hand received the "Palmer's kiss. . . ."

But Rossi had certainly kissed his Juliet "fully on the mouth" as early as 1876.[62]

Fanny Kemble's manner of receiving "the parting salutations of the guests" was admired. Her "first curtsy" was merely to Benvolio. Her second, to Mercutio — whom Garrick had substituted for the unknown "Petruchio" — was "distinctly marked, as though in him she recognized the chosen friend of Romeo." And "in the third" there was a "bashful sinking of the whole figure" and a "conscious drooping of the eyelids," followed by "the hurried, yet graceful recovery of herself as she exclaims —

> 'Who's he that follows there that would not dance?' "

How, by the way, Angelica knows —

> His name is Romeo, and a Montague —

needs no explaining save to the literal-minded. But Kemble had
her leave the stage for an instant, at "Go ask his name," and Phelps
introduced "3 Musicians," who are on their way out when "stopped
by Nurse, who whispers them." [63] "If he be married," Juliet continues, as she waits for the answer,

> My grave is like to be my wedding bed.

And as Adelaide Neilson's gaze "followed the vanishing *Romeo*
she suddenly raised her left hand and kissed the spot that he, a
moment earlier, had kissed, in parting from her." [64] Of an earlier
Juliet, Miss O'Neill, we read that she seemed

rivetted to the ground, and wholly absorbed in the idea of him who
has left her. In vain the garrulous nurse interrupts her reverie; still
fixed to the pleasing spot, she remains till her loquacious attendant
drags her away. Even then her eye is seen to look to the door through
which he past.[65]

Shortly after Miss Nossiter, a *protégée* of Barry's, made her
début at Covent Garden (October 10, 1753), an anonymous *Letter*
was addressed to her, which contains the earliest detailed criticism
we possess of an actress as Juliet. Its terms are adulatory, for the
most part.

In the favorite Scene of the Balcony . . . she appears at the Window,
not as if she sat there only to take the Air. . . . Her whole Carriage
discovers an Uneasiness of Soul, and then she sighs, and with a peculiar
Grace . . . leans upon her Hand with such a natural Ease that ROMEO's
observation
> *See how she leans her Cheek upon her Hand*,
seems an extempore Remark, dictated immediately by her Action.

It was Garrick's idea, too, that she should appear at a window.
Only much later did Kemble provide the still familiar balcony
which is so often too low — or too high — and is sometimes pre-
cariously flimsy as well.[66] As for Barry, Miss Nossiter's Romeo,
he is compared to his disadvantage with Garrick, in "the garden
scene." Macklin writes:

Barry comes into it, Sir, as great as a lord, swaggering about his love, and talking so loud, that, by G—, Sir, if we don't suppose the servants of the Capulet family almost dead with sleep, they must have come out, and tossed the fellow in a blanket. . . . But how does Garrick act this? . . . he comes creeping in upon his toes, whispering his love, and looking about him *just like a thief in the night.*

The gustiness of Macklin's phrasing is perhaps the chief merit of his criticism here; though some sense of Romeo's peril may well be shown by the lovers. Madame Modjeska's "repeated and cautious look round the garden" is noted by Westland Marston, who recommends that it be adopted by other actresses. Of her performance, he writes further: "As the passion deepens, and Juliet . . . so leans from the balcony that her outstretched finger-tips almost touch Romeo's, a point of intensity is reached by an action all the more successful because its simple eagerness has a touch of the humorous." [67]

Adelaide Neilson was, according to Winter, the inventor of a "pretty and expressive" piece of business at the end of the scene when, "she impulsively snatched a handful of flowers from her girdle, pressed them eagerly to her lips, dropped them into the upstretched hands of her lover, and darted into the chamber." Rossi's Juliet, for variation, "kissed the scarf she let down to him." Mr. George R. Foss sternly protests against this sort of thing. At the close of their interview, he urges, there should be perfect contentment; and "anything like throwing flowers or trying to touch one another destroys the scene, which should fade away in placid bliss." [68]

Like Oswald in *King Lear*, the Nurse's man, Peter, used often to be thrust into uncalled-for prominence. "Stage policy," wrote Francis Gentleman in 1770,

to please the upper regions, generally presents Peter as bearing an enormous fan before his mistress; skipping also and grinning like a baboon: the beating which he gets, for not resenting Mercutio's raillery, is a very mean, pantomimical, yet sure motive of laughter.

"Little" Simmons at Covent Garden, February 25, 1811, is sharply taken to task for his "mummery" in the part: "the act of his falling down, when he is going off fanning his Nurse, is a low violation of the dignity of the scene"; and an Edinburgh comedian, Mr. Boddie, "disgraced himself" twelve years later "by practising *Squire Richard's* joke of catching flies upon the wall." [69] Squire Richard, the booby son of Sir Francis Wronghead in Cibber's old play, *The Provoked Husband*, has a great deal of waiting about to do during the second act and may have resorted to this diversion out of sheer boredom. Boddie had played the part, a new one for him, on October 12, 1822. Many years were to pass before the business turns up again. But one of Otis Skinner's "early memories of the theatre" was of an American Peter who, in the same scene, went "up to the back flats" and caught "flies from the church steeple painted in perspective a block away." For contrast, Irving's Peter — that excellent actor Mr. A. G. Andrews — seized the opportunity, while Angelica is talking with Romeo, "to stretch his limbs and bask in the sunshine." [70]

Irving avoided the supposed difficulty of "Romeo's non-recognition of the Nurse whom he perfectly well knows," simply by not seeing her "till after the careless words, 'I am the youngest of that name for want of a better,' being engaged with his back turned in easy conversation with Benvolio." [71] Romeo's changed mode of address, "nurse" instead of "gentlewoman," the instant he is alone with her, is perhaps the clue here, and if he really knows the old dame and only pretends not to, business is of course unnecessary. At Mercutio's exit, the Cushman Promptbook reads: "Peter titters as Mercutio pretends to hold up his tail. Nurse strikes him with fan" — later, when he is dozing, she "slaps his face."

After going through the form of refusing — "No, truly, sir; not a penny" — Angelica of course accepts Romeo's present. As Cumberland's edition puts it: "Nurse, *looking a contrary way, takes the purse.*" At Sadler's Wells, the lover had to force it into her hands: "Nurse continues repeating 'Not a penny' until she gets the Purse fully in her possession." Very pleasant is the account given by Mary Anderson of Mrs. Stirling's business here. In refusing the gift, she stood,

with her hands behind her back. Then, when she had taken the money, she would cross the stage, chinking the coins as she went, with her hands under her chin, until "Peter" was within reach of her stick. Then it was thwack! thwack! thwack: — chink, chink, chink — quite legitimate business, that every night would set the house in a roar.[72]

This stick of hers was old, by the way. "Nurse with a Crutch stick," figured in Garrick's *Jubilee* (1769).[73]

Ellen Terry revolted against the "tradition" that "Juliet must go on coquetting and clicking over the Nurse to get the news." Instead, she made Juliet angry with her, Mrs. Stirling reluctantly accepting the change. Early nineteenth century Juliets were sometimes blamed for petting their Angelicas to excess. In 1815, Miss Kelly's "hugging the Nurse for so long a time, after they had made up their difference, was somewhat ludicrous"; and, in 1821, Miss Dance's action was "redundant . . . impetuous, and indeed boisterous. Why should her 'honey *Nurse*' be well nigh dragged to the ground?" [74] "Juliet *runs for a chair*," is the stage direction in Cumberland's edition (1829) when the old woman complains of weariness, and "Nurse *sits down*." At line 63 ("O God's lady dear!" as Shakespeare wrote it), she "*rises in a passion, and pushes the chair away*," but at the end of the speech "*sits sulkily in the chair again*." Juliet "*kneels behind* Nurse's *chair; then creeping round to the front, she lays her face on* Nurse's *knee, and looks tenderly in her face*," and Nurse "*overcome with* Juliet's *affection, relents, and embraces her*." In French's edition, "*Nurse flaunts round*" when Juliet "*passes behind chair to* L." but is mollified when she "*steals round to* R., *and throws herself at Nurse's feet*." A variation on this business is found in the Cushman Promptbook, where

Juliet touches the Nurse on each shoulder she turns away crossly — Juliet stands behind her and puts her hands on each cheek Then comes round and kneels R. H. looking up tenderly in the Nurses face — Nurse drops her stick and embraces her — Juliet picks up the stick and gives it to her.

Julia Marlowe, after trying in vain to appease her, first on one side then on the other, only to be flung back, stopped to think. "With her bunch of roses she leans over and touches the *Nurse* on her left cheek. She flings herself over . . . into *Juliet's* waiting arms and the quarrel is over." [75] I must add that when the play was last given in New York Dame May Whitty perceptibly sniffed before remarking, "What, have you din'd at home?" [76]

No part of the marriage ceremony used to be shown, at the end of the act. Enough (as in Cumberland's edition) for the Friar to come between the lovers and take "*a hand of each*" as he led them from the stage. In 1849, however, when Fanny Vining played Romeo to Mrs. Mowatt's Juliet, at the Marylebone Theatre, "some new pictorial effects" were introduced, "in particular one at the end of the second act, — the scene opening into an inner chapel wherein the Friar performs the marriage ceremony, while the curtain falls." This new ending commended itself at once, and something like it — if only the kneeling of the lovers to receive the Friar's blessing — is still customary today. In Rossi's edition the text caught up with the business. Romeo and Juliet kneel. Friar "Lorenzo" says "*Dio vi benedica, come io vi benedico*" — picture — and the curtain falls. It should be added, I suppose, that when Margaret Mather did Juliet at the Union Square Theatre, October 13, 1885, "two monks . . . suddenly came out of the wall of *Friar Lawrence's* Cell and placed hassocks for the bride and groom to kneel on, while the service was in progress." [77]

In Theophilus Cibber's adaptation (1748), Romeo after his apology to Tybalt "*walks apart.*" In later times, he has sometimes actually left the stage, returning just as Mercutio and Tybalt are beginning to fight. By means of this arrangement, Romeo is spared the indignity of being present while his friend takes up his quarrel for him.[78] But Shakespeare appears to have been chiefly anxious so to contrive matters that Romeo may break the truce without forfeiting our respect, and the more he has to endure, meanwhile, the readier we shall be to sympathize with him when at last he rushes upon Tybalt. A silly innovation practised by Sothern at the Knickerbocker Theatre, in the autumn of 1904, but said to have originated with Kyrle Bellew, not long before, was to have Romeo snatch a cloak from a page and with it, rather than with his own rapier, attempt to separate Tybalt and Mercutio.[79] Charles Kemble's Mercutio, after saying "Ask for me to-morrow, and you shall find me a grave man," smiled:

"It was a smile to call up tears," Marston writes, "it conjured up so much of youth and the merry past, while it was well-contrasted and kept within reality . . . by the reproof to Romeo for his fatal coming between — a reproof nobly and pathetically redeemed by the loving courtesy with which he held out his hand to him, a moment after . . . a point which was, I believe, original with Charles Kemble, and which has since become an acting tradition of the character." [80]

At Drury Lane, in November 1788, Tybalt was "killed between the side scenes." This, *The English Chronicle* presumes, was "a French importation of Mr. *Kemble's*."[81] It did not last. A cautionary note is added in Cushman's promptbook to the printed direction, "*Tybalt falls and dies*": "above 2nd Groove. . . . N.B. Tybalt must either be killed above the 2nd Groove, or *die twice* to get out of the way." "Bear hence this body," the Prince orders, at the end of the scene, and in Phelps's book: "They are about to raise the body of Tybalt then $\boxed{W}$ " — that is, *whistle* for the scene to change. At Sadler's Wells, we may be confident, Tybalt would have died only once and far enough up-stage!

Romeo seems always to have killed Tybalt swiftly and with fury. When, in August 1823, Mr. Calcraft (better known as J. W. Cole, Charles Kean's biographer) was acting Romeo at the Theatre Royal, Edinburgh, he continued to strike the air with his sword after the fall of his adversary. *The Edinburgh Theatrical Observer, and Musical Review* (August 8) is disposed to accept this action as, "in the circumstances of the situation, a very natural and just one"; but the *Edinburgh Dramatic Review* (August 11) cannot abide it — and "the very idea . . . of *Calcraft* presuming to introduce so *sublime* a novelty upon the stage, is enough to make a horse laugh." Charles Kean, after running Tybalt through "faster than we can write it" assumed a "fixed posture, and look of stupid amazement at what he had done." [82] Charlotte Cushman as Romeo was frequently praised for her fencing which was "better than skilful, because it is appropriate. . . . Tybalt is struck dead as lightning strikes the pine; one blow beats down his guard, and one lunge closes the fray." [83] Irving, too, was past Tybalt's guard "in a flash." He snatched up Mercutio's sword, a detail which has symbolic value, though Romeo is not unarmed himself — Tybalt bids him "turn and draw." Scott mentions the actor's shading his eyes "to ward off the rays of the blinding sun at the beginning of the duel." [84] Finally, Otis Skinner, in 1890, is told that "his anger at the death of Mercutio is virile, but should scarcely lead him, after the first wound has been given, to pass his sword thrice through the unresisting body of Tybalt." [85]

The "Cords Scene" (II, 2) has less interest. "The upward gesture of snipping with scissors" with which Stella Colas accompanied Juliet's

> Take him and cut him out in little stars

led the usually temperate Professor Morley to growl that Shakespeare's line "to a dressy second-rate French *ingénue*, inevitably suggested millinery." Winter liked Madame Modjeska's "subtle, significant resort to the dagger" at "Vile earth, to earth resign" (line 59); but since the production of the dagger is scarcely called for here it had better be reserved for a later moment. On the other hand, one of Fanny Kemble's best lines was her

> "Tybalt is dead — and Romeo — banished!"

where, having "pronounced the last word, *banished*," she "threw herself into the arms of her nurse"; and the "affecting tenderness" of Mary Anderson's kneeling to pick up the "poor cords" which the Nurse had dropped was a remembered point in her performance, as was her burying her face in them after she had taken them up.[86]

In Romeo's "Banished Scene" action is twice called for: obviously, Romeo is to cast himself on the ground, as he cries

> then mightst thou tear thy hair
> And fall upon the ground, as I do now;

and later, when he demands of the Friar

> In what vile part of this anatomy
> Doth my name lodge? Tell me, that I may sack
> The hateful mansion,

he may well threaten to take his own life with sword or dagger. With the first action, Charlotte Cushman is particularly associated. The reckless force and wildness of despair with which she flung herself down, is commented upon by writer after writer.[87] As for the second, Poel has called attention to a direction in the 1597 Quarto — "*Nurse snatches the dagger away*" — as evidence that the "so-called 'traditional-business,' still in use," by which Friar Laurence here intervenes, "is not of Shakespeare's time." [88] The commanding dignity of the Friar and his sternly pronounced "Hold thy desperate hand" sufficiently account for the shift.

The last scene in Act III, beginning with the parting of Romeo and Juliet at dawn, then continuing (somewhat to the embarrassment of students of the Elizabethan stage) with Juliet's going down from the window and receiving her parents, was made a mere "Garden Scene" by Otway, and remained so for more than a century. A letter, dated October 20, 1750, in *The Student; Or, The Oxford and Cambridge Monthly Miscellany*, criticizes the prosaic arrangement by which the lovers were "brought in *tête à tête* [*sic*] on the platform of the stage; whereas in SHAKESPEARE they are supposed to converse together from a window." This letter, though it was reproduced in other periodicals, did no good for a long time.[89] At last, when it appeared in *The Monthly Mirror* for November 1797, the letter was accompanied by a note to the effect that "in a late performance," at Covent Garden, the objection has been removed: "the principal part of the scene is spoken from a balcony." The older staging persisted for a while longer — at Edinburgh, for example, in 1824,[90] and in the stage directions in Cumberland's acting edition of 1829 — but it was doomed. Phelps's promptbook shifts Romeo's line,

> Farewell, farewell! One kiss, and I'll descend,

so that it now precedes the Nurse's entrance; and "this line transposed to give time for Romeo to get over the Balustrade," is added by way of explanation. Later still, we find Madame Modjeska protesting against "such naturalistic details as a disarranged four-posted bed, or the turning of the key of a locked door at the nurse's entrance, or Romeo's lacing his jerkin." [91]

Meanwhile, *John Bull* (July 17, 1841) had attacked Ellen Tree for "excessive *naturalness*":

In the parting with *Romeo* . . . she clings about him, and hides her face in his bosom, and sobs away in a manner that . . . a bagman about to start on his first journey after marriage, would think very much the thing.

At this rate, the writer concludes, Shakespeare had better be "rewritten by PLANCHE or some other stage milliner, to suit the prevailing mode." Adelaide Neilson, according to Marston,

gave a telling close to the scene. As Romeo disappeared, her extended arms followed him awhile, with a desperate effort, as if her soul still pursued him; then the arms relaxed and hung supine, she turned mechanically, and lay unconscious; life had fled with him.

Mary Anderson, too, sank down "as if her life had left her," and was then "instantly withdrawn from sight by an ingenious revolution of the scenery." [92]

The *Letter to Miss Nossiter*, already mentioned, gives us somewhat fully her business while Juliet is being persecuted by Old Capulet. Saying,

> Good father, I beseech you on my knees . . .

she suited the action to the word, and "with Tears streaming from her Eyes" threw herself at his feet. As he begins his reply — "Hang thee, young baggage!" — he "throws her from him."

> Speak not, reply not, do not answer me!

he adds, an instant later.

Here, by her Action she is going to intreat him once more to hear her. . . . You would swear it was her Cue to speak, till he stops her. . . . She turns from him, with a Look that speaks, *it is in vain to try to move him*; then almost fainting, she leans upon her Nurse. . . . Every now and then, while her Father addresses the Remainder of his Speech to his Wife, JULIET casts such Looks at him as cannot be withstood. Then bursting into Tears, sinks into the Bosom of her Nurse. . . . At this he goes up to her, and, catching her by the Arm, she starts and seems frightened almost to Death.

And this scene, he adds, "has heretofore been looked upon as of no Consequence, at least as to JULIET's Part. The Father has carried off the Applause." [93]

Juliet's rising from the ground after her father's exit, her flinging herself into Angeliea's arms and clinging to the old woman, are praised in Mary Anderson's performance. In Fanny Kemble's it is her manner of speaking a single word:

Jul.   Speak'st thou this from thy heart?
Nurse.   And from my soul too; else beshrew them both.

And "Miss Kemble," Talfourd writes, "erected her head, and extended her arm, with an expressive air which we never saw surpassed in acting, and with a power like magic pronounced 'Amen!' " [94] Juliet possesses herself of a dagger:

> If all else fail, myself have power to die.

Then, in some performances, she has flung a cloak about her shoulders — and sets out to seek her ghostly confessor.[95]

At the Friar's cell, it may be expedient for Juliet to kneel at last — as Ellen Terry did — in order to be rid of Paris, whose

> God shield I should disturb devotion!

does not necessarily imply this action but gains somewhat in meaning when it is introduced. In Phelps's promptbook Friar Laurence actually "goes out & immediately returns," in obedience to her

> O shut the door! and when thou hast done so,
> Come weep with me!

Two properties are now called into service: the dagger which Juliet threatens to use against herself (Miss Nossiter's "Attitude," when the Friar stops her, was "very fine"); and the "vial" which Juliet seizes as she says,

> Give me, give me! O, tell not me of fear! [96]

"Friar blesses her" is Cushman's promptnote as the scene closes.

To a reader of the play seeing it for the first time, the Potion Scene may prove startling. Juliet will drink from the vial, he supposes, and she will be terrified by thoughts of the tomb where she must lie. But according to tradition there is a great deal more to the Scene than that. Poel, in 1889, found it often over-acted. "Our Juliets do far too much 'stumping and frumping' about." [97]

At the beginning, Phelps's promptbook has Juliet and the Nurse discovered, "Nurse shewing Garments," which agrees nicely with "Ay, those attires are best," and the lines following. Juliet's dismay when the Nurse and Lady Capulet leave the room has often found expression in terms of action. Miss Nossiter ran to the door, as if to "call them back again." Miss O'Neill, "falling on her knee," bent forward and gazed after Lady Capulet, "as if this longing, lingering look was to be her last on earth." Helen Faucit used to take up a lamp "from the table and peer into the shadows." And, to the Earl of Lytton, Mary Anderson's "look and gesture of mute appeal when the mother is about to leave the daughter without kissing her" were "most pathetic." This Juliet paid no attention to the Nurse, who, "after Lady Capulet's departure, kisses and fondles the girl's hand," but still gazed "wistfully at the spot where her mother last stood." Then, when the Nurse too has gone, "she rushes to the door to call them," afterwards drawing "the curtain over the window," where she pauses "with her hand on the curtain, half wrapping it round her . . . and stares back into the vacant chamber." [98]

The laying down of a dagger is clearly called for, a moment later, when Juliet dreads that the Friar's mixture may "not work at all." But in Cibber's adaptation, it is worth noting, she hides the dagger, instead, "*under her Robe.*" [99] Miss Nossiter, who had taken the vial from her bosom, now raised it "with a slow Solemnity . . . but just as it approached her Lips, she starts and draws it back" — "What if it be a poison," etc. Her anonymous critic praises this action:

upon looking over the Passage, it seems so visibly intended by the sudden Transition of the Thought, that it is more wonderful it was never done before, than that a Person of her Age shou'd be the first to hit it off.

Later, as she cried "Stay, Tybalt, stay!" the same Juliet was "running forward, as if the Apparition . . . was flying from her"; and here, near the end of the soliloquy, it became customary for actresses to introduce complicated miming. Tate Wilkinson, in a letter of advice to Miss Campion at the time of her first York appearance, in the seventeen-nineties, wrote: "In ye Soliloquy, you sh^d plead to Tibalt, in your Frensy, on one side, & on ye other, as to Romeo." [100] Miss Jarman, making her Covent Garden *début*, February 7, 1827, was praised for "her reeling recoil to the back of the stage at the image in her mind of the mangled Tybalt," and for "the desperate rush she made across the stage, quite to the front, and falling on her knee," as she supplicated "her cousin's ghost to spare her husband," [101] Fanny Kemble "ran down from the back of the stage to the right-hand corner of the proscenium, under the stage-box; and there threw herself into an attitude upon one knee as if driving the apparition before her." She "slides, in a manner, all across the stage," Leigh Hunt wrote; and Dunlap, looking in at the theatre to see her "great scene of madness," found it "exaggerated & the celebrated slide altogether pantomimic." [102]

Morley writes of Stella Colas, in 1864, that

she spends so much force upon the shrieking at and cowering by the bedside from Tybalt's ghost, that she can only add as an insignificant tag to the claptrap stage-effect the line in which a greater actress would have found the true climax, "Romeo, I come! this do I drink to thee." ... Instead of screaming the "Stay, Tybalt, stay," Juliet more probably whispers it. ... She drinks as from a festive bridal-cup.[102a]

Stage Juliets remained incorrigible. Marston, indeed, praises "the freezing horror" with which Adelaide Neilson "swung round, as on a pivot, with hands screening her eyes, as if recoiling from the sight, which yet fascinated her, of Tybalt's imagined shape behind her," though the "exaltation when, at last rallying herself, she raised the phial to her lips" was "perhaps the noblest feature of this powerful scene." [103] Madame Modjeska threw herself into a great chair, where "with convulsive hands" she beat off "the spectres of her imagination until love, stronger than terror, made her leap into their midst and shield Romeo from the pursuing shade of Tybalt." [104] And when, at last, restraint was tried — by Ellen Terry — Clement Scott was much dissatisfied. Her "playing of the scene was consistently graceful, but singularly incomplete. ... The 'horrible conceit of death and night' was never presented." Morley's criticism of Stella Colas is then quoted: but Morley was wrong and the scene "ought to be played" as the Frenchwoman had performed it — "nowadays it is considered that all power is rant, all screams in tragic passages are discordant." [105]

Another moment of violence was that of the actual drinking of the potion. But the introduction of sensational business here seems to have come only after the possibilities for it, earlier, had been pretty well exhausted. After all, Shakespeare had for once supplied a strong curtain! The exhaustion of Helen Faucit's Juliet as she retired to the bed is commended as a novelty — the taking of the draught was not made a climax, as it was ordinarily.[106] "Juliet should be particular to drop the vial well up stage" is a prompt note in the Cushman book, where the vial is also carefully described as "flat." Madame Modjeska's "action of catching the tablecloth" — or, perhaps, rather the bed-curtain — "and rolling herself in it as she falls," was considered "too artificial." [107] Mary Anderson's fall on the bed was also criticized, though in time she "gave up that hanging down of her head over the side of the bed, which at first caused serious apprehensions of apoplexy." But Margaret Mather rolled down some steps after drinking, and this was hailed, in *Shakespeariana*, as "an effective climax to the grandeur of the acting that had preceded it." [108] And with Julia Marlowe the sound of the vial "ringing upon the floor," when she dropped it, "startled her for one instant back to her terrors. She cast one fearful look about her, then conquered herself again, took three steps toward the bed and fell unconscious." [109]

A few additional details call for mention. Miss Nossiter spoke,

> And, in this rage, with some great kinsman's bone
> As with a club dash out my desp'rate brains,

"stamping with Rage, she flings her Arms about, then strikes her Hands with all her Force against her Forehead, as if to knock her Brains out." Similarly, Miss Jarman, at

> And madly play with my forefather's joints,

accompanied the line "with a slight indication of the action it describes, and half playing in the air with the fancied bones"; and Mary Anderson's "clutching" at the same imaginary bones is referred to in accounts of her performance. On the other hand, Olga

Nethersole, in the spring of 1895, was pouring the potion into a modern tumbler and diluting it with water from a pitcher; and, later in the year, Mrs. Patrick Campbell, "at the thought that the Friar may have 'subtly ministered' a poison to her . . . uncorks the phial and smells it to reassure herself — a little touch of exquisitely misplaced realism." [110]

In the following scenes, until we come to that in the churchyard, there is not much stage business. Two directions in Cumberland's edition, Nurse *"sits in a chair by the bed"* (at v, 5, 2) and *"Rises from her chair, and shakes her"* (at "I must needs wake her"), are perhaps worth quoting. Ellen Tree is commended in *John Bull*, July 17, 1841, for infusing "novelty into the mere *business*, as it is technically termed, of the scene. . . . She is discovered fallen on the foot of the bed, her head hanging down, the face turned towards the audience, and the body tumbled, rather than lying, cross-wise." Against the propriety of this, it is justly urged that the Nurse would now be unlikely to suppose that Juliet was merely asleep:

> The fact, we apprehend, is, that Miss TREE has here been thinking of that d—n *naturalness*, which is the bane of modern acting, and has . . . mistaken the somewhat slow operation of a sleeping draught for the instantaneous seizure of a poison.

At the conclusion of the act, Irving introduced a "procession of fair bridesmaids filing into the presence of the corpse," a novelty which Clement Scott found "singularly effective and poetical into the bargain." [111]

As for the Apothecary Scene, the Edinburgh *Theatre*, January 15, 1852, assures us that Romeo "invariably raises his voice to a great pitch in exclaiming, 'What ho!' &c., and knocks loudly against the apothecary's door." Stage directions to this effect are not wholly wanting, but they are of recent date and, though the lines themselves admit of knocking as an accompaniment, they do not demand it. John Howard Payne has a good word for the Apothecary of Meadows, at Drury Lane, February 7, 1827:

> His unconsciousness of holding the purse, in his struggle between his horror of poisoning the unknown applicant, and his dread of being starved . . . was very effectively rendered; and so was the manner in

which, as he turned away, he noticed the purse, grasped it convulsively, and flung himself, staggering, into his shop.[112]

When Romeo is opening the tomb of the Capulets he is interrupted by Paris; and in eighteenth century performances this moment was marked by a much discussed bit of posturing. Some lines, "*On seeing Mr* BARRY *and Mrs* CIBBER *in* Romeo and Juliet," in *The Gentleman's Magazine* for November 1752, refer to it:

> When *Barry* fraught with all the rage of woe,
> His accents broken, and his paces slow,
> Tow'rds *Juliet's* tomb in desperation moves,
> Each look, each motion, shows how much he loves:
> But, when, by *Paris* challeng'd to the fight,
> With hollow voice he warns the amr'ous knight,
> Starts back erect, and aims the crow on high,
> Shudders the audience, and attempts to fly.[113]

Two years later, the translator of Riccoboni's *General History of the Stage* complained that

> with us the same Scene is always play'd in the same Manner, not only by the same Actor, but by every Actor who performs it: We know, therefore, before it comes, all that we are to admire. . . . That beautiful, though perhaps not proper, Attitude of *Romeo* at the Tomb, is always the same, not only in Mr. *Barry* and in Mr. *Garrick*, every Time each plays, but 'tis the same in both.[114]

In 1755, John Hill writes of "the famous attitude in which Romeo raises the iron to dash out the intruding Paris's brains" that it is "vastly" applauded but "false." "The weapon of a gentleman is his sword, he naturally has recourse to it, and to no other." Theophilus Cibber borrowed this argument, the next year, in attacking Garrick. Romeo, he is sure,

> would immediately drop that unwieldly Instrument, the Iron Crow, and have recourse to his Sword. . . .
> But then this *Cyclopedian* Attitude wou'd be lost, in which *Romeo*, now, stands long enough to give *Paris* Time to run him thro' the Body. . . .
> No Wonder the Generality of an Audience clap, as they may well be astonished, to see my little *Romeo* wield this massy Instrument with such Dexterity: — But their Admiration would cease, when let into the

Secret, that this seeming iron Crow is really but a painted wooden one.[115]

Wilkes, who finds Garrick's attitude "very striking," remarks that it "was stolen . . . by a certain performer, who owed to his instruction many, if not most of the strokes on which was founded his great reputation in Romeo." [116] He means Barry, I suppose. At the end of the century there was still talk of scenes in which "the performer pleads a kind of prescriptive right to an attitude, as in the tomb-scene in Romeo and Juliet, the tent-scene in Richard III." [117]

According to Boaden, in 1827, Romeo in breaking open the tomb was accustomed to batter "a couple of doors fiercely with the crow in his grasp, which very naturally fly open *outwards*; and there . . . lies Juliet, above ground." Boaden calls this procedure "grossly absurd. . . . However, the *start* when she is discovered is a fine thing; the *whirling* of the iron crow is another fine thing." [118] This description is supplemented by a passage in Mrs. Mowatt's autobiography. Telling about an American performance in 1845, she refers to "some scene shifters . . . each holding a cord attached to the doors of the tomb. The cords, according to stage direction, were to be loosened at the third blow of Romeo's wrenching-iron." [119]

Sir Frank Benson remembers his disappointment when, playing Paris to Irving's Romeo, he was given no chance to display his swordsmanship:

with one hand [Romeo] seized my foil, hit me over the knuckles with his own, prodded me in the stomach with his knee, again dashed his blade against mine, said, "Die, my boy, die; down, down," elbowed and kneed me into the mouth of the tomb, and stood in front of the dying Paris, brandishing a torch.[120]

At the Lyceum, the scene now changed to the interior of the vault, and Romeo reappeared, still carrying the torch and dragging the body (a dummy had been substituted during the interval) down a flight of stone steps at the back of the stage. "The dim light and the general effect of distance were most weird and impressive," Brereton writes; and Mr. Bernard Shaw contrasts with the careful laying out of Paris, in a later production, "Irving, a dim figure dragging a horrible burden down through the gloom 'into the rotten jaws of death.' " [121]

Romeo's death does not seem to have been attended with business of any particular interest, except perhaps in the case of James Anderson who, at the Broadway Theatre in May 1847, had to roll down a flight of fourteen steps after swallowing the poison.[122] Juliet's death is another matter.

> Behold! I see thee now the dagger take,
> Roll thy wild eyes, and all thy members shake,

exclaims the author of "*On seeing Mr* BARRY *and Mrs* CIBBER *in* Romeo and Juliet"; and of Mrs. Cibber we are told further that she "introduced a shudder that affects the whole audience." [123] Miss Nossiter is described as "vigorously grasping the Dagger":

as she raises her Hand, she smiles upon the Point, and, with a Joy that commanded Tears from every Eye pronounced,
> *O happy Dagger!*
> *This is thy Sheath;*
at which she plunged it in her Breast. . . . Afraid of drawing it out, she holds it in her Breast, then turning up her Eyes with dying Agony to Heaven . . . speaks her last Words
> *There rust, and let me die.*

To the same effect is Tate Wilkinson's advice to Miss Campion: "When you have to say, 'There rest and let me die,' ye dagger s^d remain, and not be thrown away." Miss Jarman (in 1827) introduced a piece of business which, according to Payne, surprised "even those experienced in such matters," by "dragging herself across the stage to [Romeo's] body, and dying just as she had caught his hand in hers." [124] In Helen Faucit's performance "the stiffened movement of the limbs" as Juliet attempted to rise, after waking in the tomb, is commended, as is also her death scene, where "laying her face upon her husband's bosom, she raised his nerveless arms and folded them above her head." [125] Adelaide Neilson and Mary Anderson can have differed little from their predecessors, since both dragged themselves to Romeo's side and died on his breast.[126] But Mrs. Campbell did something quite new by propping Romeo's dagger against the wall of the tomb and pressing herself upon the point.[127]

It is with Romeo's dagger that Juliet stabs herself. Of that, there can be no doubt. But on the stage, a departure from Shakespeare's intention was made here — a departure which, if we are to believe Tate Wilkinson, came about as the result of accident. "For several seasons after Garrick's first revival of the piece," Wilkinson writes, no change in the prescribed business was introduced.

> But in one of her last seasons at Covent Garden, when playing Juliet with Barry, [Mrs. Cibber] fumbled and fumbled, but no dagger was to be found; at last, evidently much distressed, she held up her delicate fist (which was really so) and ideally plunged the weapon to her heart . . . and from that night, I believe, Juliet has ever trusted to her own care for that necessary plaything, the dagger. There must be many nurses . . . to the Capulet family, now existing, who can vouch whether the custom mentioned prevails in consequence of that unlucky accident.[128]

Juliet certainly began to carry a dagger of her own. "Sir" John Hill, in 1759, pokes fun at "the circumstances of the daggers": Juliet "before she takes her soporific draught, lays down one dagger upon her table, which her attendants never find. When she wakes . . . she very opportunely finds another dagger in her bosom, with which she despatches herself." So, too, in *The St. James's Chronicle*, December 6–8, 1768, "An Admirer of Shakespeare" observes that "in the Representation" Juliet is "armed even in the Tomb," and "openly snatches" a dagger "from her Pocket-Hole." Miss O'Neill used Romeo's weapon; but to do so was to run risks. Fanny Kemble tells of how when she was already irritated with her Philadelphia Romeo (December 5, 1832), she fumbled for his dagger and could not find it; whereupon, "I, Juliet, thus apostrophized him, — Romeo being dead — 'Why, where *the* devil *is* your dagger, Mr. —?' "[129] Mary Anderson, on the night of her *début*, in Louisville, Kentucky, November 27, 1875, was embarrassed by the forgetfulness of still another Romeo — and had "to despatch herself with a hair-pin." Other Juliets chose prudence as against propriety, and carried their own daggers — Mrs. Scott-Siddons, as recently as 1867. Anna Mowatt, however, once forgot what she terms "this necessary appendage of the heroine in the last act," and had recourse to Romeo's weapon — thus doing, belatedly, what mere readers of the play must have expected her to do in the first place.[130]

For stage business on a quite different plane, one this time of tragic meaning, there was Mr. Olivier's idea, three or four years ago, of having Romeo dying stretch out his hand toward Juliet, whose hand, as she stirred in her sleep, almost touched, but did not quite touch his. Star-crossed lovers, even in death!

The Roman Plays and Timon of Athens

It is conceivable that in *Julius Caesar*, given with Hart and Mohun, prior to 1672, and with a fair degree of regularity thereafter, traditions were perpetuated from pre-Restoration times. This is less likely to be true in the case of *Coriolanus*, which Restoration audiences saw only briefly in an alteration by Tate. As for *Antony and Cleopatra*, it had to wait until the middle of the eighteenth century for a revival, and did not even then establish itself as a repertory play, *Timon*, which had once been popular in Shadwell's version, faring still worse, in later times, although Samuel Phelps's production, in 1851, showed that it was by no means unactable.

On March 19, 1824, *The Edinburgh Dramatic Review* in noticing a performance of *Julius Caesar*, with Young and Vandenhoff, the night before, gave some attention to the Second Citizen: "Mackay seems to 'agnize a natural and prompt alacrity,' in being at the head of a mob. He capers and leaps, and looks like the god Pan leading on a band of satyrs." Presumably, the actor's feelings were hurt by this remark. At any rate, the critic made it clear, a week later, that he was far from denying Mackay's right to be called "a good plebeian. . . . His jumping and capering is eccentric; but, as among the lower orders, we naturally expect to find something eccentric, Mackay's jumping and capering could not well be dispensed with." In the excellent Boston Museum Promptbook (1878), "the Citizens move off stage murmuring and drooping their heads." Then, by means of a little pruning of the lines, they are allowed to hear the march heralding Caesar's approach, "which rouses them and all look off R.H."

Frederick Warde tells an amusing anecdote about a performance in San Francisco, with Booth as Brutus and McCullough as Antony. Upon Caesar's exclaiming

> Let me have men about me that are fat,

the two comedians playing the First and Second Citizens, Mr. C. B. Bishop and Mr. William Mestayer, both of very robust figures, and each turning the scales at 250 pounds at least, advanced, one on either side of Caesar, and placing their hands on their rotund and protruding stomachs, looked up at the great man as much as to say, "Well! here is just what you want."

Since "both gentlemen were great personal favorites with the public," Warde adds, their impudence went unpunished. In the same scene, Davenport as Brutus was remembered for "the deferential manner in which . . . he invariably saluted Calphurnia, and carried on a dumb-show conversation with her"; and, in Tree's production (as if Shakespeare had neglected the ominous!) girls flung down "blood-red roses in Caesar's path," at which the dictator started.[131]

In admitting the muffled men who visit his master nocturnally (II, 1), Lucius will do well to show concern. In the marked copy of Harry B. Hudson, an actor at McVicker's Theatre, Chicago, in the 'sixties, occurs the direction, "Enter [Lucius] preceeding others & Exit R 3 E — looking back frightened," and a similar note turns up in the Boston Museum Promptbook. A little further on, at "*Clock strikes*," Hudson scrawled, "Picture up stage," where the Museum prompter has: "Count ten between each stroke, and have bell very distant and full. The moment the clock strikes, a picture is formed by characters which is not broken until Cassius speaks." As the conspirators exeunt, they of course muffle their faces once more.[132]

Much business has attached itself to the Assassination Scene. Davies has a warning: "The several conspirators, pressing with eagerness to have a share in stabbing the victim, must be so regulated as to prevent confusion." There was no want of regulation, certainly, when Tieck saw Kemble's performance in 1817. Caesar was on a throne toward the back of the stage; and, while the petition was being presented, "the conspirators arranged themselves in a well-defined pyramid" of which he was "the apex." Brutus stood **far forward**, to the left. After being stabbed by Casca,

Caesar turns to the right and receives a second blow from the second of his enemies; again he staggers in affright to the left, a few steps forward, and receives a fresh wound, then the same to the right: now the free space on the stage grows larger . . . but he still goes on staggering across the stage five or six times, so as to be stabbed by the conspirators, who remain quietly standing, until he receives his death-blow from Brutus.

It was "like the most formal ballet," is Tieck's comment.[133] More exciting is the description in the Boston Museum Promptbook, where, contrary to custom, the throne is shown at one side of the stage:

When Cassius kneels. Casca rises or a little later and crosses to R.H. behind the throne. At his cue he springs upon the steps and stabs Caesar — the other conspirators rise and rush upon Caesar. excepting Cassius & Brutus. Cassius pulls Caesar from Throne. stabs & throws him over to Brutus, who then stab [*sic*] him. From the moment Casca strikes, the Citizens & Senators all rise. Cry out "Murder & Treason etc." in wild excitement.

McCullough as Brutus had shrunk from touching Caesar's hand, just before, and he made clear "the effort and his horror of it when he struck the fatal blow." Mansfield went even further. As he spoke "Et tu, Brute?" "a tremor shook his frame . . . Tenderly, sorrowfully, sacrificially the patriot laid his blade on the bleeding throat of his friend, the point directed to his own heart." [134] After Caesar has fallen, Phelps's promptbook calls for "a Violent movement of horror and confusion amongst the Citizens. clasping their hands they exclaim 'He is dead' — 'Oh Caesar.' 'Brutus!' 'Oh! horror.' 'He is slain' — 'Where is Anthony.' 'Treason!' &c" and they presently, "Exeunt in great disorder."

Brutus bids the conspirators stoop with him and bathe their hands in Caesar's blood. "Stoop then and wash," Cassius replies. But on the stage this was seldom done. What is more, the lines themselves were quietly altered, the idea underlying the changes, which vary in different editions, being always that these dignified Romans were *not* to "stoop and wash." [135] Phelps's promptnote is in part illegible, but it leaves one confident that at Sadler's Wells Shakespeare's intention was heeded — "they gather round the body of Caesar [?& stoop] their hands on it." Tree, also, used the busi-

ness (Irving's eagerly awaited comment on his production was
"H'm— yes — too much blood!") and, when Antony shakes hands
with the conspirators, "Casca with rude intent and purposeful
cruelty smirches with a crimson stain the arm of butchered Caesar's
friend." [136] At the Boston Museum, Antony after shaking hands
with Brutus advanced toward Cassius, "offering his hand to him —
pause. and Cassius gives his coldly. Antony presses and lets it fall,
turning to Audience, expressing his distrust of Cassius." [137]

Turning back for a moment to Antony's entrance, it is refreshing
to read in Tom Davies that Wilks,

> as soon as he entered the stage, without taking any notice of the con-
> spirators, walked swiftly up to the dead body of Caesar and knelt down;
> he paused some time before he spoke; and, after surveying the corpse
> with manifest tokens of the deepest sorrow, he addressed it. . . .[138]

This, I hope, was the tradition as Wilks received it. For contrast,
the objectionable violence of Lawrence Barrett must also be mentioned. As Cassius interrupts Antony —

> How like a deer, stroken by many princes,
>   Dost thou here lie!
> *Cass.*   Mark Antony —

Barrett rushed "upon Antony, passing in front of Brutus, who
seizes him by left arm and shoulder. Antony sinks almost upon his
R. knee with hands outstretched to shield himself from Cassius. —
Picture." And again, when the conspirators are leaving the stage:

> All Exeunt L.H. except Cassius who crosses threateningly to An-
> tony, who is bending over Caesar's body. Brutus as he nears L.1.E.
> turns to look for Cassius, and seeing his intent crosses to him and per-
> suades him off. as they near enterance [*sic*], Cassius turns quickly, but
> Brutus retains his hold of him.[139]

It was in this scene, too, that a finely imagined stroke was introduced by the elder Booth as Cassius. "After Caesar had been . . .
stabbed by the conspirators, and lay extended on the floor of the
Senate-house, Booth strode right across the dead body, and out of
the scene, in silent and disdainful triumph." So Gould wrote, in
The Tragedian; and Winter adds that Edwin Booth adopted, for
use in *Richard III*, his father's business "of striding, with heedless

preoccupation, across the head of the dead Caesar." [140] Tree, by
the way, closed the scene with a grotesquely un-Shakespearean
return of Calphurnia, to mourn in dumb show over the body of her
murdered lord.[141]

Voltaire addressing "Mylord Bolingbroke" in 1731, tells him of
having seen *Julius Caesar* in London:

*avec quel ravissement je voyais Brutus, tenant encore un poignard teint
du sang de César, assembler le peuple romain, et lui parler . . . du haut
de la tribune aux harangues.*

Brutus, Cassius, and the rest are directed to enter with their swords
drawn, in more than one later acting text.[142]

We usually think of Antony as swaying the emotions of his
auditors by means of words alone. Yet his oration is punctuated
by significant action. He descends from the "pulpit." He tears
away the mantle covering Caesar's body. He produces Caesar's
will. In Laura Keene's periodical, *The Fine Arts*, April 1872,
Booth's reading of "the great speech" is praised — "the quicker and
quicker delivery till it swelled to a torrent of words; finally, the
leap from the tribune (a trick, but a very clever trick), and his
thunderous denunciation of the traitors." Meanwhile, the Plebeians
have been showing their interest. Francis Gentleman refers, indeed, to a performance in which "the low comedians" had "rendered the mob totally farcical." But there is no reason to assume
that this was customary.[143] At Sadler's Wells, the supers were "to
turn to each other," repeatedly, "as if quietly getting each others
sentiments." Much was expected of them at the Boston Museum.
Thus, at

> O judgment, thou art fled to brutish beasts,
> And men have lost their reason!

"all make an angry movement towards Antony," whose "Bear with
me" would have gained point from this interruption. Later, after
Antony has shown the citizens Caesar "himself, marr'd as you see
with traitors": "All rush up Stage R&L. shouting. . . . Antony
turns and calls to them. Their impetuous course is stopped." And
the same business is repeated at

> Away then! come, seek the conspirators —

but with Antony now leaping "upon Rostrum" and calling to them "from the elevation." Tree, according to Mrs. George Cran, intrusted the parts to

a collection of intelligent actors. The man who stopped to tie his sandal at the beginning of Antony's speech first drew my attention; he was not at all interested in what the orator was going to say — Brutus had soothed him down . . . and his untied sandal wanted his attention. Suddenly . . . he jerked his head back with a nice free gesture and grew rapt in the great speech.

For a spectacular curtain Benson showed the firing of the funeral pyre: "The shouts and flames and gestures of the maddened women and the struggling men round the burning body ended the scene in tumults of applause." [144] Shakespeare's ending is very quiet indeed.

The famous Quarrel Scene must at one time have been badly over-acted. "In the fine scene betwixt Brutus and Cassius," William Guthrie wrote, in 1747, "our players have ever made a feint towards a duel or rencounter," though "nothing could be more opposite to the poet's meaning." And in Chapter LI of *Peregrine Pickle* the Knight of Malta is made to say of Quin that,

in the character of the mild patriot Brutus, he loses all temper and decorum; nay, so ridiculous is the behaviour of him and Cassius at their interview, that, setting foot to foot, and grinning at each other, with the aspect of two cobblers enraged, they thrust their left sides together with repeated shocks, that the hilts of their swords may clash for the entertainment of the audience.

What is more, Leonard Digges in commendatory verses which he contributed to the 1640 edition of Shakespeare's *Poems* speaks of Brutus and Cassius as "at halfe-sword parley," obviously referring to this same scene. Was Quin's, then, the traditional way? It is a relief, turning to Cibber's *Apology*, to learn that "when the *Betterton Brutus* was provok'd in his Dispute with *Cassius*, his Spirit flew only to his Eye; his steady Look alone supply'd that Terror which he disdain'd an Intemperance in his Voice should rise to." [145] Two further pieces of business — concerning Charles Barron as Brutus and Barrett as Cassius — are recorded in the Boston Museum Promptbook. At "For your life you durst not,"

Brutus has his back to Cassius. who now angrily advances to him, as if to strike him. Brutus quietly looks over his shoulder at Cassius. his face devoid of any anger or rage which instantly checks Cassius movement.

And, after Cassius has offered Brutus his dagger, crying that his friend loved Caesar better than he loves him: "Cassius has thrown his dagger before Brutus and now falls upon his knee before him. Brutus quietly lifts up dagger and places hilt of it in Cassius hand." Finally, Hackett was profoundly moved by Young's manner of "turning slowly and facing Cassius" as he uttered, "O Cassius, I am sick of many griefs,"

and then slowly approaching him, taking one hand within his own and resting the other on *Cassius's* shoulder and pausing a little and fixing his gaze upon the face of *Cassius*, and then with a faltering voice, and a suffused eye . . . added — *"Portia — is — dead!"* and closed his eyes.

To Hackett's compliment after the performance (in 1827), Young "modestly remarked" that he owed his conception "to the late Mr. Kemble's performance of *Brutus*." [146]

The treatment of the Ghost follows a now familiar pattern. In the 1719 adaptation of *Julius Caesar*, he *"Rises"* — by means of a trap, of course — and *"Ring down"* is prelude to his departure.[147] In a promptbook of the Garrick Period, his entrance is merely "PS," though at his exit we have "®Trap Bell to sink Ghost." And this arrangement, authorized by Brutus's own words — "Ha! who comes here?" and "thou vanishest" — presumably lasted for many years. Then, as might be expected — gauzes. "As Brutus turns to trim taper," reads the Boston Museum Promptbook,

the Gauze at back is illuminated and Ghost of Caesar discovered almost centre. . . . The Ghost moves slowly across. it's [*sic*] hands outstretched — pointing to R.H — but its eyes fixed upon Brutus. who has risen and is in Centre of stage. back to Audience . . . Ghost . . . at it's last word vanishes — that is to say — Calcium is taken off and footlights are turned ¾ up.[148]

Last of all, there is the meaningless sophistication of Mansfield's "vaporous shadow in a lurid light, out of which the voice floated." Trapwork — gauzes — nothing at all!

As for Brutus, "the inexpressible tenderness of manner" with which Davenport covered "the boy Lucius with his own mantle," when he found him asleep, was "never to be forgotten." [149] At the end of the scene, "when Brutus finishes speech — he staggers grasps convulsively and falls upon stool." Lucius kneels beside him. "Ring quickly." And to this promptnote, in the Boston Museum book, once more, is added in pencil: "Don't ring till Mr. Booth about to sit."

Cassius in the 1719 adaptation, and often subsequently, has fallen on his sword instead of being stabbed by Pindarus. Creswick, the old Sadler's Wells actor, "treated the gallery to one of the straightest 'backfalls'" Godfrey Turner, an authority on the subject, had ever seen — a "backfall," as he defines it, being "a voluntary fall backward, in rigid form, from heels to shoulders." [150] As Brutus, Mansfield sat at the foot of a shattered tree and,

drawing his shield before his breast and face, his sword slowly searched his heart. There was the fortitude of a general in the convulsion of the whole frame as he withdrew the blade. He slowly lowered the shield, and the sword fell from his fingers as they groped straight before him.

Then, after saying "Caesar now be still . . ." his "head dropped upon his breast, and here Octavius and Antony found him dead." Barron had been caught by Trebonius, "as he falls upon one knee. a shrill Trumpet is heard. Brutus starts up and then falls back dead." [151]

In the Jarrett-Palmer production at Booth's Theatre, in December 1875, the play closed with "a tableau pictorial of the pyre erected for the incineration of the body of *Brutus*." This tableau, which included, it appears, "a number of long sections of stove piping . . . painted to represent logs of wood," had been used originally in Forrest's revival of *Coriolanus* in 1863.[152] But it was quite as appropriate for the one tragedy as for the other.

When Kemble entered, in the opening scene of *Coriolanus*, saying

What is the matter, you dissentious rogues?

"the crowd of mob-Romans fell back as though they had run

against a mad bull, and he dashed in amongst them in scarlet pride, and looked, even in the eyes of the audience, sufficient 'to beat forty of them'." It was "impossible," we read,

not to admire the noble proportions and majestic *contour* of his figure; the expression of his face . . . his right arm erected in conscious authority; his chest thrown forward, and his head slightly back; his right leg fearlessly advanced, and firmness in all his attitude.[153]

Against the lines in which Marcius chides the Plebeians,

> And call him noble that was now your hate,
> Him vile that was your garland . . .

Macready noted: "As Coriolanus advances — at every step [the] Citizens recede a step . . . shrinking with fear from him." [154] In Phelps's promptbook, "they are retiring," just before the entrance of the hero; but when Menenius hails him, the Citizens "turn saying 'Where,' 'Where is he.' menacingly — until Coriolanus on — when they cower." And, at the beginning of the sixth scene, occurs the not uninteresting direction: "18 Roman Troops Enter P.S. 2 & 3rd Es looking back and walking as if fatigued — not in marching order." There was no want of imagination in the productions of Shakespeare at Sadler's Wells.

Sir Walter Scott cites as an instance of the ability of Kemble to employ "instant and precipitate exertion," when it was required, "the mode in which he rushed on the stage," in Scene 6, "with the half breathless cry, 'Am I too late?'" [155] Salvini was admired, three scenes later, when Marcius, begging in behalf of his "poor host" and suddenly overcome by weariness, is asked the man's name. The actor staggered and put his hand to his brow, then, shaking his head, answered: "By Jupiter, forgot! . . . Have we no wine here?" [156]

When, in Act II, Kemble's Coriolanus solicited the "voices" of the Citizens, "Little Simmons," the comedian, "used to peer about for Kemble's wounds like a flimsy connoisseur examining a statue of some mighty Roman"; and, a little further on, having "caught the peculiarities of the great tragedian, and transferred them to his own small person . . . he waved his hand in imitation of the would-be consul, and exclaimed, 'Your voices! your most sweet voices!' " [157] Of another distinguished Coriolanus, Vandenhoff, at the Theatre Royal, Edinburgh, in 1824, we hear that "supercilious disdain was never more powerfully expressed" than it was by him "when a citizen (*Mackay*) makes the attempt to shake hands with him." [158] The same attempt is called for in the "Ludlow and Anderson" Promptbook after the First Citizen has promised Coriolanus his vote — "you shall ha't, worthy sir" — and Coriolanus has replied "A match, sir": "First citizen offers to take his hand."

I have little to tell about the first two scenes in Act III. A stage direction of Kemble's, "All rush tumultuously towards L" is in keeping with the Tribune's command,

> Pursue him to his house and pluck him thence (iii, 1, 309),

and gives point to Menenius's "One word more, one word!" [159] Earlier in the scene, when the Tribunes are attempting to stop Coriolanus on his way to the market place, Phelps's promptbook reads: "Lictors wheel from Centre to RH Wings up Stage and place themselves in a posture of defence — Fasces lowered waiting for Orders. Coriolanus is urged by Com^s — & Lartius &c — R corner . . ." this business helping to cover the interval between the summoning of the Plebeians and their arrival. Another pause, in the next scene, is filled even more effectively.

Cor.   Must I
> With my base tongue give to my noble heart
> A lie that it must bear? Well, I will do't.

"Volumnia looks at Coriolanus" is Phelps's promptnote at the break in the last line.

The great speech in the Banishment Scene —

> You common cry of curs, whose breath I hate
> As reek o' th' rotten fens —

will ever be a challenge to the actor. C. R. Pemberton writes, in 1834, that "Kemble here exhibited stately scorn, indignation and high anger. . . . He accompanied the 'I banish you!' with a stately sweep of lifted arm"; whereas Macready, whose conception seemed to Pemberton more thoughtful, did without "the arm's sweep." Of Phelps, at Sadler's Wells in 1860, Morley tells us:

When the mob raising their staves expel him from city he mounts proudly the steps from which as from his mental height he looks down on them. . . . With a sublimity of disdain he retorts on them that "I banish you," which Edmund Kean erred in delivering with an ungovernable passion.

As for Forrest, "his eyes flashed, his form lifted to its loftiest altitude. . . . As the enraged mob pressed yelping at his heels, he turned, and . . . calmly looked them reeling backwards." [160]

From more recent times comes a detail, recorded by Dickins, concerning the Sicinius of Oscar Asche in Benson's revival of the play in 1901: "I can still see him, after the expulsion of Coriolanus, seated on a stone in the Roman street, contentedly peeling and eating an orange." [161] *Coriolanus* needs such homely touches as this — and the business is in character too.

"*Throwing off his cloak*," a stage direction frequently met with in early nineteenth century stage texts, when the hero makes known his identity to Aufidius, brings to mind Kemble's business at "This is I, Hamlet the Dane"; and among the items of dress listed in Macready's *Coriolanus* promptbook is a "Large dark Cloak — Hamlet's." [162] A truncheon was one of the properties.

There may be danger in suiting the action to the word. In a searching criticism of Vandenhoff at Covent Garden, *John Bull*, September 30, 1838, cites a passage from the climactic scene outside Rome:

after embracing his wife, [Coriolanus] recollects that his mother is a suppliant before him —

> "You gods! I prate,
> And the most noble mother of the world
> Leave unsaluted. *Sink, my knee, i' the earth*;
> Of thy deep duty more impression show
> Than that of common sons."

Whereupon Mr. VANDENHOFF literally clutches hold of his knee, forces it down as if it recalcitrated at volition, and apostrophises it! Now *Coriolanus* surely means — "I'm kneeling, mother, bless me!"

More inspiring is a bit of business in Phelps's performance. When the child is presented, and Volumnia says "Your knee, sirrah," the Sadler's Wells prompter wrote: "Young Marcius about to kneel

Coriolanus catches him up. Kisses him." "That's my brave boy!" he cries; then he gives the child back to Virgilia.

Godfrey Turner brings Phelps vividly before us, at the moment when Coriolanus is taunting his country's enemies:

> like an eagle in a dovecote, I
> Flutter'd your Volscians in Corioles:

A fine action of Phelps's accompanied his utterance of the word "fluttered," which came after a seemingly enforced pause, and with that lifted emphasis and natural break in his voice, remembered, I daresay, by all who admired him in his prime. Lifting his arm to its full outstretched height above his head, he shook his hand to and fro, as in the act of startling a flock of doves.[163]

The hero's death follows swiftly. Scott praises Kemble's

command of muscle and limb . . . when the Volscian assassins approaching him from behind . . . seemed to pass their swords through the body of Coriolanus. There was no precaution, no support; in the midst of the exclamation against Tullus Aufidius, he dropped as dead and as flat on the stage as if the swords had really met within his body. We have repeatedly heard screams from the female part of the audience when he presented this scene, which had the most striking resemblance to actual and instant death we ever witnessed.[164]

Again, as in *Hamlet*, the tragedy ends austerely with the bearing away of the hero's body. In Macready's production, in 1838, "the last effect of all" was gained through "a simple adherence to Shakespeare's own stage directions. . . . The warriors around lift up the dead body of the conqueror on their shields, hang around it the splendidest trophies of war, and trailing their steel pikes in sorrow, move with it up the stage to the sound of mournful music." [165] So the scene was played at Sadler's Wells. But an age of spectacle and melodrama demanded something more exciting; and when Forrest appeared in *Coriolanus* at Niblo's Garden, November 2, 1863, "the performance closed with a tableau showing the incineration of the body of *Coriolanus* upon a huge funeral pyre — a lurid and imposing picture." [166]

Whatever *Antony and Cleopatra* was like on the Elizabethan stage — and Mr. Granville-Barker's *Preface* gives reason to suppose that it could have left little to be desired as an acting play — its history in the theatre, since the introduction of heavy scenery, is profoundly discouraging. It was still possible to make *Antony and Cleopatra* into a spectacle, but to do so was to sacrifice its identity as one of Shakespeare's greatest tragedies.

Such attempts at revival as were made, have yielded little of interest, so far as stage business is concerned. Lacy's edition, "as Performed at the Princess's Theatre, on Wednesday, May 15th 1867," with Miss Glyn, once famous as Cleopatra at Sadler's Wells, heading the cast, is notable for the fullness of its stage directions, and a fair number of them are worth recording here. Thus, in the third scene when Cleopatra, seeing Antony approaching, decides to be "sick and sullen," she "*affects to fall into the arms of* Charmian." ("Help me away, dear Charmian!" are the next words she speaks.) Later, when Antony, referring to Fulvia, says, "See when and where she died," it is "*offering letters*," which Cleopatra, taking, returns "*scornfully*" — "O most false love!" And, at "Cut my lace, Charmian, come," "Attendants *hurry to* Cleopatra"; then, as she adds, "But let it be," "*they retire up*." Benson, at Stratford in 1898, had roses strewn before the lovers at their farewell.[167]

Miss Glyn's Cleopatra struck down the Messenger while he was kneeling but, when she drew a dagger against him, Charmian caught her arm (II, 5). Mrs. Langtry struck him "in the face with the jewels unclasped for the purpose of rewarding his expected intelligence." [168]

Two further details come from Lacy's edition. "*They all rise and come forward, waving their goblets*," is supplied after the first of these lines:

Pom.   This is not yet an Alexandrian feast.
Ant.   It ripens towards it. Strike the vessels, ho!
      Here's to Caesar!

And in the scene of Antony's arming — a scene shot through with allusions to the action in progress — at,

      So, so. Come give me that! This way. Well said,

Antony "*puts on helmet*" and "Cleopatra *gives shield the wrong way*."

Capell, having accepted too literally the hero's words at IV, 14, 23, "She has robb'd me of my sword," makes Antony use the sword of the faithful Eros in taking his own life; and it is this sword, accordingly, which Dercetas now carries away to show Octavius! [168a] In the Drury Lane production with Anderson and Miss Wallis, in September 1873, the suicide of Eros (Howard Russell) is described as "well arranged, contrasting admirably with the bungling effort of Antony." But regret is expressed that "the stage direction" was not "literally followed. Falling on a sword is a more easily realizable form of suicide than thrusting the weapon with a violent effort into the side." Mr. Bernard Shaw writes of Louis Calvert at Manchester in 1897:

> His one really fine tragic effect is the burst of laughter at the irony of fate with which, as he lies dying, he learns that the news of Cleopatra's death . . . is only one of her theatrical, sympathy-catching lies.[169]

In Lacy's edition, the business of 'heaving Antony aloft to Cleopatra' was shirked, and instead he is merely borne in by guards who *"place him on couch."* [170] This was not the case, according to Lady Benson, when her husband's company did the play at Stratford in 1898:

> "Cleopatra" and her maids were discovered on a high balcony, and when the dying "Antony" was brought in . . . we used to lower strips of linen, which the guards wound round "Antony," and raising him on the butt-ends of their halberts, helped us to hoist him over the balcony. This was no easy task . . . but it was a realistic and effective piece of business.[171]

The surprising of the Queen in her monument — an episode hard to visualize in terms of the Elizabethan stage — was effected in Miss Glyn's production by means of a window. While Cleopatra is negotiating with Proculeius at *"a grated door,"* Gallus and two soldiers steal away and presently *"appear at the window, they gently enter and descend to the stage, throw back bar of grated door, R.3 E., and let in* Proculeius *and* Soldiers." [172] Later in the scene, Capell has Cleopatra "flying" at Seleucus — "Slave, soulless villain, dog! / O rarely base!" — and Caesar *"interposing."*

From Lacy's edition, once more, we learn that when Charmian enters shortly before the coming of the "rural fellow" with his figs, *"she whispers to* Cleopatra" — as if telling her that the mission she was sent on had been accomplished. "Now, Charmian!" Cleopatra exclaims; and the words might be so spoken as to bring out the added tension and significance which this business imparts to them. Then Iras "*goes behind screen for robes*, &c."

Mrs. Langtry's death, as Cleopatra, was, to *The Athenaeum* critic (November 22, 1890), "a most effective result of stage management; the aspect of the queen, motionless and erect in her robes, with her handmaidens prostrate and dying before her, is superb"; whereas *The Saturday Review* finds that "the stage business might be improved. 'Falls on a bed and dies,' is the stage direction; but Cleopatra here sits on her throne." The idea of the baby at her breast "that sucks the nurse asleep"; Charmian's "wake her not"; Caesar's "she looks like sleep" . . . and his "take up her bed" — all are against this rigid posture. Rather, she is again lying luxuriously, as once she lay in her barge upon the river of Cydnus "when she first met Mark Antony." [173]

Most of what I have been able to discover about the stage business in *Timon of Athens* comes from a single source. This is the Sadler's Wells Promptbook (now preserved in the Folger Library), used seemingly both in 1851, when Phelps bravely revived the play, and in 1856. The notes possess the characteristics which I have come to associate with Phelps — fidelity to what Shakespeare wrote, as fidelity was then understood, and a careful attention to detail, without fussiness.

Thus, in the first scene, "Old Athenian shakes hands with Lucilius very cordially," to seal the matrimonial bargain arranged by Timon. In Scene 2 — a discovery, of course — there is a general "bowing" to Timon, at frequent intervals. Apemantus, sitting by himself, "pushes away the Goblet & fruit on Table," as he expresses wonder that men should "dare trust themselves with men" when he who sits next you is "the readiest man" to take your life — " 'T has been proved." A moment later (at line 58), he "takes from his Wallet a small wooden Bowl & pours from a Gourd (suspended from his girdle) water — and eats part of a head of celery which he takes out of Wallet." [174] And, at the beginning of Act II, Scene 2, the fact that Timon is returning from hunting is brought out by the entrance of "Alcibiades & Timon in Hunting Dresses with skins of animals as Drapery Spears and one Attendant who receives Timon's spear & Exits."

Edmund Kean, playing in an adaptation of the play in 1816, found opportunities for the passionate effects upon which so much of his fame rests. "The first burst of passion which the character afforded" writes a correspondent to *The Theatrical Inquisitor*, "was ... in the short, but pithy dialogue with the creditors" (III, 4). The following speeches are then quoted:

> Cut my heart in sums! ...
> Tell out my blood! ...
> Five thousand drops pays that. What yours? and yours? ...
> Tear me, take all, and the gods fall upon you!

And the writer continues: "Mr. Kean gazed at the blood hounds who were preying upon his existence, tore open his vest to enforce the offer he had urged, and at length broke from the clamours his distraction could not silence, with an imprecation of tremendous horror on the throng that assailed him." [175]

In Act IV, Scene 3, Phelps as Timon was "discovered seated on Bank, with Spades." He has a "Wallet around neck," into which he later puts some of the gold. Moreover, to the printed direction, "*Digging the Earth*," at line 23, is added in the promptbook, "and shovelling it aside. pulls out the Urn of Gold." As for Kean, his business at another moment in the same scene is memorably described in *The Examiner*, November 3, 1816:

> *Timon*, digging in the woods with his spade, hears the approach of military music; he starts, waits it's approach sullenly, and at last in comes the gallant *Alcibiades* with a train of splendid soldiery. Never was scene more effectively managed. First, you heard a sprightly quick march playing in the distance; — KEAN started, listened, and leaned in a fixed and angry manner on his spade, with frowning eyes, and lips full of the truest feeling, compressed but not too much so; — he seemed as if resolved not to be deceived ... the march threw forth its gallant notes nearer and nearer; — the Athenian standards appear, then the soldiers come treading on the scene with that air of confident progress which is produced by the accompaniment of music; and at last, while the squalid misanthrope still maintains his posture and keeps his back to the strangers, in steps the young and splendid *Alcibiades* in the flush of victorious expectation. It is the encounter of hope with despair.

Bibliographical Notes

Titles marked with an asterisk I have found particularly useful.

Chapter 1. The Comedies

TWELFTH NIGHT

Promptbooks

(a) * John Moore's Promptbook (Harvard).

[Inscribed, and dated "1840." According to a memorandum by Moore in the Harvard Extra-Illustrated *Ireland*, II, pt. 18, p. 53, he was born in England in 1814 and came to Park Theatre in September 1848. In 1853-4 he was at Burton's (Odell's *Annals*), and "Burton" is often named in this book (cf. *Twelfth Night* production in 1852). Later he was with Daly. In obituary notice in *N. Y. Herald*, January 12, 1893, he is said to have managed companies "in all the British possessions" before coming to America. Probably not the "Mr. Moore" who appeared at C. G. in 1840. See also *Othello* "g."]

(b) * Mrs. Shaw's Promptbook, c. 1850 (Harvard).

[Twice inscribed: on p. 1, "Mʳˢ M. A. Hamblin's Prompt Book," in hand which signed a later note "J. B. Addis" — Addis was for "eleven years" prompter and stage manager at Bowery (Brown, *History of the American Stage*, s.n.); on t. p., "Eliza M. A. Hamblin." Mrs. Shaw became Mrs. Hamblin in 1849. See also *King John* "b."]

(c-d) * Two Promptbooks marked by George Becks (N. Y. P.).

[The first, Accession Number 285350, dated "1864"; the second, Accession Number 343034, identified by note opposite Feste's concluding song, "This is general version & as followed by Neilson." Seemingly "1864" is in part by an earlier prompter.]

The "William Warren Edition," Boston [1907], is "based upon the Prompt-Book of Miss Julia Marlowe."

MUCH ADO ABOUT NOTHING

Promptbooks

(a) * Warren and Wood's Promptbook (Harvard).

["Warren & Woods" on first page of text (Bell's ed.). A number

of the named singers and minor actors were with the company in
1810 — cf. James, *Old Drury of Philadelphia*, 15. "Lamps down,"
p. 351; cf. first use of gas in 1815 — Wood, *Personal Recollections*,
206.]

(b) * F. Vining's Marked Copy, 1833 (Harvard).

[Signed, and dated "Haymarket May 1833." *M. A.*, with Vining as
Benedick, closed the season May 15 — *Theatrical Observer*.]

(c) * "Cut, marked, corrected, &c &c as acted at the TR. DL under
the management of Mr Macready" (Harvard).

[Dated on t. p. "1845." But Macready was not at D. L. that year,
and probably a mistake for "1843," when *M. A.* was given, February 24, with Miss Fortescue, Hudson, and Stanton, all of whom are
named in a "calls" pamphlet loosely inserted.]

(d) * James E. Murdoch's Inscribed Promptbook (Univ. of Penna.).

["French's Standard Drama" ed. with 1845 printed cast.]

(e) George Becks's Marked Copy "As done by H Irving Esq."
(N. Y. P.).

[Inserted programme cast of N. Y. performance "March 31ˢᵗ"
(1884).]

(f) * Promptbook and Marked Copies for Fanny Davenport's Production, 1886 (Harvard).

[The copies are marked "Benedick" (with "Barnes" added in pencil), "Don Pedro" ("Buckly"), "Borachio," "Conrad." All are
"Property of Miss Davenport," as is the promptbook. For her American tour in 1886–87, see J. H. Barnes, *Forty Years on the Stage*, 162.]

(g) Promptbook "Used on the Booth-Barrett Transcontinental Trip"
(Harvard).

[Description from H. C. L. card. Book signed "G. W. Riddell."
Business notes at times echo phrasing of "C."]

(h) * Daly Promptbook (N. Y. P.).

[Accession no. 686459. Daly, 1897, ed. Gift of Ada Rehan.]

THE MERCHANT OF VENICE

Promptbooks

(a) * "Marked from Mr C Keans prompt book (by J W Edmonds),
prompter, Princess' Theatre 1850/51" (N. Y. P.).

[Accession no. 342960.]

(b) * Inscribed Promptbook of Mrs. George Vandenhoff (Harvard).

["Modern Standard Drama" ed. Also signed "Miss M. E. M.

Makeah," her maiden name. She married Vandenhoff, August 20, 1855, not long after her début.]

(c) * J. Wallack's Promptbook, 1858 (N. Y. P.).

[Accession no. 342979. Inscribed Jm^s Wallack from his brother H. J. Wallack," with partial cast, "Wallacks Theatre, N. Y. 1858."]

(d) Promptbook "as Played by E. L. Davenport" (N. Y. P.).

[Accession no. 164543. "Property of E. F. Taylor." Version in three acts.]

(e) * Barrett-Booth 1887 Promptbook (Harvard).

[Inscribed: "Property of Lawrence Barrett . . . Marked by Oliver Doud. 1887," and, on flyleaf, "Miss Elizabeth Robins." She was with Booth during tour of 1887–88.]

(f) J. R. Pitman's Promptbook (Furness).

[1881 Booth-Winter ed. At end of Trial Scene: "Ring when Mr. Booth strikes the door." Pitman was long prompter at the Boston Museum. Some hastily-made pencilled additions may be of much later date, and Castle Square Theatre programmes of performances in 1901, 1903, under Pitman's direction, are inserted.]

As You Like It

Promptbooks

(a) ? Eighteenth Century Promptbook (N. Y. P.).

[Bell ed. annotated in old hand. What looks like "Carvers Gar:" (*sc.* "Garden") at beginning of I, 1 — cf. Robert Carver, the scene-painter, died 1791. Very few properties — e. g., a single "gilt chair" in I, 2.]

(b) Marked Copy of 1794 acting edition (Harvard).

[Old hand and faded ink. An actor's name (?) against "Oliver," p. 63, but this is in pencil and perhaps later, as is "write this myself," p. 51.]

(c) Aberdeen 1806 Promptbook (N. Y. P.).

[1775 ed. inscribed "Aberdeen Jany 1806."]

(d) "Prompt Book Theatres Sheffield & Doncaster. Novr 1834" (N. Y. P.).

[The "Sheffield &" are added, as if originally used at Doncaster. Later printed casts inserted, of Birmingham (1847) and Boston (1856) performances.]

(e) * "Prompt Copy Marked & Corrected by Robert Jones Stage Manager Howard Athenaeum Boston 1852" (N. Y. P.).

[Jones became stage manager at the opening of the season of 1852–53 when *As You Like It* was played with Miss Kimberly as Rosalind, Oct. 4 and 15 — Van Lennep.]

(f) * Buckstone's Haymarket 1867 Inscribed Promptbook (A. C. S.).

[Stage directions in Lacy's Acting Edition almost invariably retained. Some pencilled additions refer to Manchester performances.]

(g) * Lester Wallack's Promptbook (N. Y. P.).

[Pencilled cast that of the important revival Sept. 30, 1880 — see Odell, xi, 220. Twice described as "Wallack's Copy."]

(h) James L. Carhart's Marked Copy (Harvard).

[Ed. "As Played by Mrs. Langtry," New York and London, c. 1883, with printed cast including Carhart as Duke. This part and that of Adam are marked.]

(i) * Fanny Davenport's 1886 Promptbook (Harvard).

[Handwriting, cuts, business, etc. identify it with "j" and the Fanny Davenport — J. H. Barnes tour of 1886–87. See *Much Ado* "f."]

(j) Wilton Lackaye's Marked Copy (Harvard).

["Property of Miss Davenport," and "Oliver" (in pencil, "Lackaye") on cover. Lackaye appeared with Miss Davenport on 1886–87 tour. Two other marked copies are for "Phoebe" and "Banished Duke."]

(k) * James Lewis's Marked Copy (Harvard).

["French's Standard Drama" ed. "James Lewis" on wrapper, and the part of Touchstone marked throughout. He played it, under Daly, in 1889.]

The "William Warren Edition," Boston [1907], is "based upon the Prompt Book of Miss Julia Marlowe."

THE TEMPEST

Promptbooks

(a) * ?Eighteenth Century Promptbook (N. Y. P.).

[Bell's ed. "Carver's Rock" or "Rocks" several times mentioned — also, "lamps," p. 238. See *A. Y. L.* "a."]

(b) Becks's Copy of J. B. Wright's "Broadway Theatre" Promptbook (N. Y. P.).

["French's American Drama" ed. (c. 1856), which is based on Wright's promptbook. Becks's date, "October 22, 1863," is presumably that of his transcription. Wright, the Boston stage manager, had left The Broadway by 1854, but perhaps the *Tempest* had been got up for performance there — though not given — before his departure? Or Becks thought that it had been given there?]

MERRY WIVES OF WINDSOR

Promptbooks

(a) Marked Copy, "Corrected and cut according to Prompt book T. R. D. L." (Harvard).

[N. Y., 1817, ed. On p. 1 is written: "From Wilmotts correction T. R. D. L."]

(b) * Bartley's 1840 Promptbook (N. Y. P.).

[Copied by William F. Owen, by permission of Edward Hastings, "for many years the Stage Manager of the Haymarket Theatre." Originally used 'at Covent Garden, Sept. 7, 1840.' Gift of Owen's to Becks.]

(c) * Promptbook "Marked from Mr. Hackets book" (Harvard).

[Dated "Dec. 11, 1840" or "1849" — illegible. "John H. Oxley's book." References also to "Mr. Hamersly," and "R. Baldock." Opposite p. 21, is the note, "Out at Park Theatre." Oxley's N. Y. *début* was in August 1836 — see Odell's *Annals*, iv, 68. Park Theatre was destroyed in 1848; but the allusion to it may be retrospective. "1840" seems a little likelier than "1849."]

A MIDSUMMER NIGHT'S DREAM

Promptbooks

(a) * Samuel Phelps's Inscribed Promptbook (Folger).

[It contains note: "Produced Oct 1853/55–/56–/61."]

(b) * J. B. Wright's "Broadway Theatre, N. Y., 1854," Promptbook (N. Y. P.).

[Accession no. 343412. Inscribed as above, in faded ink on the paper wrapper. See also, Odell, " 'A Midsummer Night's Dream' on the New York Stage," *Shaksperian Studies*, N. Y., 1916.]

(c) Selwyn's Theatre, Boston, 1869, Promptbook (Harvard).

[Identified through references to "Selwyn," "Mrs. B" (sc. Barry) as Oberon, "Tuesday, November 16," and Miss Savory as Second Fairy. Stuart Robson was Bottom in this production.]

THE TAMING OF THE SHREW

(a) * J. P. Kemble's Marked Copy (Furness).

[Dated "1808." Gift of Fanny Kemble to Furness.]

(b) * Walnut Street, Philadelphia, 1848, Promptbook (Univ. of Penn.).

[Inscribed: "G. W. Lewis. Prompter Walnut Street Theatre Phila 1848." James E. Murdoch Collection, and his name on cover.]

(c) Davidge's Marked Copy (Harvard).

["W. Davidge" stamped on copy of early acting edition.]

(d) * George Becks's Promptbook of Daly's 1887 Production (N. Y. P.).

[Daly's 1887 edition very fully annotated, with calls, lights, and a programme inserted.]

CYMBELINE

Promptbooks

(a) Marked Copy of G. F. Cooke, 1806 (Harvard).

["Mr Cooke" on t. p. and Iachimo's part marked. MS. cast headed "Covent Garden, Sat. Jan. 18, 1806."]

(b) * Adelaide Neilson Promptbook (Harvard).

[Identified by "Diagram for Miss Neilson" at beginning of Chest Scene. "Calcium" moonlight and "M trem." — i. e. music tremolo — are called for.]

MEASURE FOR MEASURE

Promptbook

* Sadler's Wells Promptbook (Folger).

[On paper cover, "Prompt Book Theatre Royal Sadlers Wells," and obviously designed for Phelps's production.]

THE WINTER'S TALE

Promptbook

* Eighteenth Century Promptbook of *Florizel and Perdita* (Harvard).

[1758 ed. of Garrick's adaptation much annotated in an early hand. Added passages include some from *The Sheep-Shearing*, some from Shakespeare; and some may be original. Bohemia is "Bithynia" throughout. On p. 3, a note begins: "If Perdita do not sing. . . ."]

THE COMEDY OF ERRORS

Promptbook

* Ludlow and Smith Promptbook (Furness).

["Ludlow and Smith" — the Southern managers, 1835–1853 — on first page of text.]

THE TWO GENTLEMEN OF VERONA

Promptbook

Sadler's Wells 1857 Promptbook (Folger).

[Ms. cast including Lewis Ball as Launce. Not interleaved and not heavily marked.]

LOVE'S LABOUR'S LOST

Promptbook

* Sadler's Wells 1857 Promptbook (Folger).
[Ms. cast includes Phelps as Armado, Ball as Costard, Marston as Berowne, Rose Will[iams] as Moth.]

ALL'S WELL THAT ENDS WELL

Promptbooks

(a) Inscribed Promptbook of William B. Wood (N. Y. P.).
[Kemble 1793 ed.]

(b) Promptbook "Marked for M^r H Edwards by Joe T. Downey Sydney 1858" (Harvard).
["Hy. Edwards" appears on p. 7 — i. e. Harry Edwards, the actor, manager, and entomologist, who died in 1891.]

Chapter II. The Histories

HENRY VIII

Promptbooks

(a) "Cut, quoted and adapted, with the Entrances and Exits properly mark'd, To the Use of the Edinburgh Theatre, Anno Domini 1761" (Furness).
[Manuscript.]

(b) * Cooke-Cooper Promptbook (Harvard).
[MS. cast of New York performance October 2, 1811 — Odell, *Annals*, II, 377, 378.]

(c) * Jarrett and Palmer 1878 Promptbook (N. Y. P.).
[For the production, with Vandenhoff and Geneviève Ward, see Odell, x, 568.]

(d) Marked copy inscribed Russell Bassett (A. C. S.).
[French's Standard Drama ed. See page 78, above.]

I HENRY IV

Promptbooks

(a) William B. Wood's Marked Copy (N. Y. P.).
[Kemble 1815 ed. inscribed.]

(b) * Sadler's Wells 1856 Promptbook (Folger).
[1709 ed. MS. cast includes Phelps, Bennett (King), Creswick (Hotspur), and Marston (Hal).]

(c) Joseph E. Nagle's Marked Copy (Harvard).
[Inscribed by Nagle, and also "F. Chippendale from Mary Shaw December 1857." Nagle's name stands against Hotspur in cast, and the only notes concern Hotspur's part. For Nagle, see Odell, *Annals*, vols. vii–viii. He played Ford to Hackett's Falstaff, at The Broadway, Sept. 24, 1866, and is a likely guess for Hotspur, later in the same engagement.]

2 HENRY IV

Promptbook
Garrick's Marked Copy (Folger).
[See Furness *Variorum*, 652.]

RICHARD III

Promptbooks
(a) William B. Wood's Marked Copy (N. Y. P.).
[Accession no. 164553.]

(b) Promptbook inscribed Stanley Charles Ferrers (N. Y. P.).
[Accession no. 342963. "Stage Manager & Prompter of the Theatres Royal, and Adelphi, — Edinburgh. 1836." Forrest and "Mr C. Kean. 1839" are mentioned in the notes, also "Mr. E. Kean's book."]

(c) * "Sadler's Wells Promptbook March 1845" (Folger).
[So inscribed near beginning; at the end, "Marked under the direction of W C Williams T R Sadlers Wells. for S Phelps Esqre." Contains delightful pen-and-ink sketches of scenes.]

(d) * George Becks's Promptbook (N. Y. P.).
[Accession no. 342980. Forrest (1860) ed. The inserted matter includes a Niblo's Garden, Oct. 20, 1864, printed cast, headed by Forrest, with Becks as Mayor.]

(e) Edwin Adams's Promptbook (Harvard).
["Marked for Edwin Adams Esq. By W^m H Daly Mc Vickers Theatre Feb 1866."]

(f) * Edwin Booth's Promptbook (Players).
[Cibber version. Cast of 1886–1887 tour.]

(g) Lawrence Barrett's Promptbook (Harvard).
["French's Standard Drama" ed. Barrett's name stamped on cover. "Mr. B." often mentioned.]

(h) * Louis James's Promptbook (Furness).

[Cibber version. "Property of Louis L James June — 17 — 1881." His *Hamlet* book is bound with this.]

(i) * Becks's Marked Copy of Mansfield's 1889 Edition (N. Y. P.).

[Accession no. 342934. See page 100, above. Notes are clearly in Becks's hand.]

KING JOHN

Promptbooks

(a) William B. Wood's Marked Copy, 1804 (N. Y. P.).

[Contains a ms. cast of 1807, with Fennell as John, Wood as Faulconbridge.]

(b) * Promptbook prepared by J. B. Addis (Harvard).

[The hand is clearly that of Addis — cf. *Twelfth Night*, "b." On a label on cover is, "E. M. A. Shaw," i.e. Eliza M. A. Shaw who became Mrs. Hamblin in 1849. She did Constance and Hamblin John at The Bowery, October 16, 1843 (Odell, v, 21), and the names of both players figure in these notes.]

(c) "Bowery Theatre New York 1858" Promptbook (Harvard).

[Above this inscription, but in a different hand, is the name "W. H. Stephens," who was at this theatre in 1860 — Odell, vii, 326. In almost every case, the "Modern Standard Drama" directions are underscored, as used.]

(d) Promptbook inscribed "Robt John Preston" (Harvard).

[For a production at the California Theatre, April 1875.]

Helen Faucit's MS. Part, Constance (Furness).

[See page 112, above. "Just as she must have handled it when she acted it in 1842–3" — ms. letter from Sir Theodore Martin.]

HENRY V

Promptbooks

(a) "Prompt Book 1852–5–8 Theatre Royal Sadlers Wells" (Folger).

(b) Charles Kean's Marked Copy (Harvard).

[All notes in pencil. Handwriting probably Kean's. "Mrs. K." twice mentioned, and "the first night." Opposite p. 45 is a comparison with battle sounds in *John* and *Lear*.]

RICHARD II

Promptbooks

(a) Promptbook inscribed John Roberts, 1727 (Folger).

[Two excellent drawings of scenes. Little or no business.]

(b) * Booth's Promptbook, inscribed "Lyceum Theatre N. Y. 1877" (Players).
[Typewritten. The copy used for Booth-Winter Edition.]

Chapter III. Hamlet

Promptbooks

(a) * Crow Street "Promptbook" (Folger).
[Described in Hand "H" (neat and slanting) as "The Prompter's Book, of the Theatre Royal, Crow Street, when under the management of Richard Dailey Esqre — " i.e. 1788–1797. A second hand ("B") is probably the earlier of the two (see especially, p. 47). Many of "H's" notes are literary; and rather a "marked copy" than a promptbook? Holman is mentioned.]

(b) * Brighton Promptbook (Folger).
[Ms. note on t.p., "M^r. Young. Brighton Septr 19. 1809." Kean, Kemble, and Cooper are also mentioned, casually.]

(c) E. Lambert Stirling's Marked Copy (Harvard).
[Dolboy's British Theatre, 1825, ed. Theatres Royal "Richm[ond]" and "Dundee" mentioned. For Stirling's beginnings as a provincial actor, c. 1828, see Percy Allen, *Stage Life of Mrs. Stirling*, 32 note.]

(d) James E. Murdoch's Promptbook (Univ. of Penn.).
[822c, Vol. 47, Oxberry, 1822, ed.]
$\overline{\text{M945}}$

(e) * Henry B. Phillips's Promptbook (N. Y. P.).
[Mod. Standard Drama, 1847, ed. Astor Place, 1848, ms. cast headed by Macready. Some later casts in pencil.]

(e¹) "Marked for J W Wallack as played by him by Henry B Phillips Prompter Wallacks Theatre New York 1856" (N. Y. P.).

(f) * George Becks's Marked Copy (N. Y. P.).
["Forrest" (1860) ed. Introductory note is headed, "A Memory of Some of Forrest's business and manner in Hamlet," and begins, "Having played different parts in the play with him every time he played the part within four consecutive seasons — much has lived with me. Never could I forget it."]

(g) Booth's Marked Copy ("Players").
[Booth, 1866, ed. Marked "Private." Interesting notes on Acts I–II; few thereafter.]

(h) * Booth's Promptbook (Harvard).

["TS 2272.73." Identified by "Call Mr. Booth," p. 60 — and cf. 119. Full, untidy notes in two hands.]

(i) * Lawrence Barrett's Promptbook (Harvard).

["TS 2272.78." Cover label: "Hamlet/Lawrence Barrett," and, on p. 75, "Mr. Barrett will explain fight." Notes not in his hand.]

(j) James Taylor's Marked Copy (Harvard).

["TS 665.9.5." Initialled notes contributed by Booth and Barrett, with whom Taylor acting in 1890.]

(k) * Irving's Promptbook (Harvard).

["TS 2272.75." At end of Act I is written "I.H. Allen. Lyceum March 1877" — Irving's prompter. Valuable diagrams, as well as very full notes.]

(l) Louis James's Promptbook (Furness).

[Inscribed "Louis James 1882 & 3." Text pasted in scrapbook containing also James's prompt copy of *Richard III*.]

Chapter IV. Othello

Promptbooks

(a) John Palmer's Promptbook (Folger).

[1761 ed., inscribed, and dated "1766."]

(b) * Cooke-Cooper Promptbook (Harvard).

[Boston, 1807, ed. with ms. cast headed by Cooke as Iago, Cooper as Othello. The inclusion of Hallam, as the Duke, and Hilson, as Roderigo (cf. Odell, *Annals*, II, 367, 378) points to 1811 and probably to the performance on May 8.]

(c) Kean: "Corrected from the Prompt-Book by G. C. Carr, Prompter, Theatre Royal Drury Lane" (Folger).

[Kemble, 1818, ed.; Carr died in May 1823.]

(d) Charles Durang's Promptbook (Harvard).

[Inscribed: "Charles Durang Chestnut St. Theatre." Dated on cover "1828."]

(e) * Stanley Charles Ferrers's Promptbook (N. Y. P.).

[Accession no. 343041. After F's signature is written: "Stage Man^r & Prompter of the Theatres R. Edinburgh. 1836, 1837." Several American actors (Booth, e.g., and Hamblin) are mentioned on p. 37. George Becks has made additional notes, readily distinguishable.]

(f) "Correctly Marked as play'd by J. Murdoch, Geo. W. Lewis Prompter. W[alnut] S[treet] T[heatre] Phil^a 1845" (Univ. of Penn.).

[James E. Murdoch Promptbooks, vol. 55a.]

(g) * John Moore's Promptbook (Harvard).

[Signed "J. Moore." References to "Brighton," and to Forrest and Graham together (pp. 50, 64) point to a performance there, August 2, 1845 (cf. H. C. Porter, *History of the Theatres of Brighton 1774 to 1886*, p. 81). But Hamblin is often mentioned, and "Park 1848" is pencilled on end paper. Other players mentioned include: Cathcart, C. Kean, Mrs. Warner (Emilia), Anderson, (Emmerline?) Montague, (Rose) Telbin. In original state probably used in English provinces; later in New York. See also page 335.]

(h) George W. Lewis's Promptbook (N. Y. P.).

[Accession no. 342999. "Mod. Standard Drama," N. Y., 1848 ed. inscribed "Broadway Theatre New York 1851"; and again, "Marked as played at Broadway Theatre — Walnut Street Theatre — by — Mr. Forrest — Booth &c." Derivative of "e" — see, e.g., p. 37. Brooke is often mentioned.]

(i) * Clarke-Forrest Promptbook (Harvard).

[Forrest 1860 ed. inscribed: "Property of George H. Clarke November 1868." A ms. cast, headed "Niblo's," includes Forrest and Clarke (Iago). Cf. Odell, *Annals*, VIII, 442 for Forrest-Clarke performances October 21, 22, 1868.]

(j) McCullough Promptbook (Harvard).

["John McCullough" on cover label, and inscribed, at the end, "Prov[idence] Dec. 19." Several hands are discernible. Dr. William Van Lennep identifies one of them as figuring also in a *Macbeth* (Barton Hill) promptbook, c. 1873–1877, and the same interleaving paper was used for both promptbooks.]

(k) * Charles D. Herman's Promptbook (Harvard).

["French's Standard Drama" ed., inscribed "Chas. D. Herman. San Francisco Calif. Aug. 14th 1902." *Othello* was acted there, August 8, with Frederick Warde and Herman (Iago) — information supplied by Dr. Van Lennep.]

Chapter V. Macbeth

Promptbooks

(a) "Adapted to ye Edinburgh Theatre Anno 1761" (Furness).

[Wholly ms. Cast includes Aiken and Mrs. Hopkins. Significant words often underscored. Little business.]

(b) * West Digges (Harvard).

[Edinburgh, 1753, ed. A ms. note of 1803 associates book definitely with Digges's Edinburgh days. His first Macbeth there was in 1757. Perhaps, used not long after?]

(c) ? Eighteenth Century Promptbook, from Sir Henry Irving's Library (Folger).

[1773 acting ed. G. W. Stone, "Garrick's Handling of *Macbeth*," S.P., October 1941, suggests it may be "Gentleman" Smith's text. Notes in ink and (later?) pencil. Little business.]

(d) * H. Charnock's Boston Promptbook, c. 1810–1826 (Furness).

[1794 London acting ed. "1810" on first page of text; "Fall of 1826" on p. 43, when Macready in Boston. He is twice mentioned. For Charnock, cf. Clapp, *Record Boston Stage*, 223, 254.]

(e) * Sadler's Wells Promptbooks (Folger).

[One is dated on cover 1847 – the "7" indistinct, but cf. cast and inclusion of Macbeth's head on pole.

The other – usually preferred by me – contains "Super Plot 1860," though it continued to be used for some years after that date. Leather label on cover is stamped "Theatre Royal Sadlers Wells S. Phelps."]

(f) * "Mark'd & Corrected by Robt Jones Stage Manager Howard Athenaeum Boston 1852" (N. Y. P.).

[Accession no. 343040. "Modern Standard Drama" ed.]

(g) * George Becks's Marked copy (N. Y. P.).

[Accession No. 342970. "Forrest" ed. Some actual prompt directions, in early part only. Many descriptive notes concerning Forrest and Madame Ponisi.]

(h) * George H. Clarke's Promptbook (Harvard).

["Forrest" ed. In 1868–69, Clarke was stage-manager for Forrest, who is often mentioned in this book.]

(i) * Henry Irving's Marked Copy (Furness).

["Clarendon Press Series," 1874, ed. Irving's own pencilled notes, and possibly the copy in which he "studied the title role." Cf. Charles Rann Kennedy, "An Unique Copy of 'Macbeth,' " *The Theatre* (N. Y.), April 1916.]

(j) J. H. Barnes's Promptbook, 1882 (Harvard).

[Initialled slip has: "Prompt Book of Macbeth as played at Drury Lane Theatre by me 1882." For the production, with Madame Ristori, see Barnes's *Forty Years on the Stage*, 135.]

The "William Warren Edition," Boston, 1915, is printed from the promptbook of the Boston Museum Company, ed. Kate Reignolds-Winslow, who was with them in the early eighteen-sixties.

Chapter VI. The Other Tragedies

KING LEAR

Promptbooks

(a) * J. P. Kemble's Marked Copy (Harvard).

[Kemble, 1808, ed. with annotations in his hand.]

(b) * Cooke Promptbook (Harvard).

[A ms. cast including Cooke and Mrs. Mason, who was in America 1809–1811 (see Odell, *Annals*, II, 330, 377), is perhaps that of Park performance, February 22, 1811.]

(c) "Marked from Mr Kean's Book . . . by G. C. Carr Prompr TRDL S. C. Ferrers T. R. Glasgow April 1827" (Harvard).

(d) Promptbook inscribed "R. I. Collier T R. Hull 1830" (N. Y. P.).

(e) H. C. Charnock's Promptbook (Furness).

[Dublin 1758 ed. "Mr Bartn dresses," before IV, 7. Cf. the Barton who made American *début* at The Park, March 1831 (Odell, III, 499), played Lear at The Bowery, Sept. 1832, and was later at New Orleans. See also *Macb.* "d."]

(f) * Forrest Promptbook (N. Y. P.).

[Accession no. 343043. Forrest ed. marked by Becks. Photograph of Becks as Oswald inserted. M'me. Ponisi mentioned, p. 14.]

(g) * Samuel Phelps Promptbook (Folger).

[Inscribed "Sadlers Wells. 1861 . . . G.H. Gates. Prompter." Used also at D.L. 1864–1866.]

(h) * "Copied from P.B. of Jas Wallack Jr" (N. Y. P.).

[Accession no. 342948. Shakespeare's tragedy was given by Wallack at The Bowery, October 29, 1849, and in the following spring – Odell, V, 534, 537, 538.]

(i) Charles Kean's Promptbook (Harvard).

[Dated "April 1858," and has ms. cast. A curious note is "Look thro' for Caius." A lighting and music plan included. Act I much more fully annotated than the rest.]

(j) * Edwin Booth's Typescript Promptbook ("Players").

[Winter ed. Computations of acting time are included for performances January 10, Sept. 13, 1877.]

(k) McCullough Promptbook (Harvard).

[Forrest (1860) ed. Identified by: "Ring when Mr McCullough drops straw," p. 39.]

(l) "Lawrence Barrett's Ms. copy Marked from Mr John McCullough's Prompt Book by R. J. Preston, 1876" (Harvard).

ROMEO AND JULIET

Promptbooks

(a) (?) Eighteenth Century (N. Y. P.).

[Accession no. 709397. Bell ed.]

(b) Henry Betty's Marked Copy (Folger).

[Cumberland ed., repeatedly inscribed. Unimportant.]

(c) * Sadler's Wells Promptbook (Folger).

[Dated "Sept. 15th 1846." No cast given.]

(d) * Providence, 1852, Promptbook (Harvard).

[N. Y. (Taylor) ed., signed "Asa Cushman Prompter." Date (March 5, 1852) and cast (Charlotte Cushman as Romeo, Mrs. Forbes as Juliet) from inserted play bill.]

JULIUS CAESAR

Promptbooks

(a) Promptbook of Garrick Period (Folger).

[Notes identified by Dr. Van Lennep as in hand of the person (Peter Garrick?) who kept the Drury Lane Diary 1760-1769.]

(b) W. B. Wood's inscribed Promptbook (N. Y. P.).

[Kemble, 1814, ed.]

(c) * Phelps, 1846, Promptbook (Folger).

[Reference to "Procession 1846"; ms. cast including Phelps as Brutus, Bennett, Cassius, perhaps that of May 5.]

(d) "Marked from G. Bennett Esqs Book" (N. Y. P.).

[A long inscription, beginning "W. Waller Theatre Royal Sadlers Wells," is dated "Nov. 28th 1850"; other owners are named; business often that in Lacy's ed.]

(e) Harry B. Hudson's Marked Copy, 1867 (A.C.S.).

[French's Standard Drama ed., inscribed and dated "Chicago, Ill., 1867." The parts of Trebonius and Lucius are marked. Hudson was "juvenile man" at the Boston Museum in 1867-1868, coming there from McVicker's Theatre, 1865-1870 — Van Lennep.]

(f) * Boston Museum Promptbook (Furness).

[French's Standard Drama ed., inscribed on cover "Property of J. R. Pitman." MS. cast, including Barron as Brutus, Barrett, Cassius, Cotter, Antony, seems that of performance March 18, 1878. Mention of "Mr. Booth" (see page 326, above) may refer to his appearance with Museum Company, January 25, 1886.]

CORIOLANUS

Promptbooks

(a) Kemble's Marked Copy (Folger).

[Kemble, 1806, ed. marked in his hand.]

(b) Dowton's Marked Copy (Folger).

[Kemble, 1814, ed. Menenius's part marked. Unimportant.]

(c) * Macready's Marked Copy (Folger).

[Inscribed "William Charles M'Cready T.R. Covent Garden." Notes in two hands, one of them Macready's.]

(d) "Ludlow and Anderson" Promptbook (Furness).

[Philadelphia, 1823, ed. "Ludlow and Anderson" stamped on cover. Ludlow was associated with Smith in theatrical management at New Orleans. Was Anderson the English tragedian who did *Coriolanus* there in 1845? (Ludlow, *Dramatic Life*, 611).]

(e) * Sadler's Wells Promptbook (Folger).

[Dated on cover "1845-50-57"; opposite p. 204 is reference to 1860.]

TIMON OF ATHENS

Promptbook

Sadler's Wells Promptbook (Folger).

[Contains ms. casts of 1851, 1856.]

Notes

IN ORDER to cut down the number of notes as much as possible, references to authorities have frequently been grouped in sequences corresponding to those of the text, with semicolons used to distinguish one set of references from another. Thus, on page 66 of the text, I have written.

> Mamillius, early in the nineteenth century, was contented with such playthings as a horse and drum. But Ellen Terry, playing the part in Charles Kean's production, drew about a toy cart "from an actual one, in terra-cotta, preserved in the British Museum." [232]

Note 232 reads: "Oxberry's edition; Kean's edition, William Archer, "The Winter's Tale," *The Nineteenth Century*, October 1887, Ellen Terry, *The Story of My Life*, photograph opposite page 12, etc." Here "Oxberry's edition" is my authority for the early toys; whereas "Kean's edition" and the other two citations refer to Ellen Terry's go-cart.

I do not pretend that the method followed is an ideal one. It has very practical advantages, nevertheless, and should not, I am persuaded, lead to confusion on the reader's part.

All Shakespearean references are to G. L. Kittredge's edition, Boston, etc. [1936].

NOTES TO INTRODUCTION

1. Matthews, "Shaksperian Stage-Traditions" (1916) in *The Principles of Playmaking*, New York, 1925, pp. 100, 101; Hazlitt, *The Examiner*, March 19, 1815, quoted in *A View of the English Stage* (*Collected Works*, edd. Waller and Glover, VIII, 222).

2. Yet it was "one of the strict contract rules" of Daly's Theatre that "every member of the company" should "obey, under penalty, the directions of the manager as to the performance and 'business'" (George Parsons Lathrop, "The Inside Working of the Theater," *The Century Magazine*, June 1898).

3. The example is used by H. B. Irving, *Some Thoughts on "Hamlet,"* Sydney, 1911, pp. 21–24.

4. "Characteristics of the Comic Performances of the Last Century," *The Theatrical Inquisitor*, July 1813. On this matter, see also Dutton Cook "Suit the Action to the Word" in his *On the Stage*, London, 1883.

5. "Mr. Booth's Hamlet," *Appleton's Journal*, November 20, 1875.

6. *Henry Irving*, London [1883], p. 18.

7. London, 1761 (ed. R. W. Lowe, p. 23).

8. "On Mr. Fechter's Acting," *The Atlantic Monthly*, August 1869.

9. Mrs. Gilbert writes that as a young actress she "used to make a point of asking the stars about the business that played up to them. It was really the most important part of 'it all to them. They did not so much mind how the supports did their parts as parts" (*Stage Reminiscences*, ed. Charlotte M. Martin, New York, 1901, pp. 44, 45).

10. *Reminiscences, and Selections from His Diaries and Letters*, ed. Sir Frederick Pollock, London, 1875, I, 94, 95.

11. *The Theatrical Observer*, May 18, 1824. The other "great tragedian" was pretty certainly Young (cf. April 8, 1823).

12. Philadelphia, 1827, II, 231. For the prompter's duties, see William Dunlap, *History of the American Theatre*, 2 vols., London, 1833, II, 273; also William Davidge, *Footlight Flashes*, New York, 1866, chapter xv, and Kate Ryan, *Old Boston Museum Days*, Boston, 1915, pp. 136 ff. A brief but valuable article is William S. Clark's "Restoration Prompt Notes and Stage Practices," *Modern Language Notes*, LI (1936), pp. 226–230. For further references W. J. Lawrence, "The Prompter," *Old Theatre Days and Ways*, London [1935], should be consulted.

13. *Shakespeare on the Stage* [First Series], New York, 1911, p. 21.

14. *San Francisco Chronicle*, August 9, 1902 (for this reference I am indebted to Dr. William Van Lennep of the Harvard Theatre Collection). Cf. Warde, *Fifty Years of Make-Believe*, New York, 1920, pp. 271, 272.

15. Earlier still, there had been the repeal of the monopolies in 1843 (cf. Dion Boucicault, "The Decline of the Drama," *North American Review*, September 1877).

16. "Shakesperian Stage Traditions," p. 101. See also Harry Irvine, *The Actor's Art and Job*, New York, 1942, p. 114.

17. *The Theatrical World of 1895*, London, 1896, p. 294.

18. Cf. Alfred Harbage, "Elizabethan Acting," *P.M.L.A.*, LIV (1939).

19. That the very movement of the lines is sometimes dependent upon action is brought out by Richard Flatter, "William Shakespeare the Actor," *Dublin Magazine*, XIV (1939).

20. London, 1753, p. 13.

CHAPTER I. THE COMEDIES

1. See the mid-century French and Lacy editions, the Moore, Mrs. Shaw, and Becks Promptbooks, Daly's acting edition (1893), and the "William Warren Edition," Boston, 1907 (based on Julia Marlowe's promptbook).

Madame Modjeska, at Booth's, in 1882, appeared in a boat (William Winter, *Shakespeare on the Stage*, Second Series, New York, 1915, p. 62).

2. Gordon Crosse, *Fifty Years of Shakespearean Playgoing*, London, 1941, p. 48; Henry Morley, *Journal of a London Playgoer*, London, 1891, p. 308.

3. Shaw, in Max Beerbohm (ed.), *Herbert Beerbohm Tree*, New York, [1920], p. 249, see also W. L. Courtney, *ibid.*, 255, and Percy Fitzgerald, *Shakespearean Representation*, London, 1908, pp. 73, 74; Edward R. Russell, "Mr. Irving's Work," *Fortnightly Review*, September 1, 1884.

4. *Theatrical World of 1894*, p. 30. "Malvolio *goes off in contempt, waved away by* Olivia" is the direction in Daly's edition.

5. Cf. Fitzgerald, *Shakespearean Representation*, 73, "William Warren Edition." The wand itself is called for in Mrs. Shaw's promptbook. It is doubtless older.

6. *The Leader*, October 5, 1850, quoted in *Dramatic Essays of John Forster and George Henry Lewes*, edd. William Archer and R. W. Lowe, London, 1896, p. 106; Charles Edward Russell, *Julia Marlowe: Her Life and Art*, New York, 1926, pp. 123, 124.

7. *Theatrical Notes*, London, 1893, pp. 204, 205; *What the Author Meant*, 92, 93.

8. *History of the American Theatre*, London, 1833, II, 57, 58. The performance would seem to have been shortly after Mrs. Jordan's first appearance as Viola, November 11, 1785.

9. *European Magazine*, December 1820; *Fifty Years of Shakespearean Playgoing*, 144; Charlotte Stopes, in *Poet-Lore*, VIII (1896), p. 343, and cf. page 7, below.

10. *Notes and Various Readings*, London [1779], part IV, p. 146. As Kittredge notes, "'There you lie' gives excellent sense without any such buffoonery" (Ed. *Twelfth Night*, p. 116).

11. Performance at Ogunquit, Maine, July 21, 1934.

12. Seemingly, the candle business was the more recent. Up to "or" the note is in an earlier hand; what follows, in Becks's own. His "Neilson" book has only this. Cf. also "William Warren Edition."

13. William Winter, *Ada Rehan*, New York and London, 1898, p. 191; "The Essentials of Stage Success," *Theatre* (New York), December 1901.

14. "1864" Promptbook. Mrs. Shaw's also has the tree. Great liberties have often been taken with the convention by which the presence of the conspirators remains unperceived by Malvolio.

15. *Dramatic Essays*, ed. Brander Matthews, New York [1891], p. 51 (he is writing of a performance at Drury Lane in 1790); William L. Keese,

William E. Burton, New York and London, 1885, p. 79 (for the date, cf. Odell, *Annals of the New York Stage*, VI, 209).

16. *Boston Advertiser*, April 18, 1893, in Blinn Shakespeare Scrapbooks (Harvard Theatre Collection).

That Aguecheek's "As plain as I see you now" (III, 2, 11) was prompted by his catching Sir Toby exchanging winks with Fabian is at least conceivable (see "William Warren Edition").

17. James Boaden, *Memoirs of the Life of John Philip Kemble, Esq.*, 2 vols., London, 1825, I, 57; Becks Promptbook, cf. "William Warren Edition."

18. Dougald MacMillan, ed., *Drury Lane Calendar 1747–1776*, Oxford, 1938, p. 99; *London Chronicle*, November 1–3, 1763; *Ibid.*, November 8–10. For the stage sentry as an institution, see W. J. Lawrence, *Old Theatre Days and Ways*, London, Bombay, and Sydney [1935], chapter XXIV.

19. *Theatrical Inquisitor*, for November 1820; *Edinburgh Dramatic Review*, May 17, 1825. Leigh Hunt [?] writes of Liston in *The Examiner*, November 12, 1820, that "the faintness with which he sinks back on *Sir Toby's* breast, is absolute 'dissolution and thaw.'"

20. See Becks and Mrs. Shaw Promptbooks, Lacy's Acting Edition, "William Warren Edition," and cf. Spedding, "Miss Kate Terry in Viola," *Fraser's*, August 1865. For similar business in *The Merry Wives of Windsor*, see page 47, below.

21. C[harlotte] P[orter], in *Shakespeariana*, IV (1887), 236; *New York Dramatic Mirror*, February 20, 1904.

22. At the end of III, 4, Daly introduced a new scene in which Olivia is serenaded. Clement Scott and William Winter liked it immensely.

23. William Archer, "'Twelfth Night' at the Lyceum," *Macmillan's Magazine*, August 1884, see also, *Saturday Review*, July 12, 1884.

24. *Furness Variorum*, 309; Morley, *Journal of a London Playgoer*, 139, 140.

25. *The Athenaeum*, February 9, 1901, Mrs. George Cran, *Herbert Beerbohm Tree*, London, 1907, p. 58; Russell, *Julia Marlowe*, 348, 349, "William Warren Edition," cf. Richard Dickins, *Forty Years of Shakespeare on the English Stage: August, 1867 to August, 1907*, p. 151.

26. F. Vining's Marked Copy; Macready Promptbook; Becks's Marked Copy.

27. Vining and Becks Marked Copies.

28. Macready Promptbook, Irving's Acting Edition (c. 1883), Barrett-Booth Promptbook; Fanny Davenport Promptbook (picturesque details of the same sort were introduced also, in II, 1).

29. *Macready as I Knew Him*, London, 1884, pp. 131, 132; Macready Promptbook.

30. J. T. Grein, *Dramatic Criticism*, London, 1899, p. 46; *Saturday Review*, January 10, 1891.

31. See Kittredge, ed., *Much Ado*, p. 101. The direction reappears in the Barrett-Booth Promptbook.

32. For Becks's comments on Mansfield's *Richard III*, see pages 100, 105, below.

33. *John Bull*, March 4, 1843; Daly's Acting Edition, 1897; Dickins, *Forty Years of Shakespeare*, 113, *New York Dramatic Mirror*, February 11, 1905, A. B. Walkley, *Drama and Life*, London [1907], p. 140.

34. Cumberland's *British Theatre* (c. 1830), "Modern Standard Drama," New York, 1848, etc. The second direction was kept in preparing the Barrett-Booth Promptbook.

35. Leigh Hunt, *Dramatic Essays*, edd. Archer and Lowe, London, 1894, p. 206; Macready Promptbook, Charles Dickens, "Macready as Benedick," from *The Examiner*, March 4, 1843, quoted in *Works*, "Gadshill Edition," vol. xxxv, *John Bull*, March 4, 1843.

36. [Margaret Stokes,] "Helen Faucit," *Blackwood's*, December 1885; Clement Scott, *Ellen Terry*, New York [1900], p. 16 (she used this run in making her exit at the close of ii, 3).

37. Vining's promptbook. The Warren-Wood Promptbook includes the business, but as if it were a late addition. Daly's promptbook calls for it.

38. Daly Promptbook, *Boston Advertiser*, May 4, 1897 (in Blinn Shakespeare Scrapbooks).

At iii, 2, 111, Claudio, in Miss Davenport's production, "starts towards John Pedro stops him" — Don Pedro's marked copy.

39. Claire McGlinchee, *The First Decade of the Boston Museum*, Boston [1940], p. 86.

40. At line 28 (Macready Promptbook); line 72 (Daly's edition).

41. Walter Goodman, *The Keeleys on the Stage and at Home*, London. 1895, p. 163, quoting from an anonymous article ascribed to Dickens.

42. *Sir Henry Irving*, Philadelphia [1906], p. 149, see also Harcourt Williams, in H. A. Saintsbury and Cecil Palmer, edd., *We Saw Him Act*, London, 1939, p. 236.

43. Was this inspired by Brabantio's rejection of Desdemona? Cf. page 188, below.

44. L. Clarke Davis, in *Philadelphia Inquirer*, March 19, 1884, quoted in *Furness Variorum*, 393; *Saturday Review*, October 21, 1882 (also, *ibid.*, June 18, 1887); Daly's promptbook.

45. Cf. also, Murdoch and Barrett-Booth Promptbooks, *Saturday Review*, October 21, 1882.

46. Fanny Davenport 1886 Promptbook. For the spurious lines regularly introduced here in nineteenth century performances (even Irving could not resist them!) see *Furness Variorum*, 229. One of the two issues of the play in Mrs. Inchbald's *British Theatre* (1808) contains the lines, possibly for the first time.

47. *Edinburgh Theatrical Observer, and Musical Review*, March 15, 1824.

48. *Life and Times*, second edition, 2 vols., London, 1827, I, 86, 87, cf. Cole, *Charles Kean*, II, 332. "*Takes.off his Hat*," Cumberland's direction for Benedick at line 191, reappears often in acting texts.

49. *Drama and Life*, London [1907], p. 140.

50. Benedick's Marked Copy; *John Bull*, March 4, 1843.

51. *Saturday Review*, March 10, 1891; *New York Mirror*, September 11, 1830, quoted in Matthews and Hutton, *Actors and Actresses: Kean and Booth and Their Contemporaries*, 269.

52. Cole, *Charles Kean*, II, 264, Kean's edition (1858); Clement Scott, *From "The Bells" to "King Arthur*," London, 1897, p. 169; *Boston Herald*, January 21, 1890 (in Blinn Shakespeare Scrapbooks); Alfred Ayres, in *New York Dramatic Mirror*, September 2, 1899, Daly's edition, 1898.

53. *On Actors and the Art of Acting*, New York, 1878, p. 20, see also Hazlitt, "Actors and the Public," *Works*, edd. Waller and Glover, XI, 351; *Theatrical Journal*, December 26, 1840. Shylock's staff was, after Kean's time, a regular property (cf. Gordon Crosse, *Fifty Years of Shakespearean Play-going*, 156).

54. Page 33. For Booth's own carefully planned discovery of Shylock and Bassanio, see Winter, *Shakespeare on the Stage*, First Series, p. 157.

55. *Shakespeariana*, III (1886), 524; Winter, *Shakespeare on the Stage*, First Series, p. 180; C[harlotte] P[orter], in *Shakespeariana*, IV (1887), 121.

56. William Winter, *Life and Art of Richard Mansfield*, 2 vols., New York, 1910, I, 195, II, 118, H. A. Clapp, in *Boston Advertiser*, February 24, 1897 (Blinn Shakespeare Scrapbooks); *Furness Variorum*, p. 46; *Shakespeariana*, III (1886), 525.

57. [?Theodore Martin,] "Theatrical Reform," *Blackwood's*, December 1879, puts the business earlier, but see Scott, *From "The Bells" to "King Arthur*," 166, Winter, *Shakespeare on the Stage*, First Series, p. 183, and cf. Percy Fitzgerald, *Henry Irving: A Record of Twenty Years at the Lyceum*, London, 1893, pp. 131, 132.

58. *Theatrical World of 1897*, pp. 154, 155; Barrett-Booth Promptbook (cf. Winter, 157); Winter, 184, see also Crosse, *Fifty Years of Shakespearean Playgoing*, 11, 81.

59. *The Athenaeum*, June 19, 1858.

60. *The Roscius*, January 4, 1825; Alfred Ayres, in *New York Dramatic Mirror*, September 2, 1899; Frederick Warde, *The Fools of Shakespeare*, New York, 1913, p. 119.

61. Staunton's note (1858) in *Furness Variorum*, p. 69, citing "stage tradition, not improbably from the time of Shakespeare himself." The direction "*Falls on his knees*" goes back only to Kemble. See also, Norman Hapgood, *The Stage in America 1897–1900*, New York, 1901, p. 157.

62. Cf. Warde, *Fools of Shakespeare*, 106 ff., and pencilled notes in Pitman's promptbook.

63. For full descriptions, see "American Academy of Dramatic Arts' Edition" (1902), and Pitman Promptbook. Matthews, who appears to have

the same business in mind, compares the treatment of Peter in *Romeo and Juliet*, I, 2 (*Principles of Playmaking*, 115). See also Harcourt Williams, *Four Years at the Old Vic*, London [1935], p. 39.

64. Mrs. Inchbald's *British Theatre*. Kemble's 1797 edition lacks the direction, but see, e. g., Charles Kean and Barrett-Booth Promptbooks (in the Winter-Booth Edition, the scene is outside the house).

65. Winter, *Shakespeare on the Stage*, First Series, pp. 185, 186; *Boston Herald*, December 19, 1893 (in Blinn Shakespeare Scrapbooks), Winter, *Mansfield*, II, 108; Cole, *Charles Kean*, II, 310, Clement Scott, *The Drama of Yesterday and To-day*, 2 vols., London and New York, 1899, I, 238.

66. Jessica may well carry a torch — as she does in the Barrett-Booth Promptbook.

67. There are many accounts. See, especially: *Mr. Henry Irving and Miss Ellen Terry in America: Opinions of the Press*, Chicago, 1884, pp. 27 ff., Ellen Terry, *The Story of My Life*, London, 1908, pp. 186, 187, Winter, *Shakespeare on the Stage*, First Series, pp. 176, 177, Matthews, *Principles of Playmaking*, 119, 120.

68. Clapp, in *Boston Advertiser*, December 19, 1893 (Blinn Shakespeare Scrapbooks), Winter, *Shadows of the Stage*, Third Series, New York, 1895, p. 145; Winter, *Shakespeare on the Stage*, First Series, p. 208. Both Daly and Benson adopted Irving's business within our period. For later actors, see W. Bridges Adams, "Shakespearean Tradition in the Theatre," *Quarterly Review of Speech*, XVI (1930).

69. *Lichtenberg's Visits to England*, edd. M. L. Mare and W. H. Quarrell, Oxford, 1938, p. 40; Thomas R. Gould, *The Tragedian*, New York, 1868, p. 77; Winter, *Mansfield*, II, 118; Hapgood, *The Stage in America*, 159, 160, Daly's edition.

70. Philadelphia *Mirror of Taste and Dramatic Censor*, May 1811; Fox, "W. C. Macready," *The People's Journal* (London), December 12, 1846.

71. *Dramatic Magazine*, May 1, 1830; *Tallis's Dramatic Magazine*, January 1851; *Chicago Tribune*, quoted in *Mr. Henry Irving and Miss Ellen Terry in America*, 39.

72. *Shakespeare on the Stage*, First Series, pp. 190 ff. Benson poured dust on his head, at the close of this scene (Crosse, *Fifty Years of Shakespearean Playgoing*, 35).

73. "Helen Faucit," *Blackwood's Edinburgh Magazine*, December 1885.

74. Ellen Terry, *The Story of My Life*, 185, 186.

75. *Shakespeare on the Stage*, First Series, p. 218.

76. See also "American Academy of Dramatic Arts' Edition."

77. *The Jew of Venice* (1701); *Chicago Inter-Ocean*, quoted in *Mr. Henry Irving and Miss Ellen Terry*, 27.

78. *The World, or Fashionable Advertiser*, October 20, 1788; *Blackwood's Edinburgh Magazine*, December 1879, cf. also Charles Kean and Wallack Promptbooks; Daly's edition.

79. Sir Theodore Martin, *Helena Faucit*, Edinburgh and London, 1900,

pp. 326, 327, cf. also Mrs. Vandenhoff and Wallack Promptbooks, Winter-Booth Edition.

80. Cole, *Charles Kean*, I, 322 (see also page 29, below); Joseph Knight, *Theatrical Notes*, London, 1893, p. 303, cf. also Odell, *Shakespeare from Betterton to Irving*, II, 423, Scott, *From "The Bells" to "King Arthur,"* 167; *Random Recollections*, London [c. 1899], p. 83.

81. Winter, *Shadows of the Stage*, Third Series, p. 146, see also Clapp, in *Boston Advertiser*, December 19, 1893 (Blinn Shakespeare Scrapbooks).

82. Winter, *Shakespeare on the Stage*, First Series, p. 193; *Punch*, November 15, 1879, Percy Fitzgerald, *Sir Henry Irving*, 105, Anna B. McMahan, "Mr. Irving's Shylock," *Dial*, October 16, 1893, etc. For Booth's serpent-like gesture with his hand at line 69, see Otis Skinner, *Footlights and Spotlights*, Indianapolis, 1924, p. 93.

83. George Daniel's prefatory note to the play in Cumberland's *British Theatre*, VI (1826), p. 5. See also, for Cooke, *Mirror of Taste and Dramatic Censor*, May 1811; and, for Macklin, [J. H. Leigh,] *The New Rosciad*, London, 1785, p. 10, *The European Magazine*, April 1800, and cf. *London Chronicle*, May 7–9, 1789.

84. *The Drama; Or, Theatrical Pocket Magazine*, August 1822; Alfred Gatty, in *Notes and Queries*, December 3, 1893, Cumberland and Oxberry editions, and cf. James E. Murdoch, *The Stage: Or, Recollections of Actors and Acting*, 326, 327. The "sole-soul" conceit was often omitted in older acting editions.

85. *Furness Variorum*, 204 (and cf. *ibid.*, 384); *The Theatre* (New York), November 2, 1889, see also November 23.

86. *Monthly Mirror*, for March 1808, *Mirror of Taste and Dramatic Censor*, May 1811, William Dunlap, *Life of George Fred. Cooke*, second edition, 2 vols., London, 1815, II, 188, 189; *Furness Variorum*, 213; Martin, *Helena Faucit*, 325, [Margaret Stokes,] in *Blackwood's*, December 1885. See also, Gould, *The Tragedian*, 79.

87. *Theatrical Observer*, June 14, 1822; [Payne,] *The Opera Glass*, January 13, 1827; Winter, *Shakespeare on the Stage*, First Series, pp. 194, 195 (cf. Fitzgerald, *Henry Irving: A Record of Twenty Years at the Lyceum*, London, 1893, p. 134).

88. *Athenaeum*, June 19, 1858; *Theatrical Journal*, October 4, 1871; *Shakespearean Plays of Edwin Booth*, ed. Winter, Philadelphia, 1899 (1908). At "*kneels*," Pitman's promptbook adds, "& bares his bosom."

89. See Odell, *Annals of the New York Stage*, II, 359, Talfourd, *Shylock; Or, The Merchant of Venice Preserved* (1853), *Furness Variorum*, 222.

90. *The Theatre*, December 1, 1879, Scott, *From "The Bells" to "King Arthur,"* 168; *Mr. Henry Irving and Miss Ellen Terry*, especially the Philadelphia excerpts, pp. 7, 11.

91. *Chicago Inter-Ocean*, in *ibid.*, 25; *Shakespeare in the Theatre*, London, 1913, p. 132, *Shakespeare's Library*, ed. W. Carew Hazlitt, vol. I, part I,

p. 348; *Dramatic Magazine*, December 1, 1829, Leman Thomas Rede, *The Road to the Stage*, London, 1827, p. 96.

92. Lacy's Acting Edition, Wallack Promptbook.

93. *Boston Advertiser*, October 14, 1895 (in Blinn Shakespeare Scrapbooks).

94. February 15, 1825. See also *ibid.*, March 4, *The Opera Glass*, January 13, 1827, *The Theatre*, October 18, 1828.

95. *Dramatic Magazine*, August 1830.

96. *Theatrical Journal*, September 19, 1840, G. H. Lewes, *Dramatic Essays*, edd. Archer and Lowe, 117; *Theatrical Observer*, August 31, 1837, *John Bull*, September 3, 1837; Katherine Goodale, *Behind the Scenes with Edwin Booth*, Boston and New York [1931,] p. 312, cf. *Furness Variorum*, 229.

97. Accounts are very numerous. See especially, Dickins, *Forty Years of Shakespeare on the English Stage*, 35, and Henry Arthur Jones, *The Shadow of Henry Irving*, New York [1931], pp. 52, 53.

98. Winter, *Shakespeare on the Stage*, First Series, p. 199, and his *Richard Mansfield*, I, 279, II, 113. Calvert at Manchester allowed Shylock to reappear after the Trial Scene followed by a mob (*Punch*, October 14, 1871).

99. *Philadelphia Press*, and *Chicago Tribune*, in *Mr. Henry Irving and Miss Ellen Terry*, 12, 29; Ellen Terry, *Story of My Life*, 185, cf. Edward Gordon Craig, *Ellen Terry and Her Secret Self*, London [1931], p. 164.

100. *Random Recollections*, 84.

101. A. Darbyshire, *The Art of the Victorian Stage*, London and Manchester, 1907, p. 40, *Punch*, October 14, 1871.

102. "'*As You Like It*' à l'Américaine," *Blackwood's*, September 1890; *Dramatic Review*, February 1, 1885.

103. Daly's acting edition (1890); Lester Wallack's promptbook, "William Warren Edition."

104. "Pittite Memories," *The Theatre*, November 1, 1883; *Shakespeare on the Stage*, Second Series, pp. 278 ff.; Crosse, *Fifty Years of Shakespearean Playgoing*, 31. For an ingenious modern expedient for avoiding the danger of ridicule here, see Harcourt Williams, *Four Years at the Old Vic*, London [1935], pp. 189, 190.

105. He spoke the line as recently as 1886 (Lackaye's Marked Copy). For the gag, see Warde, *The Fools of Shakespeare*, 48.

106. 1794 Marked Copy.

107. [Margaret Stokes,] "Helen Faucit," *Blackwood's*, December 1885, cf. Helen Faucit, *On Some of Shakespeare's Female Characters*, Edinburgh and London, 1891, p. 244; Winter, *Shakespeare on the Stage*, Second Series, p. 296.

108. "William Warren Edition"; C[harlotte] P[orter], in *Poet-Lore*, 1 (1889), p. 142.

109. *The Dramatic Censor*, I, 465. James Carhart's marked copy of Mrs.

Langtry's acting edition (c. 1883) still has the knocking. It is absent in the Daly and "William Warren" editions.

110. Eighteenth Century (?) Promptbook in New York Public Library, Sheffield and Doncaster Promptbook; Howard Athenaeum and Wallack Promptbooks, Carhart's Marked Copy.

111. Cf. 1, 3, 119, and R. G. White, *Studies in Shakespeare*, Boston and New York, 1886, p. 245; and, for the crook, Howard Athenaeum and other promptbooks, Daly's edition.

112. *The Theatre*, April 1, 1880, *Athenaeum*, March 6, 1880.

113. Wallack and Fanny Davenport Promptbooks, Daly's edition.

114. "'*As You Like It*' à l'Américaine," *Blackwood's*, September 1890.

115. As, e. g., in *Love in a Forest*, where, though Orlando still says, "Come I will bear thee to some Shelter," he goes out, and later returns, merely "*leading* Adam."

116. "Eighteenth Century," Howard Athenaeum, and Wallack Promptbooks.

117. E.g., *The Monthly Mirror*, N.S., viii (1810), p. 466, *Shakespeariana*, v (1888), p. 223, J. R. Towse, *Sixty Years of the Theater*, New York and London, 1916, p. 113; Darbyshire, 77, 78; Max Beerbohm, *Around Theatres*, New York, 1930, II, 616, *Oscar Asche His Life*, London [1929], p. 119. At "Even in the cannon's mouth . . ." Daly's edition has the listeners "nod to each other."

118. Exceptions are Bell's and the "William Warren" editions. Dover Wilson has Rosalind find the verses. Kittredge has her bring them.

119. *Shadows of the Stage*, Second Series, New York, 1893 (1898), p. 251, repeated in his *Wallet of Time*, II, 155. Ada Rehan carried one paper with her and took another from the tree (Daly's edition).

120. *Dramatic Review*, September 5, 1885, Winter, *Shakespeare on the Stage*, Second Series, p. 299; *Our Theatres in the Nineties*, II, 122.

121. *The Dramatic Review*, February 1, 1885.

122. *Playhouse Impressions*, London, 1892, p. 32, Clement Scott, *Thirty Years at the Play and Dramatic Table Talk*, London [1891,] p. 216. See also, *The Athenaeum*, March 4, 1871 (on Mrs. Rousby), and the Daly and "William Warren" editions.

123. *Life Was Worth Living*, New York and London [1931], p. 71.

124. *Saturday Review*, July 26, 1890, "'*As You Like It*', à l'Américaine"; Wallack's promptbook, cf. Daly and "William Warren" editions.

125. Knight, *Theatrical Notes*, 17; Winter, *Shakespeare on the Stage*, Second Series, pp. 299, 300.

126. Cumberland's *British Theatre* (1826). Wallack's promptbook also gives her the sunflower, knife, and turnip. The sunflower is wanting in Fanny Davenport's promptbook.

127. Mary Anderson, *A Few Memories*, New York, 1896, p. 197; W. G. Robertson, *Life Was Worth Living*, 72; *The Theatre*, February 1, 1894.

See also Dutton Cook, *Nights at the Play*, 2 vols., London, 1883, 1, 247, and *The Theatre*, May 1, 1894. Much later, Elizabeth Fagan always ate "a big raw turnip," as Audrey with Benson's Company (*From the Wings*, London, etc. [1922,] p. 73).

128. L. Clarke Davis, "Gossip about Actors," *The Galaxy*, May 1873; "William Warren Edition," cf. *Poet-Lore*, i (1889), p. 144; Daly's edition. For the deer carried across the stage at many Stratford performances, in iv, 2, see C. E. Flower in "Memorial Theatre Edition," p. vi.

129. Mary Anderson's acting edition, New York, c. 1885, "William Warren Edition," cf. " '*As You Like It*' à l'Américaine"; Davenport Promptbook, Daly and "William Warren" editions; *Monthly Mirror*, xv (1803), p. 276, Daly's edition.

130. Lacy's Acting Edition (c. 1842), Howard Athenaeum Promptbook, etc.

131. *The Fools of Shakespeare*, 67, 68.

132. As reproduced in Daly's edition, the accompanying photograph of Lewis and Isabel Irving has for text the words under discussion.

133. Cf. C. D., "Audrey — A Country Wench," in *The Theatre*, May 1, 1894. Later in the scene, Daly's edition has "Touchstone *seeing* Jaques de Bois, *seizes* Audrey, *puts her arm in his, and drags her up the stage.*"

134. Mrs. Inchbald's *British Theatre* (1808), Cumberland, etc.; Hesketh Pearson (ed.), *The Swan of Lichfield*, New York, 1937, pp. 91, 92; Hapgood, *The Stage in America*, 169.

135. Tree's acting edition, 1904; Kemble's, 1806; "French's American Drama: The Acting Edition, Arranged and Adapted for Representation at the Boston Theatre, by Mr. Thomas Barry," c. 1856, Daly's acting edition, 1897. In the French edition — which is based on the promptbook of J. B. Wright, Stage Manager of the Boston Theatre — a "*large bush of flowers expands in centre, slowly, and discovers* Ariel."

136. Forster and Lewes, *Dramatic Essays*, 70, 71. Similar business is called for in the French and Daly editions.

137. Lady Benson, *Mainly Players*, 97; *ibid.*, 179, Crosse, *Fifty Years of Shakespearean Playgoing*, 31; Tree's acting edition, see also Mrs. George Cran, *Herbert Beerbohm Tree*, London, 1907, p. 68.

138. Kemble's 1806 edition; "French's American Drama"; Lady Benson, *Mainly Players*, 94; Daly's edition; Charles Kean's acting edition (1857).

139. October 21, 1838, cf. Archer, *William Charles Macready*, London, 1890, p. 118.

140. This table should be carefully distinguished from a later one which "*rises*" to tempt Trinculo and Stephano, then sinks again. Downes seems to have confused them, speaking of a scene "flying away, with a Table Furnisht out with Fruits, Sweetmeats and all sorts of Viands; just when Duke *Trinculo* and his Companions, were going to Dinner" (*Roscius Anglicanus*, ed. Summers, 34, 35). For Shakespeare's "quaint device" for the

vanishing, see John C. Adams, "The Staging of *The Tempest*, III, iii," *Review of English Studies*, October 1938.

141. *Letters*, ed. Mrs. Paget Toynbee, IV, 86. The Late Eighteenth Century Promptbook calls for "Table ready & Trap," before the appearance of the banquet, which now rises without Bell's devil attendants.

142. Cole, *Charles Kean*, II, 221; *Athenaeum*, July 4, 1857; *Shakespearean Representation*, 47 ff.

143. Kittredge and Wilson both accept this meaning, and compare V, I, 10.

144. See also Oxberry and Cumberland editions, Becks's promptbook, C. M. DeReyes, *On the Acting of Shakespeare's Plays*, London and Glasgow, 1928, p. 90, G. R. Foss, *What the Author Meant*, London, 1932, p. 45.

145. See Montague Summers, *The Restoration Theatre*, 241.

146. *Reminiscences and Diaries*, ed. Sir. Frederick Pollock, 2 vols., London, 1875, II, 151. See also *ibid.*, pp. 118, 121, 126.

147. *The Old Play-Goer*, London, 1846, pp. 33, 34, and, on Miss Horton's flying, *Theatrical Observer*, October 15, 1838, Forster, *Dramatic Essays*, 68, *John Bull*, October 21, 1838, etc.

148. Fitzgerald, *Shakespearean Representation*, 45 note, *Saturday Review*, November 4, 1871, Dutton Cook, *Nights at the Play*, I, 176. Charles Kean also had a bat ridden by Ariel (Acting Edition and Cole, II, 220). Calvert's Ariel at Manchester took the flying less literally (see Mrs. Charles Calvert, *Sixty-Eight Years on the Stage*, 70, 71).

149. Kean's acting edition, *Theatrical Journal*, August 26, 1857; *ibid.*, November 8, 1871, cf. Cook, *Nights at the Play*, I, 175; Tree's edition, *Illustrated London News*, September 24, 1904, Dickins, *Forty Years of Shakespeare on the English Stage*, III, 112.

150. *Daily Courant*, May 16, 1704, cf. Downes, *Roscius Anglicanus*, 47.

151. Dickins, *Forty Years of Shakespeare*, 105; Cumberland's *British Theatre* (1826), cf. "French's Standard Drama," c. 1855; *The Merry Wives of Windsor: A Reprint of the Prompt-Copy prepared for Use at Daly's Theatre* (etc.), introduction by Winter, New York, 1886.

152. Cf. Oxberry's *New English Drama*, 1818 (separate t. p., 1820).

153. Cf. French's edition: "Falstaff . . . *tired out* – Pistol *and* Nym . . . *laughing at him*" – after he has driven them about.

154. Charles and Mary Cowden Clarke, *Recollections of Writers*, London, 1878, p. 337, Daly's edition.

155. In French's edition the joke must needs be explained: "Ah! Jack-a-dandy, I tell you to follow my heels, not tread on my heels." Daly has Mrs. Quickly immobilized as well as Simple.

156. Cf. Daly's edition – where, by the way, Mrs. Ford and Mrs. Page are distractingly introduced listening to Falstaff and Mrs. Quickly. The gag is found earlier (e. g., in Kemble's 1797 edition). Pistol's continued presence is awkward – cf. H. C. Hart's edition, pp. 85, 91.

157. Bartley's promptbook; *New York Literary World*, March 26, 1853 (in Blinn Shakespeare Scrapbooks).

158. Bartley's promptbook, French and Daly editions.

159. *The World, or Fashionable Advertiser*, October 10, 1789; *European Magazine*, for June 1797. *The Examiner*, May 1, 1808, questions Sir Hugh's right to bring a folio with him and read from it the snatches of song. The reference is to a Covent Garden performance with Cooke as Falstaff.

160. "*They fight;*" Oxberry and Cumberland editions, at line 92.

161. *The Athenaeum*, January 12, 1901; Daly's edition. Presumably, Slender was imitating Sir Andrew Aguecheek — see page 9, above. Caius and Evans, Simple and Rugby, are still arm in arm, when we see them again in III, 2.

162. Charles and Mary Cowden Clarke, *Recollections of Writers*, 306.

163. French and Daly editions.

Miss Margaret Webster has drawn attention to the hints of something like active participation, by the women, "in the general confusion" near the close of the scene, even though they do not speak after line 222 (*Shakespeare Without Tears*, New York and London, 1942, pp. 189, 190). Kemble, however, and the editors of later acting versions, bundle them off before this.

164. Lady Benson, *Mainly Players*, 75. Dennis is very interesting on the possibilities for a great actor when Ford is listening to Falstaff's story (Epistle Dedicatory to *The Comical Gallant*, sig.A4v°).

165. *Dramatic Essays*, 171 (from *The Leader*, November 29, 1851).

166. Winter, *Shakespeare on the Stage*, Third Series, p. 411; Madge Kendal, *Dame Madge Kendal*, London [1933], p. 28.

167. Boaden, *Life of Kemble*, I, 77, 78, see also *General Advertiser and Morning Intelligencer*, November 15, 1779. There is a good account of Bartley's reading of the letter in *The European Magazine* for May 1815.

168. Bartley Promptbook, Lacy's Acting Edition; French and Daly editions.

169. "French's American Drama," Wright's promptbook. For these texts, the production to which they refer, and Burton's rival production, cf. Odell " 'A Midsummer Night's Dream' on the New York Stage," in *Shaksperian Studies*, New York, 1916. In Wright, Philostrate serves as a sort of Lord Chamberlain ("w. wand"), ceremoniously receiving Theseus, showing in Egeus, etc.

170. See pages 78, 79, 133, 134, below.

171. "Lacy's Acting Edition" (c. 1840), Charles Kean's edition (1856); Phelps Promptbook; "French's American Drama," Wright's promptbook.

172. Daly's edition (1888), G. E. Montgomery, "A Revival of Shakespeare's 'Midsummer Night's Dream,' " *Cosmopolitan Magazine*, April 1888.

173. Reynolds's adaptation, 1816, "French's American Drama"; *ibid.*, Lady Benson, *Mainly Players*, 80, Daly's edition.

174. "One night the dummy, while in full flying action, fell on the stage, whereupon in great concern for its safety, I ran on, picked it up in my arms, and ran off with it amid roars of laughter" (Ellen Terry, *The Story of My Life*, 18).

175. *Our Theatres in the Nineties*, I, 187, 188, cf. Odell, " 'A Midsummer Night's Dream' on the New York Stage," p. 153.

176 Cf. the New York *Evening Post*, November 10, 1826, quoted in Odell's *Annals*, III, 237. At line 140, Wright notes: "Bottom brays, works mouth."

177. Pencilled note in Phelps's promptbook, Daly's edition, De Reyes, *On the Acting of Shakespeare's Plays*, 38, 39.

178. "Lacy's Acting Edition." The same business is found in Charles Kean's edition, and Laura Keene's ("The Standard Drama," New York, 1859), and cf. Wright's promptbook. Phelps played all the fairy scenes behind a curtain of green gauze.

179. "French's American Drama," Wright's promptbook; Lady Benson, *Mainly Players*, 176. See also Daly's edition.

180. In "French's American Drama," "*The head flies up*"; in Wright, Robin "carries it off 2 E R."

181. *Our Theatres in the Nineties*, I, 189, cf. G. E. Montgomery, in *Cosmopolitan Magazine*, April 1888; Fred Belton, *Random Recollections of an Old Actor*, London, 1880, p. 151; "French's American Drama," Wright's promptbook.

182. November 2, 1861, cf. *The Athenaeum*, October 15, 1853.

183. Lewis, in the photograph reproduced in Winter's *Shakespeare on the Stage*, Third Series, p. 272, may, or may not be feeling for his ear.

184. Cf. also, *ibid.*, 280, and De Reyes, *On the Acting of Shakespeare's Plays*, 39.

185. *Shakspere Allusion Book* (1932), I, 174, cf. Margaret Webster, *Shakespeare Without Tears*, 157. I have seen Theseus graciously lend Thisby his own sword, when that of Pyramus could not be found.

186. Cf. "French's American Drama," Laura Keene's edition. Charles Kean gravely notes in his edition: "The lantern used by Starveling, as Moonshine, is copied from one found in Herculaneum". The Vestris properties are from "Lacy's Acting Edition."

187. Cf. Daly's edition: "*Falls on* Pyramus, *who rolls over.*"

188. Charlotte Carmichael Stopes, in *Poet-Lore*, IV (1892), p. 373.

189. Thisby stepped on the Lion's paw, when Daly's Company appeared in Boston in 1895 (*Boston Evening Transcript*, November 1, 1895, in Blinn Shakespeare Scrapbooks).

190. For Tree's ridicule of Elizabethan antiquarianism through the introduction in this play scene of placards, "This is a Forest," etc. see introduction to his acting edition of *The Tempest* (1904), p. x.

191. "Lacy's Acting Edition," *Athenaeum*, November 21, 1840, *Theatrical*

Journal, May 1, 1841; Wright's promptbook, Ellen Terry, *Story of My Life,* 17; "French's American Drama," Sir Frank Benson, *My Memoirs,* London [1930], p. 287; C. D. Linton, "Some Recent Trends in Shakespearean Staging," *E. L. H.,* December 1940, Winter, *Shakespeare on the Stage,* Third Series, p. 257.

192. *What the Author Meant,* 158. A performance of Shakespeare's play is indicated, "not later than 1663" (Spencer, *Shakespeare Improved,* 44, 83).

193. J. R. Planché, *Recollections and Reflections,* 2 vols., London, 1872, II, 83 ff.; *Athenaeum,* March 23, 1844; Morley, *Journal of a London Playgoer,* 136, 137; Daly's acting edition (1887), *Athenaeum,* June 2, 1888.

194. Morley, *Journal of a London Playgoer,* 136.

195. *Shakespeare on the Stage,* Second Series, p. 522; Kemble's 1815 edition. In recent productions of the play, I have seen the lute: (1) hanging broken about Hortensio's shoulders, and (2) planted there visibly by Kate herself (Lynn Fontanne).

196. Kemble's marked copy, etc.; Cumberland's *British Theatre* (1828), Booth-Winter edition, etc.

197. *Illustrated London News,* October 30, 1847; *Boston Advertiser,* December 27, 1893 (in Blinn Shakespeare Scrapbooks). Cf. also, Harry Irvine, "Staging Shakespeare in Schools and Colleges," *Theatre Magazine* (New York), November, December 1923, and Sir John Martin-Harvey, *Autobiography,* 414. Grumio has sometimes imitated his master in this scene and snapped a whip of his own.

198. *Theatre Magazine* (New York), November 1905, *Boston Herald,* November 28, 1905 (in Blinn Shakespeare Scrapbooks).

199. Elizabeth Fagan, *From the Wings,* 52, cf. photograph in *Illustrated London News,* May 10, 1902 (Blinn Shakespeare Scrapbooks). Sothern's Petruchio also "bore his bride away high on his shoulders" (*Boston Evening Transcript,* November 28, 1905, in *ibid.*).

200. See also, June 26, 1875, March 26, 1881 (Booth), June 6, 1885, November 6, 1897 (Tree), January 12, 1901 (Benson). The misuse of the mutton was pretty certainly older than 1870.

201. *Boston Herald,* November 28, 1905 (in Blinn Shakespeare Scrapbooks).

202. San Francisco, 1886, pp. 35, 36 (Pelby was Petruchio). See also, especially the Walnut Street and Daly Promptbooks. Of course, Petruchio deliberately trips him.

203. For the gags, see Kemble (1815), Cumberland, and Booth-Winter editions. Becks refers only to the Daly production?

204. Cumberland, French, and Booth-Winter editions, Becks Promptbook.

205. Walnut Street Promptbook, cf. Knight, *Dramatic Notes,* 49, Becks Promptbook.

206. Lady Benson, *Mainly Players,* 86. Also, in IV, 5, a donkey figured in

their performance, and Kate rode away on the donkey at the close (*ibid.*).

207. C. E. Russell, *Julia Marlowe*, 336, *Boston Herald*, November 28, 1905 (in Blinn Shakespeare Scrapbooks).

208. Hazlitt, from *The Examiner*, June 1, 1817, *Works*, VIII, 540; cf. Kemble 1810 and 1815 editions. In French's Acting Edition (Late Lacy's), c. 1864, they are "*lying on couches at a banquet.*"

209. *London Chronicle*, September 28–October 1, 1771; *Athenaeum*, February 11, 1829; *Journal of a London Playgoer*, 286, 287 — for Anderson's courtship of her, see *ibid.*, 293.

210. George Fletcher, *Studies of Shakespeare*, London, 1847, p. 99; *The Art of the Victorian Stage*, 130, 131; Russell, *Julia Marlowe*, 197; *Boston Evening Transcript*, December 7, 1897 (in Blinn Shakespeare Scrapbooks).

211. *On Some of Shakespeare's Female Characters*, p. 182, cf. II, 3, 151.

212. Cf. Capell, *Notes and Various Readings*, Part I (1774), p. 107. Kemble's editions of 1810 and 1815 have "tablets" for Iachimo.

213. Robert Farquharson, in *We Saw Him Act*, 346, 347; Martin-Harvey, *Autobiography*, 189 note; "D-G" (George Daniel), in Cumberland's *British Drama*, i (1829), p. 7.

214. Helen Faucit, *Shakespeare's Female Characters*, 185, [Margaret Stokes,] "Helen Faucit," *Blackwood's*, December 1885. The Kemble, Oxberry (c. 1821), and Cumberland editions assign the words "How now?" to Cloten, leaving Imogen only "Pisanio."

For Mrs. Siddons's superb gesture at line 130 — her right arm raised, the forefinger pointing upwards — see Gilbert Austin, *Chironomia; Or, A Treatise on Rhetorical Delivery*, London, 1806, p. 495, note, and figure 120.

215. R. Warwick Bond, "'Cymbeline' at the Lyceum," *Fortnightly Review*, November 1896, Harcourt Williams, *Four Years at the Old Vic*, 187; *The Drama of Yesterday and To-day*, 2 vols., London and New York, 1899, II, 104.

216. *The Theatre*, April 1, 1882; Henry Austin Clapp, *Reminiscences of a Dramatic Critic*, Boston and New York, 1902, p. 166, Winter, *Shakespeare on the Stage*, Third Series, p. 132. In the Neilson Promptbook, the bad old Cumberland direction "*falls back on* Pisanio" is changed to "*falls on* stage."

217. *Journal of a London Playgoer*, 287, *Shakespeare's Female Characters*, 197, 198, see also *The Saturday Review*, October 22, 1864.

218. Edward Fuller, *The Dramatic Year 1887-88*, Boston, 1889, pp. 202, 203; Towse, *Sixty Years of the Theater*, 267; *The Theatre*, October 1, 1896, cf. Christopher St. John (ed.), *Ellen Terry and Bernard Shaw: A Correspondence*, New York and London, 1931, p. 66 (Shaw's letters on the *Cymbeline* production often take up points of business).

219. Cf. Oxberry's edition (a buck) and "French's Acting Edition," c. 1864 (a deer slung on a spear).

220. *My Years on the Stage*, New York [1922], p. 59; *Shakespeare on the Stage*, Third Series, p. 132; *Our Theatres in the Nineties*, II, 211.

221. *Ellen Terry and Bernard Shaw: A Correspondence*, 42, 43. In his

analysis of the soliloquy, Shaw makes too much of Imogen's horror at the presence of the "headless man," too little of the agony with which she discovers (as she thinks) that the mutilated body is that of Posthumus.

222. The first of these directions long persisted. The second was changed (as in Mrs. Inchbald's edition and French's), so that the soldiers are raising Cloten when the curtain falls.

223. Edition of 1810, which has many directions wanting in that of 1801. "Madan *and* Locrine *support*" Iachimo, at line 149, is another Kemble thought.

223a Page 176, below; *The Stage*, 147.

224. This French edition (undated) has a separate title page, "Cumberland's British Theatre," but differs from it at several points. Kemble's appeared in 1803.

225. The Phelps Promptbook has him kneel in doing so and adds "Embracing" at line 106 ("Thanks, dear Isabel").

226. *The Old Play-Goer*, London, 1846, p. 78.

227. Kemble's edition; Oxberry and Cumberland editions.

228. 1765 edition, I, 380; New Cambridge Edition, 155, 156. For another gap in the dialogue, which the actress must fill, cf. Knight, *Dramatic Notes*, 113.

229. Kean's acting edition (1856), cf. Calvert's (1869).

230. Cumberland's ("1826," but containing a Covent Garden cast dated "1827"); Oxberry's (1824); "French's Standard Drama: The Acting Edition," New York and London (c. 1857); *ibid.*

231. Cf. Oxberry and French editions.

232. Oxberry's edition; Kean's edition, William Archer, "The Winter's Tale," *The Nineteenth Century*, October 1887, Ellen Terry, *The Story of My Life*, photograph opposite page 12, etc.

233 Oxberry's edition (presumably recording Macready's business here); French's edition.

234. Cf. pages 145, 146, below.

235. "Shakespeare's Women – Hermione," *Blackwood's*, January 1891; May 3, 1856.

236. *The Athenaeum*, April 30, 1887, Sir George Arthur, *From Phelps to Gielgud*, London [1936,] pp. 116, 117, Foss, *What the Author Meant*, 136, "'*As You Like It*' à l'Américaine," *Blackwood's*, September 1890, Mary Anderson's acting edition, London and New York [1888], etc.

237. *Nights at the Play*, II, 190; Kean's acting edition; May 10, 1856. Bell's edition, Mary Anderson's, and Viola Allen's, New York, 1905, dispense with the bear's services.

238. J. B. Wright assisted in the preparation of this edition, and the business at this point was doubtless Burton's. Furness should be read on Capell's designation of the precise moment at which Autolycus steals the purse (*Variorum Edition*, pp. XI, XII).

239. Calvert's edition, cf. Viola Allen's. In v, 2, when the Clown is put-

ting on airs, French's edition has him imitate "Autolycus' *action and manner, as in Act IV.*"

240. Page 26, cf. illustrations in Bell's *Shakespeare*, v, 138, and *Westminster Magazine*, January 1780; *Life of Kemble*, II, 314.

241. "Shakespeare's Women — Hermione," *Blackwood's*, January 1891, Martin, *Helena Faucit*, 48, and cf. 183. For Hermione's pose, see also, Cole, *Charles Kean*, II, 178.

242. Thomas Hull's adaptation, ed. Kemble, 1815. The later of two issues of Mrs. Inchbald's *British Theatre* ("1808") borrows from Kemble. Cf. page 427, note 135, below.

243. In "Spencer's Boston Theatre," he is reenforced by Servants here. This edition has, also, though in a milder form, the pursuit by "Bridget" at the end of Act III.

244. 1857 Promptbook; Kemble's edition, 1808. Speed has sometimes seen and picked up the glove on the stage.

245. *The Fools of Shakespeare*, 177. In Cumberland's *British Theatre* (1828), they exeunt at the end of the scene, "*Panthino driving Launce before him.*"

246. "Modern Standard Drama"; *Theatrical Observer*, January 17, 1822.

247. Daly's edition (c. 1895) has the Musicians arrive and depart by boat. And at IV, 2, 106, Julia (Ada Rehan) "*with a moan, falls upon a seat.*"

248. "Spencer's Boston Theatre" (c. 1858), Daly's acting editions, 1874, 1891; Daly's editions.

249. "Spencer's Boston Theatre." The wand is also assigned in "Cumberland's Acting Plays" (c. 1839), to which the Lacy, French, and Spencer editions (the last two, differing from each other only in imprint) are greatly indebted.

250. Daly's 1891 edition causes Berowne to be held by Dumain and Longaville at IV, 3, 188. For the difficulties in staging this scene, cf. Foss, *What the Author Meant*, 150, 151.

251. "Cumberland's Acting Plays," etc. Daly has "*a Tableau*" disclosed in each case.

252. Cf. Lacy and Spencer editions, Foss, *What the Author Meant*, 149.

253. Cumberland's *British Theatre* (1828), in the second instance following Kemble's edition of 1811.

254. *Dramatic Miscellanies*, II, 39, 40. Cumberland's edition, following Kemble's, has "*Dumain lifts up his hand in anger,*" at line 213, and "*Bertram lifts up his hand in anger,*" at line 269.

CHAPTER II. THE HISTORIES

1. *Roscius Anglicanus*, ed. Summers, p. 24.

2. Pages 37, 38, above; Cole, *Charles Kean*, II, 152; *Life of Cardinal Wolsey*, "Morley's Universal Library," p. 39.

3. Lewis Calvert, *Problems of the Actor*, New York, 1918, pp. 126, 127 (cf. Lowell Thomas, *Adventures Among Immortals*, 216). Tree's revival of the play was in 1910.

4. *Life Was Worth Living*, 151; Cumberland and French editions; Mrs. Inchbald and Oxberry editions (cf. Winter-Booth edition).

5. Cumberland's *British Theatre* (1826). The queenliness of Mrs. Siddons as she sat "in her great chair" is noted by Wilkinson, *The Wandering Patentee*, IV, 23.

6. [? H. A. Saintsbury,] *Letters of an Unsuccessful Actor*, Boston [1923], p. 328, Tom Heslewood, in *We Saw Him Act*, 290.

7. Cibber, *Life and Character of that Excellent Actor Barton Booth*, London [1753], p. 74. In Cumberland's edition, Sandys's dress is to be "one of extreme (antiquated) foppery."

8. Kemble's acting edition (1804). Jarrett and Palmer's promptbook has the couples pass before Wolsey "bowing or courtesying" to him, as guests might do on leaving their host.

9. Kean's acting edition (1855); *A Player under Three Reigns*, London [1925], pp. 149, 150; Jarrett and Palmer Promptbook. See also Skinner, *Footlights and Spotlights*, 201, and cf. Doris Westwood, *These Players: A Diary of the "Old Vic,"* London, 1926, p. 136.

10. *Tallis's Dramatic Magazine*, January 1851; Cole, *Charles Kean*, II, 391; Morley, *Journal of a London Playgoer*, 298, Knight, *Theatrical Notes*, 79; Winter, *Booth*, 254; Jarrett and Palmer Promptbook. Only in this last, and in Bassett, is the business definitely connected with II, 2.

11. I, 113.

12. Pages 122, 123. See also Heslewood, in *We Saw Him Act*, 289.

13. Bell's edition; Davies, *Dramatic Miscellanies*, I, 382, 383.

14. Kemble's edition. Guildford removes the cushion in Oxberry and the Cooke-Cooper Promptbook; but Boaden speaks of Katherine's "page bearing a cushion before her," in I, 2 (*Memoirs of Mrs. Siddons*, Philadelphia, 1827, p. 319).

15. For the staging, cf. Edinburgh 1761 Promptbook, Bell, Oxberry, and Cumberland editions. Oxberry has a valuable diagram.

16. H. C. Fleeming Jenkin, *Mrs. Siddons as Lady Macbeth and as Queen Katharine*, ed. Brander Matthews, "Publications of the Dramatic Museum of Columbia University," New York, 1915, p. 89. See also, especially, *Monthly Mirror*, N. S. IV (1808), 321, [James Ballantyne,] *Dramatic Characters of Mrs. Siddons* [Edinburgh, 1812], pp. 33, 34, Boaden, *Mrs. Siddons*, 320, 321, "J. H. Siddons" [J. H. Stocqueler], "Random Recollections of a Life," *Harper's Monthly Magazine*, December 1862.

17. "Shaksperian Stage-Traditions," *The Principles of Playmaking*, 116, 117. Fanny Kemble (John Coleman, in *The Theatre*, March 1, 1893) and Isabel Glyn (*Athenaeum*, December 16, 1848, *Tallis's Dramatic Magazine*, December 1850) were other noted actresses who used the business. For

Charlotte Cushman, see also Ball in Clara Clement's *Charlotte Cushman*, Boston 1882, 169, 170, and Catherine Reignolds-Winslow, *Yesterdays with Actors*, 28.

18. Henry P. Goddard, "Some Players I have Known," *The Theatre Magazine*, September 1908. For the Cushman exit, see also Winter, *Shakespeare on the Stage*, First Series, pp. 556, 557.

19. Heslewood, in *We Saw Him Act*, 289.

20. Brereton, *Life of Henry Irving*, II, 169, Winter, *Shakespeare on the Stage*, First Series, p. 548. The scene was often omitted in representation.

21. Davies, *Dramatic Miscellanies*, I, 397; Genest, *History of the English Stage*, IX, 122.

22. *Manchester Examiner and Times*, March 7, 1877, quoted in Phelps and Forbes-Robertson, *Life and Life-Work of Samuel Phelps*, 332; *Dramatic Miscellanies*, I, 400.

23. Wolsey's speech, lines 203 ff., with copious annotations by Mossop (including some minor business) is printed in *The Monthly Mirror*, VII 1799), p. 178, note. See also Winter, *Shakespeare on the Stage*, First Series, p. 541, for Charles Kean's gesture at the close of the same speech.

24. See, e. g., *The Rehearsal*, ed. Summers, 27, Odell, *Shakespeare from Betterton to Irving*, II, 102.

25. Godfrey Turner, "Show and its Value," *The Theatre*, May 1, 1884. See also, e. g., *Theatrical Journal*, June 6, 1855, "The Drama," *Blackwood's Edinburgh Magazine*, February 1856, *Athenaeum*, July 19, 1862, May 26, 1866, Odell, II, 336ff., and cf. Clara Morris, *Life on the Stage*, 49. During the song Cromwell (who for a century or so replaced Griffith here) sometimes occupied himself with the writing of the letter referred to at line 127.

26. [Ballantyne,] *Dramatic Characters of Mrs. Siddons*, 37, 38, *The Examiner*, July 5, 1812. See also, Henry Crabb Robinson, *Diary*, I, 247, and Sir Charles Bell, *Anatomy and Philosophy of Expression*, (1806) 1885, p. 83.

27. Henry Siddons, *Practical Illustrations of Rhetorical Gesture and Action; Adapted to the English Drama*, London, 1822, pp. 14, 15 (cf. 205).

28. Cole, *Charles Kean*, II, 150. Charlotte Cushman excelled in this scene — see especially M'me De Marguerittes, "Mademoiselle Rachel and Miss Cushman," *Sharpe's London Magazine*, XV (1852).

29. Davies, *Dramatic Miscellanies*, I, 427, 428. Taswell played Gardiner, September 26, 1752 (Harvard bills) and May 9, 1758 (Genest).

30. Genest, V, 586, 587, referring to a letter in the *London Evening Post* on the performance of August 29, 1777.

31. June 16, 1804. Concerning I, I, I know only that Mr. Weaver as the King, in a Boston production with Hackett, is taken to task by The *Traveller*, December 29, 1868, for carrying "a truncheon in the palace scenes" (Blinn Shakespeare Scrapbooks).

32. Cumberland and Lacy editions, *Theatrical Journal*, May 13, 1857, Joseph Hutton, *With a Show in the North*, London, 1871, p. 14.

32a. *Monthly Mirror*, XIII (1802), p. 131.

33. Cumberland. Except where otherwise indicated, the description is based on the Kemble editions. The Phelps details are from his promptbook.

34. *European Magazine*, October 1802. Cf. Cumberland: "Falstaff *repeatedly holds up his booty to survey it, and breaks into sudden and violent fits of laughter.*"

35. London, 1855, pp. 5, 6, cf. J. E. Murdoch, *The Stage*, 363.

36. *John Bull*, May 9, 1824; Hutton, *With a Show in the North*, 18.

37. Phelps and Nagle Promptbooks. Macready appears to have sat during the reading of the letter (see George Daniel's "Remarks" in Cumberland's edition).

38. *Shakespeare on the Stage*, Third Series, p. 323, Wood and Nagle Promptbooks; Wood's promptbook ("kisses her forehead" — Phelps).

39. Phelps Promptbook (cf. Cumberland's edition); *Theatrical Inquisitor*, XVI, 242, cf. XVII, 156 (see also *Furness Variorum*, 503, on Charles Kean's promptbook).

40. Cumberland, French, and Lacy editions. See also, Mrs. Mathews, *Memoirs of Charles Mathews*, 4 vols., London, 1839, II, 283.

41. "Shaksperian Stage-Traditions," 113, 114. It is wanting in Phelps's promptbook.

42. Ed. 1773, p. 9. Cf. Davies, *Dramatic Miscellanies*, i, 247.

43. *Letters and Poems by the Late Mr. John Henderson*, Dublin, 1786, pp. 142, 143.

43a. Here, too, the Hostess "curtsies," at line 319, and Hal "curtsies" in return at line 322.

44. *Dramatic Essays*, edd. Archer and Lowe, 185. Cumberland has "*Kneels*," for Hal at line 153, and the King "*rises, goes to the Prince and raises him*," at line 160.

45. The Folio has a comma after "*playing.*" For the question of whose truncheon it is, see Nichols, *Illustrations of the Literary History of the Eighteenth Century*, II (1817), p. 408, and the *Furness Variorum*, 234.

46. *Hamlet*, I, 2, 204; *Othello*, II, 1, 280; *Shakespeare's England*, I, 116. Cf. Nash, *The Unfortunate Traveller*, ed. Mc Kerrow, II, 217, Dekker, *Bellman of London*, "Temple Classics," p. 90.

47. *The Rehearsal*, IV, 1 (ed. Summers, p. 54); Steele, *Plays*, "Mermaid Edition," p. 392. See also, e. g., James Ralph, *The Touch-Stone*, London, 1728, p. 82, [? Edward Phillips,] *The Players*, London, 1733, sig. C4, [James Miller,] *Harlequin Horace*, third ed., 1735, p. 36, *Apology for the Life of Mr. T— C—, Comedian*, London, 1740, p. "26" [28], Chetwood, *A General History of the Stage*, London, 1749, pp. 164ff., John Armstrong, *Miscellanies*, Dublin, 1770, II, 49, 50, Garrick, *The Meeting of the Company* (1774), in Stern (ed.), *Three Plays*, p. 131, *Town and Country Magazine*, March 1779, pp. 145, 146.

48. June 16, 1804. "Prince Henry Truncheon" is a note in Phelps's book, referring to IV, 2.

49. The crabbedness of this note is due in part to its having been added to. The "s" in "draws" is pencilled in.

50. *Dramatic Censor*, II, 393, cf. Bell's edition, IV, 123, note, and *Furness Variorum*, 296; *Monthly Mirror*, XIV, 63.

51. *Theatrical World of 1896*, p. 147.

52. *Essay on the Dramatic Character of Sir John Falstaff*, London, 1777, pp. 24, 25, see also my *Shakespeare and the Audience*, 157, 158.

53. *Edinburgh Dramatic Review*, April 17, 1824, cf. Walter Leman, *Memories of an Old Actor*, San Francisco, 1886, p. 137.

54. Bell's edition, IV, 130; *Dramatic Miscellanies*, I, 273ff.

55. E. g. Kemble 1815 (though not 1803 or Mrs. Inchbald), Cumberland, and Lacy editions; *Edinburgh Dramatic Review*, April 17, 1824; Charleston *Morning Post*, January 17, 1787, quoted in Eola Willis, *The Charleston Stage in the Eighteenth Century*, Columbia, S. C., 1924, p. 134; *Edinburgh Dramatic Review*, July 7, 1823; *Theatrical Observer*, October 4, 1823. See also, Winter, *Shakespeare on the Stage*, Third Series, p. 337, and *Furness Variorum*, 332.

56. Sheridan's *Plays and Poems*, ed. R. Crompton Rhodes, II, 203. In 1861, Barrett at Sadler's Wells was reminded by *The Sunday Times* that Falstaff "was too fat to be always twirling and swinging his walking-stick about" (Forbes-Robertson and Phelps, *Life and Life-Work of Samuel Phelps*, 240). Cf. page 46, above.

57. Kemble's edition appeared in 1804; Cumberland's (c. 1829) has an 1821 Covent Garden cast, with Fawcett as Falstaff and Macready as the King; Lacy's, an 1864 Drury Lane cast, with Phelps doubling the King and Shallow, Barrett as Falstaff.

58. Cumberland, Lacy, and Calvert (1874) editions.

59. *Dramatic Miscellanies*, I, 307; *Fifty Years of Shakespearean Playgoing*, 55.

60. *Mainly Players*, London [1926], p. 136.

61. *Stratford-upon-Avon Herald*, March 12, 1909 (in Blinn Shakespeare Scrapbooks).

62. Montague Summers, *The Playhouse of Pepys*, 224, *Times Literary Supplement*, June 27, July 4, 1935, April 30, May 7, June 18, 1938. The possibility of a still earlier revival is not to be ignored (cf. Spencer, *Shakespeare Improved*, 132, note).

63. Finlay, *Miscellanies*, 212, see also Macready, *Reminiscences*, I, 95.

64. J. H. Siddons [J. H. Stocqueler], "Some Theatrical Recollections," *Temple Bar*, August 1879 (cf. his *Memoirs of a Journalist*, Bombay and London, 1873, p. 15); W. R. Alger, *Edwin Forrest*, 2 vols., Philadelphia, 1877, II, 747; E. F. Edgett, *Edward Loomis Davenport*, New York, 1901, pp. 63, 64; "The Old Bowery," *November Boughs* (1888), in *Complete Writings*, New

York and London, 1902, VI, 192, 193 (see also, Thomas R. Gould, *The Tragedian; An Essay on The Histrionic Genius of Junius Brutus Booth*, New York, 1868, p. 39).

65. William Dunlap, *The Life of George Frederick Cooke*, Second Edition, 2 vols., London, 1815, II, 400; Hunt, in *The Tatler*, February 1, 1831, *Dramatic Essays*, edd. Archer and Lowe, 201; *Their Majesties' Servants*, ed. Lowe, III, 413, see also, Lewes, *On Actors and the Art of Acting*, 27, and Fitzgerald, *Shakespearean Representation*, 144.

66. *Two Dissertations on the Theatres*, London, 1756, Part I, pp. 64, 65. *Punch*, XI (1846), 94, describes Richard on the stage as "continually rapping the palm of his left hand with a truncheon carried in his right," during the speaking of this soliloquy.

67. Hazlitt, *Characters in Shakespeare's Plays* (1817), 1892, p. 162, Cumberland's *British Theatre* (1829), *Athenaeum*, May 18, 1833, Lewes, *On Actors*, 20, etc.; *The Champion*, February 16, 1817, quoted in Asia Booth Clarke, *The Elder and the Younger Booth*, Boston, 1882, p. 14.

68. Charlotte Porter, in *Poet-Lore*, II (1890), p. 31. Seemingly, Mansfield's business varied, for "leans on wall" is Becks's note here.

69. Cf., on the carefully timed tolling of the bell in Irving's production, Lena Ashwell, in *We Saw Him Act*, 330.

70. *Quarterly Review*, XXXIV (1826), pp. 230, 231.

71. *Diary, Reminiscences, and Correspondence*, ed. Thomas Sadler, 2 vols., Boston [1870], I, 274; Booth-Winter Edition; Becks's marked copy — where also, at line 204, he "gathers her hand in his & lay [sic] it on his heart."

72. Gould, *The Tragedian*, 43; *Two Dissertations on the Theatres*, Part I, p. 66.

73. Russell, "Sir Henry Irving's Richard III," *Theatre*, May 1, 1897; Sadler's Wells Promptbook; Booth-Winter Edition.

74. *Henry Irving: A Short Account of His Public Life*, London, 1883, p. 161. Similarly, I recall that Mr. Hampden, in II, 1, kissed Edward's hand with dignity, then *smacked* the Queen's thrice!

75. Ed. 1700. "Prince Ed. falls in chair," is Louis James's promptnote at line 65; but this is followed, in Cibber, not by the Prince's history lesson, but by the single line,

Why at the Tower? But be it as you please.

Even with these changes, the business is melodramatic and uncalled for.

76. "Gustavus Brooke in Australia," *Theatrical Journal*, May 23, 1855.

77. March 22, 1895 (Blinn Shakespeare Scrapbooks); *View of the English Stage*, in *Works*, edd. Waller and Glover, VIII, 201.

78. *European Magazine*, March 1821, see also *Bell's Weekly Messenger*, March 18, 1821.

79. At line 57, now followed by asides between Richard and Buckingham.

80. Becks's promptbook; Francis Ormathwaite, in *The Theatre*, January

1, 1897, J. T. Grein, *Dramatic Criticism*, I, 186, cf. Crosse, *Fifty Years of Shakespearean Playgoing*, 10.

81. Wilstach, *Richard Mansfield*, New York, 1909, p. 421, cf. Charlotte Porter in *Poet-Lore*, II (1890), p. 32; *Dramatic Notes*, March 1889, Becks's marked copy.

82. Winter, *Life and Art of Richard Mansfield*, 2 vols., New York, 1910, II, 59.

83. *Boston Herald*, October 22, 1889. See also, e.g., *Dramatic Review*, March 23, 1889, Winter, *Shadows of the Stage*, First Series, pp. 313, 314.

84. Business with a truncheon is likely to figure at the end of the scene. But the closing lines were much changed by Cibber.

85. Cf. *"unfolding a scroll"* when, in this Cibber text, he later produces "a model of our battle," also, v, 2, 5. A "blank paper round Baton" is still called for in Phelps's promptbook.

86. The promptbook contains an excellent drawing of the tent. See also Phelps and Forbes-Robertson, *Phelps*, 74.

87. [H. Martin,] *Remarks on Mr. Kemble's Performance*, London, 1802, pp. 32, 33.

88. William Thew, *Poems on Various Subjects Chiefly Theatrical*, London, 1815, p. 47; *The Athenaeum*, May 17, 1832; *Theatrical Inquisitor*, XV (1819), pp. 372, 373, note (the lines referred to are, no doubt, IV, 1, 66ff., *Plays of the Restoration and Eighteenth Century*, edd. MacMillan and Jones, p. 662).

89. III, 195, 196. For Cooke's influence on Kean, see H. N. Hillebrand, *Edmund Kean*, New York, 1933, p. 330.

90. *Critical Remarks on the Astonishing Performances of Mr. Kean* [N. D.], sig. B5; Francis Wilson, *Life of Himself*, Boston and New York, 1924, p. 48.

91. Cumberland's *British Theatre* (1829).

92. See, e. g., Bell's edition (1774), Thomas Dutton, *The Dramatic Censor*, London, 1801, III, 195, *Monthly Mirror*, X (1800) p. 327.

93. Edinburgh, 1800, p. 19. Stephen Kemble is credited with the reform.

94. *View of the English Stage*, 184.

95. See also, *Bell's Weekly Messenger*, March 13, 1814, and *The European Magazine*, for March.

96. See, e. g., Cumberland's *British Theatre*, Ferrers, Phelps, and Forrest Promptbooks, Odell's *Annals*, v, 176, *The Theatre*, April 1, 1889, *Boston Herald*, October 22, 1889.

97. *A General View of the Stage*, 239; Murphy, *Life of Garrick*, 2 vols., London, 1801, I, 24 (cf. Joseph Knight, *David Garrick*, London, 1894, p. 28).

98. [John Wilson Croker,] *Histrionic Epistles*, Dublin, 1807, p. 67, note (cf. [H. Martin,] *Remarks on Mr. Kemble's Performance*, 33, 34); Theodore Martin, "An Eye-Witness of John Kemble," *The Nineteenth Century*, February, 1880. The younger Kean is said to have staggered and fallen, instead

of "sliding on his knees," Cole, *Life and Theatrical Times of Charles Kean*, I, 285.

99. *Life of Forrest*, II, 749 (for his rattling sword, see *ibid.*, I, III, II2, and C. T. Congdon, *Reminiscences of a Journalist*, Boston, 1880, pp. 192, 193).

100. Francis Ormathwaite, "*Richard III* on the Stage," *The Theatre*, January 1, 1897, cf. Hall Caine, *Richard III and Macbeth: The Spirit of Romantic Play*, London, 1877, pp. 44, 45; H. M. Walbrook, "Henry Irving: His Personality and his Art, "*The Stage*" *Year Book*, 1928, [Archer and Lowe,] *The Fashionable Tragedian*, Second Edition, London, 1877, p. 22.

101. See also, e. g. *The Theatre*, April 1, 1889, and Charlotte Porter in *Poet-Lore*, II (1890), p. 33. Winter speaks of the business as "never used before Mansfield's time" (*Life and Art of Richard Mansfield*, II, 249).

102. *Remarks on Mr. Kemble's Performance*, 34; John Bernard, *Retrospections of the Stage*, 2 vols., London, 1830, I, 20; *Times*, November 9, 1819, *Theatrical Observer*, November 17, 1821, January 27, 1824, cf. *A Critical Examination of the Respective Performances of Mr. Kean & Mr. Macready in . . . King Richard the Third*, London, 1819, p. 38.
Catesby was regularly substituted for Ratcliff here.

103. *Remarks on the Character of Richard the Third as Played by Cooke and Kemble*, Second Edition, London [1801] pp. 38ff.; *Edinburgh Dramatic Review*, December 14, 1824. For details of the battle, as it was waged in two notable productions, see Phelps Promptbook; *The Boston Herald*, October 22, 1889, Becks's marked copy. In each case, much of the fighting took place at a bridge.

104. Bell's *Shakespeare*, III, 65, note; *Memoirs of His Own Life*, York, 1790, IV, 206.

105. This epilogue, spoken at an amateur performance for the benefit of the Literary Fund, is printed also in *The European Magazine*, for April 1792.

106. *View of the English Stage*, 182, cf. Leigh Hunt, *Dramatic Essays*, 202.

107. Philadelphia *Mirror of Taste*, for March 1811, see also *The Monthly Mirror*, X (1800) p. 321.

108. See, e. g., Lord Broughton, *Recollections of a Long Life*, 6 vols., London, 1909–1911, I, 86, William Thew, *Poems*, 47 ff., *Theatrical Inquisitor*, for October 1816, cf. Genest, VIII, 495. Among other accounts of the scene, see, especially, *Examiner*, February 27, 1814, *Times*, October 17, 1815, and Hazlitt, *Table Talk*, in *Works*, edd. Waller and Glover, VI, 40 (cf. "Barry Cornwall," *Life of Edmund Kean*, 2 vols., London, 1835, II, 58).

109. *The Champion*, February 16, 1817, quoted in Asia Booth Clarke, *The Booths*, 15.

110. See, e.g., Malone, "An Actor's Memory of Edwin Booth," *Forum*, July 1893, H. D. Stone, *Personal Recollections of the Drama*, Albany, 1873, p. 175, Joseph Francis Daly, *Life of Augustin Daly*, 15, 16, Frederick Warde, *Fifty Years of Make-Believe*, 124, Francis Wilson, *Life*, 136. For the elder Booth's acting here, see especially Odell, *Annals*, III, 11ff., Matthews, *Princi-*

ples of Playmaking, 302ff.; and, for his son's, Adam Badeau, *The Vagabond*, New York, 1859, p. 288, L. C. Calhoun, in *The Galaxy*, January 1869, Winter, *Shakespeare on the Stage*, First Series, pp. 112, 113.

111. *Blackwood's Edinburgh Magazine*, January 1820, cf. *Tallis's Dramatic Magazine*, June, 1851, for the traditional "fiendish glare" at Richmond.

112. W. J. Lawrence, *Barry Sullivan*, London, 1893, pp. 44, 74, Robert M. Sillard, *Barry Sullivan and His Contemporaries*, 2 vols., London, 1901, II, 18.

113. Dickins, *Forty Years of Shakespeare on the English Stage*, 32; J. T. Grein, *Dramatic Criticism*, I (1899), p. 187; *Spectator*, February 6, 1877, quoted in Pascoe's *Dramatic List*, 184.

114. Oxberry's *New English Drama* (1818), Cumberland's *British Theatre* (1829); *Theatrical Observer*, April 19, 1823; "French's Acting Edition" (1854).

115. "French's Standard Drama." This acting edition is based pretty certainly (cf. not only the title page but also the stage directions themselves) on Kean's New York production in 1846.

116. Oxberry's *New English Drama* (1819), Addis's promptbook (c. 1843); G. B. Shaw, in *Saturday Review*, September 30, 1899 (quoted in *Furness Variorum*, p. 686ff).

117. Kemble's editions of 1803, 1814 (cf. *Furness Variorum*, 28); Hazlitt, *View of the English Stage*, 347; *My Long Life*, New York, 1896, p. 100.

118. *Saturday Review*, September 30, 1899.

119. *Autobiography and Reminiscences*, New York, 1888, p. 21, *Letters to Fanny Kemble*, New York and London, 1895, p. 176. See also *ibid.*, 55, and Walter Lacy, "Old and Young Stagers," *The Green Room*, Christmas 1880.

120. "French's Standard Drama."

121. *History of the Theatres of London and Dublin*, 3 vols., London, 1769–1771, III, 82, *Literary and Miscellaneous Memoirs*, 4 vols., London, 1826–1828, IV, 101. See also, *The Upper Gallery: A Poem*, London, 1753, p. 8, and Davies, *Dramatic Miscellanies*, I, 35, 36.

122. *Tatler*, March 28, 1831, in *Dramatic Essays*, edd. Archer and Lowe, 213 (for Mrs. Siddons, see also Boaden's *Kemble*, I, 134, *The Drama; Or, Theatrical Pocket Magazine*, March 1823, etc.); *Theatrical Inquisitor*, for December 1816; George Fletcher, *Studies of Shakespeare*, 30, 31; *Story of My Life*, 28.

123. Fletcher, *Studies of Shakespeare*, 32; Gilbert Austin, *Chironomia; Or, A Treatise on Rhetorical Delivery*, London, 1806, p. 495, note, and figure 118; Campbell, *Life of Mrs. Siddons*, 2 vols., London, 1834, I, 210.

124. Oxberry's *New English Drama* (cf. Cumberland edition).

125. *Dramatic Censor*, II, 160; Kemble editions; Shaw, in *Saturday Review*, September 30, 1899. Lacy's Acting Edition has Faulconbridge return "*with the lion's hide, and his sword bloody.*"

126. *Theatrical Observer*, November 17, 1831, cf. Fletcher, *Studies*, 39, 40;

Theatrical Inquisitor, for December 1816; [Payne,] *The Opera Glass*, January 20, 1827.

127. C. R. Pemberton, *Life and Literary Remains*, ed. John Fowler, London, 1843, p. 238; *Theatrical Journal*, November 5, 1842; *Autobiography*, 21.

128. *Saturday Review*, September 21, 1889; *ibid.*, September 30, 1899, J. T. Grein, *Premières of the Year*, London, 1900, p. 69.

129. Godwin, in Campbell's *Life of Mrs. Siddons*, I, 146, 147; Hunt, *Dramatic Essays*, 214; *Athenaeum*, February 17, 1849. Robson refers to Mrs. Siddons's "tearing the ornaments from her head" (*The Old Play-Goer*, 21).

130. *This for Remembrance*, London, 1941, p. 161.

131. *John Bull*, October 29, 1842. The throwing away of the iron figures as early as 1819 in Oxberry's edition. Cf. the daguerreotype of George Bennett as Hubert, "by Paine of Islington."

132. *Dramatic Miscellanies*, I, 70; *Saturday Review*, September 30, 1899. In French's edition, Hubert picks up the warrant before line 249.

133. Catherine Reignolds-Winslow, *Yesterdays with Actors*, Boston, 1887, pp. 52, 53. The Bowery 1858 Promptbook has in preparation for this scene, "See Arthur on Walls and Dummy Ready"; and presently, "when Arthur⁵ ready let Double Fall."

134. Cumberland and French editions, Addis's promptbook.

135. In French's edition, it is worth noting, Salisbury "*has an open letter in his hand,*" when he enters, and "*the Lords crowd round him.*" Also, Hubert "*rushes up to the body,*" before line 104.

136. *Fifty Years of Shakespearean Playgoing*, 54; French's edition, cf. *The Albion*, November 21, 1846 (quoted in Odell's *Annals*, v, 255).

137. *Good-Bye My Fancy* (1891), in *Complete Writings*, VII, 51. Both the French and Kean's own edition (1858) have the King borne in on a couch or bench, and cf. Odell, *Annals*, v, 255.

138. *Life and Literary Remains*, 240; Shaw, in *Saturday Review*, September 30, 1899, cf. Forbes-Robertson, *A Player under Three Reigns*, 280.

139. Phelps Promptbook. Charles Kean's marked copy has similar directions.

140. Lady Benson, *Mainly Players*, 174, Crosse, *Fifty Years of Shakespearean Playgoing*, 53.

141. Mrs. Charles Calvert, *Sixty-Eight Years on the Stage*, London [1911], p. 144. C. E. Newton's edition in "De Witt's Acting Plays" — "*As Produced at Booth's Theatre, New York, February 8, 1875*"— based in part on Calvert's "arrangement of the drama," adds many details here, e. g., the carrying in of scaling ladders and the firing of volleys of arrows. I am not certain how seriously to take these directions as representative of an actual, not an "ideal" performance. Cf. "French's Standard Drama: The Acting Edition" [1875].

142. Kean (1859), De Witt (1875), and Mansfield (1901) editions.

143. Kean's edition; Boaden, *Memoirs of the Life of John Philip Kemble*,

ii, 8; *Edinburgh Dramatic Review*, March 11, 1825. Waller rang down his curtain on the King still kneeling (Mrs. Clement Scott, *Old Bohemian Days in London*, New York [? 1919], p. 179.

144. *Diaries*, ed. Toynbee, i, 75; Kean's marked copy; *Fifty Years of Shakespearean Playgoing*, 53. I am not inclined to take seriously the threatening gesture toward Westmoreland attributed to Kemble in the *Attic Miscellany*, December 1789.

145. *Richard Mansfield Acting Version* (1901); Kean's edition; Phelps Promptbook.

146. New York, 1920, p. 102.

147. Charlotte Stopes, in *Poet-Lore*, viii (1896), p. 345; Lady Benson, *Mainly Players*, 148; Max Beerbohm (ed.), *Herbert Beerbohm Tree*, 248. Lady Benson has the act of disloyalty occur during the Deposition Scene, but Mr. Henry Herbert, an actor long with Benson, is certain that it came much earlier, in the scene of the Judicial Combat. Cf. Froissart, *Chronicles*, "Globe Edition," 464.

148. "Lacy's Acting Edition." Kean's own edition has similar but briefer directions.

149. *The Athenaeum*, November 18, 1899; *From the Wings*, London, etc. [1922], pp. 55, 56. For Tree's staging of this scene, see Fitzgerald, *Shakespearean Representation*, 77.

150. Morley, *Journal of a London Playgoer*, 143.

151. Henry Crabb Robinson, *Diary, Reminiscences, and Correspondence*, 2 vols., Boston [1870], i, 310, 311; Godfrey Turner, "The First Nights of My Young Days," *The Theatre*, July 1, 1887 (see also, Cole, *Charles Kean*, ii, 208, 209); Boswell-Stone, *Shakespeare's Holinshed*, 109.

152. *View of the English Stage*, 224.

153. Manuscript note in Booth's hand in a copy of the Booth-Winter edition at "The Players."

154. *Forty Years of Shakespeare on the English Stage*, 81 (when Dickins saw Benson later this effect was not attempted); W. J. L., " 'Richard II.' in the Provinces," *Sketch*, March 17, 1897.

155. Beerbohm (ed.), *Herbert Beerbohm Tree*, 179; *Times*, March 16, 1857, quoted in Pascoe's *Dramatic List*, 202.

156. *Boston Evening Transcript*, November 2, 1910 (quoted in Blinn Shakespeare Scrapbooks); James Agate (ed.), *The English Dramatic Critics*, London [1932], 253, 254.

157. *Henry the Sixth*, 1681; *The Misery of Civil War*, 1680.

158. Day and Trewin, *The Shakespeare Memorial Theatre*, 82; *Mainly Players*, 202, 203.

159. *Reminiscences and Diaries*, ed. Pollock, i, 95; Alger, *Forrest*, ii, 748.

160. *Mirror of Taste and Dramatic Censor*, for March 1811; *Boston Herald*, October 28, 1889; *Sixty Years of the Theater*, 326.

161. Wilkes, *General View of the Stage*, 236; John Foster Kirk, "Shake-

speare's Tragedies on the Stage," *Lippincott's Magazine,* June 1884, Gould, *The Tragedian,* 41. For Kean's business here, see H. Halladay-Hope, in *We Saw Him Act,* 72, 73.

162. See Winter, *Life and Art of Edwin Booth,* 216, and page 322, below. Benson dragged the body out — as the Elizabethan Richard must have done (Crosse, *Fifty Years of Shakespearean Playgoing,* 36). Mansfield left it on a curtained bed, where it was being examined by two of his Myrmidons as the scene closed (Becks's marked copy of Mansfield's acting version).

CHAPTER III. HAMLET

1. *Roscius Anglicanus,* 1708 (ed. Montague Summers, p. 21). Sir E. K. Chambers notes that Shakespeare may hardly have instructed "Taylor, who joined the King's in 1619" (*William Shakespeare,* II, 263).

2. Percy Fitzgerald, *Henry Irving: A Record of Twenty Years at the Lyceum,* London, 1893, p. 115, see also *Punch,* November 28, 1874.

3. For a provincial modification of this absurd piece of business, see Samuel Ryley, *The Itinerant,* 9 vols., 1808-1827, VI, 132, 133. Tom Taylor's edition of *Hamlet* (1873) has Francisco and Marcellus exchange salutes just before the former's exit.

4. For the staging of this episode, see W. J. Lawrence, *Pre-Restoration Stage Studies,* Cambridge (Massachusetts), 1927, pp. 104 ff. He notes that the other characters are seated, and suggests that the Ghost rose in front of them.

5. 1771 ("World's Classics" ed., p. 61).

6. *Gazetteer and New Daily Advertiser,* November 11, 1784 (also, *ibid.,* August 17, 1787, and *London Chronicle,* August 21-23, 1787). As a matter of fact, Garrick did not appear as Hamlet at Goodman's Fields (see W. J. Lawrence, *The Elizabethan Playhouse,* Second Series, pp. 229 ff.).

7. *Edwin Booth,* Boston, 1901, p. 105 (see also, e.g., Percy Fitzgerald, *Shakespearean Representation,* 11).

8. Louis James's promptbook has a precisely similar arrangement, the Ghost entering "L.1.E."

9. *Dramatic Miscellanies,* III, 32; William Cooke, *Memoirs of Charles Macklin,* London, 1804 (1806), p. 376.

10. Archer, *An Actor's Notebooks,* 61; *The Theatre,* October 4, 1828, *Theatrical Observer,* October 2, 1829, September 13, 1831, February 7, 1832.

11. Dublin, p. 13.

12. Arthur Matthison, "Theatrical Properties," *The Era Almanack,* 1882. See also Mackenzie's epilogue to *Vimonda,* 1787, in his *Works,* Edinburgh, 1808, VIII, 97.

13. *Pre-Restoration Stage Studies,* 107, 108 (for an alternative suggestion, see Hazelton Spencer, "How Shakespeare Staged His Plays," *Johns Hopkins Alumni Magazine,* XX [1932]); *Shadows of the Stage,* Third Series, p. 178.

14. This cartoon, reproduced in G. M. Godden's *Henry Fielding*, London, 1910, p. 70, is described by Lawrence, p. 119. Verses appended to it show that the artist had *Hamlet* in mind. A cock is crowing at the Ghost, who is beardless, looks disagreeable, and holds a truncheon in his right hand.

14a. October 12, 1844. H. Chance Newton states that Fechter in his later productions of *Hamlet* regularly used the singular optical illusion known as "Pepper's Ghost." If so, it would have been at this point in the play (*Cues and Curtain Calls*, 191, 192; cf. *Punch*, May 16, 1863, and [John Henry] Pepper, *The True History of the Ghost*, London, etc., 1890).

15. Cf. William Poel, *Shakespeare in the Theatre*, London and Toronto, 1913, p. 159, J. Dover Wilson (ed.), *Hamlet*, 149, G. L. Kittredge (ed.), *Hamlet*, 139. For the advantages of processions as against discoveries, see Harcourt Williams, *Four Years at the Old Vic, London* [1935], p. 96.

16. *The Port Folio* (Philadelphia) XLI (1823), p. 200.

17. John Foster Kirk, "Shakespeare's Tragedies on the Stage," *Lippincott's Magazine*, June 1884.

18. Hermann Vezin, "My Masters," *The Dramatic Review*, March 21, 1885 (see also Theodore Martin, "Shakspeare and his Latest Stage Interpreters," *Fraser's Magazine*, December 1861).

19. George Becks's marked copy of *Hamlet*; Winter, *Shakespeare on the Stage*, First Series, p. 334 (cf. W. R. Alger, *Life of Edwin Forrest*, 2 vols., Philadelphia, 1877, II, 751).

20. Edward R. Russell, *Irving as Hamlet*, London, 1875, p. 22; Ellen Terry, *Story of My Life*, 126, 127 (see also Clement Scott, *Some Notable Hamlets of the Present Time*, London, 1905, p. 30; and, for details of the procession and stage arrangements, the Irving Promptbook [1877] in the Harvard College Library).

21. *Dame Madge Kendal* [*by Herself*], London, 1933, p. 134; and, for Barrett, Edward Aveling, "Hamlet at the Princess's," *To-Day*, November 1884 (the business with the child was not, seemingly, a regular part of his performance: cf. Scott, *Some Notable Hamlets*, 65, 66; *Dramatic Notes*, 1884–1885, p. 60; *Shakespeariana*, IV [1887] 30).

22. L. G. Calhoun, "Edwin Booth," *The Galaxy*, January 1869.

23. *Shakespearean Representation*, 12. In an article, "Mr. Booth's Hamlet" in *Appleton's Journal*, November 20, 1875, the late entrance is described as a recent innovation.

24. Boston and New York [1931], pp. 175, 176. Frederick Warde had seen few Hamlets, before his own appearance as the Dane in 1881, who did not enter late —"thus securing recognition and a reception from the audience" (*Fifty Years of Make-Believe*, 206, 207; see also the Lawrence Barrett promptbook).

25. Edd. 1804, 1815; Cumberland's (c. 1826) has the rod. How early is Polonius referred to as Chamberlain? Wilson (ed. *Hamlet*, 141) mentions

Rowe, but cf. Etherege's *Letterbook*, ed. Sybil Rosenfelt, p. 104. The King, by the way, often has a staff or truncheon (e.g., in Lacy's edition).

26. *The Athenaeum*, March 23, 1861 (cf. À Beckett, *Green Room Recollections*, Bristol, [?1896], p. 23).

27. *The Athenaeum*, May 10, 1873; Sir John Martin-Harvey, *Autobiography*, London [1933], p. 74 note; and (for Tree), Scott, *Some Notable Hamlets*, 104, 105.

28. Fechter (Kate Field, in *Atlantic*, November 1870), Wilson Barrett (*Dramatic Notes*, October 1884), and Benson (*Saturday Review*, March 15, 1890). For Sullivan's consulting of the miniature, even earlier in the play, see *Theatrical Journal*, December 9, 1868.

29. *Boston Advertiser*, May 8, 1894 (in Blinn *Hamlet* Scrapbooks). Cf. also Mounet-Sully acting edition, New York [1894]. A gesture of Garrick's near the end of the soliloquy excited Lichtenberg (*Visits to England*, trans. Mare and Quarrell, Oxford, 1938, p. 15).

30. [J. T. Buckingham] *The Polyanthos*, for January 1813 (cf. Garrick, *Private Correspondence*, ed. Boaden, I, 11, 22, 25).

31. Kate Field, in *The Atlantic*, November 1870; and (for Kean), Hermann Vezin, cited in William Archer's *Masks or Faces*, London and New York, 1888, p. 192. Further business of Kean's is described in *John Bull*, January 14, 1838.

32. James Henry Hackett, *Shakespeare's Plays and Actors*, 145. Wilson Barrett sank into a chair, at line 195, and listened "gasping with fear, and leaning out on the arm" (*Shakespeariana*, IV [1887], pp. 31, 32).

33. "C. P.," in *Shakespeariana*, IV (1887), p. 33; *The Theatre*, February 1, 1879.

34. Cf. also Irving and Louis James promptbooks.

35. Kate Field, in *The Atlantic*, November 1870 (cf. Winter, *Shakespeare on the Stage*, First Series, pp. 406, 407). Many later editions have "*Enter Hamlet and Horatio, to Marcellus, who is on guard.*"

36. [Frederick Pilon] *Essay on Hamlet as Performed by Mr. Henderson*, second edition, London [1777], p. 7; [H. Martin] *Remarks on Mr. John Kemble's Hamlet*, London, 1802, p. 4; Forster, in *The Examiner*, October 11, 1835 (quoted in *Dramatic Essays*, edd. Archer and Lowe, 11); Wallack Promptbook; Winter, *Vagrant Memories*, New York, 1915, pp. 376, 377; Dutton Cook, "Stage Traditions," *On the Stage*, I, 237. According to Becks's ms. notes on Forrest: "Hamlet in cloak & hat Xs to L & back to C," at the beginning of the scene.

37. I, 48; Winter, *Shakespeare on the Stage*, First Series, 357; and cf. his *Vagrant Memories*, 376, 377 (for Forbes-Robertson).

38. No. c. Hill's critique on Wilks's acting was reprinted in the *Westminster Magazine* for October 1784 and in *The Gentleman's Magazine*, LIV (1784), pp. 569 ff.

39. Page 85. See also Garrick, *Private Correspondence*, I, 25; *St. James's*

Chronicle, February 20–22, 1772, October 17–19, 1776; Boaden's *Kemble*, I, 442, 443 (criticism by Macklin).

40. *Journal of a Tour of the Hebrides*, ed. R. W. Chapman, Oxford, 1924, p. 183 – August 15, 1773.

41. *Lichtenberg's Visits to England*, trans. Mare and Quarrell, 10; *Public Advertiser*, October 7, 1783; *Universal Magazine* for October 1783.

42. London, 1806, p. 421, cf. B. Wilson's portrait of Garrick reproduced in Churchill's *Rosciad*, ed. R. W. Lowe, 8.

42a. John Jackson, *History of the Scottish Stage*, Edinburgh, 1793, pp. 338, 339 (cf. Tate Wilkinson, *Memoirs*, IV, 114, 115, Elizabeth Stein, *David Garrick, Dramatist*, New York, 1938, p. 13).

43. Ellen Terry, *Story of My Life*, 177, Dutton Cook, *Nights at the Play*, II, 43, 44 (cf. E. R. Russell, *Irving as Hamlet*, 27, 28); Becks's marked copy (for the cloak). See also page 146, below.

Garrick's hair stood on end, and his wig-maker took credit for the effect (Frederick Reynolds, *Life and Times*, I, 88, 89). A mechanical wig which served the same purpose in Dutch performances of *Hamlet* is described in *The Gazetteer*, October 8, 1791. See also *Garrick's Looking-Glass*, London, 1776, pp. 11, 12; "The History of Manthorn the Enthusiast," *Town and Country Magazine*, March 1777; Finlay, *Miscellanies*, 220.

44. Henderson was charged with the same fault ([Pilon] *Essay on Hamlet as Performed by Mr. Henderson*, 7).

45. For Betty, see Hewson Clarke, *The Saunterer*, Newcastle, 1805, pp. 248, 249; the Manchester *Argus*, November 24, 1804, and *Townsman*, December 1, 1804; Payne's *Thespian Mirror*, March 8, 1806. Henry Betty closely copied his father here (*Theatrical Journal*, August 7, 1841, *Athenaeum*, January 4, 1845).

46. Finlay, *Miscellanies*, 220; Adam Badeau, *The Vagabond*, New York, 1859, p. 288, "Edwin Booth On and Off the Stage," *McClure's Magazine*, August 1893 (also L. G. Calhoun, in *The Galaxy*, January 1869); Emma Lazarus, "Tommaso Salvini," *The Century*, November 1881.

47. Aaron Hill, *The Prompter*, October 24, 1735; *Lichtenberg's Visits to England*, 10, 11, Garrick, *Private Correspondence*, I, 13.

48. *European Magazine*, November 1783 (a reference which would have convinced Austin Brereton that Boaden was correct in making Kemble, and not Kean, the innovator: cf. *Some Famous Hamlets from Burbage to Fechter*, London, 1884, pp. 24, 25). Creston Clarke was using Kemble's business in Philadelphia as late as 1888 ("C. P.," in *Shakesperiana*, v, 174).

49. *The Examiner*, March 27, 1814, *Bell's Weekly Messenger*, April 3, 1814, Hazlitt, *View of the English Stage*, in *Works*, edd. Waller and Glover, VIII, 188.

50. *Boston Advertiser*, January 22, 1895 (in Blinn *Hamlet* Scrapbooks). For Booth, see also Winter, "Edwin Booth," *Harper's Magazine*, June 1881. E. M. Royle states that Fechter appropriated Booth's business (*Edwin Booth*

as I Knew Him, New York, 1933, p. 31). Cf. Valentin's use of the cross-hilt in Gounod's *Faust* (1859).

51. Becks's marked copy, J. H. Stoddart, *Recollections of a Player,* 51, George D. Pyper, *The Romance of an Old Playhouse,* Salt Lake City, 1928, p. 116.

52. *Theatrical Censor,* no. IX, p. 82, *The Port Folio,* February 1, 1806; L. G. Calhoun, *The Galaxy,* January 1869.

53. *The Theatrical Speaker,* 51, see also *Hull Dramatic Censor,* February 24, 1827.

54. *The Examiner,* October 23, 1808, cf. Francis Gentleman, *Dramatic Censor,* London, 1770, I, 58, *Monthly Mirror,* N. S. III (1808), p. 131. The idea of the manuscript which the Ghost in Mr. Wopsle's performance had round its truncheon came, I suggest, from Robert Dyer's *Nine Years of an Actor's Life,* London and Plymouth, 1833, p. 23.

55. *St. James's Chronicle,* June 4–7, 1768 (cf. also *London Chronicle,* June 26–28, 1777, for Palmer's Ghost).

56. *St. James's Chronicle,* October 4–6, 1774 (cf. *Lichtenberg's Visits to England,* 12); Garrick, *Private Correspondence,* I, 13 (for this letter, see W. J. Lawrence, *The Elizabethan Playhouse,* Second Series, pp. 232 ff.). Here the Booth 1890 Promptbook has "Hamlet Kneels," and there is a similar direction in the Mounet-Sully acting edition, New York [1894].

57. Kate Field, in *Atlantic Monthly,* November 1870.

58. *London Chronicle,* June 26–28, 1777 (cf. [Pilon] *Hamlet as Performed by Mr. Henderson,* 12, 13, and Crow Street "Promptbook"); Henry B. Phillips's Promptbook (1848); *Boston Evening Transcript,* March 29, 1895 (in Blinn Shakespeare Scrapbooks).

59. Morley, *Journal of a London Playgoer,* 41 (cf. Granville-Barker, *Prefaces to Shakespeare,* Third Series, p. 54, note); Aveling, "Hamlet at the Princess's," *To-Day,* November 1884.

60. Lawrence, *Pre-Restoration Stage Studies,* 110.

61. Macready's *Diaries,* ed. Toynbee, II, 251; *Theatrical Journal,* October 5, 1844.

62. "Shakespeare's Tragedies on the Stage"; and, for Fechter, Odell, *Shakespeare from Betterton to Irving,* II, 360. "An excellently contrived arrangement of gauze" by means of which the Ghost "appeared to dissolve, as it were, into a mist" was used at the Marylebone Theatre in 1847 (*Illustrated London News,* October 16, 1847; cf. August 29, 1846).

63. *Lichtenberg's Visits to England,* 30; *Life of Kemble,* I, 98; *Punch,* November 28, 1874, January 11, 1879. For Mounet-Sully's fall, see Edmund Yates, quoted in *The Theatre: An Illustrated Weekly Magazine,* December 6, 1886; William E. Bryant in *The Boston Journal,* May 8, 1894 (Blinn Shakespeare Scrapbooks).

64. *John Gielgud's Hamlet,* ed. Rosamond Gilder, New York and Toronto, 1937, p. 49 (cf. Harcourt Williams, *Four Years at the Old Vic,*

158, 159). A stage direction in the "Edwin Forrest Edition" of *Hamlet*, c. 1860 — *"Kneels and kisses the cross of sword"*— is the earliest reference to this business I have found. It may well be somewhat older. Mr. Maurice Evans wrote on a wall with the hilt of his sword.

65. Scott, *Some Notable Hamlets*, 105, 106, Tree, "Hamlet — from an Actor's Prompt Book," *Fortnightly Review*, December 1895; *The Townsman: Addressed to the Inhabitants of Manchester on Theatricals*, January 12, 1804.

66. Wilson, *What Happens in Hamlet*, 79, 80, Ed. *Hamlet*, 163, 164; *Life of Kemble*, I, 98.

67. Marked copy of *Hamlet*. See also Wallack Promptbook (1856).

68. See also the *Morning Advertiser*, quoted in W. J. Lawrence's *Gustavus Vaughan Brooke*, Belfast, 1892, p. 89.

69. Kate Field in the *Atlantic*, November 1870, George B. Woods, "The New Tragedian," *Old and New*, April 1870.

70. See L. G. Calhoun's "Edwin Booth," "Mr. Booth's Hamlet," *Appleton's Journal*, November 27, 1875 (which probably indicates variation on the actor's part), and especially the Winter-Booth Edition. Tree would have the distinction made at "There's ne'er a villain" ("Hamlet — From an Actor's Prompt Book").

71. *Monthly Mirror*, N. S., II (1807), 142, 267 ff., III (1808), 130, Brighton 1809 Promptbook. See also Johnson's *Shakespeare*, VIII, 171.

72. See John Malone, "An Actor's Memory of Edwin Booth," *Forum*, July 1893, and E. M. Royle, *Edwin Booth as I Knew Him*, 31 (cf. also E. C. Stedman, "Edwin Booth," *Atlantic Monthly*, May 1866).

73. Russell, *Irving as Hamlet*, 31, 32; Marston, *Our Recent Actors*, I, 82; "Signor Salvini's Hamlet," *Saturday Review*, April 12, 1884.

74. Edward Lambert Stirling's marked copy of *Hamlet*; Booth (1890) and Lawrence Barrett promptbooks; A. B. Walkley, *Drama and Life*, London [1907], p. 145.

75. Ed. *Hamlet*, 1873.

76. "Hamlet — From an Actor's Prompt Book" (cf. Poel, *Shakespeare in the Theatre*, 162; Helen L. Gardner, "Lawful Espials," *Modern Language Review*, July 1938).

77. Kate Field, in *The Atlantic Monthly*, November 1870; *Public Advertiser*, October 7, 1783 (cf. Boaden's *Kemble*, I, 98, 99); H. A. Clapp in *Boston Advertiser*, January 22, 1895 (Blinn *Hamlet* Scrapbooks); *Theatrical Journal*, December 9, 1868. For Polonius to be retreating, when Hamlet alludes to the crab, is surely to obscure Shakespeare's meaning (cf. Wilson, ed., *Hamlet*, 172, and Capell, *Notes and Various Readings to Shakespeare*, London, 1779, I, 131).

78. Hazlitt, *View of the English Stage*, 188; Elizabeth Robins, "On Seeing Madame Bernhardt's Hamlet," *North American Review*, December 1900, Norman Hapgood, *The Stage in America 1897–1900*, pp. 189, 190, Winter, *Shakespeare on the Stage*, First Series, p. 433.

79. "Mr. Booth's Hamlet," *Appleton's Journal*, November 20, 1875; *Athenaeum*, November 13, 1880 (cf. Edwina Booth Grossmann, *Edwin Booth*, 177, letter dated September 27, 1868).

80. Kate Field, in *Atlantic*, November 1870, *Athenaeum*, December 4, 1869.

81. "Hamlet – from an Actor's Prompt Book."

82. Booth 1890 Promptbook; Elizabeth Robins, "On Seeing Madame Bernhardt's Hamlet," J. T. Grein, *Dramatic Criticism*, ii, 38, Dickins, *Forty Years of Shakespeare on the English Stage*, 92.

83. *Private Correspondence*, i, 27; Kate Field, in *Atlantic*, November 1870.

84. Archer, *Theatrical World of 1897*, p. 255; Winter, *Shakespeare on the Stage*, First Series, p. 433; Joseph Francis Daly, *The Life of Augustin Daly*, New York, 1917, p. 225 (Coghlan's business is referred to, however, as if it came after the soliloquy); Tree, "Hamlet – From an Actor's Prompt Book" (also, *Boston Evening Transcript*, March 29, 1895, in Blinn *Hamlet* Scrapbooks).

85. Page 343. Fechter's "magnificent sweep and clutch" at the same words are noted by George B. Woods, "The New Tragedian," *Old and New*, April 1870.

86. Coleman, *Fifty Years of an Actor's Life*, New York and London, 1904, i, 154; *The Athenaeum*, March 4, 1854.

87. See, especially, Russell, *Irving as Hamlet*, 35, Frank A. Marshall, *A Study of Hamlet*, London, 1875, p. 153, Sir John Martin-Harvey, *Autobiography*, 29, and G. R. Halkett's satirical illustration in [Archer and Lowe] *The Fashionable Tragedian*, London, 1877, p. 6.

88. "Hamlet – From an Actor's Prompt Book," Mowbray Morris, "'Hamlet' and the Modern Stage," *Macmillan's Magazine*, March 1892, Scott, *Some Notable Hamlets*, 107, 108.

88a. *Visits to England*, 16; Kirk, "Shakespeare's Tragedies on the Stage"; Asia Booth Clarke, *The Elder and the Younger Booth*, Boston, 1882, pp. 153, 154. Henry Nicholls sat throughout the soliloquy (*The Athenaeum*, March 4, 1854).

89. Austin Brereton, *"H. B." and Laurence Irving*, Boston [1923], pp. 123, 124; *Hull Dramatic Censor*, February 24, 1827; Kate Field, in *The Atlantic*, November 1870, Winter, *Shakespeare on the Stage*, First Series, pp. 407, 423 (cf. H. Chance Newton, *Cues and Curtain Calls*, 191); Royle, *Edwin Booth As I Knew Him*, 10, *Athenaeum*, November 13, 1880.

90. *What Happens in Hamlet*, 126.

91. Mrs. Charles Calvert, *Sixty-Eight Years on the Stage*, London [1911], pp. 171, 172; Warde, *Fifty Years of Make-Believe*, 109; Scott, *Some Notable Hamlets*, 108 ff., Tree, "Hamlet – From an Actor's Prompt Book," Cecil Howard, in *The Theatre*, March 1, 1892, etc.

92. Page 69; cf. Gould, *The Tragedian*, 61. Payne who was abroad at the time need not have heard of the innovation.

93. *Notes upon Shakespeare's Plays and Actors*, 155ff., see also the Pattie

acting edition (1839). Phillips's promptbook (in which Macready is frequently mentioned) has the conspirators appear at line 97. Barry Sullivan claimed, indeed, that he first showed "the reason of Hamlet's sudden change of demeanour as he discovers Polonius and the King eavesdropping" (Lawrence, *Barry Sullivan*, 28).

94. Winter-Booth Ed., L. G. Calhoun "Edwin Booth," Elizabeth Robins, "On Seeing Madame Bernhardt's Hamlet," *North American Review*, December 1900. The Forrest acting ed. has the eavesdroppers *"appear in gallery above,"* before line 103. For the two dissenters, see Scott, *Some Notable Hamlets*, 135; *Athenaeum*, May 27, 1905.

95. "An Actor's Notes on Shakespeare," *The Nineteenth Century*, May 1877; and see, e.g., Russell, *Irving as Hamlet*, 36 ff., Irving Promptbook, Scott, *Some Notable Hamlets*, 179.

96. Aveling, "Hamlet at the Princess's," *Athenaeum*, April 18, 1891, Winter, *Shadows of the Stage*, Second Series, p. 354. A mere stirring of the arras was noticed by other critics (*Dramatic Notes* 1884–1885, p. 60, *Shakespeariana*, IV [1887], p. 37).

97. *Saturday Review*, March 15, 1890. Walter Montgomery had also "peeped behind the curtain," but at line 134 (*Athenaeum*, August 12, 1871).

98. January 30, 1892; *The Spectator*, March 19, 1892, etc.

99. Payne, *The Opera Glass*, December 25, 1826, Phillips and Booth prompt-books, Lacy (1865) and Taylor (1873) editions.

100. Kate Field, in *The Atlantic*, November 1870.

101. "Edwin Booth," *The Galaxy*, January 1869. The exits appear much earlier in, e.g., the Crow St. and Brighton promptbooks.

102. *Examiner*, March 20, 1814, unidentified review in Rhys's *Forrest*, 189, cf. Leggett in *New York Evening Post*, September 18, 1832, and Serjeant Adams, in Cole's *Charles Kean*, I, 275.

103. Finlay, *Miscellanies*, 223, 224. I do not know how seriously to take Frederick Reynolds's story of Holman's kissing his Ophelia (at "To a nunnery, go") and citing Macklin for his right to do so, when Mrs. Holman objected (*Life and Times*, II, 117, 118). Garrick's rudeness is noted, *ibid.*, and see Davies, *Dramatic Miscellanies*, III, 79, and Holcroft, *Theatrical Recorder*, II (1806), 412.

104. *View of the English Stage*, 188. The fullest of the many descriptions of Kean's action is perhaps Tieck's (Theodore Martin, "An Eye-Witness of John Kemble," *The Nineteenth Century*, February 1880).

105. *Edinburgh Dramatic Review*, February 28, 1823. The elder Booth was one of those who followed Kean (*The Actor*, 69).

106. *Some Notable Hamlets*, 110. That Tree's business was invented by Barry Sullivan is implied by Sillard, I, 167. Irving's trembling hands in this scene are often mentioned.

107. Finlay, *Miscellanies*, 223; Dickins, *Forty Years of Shakespeare on the English Stage*, 86; and, for Fechter, *The Athenaeum*, March 23, 1861,

[R. G. White] "The New Hamlet," *The Nation*, February 24, 1870. The Mounet-Sully acting edition has Hamlet give *"un rouleau au premier comédien"* before the "advice."

108. *Saturday Review*, March 15, 1890. Irving's First Player waved his arm "in a peculiar manner," which lent point to Hamlet's warning against sawing the air "thus" (Towse, "Henry Irving," *Century Magazine*, March 1884).

109. There is a stage direction to the same effect in Tom Taylor's edition.

110. Gould, *The Tragedian*, 63.

111. *Monthly Repository*, January and February 1834 (quoted in *Life and Literary Remains*, London, 1843, p. 236); *Dramatic Essays*, edd. Archer and Lowe, 11. Among later accounts, see F. C. Wemyss, *Twenty-Six Years of the Life of an Actor and Manager*, 2 vols., New York, 1847, II, 388; Gould, *The Tragedian*, 62; Hackett, *Notes*, 158; N. M. Ludlow, *Dramatic Life as I Found It*, St. Louis, 1880, p. 688; Coleman, *Players and Playwrights*, I, 32.

112. *Shakespeare on the Stage*, First Series, p. 339. For Tree's by-play with a court jester here, see "Hamlet – From an Actor's Prompt Book." More attractive is Sullivan's business of nervously "opening the curtains" to make sure the stage-arrangements were right (*Theatrical Journal*, December 9, 1868).

113. Tony Aston, *Supplement to Colley Cibber's Lives*, ed. Lowe, II, 300 (Rowe's Edition has *"Lying down at Ophelia's Feet,"* at III, 2, 119).

The position of the platform on which the play is represented has varied. Most often, perhaps, it has been up-stage, with Hamlet and Claudius, downstage, opposite each other; but sometimes it has been at the side. In Garrick's day, complaint was made that the actors were turning their backs to the King (*Theatrical Review*, May 1763).

114. *Reasons Why David Garrick Should Not Appear on the Stage*, London, 1759, p. 25; Finlay, *Miscellanies*, 224, 225; [H. Martin] *Remarks on Mr. John Kemble's Performance*, 6, 7.

115. Borgerhoff, *Le Théâtre anglais à Paris*, 78; Dumas, *Mes Mémoires*, 10 vols., Paris, 1894–1900, IV, 280.

116. Kate Field, in *Atlantic*, November 1870, Dutton Cook, *Hours with the Players*, London, 1883, p. 358; *Punch*, June 12, 1874, Winter, *Shakespeare on the Stage*, First Series, p. 416 (but he makes Kemble the inventor of the "manuscript business"); Cecil Howard, in *The Theatre*, March 1, 1892, Scott, *Some Notable Hamlets*, 111, 112 – etc.

117. Whereas H. B. Irving in 1895 conned "his own copy of the manuscript" (Brereton, "*H. B.*" *and Laurence Irving*, 60).

118. Pages 43, 44.

119. *Monthly Mirror*, II, 40; *Edinburgh Dramatic Review*, February 28, 1823, January 13, 1824, Hackett, *Notes*, 178, 179. I have now seen Agate's *These Were Actors* – and Kean certainly crawled (p. 31).

120. Marston, *Our Recent Actors*, I, 82; Borgerhoff, *Le Théâtre anglais*, 78, 79 (quoting French reviews); L. G. Calhoun, "Edwin Booth" (cf. "Mr. Booth's Hamlet," in *Appleton's Journal*, November 27, 1875, and Beaumont Fletcher, "The 'Hamlet' of Mr. Walker Whiteside," *Godey's Magazine*, December 1895); Russell, *Irving as Hamlet*, 45, 46, Fitzgerald, *Henry Irving: A Record*, 68, 69, Clapp, *Reminiscences*, 226, 227; *Spectator*, April 26, 1890; Tree, "Hamlet — From an Actor's Prompt Book," Mrs. George Cran, *Herbert Beerbohm Tree*, 30; *Athenaeum*, December 29, 1866; Hapgood, *The Stage in America*, 185; Sillard, *Barry Sullivan*, II, 154 (quoting *New York Tribune*); *New York Dramatic Mirror*, July 1, 1899, Winter, *Shakespeare on the Stage*, First Series, p. 434.

121. *Dramatic Miscellanies*, III, 93, 94 (cf. Cole, *Charles Kean*, I, 282, 283). The criticism implied in Davies's remarks may have more significance than I am inclined to attach to it.

122. [H. Martin] *Remarks on Mr. John Kemble's Performance*, 7; *The Theatre*, October 4, 1828. Salvini and Tree did so, too, after scattering the leaves of their manuscripts in the air.

123. Page 227 (cf. 156, 157). There are many accounts — see especially Russell, *Irving as Hamlet*, 46, 47. À Beckett asserts that Montgomery had also seated himself on the throne (*Green Room Recollections*, 26).

124. Barrett's Hamlet then sank into Horatio's arms (see, e.g., *Dramatic Notes* 1884-5, p. 60, Scott, *Some Notable Hamlets*, 62, 63). Mr. Maurice Evans (in 1938) combined Irving's thought with Barrett's by putting on the crown of the Player King.

125. A. E. Hanford, in Brereton's *"H. B." and Laurence Irving*, 124; Becks's Notes.

126. The Tonson Edition of 1735 has Horatio's entrance — which presupposes his exit. Both are in Bell's Edition and many later acting texts. Sometimes (as in Kemble's editions) two musicians return with him.

127. Charles Dickens, "On Mr. Fechter's Acting," *Atlantic*, August 1869. Cf. The Second Quarto's *"Enter the Players with Recorders"*; Poel, *Shakespeare in the Theatre*, 168; Granville-Barker, *Prefaces*, Third Series, pp. 99, 100 note.

128. Brighton and Wallack promptbooks (cf. also pencilled note in Phillips's); Boaden's *Kemble*, I, 102.

129. Winter, "Edwin Booth," *Harper's Magazine*, June 1881 (etc.); Elizabeth Robins, "On Seeing Madame Bernhardt's Hamlet," but cf. Cook, *Nights at the Play*, II, 274.

130. *Ibid.*, II, 200, Knight, *Theatrical Notes*, 6; Aveling, "Hamlet at the Princess's," Scott, *Some Notable Hamlets*, 73, 74 (cf. *John Gielgud's Hamlet*, 59). The Irving 1877 Promptbook has merely "Throws pipe away."

131. Curtis, in *Harper's Magazine*, April 1865, *Athenaeum*, November 13, 1880; C[harlotte] P[orter] in *Shakespeariana*, IV (1887), p. 38, Winter, *Shadows of the Stage*, Second Series, pp. 355, 356; Irving 1877 Promptbook,

Cook, *Nights at the Play*, II, 43, 201. For H. B. Irving's modification of the torch business, see *The Athenaeum*, April 8, 1905.

132. Marshall, pp. 163, 166; *Saturday Review*, April 12, 1884; Winter, *Shadows of the Stage*, Third Series, pp. 177, 178.

133. *Pre-Restoration Stage Studies*, 111 ff.

134. Becks's Notes; Booth 1890 Promptbook. Cf. Crow St. "Promptbook" ("Hand B"): "he seats her, but with great deference." After stabbing Polonius, Fechter, followed by Rossi, threw his sword away (Kate Field in *Atlantic*, November 1870; Winter, *Shadows of the Stage*, Third Series, p. 240).

135. Scott, *The Drama of Yesterday and To-day*, I, 561, 562; W. H. Pollock, in *The Theatre*, October 1, 1897; Irving 1877 Promptbook (cf. Russell, *Irving as Hamlet*, 12).

136. "The Autobiography of an Actor," *The Theatre*, September 1, 1883 (cf. Fred Belton, *Random Recollections of an Old Actor*, London, 1880, pp. 76, 77).

137. Hackett, *Notes*, 182; Coleman, *Players and Playwrights*, I, 75, 76. See also, e.g., Bunn, *The Stage Before and Behind the Curtain*, 3 vols., London, 1840, III, 5, 6, M. W. Disher (ed.), *The Cowells in America*, London, 1934, p. 206, Marston, *Our Recent Actors*, I, 174.

138. Several details which do not directly affect business are omitted in this description. For the Rowe engravings, see a series of articles by R. W. Lowe in the *Illustrated London News*, beginning February 11, 1893; Odell, *Shakespeare from Betterton to Irving*, I, 209 ff.; Lawrence, *Pre-Restoration Stage Studies*, 113 ff; and, especially, Hazelton Spencer, "How Shakespeare Staged his Plays," *Johns Hopkins Alumni Magazine*, March 1932.

139. *Dramatic Miscellanies*, III, 109. Cf. "Mr. Booth's Hamlet," *Appleton's Journal*, November 27, 1875: "The ghost always comes in, as in the first scene, in armor." The meaning of the passage was slow in establishing itself (see Malone Variorum of 1821).

140. *The Connoisseur*, September 19, 1754, *Lichtenberg's Visits*, 16, 29, Thomas Goodwin, *Sketches and Impressions*, ed. R. Osgood Mason, p. 38, Payne, *Thespian Mirror*, January 4, March 8, 1806 (cf. *Polyanthos*, for February 1812), Brighton Promptbook, etc.; and, for Kean, *The Athenaeum*, January 13, 1838, Forster, *Dramatic Essays*, 45, Bunn, *The Stage*, III, 9, 10. See also, *Theatrical Journal*, April 10, 1851.

141. *The Life of Mr. Thomas Betterton, The Late Eminent Tragedian*, 74; *Reflections upon Theatrical Expression in Tragedy*, 30–32 (Hamlet's earlier start may, of course, be referred to — see page 138, above).

142. *The Actor*, 276 (cf. note 121, above); Ireland, *Letters and Poems by the Late Mr. John Henderson*, Dublin, 1786, p. 163 note; *St. James's Chronicle*, February 8–11, 1777. See also Davies, *Dramatic Miscellanies*, III, 108.

143. L. G. Calhoun in *The Galaxy*, January 1869.

144. *Town and Country Magazine*, December 1774. See also Boaden's *Kemble*, II, 117.

145. Theodore Martin, "An Eye-Witness of John Kemble," *The Nineteenth Century*, February 1880; *Miscellanies*, 229, 230.

146. [Martin,] *Remarks on Mr. John Kemble's Performance*, 7; *Polyanthos*, January 1806; Becks's Notes; Curtis, in *Harper's Magazine*, XXX (1865), 674. Mounet-Sully followed the Ghost out, and "screamed . . . in the passage" (Winter, *Shakespeare on the Stage*, First Series, p. 427).

147. Page 229. In his "Private" copy of *Hamlet*, Booth put a note of interrogation after "Lest with this piteous action" (cf. Wilson Ed., 215).

148. *St. James's Chronicle*, February 20–22, 1772 (cf. E. H. Seymour, *Remarks upon the Plays of Shakspeare*, 2 vols., London, 1805, II, 188); *Athenaeum*, November 13, 1880. Gertrude sometimes clings to her son, on the Ghost's appearance (Barrett and Louis James Promptbooks).

149. Edith McCarthy, in *Times Literary Supplement*, August 30, 1928.

150. "An Actor's Notes on Shakespeare," *The Nineteenth Century*, February 1879.

151. Cf. Martin-Harvey, *Autobiography*, 308, for his abandonment of the visible portraits.

152. IV, 2, 1ff. (cf. D. J. McGinn, *Shakespeare's Influence on the Drama of his Age Studied in Hamlet*, New Brunswick, 1938, p. 109). Emilia's pictures are obviously neither wall portraits nor thin air.

153. Irving, "An Actor's Notes on Shakespeare"; Sol Smith, *Theatrical Management in the West and South*, New York, 1868, pp. 218–220.

154. *Dramatic Miscellanies*, III, 106, 113; "Launcelot Temple," *Sketches: Or Essays on Various Subjects*, London, 1758, p. 85; February 20–22, 1772. Armstrong was born in 1709.

155. Ireland, *Letters and Poems by the Late Mr. John Henderson*, 162, 163, [Pilon] *Essay on Hamlet as Performed by Mr. Henderson*, 20, 21; *A Short Criticism on the Performance of Hamlet by Mr. Kemble*, London, 1789, pp. 16, 17.

156. *The Gazetteer, and New Daily Advertiser*, October 10, 1793, *European Magazine*, for October 1793 (also in Oulton's *History of the Theatres of London*, London, 1796, II, 157). Holman's business is criticized by "H" in the Crow St. "Promptbook"; and there is a confused account of it in Joseph Hunter's *New Illustrations of Shakespeare* (II, 256, 257) which has misled one or two later writers.

157. Crow St. "Promptbook"; *The Townsman: Addressed to the Inhabitants of Manchester*, January 12, 1804; Finlay, *Miscellanies*, 228, 229. Young "tore" Gertrude's "picture from her, and flung it upon the ground" (*Edinburgh Dramatic Review*, March 16, 1824).

158. See, e.g., *Theatrical Journal*, March 28, 1840; Dutton Cook, *On the Stage*, I, 244, Clara Morris, *Life on the Stage*, New York, 1901 (1902), pp. 166 ff; *Theatrical Journal*, October 12, 1844; Dutton Cook, "A Note on

Fechter," in *Hours with the Players*. The Ghost's occupancy of the portrait became popular (see, especially, Phillips's Promptbook, Hackett, *Notes*, 79, 80, and *The Athenaeum*, March 28, 1857).

159. Manuscript note in Taylor's interleaved copy of *Hamlet*. See also Booth 1890 Promptbook and Winter, *Shakespeare on the Stage*, First Series, pp. 346, 347.

160. See especially Frank Marshall, *A Study of Hamlet*, 166–173, Irving, "An Actor's Notes on Shakespeare," *The Nineteenth Century*, February 1879; Emma Lazarus, "Tommaso Salvini," *Century Magazine*, November 1881.

161. Knight, *Theatrical Notes*, 119, *The Theatre*, October 1, 1884 (Wilson Barrett and Benson also trampled upon the King's picture); Courtney in Scott's *Some Notable Hamlets*, 160, Brereton, "*H.B.*" *and Laurence Irving*, 60, 124, 125.

162. *The Athenaeum*, June 20, 1868.

163. "Reprints of Scarce Pieces of Shakespeare Criticism," London, 1864, p. 35 (for the authorship, cf. C. D. Thorpe in *Modern Language Notes*, December 1934).

164. *Notes*, 163. The business may go back to Young (see J. C. Young's *Memoir*, 26, 27) and Kemble (Wilkinson, *Wandering Patentee*, II, 6), though Kemble was criticized for kneeling to Gertrude at line 145 (*ibid.*, *Public Advertiser*, October 7, 1793, Boaden, I, 102, cf. also Crow St. "Promptbook").

165. *Theatrical Journal*, September 5, 1840; Becks's Notes; Kate Field, in *Atlantic*, November 1870, cf. *Theatrical Journal*, June 15, 1864, and [R. G. White,] "The New Hamlet," *The Nation*, February 24, 1870.

166. "Mr. Booth's Hamlet," *Appleton's Journal*, November 27, 1875. The business was older, it appears (see Phelps and Forbes-Robertson, *Life and Life-Work of Samuel Phelps*, 399, 400). James's gag grew longer, in time (Hapgood, *The Stage in America*, 188).

167. Russell, *Irving as Hamlet*, 49, 50, Irving 1877 Promptbook (cf. *New York Herald*, November 27, 1884, quoted in Odell's *Annals*, XII, 434); Sothern Acting Version, Hapgood, *The Stage in America*, 185, 186 (cf. Winter, *Shadows of the Stage*, Second Series, p. 355, on Wilson Barrett). Madame Bernhardt also dragged Polonius away (J. T. Grein, *Premières of the Year*, London, 1900, p. 39).

168. C[harlotte] P[orter] in *Shakespeariana*, IV (1887), *The Theatre: An Illustrated Weekly Magazine*, November 8, 1886, Aveling, "Hamlet at the Princess's"; Winter, *Shakespeare on the Stage*, First Series, 390, 391, Hapgood, *The Stage in America*, 185.

169. Edwina Booth Grossmann, *Edwin Booth*, New York, 1894, p. 21.

170. Poel, *Monthly Letters*, London, 1929, pp. 82, 83. Two photographs in the *E. H. Sothern Acting Version* show Julia Marlowe with a lute.

171. *Visits to England*, 17; *Lady's Magazine*, for June 1789; Borgerhoff, *Le Théâtre anglais*, 172 note (see also Jusserand, *Shakespeare in France*, 456,

and the charming "portrait of Miss Smithson by Valmont," there reproduced); *Punch*, November 17, 1855 (also II [1842], 31 and XI [1846], 153);
Bram Stoker, *Irving*, II, 195, Scott, *The Drama of Yesterday and To-day*, II,
61.

172. Payne, *The Opera Glass*, October 23, 1826; see also Lacy's edition.

173. Sothern Acting Version. For her innovation in offering flowers to
imaginary persons, see Russell, *Julia Marlowe*, 323.

174. Cf. *New York Evening Post*, September 18, 1832 (quoted in Moses
and Brown, *The American Theatre as Seen by its Critics*, 58), *Athenaeum*,
November 13, 1880, Louis James Promptbook.

For a sensational exit through the tapestry by Miss Eastlake, following a
suggestion of Clement Scott's "that the scene needed a dramatic climax,"
see *The Theatre*, November 1, December 1, 1884 and Aveling, "Hamlet at
the Princess's."

175. *Athenaeum*, March 13, 1886, *Saturday Review*, March 13, 1886, *The
Theatre*, April 1, 1886, *Shakespeariana*, III (1886), pp. 180, 181 (cf. Morand
and Schwab, *La Tragique Histoire d'Hamlet*, Paris, 1932, p. 253, note).

176. "The Two Tragedians, Booth and Barrett," in Edward Fuller (ed.),
The Dramatic Year 1887–1888, Boston, 1889, pp. 162, 163.

177. See also *The Theatre*, April 1, 1890, and [Elizabeth Fagan] *From the
Wings*, London [1922], p. 74.

178. Cf. Winter, *Shadows of the Stage*, Third Series, pp. 177, 178, the
Forbes-Robertson and Sothern acting editions.

179. *The Tuner*, Letter V (1755), p. 18; *Theatrical Journal*, August 24,
1853.

180. Brereton, *Life of Henry Irving*, II, 319, 320; Frederick Warde, *Fifty
Years of Make-Believe*, 129 (cf. *The Fools of Shakespeare*, 158 ff.). *Papier-
mâché* counterfeits are mentioned, as if common, in Fitzgerald, *Henry
Irving: A Record*, 313.

181. John W. Francis, *Old New York*, New York, 1858, p. 292; N. M.
Ludlow, *Dramatic Life as I Found It*, St. Louis, 1880, pp. 417, 418; Otis
Skinner, *Footlights and Spotlights*, Indianapolis, 1924, pp. 60, 61. See also
Dutton Cook, "Stage Properties," in *On the Stage*, I, 207–228.

182. *Saturday Review*, March 15, 1890. I am indebted to the late William
Parke for a description of this piece of business which was, he assured me,
that of his Fellow-Gravedigger, Rowland Buckstone.

183. *The Harlequin: A Journal of the Drama*, June 6, 1829. For the
Barrett-James business, see also Warde, *The Fools of Shakespeare*, 145.

184. *Journal of a Tour and Residence in Great Britain*, 2 vols., New
York, 1815, II, 121, 122.

185. A parallel to the Gravedigger's defoliation has been found in the
1708 edition of *The Duchess of Malfi*, V, 2. Capell's stage direction — at
"Come, my spade" — might also be cited: *"strips, and falls to digging."*
Lawrence's essay, which first appeared in *The Stage*, June 5, 1924, is in his
Speeding Up Shakespeare, London, 1937.

186. *Memoirs of Mrs. Inchbald*, 2 vols., London, 1833, I, 120 (this performance was a little *before* the restoration of *Hamlet*, at Drury Lane, April 21); John Alexander Kelly, *German Visitors to English Theatres in the Eighteenth Century*, Princeton and Oxford, 1936, pp. 95, 96.

187. Dutton, *Dramatic Censor*, III, 159, 160, of a performance with Kemble, September 29 (cf. *The Theatrical Repertory; Or, Weekly Rosciad* [1802], p. 71). The following references to the waistcoats are supplementary to those given by Lawrence: *The Townsman* (Manchester), January 12, 1804; *Theatrical Censor* (Philadelphia), no. IX — reviewing a performance, January 22, 1806, in which Blisset had "judiciously reformed the custom"; — Buckingham, *Polyanthos*, for February 1812; *Theatrical Inquisitor*, for September 1815; *The Private Theatre of Kilkenny*, p. 105; *Theatrical Observer*, October 16, December 4, 1821; *Edinburgh Theatrical Observer, and Musical Review*, March 16, 1824; *Edinburgh Dramatic Review*, December 28, 1824; Cumberland's acting edition, 1826 (costume notes); *Hull Dramatic Censor*, February 24, 1827.

188. Dutton Cook, "Stage Traditions," *On the Stage*, I, 239; *Theatrical Observer*, January 30, 1838; Bunn, *The Stage*, III, 10; *Life and Memoirs of William Warren* [Boston, 1889], p. 12.

189. See, e.g. *The Theatrical Journal*, June 21, 1854, April 13, 1870, and H. Chance Newton, *Cues and Curtain Calls*, 213, 214.

For further details of business, see especially Warde, *The Fools of Shakespeare*, 147 ff.

190. Thomas Wilkes, *A General View of the Stage*, London, 1759, p. 161; Gilliland, *A Dramatic Synopsis*, London, 1804, pp. 122, 123. Cf. *The Townsman*, January 12, 1804.

191. *The Athenaeum*, March 23, 1861, [R. G. White,] "The New Hamlet," *The Nation*, February 24, 1870, etc.

192. Winter-Booth Edition (see also *Boston Advertiser*, September 29, 1866, in Blinn Shakespeare Scrapbooks); Winter, *Shakespeare on the Stage*, First Series, p. 347, Cumberland's Edition.

193. Murdoch, *The Stage*, 256; "Hints on Stage Business," *Theatrical Journal*, December 9, 1868 (Capell's direction at "And smelt so? Pah!" is "*throws it down*"). Cf. also John Raynolds, *Dolarnys Primerose* (1606) in *Shakespere Allusion Book*, I, 160.

194. Wilson Ed., 237, 238, Fitzgerald, *Shakespearean Representation*, 30, 31.

195. Gould, *The Tragedian*, 69; Alger, *Forrest*, II, 756; Pitou, *Masters of the Show*, 76 ff. (Booth's business was sometimes even closer to that of his father and Forrest, see L. G. Calhoun, in *The Galaxy*, January 1869 and Asia Booth Clarke, *The Elder and the Younger Booth*, 154); Kate Field, in *The Atlantic*, November 1870.

196. Lacy and Winter-Booth editions, Barrett and Irving promptbooks.

197. See also Lady Benson, *Mainly Players*, 85, 86.

198. *Prefaces to Shakespeare*, Third Series, p. 162 and note (cf. Harbage,

"Elizabethan Acting" *P.M.L.A.*, LIV [1939]); *Shakspere Allusion Book*, I, 272; *Memoirs of Robert Wilks, Esq.*, London, 1732, p. 15.

199. Kemble's editions, *Edinburgh Dramatic Review*, March 22, 1825; *The Townsman*, March 27, 1804, Brighton Promptbook, *Theatrical Looker-On* (Birmingham), July 22, 1822; *Edinburgh Dramatic Review*, January 13, 1824; Hazlitt, *View of the English Stage*, 187.

200. Winter-Booth Ed.; Irving Promptbook, *The Theatre*, February 1, 1879; Kate Field, in *The Atlantic*, November 1870; *The Athenaeum*, April 12, 1884.

201. Becks's Notes, Booth 1890 Promptbook; Winter, *Shakespeare on the Stage*, First Series, p. 386, Tree, "Hamlet — From an Actor's Prompt Book" (cf. Louis Calvert, *Problems of the Actor*, New York, 1918, pp. 130, 131).

201a. Kemble, Charles Kean, Winter-Booth editions (Lacy's has, at line 289, *"puts in the ring"*), Poel, *Shakespeare in the Theatre*, 174. Cf. W. J. Lawrence, "The Poisoned Chalice," *London Mercury*, March 1938.

202. *Prefaces to Shakespeare*, Third Series, p. 176 note; Winter-Booth Edition (but the stage direction is deleted in Booth 1890 Promptbook).

203. *A Short Criticism*, 19, 20, [Martin] *Remarks on Mr. John Kemble's Performance*, 7, 8. Henry Angelo mentions in his *Reminiscences* having taught Kean the salute, for use in Hamlet (II, 275).

204. Godfrey Turner, "Scenery, Dresses, and Decorations," *The Theatre*, March 1, 1884.

205. See, especially, *Punch*, June 12, 1875; Marshall, *Study of Hamlet*, 200; *Athenaeum*, April 12, 1884; *Saturday Review*, April 12, 1884; W. H. Pollock, "Hamlets with Differences," *The Theatre*, October 1, 1897. Tree, Madame Bernhardt, and Sothern all adopted Salvini's business with little modification.

206. Beatty-Kingsford, "Rossi on Hamlet," *The Theatre*, October 1, 1884; *Furness Variorum*, II, 258; Wilson Ed. *Hamlet*, 256 (for Irving's "duelling-swords," see W. H. Pollock, in *The Theatre*, June 1, 1896).

207. *Shadows of the Stage*, Third Series, p. 178, see also H. H. Furness, *Letters*, 2 vols., Boston and New York, 1922, I, 299, 300.

Noted as a subtlety in Willard's earlier performance, as Claudius, was his "taking off his crown . . . when at length the fatal thrust is given by Laertes" (Aveling, "Hamlet at the Princess's").

208. At "set it by awhile," Irving smiled at "the pretty little cup-bearer . . . and passed his hand caressingly" over the child's "golden hair." (Bram Stoker, *Personal Reminiscences of Henry Irving*, I, 76.)

209. Directions to this effect appear, e.g., in the Cumberland and Charles Kean Editions. Pattie's (1839) has: *"She dies in chair, or is led off L. by ladies."*

210. *Private Correspondence*, I, 452; *Dramatic Miscellanies*, III, 146, 147 (but there seems small chance for a "rencounter" in the altered text, as printed by G. W. Stone, *P.M.L.A.*, September 1934).

211. Dutton, *Dramatic Censor*, III, 159 (of a Drury Lane performance, September 29); *Memories of an Old Actor*, San Francisco, 1886, pp. 173 ff. (in the Phillips Promptbook, "King draws his sword and stands on his defence").

212. Dutton Cook, *Hours with the Players*, 359, Kate Field, in *The Atlantic*, November 1870.

213. Sullivan had used it as early as 1852 (Sillard, I, 228), and was followed by Booth (as we have seen) and Lawrence Barrett.

214. Dickins, *Forty Years of Shakespeare on the Stage*, 97 (cf. Day and Trewin, *The Shakespeare Memorial Theatre*, London and Toronto [1932], p. 120).

215. Martin, "An Eye-Witness of John Kemble," *The Nineteenth Century*, February 1880.

216. *Illustrated Sporting and Dramatic News*, April 29, 1876 (in Blinn Shakespeare Scrapbooks); *Shadows of the Stage*, Third Series, p. 240 (see also Beatty-Kingston, "Rossi on Hamlet," *The Theatre*, October 1, 1884).

217. Bram Stoker, I, 76; *Masks or Faces? A Study in the Psychology of Acting*, London and New York, 1888, p. 218.

218. *The Tatler*, September 23, 1831 (in Leigh Hunt's *Dramatic Essays*, edd. Archer and Lowe, 230); *Theatrical Journal*, September 12, 1840; Becks's Notes; Lewes, *On Actors and the Art of Acting*, 231, 232 (see also Scott, *The Drama of Yesterday and To-Day*, II, 452); Dickins, *Forty Years of Shakespeare on the English Stage*, 18 (cf. Scott, *Some Notable Hamlets*, 181); Mary Cowden Clarke, in *The Athenaeum*, June 7, 1873 (on Rossi in Genoa), H. P. Phelps, *Hamlet from the Actor's Standpoint*, 160; C[harlotte] P[orter], in *Shakespeariana*, IV (1887), 40, *The Theatre*, November 1, 1884. Barrett had been anticipated to some extent by an amateur, Edgar Chalmers, at Astley's (see *Theatrical Journal*, August 31, 1864).

219. Scott, *Some Notable Hamlets*, 132 ff., cf. J. T. Grein, *Dramatic Criticism*, London, 1899, p. 190, and Fitzgerald, *Shakespearean Representation*, 103.

220. *Ellen Terry and Bernard Shaw: A Correspondence*, 207; *The Sketch*, September 15, 1897 (in Blinn Shakespeare Scrapbooks), Grein, *Dramatic Criticism*, 190, Winter, *Vagrant Memories*, New York, 1915, pp. 379 ff., etc.

CHAPTER IV. OTHELLO

1. See [Charles Lillie] *Original and Genuine Letters Sent to the Tatler and Spectator During the Time Those Works Were Publishing*, 2 vols., London, 1725, I, 255 ff.

2. Gould, *The Tragedian*, 84; Cooke-Cooper Promptbook (cf. Pattie's edition [1839], but this has Roderigo knock). Edwin Booth suggests that "Brabantio should be seen through the open window at his book or papers"

— which would "account for his appearance, instead of his servants" (*Furness Variorum*, 19).

3. Oxberry and French editions (*"checks him"*), Becks's note in Ferrers Promptbook (cf. Moore Promptbook).

4. Fechter's edition, B. W. Watkins in *Theatrical Journal*, January 8, 1862, *On Actors*, 130.

5. Lewis Promptbook (1851), *Furness Variorum*, 38, 41.

6. Mason, *The Othello of Salvini*, 5.

7. In Bell's edition (1774), he *"gives a Packet,"* at line 41.

8. *Dramatic Censor*, I, 151, 152. Charles Kemble, at the Odéon in 1827, *"gardait ses gants blancs pendant toute la durée de la pièce"* (Borgerhoff, *Le Théâtre anglais*, 134).

9. Fechter's edition, cf. Booth in *Furness Variorum*, 47.

10. Ferrers's Edinburgh Promptbook. The 1622 Quarto has *"Exit two or three"*; Bell's edition names Roderigo.

11. Gould, *The Tragedian*, 97 (cf. Edwin Booth in *Furness Variorum*, 54); Morley, *Journal of a London Playgoer*, 228.

12. *Furness Variorum*, 62 (see also Cook, *Nights at the Play*, II, 298; and cf. Mason, *The Othello of Salvini*, 13, 14 note). Sometimes, Othello has helped her off with her veil.

13. "Justus," in *Bell's Weekly Messenger*, April 2, 1797; Ferrers, Murdoch, Moore, and McCullough promptbooks, Pattie's acting edition (1839), cf. also Cooke-Cooper Promptbook ("Brabº gives Desdº to Othello").

14. *The Othello of Salvini*, 15. For his joy when Desdemona pleads to go with him, see *ibid.*, 17, 18, and Knight, *Theatrical Notes*, 21.

15. Oxberry's edition (1819), Kean, Ferrers and other promptbooks, etc.; Mason, 19, 20.

The naturalness of a supplicating gesture by Desdemona is not to be questioned; but today we do without the formal tableau.

16. *The Athenaeum*, October 26, 1861; Henry Ottley, *Fechter's Version of Othello Critically Analysed*, London, 1861, p. 10.

17. Fechter's edition; Walbrook, "Henry Irving: His Personality and his Art," *"The Stage" Year Book*, 1928 (see also *The Theatre*, June 1, 1881, Fitzgerald, *Sir Henry Irving*, 128, etc.).

Fechter's last direction in the scene is: *"breaks into a savage, ringing laugh — stops suddenly — turning quickly round, and looking on all sides, in fear that he has been overheard."*

18. Ottley, *Fechter's Version of Othello*, 11. One of the few modern touches in the Warde-Herman Promptbook is Desdemona's sitting on a "bale."

19. This business was long perpetuated in the Lacy and French editions.

20. Ellen Terry, *Story of My Life*, 206; Morris, *Essays in Theatrical Criticism*, 102. See also, especially, A. B. Walkley, *Playhouse Impressions*, London, 1890, pp. 256, 260.

21. *Works*, 4 vols., London, 1754, I, 273, 274 (letter dated October 23, 1734); "Mackliniana," *European Magazine*, September 1800. Booth's "leap from the ship to the dock" is described by Mrs. Goodale, *Behind the Scenes with Edwin Booth*, 213.

22. Lewis's 1851 Promptbook (also Fechter's acting edition, and cf. Mason, 23, and McCullough Promptbook); Moore's Promptbook; Gould, *The Tragedian*, 86, 87.

23. Booth-Winter Edition. Before Macklin and Garrick reformed the abuse, Iago's soliloquy, at line 50, used to be spoken with "a world of unnatural contortion of face and absurd bye-play" (John Hill, *The Actor*, London, 1750, pp. 282, 283). Was Colley Cibber to blame for this? (cf. page 193, below).

24. Booth, in *Furness Variorum*, 133; Ed. *Othello*, 170. Fechter's business was very similar, and cf. George Skillan's recent acting edition (London [1935]), p. 32.

25. Murdoch and Ferrers Promptbooks.

26. "My Four Favorite Parts," *The Forum*, September 1893; Booth in *Furness Variorum*, 136, Booth-Winter Edition; *Diaries*, ed. Toynbee, II, 475.

27. *Footlight Flashes*, New York, 1860, p. 61, see also *John Bull*, May 28, 1838 (on Kean's son) and Alger's *Forrest*, II, 771, 772 (but cf. Harrison's *Forrest*, 69).

28. Coleman, *Players and Playwrights*, II, 226, *Theatrical Journal*, May 25, 1848, and cf. Edward Mayhew, *Stage Effect: Or, The Principles which Command Dramatic Success in the Theatre*, London, 1840, pp. 50 ff. The cut appears as early as Bell's edition and as late as French's.

29. Fanny Kemble, "Salvini's Othello," *Temple Bar*, LXXI (1884), 375, Mason, 28.

30. Moore, McCullough, Warde-Herman Promptbooks; Ferrers, Murdoch Promptbooks (cf. Booth in *Furness Variorum*, 145); Ferrers, Warde-Herman Promptbook, Lacy's acting edition; Fechter's acting edition. Iago sometimes pushed Roderigo out.

31. *A Short View of Tragedy*, London, 1693, pp. 118, 119; *Grub-street Journal*, October 31, 1734; *Dramatic Historiographer*, 236.

32. Theodore Martin, "Shakspeare, and his Latest Stage Interpreters," *Fraser's Magazine*, December 1861.

33. Cooke-Cooper and Clarke's Forrest Promptbooks (cf. Harrison, *Forrest*, 83, 84), Mason, 31.

34. Fechter's edition; Addison Bright, in *The Theatre*, December 1, 1891; Mason, 32.

35. Fechter's edition, Mason, 34, and cf. Ferrers, Lewis, and McCullough Promptbooks.

36. *The Athenaeum*, December 6, 1856.

37. *On Actors*, 137 ff. (cf. Kate Field, *Charles Albert Fechter*, Boston, 1882, p. 189); Knight, *Theatrical Notes*, 22, Fanny Kemble, "Salvini's

Othello"; *New York Times*, January 20, 1875, quoted in Matthews and Hutton, *Life and Art of Edwin Booth and his Contemporaries*, 72; *Times*, February 17, 1876, quoted in Pascoe's *Dramatic List*, 182.

Salvini played Othello a little earlier than the date of Dillon's London performance — but in Italy.

38. Pierre Irving, *Life and Letters of Washington Irving*, New York, 1862–1864, IV, 241, 242 (cf. Harrison, *Forrest*, 98).

39. Mary Cowden Clarke, *My Long Life*, New York, 1896, p. 82 (cf. Hazlitt, *View*, 189, 272); [Richard H. Dana,] "Mr. Kean," *The Idle Man*, New York, 1821, pp. 45, 46; "Reminiscences of Edmund Kean," *Theatrical Journal*, February 19, 1868.

40. Addison Bright, in *The Theatre*, December 1, 1891 (cf. Shaw, *Our Theatres in the Nineties*, III, 158). See also page 200, below.

41. Morley, *Journal of a London Playgoer*, 229.

42. Mason, 42, 44; see also Fechter's direction at line 223. In Ferrers's promptbook, the Moor actually "takes hold of Iago," at line 162. But this was to anticipate a later, legitimate effect.

43. Booth in *Furness Variorum*, 187; Kittredge ed., 188, 189.

44. *Furness Variorum*, 188; Morley, *Journal*, 235 (cf. Fechter's edition: "*retires humbly. . . . At the door raises his shoulders in contempt*").

45. Mason, 46, 47; Fechter's edition; (cf. Kate Field, *Fechter*, 189, for the glass).

46. *Dramatic Essays*, 22.

47. *Furness Variorum*, 193, 194; Mason, 48, Salvini's acting edition. Rowe has simply "*She drops her Handkerchief*."

48. *Acting and Actors, Elocution and Elocutionists*, New York, 1894, p. 188; *On Some of Shakespeare's Female Characters*, 68 (cf. Moore Promptbook).

49. Booth, in *Furness Variorum*, 195, 196; Fechter's edition; Ferrers (and also Lewis) Promptbook. She has often put the handkerchief behind her, before Iago snatches it.

50. *Times*, May 14, 1814 (also *Bell's Weekly Messenger*, May 15); Gould, *The Tragedian*, 107.

51. *View*, 339 (see also *Edinburgh Dramatic Review*, May 17, 1824); Mason, 50, 51 (cf. *Theatrical Observer*, July 20, 1875); Booth-Winter and Fechter editions; Alger, *Forrest*, II, 774, 775.

52. *Critical Review*, for November 1765 (xx, 331).

53. Pages 28, 32. Both actors are charged with becoming jealous too early — at "Ha," line 165. Barry's collaring of Iago is mentioned in *The Theatrical Review of 1757*, p. 24.

54. Ed. 1764. For the Collaring Scene as performed by "spouters," see *Town and Country Magazine*, January 1769.

55. William Cooke, *Memoirs of Samuel Foote, Esq.*, 2 vols., New York, 1806, I, 185 ff.

"Greater than – that . . ." I still recall the earnest insistence of an old actor, once with Bandmann in Shakespearean parts, that Othello should fling down Iago here, and nowhere else.

56. See, e.g., *The Theatrical Inquisitor*, for May 1814 (and, for a dissenting opinion, *European Magazine*, January 1816); for Forrest, Alger, ii, 775, Harrison, 89, 90, Winter, *Shakespeare on the Stage*, First Series, p. 266.

57. *Liverpool Post*, quoted in Sillard, *Barry Sullivan*, i, 208 (I have been unable to identify the particular performance).

58. *Furness Variorum*, 204 (cf. *Theatrical Journal*, April 4, 1866); Winter, *Shadows of the Stage*, First Series, p. 194 (also in *The Wallet of Time*, i, 277); Bright, in *The Theatre*, December 1, 1891, cuttings from *Boston Journal*, November 25, 1893, *Boston Evening Transcript*, February 5, 1895 (cf. November 25, 1893), in Blinn Shakespeare Scrapbooks.

59. Rees thought he *"kicked him when down"* (*Life of Forrest*, 144), and Gabriel Harrison asserts ridiculously that Salvini "had the audacity in the presence of a refined audience to . . . place his foot" upon Iago's neck (*Forrest*, 91).

60. See especially Knight, *Theatrical Notes*, 22, 23, and Mason, 52, 53. Rossi, too, threatened to stamp upon Iago's head (Winter, *Shakespeare on the Stage*, First Series, p. 296).

61. Paris, 1868, ii, 105 ff.; "Shakespeare's Tragedies on the Stage," *Lippincott's Magazine*, May 1884.

Kittredge finds even the traditional business without Salvini's additions "foreign to Shakespeare's intent," since Iago's "O grace! O heaven forgive me" etc. "is not a protest against physical violence but against Othello's imputation on his honesty" (ed. *Othello*, 194).

62. *The Tragedian*, 108; Edwina Booth Grossmann, *Edwin Booth*, 263 (cf. Furness, *Letters*, i, 232); *Furness Variorum*, 208.

63. Fechter's ed.; *Furness Variorum*, 212; *Life of Cooke*, ii, 398 (cf. *Actors by Daylight*, February 16, 1839).

64. *Furness Variorum*, 214; Fechter's ed.; Mason, 60.

65. Gould, *The Tragedian*, 110; Mrs. Kendal, *Dramatic Opinions*, Boston, 1890, p. 29 (also in *Dame Madge Kendal*, 86, 87); Fechter's ed.; *Journal of a London Playgoer*, 230 (see also Kate Field, *Fechter*, 190).

66. She exits and returns, in Cooke-Cooper Promptbook and Winter-Booth edition. In Lewis's Promptbook, she either "re-enters, R. or comes forward," at line 98.

67. Mason, 67, 68.

68. Ottley, *Fechter's Version of Othello*, 27; Fechter's ed. Booth closed the scene with Desdemona kneeling,

Heaven keep that monster from Othello's mind!

69. [Charles Lillie,] *Original and Genuine Letters Sent to the Tatler and Spectator*, 2 vols., London, 1725, i, 255 ff. (cf. J. T. Kirkman, *Memoirs of Charles Macklin*, London, 1799, ii, 260).

70. At most about 250 lines are retained out of some 650.

71. Fechter's edition (cf. Ottley, *Fechter's Version of Othello*, 10, 11, and Lewes, *On Actors*, 134, 135).

72. *Furness Variorum*, 250, 251, Mason, 74 (see also, Fanny Kemble, "Salvini's Othello," *Temple Bar*, July 1884, Harrison's *Forrest*, 91); *Shakespearean Tragedy*, 184. Rymer, out of mere perverseness, I take it, speaks of Othello's "kicking her" (*A Short View of Tragedy*, 133).

73. Fechter's edition. Salvini's Moor, in making his exit, sometimes gave way to his passion, uttering "loud cries of anguish" and "wringing his hands wildly above his head" (Mason, 77).

74. Kean, Ferrers (Becks's note), and Lewis Promptbooks.

75. *Original Letters, Dramatic Pieces, and Poems*, 3 vols., London, 1786, I, 98, 99; Bernard, *Retrospections of the Stage*, I, 28, 29.

76. From his promptbook, McCullough's business must have been very similar. Salvini spoke "O Desdemona," retreating from her — "she must not even touch him" (Mason, 82).

77. Fechter's edition, Morley, *Journal*, 230, *Punch*, December 14, 1861.

78. Mason, 85, 86; Kean and Murdoch Promptbooks, Phelps and Forbes-Robertson, *Life and Life-Work of Phelps*, 323. See also Victor quotation, above.

79. *Furness Variorum*, 264. Alfred Brydome, in Oscar Asche's production, February 28, 1907, "deliberately appropriated the purse" (Dickins, *Forty Years of Shakespeare on the English Stage*, 146).

80. *New York Evening Post*, January 25, 1833; Fechter, Booth-Winter Editions.

81. *Actors by Daylight*, March 16, 1839; *Principles of Shakespearean Production*, 148; Ellen Terry, *Story of My Life*, 205.

Desdemona kneels for her protestation (line 151), and "*They raise her*" (Kemble), or "Iago assists" her "to rise" (Booth).

82. Ferrers Promptbook; *Furness Variorum*, 270.

83. Warde-Herman and Moore Promptbooks.

84. Fechter's edition. At the end of the scene, Roderigo stops, just as he is going out to speak his last line: Iago "*drags him off.*"

85. Shakespeare relies on the player's action to explain Desdemona's "Lay by these" (line 48). I have seen her give her rings to Emilia here — an idea which goes back to Capell ("*Giving her her Jewels*").

Winter, in his long career as a playgoer had heard the Willow Song only once, at Booth's in 1869 (*Shakespeare on the Stage*, First Series, p. 270).

86. January 22, 1881 (cf. Furness, *Letters*, I, 233); page 23, above, and cf. page 382, note 50.

87. See, e.g., Cooke-Cooper, Ferrers and Murdoch Promptbooks, Booth in *Furness Variorum*, 196, 287, and page 219, below.

88. *The Theatrical Repertory containing Criticisms on the Performances . . . during the Season 1801–2*, London [1802], pp. 102, 186, Oxberry's *New English Drama*, v (1819), p. 64; *Thespian Magazine* for June 1793.

89. *Punch*, May 14, 1881 (cf. Gustave Garcia, *The Actor's Art*, London, 1888, p. 183); *The Daily Telegraph*, May 5, 1881, quoted in *The Theatre*, June 1, 1881; *Athenaeum*, May 7, 1881.

90. *Life and Art of Edwin Booth*, 113, 247, Booth in *Furness Variorum*, 287 — etc. In Hinton's edition of Booth's acting version (c. 1869), Lodovico and Gratiano enter, strangely enough, where Shakespeare directs them to enter, before the stabbing of Roderigo; but in view of Winter's express statement I am not inclined to attach importance to this.

91. *Athenaeum*, March 8, 1862; Fechter's edition.

92. *The Restoration Theatre*, 144. The same door would be unlocked when Othello admits Emilia.

93. Morley, *Journal*, 231, Fechter's edition; Mason, 89.

94. In *The Theatrical Guardian*, April 2, 1791, is a curious reference to "that attempt which is generally made" on Desdemona's life at "Put out the light, and then. . . ." A dagger had figured here in Kemble's performance which the *Guardian* disapproves of.

95. Shakespeare's *Works*, (1735) London, 1773, VIII, 357.

96. *Forrest*, 92, 93. Lewis's promptbook has: "Mr. For^s disc^d at window" (and cf. Alger, II, 775). Presumably, the tragedian had changed his practice? Brooke, Booth, Fechter, and McCullough all were discovered.

97. Cooke, Kean, Murdoch, and Moore Promptbooks; Morley, *Journal*, 231. Booth, like Fechter, preferred having the bed at the side of the stage.

98. Morley *ibid.*, Fechter's edition. The business is criticized, with varying degrees of severity, by Ottley, *Fechter's Version of Othello*, 29, *The Theatrical Journal*, November 6, 1861, *Punch*, December 14, 1861, and Theodore Martin, in *Fraser's*, December 1861. See also Scott, *The Drama of Yesterday and Today*, I, 462.

99. *Dramatic Essays*, 16. See also *ibid.*, 24 (Forrest), *Edinburgh Dramatic Review*, March 17, 1824 (Vandenhoff), and Cumberland's edition.

100. *Roba di Roma*, 5th ed., Philadelphia, 1867, I, 230, 231 (see also, especially, Henry James, "Tommaso Salvini," *Atlantic Monthly*, March 1883). Cumberland's edition has *"Walks about,"* at line 40, and "Paces stage in front" (at line 32) is given in the Ferrers and Lewis Promptbooks.

101. I, 257. Cf. also *Thespian Magazine*, for September 1792.

102. Borgerhoff, *Le Théâtre anglais*, 85; *Examiner*, November 17, 1822.

103. *New York Herald*, November 1, 1881, quoted in Odell's *Annals*, XI, 451.

104. *Records of Later Life*, 630, 631, 646 (the second letter is misdated February 23 — *sc.* "25").

105. Borgerhoff, *Le Théâtre anglais*, 149; *Tallis's Dramatic Magazine*, April 1851.

106. *Daily Telegraph*, November 4, 1861, quoted in Phelps and Forbes-Robertson, *Life and Life-Work of Samuel Phelps*, 199. Forrest, too, hid the crime behind curtains (Harrison, 94). But Brooke anticipated the later emphasis on horror. His Desdemona (Miss Anderton) "struggled, in almost

an erect position, with *Othello* for her life, in a manner that made it a positive fight" (*Athenaeum*, September 10, 1853, and cf. *Theatrical Journal*, June 6, 1855).

107. "Shakspeare, and his Latest Stage Interpreters," *Fraser's Magazine*, December 1861, see also, e.g., *The Athenaeum*, November 2, 1861, *Punch*, December 14, 1861.

108. *Dramatic Opinions*, 29 (also, *Dame Madge Kendal*, 87).

109. Mason, 95. He adds that in 1873 Salvini used to take her up "bodily in his arms, and carry her off." Among the numerous other accounts, see especially R. G. White, in *The Nation*, September 25, 1873, Knight, *Theatrical Notes*, 23, 24, "Nym Crinkle," in *The Theatre* (New York), October 19, 1889, and Towse, *Sixty Years of the Theatre*, 162 ff.

110. *Shakespeariana*, v (1888), 267. Sir Frank Benson tells of his father's expostulating with him, in the 'eighties: " 'You promised, Frank, that you would strangle her behind the curtains . . . I cannot bear it on the stage' " (*My Memoirs*, 218).

111. *A Short View of Tragedy*, 140; "*Journal littéraire*, tome IX. pp. 157–216," quoted in F. A. Hedgcock, *David Garrick and his French Friends*, 198 note, see also Voltaire, *Lettres Philosophiques* (1734), *Oeuvres Complètes*, Paris, 1879, XXII, 149.

112. I, 148. There is a note to the same effect in Bell's edition (1774).

113. *Private Correspondence*, I, 599 (cf. also, 592, 593, 636, 650, II, 16). For the writer, a retired actor named George Cornelius Swan, see Boaden, *Life of Mrs. Jordan* (1831), "Grolier Society," I, 35, note, and La Tourette Stockwell, *Dublin Theatres and Theatre Customs*, 73 ff. His ms. "Dissertation" on *Othello* sounds interesting, and he had ideas of his own about the stabbing. Steevens planned to print some of his stage directions in a later edition of his own Shakespeare, but did not.

114. Helen Zimmern, "Salvini on Shakespeare," *Gentleman's Magazine*, February 1884, *Furness Variorum*, 303.

115. Frederick Rule, in *Notes and Queries*, December 6, 1884; Webster's *Complete Works*, ed. Lucas, II, 189.

116. *Sixty Years of the Theatre*, 163, 164, see also Story, *Roba di Roma*, I, 231; Marston, *Our Recent Actors*, I, 83, Forster, *Dramatic Essays*, 16.

117. Harrison, *Forrest*, 94, 95; Phelps and Forbes-Robertson, *Life and Life Work of Phelps*, 324; Fitzgerald, *Henry Irving: A Record*, 169, 170.

118. The phrase itself was cut in a number of acting editions — Bell's, for instance, Kemble's, and French's — but promptbook evidence shows that Othello often closed the curtains here, even so. The presence of the same words reduces the likelihood, without ruling out the possibility, that on Shakespeare's stage the actual murder was done behind curtains.

119. Fechter's ed. Cf. the promptnotes, "Mind Key in L.H. Door" (Moore) and "See key in L. door" (Lewis 1851). "*Unlocks the door*" is as old as Theobald's edition.

120. *Life on the Stage*, New York, 1901 (1902), pp. 182, 183. Cf. Harcourt Williams, *Four Years at the Old Vic*, 146, for his attempt to produce the same effect there, when Edith Evans was playing Emilia. The exit, which is sharply criticized in George Skillan's recent acting text, is given in the Booth-Winter edition, but I am at a loss to say how old it is.

121. Fechter Edition; Oxberry (also Cumberland) Edition.

122. Lewis's promptbook also has the sword taken "from table RH." For Emilia's kneeling, see especially W. T. Price, *Charlotte Cushman*, New York [1894], p. 159, and Mrs. Gilbert, *Stage Reminiscences*, New York, 1901, p. 99.

Salvini spoke "Are there no stones in heaven . . ." with "the full power of his voice. His arms are stretched upward; his head is thrown back; his aspect is Titanic" (Mason, 101).

123. *Theatrical Observer*, October 25, 1836; *Athenaeum*, October 6, 1849 (cf. January 8, 1848).

124. For Forrest, see Becks's note in the Ferrers Promptbook; and, for Booth, cf. the Winter edition and *Boston Traveller*, October 4, 1866 (in Blinn Shakespeare Scrapbooks).

125. Murdoch Promptbook; Booth-Winter Edition.

126. Booth, in *Furness Variorum*, 323; "Tommaso Salvini," *Atlantic Monthly*, March 1883, see also, e.g., Knight, *Theatrical Notes*, 24.

127. *Letters*, ed. Mrs. Toynbee, III, 37; *Literary Gazette*, quoted in *The Gentleman's Magazine*, March 1751 (given also in John Hill, *The Inspector*, 2 vols., London, 1753, I, 13, and Kirkman's *Macklin*, I, 339). Othello often clasped Cassio's hand here in later times.

128. Oxberry's edition (cf. also Cumberland's and Kean Promptbook). I can find no trace of the Quarto's "*Chaire*" for Cassio here. Kemble has him "*brought in by* Antonio *and* Julio."

129. Note in Ferrers Promptbook — there is a similar one by Becks in Lewis. In the Clarke-Forrest and McCullough Books, Othello merely looks at or points to the handkerchief "in Cassio's bosom."

130. Gould, *The Tragedian*, 116. For his son's business, cf. *Furness Variorum*, 326.

131. May 1814. For Kean's retirement to the bed, see also [Frances Williams-Wynn,] *Diaries of a Lady of Quality*, ed. Abraham Hayward, London, 1864, p. 113. The famous gesture with "the clasped hands, palms upward" is said to have been used once more, most tellingly, during the disclosures just before (Ottley, *Fechter's Version of Othello*, 32, and cf. Kirk, "Shakespeare's Tragedies on the Stage"). See page 195, above.

132. *Miscellanies*, 244; letter to *The Tatler*, September 23, 1831, quoted in Leigh Hunt, *Dramatic Essays*, 229 (see also Ottley, *Fechter's Version of Othello*, 32).

133. Paris, 1868, II, 123. Othello's concluding lines are likely to be wanting in acting texts from Bell's onwards.

134. "Shakespeare's Tragedies on the Stage," see also *Theatrical Observer*, November 14, 1822 (cf. *The Mirror*, February 7, 1824, on Conway, quoted in Odell, *Annals*, III, 101), *Theatrical Journal*, August 22, 1840, and Godfrey Turner, "Back-Falls," *The Theatre*, February 1, 1884.

135. Phelps and Forbes-Robertson, *Phelps*, 181; *Tallis's Dramatic Magazine*, April 1851; Furness Variorum, 332; Marie and Squire Bancroft, *The Bancrofts: Recollections of Sixty Years*, New York, 1909, p. 46.

136. *Reminiscences*, etc. II, 456. See also, e.g., Morley, *Journal*, 232; Martin, in *Fraser's*, December 1861; Pascoe's *Dramatic List*, 132, 276.

137. Salvini, "Impressions of Some Shakespearean Characters," *Century Magazine*, November 1881; Lewes, 224; Knight, *Theatrical Notes*, 24, 25, 129. See also, especially, Mason, 107. With Irving, in 1876, tradition was reestablished (Cook, *Nights at the Play*, II, 108).

138. Furness Variorum, 324, *Behind the Scenes with Edwin Booth*, 110. See also Towse, *Sixty Years of the Theatre*, 191, and Skinner, *Footlights and Spotlights*, 94.

139. *View of the English Stage*, 221; *Diaries of a Lady of Quality*, 111. The early exit and the gag are still found in French's edition.

140. *The Morning Post*, quoted by Asia Booth Clarke, pp. 21, 22; *Theatrical Inquisitor*, for February 1817; *Theatrical Observer*, November 26, 1836. See also Hazlitt, *View*, 356.

141. *Edinburgh Dramatic Review*, March 14, 1825 (for Cooke, see also *Examiner*, January 31, 1808); *Theatrical Journal*, October 10, 1840; Manchester *Sphinx*, November 27, 1869, quoted in Phelps and Forbes-Robertson, *Phelps*, 324.

142. Dickins, *Forty Years of Shakespeare on the English Stage*, 40. See also, Fitzgerald, *Henry Irving: A Record*, 170, and cf. Winter, *Booth*, 197.

CHAPTER V. MACBETH

1. *Journal*, 2 vols., Philadelphia, 1835, II, 115, 116. See also Simond's comments in his *Journal of a Tour and Residence in Great Britain*, 2 vols., New York, 1815, I, 131, 132; though some reforms seem to have been accomplished under Kemble (Odell, *Shakespeare from Betterton to Irving*, II, 92).

2. *Roscius Anglicanus*, 1708, ed. Montague Summers, p. 33. For further references to flyings by the Witches, a feature of productions of *Macbeth* in the Restoration, see the same editor's *Shakespeare Adaptations*, London, 1922, pp. xlvi, lxii. Davenant's adaptation is readily available in the appendix to the Furness Variorum *Macbeth*.

3. Cf. the interesting edition, *Newly Adapted to the Stage, with Alteration as Performed at the Theatre in Edinburgh*, Edinburgh, 1753, which has the "*Three* Witches *rise separately*" at the beginning of the scene and "*vanish*" at the end of it. "G. Trap," I take it, means Grave Trap.

4. I, 80. He returns to the attack in a footnote to the stage direction in Bell's Edition of Shakespeare's Plays (1774), *"Thunder. The Witches sink."*

5. The two printed directions first appeared in Kemble's edition of 1803, whence they passed to Mrs. Inchbald's *British Theatre* (1808) and French's *Standard Drama,* turning up as recently as 1915 in the "William Warren Edition." George H. Clarke's Forrest Promptbook (c. 1868–1869) reads: "The witches are close together as curtain rises – then they separate, as if going in different directions, before 1ˢᵗ Witch speaks."

6. *The Athenaeum,* October 2, 1847, Lloyd's *Weekly London News* (quoted in Phelps and Forbes-Robertson, *Life and Life-Work of Samuel Phelps,* 100), *Dramatic and Musical Review,* October 9 and 16, 1847. Charles Kean in his Princess's Theatre production, February 16, 1853, followed Phelps's lead in the matter of mist (see his acting edition and "Cuthbert Bede" [Edward Bradley] in *Notes and Queries,* July 13, 1889). Irving's witches were "revealed by flashes of lightning" (Knight, *Theatrical Notes,* 64, 65, cf. Towse, *Sixty Years of the Theatre,* 301).

7. Sadler's Wells Promptbooks.

8. "Facts and Fancies about Macbeth," *Gentleman's Magazine,* March 1889.

9. For the litter, see George Henry Lewes, in *Dramatic Essays,* edd. Archer and Lowe, 239, "Cuthbert Bede" in *Notes and Queries,* July 13, 1889. The Sergeant is supported by guards alone, in Cumberland's Edition. In the 1852 Howard Athenaeum Promptbook, they are reinforced by the Physician.

10. Phelps "1860" Promptbook; George H. Clarke's Forrest Promptbook, c. 1868–1869.

11. Cumberland, Oxberry, and "William Warren" Editions, Charnock's Boston Promptbook, Phelps "1860" Promptbook.

12. Traps are called for in West Digges's Promptbook (c. 1757), and the Edinburgh, 1761, Promptbook, and in Bell's Edition (1774). For the Sadler's Wells gauze curtain, see Godfrey Turner, "Scenery, Dresses, and Decorations," *The Theatre,* March 1, 1884, and Odell, *Shakespeare from Betterton to Irving,* II, 319. The Howard Athenaeum Promptbook, 1852, calls for "a dark cloud" and "a gauze clouding in front of that," which "rise during the dialogue of the witches."

13. 1847 Sadler's Wells Promptbook; the sentry figures (uniquely, so far as I know) in The Howard Athenaeum 1852 book.

14. Oxberry's *New English Drama,* 1821 – the earliest edition to contain business at this point – has the three bows. Cf. Winter-Booth direction: *"Witches join hands, move round in circle, and bow thrice."* Salvini's Edition (London, 1876) has them move with *"gesti e modi strani e diabolici."*

15. *Notes and Queries,* July 13, 1889. The Clarke promptbook was prepared about 1868–1869 and Charles Kean's production, thus, took place some fifteen years before. But in 1852 Robert Jones's book shows us that the Howard Athenaeum witches carried wands. See also, page 265, below.

16. A later note includes a *"Bagpipe"* (queried) in addition to the fifes!

The 1773 production was, of course, that in which Scottish habits were for the first time employed in *Macbeth*. The Macklin ms. was kindly placed at my disposal by Dr. William Van Lennep.

17. *Quarterly Review*, xxxiv (1826), 199. For Kemble's entrance, see also *The Kilkenny Chronicle*, October 27, 1812 (quoted in *The Private Theatre of Kilkenny*, p. 74). Bell's edition (1774) has Rowe's stage direction, Davenant's new line, and the halts. Cumberland's influential acting text (c. 1829) directs part of the army to pause on a bridge; they resume their march at the end of the scene.

18. Truncheons and shields for Macbeth and Banquo are called for in the Howard Athenaeum and Phelps (1860) Promptbooks. A notice of the actor Packer in the *Thespian Magazine*, November 1792, implies that Banquo carried a truncheon, see also *Punch*, October 20, 1855. At the time of the Astor Place Riot Macready pointed out the demonstrators to the police with his truncheon (*Diaries*, ed. Toynbee, ii, 425). This was during one of the early scenes in *Macbeth*.

19. Forster would have the business at the earlier moment (*The Examiner*, February 12, 1837, quoted in *Dramatic Essays*, edd. Archer and Lowe, 33). James E. Murdoch puts it at lines 136–137 (*The Stage*, Philadelphia, 1880, p. 326).

20. *Shakespeare on the Stage*, First Series, p. 480. Adam Badeau records a more sensational entrance by Booth, "leaping from the rocks" ("Edwin Booth On and Off the Stage," *McClure's Magazine*, August 1893). He carried a spear when Katherine Goodale was with him in 1886–1887 (*Behind the Scenes with Edwin Booth*, 26).

21. *Early Stages*, N. Y., 1939, p. 168. Partridge's drawing is reproduced in Ellen Terry, *The Story of My Life*, p. 305. For Irving's soldiers in this scene, see Bram Stoker, *Personal Recollections of Henry Irving*, i, 24.

22. Barnes's Promptbook; *The Theatre*, August 1, 1882.

23. *The Dramatic Censor for the Year 1811*, 372. Cumberland's stage direction follows closely that in Oxberry, which is several years earlier. Charnock's Boston Promptbook, used during Macready's visit in 1826, has it too.

24. In the Howard Athenaeum Promptbook, this was done at each of the three hails; in Phelps's "1860" book only at the word "King." Clarke's Forrest Promptbook has at this last hail: "1st & 3rd Witches kneel – 2nd Witch stands, hands raised."

25. Hunt, in *The Tatler*, March 15, 1831, quoted in *Dramatic Essays*, edd. Archer and Lowe, 210; FitzGerald, *Letters to Fanny Kemble*, New York and London, 1895, p. 55; "Cuthbert Bede" in *Notes and Queries*, July 13, 1889; Clarke's (for the vanishing) and Becks's Forrest Promptbooks.

26. "1860" Promptbook. In Margaret Webster's recent production, Macbeth had been given a parchment, which he pretended to examine during the speaking of the aside, but "I thank you, gentlemen" was not accompanied by special business.

27. *Players and Playwrights I have Known*, London, 2 vols., 1888, i, 39.

Irving's marked copy has at Duncan's "My worthy Cawdor," "offers his hand." Did Irving's Macbeth by any chance avoid taking it? Davenant's stage direction at line 47 is perhaps worth quoting: "Macbeth *going out, stops, and speaks whilst the King talks with* Banq. &c."

28. *The Tatler*, March 15, 1831 (in *Dramatic Essays*, edd. Archer and Lowe, 212). Cf. *The Examiner*, October 21, 1817, on a Drury Lane actress, Miss Campbell.

29. Clara E. Clement, *Charlotte Cushman*, 173, 174; Beck's Forrest Promptbook; Winter, *Shadows of the Stage*, Second Series, p. 36 (also, *Shakespeare on the Stage*, First Series, pp. 504, 505).

30. *Ricordi e Studi Artistici*, Second Edition, Turin, Rome, and Naples, 1888, pp. 216, 217. Madame Ristori's accounts of her own stage business are given, throughout, in greatly abridged paraphrase.

31. *Notes and Queries*, July 13, 1889; Coleman, "Facts and Fancies about Macbeth," *Gentleman's Magazine*, March 1889; Winter, *Other Days*, New York, 1908, p. 156. The Winter-Booth Edition has, at "unsex me here," "*Touching her heart.*"

32. *Dame Madge Kendal, by Herself*, London [1933], p. 90. The Edinburgh 1753 edition, "*Newly Adapted to the Stage*," and Bell's Edition follow Rowe.

33. Becks's Forrest Promptbook has a similar direction; Clarke's, "rushes into his arms." Mrs. Kean, "at 'Great Glamis!' . . . hastily advanced to meet her husband, and fondly embraced him" ("Cuthbert Bede" in *Notes and Queries*, July 13, 1889).

34. Philadelphia [1874], pp. 259–261.

35. Becks's Forrest Promptbook has at "To-morrow, as he purposes", "drops his eyes: and turns away."

36. "J. H. Siddons," "Random Recollections of a Life," *Harper's Monthly Magazine*, December 1862.

37. Fleeming Jenkin, "Mrs. Siddons as Lady Macbeth," *The Nineteenth Century*, February 1878 (also, ed. Brander Matthews, "Publications of the Dramatic Museum of Columbia University," New York, 1915).

38. *The Journal of a London Playgoer*, 159. In the Phelps "1860" Promptbook, "Lady Macbeth goes R turns and perceives Macbeth abstracted, returns to him and urges him off." Charlotte Cushman's "pointing beyond" Macbeth to "the coming *Duncan* who 'must be provided for,'" greatly impressed Winter (*Shakespeare on the Stage*, First Series, p. 502).

39. Fleeming Jenkin, "Mrs. Siddons as Lady Macbeth"; Clara Erskine Clement, *Charlotte Cushman*, 114 (quoting the *New York Tribune*).

40. See page 150, above.

41. This was when Bell saw her (Fleeming Jenkin, "Mrs. Siddons as Lady Macbeth"). Kean's gesture is described in *The Times*, November 7, 1814. At Macbeth's difficult "And falls on the other . . ." Becks's Forrest Promptbook has: Lady Macbeth "touches him on the shoulder – He starts."

42. Hunt, in *The Tatler*, November 7, 1831 (quoted in *Dramatic Essays*,

edd. Archer and Lowe, pp. 231, 232); *Shakespeare on the Stage*, First Series, p. 511; *The Spirit of the Times*, January 26, 1889. Salvini embraced his Lady Macbeth "rapturously" when she unfolded her plan (Towse, *Sixty Years of the Theatre*, 178).

43. Winter-Booth Edition; Phelps "1860" Promptbook. Sir E. K. Chambers has a wise note on the passage, in his edition of the play (Boston, 1901).

44. *Diaries*, ed. Toynbee, I, 346. The Macklin Ms., the Charnock Promptbook, and the Winter-Booth Edition have the ring; cf. also *Punch*, xxvi (1854^1), 95.

45. *Private Correspondence*, ed. Boaden, II, 363.

46. James Boaden, *The Life of Mrs. Jordan* (1831), "Grolier Society Edition," I, 241, also *The Theatrical Inquisitor*, for August 1819.

47. Genest, *Some Account of the English Stage*, IX, 223.

48. Fleeming Jenkin, "Mrs. Siddons as Lady Macbeth" (cf. *European Magazine*, February 1815); *European Magazine*, September 1815.

49. *The Theatrical Observer*, October 31, 1822 (cf. *The Theatre*, October 11, 1828). Holman, too, had peered about the hall, after searching it first for concealed spies! (*The Columbian*, May 22, 1813, quoted in Odell's *Annals of the New York Stage*, II, 406).

50. For Kemble, see *The Times*, September 19, 1811; for Kean, Henry Crabb Robinson, *Diary*, December 1, 1814. Compare *John Bull*, May 26, 1839, on Macready: "suddenly raising his hand, he sees the dagger — and starts according to prescribed rule."

51. Fleeming Jenkin, "Mrs. Siddons as Lady Macbeth."

52. *Lloyd's Weekly London News*, on Phelps's recent performance at Sadler's Wells, September 27, 1847 (quoted in Phelps and Forbes-Robertson, *Life and Life-Work of Samuel Phelps*, 101). Forrest stood looking at the floor for some time, "buried in thought," then, "lifting his head, at last," saw the dagger, winked rapidly and rubbed his eyes (Alger, *Life of Edwin Forrest*, II, 742).

53. *The Dramatic Review*, January 5, 1889.

54. *Shakespearean Representation*, 143.

55. *Tallis's Dramatic Magazine*, November 1850; *ibid.*, June 1851.

56. Quoted in Pascoe's *Dramatic List*, 181. For the averted hands, cf. *Figaro* quotation in Brereton, *Life of Henry Irving*, I, 190.

The assertion of a writer in *The European Magazine*, March 1801, that the *"ideal dagger"* used to be represented objectively on the stage (he himself had seen it "within these few years") should be taken, it seems to me, with more than a grain of salt (cf. also *The Monthly Mirror*, New Series, II [1807], 438).

57. Fleeming Jenkin, "Mrs. Siddons as Lady Macbeth"; *The Morning Chronicle*, October 21, 1802 (quoted in Odell, *Annals of the New York Stage*, II, 153). Henry Crabb Robinson praises Kemble: "In his eye you could see when he lost sight of the dagger" (*Diary*, December 1, 1814).

58. *The Examiner*, January 15, 1809; "Facts and Fancies about Macbeth"; Winter, *Shakespeare on the Stage*, First Series, p. 469; Gordon Crosse, in *Notes and Queries*, July 8, 1916. In speaking the last line, Macready had pointed "upwards at the word 'heaven' — and *vice versâ*" (*John Bull*, May 26, 1839).

59. Forster, in *The Examiner*, February 12, 1837 (quoted in *Dramatic Essays*, 35); Winter, *Shakespeare on the Stage*, First Series, pp. 475, 476 (cf. Clarke's Forrest Promptbook).

60. E. R. Russell, "Mr. Irving's Interpretations of Shakspeare," *Fortnightly Review*, October 1, 1883.

61. J. H. Stocqueler, *The Memoirs of a Journalist*, Bombay and London, 1873, p. 17 (cf. Fleeming Jenkin, "Mrs. Siddons as Lady Macbeth"); Winter, *Shakespeare on the Stage*, First Series, p. 502. Unless I am mistaken, the photograph of Charlotte Cushman, *ibid.*, 508, shows her at this moment in the play.

62. According to Kemble's "institutes," the account proceeds, "Macbeth closes the .door with the . . . caution of a practised housebreaker," and in what follows is "awake to the suggestions of the lowest kind of cunning." Professor Bell's annotations are scarcely reconcilable with this (Fleeming Jenkin, "Mrs. Siddons as Lady Macbeth").

63. Towse, *Sixty Years of the Theatre*, 42. Contrast the Winter-Booth Edition, before "This is a sorry sight": *"Looking on his hands . . . in one of which he grasps two blood-stained daggers."*

64. *The Theatrical Inquisitor*, November 1814 (cf. Hazlitt, *View of The English Stage*, 207, and, on Holman, *The Columbian*, May 22, 1813, quoted in Odell's *Annals*, II, 406). The author of the "Notes, Explanatory, &c." tells us that "many actors . . . make a tremendous noise with the door" to announce their return (*European Magazine*, February 1815).

65. *Theatrical Observer*, December 3, 1836, see also Alger, *Life of Forrest*, I, 313, 314, II, 743.

66. See also Clarke's Promptbook and *The Athenaeum*, March 1, 1845.

67. The "William Warren Edition" has merely, *"Starts."* Macready made much of the return from the murder. Having rushed on, he stood bent backwards, as if he had been "shot through the breast by an arrow" (*Tallis's Dramatic Magazine*, November 1850; see also the Birmingham *Theatrical Looker-on*, II, 73 [July 21, 1823], and *The Theatrical Journal*, August 4, 1840).

68. E. R. Russell, "Mr. Irving's Interpretations of Shakespeare." A winding staircase must have contributed to the effect (Percy Fitzgerald, in *The Theatre*, February 1, 1888). See also O. B. Clarence, in *We Saw Him Act*, 92.

69. Fleeming Jenkin, "Mrs. Siddons as Lady Macbeth."

70. Mrs. Pritchard (Davies, *Life of Garrick*, II, 183, 184); Mrs. Siddons (*The London Chronicle*, February 5, 1785, Fleeming Jenkin, "Mrs. Siddons as Lady Macbeth", *Bell's Weekly Messenger*, October 18, 1818, Campbell, *Life of Mrs. Siddons*, II, 20, 21); Mrs. Pope ("Timothy Plain," *Letters Respecting the*

Theatre Royal, Edinburgh, August 6, 1798); Miss O'Neill (William Thew, *Poems on Various Subjects Chiefly Theatrical,* 56); Charlotte Cushman (William T. W. Ball, in Clara Clement's *Charlotte Cushman,* 175); Madame Ristori (*Theatrical Journal,* July 15, 1857); Miss Bateman (Brereton, *Life of Henry Irving,* I, 189); Ellen Terry (E. R. Russell in *The Liverpool Daily Press, ibid.,* II, 144); Mrs. Langtry (*The Spirit of the Times,* January 26, 1889); cf. Booth-Winter Edition.

71. Edward Fuller (ed.), *The Dramatic Year 1887-88,* Boston, 1889, pp. 152, 153.

72. It had, of course, been challenged, as early as the eighteen-forties, by Helen Faucit.

73. *The Spirit of the Times,* January 26, 1889 (reviewing Mrs. Langtry's performance, at the Fifth Avenue Theatre, the Twenty-first); Fleeming Jenkin, "Mrs. Siddons as Lady Macbeth." A "curious curdling touch of detail" was introduced in Ellen Terry's performance on her return "from depositing the daggers": she lifted "by the tips of her fingers only the robe which lies fallen on the ground" (Russell in *The Liverpool Daily Post,* quoted in Brereton's *Life of Irving,* II, 144).

74. Gould, p. 126; Fleeming Jenkin, "Mrs. Siddons as Lady Macbeth."

75. It was followed by Cooper (*The Morning Chronicle,* quoted in Odell's *Annals,* II, 166) and Vandenhoff (*Edinburgh Theatrical Review,* January 1, 1824, *Edinburgh Theatrical Observer, and Musical Review,* February 10, 1824). See also *The Private Theatre of Kilkenny,* 74, Charnock's Boston Promptbook, the Cumberland, French, Edwin Forrest, and "William Warren" editions.

76. *Our Recent Actors,* I, 78; Clara Clement, *Charlotte Cushman,* 175 (cf. Coleman, *Fifty Years of an Actor's Life,* I, 301). In Becks's Forrest Promptbook, Lady Macbeth "seizes him to pull him off," at line 72.

77. "Cuthbert Bede" in *Notes and Queries,* July 13, 1889; Russell, "Mr. Irving's Interpretations of Shakespeare"; Adelaide Ristori, *Ricordi,* 218 (see note 30, above).

78. Winter-Booth Edition. Kemble started the practice of having poor Seyton get the blame for keeping Macduff waiting. For a yawning, fumbling Porter without his speech — "which is too coarse for our taste" — see Tom Taylor, New Shakspere Society *Transactions,* 1874, p. 271.

79. *Quarterly Review,* XXXIV (1826), 219. Mr. Walter Hampden's Macbeth, I remember, *looked at his hands,* when he got a chance.

80. *New York Evening Post,* February 19, 1833.

81. See Kittredge (ed.), *Macbeth,* p. 142. French's Standard Drama, as usual, and The "William Warren Edition" have Cumberland's direction, "*Throwing open the door leading to the King's bedchamber,* R."

82. *Principles of Shakespearean Production,* 198; Phelps "1860" Promptbook ("1847" is to the same effect but less full). See also *Lloyd's Weekly London News* (quoted in Phelps and Forbes-Robertson, *Life and Life-Work*

of Samuel Phelps, 100). In the "William Warren Edition," Macduff, while speaking lines 78ff., "*beats the various doors*"; then, when his words have taken effect, he "*falls on* Banquo's *shoulder.*"

83. Coleman, "Facts and Fancies about Macbeth."

84. *Dramatic Miscellanies*, II, 152, 153. Mrs. Porter retired in 1743.

85. *The Journal of a London Playgoer*, 292 (cf. *ibid.*, 160).

86. *Boston Evening Transcript*, November 7, 1866 (Blinn Shakespeare Scrapbooks); also, the Ristori acting editions of 1857 and 1875. Cf. "Lacy's Acting Edition" (?1865): "*Pretending to faint.*"

87. *The Spirit of the Times*, January 26, 1889, cf. Winter, *Shakespeare on the Stage*, First Series, pp. 492, 493.

88. E. R. Russell in *Liverpool Daily Post*, December 31, 1888, quoted in Brereton's *Life of Irving*, II, 145 (cf. *Furness Variorum*, 124).

89. *My Memoirs*, London [1930], pp. 227, 228. At the time of which he writes, Janet Achurch was his Lady Macbeth.

90. Davies has some general reflections on the acting of the scene, which are not without interest (*Dramatic Miscellanies*, II, 158; cf. p. 153).

91. *Journal of a London Playgoer*, 291 (see also Doran in *Dublin Evening Mail*, December 23, 1864, quoted in Theodore Martin's *Helena Faucit*, 277).

91a. When Macbeth breaks off his account of the tales that are being told abroad (line 33), the same edition has Lady Macbeth leave the ladies with whom she has been engaged and take his hand, to stop him.

92. Clarke's Forrest Promptbook has at line 44: "All back out C. D", Seyton last." Irving argues elaborately that the Servant who figures in this scene is the mysterious Third Murderer ("An Actor's Notes on Shakspeare," *The Nineteenth Century*, April 1877).

93. *Shakespeare on the Stage*, First Series, p. 488. For the murderers, see Kittredge (ed.), *Macbeth*, 157.

94. Morley, *Journal of a London Playgoer*, 291 (December 3, 1864).

95. C[harlotte] P[orter], "Modjeska's Lady Macbeth," *Poet Lore*, IV (1892), 44. Mrs. Siddons, of course, interpreted the scene in the same way, as far as Lady Macbeth's *knowing* is concerned.

96. *The Athenaeum*, July 11, 1857; *John Bull*, May 26, 1839; Otis Skinner, *Footlights and Spotlights*, 93.

97. E.g., the Edinburgh 1753 Edition and 1761 Promptbook, Kemble (1815) and French Editions. Rowe has a scuffle, and Banquo's death, on stage. The Irving and Booth-Winter Editions omit the scene.

98. See especially a letter of Granville-Barker's in Harcourt Williams, *Four Years at the Old Vic*, 65, 66, and the notes on this scene in Kittredge's edition.

99. *Records of Later Life*, 637, 638. Macready, she goes on, insisted on having a long table "at the foot of the steps in front of the dais," which was very much in her way.

100. The diagram shows, however, a third table — just where Macready

placed his. Charnock's Boston Promptbook has a similar diagram (except that it puts Macbeth's chair nearer.the centre), and the stage directions in Cumberland's Edition imply the same general arrangement. Macklin in his Memoranda prefers a "horse-shoe" table. See also, *The Theatrical Censor* (Philadelphia), Number x.

101. See *The Athenaeum*, October 2, 1847, and October 5, 1850. There are interesting diagrams, for this scene, in the Howard Athenaeum and J. H. Barnes Promptbooks.

For the eccentric position of the chair, see also a further communication by "Umbra," "More Ghost-Playing," in *The London Magazine*, July 1824.

102. Cibber's *Apology*, ed. Lowe, I, 133, 134, *The Tatler*, July 16, 1709, Davies, *Dramatic Miscellanies*, III, 92, 93, etc.

103. *Boston Traveler*, January 29, 1867; *Boston Advertiser*, October 13, 1875 (cuttings in Blinn Shakespeare Scrapbooks).

104. John Munro, "More Shakespeare Allusions," *Modern Philology*, January 1916. Higden's *"Bancoe"* is very like Simon Forman's "Banko" and "Banco." Query, was the word so pronounced by the old actors? Forman's puzzling account of the play, c. 1611, may be read for what it is worth in Kittredge's edition of *Macbeth* (see also E. E. Stoll, *Shakespeare Studies*, 215, and note 125 below).

105. Cf. Rowe's direction: *"As he is drinking, the Ghost rises again just before him."* Bell adopts Capell's over-symmetrical *"rises . . . vanishes . . . rises . . . vanishes."* In the early promptbook, once Irving's, in the Folger Library, these directions become "Rise Trap OP" and "Sink T: OP," in the first two instances.

106. *Diary*, ed. James Greig, 8 vols., London, 1922–1928, VII, 59. I do not understand the "7 years." The Ghost had been restored at Covent Garden by November 25, 1807 (*Monthly Mirror*, N. S. ii [1807], 438). See also, e. g.: Wally Chamberlain Oulton, *The Busy Body*, February 26, 1787, and *The History of the Theatres of London*, 2 vols., 1796, II, 140; *The Morning Chronicle*, April 24, 1794, September 19, 20, 1798; *The Monthly Mirror*, v (1798), 112 note, 170, 301; xv (1803), 333, XVI (1803), 413, XVII (1804), 188; *The Times*, September 19, 1811; Boaden, *Life of Kemble*, II, 120; John Adolphus, *Memoirs of John Bannister*, 2 vols., London, 1839, I, 333.

107. *New York Evening Post*, October 28, 1829 (cf. *Athenaeum*, March 1, 1845, and Clarke's Promptbook). For the Booths, see Gould, *The Tragedian*, 129; Booth-Winter Edition; Malone, "An Actor's Memory of Edwin Booth," *Forum*, July 1893; Winter, *Life and Art of Edwin Booth*, 190.

108. *Barry Sullivan and his Contemporaries*, I, 211. Shades of John Philip Kemble!

109. *Ibid.*, II, 166. For Sullivan, see also Knight, *Theatrical Notes*, 162, and Coleman, "Facts and Fancies about Macbeth."

110. Brereton in *The Theatre*, October 1, 1895. See also *The Dramatic Review*, January 5, 1889; Odell, *Shakespeare from Betterton to Irving*, ii, 440;

Georges Bourdon, *Les Théâtres Anglais*, Paris, 1903, pp. 38, 39; Winter, *Shakespeare on the Stage*, First Series, pp. 484, 485; and note 116, below.

111. January 30, 1858. See also *The Times*, November 7, 1814 (cf. *The Drama; Or, Theatrical Pocket Magazine*, October 1824).

112. *Tour in England, Ireland, and France*, Philadelphia, 1833, p. 219. When, years later, Macready was acting with Mrs. Butler at the Princess's, the masking was done by "six cup-bearers" (*Theatrical Journal*, March 16, 1848).

113. W. W. Clapp, *A Record of the Boston Stage*, Boston and Cambridge, 1853, pp. 460, 461. The screening of the Ghost figures in two contemporary American promptbooks (not otherwise used by me). Both are in the Becks Collection: Accession Number 342940, signed "G. W. Lewis Prompter Broadway Theatre New York . . . 1852"; and, Accession Number 285353, signed "J. B. Wright Broadway Theatre N. Y. — 1854." Phelps's production was in 1847.

114. *Theatrical Observer*, May 22, 1841 (Mr. H. Wallack as Banquo). See, also, page 130, above.

115. *The Athenaeum*, June 9, 1849.

116. "Cuthbert Bede," in *Notes and Queries*, July 13, 1889. See also, Kean's Edition; *The Athenaeum*, February 19, 1853; Godfrey Turner, "The First Nights of my Young Days," *The Theatre*, June 1, 1887; Coleman, "Facts and Fancies about Macbeth"; Fitzgerald, *Shakespearean Representation*, 39, 40; James R. Anderson, *An Actor's Life*, ed. W. E. Adams, London and Newcastle-on-Tyne, 1902, p. 256.

Irving's Ghost in 1875 was, according to correspondence reprinted in *The Boston Advertiser*, October 13, 1875, "a painted effigy, on which the green light appropriated to spectral illuminations is thrown." Clement Scott speaks of it as "new practical and transparent" (*From "The Bells" to "King Arthur*," 77).

117. Coleman, "Facts and Fancies about Macbeth," see also *The Athenaeum*, March 15, 1884 (cf. Winter, *Shakespeare on the Stage*, First Series, p. 488). For some admirable reflections on the introduction of the Ghost, see G. Wilson Knight, *Principles of Shakespearean Production*, 104, 105.

118. *Private Correspondence*, I, 19, 134, 136 (letters dated January 17, 1744, January 22, 24, 1762).

119. Why, "to his Chair" — unless, perhaps, the trap was there? Ross played Banquo to Mossop's Macbeth, October 16, 1752 (Genest). *The New York Magazine; Or, Literary Repository*, for January 1795, speaks of the Ghost's 'retiring before' Mr. Hodgkinson's Macbeth.

120. *Theatrical Observer*, June 11, October 31, 1822. The bullying of the Ghost is deplored, lengthily, by W. H., "Notes, Explanatory, &c. &c. on the Tragedy of Macbeth," *European Magazine*, for March 1815.

121. Finlay, *Miscellanies*, 282, see also, on Kemble, *The English Chronicle and Universal Evening Post*, October 21–23, 1788, [John Williams] *The Chil-*

dren of Thespis, 13th ed., 1792, p. 50, Fleeming Jenkin, "Mrs. Siddons as Lady Macbeth."

122. *Morning Herald*, June 10, 1820 (quoted in Macready's *Reminiscences*, ed. Pollock, i, 214, note), *Theatrical Inquisitor*, for June 1820, *Theatrical Observer*, April 8, 1823, May 18, 1824, *Examiner*, April 13, 1823, Pückler-Muskau, *Tour of England*, 219, whose account is silently incorporated in Professor Bell's notes ("Mrs. Siddons as Lady Macbeth"). Davenport and Salvini were both influenced by Macready here (Winter, *Shakespeare on the Stage*, First Series, pp. 470, 488). Vandenhoff's business sounds more like Kean's (*Edinburgh Theatrical Observer, and Musical Review*, February 10, 1824, and *Edinburgh Dramatic Review* of the same date).

123. Becks's Forrest Promptbook ("tormentor" is of course in the technical sense). For Dillon's eccentric business of tearing his collar, see Marston, *Our Recent Actors*, ii, 184, cf. Ball, *The Amazing Career of Sir Giles Overreach*, 72.

124. Correspondence in *The Boston Advertiser*, October 13, 1875 (Blinn Shakespeare Scrapbooks), for this detail. See also, *Theatrical Observer*, October 9, 1875, Scott, *From "The Bells" to "King Arthur,"* 77.

125. J. Q. Adams, using these lines, points out a discrepancy in Simon Forman's account of the scene (ed., *Macbeth*, 297).

126. "British Essayists," ed. Chalmers, xxv, 177; see also, p. 203 (where again the glass is "dashed down"). Cf. Andrew Erskine's "Ode to Fear," *London Magazine*, April 1763 (also, *Gentleman's Magazine*, April 1763).

127. *Some Account of the English Stage*, vi, 338. "Stanley" is the authority. Is this the actor? See *ibid.*, viii, 693.

128. Davies, *Dramatic Miscellanies*, ii, 167; Boaden, *Memoirs of Mrs. Siddons*, 260; Campbell, *Life of Mrs. Siddons*, ii, 27. Mrs. Siddons imagines that on the second appearance of the ghost Lady Macbeth saw it, too!

129. *The London Chronicle*, February 5, 1785; *Bell's Weekly Messenger*, July 5, 1812 (also in *The European Magazine*, for July); Charles Lamb, "On the Tragedies of Shakespeare" (1811), in *Dramatic Essays*, ed. Brander Matthews, 195. For details of her acting in this scene, see Fleeming Jenkin, "Mrs. Siddons as Lady Macbeth."

130. Morley, *The Journal of a London Playgoer*, 160 (under date of July 25, 1857). In 1935, Miss Gladys Cooper, I remember, sat down on the stool which the ghost had occupied — as if thereby to prevent a return of Macbeth's hallucination.

131. Towse, *Sixty Years of the Theatre*, 211, 212, cf. Winter-Booth direction, "*Sinks on her bosom*" at "Shall be the maws of kites." Charles Kean had "clung in terror to his wife" at the beginning of the speech ("Cuthbert Bede," in *Notes and Queries*, July 13, 1889).

132. *The Commercial Advertiser* (New York), November 18, 1799, *The Athenaeum*, September 26, 1868, *Poet-Lore*, iv (1892), 44, 45.

133. [Margaret Stokes,] "Helen Faucit," *Blackwood's Magazine*, December

1885, cf. Theodore Martin, *Helena Faucit*, 313, 314. *The New York Dramatic Mirror*, February 26, 1898, praises Madame Modjeska's "dejection and weary despair after the banquet, when stripping herself of the insignia of her rank. . . ."

134. Towse, *Sixty Years of the Theatre*, 187, see also, Winter, *Life and Art of Edwin Booth*, 191, 245, and Winter-Booth Edition.

135. See also Winter, *Shakespeare on the Stage*, First Series, p. 484. I do not know at what date Lady Benson introduced the anticipatory action of rubbing her hands, at

> You lack the season of all natures, sleep

(*Mainly Players*, 269, 270, cf. *Poet-Lore*, viii (1896), p. 344).

136. *Theatrical Journal*, April 27, 1853 (also, *The Times*, February 15, 1853, quoted in Pascoe's *Dramatic List*, 274); [Margaret Stokes,] "Helen Faucit," *Blackwood's Magazine*, December 1885; Becks's Forrest Promptbook; Edward Fuller, *The Dramatic Year 1887-88*, p. 153; Kate Field, "Adelaide Ristori," *Atlantic Monthly*, April 1867 (cf. her review in *The Boston Transcript*, November 7, 1866, Blinn Shakespeare Scrapbooks).

137. *Ricordi*, 224, 225. For his recoiling from her, "as from another spectre," a little earlier, see Morley, *Journal of a London Playgoer*, 161.

138. Russell in *Liverpool Daily Post*, December 31, 1888 (quoted in Brereton's *Irving*, ii, 145); Winter, *Shakespeare on the Stage*, First Series, p. 485.

139. *Morning Chronicle*, April 22, and April 24, 1794 (Oulton's familiar account, in his *History of the Theatres of London*, borrows from this).

140. W. J. Fox, "W. C. Macready," *The People's Forum*, December 19, 1846; *Theatrical Register for the Year 1788* (York), no. vii. "A less liberal employment of fireworks in the brewing of the magic 'gruel'" is recommended to Irving by Knight, *Theatrical Notes*, 65.

141. See also J. H. Stoddart, *Recollections of a Player*, New York, 1902, p. 16, writing of a performance at Edinburgh, c. 1832.

142. Cf. stage directions in the Folio and in Rowe's Edition; also, W. J. Lawrence, "Early Stage Traps," *Pre-Restoration Stage Studies*, 145 ff.

143. xvi, 414. Oxberry's Edition (1822) has the First Apparition rise *"from a trap in the middle of the stage"*; Cumberland's (1829) has each of the three rise *"through the cauldron."* *The Theatrical Observer*, December 20, 1821, reports that at Drury Lane two days before, the cauldron had nearly been "knocked over by the little boy who was pushed up it."

144. Cf. James R. Anderson, *An Actor's Life*, 146, J. H. Stoddart, *Recollections of a Player*, 16.

145. *Behind the Scenes with Edwin Booth*, 27 ff.; Winter-Booth Edition; Robert Jones's Promptbook.

146. Irving, in 1895, substituted "a crater in a mountain top" for the cauldron (Towse, *Sixty Years of the Theatre*, 301, 302); and Peter Paterson tells of how the cauldron was dragged off by ropes — but that was at a performance by strollers (*Glimpses of Real Life as Seen in the Theatrical World*,

London, 1864, pp. 3 ff.). For the Elizabethan staging of the "shew," see J. C. Adams, *The Globe Playhouse*, 189–191.

147. *Quarterly Review*, XXXIV (1826) p. 227. Gauzes figure in the Phelps, Howard Athenaeum, and Barnes Promptbooks. Another Kemble stage-trick — a succession of flashes of light upon a single object — is noted in *The Monthly Mirror*, XVI (1803), p. 414.

148. *Shakespearean Representation*, 38; *Theatrical Censor*, January 27, 1806.

149. *Dramatic and Musical Review*, October 22, 1842; Winter, *Shakespeare on the Stage*, First Series, pp. 488, 489 (also, Coleman, "Facts and Fancies about Macbeth").

150. *Fifty Years of an Actor's Life*, I, 155, 156.

151. Pages 141, 146, above. Both Phelps Promptbooks and also the "William Warren Edition" have "Kneeling". at "And braggart with my tongue" — the last speech in the scene.

152. *London Chronicle*, April 18–20, 1786, *New York Magazine; Or, Literary Repository*, October 1791, *Theatrical Journal*, I (1839), 22, 32 (where the actress whom Delia imitates has become Mrs. Warner!). It is also printed in Pratt's *Miscellanies*, 4 vols., London, 1785, III, 101 ff.

153. Fleeming Jenkin, "Mrs. Siddons as Lady Macbeth."

154. Campbell, *Life of Mrs. Siddons*, II, 38. For the candle, see also *The Green-Room Mirror*, London, 1786, p. 63, and "Lord Harcourt's judgment of Mrs. Siddons, on her first appearance," in Walpole's *Letters*, ed. Peter Cunningham, VIII, 317. An engraving in *The Universal Museum*, April 1768, shows Mrs. Pritchard holding the candle in her left hand. The Doctor and Gentlewoman are huddled together at the side.

155. Number XVI, p. 144. Cf. *Mirror of Taste* (Philadelphia), March 1810. *The Theatrical Censor* was equally unaware of the origin of Fennell's "Did you not speak to it" (*Hamlet*, I, 2, 214), a famous point of Kemble's.

156. Number I, January 24, 1807 (*Salmagundi*, third edition, New York, 1820, I, 21).

157. Z. B. Gustafson, *Geneviève Ward*, London [1881], p. 115 note. See also e. g., the Charnock, Howard Athenaeum, and Clarke Promptbooks, Talfourd's *Macbeth Travestie* (1853), De Reyes, *On the Acting of Shakespeare's Plays*, 79.

158. *Memoirs of Mrs. Siddons*, 262, see also *The Morning Chronicle*, September 19, 1798.

159. N. S., I (1807), p. 358; VII (1810), p. 387; cf. II (1807), 438. A letter from Bernard Shaw, quoted by Mrs. Patrick Campbell (*My Life and Some Letters*, New York, 1922, p. 185), warns her against rubbing her hands "realistically (drat the blood, it won't come off)." Those who saw Miss Judith Anderson's Lady Macbeth, in 1941, will recall the appalling sense she gave of the blood's having got *deep in*.

160. Leigh Hunt's *London Journal*, I (1834), 118, cf. *Autobiography*, 2

vols., New York, 1872, I, 159; and, for the over-elaboration of the washing, *Dramatic Essays*, edd. Archer and Lowe, 235. Mrs. Cibber "seem'd to smell to her fingers," [Bonnell Thornton] *Have at You All; Or, The Drury-Lane Journal*, March 19, 1752.

161. [Edward Mangin] *Piozziana*, London, 1833, p. 127 (see also *ibid.*, 85 and *Diaries of a Lady of Quality*, ed. A. Hayward, London, 1864, p. 105). Mrs. Duff's "retiring backwards" is noted by *The Albion*, September 13, 1823 (quoted in Odell, *Annals of the New York Stage*, III, 89).

162. *Some of Shakespeare's Female Characters*, 231; *Liverpool Post*, quoted in Theodore Martin, *Helena Faucit*, 314. Fanny Kemble's business, on the contrary, was her aunt's (see *The Manchester Dramatic and Musical Review*, February 27, 1847).

163. *Ricordi*, 226–229, Morley, *Journal of a London Playgoer*, 159, 161, *The Athenaeum*, July 19, 1873, Kate Field, "Adelaide Ristori", and *Spectator*, January 5, 1889.

164. *The Spirit of the Times*, January 26, 1889. Perhaps, her putting out her candle just before was an innovation?

165. Geneviève Ward and Richard Whiteing, *Both Sides of the Curtain*, London (etc.), 1918, p. 164; *The Athenaeum*, July 12, 1884; Lady Benson, *Mostly Players*, 269.

166. In his 1815 edition Kemble made the gentleman a *"Marshal."* Winter mentions Mantell's truncheon, *Shakespeare on the Stage*, First Series, p. 496.

167. Clarke's Promptbook. "Seyton bows rebuked," at line 34, is another interesting detail.

168. E.g. Bell, Kemble, Oxberry, Cumberland, French, Booth, Salvini, and "William Warren" Editions.

169. *Theatrical Observer*, November 7, 1837; also, *John Bull*, November 12, 1837.

170. Cf. Charles Kean's Edition: *"Trumpet heard; the boughs are thrown down and the Army discovered."*

171. *Opera Glass*, December 1895 (Blinn Shakespeare Scrapbooks). Booth's soldiers set out *"with axes, etc.,"* at v, 4, 7, returning swiftly *"with boughs."*

171a. *Dame Madge Kendal*, 7.

172. "1860" Promptbook; *Shakespeare on the Stage*, First Series, p. 469; "Cuthbert Bede" in *Notes and Queries*, July 13, 1889; Emma Lazarus, "Tommaso Salvini," *The Century*, November 1881.

173. *The Examiner*, February 12, 1837 (quoted in *Dramatic Essays*, 36); *London Spectator*, March 8, 1845 (quoted in *A Rejoinder to "The Replies from England*," New York, 1849, p. 66).

174. London, 1764, p. 12.

175. London, 1817, pp. 110, 111, note. It might be urged with equal force that the presence of the direction in Rowe points to Betterton's practice.

176. Macready, *Reminiscences*, I, 148. Rowe's direction is wanting in many nineteenth-century acting editions, following Kemble's, but is retained in

Charles Kean's, Lacy's, and Salvini's. Talfourd's *Macbeth Travestie* (1853) equips the hero with *"a truncheon"*; as for the messenger – he *"punches his head."*

177. *Theatrical Journal,* July 22, 1843, Murdoch, *The Stage,* 105.

178. Forster in *The Examiner,* February 12, 1837 (quoted in *Dramatic Essays,* 36, 37); St. John Ervine, *The Theatre in my Time,* London, [1933], p. 48. Possibly there was still further business with a truncheon later in the scene. In O'Keefe's *Beggar on Horseback* (1785), II, 4, Mrs. Mummery, thinking of engaging Codger as a provincial actor, says to him: "Well, Macbeth – here['s] a truncheon . . . 'Blow wind, burst rack, at least we'll die with harness on our back' " (*Dramatic Works,* 1798, III, p. 466).

179. E. R. Russell in *The Liverpool Daily Post,* December 31, 1888 (quoted in Brereton's *Irving,* II, 147); "The William Warren Edition" – which has also, at "The Queen, my lord, is dead," *"All express sorrow.* Soldiers *reverse their arms,"* a direction which at least sets one thinking.

180. *Masters of the Show,* New York, 1914, pp. 109, 110 (cf. Fitzgerald, *Shakespearean Representation,* 98, 99). Bell's *Shakespeare* has *"a grand battle is fought across the Stage,"* at the beginning of V, 7.

180a. *Footlights and Spotlights,* 175.

181. Lyon, 1760, pp. 215–217. It is accepted as referring to Macbeth by G. W. Stone, "Garrick's Handling of *Macbeth,"* *Studies in Philology,* October 1941.

182. H. C. Robinson, *Diary,* I, 297, John Brown, *The Stage,* London, 1819, p. 35. Hazlitt notes that Kean fell "with his face downwards" (*View of the English Stage,* 207).

183. *The Examiner,* October 4, 1835 (quoted in *Dramatic Essays,* 6, 7), cf. *The Theatrical Journal,* August 4, 1840, April 2, 1842, *John Bull,* May 26, 1839 – for his rising on one knee. Charnock's Boston Promptbook enumerates the blows to be exchanged during the combat. For Charles Kean, see *Theatrical Journal,* April 27, 1853.

184. *The Morning Star,* quoted in Sillard, *Barry Sullivan,* II, 36 (see also, Ellen Terry and Bernard Shaw, *A Correspondence,* pp. XXII, XXIII); Winter, *Shakespeare on the Stage,* First Series, p. 479.

185. E. R. Russell, in *Liverpool Daily Post,* December 31, 1888 (quoted in Brereton's *Irving,* II, 147), W. H. Pollock, "Stage Swordsmanship," *The Theatre,* June 1, 1896.

186. Cf. Francis Gentleman, in Bell's *Shakespeare:* "If deaths upon the stage are justifiable, none can be more so than that of *Macbeth. Shakespeare's* idea of having his head brought on by *Macduff,* is very censurable."

187. *The Athenaeum,* October 2, 1847, notices quoted in Odell, *Shakespeare from Betterton to Irving,* II, 274, and Phelps and Forbes-Robertson, *Life and Life-Work of Samuel Phelps,* 99, 100, "The Drama," *Blackwood's Edinburgh Magazine,* LXXIX (1856), p. 227.

188. Godfrey Turner, "Scenery, Dresses, and Decorations," *The Theatre,*

March 1, 1884; *Our Recent Actors*, ii, 40. A ms. note by Booth on the direction, "with Macbeth's head on a pole," in James Taylor's interleaved copy of the play, is not I think to be taken too seriously: "should never be omitted. . . ."

189. The raising on a shield figures in Madame Ristori's Editions, and was, I believe, introduced also by Irving (cf. Brereton, *Life of Henry Irving*, ii, 147).

CHAPTER VI. THE OTHER TRAGEDIES

1. Spencer, *Shakespeare Improved*, 75.

2. *Fifty Years of Shakespearean Playgoing*, 8 (see also, e. g. Edward Russell, "Irving's 'King Lear'," *The Nineteenth Century*, January 1893). Young's tottering step and "the quick clutching of his hands" are noted in *Piozziana*, London, 1833, pp. 165, 166.

3. Cooke and Forrest Promptbooks; Kemble's marked copy of *Lear*; Booth-Winter Edition; Kean's promptbook.

4. Kemble's marked copy; Towse, *Sixty Years of the Theatre*, 176; H. J. Jennings, " 'King Lear' at the Lyceum," *Gentleman's Magazine*, December 1892.

5. Forrest Promptbook. In Ferrers, Gloster has "a wand" — again like Polonius (see page 134, above).

6. *John Bull*, February 4, 1838 (Miss Huddard's being referred to as Cordelia is obviously a slip), see also Lacy's edition. Cordelia still "throws herself at his feet and seizes his robe," in Wallack's Broadway production, ten years later.

7. *The Hospital*, quoted in *King Lear at the Lyceum: Some Extracts from the Press*, London, 1893, p. 94; *The Fools of Shakespeare*, 190, 191.

8. *Notes*, 98; *Dramatic Miscellanies*, ii, 273; McCullough and Forrest Promptbooks. Kemble's edition has Oswald enter "*singing, and passing King Lear carelessly.*"

9. *Henry Irving*, New York and Toronto, 1930, pp. 107-109; *Autobiography*, 69.

10. Macready's fondling of the Fool on the latter's entrance is praised by Forster (*Dramatic Essays*, 51, 52). In Wallack's promptbook, at line 211: "Goneril turns frowningly looking at the Fool — who archly peeps over Lear's shoulder."

11. Phelps Promptbook (but cf. Phelps and Forbes-Robertson, 81, 82), Winter-Booth and Irving Editions; *The Prompter*, October 7, 1735. Was the actor Stephens, who, according to Genest, played Lear for his benefit, April 10, 1735? Hill speaks of the performance as "some time since," before "a numerous and elegant Audience."

12. Page 31.

13. See *ibid.*, Foote, *Treatise on the Passions*, 17, Theophilus Cibber, *Two Dissertations on the Theatres*, London, 1756, part II, p. 33, *Monthly Review*, August 1769, *St. James's Chronicle*, September 26, October 3, 1769.

14. *Dramatic Miscellanies*, II, 280; C. R. Leslie, *Autobiographical Remains*, ed. Tom Taylor, Boston, 1860, p. 98. Thomas Dibdin had among his possessions "the crutch-headed cane which Mr. Sheridan used, when performing Lear" (*Reminiscences*, 2 vols., New York, 1828, I, 124).

15. See, especially, Kemble's marked copy, *The Times*, October 15, 1810. For Miss Siddons's practical demonstration of her brother's "sacrifice of energy of action to grace" here, see Sir Walter Scott, in *The Quarterly Review*, XXXIV, 216, and cf. Boaden's *Mrs. Siddons*, 380.

16. Cooke Promptbook, Dunlap, *Life of Cooke*, I, 212; Hazlitt, *London Magazine Essays*, 446; Forster, *Dramatic Essays*, 52, 53, *Theatrical Journal*, September 27, 1845; Cole, *Charles Kean*, II, 255, Winter, *Shakespeare on the Stage*, Second Series, pp. 426, 427.

17. Alger, *Forrest*, II, 786; Forster, *Dramatic Essays*, 27; Hackett, *Notes*, 99, 100; see also *Punch*, VIII (1845), 138. The sympathetic account by Henry Munroe Rogers, *Memories of Ninety Years*, Boston and New York, 1928, p. 41, adds one or two vivid details.

18. *Boston Herald*, January 13, 1883, quoted in Blinn Shakespeare Scrapbooks; *Shakespeariana*, I, (1883), 58.

19. Forrest Promptbook; *Daily Chronicle*, quoted in *King Lear at the Lyceum: Some Extracts from the Press*, 29.

When, in II, 1, Edmund says "Look, sir, I bleed," Kemble's marked copy has "Wraps his arm up in his handkerchief." Booth's typescript promptbook furnishes him with "Blood on Sponge," but the words are scored through in pencil.

20. "Throws away his Staff" is an earlier direction here. Kent has a staff and scroll in Booth's book.

21. *Random Recollections*, 65, 66.

22. I, 356, 357; Bell's *Shakespeare*, II, 28.

23. The business figures also in the Oxberry, Cumberland, and "Modern Standard Drama" editions, and, merely as "Oswalds bus," in Wallack's promptbook.

24. For the authorship, see Wood, *Personal Recollections*, 169. Davies mentions Garrick's throwing himself "on both knees, with his hands clasped," as he spoke "this touching, though ironical, petition" (*Dramatic Miscellanies*, II, 292).

25. See also, e.g. Cumberland and Booth-Winter editions and Ferrers's promptbook.

26. *Dramatic Essays*, 53. Cf. "*leans on her bosom*" at line 139 (Lacy and Pattie editions).

27. Lacy's edition; Wallack's promptbook (at lines 254, 258). The business is found, e.g., in Kemble's marked copy and in Cumberland's edition. Lear in Shakespeare is, of course, bareheaded in the storm.

28. *Two Dissertations on the Theatres*, part II, pp. 34, 35; Lacy's edition (cf. Pattie's, and *The Athenaeum*, April 30, 1864); Pollock, *Impressions of Irving*, 109, 110; *Daily News*, quoted in *King Lear at the Lyceum*, 25 (cf. also, *ibid.*, 95).

29. Page 146, above; Emma Lazarus, "Salvini's 'King Lear'," *The Century*, May 1883. Macready has the Fool "*shivering*," at line 74 (Lacy's edition).

30. Kemble's copy. In the Winter-Booth Edition, the three Storm Scenes form an unbroken sequence. I once saw them played so, and found them very nearly unendurable.

31. Booth-Winter Edition. In the "Players" Booth Promptbook, Edgar is to have a "straw wreath," a "wooden spike or thorn," a "staff," and a "horn," in this scene.

A pencilled note in Cooke's book, "strikes ground" (with his staff?) at line 146, is attractive.

32. *Treatise on the Passions*, 21. See also Lacy's edition, Wallack Promptbook, Harrison's *Forrest*, 124, *Theatrical Journal*, June 2, 1858, *The Evening News*, and *Aberdeen Free Press*, quoted in *King Lear at the Lyceum*, 39, 40.

33. Lacy's edition, Forrest Promptbook; Cooke Promptbook (hat), Cumberland's edition (headdress), etc.

34. Kean's edition; Kemble's copy; Kirkman's *Memoirs of Charles Macklin*, II, 260; *Daily Graphic* and *Liverpool Daily Post*, quoted in *King Lear at the Lyceum*, 34, 35, 49. Haviland (Irving's Fool), as he spoke his last line in the play, sank "wearily on the floor by the side of Lear's couch" (Crosse, *Fifty Years of Shakespearean Playgoing*, 16).

35. In Tate, Gloster's eyes are put out *coram populo*. Later, when the scene was included, the actual blinding was regularly done off stage (Davies, *Dramatic Miscellanies*, II, 304, Colman, Bell, Kemble, and Cumberland editions).

36. The cutting would seem to be necessary, but in Irving's edition Edgar, after catching Gloster, still talks about his father's miraculous escape!

37. *Garrick's Looking Glass*, 13. See also Benjamin Victor, *Original Letters*, I, 242, *The Universal Museum*, for April 1762, *The Spouter's Companion; or, Theatrical Remembrances*, London [c. 1777], p. 93, Hazlitt, *View of the English Stage*, 174, etc.

38. Pages 34, 35. He is replying to Foote's *Treatise on the Passions*.

39. Kemble's copy, Edward Mangin, *The Parlour Windows*, London, 1841, p. 123; Cooke's promptbook.

40. Forster, *Dramatic Essays*, 30 (see also, Alger, I, 312, and especially Winter, *Shakespeare on the Stage*, Second Series, p. 443); *Theatrical Journal*, June 26, 1861 (cf. Phelps Promptbook); *The Athenaeum*, February 19, 1881.

At "bring up the brown bills" (line 91) Forrest's promptbook has the interesting note, "Ed marches as a soldier."

41. "Tommaso Salvini," *Atlantic*, March 1883. See also, e.g., Emma Lazarus, "Salvini's 'King Lear'," *Century*, May 1883, *The Athenaeum*, March 8, 1884.

42. Wallack Promptbook; Irving, and Booth-Winter editions; Winter, *Shakespeare on the Stage*, Second Series, p. 448.

43. Quoted in *King Lear at the Lyceum*, 50 (see also, *ibid.*, 66), *Fifty Years of Shakespearean Playgoing*, 9.

44. *Prefaces to Shakespeare*, First Series, p. 212 note, Forrest Promptbook. Rowe has Edgar knock the Steward down — with his cudgel, presumably.

45. See also Lacy's edition. Bell was anticipated here by Capell, and Malone has similar directions.

46. Joseph Pittard, *Observations on Mr. Garrick's Acting*, London, 1758, p. 19, [Hugh Kelly,] *Thespis: Or, A Critical Examination into the Merits of all the Principal Performers belonging to Drury-Lane Theatre*, London, 1766, p. 3; O'Keefe, *Recollections*, I, 81. See also Davies, *Dramatic Miscellanies*, II, 317, 318. The Folio's *"chaire"* is well defended by Granville-Barker, *Prefaces*, 182.

47. Brereton, *Life of Henry Irving*, II, 175 (see also *King Lear at the Lyceum*, 102, and cf. *ibid.*, 91); *The Standard*, quoted in *ibid.*, 27.

48. Hazlitt, *London Magazine Essays*, 450 (in Ferrers's promptbook he falls here "into the arms of the 2 Knights"); C[harlotte] P[orter], in *Shakespeariana*, V (1888), p. 134.

49. *Theatrical Observer*, January 26, 1838 (see also *Diaries of a Lady of Quality*, 300, and cf. Wallack Promptbook); Phelps Promptbook; Kemble's copy.

Kemble furnished Albany with a truncheon and the captives with chains.

50. Cumberland's edition. I cannot help questioning the rightness of *"kisses her"* (at "Look on her! look! her lips!"), another direction in the same text.

51. *Journal*, 227; Lazarus, "Salvini's 'King Lear'," see also Helen Zimmern, "Salvini on Shakespeare," *Gentleman's Magazine*, February 1884.

52. C[harlotte] P[orter], in *Shakespeariana*, V (1888), 134; *Liverpool Daily Post*, quoted in *King Lear at the Lyceum*, 51, H. J. Jennings, " 'King Lear' at the Lyceum," *Gentleman's Magazine*, December 1892, etc.

53. *New York Evening Post*, November 27, 1829; "The Truth of Masks" (1891), in *Works*, "Sunflower Edition," III, 201, see also, Emma Lazarus, "Salvini's 'King Lear'."

For Irving's anxieties about the feather, see W. Graham Robertson's *Life was Worth Living*, 169.

54. Morley, *Journal*, 227; Alger, *Forrest*, II, 790, 791; Phelps Promptbook; *The Standard* and *The Eastern and Western Review*, quoted in *King Lear at the Lyceum*, 27, 101.

55. Scott, *From "The Bells" to "King Arthur,"* 233; *Personal Reminiscences of Henry Irving*, I, 98, 99. For the right weapons to use in this play, as they were introduced at a Prince of Wales matinée in May 1896, see W. H. Pollock, "Stage Swordsmanship," *The Theatre*, June 1, 1896.

56. Fitzgerald, *Henry Irving: A Record*, 304; *The Athenaeum*, November 4, 1884.

57. *"Guardando per terra vede spade e mantelli."* Irving appropriately carried a book in this scene (Ellen Terry, *Story of my Life*, 213).

58. Phelps Promptbook; Scott, in *The Theatre*, April 1, 1882 (also, H. R. Pettitt, in *We Saw Him Act*, 225).

According to Matthews, the same "succession of ironic salutations" indulged in at Gobbo's expense were used here, at Peter's (*Principles of Playmaking*, 115). See page 22, above.

59. *Essays and Addresses*, London, 1939, p. 21; Earl of Lytton, "Miss Anderson's Juliet," *Nineteenth Century*, December 1884.

60. *Dramatic Notes 1881–1882*, p. 18. For her coquettish avoidance of Romeo by dodging behind a post — in this scene, I take it — see *The Theatre*, October 1, 1880.

61. E. R. Russell, " 'Romeo and Juliet' at the Lyceum," *Macmillan's Magazine*, August 1882.

62. *Theatrical Observer*, November 22, 1822 (described as "by the Author of 'Theatrical Portraits' "); Knight, *Theatrical Notes*, 130. Cf. also, *Athenaeum*, November 8, 1884 (on Mary Anderson).

63. Mrs. Jameson, "Sketches of Fanny Kemble in Juliet," in *Sketches of Art Literature and Character* (1834), Boston and New York, 1888, p. 484; Kemble's 1811 edition; Phelps Promptbook.

64. Winter, *Shakespeare on the Stage*, Second Series, p. 154. Madame Modjeska criticized the Neilson's business as "unnecessarily borrowed from a modern French play" (*Memories and Impressions*, 324). What play is meant, I have been unable to learn — *La Dame aux Camélias*, perhaps?

65. C. I. Jones, *Memoirs of Miss O'Neill*, London (1816), 1818, pp. 13, 14.

66. *A Letter to Miss Nossiter*, London, 1753, pp. 8, 9; Kemble's 1811 edition. On the practical disadvantages of the balcony, cf. Fitzgerald, *Shakespearean Representation*, 95, 96. Though it seems to me probable that on the Elizabethan stage Juliet had appeared at a window, Otway's Lavinia, at the corresponding point in *Caius Marius*, enters *"in the Balcony."*

67. Cooke, *Memoirs of Charles Macklin*, 205; "Modjeska in England," *The Critic*, June 4, 1881.

68. *Shakespeare on the Stage*, Second Series, p. 155 (see also Modjeska, *Memories and Impressions*, 324, and cf. *The Theatre*, February 1880); Knight, *Theatrical Notes*, 130; *What the Author Meant*, 105. Romeo *"Kneels to pick up rose"* concludes the scene, in Maude Adams's acting edition.

69. *Dramatic Censor*, I, 180; Williams, *Dramatic Censor for the Year 1811*, p. 174; *Edinburgh Dramatic Review*, August 5, 1823.

70. Personal letter, Skinner, *One Man in his Time*, 161 (cf. *Footlights and Spotlights*, 77); *Athenaeum*, March 11, 1882.

71. E. R. Russell, " 'Romeo and Juliet' at the Lyceum."

72. Phelps Promptbook; Percy Allen, *The Stage Life of Mrs. Stirling*, London [1922], p. 215 (cf. also, 213, 223).

73. Garrick, *Three Plays*, ed. Elizabeth Stein, New York, 1926, p. 90. In Maude Adams's edition, the Nurse *"pokes"* Peter *"with cane"* at line 228.

At the beginning of the scene, Fanny Kemble was discovered "in a picturesque attitude" looking out of a tall window (Charles and Mary Cowden Clarke, *Recollections of Writers*, London, 1878, p. 72, Mrs. Jameson, *Sketches of Art*, 487).

74. *Story of my Life*, 211; *Theatrical Inquisitor*, for January 1815; *Examiner*, May 6, 1821.

75. Russell, *Julia Marlowe*, 234, 235.

76. Laurence Olivier's production, May 1940.

77. *The Athenaeum*, April 28, 1849; Winter, *Shakespeare on the Stage*, Second Series, p. 180.

78. See, e.g., Oxberry, Cumberland, French, and Maude Adams editions. Tybalt, too, has sometimes gone out, only to be called back by Mercutio.

79. *The Theatre* (New York), December 1904, July 1905.

80. *Our Recent Actors*, I, 125. Othello's giving his hand to Cassio may have suggested this gracious action. See page 219, above.

81. *The English Chronicle; and Universal Evening Post*, November 15–18, 1788.

82. *The Theatre*, December 27, 1828, *John Bull*, July 17, 1841.

83. Emma Stebbins, *Charlotte Cushman: Her Letters and Memories of her Life*, Boston, 1878, p. 62 (cf. *The Times*, quoted in Price, *Charlotte Cushman*, 135). Vandenhoff had given her "some useful fencing hints for the killing of Tybalt and Paris" (*Leaves from an Actor's Notebook*, 202).

84. Henry R. Pettitt, in *We Saw him Act*, 226; Russell, "'Romeo and Juliet' at the Lyceum" (the same business appears in the Maude Adams Edition); *From "The Bells" to "King Arthur*," 238.

85. *The Athenaeum*, June 21, 1890.

86. *Journal*, 277; *Wallet of Time*, I, 384, 385; Mrs. Jameson, *Sketches*, 489; Lytton, "Miss Anderson's Juliet"; G. E. Humphreys, "Voice and Emotion . . . The 'Juliet' of Miss Mary Anderson," *National Review*, February 1885.

87. E.g., *The Dramatic and Musical Review*, January 3, 1846, Marston, *Our Recent Actors*, II, 76, Godfrey Turner, in *The Theatre*, July 1, 1887.

88. *Shakespeare in the Theatre*, 50.

89. *The Ladies Magazine*, November 17–December 1, 1750, *Universal Museum*, October 1762 (cf. also *The Gazetteer*, September 23, 1788). In Shakespeare's lines the references to Romeo's descending were of course removed.

90. *Edinburgh Dramatic Review*, April 20, 1824.

91. *Memories and Impressions*, 138. Modjeska's own Romeo was "repeatedly" made to "re-ascend the ladder" to kiss Juliet (*The Theatre*, October 1, 1880).

92. *Our Recent Actors*, II, 237; Lytton, "Miss Anderson's Juliet." Sometimes Juliet has gone to the window just before she cries that it is day (see Russell, *Julia Marlowe*, 235, and Maude Adams's edition).

93. Pages 23–26.

94. Lytton, "Miss Anderson's Juliet"; Talfourd, "First Appearance of Miss

Fanny Kemble," in *Critical and Miscellaneous Writings*, Philadelphia, 1848, pp. 118, 119 (see also Mrs. Jameson, *Sketches*, 490, *The Athenaeum*, March 6, May 1, 1847).

95. Helena Faucit, *On Some of Shakespeare's Female Characters*, 140, Winter, *The Wallet of Time*, I, 385 (on Modjeska), Maude Adams Edition; Lytton, "Miss Anderson's Juliet," Russell, *Julia Marlowe*, 237.

96. *Story of My Life*, 222; *A Letter to Miss Nossiter*, 27. For the seizing of the vial, cf. Helena Faucit, *Shakespeare's Female Characters*, 141, Mrs. Mowatt's *Autobiography*, 239, Winter, *Shakespeare on the Stage*, Second Series, p. 182 (on Margaret Mather).

97. *Shakespeare in the Theatre*, 148.

98. *Letter to Miss Nossiter*, 30; *Private Theatre of Kilkenny*, 126; Helena Faucit, *Shakespeare's Female Characters*, 143; "Miss Anderson's Juliet," *Nineteenth Century*, December 1884. Cushman's promptbook has: "Runs & pushes door ½ open."

99. See page 318, below. The direction, "*Lays down the Dagger*" occurs as early as Otway's *Caius Marius*.

100. *Letter to Miss Nossiter*, 31 ff.; Raymond, *Elliston*, 14. Miss Campion (the later Mrs. Spencer and Mrs. Pope) made her *début* at Dublin in 1792 (*D.N.B.*), and was still there in June 1794 (Mrs. Mathews, *Memoirs of Charles Mathews*, I, 87; cf. 145). Her York appearances seem to have come between this date and October 13, 1797, when she acted Monimia at Covent Garden.

101. [Payne], *The Opera Glass*, February 10, 1827. Mrs. Duff while she drank "the potent liquid" flung out her arms as if to protect Romeo from Tybalt (Ireland, *Mrs. Duff*, 53).

102. Cole, *Charles Kean*, I, 185, 186; *Dramatic Essays*, 149; *Diary of William Dunlap*, New York, 1930, III, 654 (February 7, 1833). Mrs. Jameson calls her speaking of the first part of the soliloquy, seated, an innovation (*Sketches*, 491).

102a. *Journal of a London Playgoer*, 278 ff.

103. *Our Recent Actors*, II, 238, 239. For her over-acting of the scene, cf. L. Clarke Davis, "Gossip about Actors, Old and New," *The Galaxy*, May 1873, and M. A. De Leine, *Lilian Adelaide Neilson*, London, 1881, p. 32.

104. Marston, "Modjeska in England," *The Critic*, June 4, 1881. See also, e.g., DeKay, in *Scribner's Monthly*, March 1879 and Towse, *Sixty Years of the Theatre*, 205.

105. *The Theatre*, April 1, 1882 (the discussion of Morley's theory is in "Our Omnibus-Box," *ibid.*), cf. Foss, *What the Author Meant*, 106.

106. [Margaret Stokes] "Helen Faucit," *Blackwood's*, December 1885.

107. *The Theatre*, October 1, 1880, *Punch*, April 9, 1881 (where there is a sketch of her doing it). Cf. the stage direction in Rossi's edition, and *Boston Transcript*, March 28, 1895 (in Blinn Shakespeare Scrapbooks).

108. G. E. Humphries, "Voice and Emotion," *National Review*, Febru-

ary 1885, (cf. Lytton, "Miss Anderson's Juliet"); *Shakespeariana*, II (1885), 545, Odell, *Annals*, XIII, 25.

109. Russell, *Julia Marlowe*, 237, see also H. R. Van Law, "Five Actresses whom I have Seen as Juliet," *The Theatre* (New York), July 1910. In "The Essentials of Stage Success" (*Ibid.*, December 1901), Julia Marlowe writes interestingly of the growing restraint in her own playing of this scene. When the Nurse's Discovery Scene is cut, as in Maude Adams's edition, no harm is done, I suppose, if Juliet falls beside the bed rather than "*within the curtains.*"

110. *Letter to Miss Nossiter*, 34, 35; *The Opera Glass*, February 10, 1827; *Saturday Review*, November 8, 1884, Lytton, "Miss Anderson's Juliet"; *Boston Herald*, March 28, 1895 (in Blinn Shakespeare Scrapbooks); *Theatrical Year of 1895*, p. 292.

111. *The Theatre*, April 1, 1882 (cf. Harcourt Williams, *Four Years at the Old Vic*, 38).

112. Rossi and Maude Adams editions; *The Opera Glass*, February 10, 1827.

113. Also in *The Ladies' Magazine*, February 17, 1753, signed "Rider."

114. Second edition, pp. XIV, XV.

115. *The Actor*, 1755, p. 283; *Two Dissertations on the Theatre*, part I, pp. 69, 70. Cibber also ridicules Garrick's start "at the Sight of a Monument, he went to look for."

116. *General History of the Stage*, 251. See also Lloyd, *The Actor*, 7, and *The Critical Review*, for April 1760.

117. *The New Thespian Oracle*, London, 1791, p. 16, also in *The School of Roscius*, 1791, pp. 6, 7, and *The Theatrical Speaker*, 1807, p. 1.

118. *Memoirs of Mrs. Siddons*, 329, 330. Dr. J. C. Adams maintains that on the Elizabethan stage Romeo burst open one of the stage doors (*The Globe Playhouse*, 206, 207). Lawrence, noting the First Quarto direction, "*She rises,*" would have a trap prised open (*Pre-Restoration Stage Studies*, 155).

119. *Autobiography of an Actress*, Boston, 1854, pp. 237, 238.

120. *My Memoirs*, 173, 174. In several later productions the fighting was with daggers, though Friar Laurence finds "gory swords" beside the tomb. See *Boston Advertiser*, December 14, 1897 (Blinn Shakespeare Scrapbooks), Maude Adams acting edition, Winter, *Shakespeare on the Stage*, Second Series, 192, 193.

121. *Life of Henry Irving*, I, 356; *Our Theatres in the Nineties*, I, 212. See also, especially, Stoker, *Irving*, I, 96 ff., Ellen Terry, *Story of My Life*, 215.

122. Anderson, *An Actor's Life*, 147, 148 (for the date, cf. Odell, *Annals*, V, 342, 343). Scott refers irreverently to the "interminable death-rattle, and colicky kickings" of Charlotte Cushman's Romeo (*The Theatre*, February 1, 1883, p. 123).

123. *Gentleman's Magazine*, for November 1752 (see also note 113); *ibid.*, October 1750.

124. *Letter to Miss Nossiter*, 45, 46; Raymond's *Elliston*, 14; *The Opera Glass*, February 10, 1827 (cf. *John Bull*, February 11).

125. Martin, *Helena Faucit*, 279; [Margaret Stokes], "Helen Faucit," *Blackwood's*, December 1885.

126. L. Clarke Davis, in *The Galaxy*, May 1873 (cf. *Athenaeum*, December 24, 1870); Lytton, "Miss Anderson's Juliet." See also, for Margaret Mather, *Shakespeariana*, II (1885), 545.

127. *Shakespeare on the Stage*, Second Series, p. 138, see also *Ellen Terry and Bernard Shaw: A Correspondence*, 17.

128. *Monthly Mirror*, XIV, 337 (November 1802). In Garrick's version, the direction *"Draws a Dagger"* might be held to imply that Juliet has one of her own, but cf. the manuscript addition in Cushman's promptbook, "From Romeo's Belt."

129. *A Letter to the Hon. Author of the New Farce Called The Rout*, 36, 37; *Theatrical Observer*, September 25, 1832; *Journal*, II, 17 (a similar mishap befell Fanny Kemble in Baltimore, January 7, 1833, see *ibid.*, II, 83).

130. Mary Anderson, *A Few Memories*, 58; Cook, *Nights at the Play*, I, 8; Mrs. Mowatt, *Autobiography*, 237.

131. *The Fools of Shakespeare*, 126, 127; H. P. Goddard, "Recollections of Edward L. Davenport," *Lippincott's Magazine*, April 1878; *Times*, January 24, 1898, quoted in Odell, *Shakespeare from Betterton to Irving*, II, 452.

132. This direction goes back to Kemble's time.

133. *Dramatic Miscellanies*, II, 237, 238; Martin, "An Eye-Witness of John Kemble," *The Nineteenth Century*, February 1880.

134. Winter, *Shakespeare on the Stage*, Second Series, p. 609; Wilstach, *Mansfield*, 398 (cf. Winter, *Mansfield*, II, 161, 162, who notes that Booth, also, had "delivered a perfunctory stroke, and momentarily seemed to recoil from the deed").

135. See Kemble, Oxberry, Cumberland, French, and Winter-Booth editions for one version; the first issue of Mrs. Inchbald's *British Theatre* (72 pages, frontispiece dated "1806") for another. In Bell's edition, lines 111ff. (including Rowe's direction, "Dipping their swords in *Cæsar's* blood") are quoted, as "seldom delivered on the stage."

136. Lena Ashwell, in *We Saw Him Act*, 330; Maud Tree in Beerbohm's *Herbert Beerbohm Tree*, 107, 108.

137. It is pleasant to find Brutus raising Antony's kneeling servant – sometimes at line 138 (Wood's promptbook), sometimes at 125 (Oxberry's edition, Phelps Promptbook).

138. *Dramatic Miscellanies*, II, 241. Cooper used a slightly elaborated version of the same business (*Mirror of Taste and Dramatic Censor*, May 1810).

139. Boston Museum Promptbook, and for the later moment Winter, *Shakespeare on the Stage*, Second Series, p. 595. Charles D. Herman adopted

the same business here (*Boston Herald*, December 5, 1893, quoted in Blinn Shakespeare Scrapbooks).

140. *Tragedian*, 152; *Life and Art of Booth*, 216, see also page 126, above.

141. Shaw, *Our Theatres in the Nineties*, III, 316.

142. "Discours sur la tragédie," *Oeuvres Complètes*, Paris, 1877, II, 316, 317; Mrs. Inchbald (second issue), Cumberland, and Lacy editions.

143. Bell's edition, p. 42 note.

144. *Herbert Beerbohm Tree*, London, 1907, p. 53; Benson, *My Memoirs*, 301 (cf. *Times*, January 24, 1898, quoted in Odell, II, 452, on Tree's production).

145. *An Essay upon English Tragedie* [London, 1747], p. 33, also, in *Town and Country Magazine*, July 1774; *Shakespere Allusion Book*, I, 456 (cf. *ibid.*, 318); *Apology*, ed. Lowe, I, 103, 104. "*Half draws his sword*," for Cassius at line 12, appears in several nineteenth century acting editions.

146. *Notes*, 136, 137. In the acting editions are one or two interesting directions concerning the drinking and sitting down at table: Lacy's, e.g., has at "Why, farewell, Portia" (line 190), "*they all rise and advance* — Titinius *draws his chair near the wing*, R., *and leaves it ready for* Lucius."

147. For a second appearance of the Ghost in this version, referred to also late in the century, see Odell, *Shakespeare from Betterton to Irving*, I, 237.

148. Alternative directions are given for performances in which "the gauze effect is not used," arches then figuring. "When the Arches are dispensed with" the "first entrances R. and L." were used by the Ghost.

149. Wilstach, *Mansfield*, 399, see also Winter, *Mansfield*, II, 162; Goddard, "Recollections of Edward L. Davenport" (McCullough is praised for the same action by Winter, *Shakespeare on the Stage*, Second Series, p. 609).

150. *The Theatre*, February 1, 1884, April 1, 1887.

151. Wilstach, 399, see also *Oscar Asche his Life*, 110; Boston Museum Promptbook.

152. Winter, *Shakespeare on the Stage*, Second Series, p. 603, Frederick Warde, *Fifty Years of Make-Believe*, 137.

153. "Mr. Kemble," *London Magazine*, April 1823; J. A. Williams, *Memoirs of John Philip Kemble, Esq.*, London, 1817, p. 77.

154. Macready's promptbook; see also Ludlow-Anderson Promptbook.

155. *Quarterly Review*, XXXIV (1826), 223. When Cominius asks, "Where is he?" (line 41), Kemble's edition has: "*The* Officer *advances, and the* Soldiers *prepare to seize him*." "Call him hither" has now to be cut, but there is gain in our *seeing* the man saved. The edition of 1789 has a similar direction.

156. *Shakespeariana*, II (1885), 587, 588, Winter, *Shakespeare on the Stage*, Third Series, p. 230.

157. *London Magazine*, April 1823; Robson, *The Old Play-Goer*, 193. Dennis, in *The Invader of his Country* (1720) has: "*The Citizens pass by*

Coriolanus, *each making a singular awkward Bow, and a different ridiculous gesture.*"

158. *Edinburgh Dramatic Review*, January 6, 1824.

159. Kemble's marked copy. A similar direction persisted through the Oxberry and Cumberland editions to French's.

160. *Literary Repository*, January and February 1834, quoted in Pemberton, *Life and Literary Remains*, 245; *Journal*, 217; Alger, ii, 763. *"Rushes forward to C"* precedes line 120 in Cumberland and other acting editions.

161. *Forty Years of Shakespeare on the English Stage*, 99.

162. E.g., Oxberry, Cumberland, and French editions; page 176, above. Kemble's version, which is much rewritten at this point, has the hero discovered standing at the foot of a statue of Mars; and this idea of a striking discovery affected even Phelps, who begins a new scene at IV, 5, 58, with Coriolanus "seated by the glowing embers of the brazier that represents his enemy's hearth" (Morley, *Journal*, 217).

163. "The First Nights of my Young Days," *The Theatre*, June 1, 1887, cf. on Vandenhoff's gesture of describing two or three circles with his hand, *Edinburgh Dramatic Review*, April 6, 1824.

164. *Quarterly Review*, xxxiv (1826), 224. For a much less favorable account, cf. *Theatrical Inquisitor*, for May 1817. Cooper "in the act of dying . . . covered his face with his garment" (Isaac Harby, *Miscellaneous Writings*, Charleston, 1829, p. 279).

165. Forster, *Dramatic Essays*, 60, 61, cf. W. J. Fox, "W. C. Macready," *The People's Journal*, December 19, 1846, and Coleman, *Players and Playwrights*, i, 19, 20. For an amusing monologue, introducing Vandenhoff rehearsing the end of *Coriolanus*, see Henry Valentine, *Behind the Curtain*, 91, 92.

166. Winter, *Shakespeare on the Stage*, Third Series, p. 219. See page 326, above.

167. Lady Benson, *Mainly Players*, 158. Mrs. Langtry had had them arrive (in i, 1) on a slowly moving barge.

168. Lacy's Acting Edition (1867); *The Athenaeum*, November 22, 1890.

168a. *Furness Variorum*, 304; Capell's adaptation, 1759 (in Mrs. Inchbald's *British Theatre*). In Lacy's edition, Eros *"stabs himself with the sword — then throws it convulsively at the feet of* Antony *as he staggers back and falls."* His body is presently removed by the Guard; and, at the end of the scene, they go out *"bearing and supporting* Antony *on a shield."*

169. *The Athenaeum*, September 27, 1873; *Our Theatres in the Nineties*, iii, 84.

170. Cleopatra is kneeling at the close: *"with her arms extended aloft as invoking the protection of the gods —* Iras *and* Charmian *in great despondency — Tableau."*

171. *Mainly Players*, 158, 159. Capell has "Cleopatra *and her Women throw out certain Tackle, into which the People below put* Antony *and he*

is drawn up." At the beginning of the scene, she enters *"at a Window above."*

172. Line 35 ("You see how easily she may be surpris'd") is moved back so as to follow line 21. Mrs. Langtry's edition sounds as if the same strategy was employed in her performance.

173. For a different interpretation, see Knight, *Shakespearean Production,* 228 note.

174. It is celery again which he offers Apemantus at IV, 3, 282. He lies down, just before, at "Thou hadst been a knave and flatterer," and Apemantus sits.

175. October 1816. For Kean's version, see Odell, *Shakespeare from Betterton to Irving,* II, 77 ff.

I have no business to record in the case of *Pericles* and *Titus Andronicus.* Dryden's *Troilus and Cressida* (1679) has one interesting stage direction, in V, 2: *"Enter* Diomede; Troilus *and* Ulysses *appear listening at one door, and* Thersites *watching at another."*

INDEX OF ACTORS AND PROMPTERS

This index is primarily one of persons. It includes references only to the principal passages concerning promptbooks and works written or edited by actors.

Achurch, Janet, 411 (n.89).

Adams, Edwin, 342.

Adams, Maude, 424 (n.92), 425 (n.95); as Maria (*Twelfth Night*), 7.

Addis, J. B. (prompter), 335, 343.

Addison, Laura, 258.

Aherne, Brian, 209.

Aikin, James, 346.

Aldridge, Ira, as Othello, 202, 214.

Alexander, Sir George, as Benedick, 12.

Allen, I. H. (prompter), 345.

Allerton, Mr., as Hamlet, 169.

Anderson, James, 350; as Antony, 332; Jack Cade, 125; Romeo, 317.

Anderson, Judith, 416 (n.159).

Anderson, Mary, 38, 298, 303, 304; as Hermione, 67; Juliet, 299, 307, 309–311, 313, 317, 318; Rosalind, 33, 35, 37.

Anderton, Sarah, as Desdemona, 401 (n.106).

Andrews, A. G., 21; as Fluellen, 121; L. Gobbo, 21; Peter, 303.

Archer, Frank, 130.

Arthur, Julia, as Viola, 9; production of *As You Like It*, 40.

Asche, Oscar, 33; as Falstaff (*Merry Wives*), 48; Jaques, 35; Sicinius, 329.

Ashton, Antoinette, xxi.

Bankhead, Tallulah, xvi.

Bannister, John, 286.

Barnes, J. H., 230; as Benedick, 16; promptbooks of, 336, 338, 347.

Barrett, Henry M., as Falstaff (*2 Henry IV*), 372 (n.56).

Barrett, Lawrence, 173, 345, 349, 350; as Cassius, 322, 324, 325; Hamlet, 154, 181, 395 (n.213); Shylock, 20; promptbooks of, 336, 337, 342, 345, 349.

Barrett, Wilson, 136, 137, 194; as Hamlet, 133, 142, 154, 160, 161, 170, 184, 381 (nn.28, 32), 388 (n.124), 391 (n.161); Othello, 195, 200.

Barron, Charles, 350; as Brutus, 324–326.

Barry, Mrs. (Mrs. Dancer), as Constance, 113.

Barry, Spranger, 90, 301, 317; as Lear, 289, 292; Macbeth, 242; Othello, 190, 198, 199, 204, 205, 216; Romeo, 301, 302, 315, 316, 318.

Bartley, George, as Falstaff (*Merry Wives*), 46, 48; promptbook of, 339.

Barton, J. H., 348.

Bassett, Russell, 78, 341.

Bateman, Kate, as Lady Macbeth, 409 (n.70).

Becks, George, 12, 100, 105, 287; promptbooks of, Bibliographical Notes *passim*.

Bellew, Kyrle, as Romeo, 305.

Bennett, George, as Caliban, 41; Hubert, 377 (n.131); promptbook of, 349.

Bensley, Robert, as Malvolio, 8.

Benson, Sir Frank, 174, 316, 329, 402 (n.110); as Caliban, 41; Hamlet, 154, 159, 182, 183, 381 (n.28), 391 (n.161); Macbeth, 247; Orlando, 33; Paris, 316; Petruchio, 57; Richard II, 121–125; Richard III, 379 (n.162); Shylock, 357 (nn.68, 72);

productions of, 6, 7, 22, 41, 47, 60, 118, 125, 156, 173, 324, 331, 365 (n.206).

Benson, Lady, as Cleopatra, 332; Lady Macbeth, 272, 414 (n.135); Margeret (*3 Henry VI*), 125.

Bernhardt, Sarah, 173; as Hamlet, 147–149, 159, 391 (n.167), 394 (n. 205); Lady Macbeth, 272.

Betterton, Mrs., 268.

Betterton, Thomas, xxiv, 76, 198, 276, 281, 283; as Brutus, 324; Hamlet, 127, 138, 157.

Betty, Henry, 349, 382 (n.45).

Betty, William Henry West, as Hamlet, 140.

Bishop, C. B., 320; as Pistol, 121.

Blanchard, William, as Speed, 72.

Blisset, Francis, 393 (n.187).

Boddie, Mr., as Peter, 303.

Booth, Barton, as Ghost in *Hamlet*, 130; Henry VIII, 81; Othello, 198.

Booth, Edwin, xvii, xviii, xxi, 94, 97, 166, 173, 174, 201, 266, 277, 320, 345, 350, 419 (n.188); as Antony (*Julius Caesar*), 323; Brutus, 326, 427 (n. 134); Hamlet, Chapter III *passim*; Iago, Chapter v *passim*; Lear, 286, 291, 294–297; Macbeth, 229, 230, 243, 248, 250, 254, 257, 264, 278, 406 (n.20); Othello, Chapter v *passim*; Richard II, 122–124; Richard III, 97, 99, 126, 322, 323; Shylock, 19–21, 24, 27–30, 356 (n.54), 358 (n. 82); Wolsey, 78; comments of, on *Merchant of Venice*, 19; *Othello*, 188, 196, 205; promptbooks of, 336, 337, 342, 344, 345, 348.

Booth, J. B., xviii, 174, 187; as Cassius, xv, 126, 322, 323; Hamlet, 153, 156, 177, 386 (n.104); Iago, 185, 190, 201, 222, 223; Macbeth, 244, 257; Othello, 195, 202, 220; Richard III, 95–97, 106, 126; Shylock, 23.

Bosworth, Hobart, as Charles the Wrestler, 32.

Bracegirdle, Anne, as Portia (*Merchant of Venice*), 31.

Bransby, Robert, as Ghost in *Hamlet*, 142.

Brooke, Gustavus Vaughan, 209, 346; as Hamlet, 145; Othello, 192, 221, 401 (nn.96, 106); Richard III, 98; Shylock, 24.

Brough, Lionel, as Touchstone, 34.

Brougham, John, 114.

Brown, Mr., as Bishop Gardiner, 83.

Brydome, Alfred, 400 (n.79).

Buckstone, John Baldwin, as Aguecheek; 10; promptbook of, 338.

Buckstone, Rowland, 392 (n.182).

Burbage, Richard, xxiv, 178.

Burton, William E., 335; as Autolycus, 367 (n.238); Bottom, 53; Falstaff (*Merry Wives*), 46.

Butler, Sam, as Hamlet, 150.

Byford, Roy, 86.

Calcraft, J. W., 79; as Romeo, 306.

Calvert, Charles, 69, 288; productions of, 28–29, 31, 69, 118, 359 (n.98), 362 (n.148), 377 (n.141).

Calvert, Mrs. Charles, 152.

Calvert, Louis, as Antony, 332; Pandulph, 116.

Campbell, Mrs. Patrick, 416 (n.159); as Juliet, xxiii, 314, 317, 318.

Campion, Miss. *See* Mrs. Pope.

Carhart, James L., 338.

Carr, G. C. (prompter), 345, 348.

Chalmers, Edgar, 395 (n.218).

Charnock, H. C., 347, 348.

Cibber, Mrs., 315; as Constance, 109, 110; Juliet, 317, 318; Lady Macbeth, 416 (n.160); Ophelia, 171.

Cibber, Colley, 94–96, 100, 102, 103, 114, 126, 138, 193, 315, 316; as Iago, 193; Shallow (*2 Henry IV*), 92; Wolsey, 81.

Cibber, Theophilus, 96, 97, 290, 291, 305, 311.

Clarke, Creston, 382 (n. 48).

Clarke, George H., promptbooks of, 346, 347.

Clarke, Wilfred, as L. Gobbo, 21.

Coghlan, Charles, as Hamlet, 149.

Colas, Stella, xvii; as Juliet, 307, 312, 313.

Coleman, John, 150, 226; as Macduff, 268.

Collier, R. I., 348.

Compton, Henry, as Gravedigger, 176.

Cooke, George Frederick, 174, 194, 208; as Falstaff, 89; Henry VIII, 77, 79, 81; Iachimo, 61; Iago, 194, 196, 201, 207, 223; Lear, 282, 286, 289–293, 295, 296; Richard III, 95, 102, 105, 106, 126; Shylock, 20, 23, 24, 27–29; promptbooks of, 340, 341, 345, 348.

Cooper, Gladys, 414 (n.130).

Cooper, John, as Ghost in *Hamlet*, 130; Henry IV, 87; Theseus, 53.

Cooper, Thomas Abthorpe, 241, 270; as Antony (*Julius Caesar*), 427 (n.138); Coriolanus, 429 (n.164); Hamlet, 137, 144, 159, 166, 168; Macbeth, 240, 410 (n.75); Othello, 218, 219; Wolsey, 79; promptbooks of, 341, 345.

Creswick, William, as Cassius, 326.

Cushman, Asa (prompter), 349.

Cushman, Charlotte, 78, 229, 349, 424 (n.83); as Lady Macbeth, 232, 233, 241, 244, 407 (n.38), 409 (n.70); Queen Katherine, 80, 370 (n.28); Romeo, 306, 307, 426 (n.122).

Daly, William H., 342.

Dance, Miss, as Juliet, 304.

Davenport, Edward L., as Brutus, 320, 326; Macbeth, 275, 414 (n.122); Richard III, 95; promptbook of, 337.

Davenport, Fanny, 11, 18, 38, 39; promptbooks of, 336, 338.

Davidge, William, as Bottom, 52; marked copy of *Catharine and Petruchio*, 340.

Davison, Mrs., 265.

Delaval, Francis, as Othello, 219.

Devrient, Emil, as Hamlet, 142.

Digges, West, promptbook of, 255, 347.

Dillon, Charles, as Macbeth, 414 (n. 123); Othello, 194.

Dodd, James, as Aguecheek, 6; Roderigo, 208.

Doggett, Thomas, xxiii, 19.

Doud, Oliver (prompter), 337.

Downes, John (prompter), 76, 127, 225, 297, 361 (n.140).

Downey, J. T., 341.

Dowton, William, 143, 350; as Falstaff, 91; Shylock, 27, 29; Witch in *Macbeth*, 227, 228.

Doyne, Henry (prompter), 59.

Drew, John, 62, 63; as Petruchio, 57.

Duff, Mrs., as Juliet, 425 (n.101); Lady Macbeth, 417 (n.161).

Durang, Charles, promptbook of, 345.

Dyer, as Surrey, 81, 82.

Eastlake, Mary, as Ophelia, 137, 392 (n.174).

Edmonds, J. W. (prompter), 336.

Edwards, Harry, promptbook of, 341.

Edwin, John, as Sir Hugh Evans, 47.

Elliston, Robert, 143.

Emery, John, as Barnardine, 65; Caliban, 42.

Evans, Edith, 403 (n.120).

Evans, Maurice, xxii, 21, 123, 168, 383 (n.64), 388 (n.124).

Fagan, Elizabeth, 122, 360 (n.127).

Fagan, James, 93, 94.

Faucit, Helen, 69, 70, 172; as Beatrice, 13; Constance, 110; Cordelia, 283; Desdemona, 197; Hermione, 67, 69, 70; Imogen, 61, 62; Juliet, 311, 313, 317; Lady Macbeth, 246–249, 264, 271, 272, 410 (n.72); Ophelia, 172; Portia (*Merchant of Venice*), 24–28; Rosalind, 33, 37; manuscript part of Constance, 112, 343.

Fawcett, John, as Gravedigger, 175, 176.

Fearon, Mr., as Duke in *Merchant of Venice*, 26.

Fechter, Charles Albert, xvii, xviii, 132; as Hamlet, Chapter III *passim*; Othello, xvi, Chapter V *passim*.

Fennell, James, 343; as Hamlet, 135, 141, 416 (n.155); Othello, 212, 218.

Ferrers, Stanley Charles (prompter), 342, 345, 348.

Fisher, Charles, as Malvolio, 8.

Fisher, Clara, as Beatrice, 18; Richard III, 105.

Fontanne, Lynn, 365 (n.195).

Forbes, Norman, as Aguecheek, 4.

Forbes-Robertson, Sir Johnston, 78, 86; as Buckingham (*Henry VIII*), 78; Hamlet, 127, 133, 137, 149, 153, 156, 184; Orlando, 38.

Forrest, Edwin, 100, 151, 157, 229, 230, 326, 330, 342; as Coriolanus, 329; Hamlet, 133, 135, 145, 146, 154, 160, 166, 169, 177, 184, 381 (n.36), 383 (n.64); Lear, 283, 284, 286, 287, 293, 294, 297; Macbeth, Chapter v *passim*; Othello, 196, 197, 199, 205, 206, 210, 211, 216, 217, 219, 401 (nn.96,106); Richard III, 95, 99, 104, 126, 375 (n.99); promptbooks of, 342, 344, 346–348.

Ganthony, Robert, as Oswald, 287, 288; in *Merchant of Venice*, 27, 30.

Garrick, David, xviii, xxiv, 60, 90, 110, 129, 137, 139, 166, 171, 181, 215, 301, 397 (n.23); as Benedick, 17; Hamlet, 138, 139, 142–145, 148, 150, 157, 159, 164, 168, 381 (n.36), 382 (n.43); King John, 114; Lear, 286, 287, 289–293, 295, 420 (n.24); Macbeth, 228, 236, 241, 242, 259, 275, 276, 278; Othello, 204, 216; Posthumus, 63; Richard III, 104, 126; Romeo, 301, 302, 315, 316, 426 (n.115); *Essay on Acting*, 238, 239, 259–261; promptbooks of, 342; Shakespearean versions of, 55–57, 59, 68, 86, 175, 181, 279, 300, 339, 340, 427 (n.128).

Gates, G. H. (prompter), 348.

Gielgud, John, xiv, 134, 144, 230.

Gilbert, Mrs., 352 (n.9).

Glover, Miss M., as Ophelia, 172.

Glyn, Isabel, as Cleopatra, 331; Constance, 113; Emilia, 217; Queen Katherine, 369 (n. 17).

Goodale, Katherine, 222; in *Macbeth*, 266.

Goodwin, Nat, as Shylock, 23.

Gould, Nutcombe, as Shylock, 20.

Graham, John, as Antonio, 28.

Greet, Sir Philip Ben, 20, 156; as Touchstone, 35, 36.

Hackett, James H., 153, 169, 284, 325; as Falstaff (*Merry Wives*), 45, 48, 49; promptbook of, 339.

Hamblin, Thomas S., 343, 346.

Hamblin, Mrs. *See* Mrs. Shaw.

Hampden, Walter, xiv, 373 (n.74), 410 (n.79).

Harley, John Pritt, as L. Gobbo, 22.

Hart, Charles, 319.

Hartley, Elizabeth, as Hermione, 69.

Hastings, Edward, 339.

Haviland, William, as Fool in *Lear*, 421 (n.34).

Haworth, Joseph, as Hamlet, 141, 147; Richard III, 98.

Hayes, Helen, 4.

Henderson, John, 137; as Falstaff, 90; Falstaff (*Merry Wives*), 49; Hamlet, 137, 142, 144, 145, 168, 382 (n. 44); Lear, 289; Macbeth, 241.

Herbert, Henry, viii, 22, 176, 378 (n.147).

Herbert, Sidney, as Shylock, 23.

Herman, Charles D., as Cassius, 427 (n.129); promptbook of, xxi, xxii, 346.

Hill, Barton, 346.

Hippisley, John, as Bishop Gardiner, 82.

Hodgkinson, John, as Macbeth, 240, 413 (n.119).

Holland, Charles, as Hamlet, 139.

Holloway, Baliol, vii.

Holman, J. G., 344; as Hamlet, 135, 139, 155, 168, 386 (n.103); Macbeth, 260, 408 (n.49).

Holt, Maud, as Ophelia, 171.

Hopkins, Mrs., 346.

Horton, Priscilla, as Ariel, 44.

Howard, Leslie, 154.
Huddard, Miss. *See* Mrs. Warner.
Hudson, Harry B., 320, 349.

Irving, H. B., as Hamlet, 146, 151, 160, 169, 387 (n.117), 388 (n.131).
Irving, Sir Henry, xviii, 31, 35, 94, 174, 206, 285, 322, 336, 422 (n.53); as Benedick, 11–14, 16, 355 (n.46); Hamlet, Chapter III *passim*; Iachimo, 61; Iago, 189, 191, 206, 208, 209; Lear, 282, 283, 286, 287, 291, 294, 295; Macbeth, Chapter V *passim*; Malvolio, 4, 10; Othello, 194, 216, 404 (n.137); Richard III, 97–100, 104, 107; Romeo, 299, 300, 303, 306, 316, 317, 423 (n.57); Shylock, 20–24, 27–30, 208; Wolsey, 77, 79, 81; productions of, 15, 16, 18, 26, 27, 227, 276, 277, 297, 298, 314; promptbooks of, 345, 347; quoted, on *Hamlet*, 154, 166.
Irving, Isabel, as Audrey, 38.
Irving, Lawrence, as Shallow (*2 Henry IV*), 93.

James, Louis, as Hamlet, 170; Othello, 196, 197, 214; promptbooks of, 343, 345.
Janauschek, Madame, as Lady Macbeth, 243, 244, 263, 264.
Jarman, Miss, as Juliet, 312, 313, 317.
Johnson, Benjamin, as Bishop Gardiner, 82.
Jones, Mr., as Prince Hal, 88.
Jones, Robert, promptbooks of, 337, 338, 347.

Kean, Charles, 69, 71, 176, 221, 258, 342; as Benedick, 16; Ford, 49; Hamlet, xvii, 133, 135, 162, 163, 168; King John, 116; Lear, 282, 283, 286, 292; Macbeth, 231, 245, 264, 275, 414 (n.131); Posthumus, 63, 64; Richard II, 123, 124; Richard III, 96, 374 (n.98); Romeo, 306; Wolsey, 76, 78, 79; productions of, 19, 21, 43, 44, 51, 66–68, 78, 82, 109, 116–122, 226–228, 246, 259, 280, 284, 292, 362

(n.148), 364 (n.186); promptbooks of, 336, 343, 348.
Kean, Mrs. Charles, 71; as Beatrice, 16; Constance, 110; Hermione, 67; Juliet, 308, 309, 314; Lady Macbeth, 232, 245, 407 (n.33); Portia (*Merchant of Venice*), 30; Queen Katherine, 82; Queen of Richard II, 124; Viola, 5.
Kean, Edmund, xviii–xx, 227, 266, 279, 394 (n.203); as Coriolanus, 329; Hamlet, 140, 141, 147, 155, 158, 159, 165, 168, 178, 183; Iago, 208, 222, 223; Lear, 286, 287, 296; Macbeth, 235, 238, 242, 243, 260, 274, 278, 418 (n.182); Othello, 192, 194, 195, 197, 199, 211, 217, 219, 220, 403 (n.131); Richard II, 123; Richard III, 95–99, 102, 104–107, 126, 278; Shylock, 19, 24, 27–30; Timon, 334; promptbooks of, 345, 348.
Keeley, Robert, as Verges, 15.
Kelley, Miss F. H., as Juliet, 300.
Kelly, Lydia Eliza, as Juliet, 304.
Kemble, Charles, as Benedick, 13, 16; Cassio, 191; Falstaff, 85, 90, 91; Faulconbridge, 108, 109; Hamlet, 151, 158, 159; Macbeth, 237, 245, 262; Mercutio, 305, 306; Othello, 211, 220, 396 (n.8); Shylock, 24.
Kemble, Fanny, 212, 213, 224, 251, 318, 427 (n.129); as Constance, 113; Desdemona, 212, 213; Juliet, 300, 307, 310, 312, 318, 423 (n.73); Lady Macbeth, 417 (n.162); Queen Katherine, 369 (n.17).
Kemble, John Philip, xix, 64, 80, 220, 241; acting editions of, 68, 108, 111, 187, 189, 226, 247, 248, 288, 289, 301, 328, 428 (n.155); as Brutus, 325; Coriolanus, 326–328, 330; Hamlet, Chapter III *passim*, 329, 416 (n.155); Henry V, 119, 378 (n.144); Hotspur, 84; King John, 108, 111, 112, 116; Lear, 283, 286, 290, 292, 293; Macbeth, 229, 234, 235, 237, 238, 240, 244, 245, 260, 273, 276, 408 (n.57), 409 (n.62); Othello, 194, 401 (n.94); Richard III, 95, 101,

104, 105; Wolsey, 78, 79, 81; marked copies of plays, 57, 339, 348, 350; productions of, 97, 230, 231, 256, 257, 265–267, 306, 320, 321, 429 (n.162); quoted, on *Macbeth*, 276.

Kemble, Stephen, 374 (n.93); as Falstaff, 83–85, 89.

Kendal, Dame Madge, 202, 233; as Desdemona, 202, 214; Lady Macbeth, 233; Rosalind, 36.

King, Thomas, 175.

Knight, Edward, as Francis in *1 Henry IV*, 85.

Kynaston, Edward, 94.

Lackaye, Wilton, 338.

Langford, Mr., as Macbeth, 279.

Langtry, Lily, 38, 338; as Cleopatra, 331, 333; Lady Macbeth, 236, 244, 247, 272, 409 (n.70); Rosalind, 36, 37.

Lea, Marion, as Audrey, 38.

Leech, John, as Slender, 47, 48.

Leman, Walter, as Claudius, 182; in *Taming of the Shrew*, 58, 59.

Lemon, Mark, as Falstaff, 85.

Lewis, G. W. (prompter), 339, 346, 413 (n.113).

Lewis, James, as Bottom, 364 (n.183); Costard, 74; Launce, 72; marked copy of *As You Like It*, 33, 39, 338.

Liston, John, xix; as Aguecheek, 6, 9, 354 (n.19); Cloten, 60.

Love, James, as Falstaff, xviii.

Lowin, John, 76.

Ludlow, N. M., 340, 350.

McCullough, John, 229, 320; as Brutus, 321, 428 (n.149); Othello, 200, 400 (n.76), 401 (n.96); promptbooks of, 346, 349.

Mackay, Mr., in *Coriolanus*, 328; *Julius Caesar*, 319.

Macklin, Charles, 199, 219, 225, 246, 292, 301, 302, 397 (n.23), 405 (n.16); as Macbeth, 228, 237, 275; Shylock, 20, 23, 27, 28; notes on *Macbeth*, 228, 235–237, 277, 405 (n.16), 411 (n.100).

Macready, William Charles, xix, 44, 64, 99, 114, 191, 192, 213, 221, 231, 232, 251, 263, 271, 272, 281, 283, 406 (n.18); as Benedick, 12–14, 16, 18; Coriolanus, 327–329; Ghost in *Hamlet*, 130; Hamlet, Chapter III *passim*; Henry V, 120; Hotspur, 371 (n.37); Iago, 191, 192, 223; King John, 108, 112, 116; Lear, 286, 290, 291, 297, 419 (n.10); Leontes, 69, 70; Macbeth, xx, Chapter V *passim*; Othello, 186, 197, 199, 212, 213, 216, 220, 221; Richard III, 99, 106, 107; Shylock, 30; Wolsey, 78; productions of, 11, 12, 15, 40, 41, 44, 257, 258, 265, 273, 274, 296, 330; promptbooks of, 336, 344, 347, 350; stage accidents in performances of, 119, 143, 182, 236.

Makeah, Miss. *See* Vandenhoff, Mrs. George.

Mansfield, Richard, 21, 117, 121, 343; as Brutus, 321, 326; Richard III, 96, 97, 100, 104, 105, 107, 126, 379 (n.162); Shylock, 20, 22, 23, 27, 30; productions of, 100, 118, 119, 325.

Mantell, Robert B., 273.

Marlowe, Julia, 7, 57, 86, 426 (n.109); as Imogen, 61; Juliet, 304, 313, 426 (n.109); Katherina, 58, 60; Ophelia, 172, 391 (n.170), 392 (n.173); Rosalind, 33; Viola, 5, 7; promptbooks of, 335, 338.

Marston, Henry, as Orlando, 32.

Martin-Harvey, Sir John, 153, 285, 390 (n.151).

Mason, Mr., 265; as Aguecheek, 9.

Mason, Mrs., 348.

Mather, Margaret, as Imogen, 61; Juliet, 305, 313.

Mathews, Charles (the elder), as Aguecheek, 9.

Mead, Thomas, 130.

Meadows, Drinkwater, as Apothecary, 314, 315; L. Gobbo, 21.

Melmoth, Mrs., as Lady Macbeth, 270.

Merry, Mrs. *See* Mrs. Wignell.
Mestayer, William, 320.
Miller, Mr., 17.
Modjeska, Madame, 423 (n.64); as
    Imogen, 62; Juliet, 299, 302, 307,
    308, 312, 313, 424 (n.91); Lady
    Macbeth, 235, 236, 250, 414 (n.133);
    Portia (in *Merchant of Venice*),
    19; Queen Katherine, 80; Viola, 9,
    353 (n.1).
Mohun, Michael, 319.
Molony, Kitty. *See* Goodale, Kath-
    erine.
Montgomery, Walter, as Hamlet, 159,
    386 (n.97), 388 (n.123).
Moore, Adelaide, as Juliet, 300.
Moore, John (prompter), 335, 346.
Morris, Clara, as Emilia, 216, 217.
Mossop, Henry, 370 (n.23); as Lear,
    289; Macbeth, 241.
Mounet-Sully, as Hamlet, 135, 182,
    390 (n.146).
Mountfort, William, 94.
Mowatt, Mrs., 316; as Juliet, 305, 318.
Munden, J. S., as Bishop Gardiner,
    83.
Murdoch, James E., 63; promptbooks
    of, 336, 339, 344, 346.
Murray, Leigh, 130.

Nagle, Joseph E., 342.
Neilson, Adelaide, as Imogen, 62–63;
    Juliet, 301, 302, 309, 312, 317; Rosa-
    lind, 38; named in promptbooks,
    335, 340.
Neilson, Julia, as Constance, 113.
Nethersole, Olga, as Juliet, 313, 314.
Newcombe, Miss, as Arthur, 114.
Nicholls, Henry, as Hamlet, 150, 385
    (n.88a).
Nicholson, H. O., as Davy, 94.
Nicol, Mrs., as Audrey, 37.
Nossiter, Miss, as Juliet, 301, 309–311,
    313, 317.

Ogilvie, Mrs., as Queen Katherine,
    xix, xx.
Olivier, Laurence, 319.
O'Neill, Miss, as Constance, 110; Ju-
liet, 301, 311, 318; Lady Macbeth,
    409 (n.70).
Owen, William F., 339; as Falstaff,
    86.
Oxley, John B., 339.

Packer, John, 406 (n.18).
Palmer, John, as Sir Toby, 6;
    promptbook of, 345.
Parke, William, 392 (n.182).
Parsons, William, as Bishop Gardi-
    ner, 83.
Pelby, William, 365 (n.202).
Phelps, Samuel, 64, 94, 233, 248; as
    Bottom, 52–55; Coriolanus, 327–
    330; Falstaff, 85–88; Hamlet, 168;
    Iago, 223; Lear, 286, 294, 297; Mac-
    beth, 231, 238, 242, 275, 277, 279;
    Malvolio, 10; Othello, 213, 216,
    221; Richard III, 96, 99; Shylock,
    30; Timon, 330, 331; Wolsey, 78,
    79, 81; productions of, at Sadler's
    Wells, 55, 56, 74, 75, 89, 98, 99, 101,
    117, 118, 132, 143, 226, 227, 246, 252–
    254, 258, 267, 274, 279, 296, 297, 306,
    321, 323, 327, 328, 333, 364 (n.178),
    429 (n.162); promptbooks of, 339–
    343, 347–350.
Phillips, Miss, as Imogen, 60.
Phillips, Henry B. (prompter), 344.
Pitman, J. B., 337, 350.
Pitou, Augustus, 277.
Ponisi, Madame, 347; as Lady Mac-
    beth, 232, 264.
Pope, Mrs. (*née* Campion), 425 (n.
    100); as Juliet, 311, 312, 317; Lady
    Macbeth, 409 (n.70).
Pope, Mrs. (*née* Younge), as Des-
    demona, 188; Imogen, 60.
Porter, Mary, 246.
Powell, William, 267; as Othello, 215.
Preston, Robert John, 343, 349.
Pritchard, Hannah, as Gertrude, 166;
    Lady Macbeth, 243, 262, 263, 268–
    271, 409 (n.70), 416 (n.154).
Proctor, Joseph, as Macbeth, 254.

Quin, James, 128; as Brutus, 324; Fal-
    staff, 87, 90; Othello, 187, 198, 199.

Reddish, Samuel, as Macbeth, 241.
Rehan, Ada, 336; as Beatrice, 16; Julia, 368 (n.247); Katherina, 56; Portia (in *Merchant of Venice*), 19, 26; Rosalind, 32, 35–37, 360 (n. 119); Viola, 7.
Rich, John, xvi.
Reignolds-Winslow, Kate, 229, 347; as Arthur, 114, 115.
Righton, Mr., as Flute, 53.
Ristori, Adelaide, xvii, 230, 347; as Lady Macbeth, 232–235, 247, 250, 263, 264, 271, 272, 409 (n.70); *Ricordi*, 232, 245, 264, 407 (n.30).
Roberts, John, 343.
Robeson, Paul, 197, 198.
Robins, Elizabeth, 337.
Robson, Stuart, as Touchstone, 39.
Ross, David, 260.
Rossi, Ernesto, xvii, 305; as Hamlet, 161, 169, 180, 183, 184, 389 (n.134); Othello, 212, 399 (n.60); Romeo, 298, 300.
Russell, Howard, as Eros, 332.
Ryder, Corbet, as Falstaff, 91.
Ryder, John, 143; as Buckingham (*Henry VIII*), 78; Iago, 189.

Saker, Horatio, as Flute, 53.
Salvini, Tommaso, xvii, 259, 274; as Coriolanus, 327; Hamlet, 140, 146, 158, 161, 178, 179, 184, 388 (n.122); Lear, 282, 291, 294, 296; Macbeth, 248, 249, 267, 407 (n.42), 414 (n. 122); Othello, Chapter v *passim*.
Sandford, Samuel, 94.
Scott-Simmons, Mrs., as Juliet, 318.
Sefton, Ann. *See* Wallack, Mrs. James W.
Shaw, Mrs., promptbooks of, 335, 343.
Sheridan, Thomas, as Lear, 289, 420 (n.14); Macbeth, 241, 242; Richard III, 105.
Sheridan, William E., as Lear, 287.
Shuter, Edward, as Bishop Gardiner, 83.
Siddons, Mrs., 64, 231, 256, 262, 420 (n.15); as Constance, 108, 110, 111,

377 (n.129); Hermione, 69; Imogen, 366 (n.214); Isabella, 66; Lady Macbeth, 224, 232–235, 241, 243, 244, 263, 269–272, 409 (n.70), 411 (n.95); Queen Katherine, 80, 82, 369 (n.5); Rosalind, 39, 40; "Remarks on the Character of Lady Macbeth," 263, 270, 414 (n.128).
Simmons, Samuel, as Peter, 302, 303; in *Coriolanus*, 327.
Skinner, Otis, 303; as Macduff, 277; Romeo, 300, 306, 307; Shylock, 29.
Smith, Mrs., as Ophelia, 171.
Smith, Sol, 340.
Smith, William, 90, 347; as Hamlet, 142.
Smithson, Harriet, as Desdemona, 213; Ophelia, 171.
Sothern, E. H., as Hamlet, 159, 170, 171, 394 (n.205); Malvolio, 10, 11; Petruchio, 57, 365 (n.199); Romeo, 305.
Stephens, Mr., 419 (n.11); Othello, 190.
Stephens, W. H., 343.
Stirling, Mrs., as Nurse, 299, 303, 304.
Stirling, Edward Lambert, 132; marked copy of *Hamlet*, 344.
Suett, Richard, as Gravedigger, 175, 176.
Sullivan, Barry, 151, 152; as Hamlet, 147, 151, 152, 157, 159, 177, 381 (n.28), 385 (n.93), 386 (n.106), 387 (n.112), 395 (n.213); Macbeth, 257, 276, 278; Richard III, 102, 107.
Swain, Lillian, as Puck, 51.
Swan, George Cornelius, 402 (n.113).

Taswell, Mr., as Bishop Gardiner, 82, 83.
Taylor, E. F., 337.
Taylor, James, marked copy of *Hamlet*, 141, 345.
Taylor, Joseph, 127.
Terriss, William, as Henry VIII, 81.
Terry, Daniel, as Malvolio, 10.
Terry, Ellen, 364 (n.174); as Arthur, 110; Beatrice, 11–13, 16; Cordelia, 284, 295; Desdemona, 206; Imogen,

61–63; Juliet, 304, 310, 312; Lady Macbeth, 243, 247, 409 (n.70), 410 (n.73); Mamillius, 66, 67; Ophelia, 137, 172; Mrs. Page, 49; Portia (*Merchant of Venice*), 19, 25, 30; Puck, 51; Queen Katherine, 80.

Terry, Kate, as Boy in *Henry V*, 118, 119; Viola, 4; York (*Richard III*), 98.

Tilbury, W. H., as Doctor in *Macbeth*, 263, 264.

Tree, Ellen. *See* Kean, Mrs. Charles.

Tree, Sir Herbert Beerbohm, 364 (n. 190); as Benedick, 13, 18; Caliban, 41–44; Falstaff, 90, 91; Falstaff (*Merry Wives*), 49; Hamlet, Chapter III *passim*; King John, 112, 114, 116; Malvolio, 4, 5, 10; Richard II, 122, 124; Wolsey, 76; productions of, 12, 13, 40–44, 45, 55, 108, 320–324; quoted on *Hamlet*, 147, 148.

Tree, Lady, 113.

Tree, Viola, as Queen to Richard II, 124.

Vail, Mr., as Gravedigger, 175.

Vandenhoff, George, 341, 424 (n.83); as Wolsey, 78.

Vandenhoff, Mrs. George, promptbook of, 336, 337.

Vandenhoff, John, 267, 319, 429 (n. 165); as Coriolanus, 328, 329, 429 (n.163); Hamlet, 155, 159, 178; Henry V, 119; Iago, 206; Macbeth, 238, 410 (n.75), 414 (n.122).

Vestris, Madame, production of *Midsummer Night's Dream* by, 52, 54, 55.

Vezin, Mrs., as Gertrude, 166.

Villiers, Mrs., as Lady Macbeth, 270.

Vining, Mrs., as Elinor, 111.

Vining, Fanny, as Romeo, 305.

Vining, Frederick, as Benedick, 11, 14; promptbook of, 336.

Waddy, Mr., as Claudius, 181.

Wallack, H., 413 (n.114).

Wallack, James ("*the* Wallack"), as Hamlet, 137; promptbooks of, 337, 344.

Wallack, James W. (the younger), as Lear, 283, 290–292, 294, 297; Macbeth, 240, 249, 277; Othello, 213, 221; promptbook of, 348.

Wallack, Mrs. James W., as Lady Macbeth, 249.

Wallack, Lester, 78; promptbook of, 338.

Waller, Lewis, as Henry V, 119.

Waller, W., 349.

Wallis, Miss, 332.

Ward, Geneviève, 341; as Lady Macbeth, 270–272.

Warde, Frederick, xxi, 39, 121, 320, 346, 380 (n.24); as Othello, 219; production of *Lear*, 284.

Warner, Mrs., 258; as Emilia, 217; Lady Macbeth, 242, 416 (n.152).

Warren, William, 335.

Warren, William (of the Boston Museum), as Dogberry, 14; Gravedigger, 176.

Weaver, H. A., 370 (n.31).

Webster, Ben, as Petruchio, 57; production of *Taming of the Shrew* by, 55, 56.

Webster, Margaret, 89, 205, 363 (n. 163), 406 (n.26).

Weir, G. R., as Bottom, vii, 53; Falstaff (in *2 Henry IV*), 94; Gravedigger, 174.

Welles, Orson, xxiii.

Wemyss, Miss, 234.

Whitty, Dame May, 304.

Wignell, Mrs., as Desdemona, 212.

Wilde, James (prompter), xx.

Wilkinson, Tate, 311, 312, 317, 318.

Wilks, Robert, as Antony (in *Julius Caesar*), 322; Hamlet, 127, 138, 140, 157, 167, 168, 178.

Willard, E. S., 131; as Claudius, 394 (ŋ.207); Hamlet, 161, 180.

Williams, W. C., 342.

Willmott, John (prompter), 339.

Wilson, George, 14.

Wood, W. B., promptbooks of, 335, 336, 341–343, 349.

Woodward, Henry, xvi.
"Wopsle, Mr.," 140, 163, 164, 172, 176, 177, 383 (n.54).
Wrench, Benjamin, xix.
Wright, J. B. (prompter), 338, 339, 361 (n.135), 367 (n.238), 413 (n. 113).

Yates, Mrs., as Constance, 113; Lady Macbeth, 269.

Young, Charles Mayne, 130, 319; as Brutus, 325; Hamlet, 135, 143, 145, 159, 178, 179, 390 (n.157), 391 (n. 164); Iago, 223; Lear, 419 (n.2); Macbeth, 237, 238, 240, 260, 352 (n.9); Shylock, 28; Wolsey, 81; promptbook of, 344.
Younge, Elizabeth. *See* Mrs. Pope.

ADDENDA

Page 9: line 12. At the end of January 1821, the Dublin *Theatrical Observer* complains of Mr. Chippendale's "climbing up the side at the conclusion of the fight." The gods were amused, but did not consider "that Sir *Andrew* is a Gentleman, as weak in person as in mind," and quite incapable of the feat (i, 38, 42).

Pages 44: line 32, and 82: line 11. For Charles Kean's "mechanical contrivance," by means of which "his Ariels and angels" were made to "float in the apparent air," see Herman Charles Merivale, *Bar, Stage and Platform*, London, 1902, pp. 137 ff.

Page 85: line 5. How "the *player* Falstaff" was accustomed to rise belatedly and be at last "goaded off the stage, like a fat ox" is described with relish by Morgann (*Essay* [1777], 1820, pp. 131, 132).

Page 86: line 8. Cooke's Falstaff as he began "By the Lord, I knew ye" laughed; "and Mr. Harwood [the box-keeper at the Providence Theatre] used to protest that he saw the laugh come rippling into sight at his ankles, and then spread over his body until his face was all ablaze with drollery, and his frame shaking like jelly. 'I saw his ankles laugh,' said Harwood" (George O. Willard, *History of the Providence Theatre*, Providence, 1891, p. 63).

Page 146: line 2. It is perhaps significant that in *The Spanish Tragedy* (ii, 1) Pedringano takes an oath on "this cross . . . this very sword."

Page 164: line 3. As lately as January 30, 1847, the *Theatrical Times* was trying to dissuade Mr. Cowle at the Marylebone from continuing to wear "the ungartered stocking."

Page 164: line 6. The *Laureate* (1740) says of Betterton that at the Ghost's appearance "every Article of his Body seem'd to be affected with a Tremor inexpressible" (pp. 31, 32).

Page 176: line 20. Although Harley at the Haymarket had broken with the evil custom on September 12, it lingered on at Covent Garden. There, when *Hamlet* opened the season three weeks later, the *Owl* was "glad to observe strong symptoms of disapprobation at the grave diggers stale trick of disencumbering himself of the superfluity of garments."

Page 176: line 29. Mr. Allan Wilkie writes me that during his first Shakespearean engagement he "played the second gravedigger to an old actor, one Alfred Tate, who went through the business of stripping off half a dozen garments much to the delight of the galleryites."

Page 210: line 8. The Boston *Emerald*, February 20, 1808, raised objection to Cooper's entering "in the last scene, with a *drawn* sword."

Page 231: line 27. Sheridan Knowles suggests that Macbeth is absent-mindedly thanking them a second time, after they have drawn apart with Banquo (*Lectures on Dramatic Literature: Macbeth*, London, 1875, pp. 9–11). If so, no business is needed.

Page 239: line 14. Instead of gazing fixedly at the dagger until it disappeared, Fennel in Boston, February 20, 1807, is described by the *Emerald* as starting "suddenly at the sight of the dagger — he endeavours to seize it, is disappointed, and on the suggestion of its being a false creation . . . seems for a moment to lose it" — as again at "Mine eyes are made the fools o' th'other senses."

Page 254: line 14. The manuscript "Dramatic Register" of Charles Rice in the Harvard Theatre Collection has good material on Macready, Forrest, and the young Phelps. Rice is severe in his criticism of Forrest's Macbeth at Drury Lane, February 23, 1837, but one detail he liked: "the holding of his cloak by Mr. Forrest before the face of the first murderer, when he enters at the banquet, to conceal the blood thereon from the company."

Page 264: line 20. Robert Louis Stevenson finds "something really childish in the way" Salvini's Macbeth "looks about the room, and, seeing nothing, with an expression of almost sensual relief, plucks up heart enough to go to bed" ("Salvini's Macbeth" [1876], in *Lay Morals and Other Papers*, London, 1920, p. 184).

Page 294: line 8. Labouchere in *Truth*, February 24, 1881, noticed that in this scene Booth "represented justice and the thief by two straws plucked from his maddened costume, and changed them about 'handy-dandy'."

Page 344: line 3. For an interesting promptbook, marked from Edmund Kean's, see Sprague, "The First American Performance of *Richard II*," *Shakespeare Association Bulletin*, July 1944.

Page 358: note 84. The author of the lines on Kean was Harry Van Dyk — see his *Theatrical Portraits*, London, 1822. Cf. page 423, note 62.

Page 393: note 187. Add: The *Emerald*, November 7, 1807; Knowles, *Lectures on Dramatic Literature*, London, 1873, pp. 138, 139.

Page 425: note 100. Mrs. Spencer was in fact with Wilkinson during the season of 1795–1796 (Sybil Rosenfeld, in *Theatre Notebook*, January 1947).